GREAT BIG BOOK *on* Real Estate Investing

Everything You Need to Know to Create Wealth in Real Estate

Stuart Leland Rider

EP Entrepreneur® Press

Editorial Director: Jere L. Calmes
Cover Design: Beth Hansen-Winter
Editiorial and Production Services: CWL Publishing Enterprises, Inc., Madison, WI, www.cwlpub.com

ISBN 1-932531-51-3

Library of Congress Cataloging-in-Publication Data

Rider, Stuart Leland.
Great big book on real estate investing / by Stuart Leland Rider.
p. cm.
ISBN 1-932531-51-3
1. Real estate investment—United States. 2. Housing rehabilitation—Economic aspects—United States. I. Title.
HD255.R5254 2005
332.63'24'0973—dc22

2004061985

10 09 08 07 06 05 10 9 8 7 6 5 4 3 2 1

Printed in Canada

Contents

Preface

Real estate and the practice of investing in real estate are similar to any other new endeavor. There's nothing mysterious about real property, and with professional advice, you can easily acquire the skills and knowledge necessary to become a successful real estate investor.

This book is intended to be an organizational tool for you to pursue making money by investing, first of all, in your own home, then, perhaps, expanding that idea to encompass other potential opportunities in your own area and in other areas of the country. Through this book I want to provide you with a methodology you can use to approach the process of investing and prospering through real estate. The most important tool in the process is your own common sense, and you're already equipped with that.

I have been using the approach outlined in this book for almost 30 years, and I know it works. It is not a get-rich-quick book, and you are not going to get something for nothing. I don't advocate buying property for no money down. There are opportunities to purchase distressed real estate for little or no money down, but these opportunities seldom lead to wealth.

The methodical step-by-step approach described in the pages that follow, with limited financial exposure along the way, seems to me to be the most prudent and surefire way to succeed. It works for me, and I hope it will work for you, as well.

Acknowledgments

No one works in a vacuum, and to succeed, I have shamelessly called upon the considerable talents of people I trust and who are experts in their own fields. The sketches in this book were generously contributed by my architect of 25 years, Bozidar Rajkovski. I have lost track of exactly how many projects we have done together; he is a man of many talents and a good friend. When I am looking at a piece of real property, I use the filter of 25 years' experience to decide whether to proceed, and if I like it, I call my good friend, David Kipnis, of Marketing Solutions to make sure I have decided on a winning site. He can prove through research what my gut tells me. He has yet to give me a bum steer and has provided most of the statistics you see in this book.

Finally, my daughter, Tarah Rider Berry, of South Mountain Studios provided the photography. Her talent with a camera is not necessarily discernable with the subject matter in this book, but you can sample her full range of accomplishments by logging on to her web site www.southmountainstudios.com.

To these people I offer sincere thanks, and to all the partners, investors, lenders, and consultants I've had the privilege of working with over the past 25 years, I say I couldn't have done it without you. Last, but not least, I must thank my partner of 43 years, my wife, Christine, who has always served as my devil's advocate. Her advice and counsel has helped avert some potential disasters over the years. Two sets of common sense are always better than one!

—Stuart L. Rider

About the Author

Stuart Leland Rider is a commercial real estate developer, commercial general contractor, lecturer, and author.

Since 1975 he has successfully developed 785,000 square feet of commercial office space and 525,000 square feet of retail shopping center space.

Current projects include 75,000 square feet of office and 425,000 square feet of retail space.

As a general contractor, he has managed the construction of one hotel, one paper manufacturing plant, eight restaurants, three office buildings, three commercial subdivisions, and 23 miscellaneous buildings.

Before becoming a real estate developer, Mr. Rider worked as a construction superintendent and, later, as a real estate analyst for a major life insurance company in its real estate investment department. His area of responsibility included company-owned real estate (foreclosed properties) and new joint ventures.

He continues to be active in real estate development and consulting, and offers seminars in real estate development and investment in Arizona.

SECTION

I

ENTREPRENEURSHIP *and* INVESTMENT

CHAPTER

1

Entrepreneurship *and* Real Estate

You have lived your entire life in and around other people's money-making investments. You were born in one, went to work in one, lived in one, played in one, and will most likely die in one and be buried in one. Yes, people who build cemeteries do so for a profit!

It's about time you took a good look around and understood the implications of this.

Almost everyone who deals with investments of any type is involved in real estate. According to the *Kiplinger Report*, over 65 percent of the people in our country own a private residence, and real property is an integral and essential part of everyone's daily life. The sad fact is that most people seem oblivious to the fact that every structure involved in their daily lives is a money-making enterprise for someone else. Even the majority of people who own their own homes seldom spend any time thinking about real estate as a pure investment opportunity.

They say that a home is the single largest purchase that most people will make in a lifetime, and yet it is amazing how little thought to the investment aspects of the transaction goes into the decision to make that purchase. You would think that if someone was spending that amount of money, he or she might be a touch more analytical about the purchase. If someone were buying an office building or a shopping center, I'm sure there would be a more complex analysis of the potential of the property purchase. I believe that analytical thinking should be applied to all aspects of life, and especially to major investments. I define this as the beginning of entrepreneurship.

Webster's dictionary (1976 edition) defines entrepreneurship as "the organization, management, and assumption of risk of a business enterprise"; hence, an entrepreneur is one who does exactly that. My own definition is a little more whimsical: I define entrepreneurship, correctly applied to deal making, as trying to see around all the corners of a deal. What exactly does this mean to me? This question is the subject of my book, and the answer to this question has become the philosophy by which I try to live my life. Simplistically, I'm a professional pessimist. I attempt to identify the worst plausible scenario in a transaction and evaluate whether I can live with this potential eventuality. If I can, then I proceed to the next step. The unique spin that I give to a deal is to imagine every potential direction the deal may take, and then pursue them all relentlessly. I then have the option to take the most profitable direction offered by the deal, as it evolves. In my day-to-day life, I tend to be analytical about most actions, but perhaps less sanguine than I am when looking at a purely financial transaction.

Real Estate

How does this philosophy apply to a real estate investment or a real estate investment career? I look at it as a fail-safe approach to all transactions. When most people buy a home, they look at where it is in relation to their work, shopping, schools, and entertainment and the area that best reinforces their self-image. The entrepreneur also looks at it as a business deal with a view to maximizing the return on investment (ROI) over a specific period of time. That is not to say that the decision will rest solely on the business aspects of the home, but that all factors will be taken into consideration prior to the purchase. The true entrepreneur is always looking at the bottom line, aka the ROI.

DEFINITION

ROI is the acronym for return on investment; also known as (aka) the rate of return or the percentage yield on cash invested.

There are many ways to look at the value of an investment, and in this area, I am a purist. I have no use for the discounted rate of return, the present worth of the dollar, or after-tax rates of return. I believe that the only true measure of a deal is cash return on cash invested, aka the cash-on-cash return. If that works for you, all else is gravy.

What This Book Covers

This book is intended to show you how you can become wealthy without undue risk. It will require hard work, diligence, perseverance, and analytical thinking. The major topics of discussion will be:

- Profiting from your personal residence
- Investing in housing
- Renovation and expansion of residential and commercial real estate
- Purchasing investment-grade real estate
- Managing income properties for a profit
- Real estate development from raw land to large multiuse properties
- Portfolio building and strategies for wealth

Along the way, we will be discussing all the basic tools you will need to achieve these goals.

You cannot neglect the basics and there are no shortcuts. If you do not do the work, you will be disappointed in the results.

Housing vs. Investment Property

I began the discussion of real estate investment with the topic of personal housing because it is a subject and an investment that most people have in common. If you can adjust your thinking about your personal housing, then, treated properly, your new mindset can become a foundation of investment philosophy that can carry through to other investments and other aspects of your life. You should show a profit, personal or financial, in everything you do, and with a little thought and planning, you can do it consistently. A house is not just a home; it should also be a serious income-producing asset. It can and should be the primary stepping-stone for your wealth-building plan.

Once you have it made financially, you can treat your next home as a reward for a job well done, but while you are working on building a solid net worth, you cannot afford to neglect your primary financial asset. Many people, in fact, make a career out of housing in many different ways.

FIGURE 1-1. UPSCALE SUBDIVISION PLAN

Investment property, by its very nature, demands analytical thinking. It is somewhat difficult for most people, all of a sudden, to become analytical. You must study it and practice it daily so that it becomes second nature to you. Then, whenever you are called upon to be analytical, you can take your everyday mindset and ramp it up to suit the occasion.

What to Look For

If you are buying a home, you will need to examine all the usual aspects of the home as they relate to your life and your future plans. In addition, I want you to ask yourself some additional questions that pertain to the potential investment, itself, rather than the housing aspects of the purchase.

- How long am I going to live there?
- How much can I expect to profit from this house and where is the profit going to come from?
- Where will the area be in ten years?
- Is the house in the path of growth or in an established neighborhood?
- Can the home be upgraded or expanded?
- Will the area support improving and expanding the home, or will doing so over-improve the home?
- How should I pay for the house?

These are the types of questions that you would ask yourself if you were buying an apartment complex, an office building, or a retail building, so why not apply a little entrepreneurial thinking to your home as well?

FIGURE 1-2. SUBURBAN OFFICE BUILDING

Some people make money on a home before they are required to purchase it. A common occurrence when a developer opens up a new tract for sale is that early buyers get a better price on the homes and more freebies; once the tract has been accepted and sales accelerate, prices rise. The normal turnaround time for a builder in a tract is six months from purchase to move in. During this time, it is not uncommon in areas that are experiencing growth for prices to have increased 10-15 percent or more during that period. There are cases today where people resell the home before they buy it, making a handsome profit on their initial earnest money deposit. Currently, this is an increasing trend in growth areas.

In an article excerpted in the *Arizona Republic* (August 1, 2004) by Glen Creno and Catherine Reagor Burrough, there is a discussion of the growing impact of this investment trend and the industry's reaction to it. The developers have found that this type of investor behavior hurts their developments and significantly raises the housing price to the public. They now, in both the Las Vegas and Phoenix markets, are starting to require that all buyers must actually move into the home if they are purchasing it. No move, no sale. At the very least, most housing builders are limiting the number of investor sales in their new tracts.

What can you glean from this article? My take on this is that these people have too little imagination and are trying to jump on a train that has already left the station. They are lazy and guilty of sloppy thinking. The people who started this trend have already moved on. The situation cited in the article above is symptomatic of an environment where prices are rising in the face of consistent demand. Currently, we are building 60,000-plus homes a year in the Phoenix area. When rampant speculation like this occurs, it's best to look for another area or another type of home. The very nature of a residential tract will limit your increased value to normal appreciation. Because of the uniformity of the typical tract, there are limits on what you can do to a home without over-improving it. You will also compete with all other homes that are the same model. If you look in areas of custom housing, your opportunities are infinitely greater.

TIMING

The most important aspect of entrepreneurial thinking is to be on the front end of the curve. Some specific examples from my own career that will give you an idea of how good projects evolve are the following.

War Stories

MY FIRST REAL ESTATE DEAL

In 1976, for my first real estate development transaction, I optioned a piece of property in San Ramon, California, from Boise Cascade Corporation. We were able to negotiate a two-year option at a specific price to give ourselves

FIGURE 1-3. SAN RAMON SHOPPING CENTER

a chance to get the required governmental approvals and pull the project together. Because my financial partner had limited funds, we were very careful about our front-end expenses. Accordingly, we offered our architect a fee plus a percentage if he would defer the fee until such time as the project started construction, and our option price to Boise Cascade was paid with letters of credit rather than cash.

By the end of the two-year period, we had secured all the approvals necessary for the project, including a building permit, and had executed leases for 97 percent of the leasable space, and our total investment was $13,000 in cash and $50,000 in letters of credit. It was time to build. In the meantime, another developer approached us to inquire whether we would sell him the project as is. After several months of negotiating, we agreed on a price, with the new developer assuming all outstanding obligations, including the architect. We concluded that we could not do better on a rate of return than the price we negotiated. Our total investment was $63,000. Our yield was money back and $750,000. Our entrepreneurial approach to the front end resulted in an ROI of 1190.47 percent over the two-year period or a 595.23 percent annual ROI.

New Policy

As a result of this deal, our company policy was changed to accommodate this type of marketing for every project we would undertake. Since that time our projects have been both for lease and for sale from the moment we open the escrow. The result has been that, on projects sold before construction (approximately 50 percent of our projects), we have averaged a 300-plus percent annual ROI, and on projects actually built, we have averaged 180 percent annual ROI. Our project rates of return are calculated from the time we start spending money on a deal to the time when the project achieves a 95 percent occupancy and rent payment. The resulting NIBDS was capitalized at the then market rate and the costs were deducted to determine the development or entrepreneurial profit.

DEFINITION

NIBDS is the acronym for net income before debt service.

From that point on, the development phase is over and the operating phase begins. That is another project category I refer to as Continuous Redevelopment©, and it is a constant condition until the project is sold. I will discuss this more later in the book.

A New Idea

While this deal was going on, we were looking for a home for our operation and, in the process, we discovered that the only truly professional office locations were in the city, approximately a 45-minute commute from where I lived. It occurred to me that if I did not want to commute to the city, then there were probably many other people who shared my sentiments. Accordingly, I optioned a piece of property along the freeway between our residential area and the city. It took us only six months to lease the building to break even, and we were only part way through the governmental approval process. I realized that we had struck a gold mine and quickly optioned six more properties in our general area in similar locations. The intercept theory had been born, at least in my area. I'm sure that there were other people doing this, but I had not noticed and they were not doing it in my area. Within a year of opening our first fully leased building, other developers started following us around. Whenever we built a building, three or more competitive buildings would follow ours in quick succession. I rapidly realized that the first building got the best tenants. Since then, we have developed offices in towns where we were the first modern office building in town. Our tenants were inevitably the local movers and shakers who realized that to stay on top they needed the best location and a professional setting. We left the overflow to others. We also liked to build rather modest-sized buildings so that our lease-up process was relatively easy.

Here's what I took away from this experience:

- Locate a good suburban market and be the first one there.
- Do not overbuild the market; err on the small side.
- Pick a location that will always be a solid one.
- Build a good "grade B" building with no frills, as it will always be able to compete with any future competition.

Synergy

Another aspect of our office property development program that derived from this experience was to maximize the land yield and create a more synergistic development. We realized that to make each project easy to lease, we should not build to the maximum capacity of the market. In most instances we were going to have more land than we needed for the office building. We discovered that by subdividing the property into an office building, a bank property, and a restaurant site, we were able to sell off the bank and restaurant pads for enough money to pay off the office building pad. This left us with little or no equity in the office property, thus increasing our yield on investment. Further, it also made the property easier to market to all three, as the synergy among offices, restaurant, and financial institution gave each part of the development a built-in list of customers.

This all occurred in the mid- to late 1970s and I'm still in the business. So what did this early experience teach me about entrepreneurship?

First of all, the early lessons helped me to establish a pattern of thinking that has served me well in my career. I'm not suggesting that you copy my M.O., but rather that you develop your own, based on your personal experiences as you go along. The important thing is to pay attention to what is going on and incorporate a continuous pattern of analytical thinking as you learn and grow.

A Short Ride

In 2000, I started giving seminars about real estate development. In my first class there was a man who was involved in high-tech development. I had never heard of this, and by the time I understood the potential, the bloom was off the whole idea. He, however, rode the dotcom wave to great profit and got off before the bubble burst. His idea was simple. He located all the high-speed fiber optic trunk lines in our area, bought or built office buildings on top of them, and offered office space with high-speed access to the dotcom companies. It turned out that there was so little of this type of space available that the dotcom companies would take it at a premium, with little or no tenant improvements from the landlord. His smart move was to sell each project as soon as it was completed and leased up to people who wanted to ride the new high-tech wave. When the dotcom boom collapsed, many of these buildings suffered. They are since filling back up, but his innovative thinking made him a bundle in a three-year period.

The Long-Term Mindset

I am in no way suggesting that you look for the "once in a lifetime opportunity" and base a career on it, but rather that you keep your eyes open to a possibility that might come along, then take advantage of it without putting all your eggs in one basket. This type of a deal is nothing to build a career on. What I'd like you to take on board for your analytical toolkit are the following concepts:

- Research the market; update your findings annually.
- Look for the best location for every project.
- Re-examine the market; test your conclusions.
- Look at every deal in every conceivable way.
- Work all the possibilities simultaneously.
- Do not fall in love with any particular piece of real estate.
- Do not specialize in one particular product unless there is no discernable competition around; if you do, when competition appears, get out of it.
- Approach every transaction as if it is the most important transaction of your career.
- Do not take on too much work, as delegating important decisions can bankrupt you.
- Sign all your checks—no exceptions, unless you have become so large and successful that it doesn't matter to you.
- Make sure that all of your key people have a piece of the action and that their real compensation is tied directly to your deal's profitability.
- Do not delegate negotiations on financial matters to others, especially attorneys. It's your wallet on the line; make your own mistakes.

- Hire good consultants, listen to them, and then make the decisions yourself.
- If you make a mistake, correct it immediately and move on. Forget about blame—there's no profit in it.

With this as a basis for your thinking, you can approach any real property transaction with a healthy mindset. I have always said that real estate development or investing is not rocket science; even people with an eighth-grade education have become multimillionaires at it. One friend of mine made it big after escaping to the U.S. from the East German coal mines. He had a fourth-grade education. He retired from the housing business as a multimillionaire.

HEADS UP

Real estate is hard, painstaking work, but it can be indecently lucrative if you do it right.

The Process

Any real property transaction is relatively simple and impossibly complex at the same time. It is really what you make of it. The unconscious mind looks at it like this.

Housing

Find what you like, buy it, move in, and live there.

Income Property Investment

Find a property you like, arrange for the financing, buy it, and hope your tenants stay and pay rent.

Real Estate Development

Find a piece of vacant dirt or one with a disposable building on it, buy it, design a building, build it, and fill it up.

If this is your view of the real estate investment and development process, don't bother with the rest of this book. I can't help you. If, however, you want to know what it's really like, if you want to make some serious keeping money, and if you are willing to learn and work hard, real estate investment and development may be the vehicle most suitable for making your fortune. At the very least, you will be able to make money consistently on your own home.

CHAPTER

2

The Case *for* Real Estate Investment

Traditional Investments

Today, more than ever before, the average person has more choices of where to put his or her investment money. The three major venues for investment have always been stocks, bonds, or real estate. This is still true, but in each field the available choice of investment vehicles is staggering. At one time you had common and preferred stock; you now have warrants, hedges, options, futures, and a host of other derivatives. They all scare me to death. I have never owned one share of publicly traded stock. I have never felt that any investor has any control over the fate of a stock investment.

Stocks

Most people have neither the time nor the inclination to sort out this menu of investment choices. They prefer to leave the work to the self-proclaimed experts. For the individual with no desire or time to analyze all these choices, this multiplicity of investment vehicles has given birth to yet another class of investment, called the *mutual fund*.

A mutual fund is a company formed to own shares in other companies. The theory behind this is to spread the risk and to average gains and losses by owning a broad range of companies. There are funds that trade only certain stocks, such as high-tech companies, single industries, foreign companies, foreign currencies, certificates of deposit, or treasury bills—the list is endless. There is also another class of funds, *index funds,* that trades in a collection of stocks. These funds are based on all the stocks in an index, such as the Dow Jones Industrial Average, the S&P 500 Composite Stock Price Index, the Russell 2000 Index, or the Wilshire 5000 Total Market Index. The value of an index fund fluctuates with the index. The Dow Jones Industrial Average is a collection of 30 stocks representative of the broad range of industry. From the Dow's official web site: "The Dow's durability is in the selection of companies that make up the industrial average. Though there is occasional criticism on this assemblage, collectively, the 30 Dow industrial stocks represent every important sector in the stock market (except transportation and utilities), and they respond to every important factor in the economy." Suffice it to say, there is something for everyone.

There are even funds that hold shares in other funds, resulting in multiple layers of management charges, thus diluting the potential return on investment even further.

What Makes the Market

The average person's perception of the stock market is that it is fueled by earnings and opportunities for expansion. This is only partially true. In fact, the market is driven by the large investor; the small stockholder is merely along for the ride. The reality is even worse than that.

The Bigger Fool Theory

In the past, when people purchased stock as an investment, the price was generally based on the per-share earnings as determined by the *P/E (price/earnings) ratio* of the company's common stock. Traditional P/E ratios varied from a multiple of six times earnings for the least creditworthy stocks to 12 and up for the more elite investments. Emotion and conjecture were involved, but the investor was usually assured that his or her investment would pay an annual dividend while also retaining the potential for gain in the event the fortunes and earnings of the company increased.

Professional underwriters have historically shouldered the heavy risks and inordinate profits associated with capitalizing new or existing companies undergoing an initial public offering (IPO) of company stock. They tended to set the price and then parceled the stock out to their list of large preferred clients, who in turn made a killing when the stock was opened to public trading. Their day-to-day involvement in financial markets associated with the industries in question and the staggering amounts of capital required to fulfill this underwriting function effectively exclude the individual investor. These people are investment bankers, brokerage houses, and very sophisticated daily investors in the specific industry in question.

Starting in the 1990s, P/E ratios have increased to 50 or more times earnings, with seemingly no upper limit. People no longer buy stocks with the expectation that they will get an annual return on investment. They are now counting on the bigger fool theory to make money. This theory rests on greed as well as supply and demand, overriding investment considerations, turning people into speculators rather than investors. A modern stockholder is counting on someone else to come along who will pay more for the stock than he or she did.

Fueled by the imminent retirement of the postwar "baby boom" generation, this increasingly insatiable demand for a place to put capital, the stock market currently reflects the bigger fool theory very dramatically. The daily volatility and lack of clear direction of the stock market are indicative of an increasingly prevalent, unsound reasoning when buying and selling stocks.

Individuals who want to return to the posture of legitimate investors must take a good look at real estate as an investment vehicle: it trades on a multiple of cash flow to establish value, while retaining the added attraction of appreciation, with the interim benefit of depreciation. In short, it is a more constant and reliable vehicle for investment. In some cases, it can be a vehicle for speculation as well. One very poignant advantage that real estate has over stocks and other investment vehicles is that it is a finite commodity. Other than volcanic eruptions at sea and reclamation projects, there has been no real estate created for several million years. (*Note:* the cost of reclamation far exceeds the cost of a comparable acquisition.) The continued growth of the world's population virtually ensures appreciation as available land is absorbed.

Notes or Debt Instruments

Debt instruments (notes) are income- and credit-based. You earn a specific rate of interest annually until maturity, the date on which the debt becomes due for payment. These pieces of paper are unsecured and the values are based only on the creditworthiness of the makers. They are traded on percentages of face value, based on supply, demand, and the fate of the individual maker. The sad fact is that when you are finally paid off, your money is worth considerably less than when you invested it. Inflation has eroded your capital. This is only one of the downsides of all debt instruments; in addition, you pay ordinary income taxes on the interest while you hold these notes, thus eroding your real rate of return.

These notes are unsecured and are sold by governments and corporations. The federal government sells treasury bonds and savings bonds, short and long term. These notes are backed by the "full faith and credit" of the U.S.—by you and me. Corporations sell notes, debentures, and annuities. A *debenture* is unsecured debt; it is backed only by the integrity of the corporation, not by collateral, and documented in an agreement called an *indenture*. An *annuity* is a debt instrument that provides a specific income for a specific period of time, using a combination of income and capital to provide the annuity income. There is little or no salvage value unless you are in a constantly rising market.

Corporate Responsibility

In a perfect world, all notes would be repaid—but we do not live in a perfect world. The last call on a company's cash in the event of a financial crisis such as bankruptcy is the unsecured note. After taxes and unpaid wages, the hierarchy of payback starts with secured loans, then progresses to monies owed to employees and the government, then to suppliers and general creditors. This makes the investment in commercial paper less than secure. With no call on assets, redemption of the notes, even in part, in the event of a financial meltdown, is problematic.

Income vs. Equity

The major difference between stocks and bonds is one of equity. With stock, you can profit from the company's success or lose based on the company's failure. Your stock certificate is an equity instrument, meaning that you actually own a piece of the company, and the value of the stock can be directly related to the company's liquidation value or its earnings—or can it? The major drawback to investing in notes is the inability to build equity. Treasury bills and corporate notes pay an annual rate of return on the purchase price, with little or no potential for appreciation. Another significant downside is the inability to keep the notes, as the maker can call them (redeem before scheduled maturity) and the holder cannot extend them. They are what are known as "unsecured borrowings," generally acknowledged as the riskiest form of investment. They are not asset-backed securities; rather, they are backed solely on the general credit of the maker of the note.

Secured Investments

Traditional secured investments come in the form of mortgages or chattels secured by real or personal property.

Chattel Notes

A chattel note is a note secured by personal property and is common in industry. Equipment loans are an industry in itself; you can either make a loan directly or invest in a company that makes these loans in bulk. For instance, most jet aircraft are financed this way, as well as ships and other large pieces of equipment. Almost anything that will become worn out and/or obsolete in time is financed this way.

Mortgages

Mortgages are loans on real property and are evidenced by notes secured by mortgages or deeds of trust recorded against the title of the real property. All home loans are mortgages; some are primary or in first position, while others are in second position, aka *seconds*, such as home equity loans.

For the individual investor, placing money in mortgages is relatively easy. There are companies that pool funds and bundle mortgages into securities and sell shares. This spreads the risk for the small investor. You can also lend directly through some local companies that locate and make second mortgages. Some of these firms are called *hard money lenders* because they are expensive and are often lenders of last resort. A typical hard money deal is a 50 percent of value loan, 4 to 5 points up front, and an interest rate 4 points above the conventional mortgage market. This is expensive for the borrower but very profitable and secure for the lender.

Other Investments

Some other traditional investments are in precious metals, such as gold and platinum, or rare coins and art. These are secured investments, and rare coins and art seem to be good investments over the long pull. Precious metals are traded in the market and vary in value with supply, demand, and the public's view of the current economic outlook. In bad times, precious metals go up because people see these commodities as a hedge against disaster; in good times the values go back down to the approximate cost of mining them.

Real Estate Investment Properties

The other traditional area of investment has been real estate. There are characteristics of real estate investment that are not shared by any other investment type. When added together, they create a formidable argument in favor of investing in income-producing real property. There is also ample argument for investing in raw land for the long pull. There will be more on this later in the book. The characteristics that are inherent in real property investments are as follows:

- Real estate is a finite commodity. There will be no more manufactured; therefore, it appreciates over time, because it is becoming increasingly scarce. So long as people continue to immigrate here and people continue to have babies, demand will be constantly increasing. Some areas of the country benefit more from this demand than others.

- Annual rate of return.
- Each piece is unique.
- Income property sells for a cap rate on actual earnings, so you can generate a cash flow with a specific return on equity from day one.
- Your asset may be depreciated; the resulting write-off shelters your annual income. Properly purchased income property can have an income from which 70 percent of the cash flow is tax-sheltered. This dramatically increases your annual ROI.
- When you decide to sell real estate, you can exchange it into another property, deferring the taxes indefinitely.

If you want to cash out, your profits are taxed as capital gain at the current federal rate of 15 percent.

I am not aware of any other single investment that shares all of these characteristics.

Unique Aspects of the Investment

Another facet of real property is its uniqueness. Other than the tract home, all real estate is unique. First, the location is unique. Second, the buildings on the land are unique. This aspect lends a certain cachet to each and every piece of real property.

The single overriding characteristic that has contributed to value in real property is location. The old saw lists the three most important characteristics of a piece of real estate as "location, location, and location." This is as true today as ever. The definition of location has, however, changed with the times. In the old days, the 100-percent location in any town was at the intersection of Central and Main. When large department stores in downtown locations were popular, the best location for a small merchant was adjacent to the department store. That is still true today in the regional malls and the community-sized centers. Location, in general, however, is now defined by our mobility. The most important characteristics of location are now *visibility* (from vehicles) and *accessibility* (by vehicles). This is true of any type of real property. The better these characteristics are, the more the property is worth. The other factor that affects real property—as any commodity—is supply and demand.

Why Build?

You might wonder why anyone would build in a particular location. The simple answer is profit. There are a few exceptions to this, such as government buildings, but by and large profit is the engine that drives all commerce, development or otherwise. There may be an alternative motive for a homeowner building his or her own home, but they all know that if they do it themselves they can save money, ergo, profit from the action.

People who do this for a living market their product to a variety of clients. They lease to tenants, sell to occupants, sell to investors, and exchange the properties for more raw land and start over. The market for real estate product is limited only by the demand; since demand is ever increasing, there does not seem to be a limit on what you can do.

The essential ingredient to profitability, however, is timing and market. You need to produce the correct product at the correct time. If you are not going to build, but merely invest, you need only to access the market correctly and buy astutely. Sounds simple, doesn't it? It's not brain surgery, but you had better do your homework and know your way around the real estate market.

WHO BUILDS AND WHY?

People who keep up with the news are familiar with the names Donald Trump, Del Webb, William DeBartolo, The Rouse Company, Gerald Hines, Continental Homes, US Homes, and The Taubman Company. They have built some of America's most visible, well-publicized projects within the commercial real estate development industry. However, what these people do for a living is no different, except in scale and notoriety, from what local developers do in every town in America. The local developer might not be known in the area where he or she builds, but the entrepreneurs who build the bank buildings, office buildings, and local grocery stores are working at the same trade as Donald Trump and the others, only on a more practical and mundane level. Without these people, the world as we know it would not exist.

Commercial real estate development is defined as the creation of real property investments, "realty," as opposed to personal property or "personalty." Buildings are permanently attached to the land and, therefore, are forever part of the real estate.

Commercial development is the business of creating this income-producing real estate. Why and how is this done? What prompts builder, buyer, and tenant to get involved is the attraction of using leverage to increase their profit?

WHAT'S GOING ON UNDER YOUR NOSE?

Seldom does the grocery chain own the grocery store; if it started out that way, it was subsequently purchased by an investor group formed for the express purpose of owning quality investment-grade real estate. The business of selling groceries is often at odds with the business of owning buildings for investment. Most companies in the grocery business need all of their money to improve and enhance the process of putting groceries in the hands of the buying public. In this ever-increasing competitive field, their emphasis must be on the volume of sales and the profitability of those sales. The buildings, themselves, become leased investments whose desirability as investments depends directly on the creditworthiness and diversity of the tenants in residence on the real estate.

This process creates two types of real estate investors: those who develop the properties and those who purchase the properties as investments. In both instances, opportunity exists for profit. The profitability in each instance will be a function of the expertise of the party involved. In the case of the developer, his or her entrepreneurial talents will be involved. In the case of the investor, his or her skill and knowledge will determine the outcome.

REITS

Miraculously, there is even a security or a mutual fund, if you will, called a *real estate investment trust* (REIT) formed for the express purpose of allowing the public to invest in real estate. During the 1970s, the REIT was created to give the individual small investor the opportunity to own an undivided interest in a variety of large commercial real estate projects.

WHO OWNS THE REAL ESTATE?

Since the advent of the REIT, the public has become more aware of the possibilities of real estate development. The notion persists to this day, however, that the real estate investor is, by necessity, a very well-heeled individual. This can be true in many cases, but it is by no means the rule anymore. Many individuals, primarily professionals, have pooled their pension plans and formed small, self-directed REITs. These groups have not formed publicly traded REITs, but rather have formed partnerships and companies to own and operate these assets. They build, buy, sell, and exchange these investments regularly to maximize their portfolios much the same way any investor does with a stock portfolio.

In every building project, there are different functions for both owner and occupant. Each function is vital to the process. One person or entity may fill all the available functions in a transaction; however, in most transactions, there are many participants involved in the various functions. The owner may be the initial developer or someone who buys it after completion. Some buildings change hands many times during their useful life. The initial occupant can be the developer, the owner, and the tenant. In the case of multitenant buildings, the tenants may be unrelated to the owner and usually are. The tenant, or tenants, as the case may be, may later buy the building. The tenant may be the developer, but not the eventual owner. For the tenant, the lease is also an asset as well as a liability. The right to occupy a specific premises can, under certain conditions, be assigned and, therefore, sold.

There are many roles in this scenario for everyone. All involve real estate investment.

DEFINITION

A ***premises*** is a specifically and legally defined, usually co-mingled, leasable space.

Commercial Real Estate

Commercial real estate properties are most often created by a real estate developer. It is usually that individual's primary occupation, so he or she must do it well enough to create a profit. Sometimes a commercial real estate property is created by the occupant and later sold to an investor. No matter who creates them, these properties are everywhere you look. The home you live in was created by a developer and sold to you or the original occupant at a profit. The corner grocery store and the dentist's office building are other examples. Almost every structure not owned by the government can be classified as a real estate investment of one kind or another. Some public facilities, such as stadiums, paid for by cities, are investments in the long-term prosperity of the cities, paying dividends well into the future. Without real estate investment and development, we'd still be living in caves.

HEADS UP

Investment-grade real estate is real property worthy of being categorized as an investment rather than as a purchase only.

Who Are the Developers?

The public is usually aware of the larger development companies in our country, but small developers and investors create the bulk of real estate investment. These are people who start out building one to six houses per year and graduate to apartment buildings and condominiums. They might start by building a small office building for their own company and add some extra, unneeded space to lease in order to help pay the mortgage. A group of local businesspeople might pool their resources and build to house a bank or an automobile dealership.

These are all real estate developments. They are created by people who have never done this before and who have never invested in anything similar. Are they nuts? No. On the contrary, they are people who are smart enough to have seen the potential for profit. In old urban areas known as the "Rust Belt," people are tearing down obsolete factories and building homes and shopping centers. In the West, the great American migration keeps fueling an ever-expanding real estate market for housing, retail stores, offices, industrial buildings, marinas, airports, and other real estate products. They are all real estate investments, owned by individuals, companies, REITs, banks, and partnerships. How do these people know how to do this?

HEADS UP

This is not a proprietary or arcane process! Anyone who seeks to learn how to work in this market may do so, and you can hire the rest of what you need.

I have always worked with the theory that if someone else can do it, then I can do it. By learning as you go, and not biting off more than you can chew, you can, too. What you don't know, you can find out; what you cannot do, you can hire to do. You can find partners, consultants, employees, and experts to fill in all the gaps in your knowledge. All you need is the desire and some common sense and you will be well on your way to becoming a real estate investor or even a developer.

The business of development and/or investment as I define it is the business of taking calculated risks and the process is one of winnowing the list of unknown risks to the point where the individual involved is comfortable making the go-or-no-go decision for the project.

You will notice considerable repetition as you progress through this book. This is intentional. Many of the topics, if not all of them, are discussed from a variety of viewpoints with different considerations in mind. As each topic is examined, the repetition is intended to cause you to recall the previous associations. The single elements of real estate investment and development can be summed up in one paragraph, but the ramifications, choices, considerations, and alternatives involved in the decision-making process must be examined and implemented from multiple viewpoints.

HEADS UP

As you read through this book, you will be constantly changing hats, from buyer to owner, from investor to seller, from builder to manager. Before you're done, your hat rack will contain an amazing variety of hats, some comfortable and some decidedly not so. Wear those that are comfortable and hire someone to fill the ones that don't fit you.

Housing—The Prime Mover

The single most important force behind the real estate market in the U.S. is the desire of all Americans to own their own home. Home ownership is considered the cornerstone of the traditional "American Dream." It has been the average family's way to get ahead and save for the future. About 65 percent of American families own their homes. After World War II, the U.S. Congress passed a series of laws enabling most citizens to own housing. The law enabling the VA and FHA loan system has been further reinforced with government-backed home mortgage securities known as Fanny Mae, Freddie Mac, and Ginny Mae loans. Without boring you with details, these laws enabled people to buy homes with as little as zero dollars down (in the case of the VA loan). The banks that make these loans bundle them together to create investment securities, which they then trade on the market to investors, both large and small. The sheer volume of money made available by this process is what enables the average American to own a home. The more we build, the more affordable they are and the faster they sell. The absorption of housing is what prompts the creation of everything else in real estate. People need to eat, play, and work, and all these activities require buildings. These buildings are all real estate investments. Believe me, Donald Trump does not build them all. People like you and me create them. I think that's why you're reading this book. If you don't want to build, you might like to buy. You can make money either way.

Purchasing Your Own Home

Individual home ownership has proven to be the most widely used and popular form of savings for the average family. Since everyone needs a place to live and paying a mortgage is not much different from paying rent, most people find that the only obstacle is the down payment. The government-backed mortgage has solved this problem by lowering the down payment from the 20 percent required for a conventional loan to as little as 3 percent for an FHA loan. The benefits are many: the interest is deductible from your gross income for tax purposes and the house appreciates in value while you live there. When people pay for a house, through the down payment and through mortgage payments, they are acquiring equity. They can then use the equity in their homes for any purpose they wish. It has become common to use it to pay for a college education for their children or to purchase cars and boats. Sadly, a great many people accumulate credit card debt and then use their equity loans to pay off their debt. People who accumulate high-interest debt are unlikely candidates for a serious real property investment program.

Rentals

People who have surplus funds often find that they can look at investing a modest sum in another house for rental purposes. Many a real estate empire has started that way. The rent collected allows the landlord or landlady to pay the mortgage and thus build equity in the second house. When the owner parlays this investment into several more, it often leads to exchanging ownership in several houses for ownership in an apartment complex or small office building. Thus, a real estate investment program can be grown into a significant real estate portfolio.

Leverage

If ownership is good and profitable, using leverage merely compounds the profit. Leverage is the most common way to use other people's money (OPM) to make more money on your own money. This is the best characteristic of investing in real property. It makes your return even better.

A simple example of leverage occurs when people use a mortgage to buy a home. If you buy a home for $100,000, using a conventional down payment of 20 percent, you need to borrow $80,000 to complete the purchase. Simplistically, if you sell the house for $120,000, you have made a gross profit of $20,000. However, the deal is better than it appears, as you have used the leverage of the borrowed $80,000 to increase the rate of return on your cash invested from 20 percent on the gross price of the house to a 100 percent rate of return on the $20,000 cash down payment.

A more realistic look at a typical home sale and the realistic impact of leverage is shown in Table 2-2.

Item	Purchase Price	Sales Price	Cash Yield	ROI
Home	$100,000	$120,000	$20,000	20% on price
Down Payment	$20,000		$20,000	100% on equity

TABLE 2-1. RATE OF RETURN ANALYSIS

Item	Cash Transaction	Leveraged
Purchasing the home	$100,000	$20,000
Debt	$0	$80,000
Interest for 2 years at 7% simple	$0	$11,200
Net sale price	$130,000	$130,000
Total cash invested	$100,000	$31,200
Gross profit	$30,000	$30,000
Net profit	$30,000	$18,800
Return on cash invested	30%	60%
Annual rate of return	15%	30%

TABLE 2-2. LEVERAGE AND THE SINGLE-FAMILY HOME

There you have it—the background, the reasons the market is what it is, and the cast of characters. By the end of this book, you will have a pretty good idea where you can fit into the picture and how you can profit by doing so. Let's start with housing.

CHAPTER

3

Real Property Characteristics

Every pursuit or discipline has its own particular language and methods of operation; real estate is no different. Real property, aka *real estate* or *realty*, involves the improvement, management, purchase, and sale of real property. There are many terms and actions involved in real property transactions that, while not unique to real estate, are routine in the daily control and manipulation of real estate assets.

Land Descriptions

Land is described in many ways, the most common of which for small properties is a *lot*. A lot is pictorially represented by a *plat*. An example of a plat can be seen in Figure 3-1.

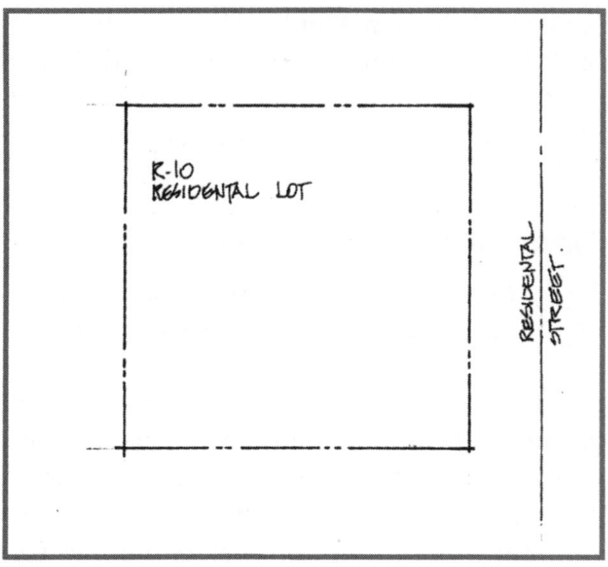

FIGURE 3-1. A TYPICAL PLAT

Lots are typically less than five acres in size. Larger size lots are called *parcels*. A square mile is composed of 640 acres, aka a *section;* when a section is broken down into parcels of 160 acres, each of the resulting four parcels is known as a *quarter section*.

There are several ways in which pieces of land are described, depending upon where you are in the country. In the eastern United States, settled long before we had a centralized government, early land descriptions were described using the physical characteristics of the terrain. An example of this might be "from the large rock adjacent to Main Street on the north side, 5 mi. south of the city limits, then north 800 ft. to the large elm tree, then 600 ft. west to the stream, south along the stream 700 ft., and then east to the point of beginning."

As cities and towns became more formalized and modern surveying techniques were created, land description became a more professional science. This can be seen, especially in the western part of the United States, settled after the advent of modern surveying techniques. In this area, the United States Geological Survey (USGS) set standards for land description based on large geographical sections of land. These divisions were called *sections, townships,* and *ranges* and all property was legally described within this unified system.

EXHIBIT 1

THE EASTERLY half of that portion of the Southeast quarter of Section 34, Township 1 North, Range 7 East of the Gila and Salt River Base and Meridian, Maricopa County, Arizona, described as follows:

BEGINNING at the Southeast corner of said Section 34;

THENCE North along the East boundary of said Section 34, a distance of 105 rods;

THENCE Westerly and parallel with the South boundary of said Section 34 to the center line of said Section 34;

THENCE South and parallel with said Easterly boundary of said Section 34, a distance of 105 rods to the South boundary of said section;

THENCE Easterly along the South boundary of said Section 34 to the point of beginning;

EXCEPT that portion conveyed to the City of Mesa, a municipal corporation, recorded in Instrument No. 91-0456905 and re-recorded in Instrument No. 92-0567093; and also

EXCEPT that portion condemned unto Maricopa County, a political subdivision, by Final Order of Condemnation entered in the Superior Court of the State of Arizona in and for the County of Maricopa, Case No. CV 91-25803, a certified copy of which was recorded in Instrument No. 93-0220881.

FIGURE 3-2. LEGAL DESCRIPTION

Metes and Bounds

Today there are basically two methods of identifying property. Large parcels of land are described by *metes* and *bounds*. These are similar to the old Eastern system, but use modern geometrical location points and compass headings based on the range and township principles. This system has recently been replaced by a system using Global Positioning System (GPS) information. In Figure 3-2 you'll find a typical example of a partial description.

The legal description in Figure 3-2 is very common and describes a parcel of land of approximately 20 acres. In addition to its legal description, each municipality assigns to each individual parcel a tax identification number, or parcel number (PN) for short.

Parcel Numbers (Tax) and Local Government Budgets

The purpose of these tax ID numbers, in addition to providing a legal description for a parcel of land, is to simplify the collection of real estate taxes for the local municipal and county governments. This enables a uniform basis for taxation and land identification. Once a large parcel of property has been broken up, aka *subdivided*, new parcel numbers are given to the newly created individual parcels of land. This enables the local government to identify and tax each individual parcel of land. This also simplifies identification of individual parcels for the purposes of buying and selling land. A typical tax parcel number is similar to a Social Security number. If you look at the tax bill in Figure 3-3, you will see not only how the government identifies each parcel but also how it prorates taxes on each parcel of land.

On this particular tax bill, you can see not only how the parcel is identified, but also the components of the taxes and how they are allocated to this particular parcel.

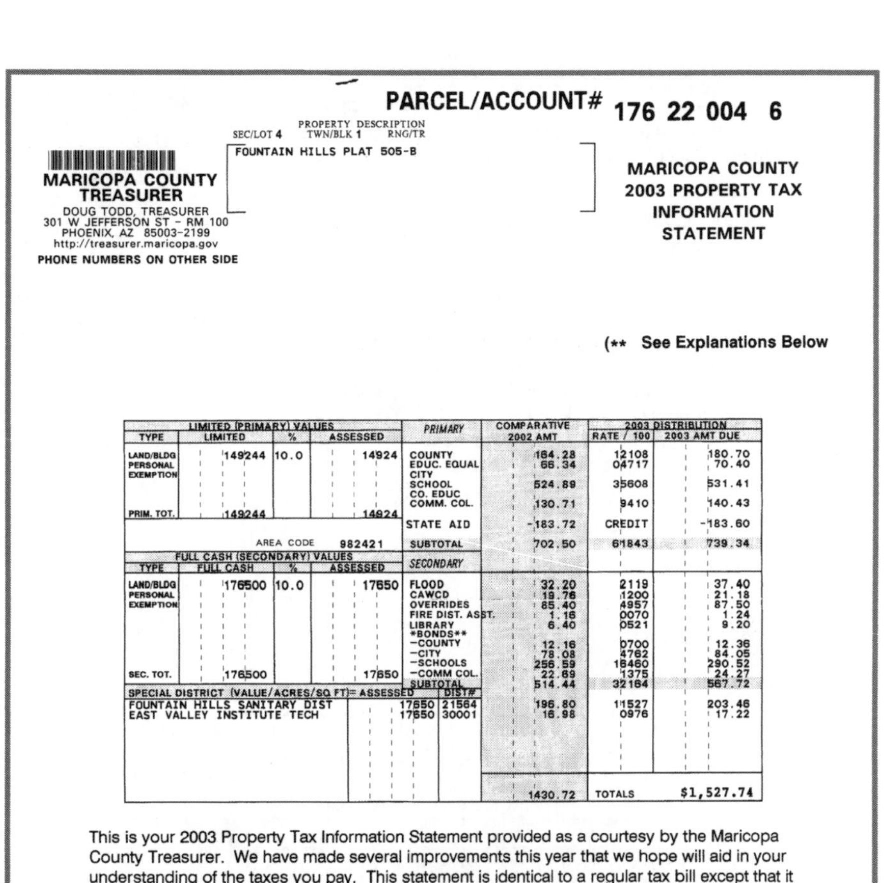

PARCEL/ACCOUNT# 176 22 004 6

PROPERTY DESCRIPTION
SEC/LOT 4 TWN/BLK 1 RNG/TR
FOUNTAIN HILLS PLAT 505-B

MARICOPA COUNTY TREASURER
DOUG TODD, TREASURER
301 W JEFFERSON ST - RM 100
PHOENIX, AZ 85003-2199
http://treasurer.maricopa.gov
PHONE NUMBERS ON OTHER SIDE

MARICOPA COUNTY
2003 PROPERTY TAX
INFORMATION
STATEMENT

(** See Explanations Below

LIMITED (PRIMARY) VALUES			
TYPE	LIMITED	%	ASSESSED
LAND/BLDG	149244	10.0	14924
PERSONAL			
EXEMPTION			
PRIM. TOT.	149244		14924
AREA CODE			982421
FULL CASH (SECONDARY) VALUES			
TYPE	FULL CASH	%	ASSESSED
LAND/BLDG	176500	10.0	17650
PERSONAL			
EXEMPTION			
SEC. TOT.	176500		17650

SPECIAL DISTRICT (VALUE/ACRES/SQ FT)= ASSESSED		DIST#
FOUNTAIN HILLS SANITARY DIST	17650	21564
EAST VALLEY INSTITUTE TECH	17650	30001

PRIMARY	COMPARATIVE 2002 AMT	2003 DISTRIBUTION RATE / 100	2003 AMT DUE
COUNTY	164.28	12108	180.70
EDUC. EQUAL	66.34	04717	70.40
CITY			
SCHOOL	524.89	35608	531.41
CO. EDUC			
COMM. COL.	130.71	9410	140.43
STATE AID	-183.72	CREDIT	-183.60
SUBTOTAL	702.50	61843	739.34
SECONDARY			
FLOOD	32.20	2119	37.40
CAWCD	19.76	1200	21.18
OVERRIDES	85.40	4957	87.50
FIRE DIST. ASST.	1.16	0070	1.24
LIBRARY	6.40	0521	9.20
*BONDS**			
-COUNTY	12.16	0700	12.36
-CITY	78.08	4762	84.05
-SCHOOLS	256.59	16460	290.52
-COMM COL.	22.69	1375	24.27
SUBTOTAL	514.44	32164	567.72
FOUNTAIN HILLS SANITARY DIST	196.80	11527	203.46
EAST VALLEY INSTITUTE TECH	16.98	0976	17.22
	1430.72	TOTALS	$1,527.74

This is your 2003 Property Tax Information Statement provided as a courtesy by the Maricopa County Treasurer. We have made several improvements this year that we hope will aid in your understanding of the taxes you pay. This statement is identical to a regular tax bill except that it does not include payment stubs. On the back of this statement is a list of phone numbers **for you to call** if you have questions about the tax levied by a particular jurisdiction.

IMPORTANT

** If you have refinanced or paid off your mortgage and are now responsible for property taxes on the above parcel, please submit either the full amount or half of the total tax indicated above by November 3, 2003 to avoid interest charges. For Property taxes of $100.00 or less the full year payment is due by November 3, 2003. If you pay half, we must receive the remaining half by May 3, 2004 to avoid interest charges. **No other notice will be mailed.**

** If you have a mortgage but are not sure if you should pay your taxes, please contact your lender before remitting payment.

** Please contact our STAR Call Center at (602) 506-8511 and let us know of any address changes.

** Include the parcel number or a copy of this statement with any correspondence to our office.

** **This is the only notice you will receive.** Arizona Revised Statutes mandate an assessment of simple interest at the rate of 16% per annum on any tax not paid by the delinquent date.

Correspondence address:
Maricopa County Treasurer
301 W. Jefferson St. - Rm. #100
Phoenix, AZ 85003-2199

Remittance address:
Maricopa County Treasurer
P O Box 78574
Phoenix, AZ 85062-8574

(OVER FOR IMPORTANT PHONE NUMBERS)

FIGURE 3-3. TYPICAL TAX BILL (CONTINUED ON NEXT PAGE)

If you have questions concerning your valuation, classification or payment of your taxes, please contact the STAR INFORMATION CENTER at (602)506-8511.

The following rates are per $100 of assessed value.

TAXING JURISDICTION NAME	TELEPHONE	PRIMARY TAX RATE	SECONDARY TAX RATE	(A) BONDS RATE	(B) BONDS RATE	OVERIDE RATE
GENERAL COUNTY FUND	(602)506-8511	1.2108		.0700		
EDUCATION EQUALIZATION	(602)506-8511	.4717				
CITY OF FOUNTAIN HILLS	(480)837-2003			.4762		
FOUNTAIN HILLS ELEMENTARY	(480)664-5000	3.5608		1.0847	.5613	.4957
MARICOPA COUNTY COMM COLLEGE	(480)731-8621	.9410		.1375		
FLOOD CONTROL OF MARICOPA CTY	(602)506-1501		.2119			
CENTRAL AZ WATER CONSV DIST	(623)869-2333		.1200			
VOL. FIRE DIST ASSISTANCE	(602)506-8511		.0070			
COUNTY LIBRARY	(602)506-8511		.0521			
FOUNTAIN HILLS SANITARY DIST	(480)837-9444		1.1527			
EAST VALLEY INSTITUTE TECH	(480)461-4173		.0976			

1. Check property description or situs location with your records to make certain you are paying on the correct parcel or account.
   The Treasurer's Office is not responsible for payment on the wrong parcel or account.
2. Checks do not pay taxes. Legal payment exists only when checks have cleared banks.
3. If your check does not clear upon deposit, taxes will be returned to an unpaid status without further notice and a $25.00 fee will be assessed.
4. The Treasurer's Office is not permitted to accept postdated checks.
5. Payment of taxes should be in United States Funds Only. Please enclose the appropriate payment coupon.
6. Valuations and property classifications are established by the County Assessor.
7. Arizona property taxes are levied on a calendar year basis (January 1 through December 31).
8. Recent changes in the law allow payment of the full year by December 31, 2003, without interest on the first half.

FIGURE 3-3. TYPICAL TAX BILL (CONTINUED)

Encumbrances

In addition to describing a piece of real property, there are other conditions imposed on individual pieces of property that will appear in the property's title report, or abstract, if you are in the eastern part of the country. These items are known, in general, as *encumbrances*, and can be liens, easements, or public encumbrances, such as assessments, rights of way, and utility easements. These can also be depicted graphically, such as shown in Figure 3-4, wherein a residential lot is depicted with easements and setbacks in the locations shown.

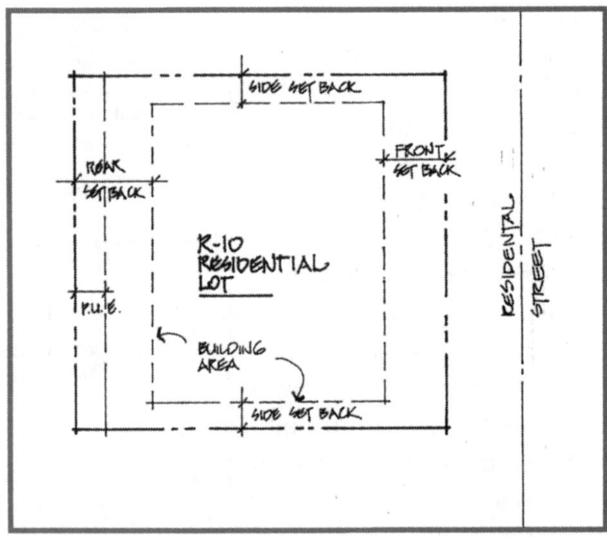

FIGURE 3-4. PLATTED LOT WITH EASEMENTS

You'll notice in the platted lot drawing in Figure 3-4 that there are both easements (public utility easement, PUE) and setbacks. Setbacks are government-imposed requirements.

In addition to the above, it is not uncommon to also have deed restrictions, zoning restrictions, and general subdivision requirements, such as covenants, conditions, and restrictions (CC&Rs).

DEED RESTRICTIONS

Deed restrictions are recorded conditions, put in place against a piece of property that can restrict or impose conditions on what may be built or housed on that particular piece of land. There may be, for instance, a restriction that you can only have one horse per acre and no farm animals. Or, there may be restrictions against the construction of two-story houses or houses smaller than 3000 square feet. The restrictions are enforceable and are voluntarily imposed on a piece of land by the owners. These restrictions are then passed along with the land to any successive owners.

ZONING RESTRICTIONS

Zoning restrictions are imposed by the city, town, or county and they are imposed on classes of property rather than specific parcels of land. They spell out, among other things, height restrictions, setbacks, and allowable lot coverage.

COVENANTS, CONDITIONS, AND RESTRICTIONS

Covenants, conditions, and restrictions (CC&Rs) are restrictions imposed upon a subdivision by the developer, to ensure uniformity during development and ownership. These generally spell out minimum house sizes, exterior finishes, parking restrictions, landscaping requirements, and restrictions for pets and other animals. They may, in some instances, also restrict your ability to rent the property to an unrelated third party.

Public Restrictions

Public restrictions on private property deal primarily with the issues of zoning and issues that deal with the *uniform building code* (UBC) as it is applied to each class of property.

These property classifications are relatively simple to understand. They separate real property into industrial, commercial, residential, and public or governmental property classifications. Within each classification, there are additional breakdowns, such as R-1, R-3, and R-143. These classifications simply outline the density of the dwelling units per acre or, in the case of commercial and industrial property, the total square footage per acre permitted in each zoning category.

THE LAW OF EMINENT DOMAIN

Another right that the public holds over private property is the right of *eminent domain*. This right allows that, for the public good, public agencies may take private property with compensation for use for public projects. In some instances, it may take private property, reclassify it, and resell it to private individuals for development. This is the case in urban redevelopment. Condemnation of property (the actual taking) is very common in areas where highways are being expanded and widened. The only control the individual property owner has over this particular process is that he or she may bring suit against the government or institute an appeal for a better price on the property taken.

GENERAL PLAN

Uniformly, in all areas of the country, property is broken down into property classifications governed by an overall master plan for that particular area known as a *general plan*. A general plan is not a fixed plan of development; rather, it is a work in progress that is periodically updated and frequently changed as the community expands. Individuals may effect changes in the general plan by making application to the local governing body, such as the town council, city council, or county board of supervisors. This is a relatively straightforward process and requires a submission of plans and the payment of fees. There may be additional studies required, such as traffic studies and, in the state of California, an *environmental impact statement* (EIS) or *environmental impact report* (EIR). This is a relatively straightforward process that will require input from the planning staff and hearings before the planning commission, city councils, or county boards of supervisors.

Within the general plan, property classifications are broken down into individual zoning areas.

ZONING

Zoning classifications are, as mentioned earlier, defined as industrial, commercial, residential, and public. Typical industrial zoning is I-1 or M-1. Typical commercial zoning varies: C-0, C-1, C-2, and C-3. The C classifications shown here stand for commercial office and commercial 1, 2, and 3. The differences in the C classifications are that C-0 provides only for the construction of office space, whereas C-1, C-2, and C-3 provide for both office and retail developments. The differences may lie in the individual uses permitted and restrictions on such design criteria as setbacks, building height, and drive-through facilities. Typical residential classifications are broken down by density. For example, one classification, designated as R-143, means that only one home per acre is permitted. R-3 and R-5 usually mean that 3,000 or 5,000 square feet of land is required per dwelling unit. Each area has different breakdowns. You should refer to your town's or county's zoning code to determine the specific residential classifications for your area.

SPECIFIC ZONING

The specific zoning classifications are covered in your town's manual and spell out at least the following criteria for development:

- Maximum building coverage
- Maximum building heights
- Maximum lot coverage
- Maximum stories
- Setback requirements
- Parking requirements
- Livestock restrictions
- Landscape restrictions
- Use restrictions
- Architectural standards
- Permitted building materials
- Slope ordinances

UNIFORM BUILDING CODE AND LOCAL BUILDING CODES

The uniform building code (UBC) is a national code that dictates minimum standards for a variety of construction types. It spells out minimum structural standards, finish standards, and safety standards. It is also linked to OSHA, the federal Occupational Safety and Health Administration. OSHA spells out working condition standards that must be maintained during the construction of anything. The UBC is supplemented by additional codes imposed by local municipalities. Local code enforcement takes precedence over the national code and the municipality always has the last word. It is its responsibility to interpret the code and enforce it as it sees fit. In times of dispute, the municipality almost always wins. After being in the business for almost 30 years, I am unaware of anybody successfully challenging a municipality in court over the interpretation of the building code.

PUBLIC UTILITY EASEMENTS

Public utility easements (PUEs) are self-explanatory. They are most often found along the front property line (the street side) of the individual pieces of real estate and they provide room for the construction of public utilities such as water, sewer, electricity, gas, and cable TV for the properties. Sometimes these easements will go along the side of the property line so that the utilities can access property in the rear of a particular piece of land. This situation is commonly found in subdivisions utilizing small lots or in areas of challenging terrain.

Private Restrictions

Private restrictions imposed on individual pieces of property are primarily deed restrictions. These can be *individual* deed restrictions imposed by the current owner or *general* deed restrictions, such as CC&Rs, imposed by the original developer of the property. A deed restriction can cover almost any restriction you might want to impose. They can be similar to those imposed under the zoning code. For instance, you might own several lots that are adjacent and wish to restrict construction on the lots on either side of your home so that no one can build a two-story home. This will ensure the privacy of your back yard and the uniformity of construction in your immediate area. Deed restrictions of this nature survive the transfer of real estate and cannot be lifted without the consent of the beneficiary parcel's owner.

EASEMENTS

You may also have easements imposed on property that deal with rights rather than restrictions. For instance, you might own a piece of property that is landlocked, with no direct frontage on a street. Since this lot would be illegal if it did not have access to a street, this lot would generally have an access easement across the parcel of land that lies between it and the street. This is called an *easement of access and egress*. Your parcel would have the *dominant* easement, because it benefits from the access and egress, and the parcel across which you have the access would have the *servient* easement.

MISCELLANEOUS ENTITLEMENTS

Two entitlements that can be placed on the land are *use permits* and *variances*. Both these entitlements are granted by the typical public hearing process.

A use permit is granted by a city, via the public hearing process outlined below, and permits a property owner to use his or her property for a use not specified under the property's zoning definitions. Examples of this are bed-and-breakfast businesses, day care facilities, and nursing homes. These entitlements expire when the property changes hands or the use is discontinued.

The other entitlement is a variance. A property owner may apply for a variance from the zoning restriction; if this variance is granted, it will be passed on in perpetuity with the land. A typical variance would be to modify a side yard setback to accommodate a roof overhang that would normally be an encroachment into the setback area. Typically, these variances require the written consent of the property owner whose rights will be encroached upon.

The Entitlement Process

All of the property rights inherent in any piece of property are known collectively and individually as *entitlements*. These rights are granted initially under the general plan and the specific zoning. These rights can also be acquired by the process of changing the master plan and/or changing the zoning for a specific parcel of land.

This process starts with an application and specific design drawings for your proposed changes. As mentioned above, it may also entail such studies as traffic, impact, and/or environmental impact. The application, usually accompanied by a sizable fee, is submitted to the planning staff. After extensive staff review and, more often than not, requests by staff for you to modify your designs, the application is then forwarded to the planning commission for review and recommendation. The recommendation of the planning commission then goes to the city council or county's board of supervisors to enact or reject. This is a relatively standard process and is common to most towns, cities, and counties in the United States.

Subdivisions

Large parcels of land are broken into smaller, more usable parcels by the process known as *subdivision*. This process takes place "in the public eye." That is to say that the public, most specially the adjacent landowners, will have a say in the process and input into the final product. The rationale behind this is to protect the public at large and the adjacent property owners, in particular, from a use or a design that may adversely affect the property values in the area. A subdivision can be as large as a master-planned community or as small as the creation of more than five lots from the original parcel. A master-planned community generally occurs where a large piece of farmland is broken into individual parcels covered by its own master plan, comprising parcels with many different specific zoning categories. Smaller parcels of land are broken into usable parcels—industrial, commercial, or residential—by the subdivision process.

The Process

The subdivision process is relatively standard, coast to coast, and is a two-stage process. In the first stage, the applicant is required to produce an engineered drawing showing the size and location of specific parcels of land, their intended use, and the public improvements required to produce these parcels, such as streets and/or utility extensions. There may be requirements, for instance, for the developer to set aside land for public uses such as schools, fire stations, and hospitals. In addition to these plans, there may be additional requirements for traffic reports and environmental impact studies.

These plans are then reviewed by the county or municipality staff; there are always negotiations related to the particulars included in the plans. Items such as public dedication, density, lot sizes, drainage, and grading are all reviewed and negotiated with the applicant. When this process is finished, the preliminary subdivision plat is referred to the planning commission for recommendation to the city council and/or the county board of supervisors. If the application is approved, the applicant is then directed to prepare the final plat for the parcel of land. The final plat will include all civil and mechanical engineering required for the onsite and offsite improvements and parcel descriptions. When this is prepared, it is resubmitted to staff, heard again by the planning commission, and finally approved or rejected by the city council or the county board of supervisors.

The Subdivision Report aka the Public Report

In addition to the local process of master planning and zoning, each county requires a subdivision report for residential housing. This is a public report that must be given to each potential buyer prior to sale of any individual lot within the subdivision. No lots can be offered for sale prior to the approval of the subdivision report.

Property Condition and Title Reports

During the buying and selling process, the legal condition of any individual piece of land is ascertained and presented to potential buyers and sellers alike by a process known as the *preliminary title report* in the western part of the country, and an *abstract of title* in the eastern part of the country. This report deals with the chain of ownership and any recorded and/or known restrictions and property rights pertaining to the individual parcel of land. In all cases, this is known as a *preliminary (prelim) title* or *abstract*.

The Prelim

The prelim or abstract deals with things like water rights, the restrictions, easements, mining rights, recorded leases, mineral rights, and anything else that may be recorded against the property by the individuals involved. It will also show any liens recorded against the property, such as *assessments*, mortgages, second mortgages, third mortgages, or judgments.

A typical title report is broken into three sections. Section one, or exhibit "A," is usually the legal description of the property. Exhibit "B" is generally the deed restrictions and liens recorded against the product. Exhibit "C" generally spells out the conditions needed to be satisfied to transfer *clean* (acceptable to the buyer) title to the prospective buyer. This section usually deals with paying off liens or removing deed restrictions to which the buyer objects. This is known as a *standard* title report or abstract, which is then converted, at the time of closing, into a standard insurance policy known as *standard title insurance*. In most instances, lenders and knowledgeable buyers require an extended form of title insurance known as an American Land Title Association (ALTA) policy or extended coverage policy.

> **DEFINITION**
>
> ***Assessments*** are financial liens recorded against a parcel of land to put the public on notice that the owner of that parcel of land is responsible for payment. They can be public, as when there are road improvements that are assessed against the property owners benefiting from the improvements, or they can be private, such as when a homeowners association levies assessments to pay for improvements to its members' common property.

ALTA Extended Coverage Title Insurance

This extended coverage policy ensures the buyer and the lender against adverse conditions not specifically recorded against the property. These conditions might include unrecorded leases, undisclosed hazardous conditions, encroachments, or potential suits for adverse possession.

Adverse possession is a legal term that denotes a potential right over a particular piece of property acquired by a third party by way of historical use and/or continuous and uninterrupted use over a specific period of time. This can occur if someone has been cutting across a piece of property for a long enough time to have acquired the permanent right to do so. Adverse possession may also occur when a fence has been placed inside a particular property line and the adjacent neighbor has been using the property outside the fence for an extended period of time. The adjacent property owner might have acquired legal title to the property through the legal principle of adverse possession by a right of continuous and uninterrupted use. Sometimes you'll notice in a large city such as New York the sidewalk in front of a building has been blocked off by barriers for a day or two. This is done to reinforce the individual building owners' rights to the sidewalk over the public's right to use the sidewalk. By interrupting the public's "continuous and uninterrupted" use of the sidewalk, the building owners prevent the possibility of adverse possession. This is especially crucial for areas of the building that may need to overhang the sidewalk in the future. A building's overhanging parts, such as roofs or awnings, cannot by law encroach on another's property. If the public acquired title to the sidewalk by adverse possession, then the overhangs could become illegal.

Lot Splits

Smaller parcels of land may be broken up into even smaller pieces by an administrative process known as the *lot split*. This is generally done by furnishing the local planning department with an engineered plot plan showing the two new parcels formed from the single existing parcel. In some areas, parcels exceeding five acres may also be split into five or fewer parcels by this process. The law governing this process will vary from municipality to municipality and state to state. All required engineering must be done in the same manner as the formal subdivision, but the applicant is spared the necessity of the public hearing process.

How Property Is Bought and Sold

What is the real estate market exactly? Simply put, it comprises every piece of real property in the country. It sounds rather intimidating, so how do we get a handle on it?

First of all, we need to think of the marketplace as broken down into manageable segments: East and West, North and South, state by state, city by city, town by town, down to specific neighborhoods. It is not necessary to have a specific grasp of the total picture; just a general overview will serve to make you a more informed participant.

The East is the old established area of the country, first settled and industrialized. The central part of the country, with the exception of Chicago, is the rural breadbasket of the country. The West is the frontier. Sounds simple, but it's not quite that simple. You need to understand the implications of these facts and what they mean to the marketplace. Over 50 percent of the country's population lives within a 500-mile radius of the city of Cincinnati, Ohio. That is a staggering fact—and that demographic has a dramatic impact on supply and demand for real estate within that circle.

Where to Live

The choice of where to buy a home is relatively simple. You should look where you want to live and work. Once that is settled, you need to examine the area for neighborhoods that meet your criteria for day-to-day living. Then there is your budget to consider. Finally, what you want to accomplish by purchasing a home. We will deal with this in more detail in the residential portion of this book. That sounds like a good place to start, doesn't it? It's not really the whole answer. Read on.

Where to Invest

This is yet another type of question, and the answer may well be at odds with where you are looking to buy a home. How can this be?

If you are living in an area that has little or no growth and declining demand, the odds are that this will not be a great place to invest your money, as the potential for profit will be limited by the lack of demand. Housing may be affordable, but prospects for appreciation and future profit may be quite dim. So how do you go about deciding where to make your play, not only in the housing market, but also when the time comes to make an investment separate from your own home? You need to look at the country's real estate markets and decide where you are the most comfortable living, working, and investing.

Real Property Transfers

Who are the players in the real property market? They include the following people:

- Buyers and sellers
- Real estate brokers
- Attorneys
- Title companies
- Construction companies
- Consultants
- Architects and engineers
- Managers
- City planning departments
- Public utility companies

The Professionals

The professionals listed above make their living in and around the creation, transfer, and ownership of real property. Some have highly specialized and responsible tasks within this business matrix.

County Recorders

County recorders' offices, coast to coast, record every transfer of property within their individual jurisdictions. In addition, your local recorder's office also records any new liens and deed restrictions placed on any individual piece of property within its jurisdiction. These documents are generally prepared by attorneys and/or title companies and are given to the recorder's office to record. The chain of title, assessments, easements, and deed restrictions comprise a property's history and legal entitlements as well as its financial encumbrances. There's usually a nominal fee (in my area it's $8.00) for recording a document. There are now standard preparation criteria for recordable documents. In the past there were so many documents recorded that are, today, almost illegible that most recorders' offices have now set standards for documents to be recordable. In my county, the document must be prepared on 8½-by-11-inch paper with minimum margins of one and one half inches, the typeface must be a minimum of 12 points in size, and the document must have a cover sheet for the recorder's information. This ensures that, after recordation, copies will always remain legible.

Real Estate Brokers

Real estate brokers are, in reality, companies composed of a managing broker who manages the company, salespeople who work under the broker's license, and a staff that prepares and processes the paperwork. Salespeople can be either licensed salespeople or other brokers doing business with and for the managing broker. They take commissions on each transaction that closes. Brokerage commissions, by law, are not standard: they are supposed to be negotiable. However, if you ask anybody what real estate commissions are in a certain area, you will be quoted a specific percentage that all brokerage houses seem to adhere to. In reality, today, you can most likely negotiate a reduction from the prevailing rate. Your success in negotiating a reduction will most likely depend upon your giving up some of the services included by most brokerage companies in their standard sales package.

SALES

Most real estate sales are handled by two separate brokerage houses. This is not always true, inasmuch as brokerage houses can handle both the listing and the sale of any property. It is most common, however, that one company will list the property for sale and another company will bring a buyer to the transaction. This process is known as *co-brokerage* or *cooperation*. At closing, the two brokerage houses split the sales commission 50/50. In residential brokerage, the marketplace is generally composed of the regional or area multiple listing service (MLS). Activity within the *multiple listing service* is governed by rules and regulations that the members must follow. They cover such items as agency, commission splits, ethics, and duties and obligations of the agents involved in the MLS.

> **HEADS UP**
>
> The law of agency provides that any sales agent must disclose to a buyer or seller in writing who he or she is working for. In the instance where a sales agent wants to represent both sides of the transaction, he or she must get written permission from both buyer and seller.

Commercial properties, however, do not have an established multiple listing system. There are several making an attempt to provide this service, but most commercial brokerage houses seem to resist participating in a multiple listing service. Commercial property markets are considerably smaller than residential markets and in most areas and regions buyers and sellers are known to most commercial brokerage houses. In their minds there still are no advantages to a multiple listing service. Hopefully, this will change in the future, as it is demonstrated that an effective multiple listing service accelerates all real estate transactions.

LEASING

Another function of real estate brokers is the leasing of commercial properties. While some landlords put a sign on the property to attract tenants, most commercial properties are leased by commercial real estate brokers. An emerging trend in the commercial brokerage business is that all tenants, especially retail tenants, seem to prefer being represented by a specific broker in a certain geographical area. As a result, most landlords have to go through commercial brokers to get at the commercial tenants.

Lawyers

A big player in the commercial real estate market is the real estate attorney. Attorneys are, in my mind, a necessary evil. A property owner buying, selling, or managing a piece of property can best benefit from the use of an attorney by confining the attorney's activity to specific chores related to the legality of what is going on, rather than delegating negotiating rights to the attorney or allowing the attorney to make business decisions. An attorney is deemed an expert in the law and is not necessarily a competent businessperson. To entrust an attorney with negotiating rights or business decision rights is like handing your wallet to a stranger and hoping for the best!

CONTRACTS AND THE LAW

All enforceable rights related to real property are governed by contracts. Under United States contract law, specifically the statute of frauds, to be legal and enforceable, contracts need to meet certain tests:

- They must be of legal intent.
- They must involve competent parties.

- Consideration must pass between the parties.
- They must be in writing and fully executed.

While oral contracts, in general, are not enforceable in real property transactions, there are some minor exceptions, pertaining to leases, especially in residential properties. All major issues, to be enforceable, must be dealt with by contracts in writing.

RECORDING CONTRACTS

Written contracts regarding real property may be recorded against the property in question. Every part of the country has different requirements that must be met for recordation; you need to check with your attorney for the rules in your area. The effect of recording is twofold: first, it puts the public on notice that there is an agreement involving that specific parcel of land, and second, it clouds the title and makes transferring that parcel of land a problem for any third party.

Property Transfers

When a real estate property changes hands, the transfer is handled in one of two ways. In the East, it is handled by real estate attorneys who specialize in this practice. In the West, real property transfers are expedited by title companies. In the East, property contracts are drawn up by attorneys. In the West, purchase and sale contracts are done uniformly by real estate agents and/or title companies. Both systems seem to work quite well.

TITLE COMPANIES

When real estate changes hands, the buyer is furnished, at the seller's expense, with a standard form of title insurance. This is true primarily in the West. In the East, the attorney's abstract of title is underwritten by similar insurance companies. In either case, buyers are assured, via the vehicle of title insurance, that they can enjoy quiet title and use of the property they have purchased. United States title companies have also recently branched out and are doing business in Mexico. Americans who purchase property in Mexico can, in some instances, purchase United States title insurance. This has led to increased purchases of second homes in northern and western Mexico by United States citizens.

What Affects the Real Estate Market?

Before embarking on your quest for real estate investments of any kind, I recommend that you look at all potential choices available to you regarding where to invest and what to invest in. Today's real estate market is such that you can choose from available sites anywhere in the U.S. and overseas. Wherever you decide to invest, it is prudent that you know the marketplace in which your potential development will need to compete. The most obvious location to examine first is the geographical area you are most familiar with. If you live in a small town, chances are that you are part of a larger *standard metropolitan statistical area* (SMSA) or *metropolitan statistical area* (MSA).

Any MSA can be divided into quadrants that can be charted, as shown in Figure 3-5, almost uniformly throughout the United States. The NE quadrant usually contains the most expensive residential areas, the SE quadrant the medium-priced homes, and the NW quadrant the "starter" or "blue collar" homes. The SW quadrant is composed of the old core city area and/or the industrial area of the MSA. Why is this and why is it consistent throughout the country? The

DEFINITION

SMSA and ***MSA*** are acronyms for *standard metropolitan statistical area* or *metropolitan statistical area.* The terms are interchangeable.

A metropolitan area consists of a large population center and adjacent communities (usually counties) that have a high degree of economic and social interaction with that center. Metropolitan areas sometimes contain more than one central city and/or cross state lines.

simple answer is that wealthy people do not drive to and from work with the sun glaring in their faces through the windshield. This rule seems to hold true all across America unless there is some natural or historic barrier such as a mountain, ocean, or river to prevent it. Obviously, there are exceptions and your community may be one of them. The important thing is that if you intend to invest your hard-earned cash in any community, you had better know what is where, and how, and why the area is prospering, stagnating, or declining.

If you live in a rural farming community, there will be little or no opportunity for investment and you will have to compete with the established local movers and shakers for what limited opportunities there are. You are better off searching in areas of growth and consistent demand. The best examples of this type of area are found in the Sun Belt states, as they are the ones experiencing consistent, annual, net in-migration. It is the demand stimulated by a steadily increasing population that creates the most reliable and consistent demand.

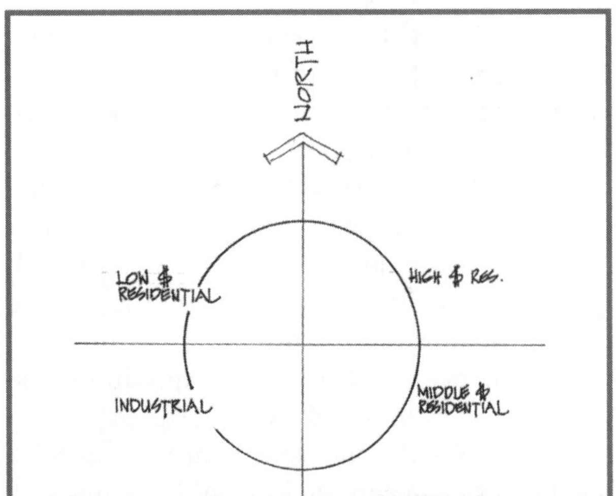

FIGURE 3-5. THE CITY QUADRANT MAP

HEADS UP

Supply and demand govern the price and availability of every commodity in every market.

Some specific areas of additional opportunity lie in states that experience high rates of population turnover. Transient areas, such as Arizona, Nevada, and Florida, breed demand for diverse real estate products that cater to this facet of the population demographic. An example of this would be a higher-than-average demand for rental housing.

The Market

Now that you know what to look for, it is time to examine the market in more detail. You need to understand the implications of existing and future transportation corridors, where new residential growth is heading and the annual absorption of new homes, and the sizes of the office, industrial, and retail markets and their respective absorption rates. Armed with these facts, you can then place any potential real estate investment, including your prospective new home, into its proper context within the target marketplace. These observations will also give you a pretty good idea of the employment market and the overall prospect for earning a living in your chosen area.

Economic Cycles

Another factor that affects real property and its market is the national economy's cycles of growth, stagnation, and recession. Since the early 1990s, the United States economy has achieved a new pattern of growth that has perhaps put our old cycles to bed for good. The effect of the Reagan and Bush presidencies and the supply-side economics of that era caused a sustained prosperity and economic boom that lasted over ten years, putting to bed the traditional three-year cycle theory. In the past, our economy had grown and retreated in three-year cycles. Smart money purchased land and buildings during the down cycles and sold at the top of the growth curve or built new properties into an improving market. This is still good practice, but our traditional cyclical pattern may have changed forever. Real estate markets have gone from scarce to overbuilt in a fairly predictable pattern.

The Economy in the New Millennium

What, then, is this new economy like? I doubt that anyone knows for sure, except perhaps God or Alan Greenspan. The latter and the Federal Reserve Board are attempting to control growth and prices to keep inflation under control and the economy rolling along in a steady and organized manner. The early 2000s seem to be stronger than anyone expected and there is no apparent end in sight. The stock market, however, does not seem capable of any sustained direction, advancing and retreating around the 10,000 mark. Periodic problems come from political instability and regional conflicts, most strongly felt in the area of energy and international trade. My take on the situation is somewhat in line with Alvin Toffler's view that we have put behind us the Industrial Age and have gone roaring into the Information Age. Our government is always a step behind, as usual, attempting to apply Industrial Age solutions to an Information Age situation. Periodic regional conflict and worldwide terrorism seem to be here to stay for the foreseeable future.

My Crystal Ball

Anyone who is an observer is entitled to an opinion about what the future holds. Therefore, let me say that I believe, as far as the United States is concerned:

- Sustained population growth is here to stay, fueled by natural population increase and immigration.
- Immigration to the U.S. will flourish as the U.S. continues to dominate this new technological era.
- The U.S. will become the focal point of innovation and growth for the near future.
- Third-World countries will take over the manufacturing of almost all consumer goods and their standard of living will escalate rapidly, providing an ever-increasing market for U.S. high-tech goods and services.
- The U.S. will become a better place to live, with an international presence beyond your greatest expectations.
- Our sunshine states will continue to evolve into meccas of living and recreation for the world's moneyed elite.

Global Impacts

What effect will the rest of the world have on our economy? My prognostication continues. When China, Africa, Asia, and the rest of the Third World start their inevitable growth spiral, the U.S. will accelerate the wholesale importing of educated people from all over the world to fill the insatiable demand for technologically educated people. This will spawn opportunities for new styles of living to accommodate these people's traditional ways of life. Areas such as Chinatown or Little Saigon in California will continue to proliferate all over the country, creating new opportunities for investment and growth. There are areas of ethnic concentration springing up throughout the country as people import their cultures and lifestyles along with their skills. There will be new patterns of commerce, living, recreation, and, therefore, completely new types of real property developments. It is exciting—and people with vision and entrepreneurial spirit should do quite well participating in this changing financial environment.

What Does This Mean to You?

This is not a light question. What you do for a living, how you invest, where you live: all are very pivotal facets of your economic lifetime. Experts agree that the average person born today will have three to four careers in a lifetime, necessitating retraining and education for each new venture. Increased savings and astute investment will become an economic necessity for all those who aspire to economic independence. You can no longer start out without a plan and hope for the best or you might find yourself washed up and out of work at 30. The one constant in our life is change; if you act and plan with that as a given, then you will have the required mind-set for the future.

Examine your investment pattern as part of your career and you should be able to make some clear, easily defined, and flexible plans for your future. Real property, from housing to investment-grade real estate, should be an important part of your financial plan.

CHAPTER

4

Investment Variety *and* Brokerage

There are an infinite variety of real estate investments available to you. The easiest way to make sense of this is to break them down into manageable segments. The two major categories are housing and commercial; within each of these there are various potential investment properties. While examining the individual potential investments, I'd also like to cover how the real estate brokerage industry deals with each real estate product.

The common thread that runs through all real estate products is obviously the land. While land is the major component of residential as well as commercial, I have placed the treatment of the investment land itself in the commercial category. This is fairly arbitrary on my part, but I would like you to think of land as separate, apart from housing and commercial investment projects.

The Housing Market

The housing market is defined not only by the type of housing but also by its location. Housing is located almost anywhere in our country and, depending upon its location, it may represent a range of investment opportunities.

Single-Family Residences

The single most popular form of housing in the United States is the detached single-family residence. This type of housing is found in the country (rural), the suburbs, and all major cities in the United States.

The most common detached single-family residence is typified by a three-bedroom, two-bath, two-car garage home on a quarter-acre lot. Since World War II this has been the most popular new or used home in the country. In recent years, since the mid-1990s, the most popular new home has been a variation on this house. The new home is a four-bedroom, two-and-a-half- or three-bath, three-car garage, on lots ranging in size from seven to 10,000 square feet. This type of house would probably be described as the most conservative investment in housing. It is the most popular, the most commonly constructed, and the easiest to resell. It is readily found in all three potential locations and its architectural variety is primarily dictated by the region in which you find it.

Rural Settings

In rural settings the detached single-family home is most often found on large lots. By "large" lots, I mean lots that are a minimum of one half acre. This rural home can be found on lots of multiple acres, as many as are contained in the average family farm. The additional land that comes with rural housing presents an investment opportunity separate from the value of the house itself. As populations expand into the country, areas that were traditionally rural are now being absorbed into suburbia. When this occurs, not only does the rural detached single-family home go up in value, but the excess land becomes a potentially separate investment. In many cases it is possible to subdivide the excess land, whether it's several acres or 600 acres, to provide for additional new housing. We will cover this in some detail in the section of the book that deals with land subdivision.

Suburbia

Suburban housing has traditionally been predominantly detached single-family houses. However, today, we're seeing more multifamily attached dwellings appearing in suburban settings. The typical suburban subdivision in the past has been characterized by the very popular quarter-acre lot. In more recent years, as both land and housing costs escalate, developers have been creating new subdivisions with lots as small as 6,000 square feet for detached single-family homes. This virtually eliminates any potential for land subdivision as part of the single-family home investment.

In some areas, where older, established neighborhoods are being taken over and redeveloped, it is possible to find large lots that can be divided into smaller lots. When this occurs, the investment potential lies in the land rather than the house itself. To create a new subdivision with smaller lots, it is almost always necessary to demolish the older homes. This can potentially be a profitable venture; however, you must be aware that for this to be effective, you must assemble enough lots to make the subdivision a viable entity.

Urban Areas

The urban version of the detached single family home is becoming increasingly rare. It is seldom found in hard-core inner-city areas; it's more generally in the less dense transition zones between the inner-city core and the surrounding suburbs. The single-family homes in urban areas are most likely destined for teardown and redevelopment. In smaller cities it is most likely that these neighborhoods will survive, participating in the cycle of deterioration and rebirth that is characterizing the modern cities today. For you to make an astute investment in this type of property, you should be very sure in which direction your city is going. While the trend today seems to be revitalizing old urban cores, there are and will remain exceptions to this general rule. One thing is certain, that as the cost of gasoline rises American cities will start to resemble their European cousins: more and more people will become interested in living within a revitalized urban core or in areas that are accessible to mass transit.

This type of transition offers opportunities to those people who can see the trend coming or have no fear in attempting to establish a trend on their own. One way to monitor this potential situation is to pay close attention to the transportation plans under way in your urban area. While these types of developments take many years to complete, you can see the potential results far in advance of the actual construction of the new transportation facilities. In our business we call this being ahead of the curve.

Patio Homes

The next step up the ladder from the detached single-family home is the patio home. The patio home is a detached single-family home, with one wall of the structure constructed at or on the lot line. Figure 4-1 shows a series of single-family dwellings constructed as a neighborhood, utilizing the "zero lot line" development technique.

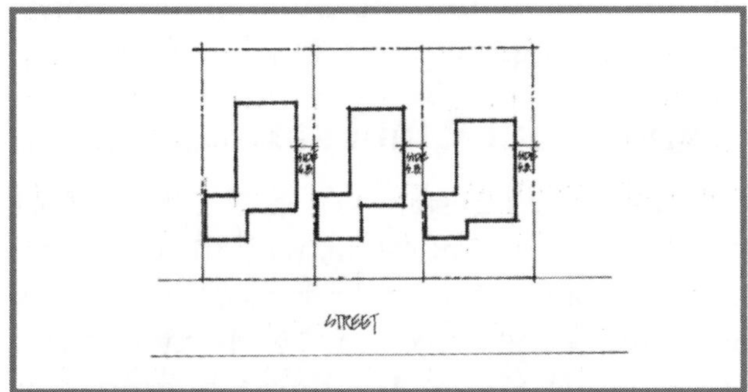

FIGURE 4-1. ZERO-LOT-LINE PLOT PLAN

This requires a variation in the standard single-family zoning. It is commonly found in areas of multifamily construction. This type of housing has all the benefits of the detached single-family home and some of the best benefits of condominium housing. Typically, in a patio home development, the exterior building and front yards are maintained by the homeowners association. This is not always the case, but in most instances, this is the great appeal of this type of housing. It is becoming increasingly popular with people as they approach retirement age. The allure of decreased maintenance and communal living has a great appeal to retirees and people who would like to travel. In my neck of the woods, this type of housing is commanding a $30-$50-per-square-foot premium over the single-family home. While there is no particular size constraint on this type of dwelling, they seem to fall in the 1,400-to-2,000-square-foot size range. The densities for this type of development seem to be in the range of six to eight per acre.

Multifamily Housing

Various housing types fall into the multifamily housing category. They include the following:

- Apartments
- Condominiums
- Townhouses
- Co-ops

Each of these types of housing has a separate and distinct form of ownership. Most people assume that the shape or size of the dwelling determines the category that it is in, but this is not the case.

Apartments

Apartment buildings are characterized by multiple dwellings within a single building. They can be as small as a fourplex and as large as an urban high-rise. The overriding characteristic of an apartment complex is that all units are under a single ownership and the people who live there are tenants rather than owners. In some cases, apartment complexes are designed and built as condominium units with a view to converting them to condominium-type ownership at a later date. The primary difference between an apartment building and a condominium building is individually metered utilities and garage parking. The ability to separately meter utilities is absolutely necessary for a condominium project. On the other hand, garage parking, while extremely preferable to open parking or carports, is not necessarily always found in condominium projects. Savvy investors are always on the lookout for apartment complexes that can be potentially converted to condominium units. The difference in value between an apartment and a condominium unit is usually a minimum of 100 percent. This potential increase in value is what makes condominium conversion a potentially lucrative business.

Condominiums and Town Houses

A condominium is a dwelling that has elements of shared ownership with other dwelling units. The most common form of condominium is known as an *air rights subdivision*. In this form of subdivision the land is separated from the housing itself. This is a dramatic exception to the rule that ownership of land includes ownership of all things permanently attached to the land. By recording an air rights subdivision, the developer is able to separate ownership of the land from ownership of the buildings. The buildings are then described by what is known as a *horizontal regime*. In this manner, the homeowners association retains ownership of the land and individual homeowners are able to take title to their specific dwelling units. In this form of home ownership, there is always a common area maintenance fee. This fee provides for, in general, the maintenance of all building exteriors, landscaping, streets, and common recreational facilities.

Condominiums may be found in many shapes and sizes. They may be single-story, two-story, three-story, or any combination thereof. The town house is probably the most ubiquitous example of the condominium. It is a two-story attached dwelling. Single-floor dwellings in multiple-story buildings are referred to as *flats* and are legally defined as condominiums or co-ops.

Co-ops

An urban variation on the condominium is the co-op. In this scenario, the co-op association owns the land and building and the individual owners own literally "from the wallpaper in." The other aspect of this type of housing is that the individual residents have control over who lives there. The co-op association must vote to admit residents to the building. This type of housing is found exclusively in major urban areas such as New York and Chicago. Costs associated with this form of housing reflect its location and its cachet of exclusivity and therefore tend to be very high. As an investment, it may be limited in its potential by the restrictions on selling.

Commercial Real Estate

Commercial real estate is separate and apart from residential real estate, with the exception that development of land for residential uses is generally considered to be a commercial endeavor. These are the broad categories of commercial real estate:

- Land
- Industrial
- Retail
- Office
- Specialty
- Mixed use
- Governmental

Land

Investment in large pieces of land has always been a long-term, conservative investment. While this is a general statement, it seems to hold true no matter where you are in the country. It is especially true in areas that experience consistent growth. Even in rural areas, agricultural land continues to appreciate in value. In semi-rural areas, land is always in demand as the suburbs expand into the farming areas. Land in and around natural recreation areas such as oceans, rivers, lakes, and mountains will always be in demand. Land in areas that are experiencing growth is in constant demand. Perhaps the most "no-brainer" investment type is raw land in the path of growth. It is simply a matter of time before this type of investment pays off handsomely. Residential land investment comes in many forms, including the following:

- Speculation
- Subdivision
- Lot splits
- Mobile home parks

Each of these types of investments is unique and potentially profitable.

Speculation

Speculation in raw land comes in several varieties. There is a form of speculation that entails simply buying or optioning a piece of land and holding onto it for a period of time. The first variation on this theme is the purchase of a parcel of land and entitlement of the land for specific development; this is known as a *rollover* deal. The second variation is *flipping*; this involves purchasing an option on a piece of land and reselling it before you have to buy it. Each form of investment is profitable in its own way. If we take the same piece of land and look at it in four ways, you will be able to see the variety of rates of return, depending upon your approach.

Let's assume that we're going to take a 640-acre (section) tract of land and handle it four ways. For the purpose of this chapter, we will use the following assumptions:

- Land size is 640 acres.
- The time period will be 24 months.
- We will ignore taxes.
- The purchase price for the land is $5,000 per acre.

In our first scenario, we will purchase the land for cash, hold it for two years, and resell it for $10,000 cash per acre. The economics are shown in Table 4-1.

If we look at the previous transaction as a leveraged deal, we see by Table 4-2 that our rate of return can be dramatically increased. Let's assume that we put down 25 percent of the purchase price in cash and the seller carried

Item	Unit Price	Purchase/ Sale Price	Carry Cost/ Sales Cost	Totals
640 Acres	$5,000	$3,200,000	$0	$3,200,000
Land Sale	$10,000	$6,400,000	($384,000) Commission	$6,016,000
Profit	$5,000		Net Profit: $2,816,000	
ROI		$3,200,000	88% or 44% per year	

TABLE 4-1. LAND SPECULATION

Item	Unit Price	Purchase/ Sale Price	Carry Cost/ Sales Cost	Totals
640 Acres	$5,000	$800,000	$480,000	$1,280,000
Land Sale	$10,000	$6,400,000	($384,000) Commission	$6,016,000
Profit	$5,000		Net Profit: $2,816,000	
ROI		$1,280,000	220% or 110% per year	

TABLE 4-2. LEVERAGED SPECULATION

the difference ($2,400,000) at 10 percent interest for two years.

As you can see from Table 4-2, the total profit is reduced by $480,000 of interest payments. At the same time, the investment was reduced from $3,200,000 to $1,280,000. This change in investment resulted in less profit, but increased the rate of return on our reduced investment to 220 percent, or 110 percent per year. This is what leverage can do for you.

In the next scenario, we take the same piece of land and process it through the local government as a housing subdivision. Since I'd like to keep this example realistic, we're going to assume that the developer/investor is going to use the same leverage as in the scenario in Table 4-2. Taking a look at the Table 4-3, we see one significant change: the land that we are selling is now entitled as a residential subdivision and can be sold for $20,000 per acre. This changes the entire picture on the rate of return.

If we look at the same transaction as a flip and include the use of entitlements to enhance the value, we see an even more profitable transaction. For the sake of this example, we will assume that the cost of our option on the property for a two-year period is $500,000.

As you can see in Table 4-4, there are some potentially spectacular returns with land speculation. What you need to do before jumping off the cliff and starting to do flips left and right is examine the downside. When you purchase land for all cash, the only downside is that you might not make as much money and the land may take more time to sell. When you leverage the speculation, the risk is that you do not have the rest of the land purchase money at the end of the two-year period if the land is not sold. You could, therefore, lose your entire investment. This is uniformly true of leveraged investments, in general. The rates of return are

Item	Cash	Other Costs	Sales Price	Commission
640 Acres	$800,000			
Engineering		$250,000		
Permits/fees		$25,000		
Interest		$480,000		
Commissions			$12,800,000	$768,000
Total costs	$3,200,000	$755,000		$768,000
Cash invested	$800,000	$755,000	Total cash invested $1,555,000	
Gross profit			$12,032,000	
Less costs			($4,723,000)	
Net profit/ ROI			$7,309,000	470% or 235% per year

TABLE 4-3. LEVERAGED ROLLOVER

Item	Cash	Other Costs	Sales Price	Commission
640 Acres	$500,000			
Engineering		$250,000		
Permits/fees		$25,000		
Interest		$480,000		
Sales commission			$12,800,000	$768,000
Gross profit	$12,032,000			
Total costs	$500,000	$275,000	Total investment $775,000	
Total profit	$8,057,000			
ROI on cash		1039% or 51.9% per year		

TABLE 4-4. FLIP

much greater, but so is the downside. If you are fortunate enough to have the money to pay cash for the land, you can then choose to leverage your purchase, knowing that you have the ability to make the payment in the event that the land does not sell within your chosen timeframe. The flip is universally considered, by most real estate professionals, to be both the riskiest and potentially the most profitable transaction in real estate investment.

SUBDIVISIONS

Subdividing land is the most common way to make money on land without speculation. In this sense, subdividing land is also a speculation: you are speculating that there will be people or builders who wish to buy individual building lots rather than a large piece of unimproved land. This is less risky than speculation and it takes more time and more cash. If you look at Table 4-3, the leveraged rollover, you'll see that we thought that the land price, when the 640 acres are sold intact, would be $20,000 per acre. If we, in fact, subdivide the land into four building lots per acre in a normal market, these lots fully improved would sell for approximately $40,000 per lot. This would be a yield of $160,000 per acre. In addition to the entitlement costs shown in Table 4-3, we would have improvement costs of approximately $15,000 per lot. For practice, do a short table showing the impact of selling finished lots.

> **DEFINITION**
>
> ***Improved***, in this case, would mean having streets and utilities to each and every lot within the subdivision.

LOT SPLITS

A much smaller proposition in investing in land would be taking smaller pieces of property, between five and 40 acres, and splitting them into five parcels or fewer. In many parts of the country, this is a simpler and less costly proposition than doing a full subdivision.

In most places you will need to do the engineering at the same level of detail as for a subdivision, but you are generally spared the public hearing process. Once the engineering is improved, you may put in the site improvements and sell the lots. In most jurisdictions, you are allowed to break a parcel of any size into five or less legal building lots. Obviously, if the legal building lot in your area is one acre per dwelling unit, you must have at least five acres to start with. If you start with 40 acres, you may still create only five lots. In all cases, the minimum size of a lot will depend on the zoning that governs your specific parcel of land.

> **HEADS UP**
>
> If you split a 40-acre parcel into one 20-acre parcel and four 5-acre parcels, the new buyers can, in turn, re-split the lots. You, as the original seller, are legally restrained from doing so. This law is intended to stop people from circumventing the subdivision laws.

MOBILE HOME PARKS

Another way to invest in land is to create a mobile home park from a parcel of raw land. This process is the same as a subdivision, with the addition of some common area amenities for the park. Most mobile home parks lease the lots to renters for their mobile home units. In some cases these lots are sold as individual parcels for the mobile homes. This process is virtually identical to that used to create single-family lots for home construction. The main difference is in the density, as mobile home parks can accommodate 8 to 12 units per acre. The yield on this type of an investment would be roughly equivalent to that from a normal single-family subdivision. The land for mobile home parks generally sells for less as raw land and each lot sells for less than a single-family home lot.

Industrial

When dealing with commercial land, the lowest economic use for a parcel of land would be industrial. Within the industrial category, land is classified as heavy, light, or business park.

HEAVY INDUSTRY

Heavy industrial land is land that is primarily dedicated to "dirty" industry, such as manufacturing or shipping or both. This type of land will be found in areas in any municipality that would be classified as the least desirable. If you refer back to our quadrant map, Figure 3-5 in Chapter 3, you'll remember that these areas are generally located in the southwest quadrant of most cities. Most of these areas are served by railroads, major freeways, and sometimes port facilities. Due to the nature of this type of "dirty" use, there are limited opportunities to invest in this type of land unless there is turnover or obsolescence occurring within the area's industrial base. These areas that have, through natural commercial attrition, been made available for investment are in what is known as the Rust Belt. The Rust Belt is primarily in the Eastern and Midwestern cities from which heavy industry has moved to the South or overseas. This has created both blight and opportunity in these cities. Most municipalities who have experienced this phenomenon have tried desperately to find or create other uses for this newly vacated land. It is the nature of the past heavy industrial uses of these pieces of property that has caused problems in recycling these properties, as many of these sites are severely polluted with hazardous materials and industrial waste. In many instances, the municipalities lack the resources to return these pieces of property to the original, environmentally sound condition. Investment in these Rust Belt areas remains a risky proposition.

LIGHT INDUSTRIAL USES

Light industrial areas are those areas that are designated for use by companies with the so-called clean businesses, with "clean" defined as nonpolluting and low impact. Most of the high-tech businesses would fall into this category. None of the old factories such as steel, coal, and power generation would be able to utilize land zoned for light industry. Warehousing, specifically public warehousing, can be put into a light industrial area because it does not involve any manufacturing processes. Warehousing, in general, requires limited use of rail and perhaps port facilities.

BUSINESS PARKS

An offshoot of light industrial uses can be seen in the modern business park, where light industrial uses are combined with suburban style office buildings in nicely landscaped park-like subdivisions. Typical types of buildings found in this environment are pure warehouse, light manufacturing, combination office/warehouse, and pure office buildings. In most cities you'll also find some limited retail uses, such as banking and restaurants as support facilities for the indigenous population. This type of development came into being in the early 1970s on the West Coast and spread rapidly throughout the entire country. Today this is an accepted form of development and considered very desirable by the municipalities where they are located.

Retail

Another major type of commercial development is retail development, comprising the following types of developments:

- Strip centers
- Neighborhood centers
- Community centers
- Power centers
- Regional shopping malls
- Super-regional centers

As a general description, retail centers are areas that provide housing for businesses selling goods and services to the local population. Most retail centers are *anchored* by a store that is either a national or a regional *credit tenant*. The stores provide two things to the center. First, they help the developer with the credit portion of the deal, making it easier to provide financing for the center. Second, they provide a built-in draw based on their national or regional reputation, which can feed the smaller, more local tenants.

STRIP CENTERS

Strip centers are generally small, three acres or less, and are usually not anchored. These centers are typically found on busy highways and are designed to cater to people headed to and from work. The tenants specialize in convenience items, such as fast food, dry cleaners, cafes, and video rental. They are generally less expensive to build than other centers and sell for a lower price per square foot due to the lack of credit tenants. Properly done, this type of center can be a great little investment.

NEIGHBORHOOD CENTERS

Neighborhood shopping centers are historically anchored by grocery stores, drugstores, and banks. In addition to the anchor tenants, there are usually a number of "mom-and-pop" local tenants providing a variety of goods and services. This type of center is probably the most common shopping center in the United States and can be found in communities with populations of 8,000 to 20,000 people or more. In areas of greater population, you can even find two or more on the same intersection.

COMMUNITY CENTERS

A community shopping center is an overgrown neighborhood center with either a discount store or a junior department store added to the tenant mix.

This type of center seems to be replacing the traditional neighborhood center coast to coast. Retailing has always been an ever-changing industry, marked by the change in direction

DEFINITION

A ***junior department store*** is a store similar to Mervyn's or a small Sears or J.C. Penney store. A *discount store*, aka a *box store*, is a retailer that specializes in selling discounted merchandise in a warehouse-type setting. Examples of this would be Costco, PETsMART, OfficeMax, or Ross Dress For Less.

taken, almost every decade, by every type of store under the sun. Stores are either designing larger or smaller prototypes, or adding and/or subtracting merchandise categories on an annual basis. Every retailer seems to be looking for the magic formula to attract buyers. The abandoned box store is becoming a reality in almost all parts of the country. Community centers, however, seem to be very popular with the shopping public, and I would prognosticate that they will become more common and larger in size and numbers of tenants.

Power Centers

The recent addition to the mix is the power center, populated by rows of discount, warehouse-type retailers. They are everywhere, even in the super-regional developments. As retailers shuffle for market share, these boxes are abandoned and re-tenanted on a regular basis. In fact, these discount centers account for a major portion of our retail sales.

Regional Shopping Malls

The "Big Daddy" of retail is the regional shopping mall, anchored by four or more major department stores and populated by stores from every national retail chain in the country. There are generally multiple stores in every type of merchandise category. The newest wrinkle in regional shopping mall development is the addition of extensive recreational facilities, including ice rinks, tennis courts, jogging tracks, casinos, and hotels. This particular type of development and/or investment is for only the very wealthy. It is truly big business.

Super-Regional Centers

The super-regional center is not really a shopping center at all, but a larger land area (hundreds of acres) generally enclosed by a loop road, the center point of which is the regional shopping center. Surrounding the regional mall you'll find a proliferation of discount stores and entertainment complexes. This is truly a mega-development, costing hundreds of millions of dollars. A project of this nature can take up to 20 years from start to finish. Once the regional shopping center is in place, the surrounding land becomes indecently valuable and, therefore, hugely profitable.

Office Buildings

Office developments, too, come in a variety of shapes and sizes, from the single-user building to high-rise (class "A") buildings. Office development offers a variety of investment opportunities, from buying the land, doing a build-to-suit for an individual tenant, to designing and building a multitenant high-rise structure.

Single-User Buildings

The single-user building is all around you, from the supermarket to the local bank to the automobile dealership. These buildings are single-tenant buildings and, at the same time, single-use buildings. Single-use buildings are defined as buildings for which it is impossible or prohibitively expensive to change the uses. These buildings have their pluses and minuses for investors. If you're lucky enough to have the bank as a single tenant, you have two things going for you: one, a financial institution with stable credit, and two, a tenant that will be in business at that location for an extended time. Both of these attributes would make this building a dynamic investment. If, on the other hand, you have invested in a used-car dealership, you might have neither a good credit tenant nor a tenant with long-term operational capability. This situation would make this type of investment a dubious one.

SUBURBAN VS. URBAN LOCATIONS

In a rural setting there is little or no demand whatsoever for office space, so office buildings are confined to suburban or urban areas. Within these settings the buildings fall into three categories: low-rise, mid-rise, and high-rise. Other than singletenant buildings, all office buildings are multitenant. In general, an investment in a multitenant building is a more conservative investment than one in a single-tenant building. The theory behind this is that of spreading the risk of loss of income from a single tenant over a larger number of tenants.

Like multifamily buildings, office buildings can be owned either individually or as condominiums by the tenants in the buildings. Any buildings, including those in excess of one-story, can be made into condominiums by the vehicle of the "air rights subdivision" and the "horizontal régime." By definition, low-rise buildings are one to three stories in height, mid-rise buildings are buildings up to seven stories high, and high-rise buildings are eight floors and above. The breakdown is arbitrary within the industry for low-rise and mid-rise buildings, but for high-rise buildings the definition becomes a function of the building code and the firefighting capability of the local fire department. The maximum height for firefighting capability for truck-mounted fire brigades is seven floors. Beyond that height, the firefighting ability must be built into the building itself.

The desirability for investment among low-rise, mid-rise, and high-rise is not as clear-cut as you might think. Obviously, the larger high-rise, class "A" building is a more expensive investment, but, due to the nature of the tenancy, it may be a less conservative and more speculative investment than a smaller suburban low- or mid-rise structure. We will be analyzing buildings for their desirability as investments later on in the book when we deal with purchasing investment-grade real estate.

Specialty Developments

Specialty developments include the following types of property:

- Recreational
- RV parks
- Mini-storage buildings
- Marinas
- Amusement parks
- Multiuse facilities

RECREATIONAL

Recreational properties come in all sizes and shapes. Their desirability as investments is directly proportional to the amount of experience you have in that type of recreational industry. Recreational property includes such uses as bowling alleys, trap and skeet fields, ballparks, ski areas, amusement parks, ice-skating rinks, and movie theaters. I have absolutely no experience with this type of property and I recommend you leave it to people with a great deal of experience in these individual fields.

RV PARKS

RV parks are much like motels or short-term rental apartment complexes. They cater to a clientele that is temporary and transient, merely passing through. Operating an RV park is about the same as operating the average motel, with the exception that building maintenance is considerably lower and traffic hazards are considerably greater.

MINI-STORAGE BUILDINGS

Much the same can be said of mini-storage facilities and marinas. Neither investment can be pre-leased and is therefore hard to finance at the time of construction or purchase. Management and operating characteristics are roughly similar to apartments, RV storage facilities, and recreational parks. I would recommend you be careful when you become involved in this type of facility, as you will need the individual industry's expertise to be able to cope with the management of this type of investment.

Buying, Selling, and Managing Real Property

Real property is purchased, sold, traded, and managed by real estate professionals known as *real estate brokers*. Each principal involved in this type of action must be a licensed broker in the state where the real estate is located. A broker may employ sub-agents known as real estate salespeople or brokers doing business "with-and-for" the licensed broker. All properties listed for sale are evidenced by a *listing agreement*. These *listings* are owned by the broker; while they may be executed on behalf of the broker by the salespeople, they are not transferable or cancelable without the consent of the listing broker.

Residential and commercial properties are traded in different ways. Residential properties are usually placed in a multiple-listing system available to all residential real estate brokers working within a given area. Commercial listings are most often worked exclusively by the listing broker's company, occasionally co-brokered with other commercial brokerage firms. Within the brokerage industry, there are large national firms such as Coldwell Banker, Century 21, Re/Max, and Prudential Properties, Inc., etc. These national brokerage companies tend to dominate the residential real estate field, accounting for over half of the residential brokerage companies in the U.S.

Commercial Brokerage

Commercial brokers also have national real estate firms such as Grubb & Ellis and CB Richard Ellis. While these national companies seem to be the largest companies in each region, they do not dominate the market. More than half of commercial real estate transactions are brokered by independent commercial brokerage companies serving local and regional markets.

Some brokerage houses specialize in leasing, land sales, or investment property sales. Most national companies have departments that specialize in each of the above fields, as they seek to dominate the local markets. There are arguments for and against the use of the large national companies vs. the local companies who specialize. I would not want to make a recommendation for or against either, as both have an integral part to play in the local commercial markets.

> **HEADS UP**
>
> The one thing I can say is that when you are buying or selling a piece of real property it is definitely in your best interest to use a qualified real estate broker.

FEES—CUSTOM AND PRACTICE

As I have mentioned earlier in this book, brokerage fees are not regulated by law. In fact, by law, they are totally negotiable. In reality, however, the local custom has a large part to play in real estate fees paid within a given area. In our area, for instance, raw land sales carry a brokerage commission between six and ten percent, housing is sold with a six percent commission, and investment sales seem to vary from one and one half percent to three percent. You'll most likely find this is true in the area in which you live and is likely also true in the area in which you care to invest.

CHAPTER

5

Before You Invest

Before you launch yourself into a new venture, you should take the time to organize yourself, your finances, and your plans. It makes sense to decide what you're going to do before you do it. Plans are such that you can always alter them at any time. To launch an investment program without a plan is an invitation to disaster. If you remember, in the previous chapter we spoke about the potential downside in land speculation using leverage; not planning for the final payment can result in a loss of your investment.

The Rationale

Perhaps the first step you should take is to evaluate where you are today, both personally and financially. From these facts, you should be able to formulate a rational plan of attack. The first step in establishing any plan is to look at the desired end result. What exactly are you trying to accomplish? What is your goal?

This may sound somewhat simplistic, but it is absolutely vital that your goals be reasonable and attainable. You could, for instance, say that in ten years you would like to have made $10 million after taxes. This is a pretty good goal, but if your liquid resources total $5,000, it may not be reasonable to assume that you can attain this goal within this time frame. You must seek to strike a balance between what you have to work with and where you'd like to go. Most people who are contemplating an investment program, whether it's in real estate or any other venue, have at least a modest amount of discretionary cash. The trick is to look at what you have to work with and decide realistically how best to put it to work.

How Do You Plan to Get There?

Getting there from here is the essence of a reasonable plan. You need to look at your personal and financial resources. For the sake of this exercise, we will need to make some assumptions about who you are, what you're doing, and where you'd like to go. The following is not a blueprint for you or anyone else; it is merely an example of how to go through the process and come out the other side with what you and anyone else might consider to be a reasonable plan of attack.

> **HEADS UP**
>
> There is no such thing as the right plan. My plan will not be your plan and, even though your plan might be brilliant, it most likely will not work for someone else. The trick is to make a plan that works for you, work the plan, and stay flexible.

What Have You Got to Work With?

Let's take a look at the mythical you and make some assumptions and, at the same time, let's look at some questions that you should ask and answer as part of this process. Let's say that you are 30 years old, married, with one child. You and your spouse together make approximately $120,000 per year. Like most people, you have a mortgage and a car payment. Unlike most people, you are not in debt up to your eyeballs with credit cards. You and your spouse have a plan to become financially independent by the time your children are grown and gone. This alone will set you apart from the herd, as most people seem to spend money they don't have and, therefore, are unlikely to accumulate wealth for the future.

Financial

After analyzing your financial situation, you determine that you have the following resources:

- $30,000 cash in the bank
- $25,000 per year of discretionary income
- Prospects for increased disposable earnings of another $10,000 per year in the short term.

You create a simple projection of your financial resources, as shown in Table 5-1. Looking at that table, you can reasonably assume that you have enough financial resources to start looking at investment properties.

Year	Cash Available	Cumulative Total
Today	$30,000	$30,000
Year 1	$25,000	$55,000
Year 2	$35,000	$80,000
Year 3	$35,000	$115,000
Year 4	$35,000	$150,000
Year 5	$35,000	$185,000

TABLE 5-1. PROJECTED CASH RESOURCES

The question is, do you wait to the end of year five, when you will have a more substantial cash reserve than you do today, or do you start looking around now, with a program to invest cash as it becomes available to you in regular intervals? The only way to answer this question with any degree of accuracy is to examine it in the context of your plan. Since your plan should reasonably be based on your personal background, education, and experience, what you decide to invest in, together with your available resources above, will determine the logical place to start.

PERSONAL CONSIDERATIONS

Now that we have examined and cataloged your financial potential, let's take a long hard look at the personal. In our assumption above, you are married with one child. Do you plan to have another child? How is your marriage? You must remember that in the United States 50 percent of all marriages fail. Is your spouse going to be supportive of your plans for financial independence? Will he or she continue to work if another child enters the picture? Will that affect your disposable income? You bet it will!

These are tough questions; the answers may be even tougher. It would seem pointless to launch the quest for financial independence only to lose it all in a ruinous divorce. In reality, serious wealth building can be stressful and potentially hazardous to your marriage. We have all seen the articles written about highly successful individuals who lost their families along the way.

> **HEADS UP**
>
> Making money in real estate does not have to cost you your family. Setting realistic goals, to which you and your spouse agree, will allow both of you to participate in the plan without creating undue stress in your relationship. This is probably the most crucial part of the plan that you should examine, as the financial part will most generally take care of itself. The exercise above is the single most critical thing you need to do before launching your investment program.

Establishing a Reasonable Plan

Now that we have established that you and your spouse are on a solid footing and agreed totally on your mutual plans for becoming indecently rich, we can turn our attention to your financial resources. One of the basic necessities for launching into an investment program involving real property and real property loans is good credit. You must review your credit situation and maximize it for the coming investment program.

The steps we are going to take in putting together a program that is reasonable and attainable are the following, to be performed in this order.

1. Put your personal house in order.
2. Clean up your credit.
3. Diagram your finances.
4. Perform a market survey.
5. Analyze your locale, your region, and any cities that are available to you with reasonable travel time.
6. Diagram your target area so that you fully understand what is where and the dollar value of everything.
7. Select the type of real estate product that you are comfortable with.
8. Create and finalize a ten-year (Phase 1) plan.
9. Outline your transition (Phase 2) and long-term (Phase 3) plans.

ESTABLISHING YOUR COMFORT ZONE

A more difficult aspect of real estate investment is to decide where to invest and what to invest in. If you remember what we covered in Chapter 3, you know that there are many types of properties to invest in and, in addition, there are many markets to examine. Our society is very mobile and, therefore, we can pick and choose where we live and where we invest our money. I live in Arizona, where we have many investors who live elsewhere. I'm not suggesting that you immediately take to the road and look for another place to invest. Simply be aware that you are not limited to investing where you live.

The key to deciding where to invest will lie in your marketplace analysis. Unless you live in a very rural area or in an area where the population is stagnant or decreasing, you will most likely find investment opportunities in your immediate area or in cities and towns that are readily available to you. The market will comprise everything from residential to the entire spectrum of commercial.

You should find a good Realtor® and start the process of analyzing the marketplace. You'll notice that I use the trademarked term Realtor®. This is a specialized real estate agent dealing primarily with residential properties. Realtors® belong to the local multiple listing service and to the National Association of Realtors® (NAR).

HEADS UP

Since you are inexperienced in real estate investment and your resources, while impressive, are limited, I would suggest that you look at a program of residential investment as the beginning of a long-term investment strategy.

While this advice is, in fact, generic, it is a safe place to launch a long-term program. By the end of this chapter, you will see exactly how a long-term progression can be started with the acquisition of one modest residential rental property.

National real estate markets are vital to our economy and housing is the engine that drives the entire market. The increase in the housing supply is directly related to an increase in population. It is very easy to find out what cities are growing faster than others. As a general rule, I favor locations that have built-in, reliable, and historic population growth. Investing in places like these gives you an edge that you will not find in areas of stagnant, or low population growth. The only problem with this approach is that your current job may not be in this type of area. This is a very personal decision that you will have to make early on in your investing career.

You may decide that your job is such that it has a bright future and that you are unlikely to be able to replace it by moving to a new locale. If the market where you work does not provide a built-in population increase, you might want to seriously consider investing in an area other than where you live and work.

Regional diversity is also an option. One alternative to going elsewhere with your investment money is to invest in your area and diversify your investments by location and type. That way you avoid putting all of your eggs in one basket. In any investment program, you must consider safety as well as rate of return. As a general rule, the riskier the investment, the greater the profit potential of that investment.

THE LOCAL MARKET

For the sake of this example, let's assume that you live in an area that is experiencing reasonable growth and good economic stability, so you choose to stay there and invest there. You and your local Realtor® decide to take apart the local real estate market so that you can understand what's where. In Figure 5-1 you can see a simplistic diagram charting a city. The purpose of charting is to start understanding why certain parts of this city grow faster and why properties

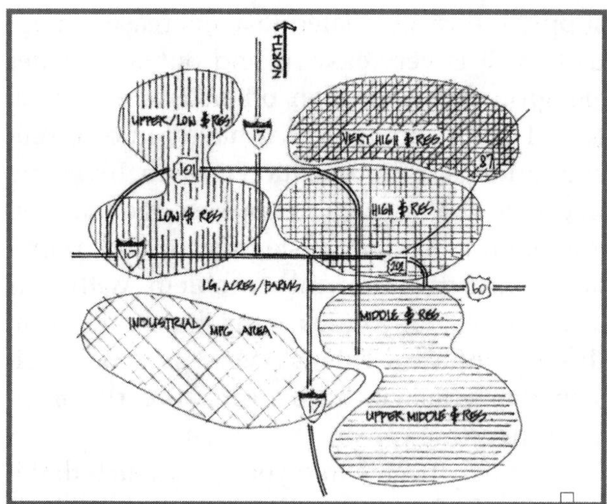

FIGURE 5-1. CITY DIAGRAM

in these areas are worth more money and seem to maintain their values better.

Diagrams cannot tell the entire story; they merely point you to areas that you need to examine further. If you have made the decision to launch your investment program by investing in housing, you need to decide where to invest your money so that your investment is secure, the properties are desirable and will remain desirable, and the prospects for the long-term appreciation of these properties are more than reasonable.

Residential Opportunities

This is not that difficult a chore. Using your diagram of the city, you can zero in on areas that have the desired potential. What you are looking for is not the area that is the hottest and most expensive new area. What you need is an area that is established, in a great location for commuting, with all the necessary services to support a prosperous residential community. In addition, it would be most desirable if this area were composed of housing that was not built as a tract. If you are not dealing in tract homes, your investment will have the added potential of upgrading by way of remodeling. We will deal with this potential in this section of the book on housing.

Let's assume, then, that you have decided to invest in a second home for lease and that you have determined that homes in the area you're interested in are valued at around $150,000.

The dollar implications of this neighborhood are that to purchase a home of this size, utilizing a conventional mortgage of 80 percent of the purchase price, you'll need a down payment of $30,000 and approximately $3,000-$5,000 for closing costs. If we refer back to Table 5-1, we can see that you will have the desired resources to purchase a home of this size in year one. If we restructure the table to allow for periodic investment in homes of this size, it will look something like Table 5-2.

Year	Cash Available	Cumulative Total
Today	$30,000	$30,000
Year 1	$25,000	$55,000
Investment	**($35,000)**	**$20,000**
Year 2	$35,000	$55,000
Investment	**($40,000)**	**$15,000**
Year 3	$35,000	$50,000
Investment	**($45,000)**	**$5,000**
Year 4	$35,000	$40,000
Year 5	$35,000	$75,000
Investment	**($50,000)**	**$25,000**

TABLE 5-2. INVESTMENT PROJECTIONS

Reflecting on Table 5-2, you'll see that based on your available cash, you will be able to make four investments over the five-year period and you will have $25,000 cash left in the bank. You may have noticed that I have withdrawn from your available cash the original $35,000 to purchase the mythical $150,000 home and then, subsequently, increased the deduction to $40,000, $45,000, and $50,000. This is because the values in that area are increasing annually and, therefore, the required down payments would increase as time passes.

We will not spend any time in this chapter discussing exactly how these investments are affecting your bottom line. It is sufficient to say that, with the givens we started with and your continuing ability to furnish additional capital, it is reasonable to assume that, at the end of five years, you could be the proud owner of four investment properties totaling at least $600,000 in value. The effect of all this will be analyzed in later chapters when we look at analyzing the impact of specific investments. At this point in the game, it is sufficient to know that your initial plan is feasible.

HEADS UP

When considering a specific area to invest in, the most important criteria you need to look at to determine its long-term potential are accessibility, historic appreciation, and desirability as an area to live in. Desirability is not easy to determine, but if all the necessary services are in place, such as transportation, schools, and shopping, the area will be deemed sufficiently desirable.

Strategy

PHASE 1

This approach to the plan will get you started, but it is not sufficient to get you all the way to wealth. Starting out, I would most likely recommend that you pursue the buy-and-lease program for a period of up to ten years. At the end of the ten years, you should have accomplished several things: you should have increased your net worth substantially, you should have gained experience in buying and managing income property, and hopefully you should have gotten a good handle on your chosen real estate market, not only the residential market, but the commercial market as well.

PHASE 2

It is at this juncture that the second phase of your investment plan should kick in. By now it should become apparent that managing multiple individual properties is somewhat unwieldy. The time is right to parlay your increased capital into a larger and more manageable piece of income-producing real estate. If you have made spectacular decisions, you may need more than one piece of real estate to absorb the capital you have been able to amass. Your choices when making this move are both residential (multifamily apartment complexes) and commercial. Due to their sheer size, these types of properties will provide ample funds for professional management. In addition, the ongoing appreciation, through periodic refinancing, coupled with your continuing savings plan, should provide ample funds to continue to invest. From here on, you are in the mature stage (Phase 2) of your investment plan.

PHASE 3

The ongoing assignment is to manage well and increase the cash flow and your portfolio. Have a good time! Remember: it's only money.

The One-Man Band vs. the Team Approach

By now you have seen your potential, what you and your spouse can do. Is this going to be enough for you? Are you going to be prepared to make the transition from managing residential renters to managing large numbers of tenants? Do you have the background and training to do your own accounting, management, and long-term planning? Is this program taking up too much of your time? Is it taking you away from your family at a time when you feel your children need more of your time? In general, do you feel like you could use a little help?

There is no specific reason why you and your spouse should go it alone, as there are many different ways you can join with others in similar circumstances to share the load, increase your diversity, and afford more professional management. There are pros and cons to taking on partners, but, in my opinion, the pluses outweigh the minuses.

While you are involved with a small number of properties, there should be no problem with the time involved in management, but once you start dealing with more substantial properties, the day-to-day demands of management and forward planning start to pile up. A larger portfolio will demand a more formalized approach to management and involve a number of professionals. At this point, at the inception of Phases 2 and 3 of your investment plan, you will be faced with the decision of quitting your day job, contracting out these chores to professionals, or joining with others to create an operation that can handle the professional management of a growing income property portfolio.

PARTNERSHIP

A logical outgrowth of this situation is to form a partnership with someone in the same situation. By combining portfolios, management skills, acquisition chores, and long-term planning, you can achieve several objectives. First of all, you can share the workload. Second, through diversification, you can strengthen your portfolio's position. Third, the combined income from your portfolio and your partner's should enable you both to afford professional management, accounting, and long-term planning. Eventually, the size of the combined portfolio would enable one of you to quit your day job and concentrate on managing the portfolio. Typical management fees for income properties are about four percent of rents collected. A gross income of $1 million would produce a management fee of $40,000 per year. Whether you choose to do it full-time or not, by sharing the chores, you'll free up more time to look for new investments and pay attention to the marketplace.

Types of Ownership

Real property working arrangements can take different legal forms. They can be *corporations*, *partnerships*, or *limited liability companies*. Let's take a look at the differences among the three entities.

This section will deal with the various forms of ownership, the requirements of the paperwork as it relates to that ownership, and the relationships between or among the parties.

Except for individual ownership, all other forms of ownership are evidenced by a written agreement between the parties and a notice, filed with the public recorder (usually the corporation commissioner), for the purpose of notifying the public of the new relationship. In essence, the recordation of the relationship provides constructive notice to the public regarding the following facts:

- The names and addresses of the owners
- The name and address of the agent for service
- The names and addresses of the managers of the entity
- A statement of the legal life of the entity

Each form of ownership will have a variation on this requirement. Also, if an entity does business out of state, most states will require that entity to register with their secretary of state as a *foreign* corporation, partnership, or limited liability company.

Corporations

Corporations are composed of stockholders who own the company. The company is created by *incorporators* who gather together to form the company and, once it is formed, select the managing executives (corporate officers) and the board of directors. The incorporators can become the board of directors as well as the officers of the newly formed corporation. Most often this is the case.

Corporations can go through transitions from small, fledgling entities to companies the size of General Motors. The typical new corporation will be owned by a few people and will have a specific purpose. Its capitalization will likely be confined to capital donated by the incorporators. The original board will authorize the issuance of stock and allocate part of the authorized stock to the incorporators and original investors in exchange for their capital or other equity contribution.

There may be two classes of stock, *common* and *preferred*. Preferred stock is generally nonvoting stock issued to investors who may have a priority over the net earnings of the company. Sometimes this stock will have the right to be converted to common stock under specific circumstances. Common stock is the voting stock; these stockholders annually elect the board of directors and the corporate officers.

The officers manage the day-to-day business of the corporation under the guidance of the board of directors. The board has the right to hire and fire the corporation's officers. While the board of directors makes mandatory annual reports to the stockholders, the directors have little or no voice in the daily management of the company. Large stockholders sometimes have enough percentage ownership to appoint board members to look out for their interests. The board members and the corporate officers have immunity from liability unless they commit fraud or negligence in managing the corporation's business.

The initial statement of incorporation is filed with the state's corporation commission, listing:

- The name of the company, and the address of its principal place of business
- The names and addresses of the incorporators
- The date of incorporation
- The names, titles, and addresses of the initial corporate officers
- The names and addresses of the initial stockholders of record holding stock in excess of 20 percent ownership
- The name and address of the agent for service

Relationships among the stockholders, the board of directors, and corporate officers are contained in a document called a *stockholders' agreement*. This document will be modified as the corporation grows and its dealings and management will become more structured and diverse. This will eventually be filed with the Securities and Exchange Commission when the company goes public, offering its shares for sale to the general public. This document can then be modified by the board of directors with the concurrence of its stockholders at the annual stockholders' meeting.

Close Corporations

Corporations, like all legal entities, evolve from formation to grow or die as the case may be. As they grow, they issue more stock to attract more capital and the ownership becomes more diluted. Few very large corporations are closely held. A corporation with ten or less stockholders is referred to as a *close corporation*. Frequently, when close corporations borrow money, the corporate officers and/or the stockholders are required to jointly and severally guarantee the loans. The reason behind this is that with so few individuals involved, the officers do not have any watchdogs looking over their shoulders. This is not a hard-and-fast rule, but most banks seem to require this added protection.

DEFINITION

Joint and several guarantee means that each guarantor of a loan assumes responsibility for the entire amount of the loan.

Subchapter S Corporations

The subchapter S corporation is a hybrid corporation whose tax situation is treated like a partnership. Unlike a regular corporation, whose net income is taxable before dividends are paid to the shareholders, the sub S corporation is treated as a partnership, with the gains and losses taxed only on the stockholders' tax returns. In all other aspects, the sub S corporation is treated as any other corporation. Once quite popular, the sub S corporation has fallen out of favor since the advent of the limited liability company.

Public Corporations

Public corporations are widely capitalized entities, managed by a stockholder-elected board of directors and an appointed slate of corporate officers. The management slate is voted in or out annually at the stockholders' meeting. Most directors represent specific investor groups holding large blocks of stock. When directors and corporate officers act lawfully and responsibly, they are immune from liability to the shareholders and the public. They are, however, held personally liable for willful negligence and fraud. The only relationship that exists among the stockholders is the right to vote their stock shares. The stockholders' total liability is the purchase price of the shares. In the event of bankruptcy, there is no liability assumed by the shareholders. If, however, shareholders elect to wind up the affairs of a corporation, dissolve the company, and distribute the assets, they will then become liable for any unpaid liabilities of the corporation.

Partnerships

Until the late 1990s, partnerships were the dominant form of ownership of investment real estate. The reasons for this were that they are not subject to double taxation (as are corporations) and capitalization and management are flexible. With profit and loss taxable at the level of the individual partners, the depreciation aspects of real estate ownership became a prime motivation factor in choosing real estate as an investment. The Tax Reform Act of 1986 changed the depreciation allowance and made real estate less viable as a tax loss investment, but it left straight-line depreciation to shelter annual cash flow. The new schedule, based on a term of approximately 31 years, allows most projects to provide their investors with some cash flow shelter. The depreciation is then added back to the profit on resale in a tax maneuver known as *recapture*. The taxes on income are, therefore, not avoided, merely deferred. The major tax benefit is that if you do not sell or if you exchange one property for another, you can defer the tax consequences indefinitely.

When partnerships are formed, the states require that *articles of organization* be filed with the secretary of state. As a general rule, the articles would include, at a minimum, the following:

- The names and addresses of the general partner(s)
- The date of formation and the expiration date
- The principal place of business
- The name and address of the agent for service
- A statement of purpose
- A termination date

Unlike corporations, which have an indefinite life, partnerships must have a termination date. The date may be extended by action of the partners and the filing of an extension, but they must have a definite termination date.

Partnership relationships are governed by a document known as a *partnership agreement*. This document sets forth the arrangement between or among the partners. It is not intended for public record. It spells out capital contributions, profit and loss allocations, dissolution procedures, assignment rights, and management rights and responsibilities. This document may be modified only by agreement of all the partners.

General Partnerships

Partnerships are self-managed. By definition, the general partner is responsible for the day-to-day business of the partnership; he or she assumes personal liability for all debts and obligations of the partnership. If there is more than one general partner, all the partners have the same joint and several liabilities. Management is distributed between them as agreed. In the event of a disagreement that cannot be resolved, the partnership generally is dissolved by the retirement of one or more general partners. To avoid the constant threat of dissolution, most partnerships have a provision that allows the general partner to act with a vote of the majority-in-interest of the partnership. If, however, the last remaining general partner elects to exit the partnership, the partnership must be dissolved and the assets disposed of. In voluntary dissolution, the individual partners assume any lingering obligations of the partnership upon dissolution.

Limited Partnerships

Limited partnerships are managed the same way as general partnerships, with one important exception: there are two classes of partners—*general,* as in general partnerships, and *limited,* as in partners whose sole liability is their investment in the partnership. Since the limited partners will not be assuming any liabilities, they are not required to be identified in the articles of organization. The exception to this rule would occur if the limited partner(s) acted to remove a general partner, for cause, and assumed the management of the partnership. The relationship between or among the partners in any partnership is called a *fiduciary* relationship; it is a legal obligation imposed on

> **DEFINITION**
>
> A ***fiduciary obligation*** requires the general partner(s) to treat the interests of the other partner(s) above their own interests. It mandates honest dealing and timely reporting. This is especially true when there are limited partners; when a general partner is dealing on behalf of passive limited partners, the regulations are even more stringent.

the partners by the law enabling the formation of the partnership.

Whenever you are dealing on behalf of anyone else's investment (including lenders' funds), I recommend that you adhere to scrupulous routines that become second nature to you over time.

HEADS UP

If you get into the habit of administering every transaction the same way, you will not go wrong.

You should always do the following:

- Create a new partnership or LLC for every transaction, regardless of common ownership.
- Open a separate checking account for each operating entity.
- Never mingle cash from one entity to another.
- Put all reports and notices in writing—every time!
- Respond in writing to all queries, however routine, from limited partners.
- Write and distribute a monthly status report—every month!—including anything of interest.
- Deliberately highlight any bad news in the status report.
- Send a copy of the status report to your lenders.
- Distribute your partners' earnings regularly and on time.
- Pay yourself last and, if you are taking fees, such as leasing fees as part of your arrangement, report them monthly.

Another piece of advice is also simple: whenever you are in negotiations or working on a dispute, put your position and responses in writing. Most people are lazy and, when confronted with your position, will tend to pick up the phone to resolve an issue. Fine, resolve it. Then, put your version of the resolution in a memo and send it off. If the dispute should ever come to court, you will find that the one with the most thorough, methodical, and complete paper trail will prevail.

HEADS UP

Why be so scrupulous? The answer is simple. If the project goes according to plan and everyone makes money, no one will ever read the paperwork. If, however, something goes wrong, you will never have a partner or lender who can say, "You never told us."

You will find that if the paperwork and the proper treatment of your partners become second nature to you, there will be few surprises that can disrupt the partnership. There will always be the outside influences, like the great recession of 1989-1991, but these events are beyond your control. If you have the confidence and trust of your partners, you will somehow survive. Sometimes there is no solution, but, if you follow the guidelines above, you can never be faulted for your treatment of your partners' interests.

Limited Liability Companies

The *limited liability company* (LLC) is a recent arrival on the real estate investment scene and it is gaining popularity in almost all forms of business. Since its advent, I have not considered forming a partnership for a new transaction. I am now conducting 100 percent of my business in the limited liability company format. The same is true for all of my contemporaries, as far as I can tell. All of the states have adopted one form or another of the LLC.

Its popularity is not confined to real estate development or investment. It seems to have invaded all endeavors, with the exception of the professional partnerships between attorneys and doctors, who seem to prefer the *limited liability partnership (LLP)* version. Since I am not familiar with the structure and rationale behind professional partnerships, I will refrain from comment and comparison.

HEADS UP

The limited liability company is the new best way to own investment real estate.

What Is an LLC?

The limited liability company is a hybrid entity combining the best features of the corporation and the partnership. The LLC offers its owners, called *members*, the liability limits of a corporation and the tax benefit of a partnership. It is, in practical terms, a streamlined version of the sub chapter S corporation. The variation in regulation and rules for formation will differ from state to state, but the essence is as outlined above.

LLCs are either member-managed or managed by an appointed manager. Member management comes in two forms: by consensus of a majority in interest or by a designated *managing member.* The most common arrangement is for the members to designate a managing member. The members do not assume the liabilities of the LLC as do the general partners in a partnership. All guarantees of loans, etc., are voluntary. It is only when an LLC is voluntarily wound up that the members assume any residual obligations. This rule seems to be consistent for all artificially created legal entities.

The paperwork for the LLC, at a minimum, involves two documents, the *articles of organization* and the *operating agreement*. The articles of organization require, at least, the following recitals for recordation with the state:

- The name and principal place of business of the LLC
- The date of formation and the expiration date
- The purpose of formation
- The names and addresses of all of the members
- The members' election for management of the LLC
- The name and address of the manager
- The name and address of the agent for service

Other requirements may vary from state to state.

The operating agreement is similar in scope to the stockholders' agreement and the partnership agreement. It must contain the operating rules, rights, and privileges of the members, as well as capital contributions, profit and loss allocation, dissolution and assignment clauses. Upon death or resignation of the last member, the LLC will be dissolved and the assets disposed of. The LLC is also required to have a definite termination date.

Benefits and Limitations

Inasmuch as the LLC is a new entity, there is a lack of established case law. It is impossible, therefore, to know with any certainty how disputes and differences will affect the investment vehicle. In general, it seems to be working quite well. In my experience, the LLC feels like a partnership on a day-to-day basis. I have not yet run into an LLC that has employees like a corporation, but as far as I know, there is no reason why an LLC cannot have employees. The problems, if any, endemic in the LLC will evolve over the next 20 years or so, as disputes between members make their way into our court system. The areas of conflict that I can foresee will involve assignment, profits and losses, and management rights. There might also be some issues with member liability. These problems are similar to those encountered in partnerships.

The LLC is similar to a partnership in the area of assignment of interest and membership. A member may assign his or her rights of ownership, but not the membership rights. For an assignee or a successor in interest to become a member, all of the other members must approve in writing. This does not diminish the assignee's rights to income or profits and losses; it merely restricts the assignee's right of management input. There is no provision in the LLC for a member to have a role similar to that of a limited partner. There is, however, a provision within the LLC structure that allows a member to have a specific allocation of profit and loss that bears no relation to the member's capital contribution.

CHAPTER

6

Investment—Residential *or* Commercial

Before getting into the specifics of how to analyze projects for purchase or development, we need to delve into the differences between residential and commercial properties. In this chapter, I will highlight the differences between residential and commercial investments and underline the similarities, in the hopes of providing you with some insight into the more subtle aspects of these investment alternatives. Besides the obvious difference in scale, there are substantive differences in planning, management, and financing.

There are at least four major investment approaches when looking at potential real estate projects:

- The quick turnaround
- The long-term cash generator
- The monthly or annual income producing project
- The long-term capital gain approach

In addition to the above, there are two other considerations, exchanges and taxes, when dealing with real property.

Project Categories

The four approaches listed above may sound alike on the surface, as they are all about making money. The differences among the four types of approach lie in how you make the money and how you pay taxes on the income.

These differences will color your judgment when deciding on how to approach making money in real estate.

The Quick Turnaround

This type of project lends itself to a fast in-and-out approach. In the residential investment field, this would be what we call the "lipstick" type project. This occurs when you buy a piece of run-down property and simply rejuvenate the finishes (décor) such as paint, wallpaper, and carpet. This quick fix takes little or no time and can result in a quick sale and a quick profit. There are opportunities for this type of approach to real estate investment in residential as well as commercial.

Keep in mind that 100 percent of the income from this type of project is taxable as ordinary income and that each individual project is a one-time, one-of-a-kind project. This type of project will find you reinventing the wheel in every single deal. That isn't to say that I'm against this type of project, just that you should know what you are in for before you approach projects of this nature.

The Cash Flow Business

There are projects that you can tackle that will generate cash flow over a longer period of time. Examples of these would be land subdivision, tract home construction, or merchant-builder commercial projects.

> **DEFINITION**
>
> A ***merchant builder*** is one who builds and sells rather than builds and holds his or her projects.

This second project type implies a need for a long-term business organization. The creation of real property projects/products for sale puts you squarely in the dealer category in terms of taxation. The tax implications of this type of project are that all income generated is forever ordinary income. Companies that engage in this type of project are commonly corporations rather than partnerships, as there is little or no tax benefit generated during the build-and-sell process. The long-term view here is to consistently generate good earnings for the corporation and dividends for the stockholders. This will raise the value of stock and provide a long-term capital gain when the stock or the company is sold.

Income Property Investment

Investment in and/or development of income-producing property is a distinctly different approach from the two above. When you buy or build, own, operate, and resell investment property, you create a scenario after 12 months in which you create more than just cash flow; you also generate long-term profit, aka capital gain. It is this type of project that actually allows real estate to produce the best possible interim and long-term results for the investor/developer.

SHORT-TERM BENEFITS

The immediate benefit from building an income-producing property is potential fee income, ordinary losses, and capital gain. Since 23 to 25 percent of the actual cost of a development project is fees, the developer has the potential for some early-on income and tax write-off against ordinary income. When the project is completed, the increase in value over cost is a capital gain or profit that is not taxed until the project is sold. In the interim, between completion and the sale of the property, this profit goes directly into the investor/developer's net worth.

MEDIUM-TERM BENEFITS

During the period between the end of the development process and the eventual sale of the property, the owner/developer/investor has the benefit of cash flow and income as well as depreciation. This combination of income and depreciation effectively improves the ROI on any project.

For example, if you are in the 30-percent tax bracket, every dollar that you shelter from your project actually produces $1.30 in real income. On average, my experience has been that between 50 and 70 percent of the cash flow on a development project is totally tax-sheltered. This makes the ownership of income-producing property a desirable financial endeavor.

LONG-TERM IMPLICATIONS

Income property, over the long term, is also a very attractive investment vehicle beyond that outlined above. When you go to sell a piece of real property that you have held in excess of 12 months, your gain is taxable at the federal capital gain rate of 15 percent. In addition, if you prefer not to pay the taxes immediately, under the U.S. tax laws, you can defer payment of capital gain by opting to effect a *1031 tax-deferred exchange*. The 1031 exchange allows owners of property to swap the property for one of "like kind" and of "equal or greater value." This triggers the start of your income and depreciation cycle again, putting off the payment of capital gain until you sell the new property. You can choose to exchange from property to property ad infinitum, rather than pay the capital gain at all. If you like, let your heirs worry about the taxes when they sell.

1031 Exchanges

The 1031 tax-deferred exchange is very common in the commercial income property and development business. A brief look at this phenomenon is in order. The way it works is relatively simple; but I strongly advise that, before you commit to a 1031 exchange, you involve an attorney who specializes in this form of tax-deferred exchange.

Here's fundamentally the way it works. You arrange to sell your property. You then assign the proceeds of the sale to an individual or business known as a *facilitator*. From the date of sale, you have six months (180 days) to locate a suitable property for the exchange. You select the property and set up the purchase so that the facilitator can buy the property on your behalf. The facilitator then "exchanges" the proceeds in his or her custody from the prior sale for the property you have selected for your exchange.

This sounds relatively simple, but it must be done very carefully to preserve the tax-deferred status of the exchange itself. Property may only be exchanged "like kind for like kind." Meeting the government's definition for "like kind" is important to preserve the tax-deferred status of this action. This is why I strongly urge you to involve experts—an attorney and a competent facilitator.

There are other issues involving the money that come into play with the 1031 exchange. If you do not spend all the money, the residual is known as *boot* and it is taxable. This is where expert guidance from an experienced 1031 tax accountant is vital. You don't want to go through the expense of the exchange process only to wind up paying taxes anyway.

TAX DISCUSSION

I do not pretend to have any expertise whatsoever in the matter of real estate taxation. Rather, I urge you at the outset to engage the services of a competent real estate tax accountant. The proper time to discuss the tax implications of a transaction is before you start the transaction. When you are buying or developing a piece of income property, the accountant can give you the potential tax treatment of every component of the deal. While this will not necessarily improve the ROI on your transaction, it will at least give you a good idea as to the financial effect of each and every action you take in the transaction.

Summary

While different styles of approach to any project can work for residential as well as commercial real estate, some projects lend themselves to one form of investment more than others.

Residential Projects

Let's first look at residential projects and put them in the light of the breakdown of project types above, factor in the tax implications, and see which approach makes the most sense for you.

While it is true that the majority of American families own their own homes, very few of them have actually sat down and analyzed precisely what the home is doing for them financially. Those people are somewhat aware of the rising values of housing in their neck of the woods, but very few have actually put on paper the real impact of owning the home.

Your Personal Residence

We will delve into this in more detail later in this book and in the section dealing with residential investment, but for now, below, you will find a quick list of the benefits of individual homeownership.

- All interest payments on mortgages and second mortgages are tax-deductible.
- If you live in the home as your primary residence for 24 months or more, all profits on the sale of the home are tax-free.
- If you maintain the home in good condition, it will continue to appreciate, keeping pace with the local market as long as you live there.
- You may borrow against your equity in the home anytime to finance other purchases. The interest on equity loans is also tax-deductible.

The Second Home

In addition to a personal residence, many people purchase a vacation home or a second home for rental purposes. These two types of second properties share many attributes, but where they differ from your personal residence is in the tax treatment. Both types of homes will appreciate, when properly maintained, with the local market. The interest on both properties is tax-deductible. A bonus with the rental home is that it can be depreciated like any other income asset. The schedule for this depreciation is slightly different than it is for commercial properties and you should check with your accountant to verify the annual write-off. When these properties are sold, the gain on the vacation property is taxable as ordinary income and the gain on the rental property is taxable as capital gain.

Renovating and Building

Another form of residential investment is renovation for profit. This type of project is a cash flow project and will be taxable as ordinary loss or gain. There are a growing number of people in the country who tackle this type of project for a living. We will deal with this in detail in Section IV.

A similar but more ambitious form of investment in residential property is building a home for your use or for resale. This process is, in reality, acquiring a home at a wholesale price. Acting as your own developer, buying the land, hiring the contractor, and supervising the construction will save you the markup normally charged by the real estate developer. This entrepreneurial profit is yours in exchange for your effort in designing and building your own home. The ultimate result of this will be in increased profit at the time of sale.

The thing to keep in mind when dealing and investing in residential property is that profits on properties held in excess of 12 months are capital gains. You may also exchange any of the investment properties for like kind under the 1031 exchange rules.

Commercial Real Estate Investment

Commercial properties are, in general, larger than residential properties. Obviously there are homes that cost as much as or more than many commercial properties. The difference is that very few people invest in these larger properties on speculation. Most of the people involved in the larger residential properties either develop the properties originally or tackle them as renovation projects.

There are two main categories of commercial properties: land and land with buildings. We will look at the basics of both types of investment.

Land

We have briefly discussed the basics of land development in previous chapters, but I would like to review the choices that are involved in land projects in a little more detail. Basic land projects break down into the following categories:

- Speculation
  - Purchase and long-term hold
  - Leveraged purchase and long-term hold
- Flip
- Rollover
- Cash flow project
  - Subdivision

SPECULATION

Pure land speculation is the purchasing of land and holding it for a period of time for profit. There are two ways to do this: either pay cash or leverage the purchase with a seller carry-back loan. Depending upon the time of sale, the leveraged version of this deal can be more profitable, based on the return on investment.

Below you will see an example of how the dollars invested in the rate of return vary between a cash deal and a leveraged deal. We will use the following assumptions:

- The land purchased is 200 acres.
- The purchase price is $5,000/acre.
- The holding time is seven years.
- The sale price is $40,000/acre.
- The land sale commission is five percent.
- Leverage available is 25 percent down and ten percent interest only, paid semiannually, with a balloon in ten years.

Table 6-1 shows a better return on the leveraged deal. The down side, however, is that if you do not have the cash at the time the balloon payment is called, you will lose your investment. This is not to say that leveraging this type of transaction is a bad idea, merely that you need to plan ahead and price the land so that it will sell within the time frame your leverage has purchased for you.

Item	Notes	Cost	Cash (Out)/In
CASH DEAL			
Land (cash deal)	200 acres @ $5 K/acre	$1,000,000	($1,000,000)
Closing costs	Nominal	$10,000	($10,000)
Holding costs	Taxes and Insurance @ 5K/year—7 years	$35,000	($35,000)
Total investment			($1,045,000)
Sale price	$40K/acre	$8,000,000	$8,000,000
Less commission	@ 5%		($400,000)
Gross cash in			$7,600,000
Net profit	Proceeds less cash out		$6,555,000
ROI		**627% or 89% per year**	
LEVERAGED DEAL			
Land (cash deal)	200 acres @ $5 K/acre	$1,000,000	($250,000)
Closing costs	Nominal	$10,000	($10,000)
Holding costs	Taxes and Insurance @ $5K/year—7 years plus interest	$35,000	($35,000) ($525,000)
Total investment			($820,000)
Sale price	$40K/acre	$8,000,000	$8,000,000
Less commission	@ 5%		($400,000)
Gross cash in	Less balance land cost		$6,850,000
Net profit	Proceeds less cash out		$6,030,000
ROI		**735% or 105% per year**	
Difference		**108% or 15.42% per year**	

TABLE 6-1. LAND SPECULATION LEVERAGE ANALYSIS

THE FLIP

The flip is a truncated version of land speculation without any improvements to the land. The steps are very simple.

1. Locate a viable market.
2. Locate a developable piece of property in the path of growth, but not too far out!
3. Negotiate a purchase agreement with a long fuse, preferable one with a seller carry-back financing option.
4. Open the escrow and put the land up for sale.
5. Review and approve the title.
6. Hope that a buyer comes along before you have to purchase the land.

THE ROLLOVER

Previously we touched on the rollover deal. I would like to expand on the process. The process of accomplishing a rollover is the first step in making improvements to a property and, contrary to the flip, which relies on timing and the "bigger fool" theory, the steps taken in a rollover transaction add real value to the property. In a rollover you take the following steps, in this order:

1. Locate a suitable market.
2. Select a developable piece of land.
3. Negotiate the purchase with enough time to do the entitlements, generally 24 months.
4. Open the escrow.
5. Review and approve the title.
6. Contract for a survey and title.
7. Create a preliminary development plan.
8. Put the property up for sale and for lease.
9. Apply to the governing municipality/county for the entitlements:
   a. Master plan change
   b. Rezoning
   c. Site plan approval
   d. Preliminary plat approval
   e. Architectural approval
   f. Final plat
10. Finalize all required approvals.
11. Sell the property to a developer prior to your scheduled close of escrow.

THE CASH FLOW PROJECT

This approach involves actually producing some saleable product for an end user. It involves all of the steps of the rollover and continues with the following additional steps:

12. Hire a contractor to build the improvements.
13. Close the escrow.
14. Build out the improvements.
15. Sell the product to the users.

This project is a cash generator and produces ordinary income. The subdivided lots, whether residential or commercial, are the end products and your buyers/users are either builders or homeowners wanting to build their own homes or commercial buildings.

Land with Buildings

BUYING VS. DEVELOPING

Real estate investment that involves buildings is broken into two separate categories: the purchase of existing property and the development of new property from raw land. The difference between the two approaches is that the purchase of existing property (buying at retail prices) and the development of new buildings (buying at wholesale prices) involve two different time frames and acquisition costs. The purchase of an existing income-producing property, when properly handled, should take between four and six months to complete. The development of new property should take about two years, on the average, from the time the property is placed in escrow until the first tenants occupy the premises. These are generalized statements; the actual time frames and costs will vary dramatically depending upon the type of project purchased or developed.

PURCHASE

Buying an existing building involves a fairly straightforward process, with the steps usually in this order:

1. Locate a suitable market.
2. Locate a viable property within that market.
3. Negotiate a price.
4. Open the escrow.
5. Evaluate the title.
6. Analyze the leases, loan documents, and contracts.

7. Negotiate a new loan.
8. Complete the financial analysis.
9. Remove all the contingencies.
10. Close the escrow and the new loan.

While this process may vary slightly from purchase to purchase, the time frames are hard to manipulate. Every process involved in this endeavor takes time to complete. You control only your own actions in the process. It is difficult to accelerate the time frame involving other people whose actions and schedules you do not control.

INVESTMENT

Once you have purchased a property, you enter a period of holding; this period is known as the period of *continuous redevelopment*. The process of redevelopment is that of cleaning up the project paperwork and improving the gross income and cash flow, while at the same time maintaining the property's physical condition to consolidate your investment and maximize your profit at the time of resale.

Holding periods for this type of investment can be as short as a year and as long as forever. During the time you own the property, your taxable cash flow will be largely offset by your allowable depreciation. If you hold the property in excess of 12 months, your gain will be taxable at the 15-percent federal capital gain rate. There will be an additional tax based on the recapture of the depreciation. To learn more about this and the actual tax impact of owning and selling income property, you need to consult a tax accountant.

Development

The wholesale version of acquiring investment property is known as real estate development. And within the development field, there are two types of developers, the *merchant developer* and the *portfolio developer*.

THE MERCHANT DEVELOPER

A merchant developer builds properties for sale to investors. The average holding time for a piece of property for a merchant developer is 12 to 36 months from the time of first tenant occupancy. The goal of the merchant developer is to maximize the cash flow prior to selling to the investors. Generally, most merchant developers will hold a property long enough to make sure that everything in the building and in the landscaping is properly completed and firmly established. During that time the developer will concentrate on completing the lease-up so that the property's cash flow is maximized. The property is then sold on the basis of the net income before debt service (NIBDS): the higher the net income, the higher the price this property will bring at the time of sale.

THE PORTFOLIO DEVELOPER

The portfolio developer's goals are very simple: build it, fill it, hold it, and enjoy as much tax-free cash flow as possible. As properties mature, rent increases kick in and cash flow increases during the period of ownership. The astute portfolio developer treats this property in the same manner as the investor who buys the property and treats it as a redevelopment project. The developer/owner strives annually to improve the paperwork and maximize the cash flow. Once the development portion has been completed, his or her primary preoccupation becomes taking care of the tenants. They are the sole source of cash flow. The happy tenant pays rent on time and does not complain about routine rent increases.

Leveraging Your Holdings

Whether you are buying or building, you need to take advantage of leverage. Leverage will not only increase the rate of return on your cash invested, but also provide cash for future deals. As your net income before debt service increases over the years, so does the value of your property. Periodically during the life of a property, you can refinance it, use the money to modernize the property to keep it competitive in the local market, and use the excess funds to acquire or develop new properties.

Properly managed properties are not only a source of income and a tax shelter, but also a source of future funds for future deals. Once the property is purchased or when the development phase is completed, it boils down to managing the property. The skills involved in development are totally different from those involved in management. While both operations require entrepreneurial functions, development and management are not necessarily compatible entrepreneurial skills. Most portfolio developers, as part of their team, maintain a separate management operation solely dedicated to taking care of the properties. These differences will be discussed in detail later in this book, when we outline the functions and responsibilities involved in the income property real estate industry.

Market Potential—Normal Appreciation vs. Capitalized Income Gain

The entrepreneurial aspects of real estate investment lie in the difference between normal appreciation and capitalized income gain. It does not matter whether you are dealing in residential real estate or commercial real estate, as in time all well-maintained properties in decent locations will increase in value. The additional increment of value, over and above that ascribed to inflation, is generated by the entrepreneur.

HEADS UP

It is your sole mission as an investor/developer/owner to increase the value of your holdings during your tenure. That is what this book is all about.

- How to buy right
- How to develop properly
- How to increase the value of what you have acquired
- How to sell it properly and move on to bigger and better things

SECTION

II

HOUSING

CHAPTER

7

The Basics of Home Ownership, Value, *and* Money

In the United States, the most common goal for most people is home ownership. Single or married, with or without children, we all strive to own our own homes. In our increasingly fast-paced world, it seems even more important than in times past. It is the only place where people can withdraw from the world and feel comforted and nurtured. Homes may be rented, leased, or owned, but the Holy Grail is to own a home.

The early parts of this section of the book will deal with your desire to improve the value of your house, prior to sale. The last part of this section will deal with the consequences of getting the house ready for sale and, then, after selling it, the question of "What now?"

Before the rash of refinancing to lower interest rates in recent years, the average mortgage was paid off in 11 years. This implies that people sold their homes, on average, in 11-year cycles. Since Americans do not generally buy a home and keep it forever, most of us will experience the opportunities and challenges of turning over real estate ownership.

Our parents and grandparents, born at the turn of the century, were conditioned to stay in one place, put down roots, buy a home, raise their children, and live their life in one community. Two world wars changed all that. People became mobile, jobs became more diverse and specialized, and the population took to the newly constructed interstates with a vengeance.

The result is a constantly changing America. Cities die off and others are created and grow like weeds. Population shifts are dramatic and frequent. People move where the opportunity is available or where the weather and terrain better suit their lifestyles. We are no longer tied to one community for life.

In that environment, what is a house? In reality, it is a home, a refuge, an investment, a tax break, an albatross, or a goldmine. It can be a reflection of your self-image, as well as all of the above. It is, in fact, what you make it. So let's make the most of it—and let's make our investment work for us.

What Is a House to You?

The answer to this question varies with the individual, but the most common element in this country is shelter and a place to raise a family. The decision to buy vs. rent is generally economic, as rent is not tax-deductible and mortgage interest is. For most Americans, this is the one big tax break of their economic lives. People who work as employees have limited tax breaks, so owning a house is their single best opportunity for a tax break and significant savings. There are other reasons to own a home: investment and long-term appreciation, location, neighborhood and amenities, schools for the children, and shopping and recreational opportunities in the area. All these components go into the decision.

Seldom does anyone think down the road to the date of sale. You might never sell, but the average American will sell in seven to 11 years. Did you take that event into consideration when you made your purchase? If you did not give some thought to eventually selling your home, then you may have neglected one of the best economic opportunities in your lifetime. The components to profit are as simple as they are varied.

- The house is shelter and home to you and your family.
- It can reflect your image and direction in life.
- The tax benefits save you money every year.
- The home appreciates annually as long as you keep it in reasonable repair. (There are exceptions to this, as we will discuss later in the book.)
- The house can be made to turn a profit with a little astute planning and investment on your part.

Tax Break

What exactly is the tax break and how does it impact on you? Most people use mortgages to pay for their homes. There are a variety of loan types that we will deal with later, but for now we'll use the conventional and most common 80-percent loan to value. If you buy a house for $150,000 with 20 percent down, you will need to borrow $120,000 from a lending institution. Conventional loans are self-amortizing.

DEFINITION

Amortization is the retirement of the principal over the period of the loan term. The *principal* is the amount borrowed. The *term* is the length of the loan and/or the amortization period.

What this means to you is that you get to deduct the amount of interest you pay during the year from your taxable income. If you were making payments on the $120,000 loan above, you would pay interest and principal monthly and the amount of each component would vary annually, even monthly over the term of the loan.

Simply, in the early years of the loan, you are paying mostly interest and a little principal, but as time goes on these amounts change so that by the end of the loan, you will be paying more principal than interest. This is based on an amortization table that allows you to make a level payment on your loan throughout the life of the loan. Your payments are determined by multiplying your loan amount by a constant percentage calculated to allow you to pay both interest and principal over the term of the loan with level payments.

HEADS UP

A mortgage with a principal amount of $120,000 for a term of 30 years at an interest rate of seven percent will require an annual loan constant of 7.99 percent. This yields an annual payment of $9,588.00 or $799.00 per month.

Here's an example. We'll say that you are in the 25-percent tax bracket, the loan on your $150,000 home is in the early years, and you paid $9,200 in interest in the tax year in question. This $9,200 deduction from your taxable income just saved you 25 percent of the interest you paid that year—$2,300. You have also paid the loan down by the difference between the total payment of $9,588 and the interest portion, $9,200—$388. So in reality, you have saved a grand total of $2,688 this year just by making your mortgage payments on time. Not too bad, but it gets better.

Appreciation

While you are going about your everyday life, your house is working at improving your net worth without any further input from you. Even in periods of low inflation, your home is gaining value each year. At the least, it will keep pace with inflation, but in reality there are other factors that cause the value of your home to increase.

- Scarcity
- The cost of construction
- New zoning restrictions
- New construction in your area
- Net in-migration
- The image of your neighborhood

While all these are factors, they only add to the basic inflation rate. If you are dealing with the original $150,000 home above, and the annual inflation rate is three percent, then your home went up in value this year by $4,500. This brings your annual savings and earnings for this year to a total of $7,188. Since you invested only $30,000 in your house initially, you have made a whopping 23-percent return on your investment this year by doing nothing except going about your normal day-to-day business. Imagine if you started working at it and improving your home. What could you really make?

HEADS UP

Appreciation is "no sweat" profit.

Shelter vs. Investment

Once you start thinking along these lines, you need to remember that the real difference between the family that rents and the family that invests in their home is profit. You have seen the results of just doing very little each year, but the real impact to you is that you were most likely paying the same $9,588 in rent before you purchased your home, so in reality you have converted this $9,588 non-deductible expense to a profit. This results in a positive effect to your net worth annually of $16,776. Most people are totally unaware of this impact on their economic well-being when they own a home.

This is just the start of the financial possibilities of home ownership. There are many ways to increase this annual yield, sometimes doubling or tripling your yield.

Most people buying a home start out with a list of things they believe they must have. During the process of looking for a home, buyers encounter a variety of things that they have never thought of or even considered. In fact, most buyers come up with homes that are significantly different from the ones they started out searching for. Why does this happen? The process of selecting a home is more an emotional experience than a test of logistics and organization. What people think they want and what they really want are seldom in line with what they can afford or even what is available. More often than not, their final choices are a result of compromise. If you are one of the organized ones, you probably started with the lists that read something like the following:

- Four bedrooms
- Three baths
- Three-car garage
- Swimming pool
- Half-acre lot
- Two-story
- Colonial
- $100,000

The only way to find out if this initial list of yours is in any way realistic is to go out and look. Like most people, you picked up the phone and called a real estate agent. The first thing the real estate agent did is to ask you what you were looking for and where in particular you thought you would like to live. This is the universal starting point. The agent searched the files of the local Multiple Listing Service® and came up with four to six houses that met your initial criteria. You got in the car and visited those houses. By the end of the trip, the real estate agent had acquired a much better feel, not for what you say you wanted, but for what you actually wanted. Where lies the difference? The difference is in the fact that buying a house is a very emotional business, more so than buying a share of stock. You are actually searching for the right place to live, to raise your children, and perhaps to grow old.

Why and how you purchased your current home is not really the focus of this book. What we're going to attempt to do throughout this book is to take the house that you currently have and improve it, so you can sell it for a profit. In reality, we are going to put your home in a condition to attract a buyer much like you. In the process, we will look at everything from a simple cleanup and paint to a major teardown, rebuild, and expand. The cost, scope, and results of this type of work will vary immensely. The decisions about what to do, when, and how to do it will depend on a variety of factors, not the least of which is your available resources.

Understanding What You've Got

What really is a house? The obvious answer is "a place to live." In reality, however, it is much more than that. The inescapable fact is that when you bought the house, you did it at a specific point in time when it reflected what you wanted at that point in time. Times have changed, people move on, neighborhoods change, economic climates and family situations change. People must change their lives to accommodate the changes around them. When you purchased your home, you obviously had some good reasons to choose not only the house itself, but the neighborhood. Your reasons were typical of the process of buying a house. Your potential buyer will most likely go through a similar process, looking at the following factors:

- Proximity to work
- Available transportation networks
- Crime rate
- Available city services
- Schools
- Churches and other religious institutions
- Shopping
- Recreation
- Weather
- Job opportunities in the community
- Space requirements
- Architectural style
- Cost and available equity and financing

Why You Bought It

Your reasons for purchasing the house you live in were personal. Everyone's decision is personal, but the components of that decision for you and for everyone else are similar and common sense. These components are definable parts of the price of the house when you purchased and its future value when you sell. To maximize your value when you sell, you must understand what makes your home worth not only what you paid, but also what you will want to get if you sell it someday down the line.

> **HEADS UP**
>
> Knowing what you know, would you buy the home you're in today? If the answer is yes, you're going to make some money when you sell.

EMPLOYMENT

One of the large components of the value of any housing unit is its location relative to major employment centers in your area. If you chose your home on the basis of a job that is outside of the normal range of employment for your area, you may have chosen a home that might be geographically incompatible with the general working patterns for your area. This is not a fatal mistake. It simply provides a limit, when the time comes for you to sell your house. All you have done by choosing a home that is out of the mainstream is limit your resale market to people who care to live and work in that area. Sometimes, it is better to choose a home that is slightly inconvenient for you than to choose one that is ideal for you but outside the mainstream.

These days, there are distinct and separate marketplaces related to employment. The historical employment base was in the traditional downtown area. However, today there is a strong suburban component to employment, as employers diversify geographically, in an effort to take advantage of available labor. The important thing for you to know and to take into account when you get ready to sell your home is the employment base your home falls into. A good realtor can help you determine this and subsequently take it into account when placing a value on your home for sale.

TRANSPORTATION

A major subset of employment is the transportation corridors that are in close proximity to your home. You must be able to get to work conveniently and have convenient access to shopping without any major stress. For major shopping, the ideal is to be within a half hour's drive.

SHOPPING

A key factor in the desirability of individual housing areas is their proximity to shopping. Shopping is broken down into two major categories: convenience and major.

The convenience category of shopping includes neighborhood centers, anchored by grocery stores, drugstores, and banks, as well as highly visible commercial centers or unanchored "strip" centers, as they are known. These centers contain stores that are convenience-oriented, i.e. readily accessible on the way to and from work. Major shopping centers lie in the expanded community centers and/or regional shopping centers anchored by three to five department stores and containing approximately 700,000 to 1,000,000-plus square feet of retail space. Auto malls are another example of a specialized major retail area.

RECREATION

Another major determinant of retail values or areas of retail values lies in their proximity or accessibility to recreational areas. Recreational areas fall into many categories. The local neighborhood recreational area could be a park, a baseball field, public tennis courts, or a high school that is available to the public for weekend use. Local urban recreational areas can be amusement parks, public swimming pools, riding stables, and entertainment complexes. Regional recreational areas include mountains, lakes, and seashores.

SCHOOLS

Schools are an essential part of the determination of value in single-family housing. Not only is proximity important, but also the quality, real or perceived, of these educational institutions is a major determinant of value. This factor will vary widely depending upon what part of the country you are in and whether the area is growing or static. In the eastern part of the country, most neighborhoods are well-established and fairly mature. However, in the western United States where growth and population expansion are the order of the day, new neighborhoods incorporate not only the necessary neighborhood commercial centers, but also the necessary schools and other infrastructures that support the new residential area.

Size Really Matters

Most people buy a home that responds directly to their current needs and somewhat to their perceived future needs. Thus, a house becomes the "family home." In the United States, however, the family is no longer the traditional mother, father, and 2.3 children. It is a single person, a single-parent household, a retired couple, a gay couple, and any other form of domestic arrangement people can come up with. Where does your house fit into this equation? It really doesn't matter, as long as you are able to value it correctly and market it to the segment of the population where it fits.

YESTERDAY'S CHOICE

If you purchased your house as a single person, it might very well be that your home is located in an area of town that is frequented by single people. If your lifestyle has changed from the time you purchased this house, that's typical. However, it would be pointless to retrofit this house, in an area that is popular among singles, to be a traditional family home. The only person who can answer this question with any degree of accuracy is your local real estate agent. When the time comes to maximize the value of your home for resale, you must be careful to take this into consideration.

TODAY'S REALITY

If you've purchased this home recently and you are part of a traditional family, you have most likely chosen a home as outlined in the section entitled "Shelter vs. Investment" earlier in this chapter, regardless of the price. This single most easily resold home in the United States used to be a house with three bedrooms, two baths, and a two-car garage on a quarter-acre lot. The only deviation from that for today's home is that the three bedrooms have now become four bedrooms. The reason for this is the proliferation of home offices. That means that the traditional three-bedroom home is a problem to sell; it has become more of a starter home than a permanent family home. You might want to take into account the possibility of adding a fourth bedroom, den, or work area before putting the house on the market.

TOMORROW'S NEEDS

If you are one of the super-organized, astute, and forward-thinking individuals, you have purchased a home that will be suitable for you and your family today and tomorrow, ideally suited to your rising affluence, your expanded collection of toys, and your self-image, not only today but also in your ultimate incarnation. If this is true, you are indeed a rare individual. This means that you have no need to move and can live in this home for the rest of your life. If this is the case, reading this section of the book will be a total waste of time for you.

Services

The basic services necessary to support any residential area are fire protection, police, and essential medical services. No matter what your circumstances, you absolutely must be in an area that contains these services. You can survive without paved streets, cable TV, and garbage service, but you must have the basic necessary services or your home will be penalized in value when you sell it.

FIRE, POLICE, AND MEDICAL

People take emergency services for granted. In older communities, such as some eastern cities, these things were not taken into account when the first housing was built. You'll find that the services somehow have been adapted into the older communities. They may not be as elegant, convenient, and economical as those found in the new communities, but I can assure you that they are there in one form or another or the residential area in question will not be a viable community and the houses will not sell easily.

SCHOOLS

If you have no children of school age, schools may not be a factor in your life or in the community in which you live. This would be a rare situation. If you are one of the few people in this situation, you will have to market directly to people who are also in this situation. In most cases, if you have changed your circumstances, you'll find that this community will no longer work for you. This is not a crisis; there is always something for everyone. You simply market to the community you used to belong to.

SHOPPING

The availability of goods and services that satisfy immediate, day-to-day needs is absolutely essential to a residential community. You can do without high-fashion clothing, automobiles, and regional shopping centers in your neighborhood. You must, however, be able to buy food, drink, toilet paper, and dog food.

RECREATION

The most immediate recreational needs for a viable housing area are local parks, a community swimming pool, some tennis courts, and a place to run. If your neighborhood contains some or all of these recreational facilities, then your home should be readily marketable to a broad spectrum of consumers. Again, you can do without Six Flags over Georgia, the ocean, the golf course view of the country club, and the ski resort, for these are all destination recreational facilities.

HEADS UP

When you are evaluating your present home, keep in mind why you chose it. Your buyer will be looking at it in the same manner. Don't lie to yourself. There is no profit in wishful thinking.

Personal Image and Selection

One of the crucial factors in owning a home is self-image. Housing styles and architecture directly address an individual's self-image. In some areas, such as New England, houses are largely constructed in a particular architectural style, such as colonial. Most areas, however, are a mix of architectural styles, sizes, layouts, and amenities. The differences in style, size, layout, and amenities are important only in that you need to understand where your home lies within the market area in which you live. Even in New England, there is a definable demand for a modern home. I would hazard a guess, having lived there for about six years, that the modern home in New England would account for less than five percent of the potential housing market. Things like this must be kept in mind when you are either buying a home or attempting to sell a home.

Architecture

Houses throughout the country come in many architectural styles. It's important that you have an understanding of your area as it pertains to architectural style. This will be valuable to you not only when you go to sell your current home, but also when you choose a new one. These are typical architectural styles:

- Colonial
- Modern
- Contemporary
- Ranch
- Spanish
- California
- Tudor
- Tuscan

Each of the styles has its place; however, they most likely do not mix well all in one neighborhood. This is a good thing to know when you start renovating. You might also benefit by taking the ugly duckling house and turning it into an architectural marvel that fits well into your neighborhood.

Size

Size matters in that your house needs to be consistent with other homes in your area. It is never a great idea to have the largest or most expensive home in your neighborhood. These are the most difficult homes to sell. If you are renovating, do not create a home that does not fit the neighborhood. Needless to say, do not buy a home that fits this description.

Layout

What exactly do I mean by "layout"? This would encompass things such as lot size, lot coverage, number of stories, sizes and types of rooms, and type of subdivision. It's not a problem if a house deviates from the norm on some of these factors. If your lot is larger than average, that will make your home very desirable for resale. If, however, you had a five-acre lot in a neighborhood of half-acre lots, you may have a problem realizing the value of your house. On the other hand, you may be able to subdivide your property and realize five times perceived value. Each situation is different and must be evaluated as such.

Amenities

Amenities fall into two categories: inside and outside the home. Interior amenities might include a wet bar, a clamshell shower, a fireplace, and fancy fittings such as upgraded windows and doors. Exterior amenities might be a swimming pool, a tennis court, a basketball court, or an oversize lot. The important thing to know about amenities is that they should be consistent with those in your neighborhood. A tract home on a quarter-acre lot with a tennis court is more of a liability than an asset. A tract home with a basketball hoop over the garage door is definitely an asset for resale.

HEADS UP

All the above factors, taken together, will be the prime determinant of the value or potential value of your home at the time of resale. Using some common sense, relying on some credible advice, and keeping things in perspective, you should have no trouble in deciding how to maximize the value of your home prior to sale.

The Economics of Ownership

As with most things in our life, housing too comes with a price tag. It is necessary when dealing with an investment of this magnitude, to understand precisely how the money works. From the price of the house right on down to *PITI,* we need to fully understand how the money works for us or against us.

DEFINITION

PITI is an acronym for principal, interest, taxes, and insurance. These are the four components of most mortgage payments.

If you've already purchased a house, which I'm assuming you have, you will remember that the purchase price was only part of what you paid for the house. In addition to the price, you paid loan costs as well as some closing costs, insurance, inspection fees, and in some cases home warranty costs. Depending upon the price of the house purchased, this could have amounted to as much as five percent to seven percent of the purchase price of the house. Why is this important? The answer is, quite simply, that by fully understanding the cash and how it flows, how it's used, and the taxable implications, you can increase your profit while you live there, and when you sell. Let's examine the components of the transaction of buying and selling and see how they relate to you and your wallet.

Price and Loans

First of all, we have the price of the house you purchased or are about to purchase. If you are an inexperienced homeowner, you may or may not have been told what your options are when purchasing a home. Depending on your status with the military, you might have the entire range of options from paying zero percent cash down to 100 percent cash. Assuming you have the cash in the bank, you might ask why you should even take out a loan. The answer is that by taking a loan of any kind, you increase your return on investment through leverage. If you purchased a $100,000 home for cash, and you sell it for $120,000, your return on investment (ROI) is 20 percent over the period you own the home. If, however, you purchased the same home with a conventional loan with 20 percent down, your actual investment was $20,000. When you sell the same house for $120,000, your ROI is now 100 percent cash on cash over the period of your ownership. The difference between paying cash and taking out a loan is called *leveraging* the money. By using someone else's money, you have increased your rate of return from 20 percent to 100 percent during the period of your homeownership.

HEADS UP

Remember leverage, because this is how homeowners make money. If you incorporate the use of leverage into your home ownership and investments, you can make your money produce much greater returns for you.

If you examine the components of the total price paid for your home, you'll see a breakdown similar to the one below.

- Price
- Loan points
- Tax impound
- Prepaid interest
- Underwriting fee
- Insurance
- Inspections
- Document preparation fee

Why should you break down the transaction in this detail? The answer is that parts of this transaction are tax-deductible in the current tax year. I'm not giving you tax advice, I am telling you to ask your accountant at tax time to look into the transaction and select those items that can be deducted from your current year's taxes. This is just one little bonus involved in home ownership. We will cover the total tax picture later in this chapter.

Down Payments

Why the difference in down payments? The answer is, that in today's housing market, you have available to you, up to and exceeding 100 percent financing. It is literally possible today to purchase a home and finance not only the house, closing costs, and loan points, but also the furniture and appliances you put in the home. Of course, this all requires excellent credit. Is this advisable? Only you can answer that in relation to your own financial picture. The following loans are listed in relation to their required down payments.

- Conventional, 20 percent down
- FHA, three percent to five percent down
- VA, for veterans only, zero percent down

For VA and FHA loans, in most cases, the seller pays the loan points. In essence you are using the seller's money to leverage your own money. Homes that sell in this price category are generally priced to accommodate the seller's paying these points, but sometimes you can get a real bargain by qualifying for an FHA or VA loan. FHA and VA loan have dollar limits that vary from state to state. The amount you can borrow this way will surprise you.

DEFINITION

VA stands for Veterans Affairs, before 1989 Veterans Administration. These loans are for veterans of military service only. *FHA* is an acronym for the Federal Housing Authority. These loans were designed to allow low-income families to enjoy the benefits of home ownership.

Additional loans, using a combination of first and second mortgages, can add up to 100 percent of the purchase price. If you live in an area where housing does not appreciate substantially every year, you should stay away from 100 percent financing altogether. If, however, you live in an area with an expanding economy, where housing increases in value ten percent to 15 percent annually, you can build up equity in your house fairly quickly with little or no money down. What this means is that if you have good credit but no cash, you can still be a homeowner and profit from your investment.

Mortgages

What is a mortgage? A mortgage is a secured loan. In the East, a mortgage is documented by a note and a recorded mortgage. In the West, mortgages are documented by a note and a deed of trust. These two documents together constitute a mortgage. The note is signed by you, as evidence of having borrowed money. The mortgage or deed of trust is recorded against your property to tell the world that you owe money on your home. This precludes the possibility of your selling the house without paying off the mortgage. Mortgages come in a variety of forms and they are, one and all, classified as liens against your property.

Liens

What is a lien? It is simply a notice that a third-party has a claim secured against your property. Liens come in a variety of forms and have a variety of priority.

What are the practical implications of priorities? In all cases, in all parts of the country, real estate taxes are in a first lien position. This means that, in the event a homeowner defaults on his or her mortgage payments, the mortgage holder must ensure that taxes are paid, to preserve the value of his or her mortgage. In a similar vein, the second, third, and fourth lienholders must ensure that the lienholders in front of them are paid in full to ensure payment of their own liens. Taxes and mortgages are the major liens. Other types of liens are *mechanics' liens* and *recorded judgments*.

DEFINITION

Priority defines who gets paid first, second, third, or fourth. The practical aspects of liens are simple. Whoever is in first position gets paid in full first. Payments then go to the second, then the third, and so on. Anybody else in line must ensure the first lienholder's payments prior to seeing any payment themselves.

DEFINITION

A ***mechanics' lien*** is a notice, recorded against your home, that a contractor has done work on your house, but has not been paid. When your home is sold, this lien will be paid before you receive any money. A *judgment* is an obligation to pay granted by the court in favor of a third party against you. Payment of this judgment may be insured by its recording against your property. It will be paid, if funds are available when the home is sold.

Payments

When you make a mortgage payment you will, like most people in this country, be making a payment that comprises four components: principal, interest, taxes, and insurance (PITI). To repay your loan amount over a specific period of time, the lender will calculate your payments using a *loan constant*. This loan constant is a composite of principal and interest on the principal. It is calculated so that each payment pays the interest on the outstanding balance of the loan at that time and enough of the principal to amortize the loan over the term of the loan. For example, a seven-percent loan for 30 years will utilize a loan constant of 7.99 percent. What this means is that the seven percent will be the interest initially on the outstanding balance of the loan and 0.99 percent will go to defray the principal of the loan. Over the years, as your payments progress, the amount of the outstanding balance of the loan will decrease, so in each payment the amount of interest paid will decrease and the amount of principal paid will increase. The result is that, at the end of the

30 years, the loan is paid in full. The payment is calculated by taking the initial loan amount, let's say $100,000, and multiplying it by 7.99 percent (.799). We get $7,990.00 per year. Divide that by 12 and you get a monthly mortgage payment of $665.83. This is the PI portion of your mortgage payment. The TI portion is also collected by your lender to ensure that you keep these payments up on a monthly basis. Experienced lenders have learned that it is difficult for the average borrower to accumulate the tax payment annually. By collecting a small portion monthly, the lender ensures that the taxes are paid. The philosophy is similar regarding insurance. The lender wants to know that its investment in your home is covered by insurance at all times. By collecting both taxes and insurance, the lender ensures that its loan is covered. Lenders don't mind lending you money, but they want to make sure that they get it back.

Equity

What is equity? It is the value of your home minus the mortgage balance. If you purchase a $100,000 home with a conventional loan, you will put down $20,000 as a down payment. This means that you are starting out with $20,000 of equity. After a few years, when you sell the house for $120,000, you will have accumulated an additional $20,000 of equity. When you sell and pay off the $80,000 mortgage, you will end up with $40,000. If you purchase the same home with zero percent down and sell it at the same time a few years later, you will have earned through ownership an equity of $20,000. Whether you pay $100,000 cash, 20 percent down, or zero down makes a difference in your ROI. In the case of all cash, your ROI is 20 percent. In the case of 20 percent down, your ROI is 100 percent. In the case of zero percent down, your ROI is infinite. In any case, if you live in an area where housing appreciates routinely, changing homes every two years will allow you to accumulate a substantial tax-free nest egg. Tax-free? Yes! Let's look at the tax implications of the average home ownership.

Tax Implications

The tax advantages of home ownership are many. They start the day you purchase a house. They are as follows:

- Portions of the purchase price are deductible from your current year taxes.
- Interest paid is deductible from your annual tax bill.
- Profits taken when you sell your home may be totally tax-free.

What are the practical implications of the above tax advantages of home ownership? Let's assume for the moment that you are in the 25-percent tax bracket. For every dollar deducted from your gross income, you save 25 percent. That means that every dollar you pay in interest, during the life of the loan, actually costs you only $.75. In addition, if you live in the home as your primary residence for a period of two years, your profit at the time of sale is 100 percent tax-free. Imagine: if you purchased and sold a home for a profit every two years, you could very easily accumulate a sizable nest egg and, conceivably, own your home free and clear in a relatively short time.

HEADS UP

This is, most likely, the one and only opportunity you will have in your lifetime to earn truly *tax-free* money. Take advantage of it as often as the law allows. If you learn only one thing from this book, this is it.

CHAPTER

8

Your Home *and* Your Money

The most basic place to start when dealing with real estate investment is your own home. Perhaps, up to now, you have not given much thought to your house as an investment. In this chapter I would like to deal with housing in several ways. First of all, let's take a look at your house. Second, let's look into a home that you may buy when you sell your house. Finally, let's look at buying another house as an investment.

A House Is Not a Home

There is a book entitled *A House Is Not a Home*. It's a basic truth. In our industry the words "house" and "home" have different connotations. Throughout the book, you may notice that I use the words differently in different contexts. When I use the word *home*, I think of it as a place where you or I live. When I use the word *house*, I think of it as a building project, a structure, a rental unit, or an investment. You need to start thinking of your home as also a house.

As I mentioned earlier in the book, your home is a bank account that you may draw upon at any time. If you have lived there for over two years, you may sell the house without paying any taxes whatsoever on your profits. The equity in your current home, as of today, is a given. What can you do to maximize that value prior to a sale? We will touch on some of these strategies later in this section of the book. For now, let's just outline what the potential can be.

- You can clean the place up, give it a new coat of paint, put up wallpaper, put down carpet, and make sure that all items of deferred maintenance are caught up. This will make the house, as is, as presentable and, therefore, as salable as possible.
- You can embark upon a renovation program, adding features desirable in today's market. This would be an upgrade, increasing the value of your home when completed.
- You can totally revamp your home through demolition and construction, taking your home to a whole new category of house. Before you embark on a program like this, however, you need to do some serious market research. This step is the biggest step in house investment, as it involves your home.

A Financial Snapshot

If you have not done an in-depth analysis of your home as a financial investment, perhaps now is an appropriate time to do so. Let us take a hypothetical home, owned by the average American today, and make some basic assumptions:

- The home was purchased five years ago for $160,000.
- It was purchased with a conventional loan (20 percent down). The terms were eight percent for 30 years.
- In the last five years, houses in the immediate area have increased on the average of ten percent per year.

Table 8-1 outlines the basic financial facts.

When you examine Table 8-1, you will realize that, over a five-year period, you have made a profit of $94,000, totally tax-free. In addition, you actually made an investment that produced 53 percent per year totally tax-free. When was the last time you made such a good investment? Hopefully this puts your personal residence in a new light for you. Who knows what the future might hold for you if, before buying a house, you actually planned to make money on it?

How to Buy a Home

Before you buy your next home, you need to decide on the most important components of your house purchasing rationale. Considerations for buying a home include the following:

- The need for shelter for you and your family
- The home's location as it relates to your work
- Services convenient to the home's location
- The area—social factors as well as economic
- The financial investment
- The potential future appreciation of the house
- Is it upgradeable?
- Is it expandable?
- Can the neighborhood/area absorb the upgrade or the expansion?
- Where is the top of the market?
- How long do you plan to keep the house?
- Is the size of your family going to remain constant?
- How does the investment in this new home fit into your long-term financial planning?
- How much of your available financial resources are you willing to commit to this purchase/investment?

Item		Dollar Value
Purchase price		$160,000
Down payment (20%)	conventional loan	$32,000
Closing costs	estimate	$3,500
Mortgage amount	80%	$128,000
Mortgage (PI) 8%/30 years (APR = 8.81%)	PI = principal and interest on $128K	$11,276.80/year $939.73/month
Appreciation (10% x 5 years)	compounded year 1	$176,000
	compounded year 2	$193,600
	compounded year 3	$212,960
	compounded year 4	$234,256
	compounded year 5	$257,682
Initial investment	down + closing costs	$35,500
Gross appreciation/ profit	end of year 5 new value less cost	$94,182
ROI	on $35,500	265% or 53%/year
Annual benefit during ownership	estimated tax write-off	$10,240

TABLE 8-1. PERSONAL RESIDENCE—ECONOMIC PROFILE

You can probably add to this list for your own particular situation. Whether you add to it or not, you need to go through this list before you purchase a new home. I recommend that, before you buy a new home, you incorporate formal investment analysis into your long-term financial planning. As you can see above, you are able to profit tax-free on the house you're currently living in. Can you find another investment that will be as advantageous? I doubt it.

The implication of this potential increase in your net worth as it relates to your housing is that it is and should always be a cornerstone of your long-term financial planning. Unless you're working with an unusually large amount of money, rotating your family home every two to three years and taking advantage of the tax-free nature of the investment might very well prove to be the single most profitable investment you are likely to make. All other investments will be taxable, either annually or at the time of sale.

Market Research

Now that you have a clearer financial picture of your home and its current and potential impact on your wallet, you need to figure out how to go about maximizing the value and the return on investment of your next home.

HEADS UP

The universal truth in real estate is that you make your money when you buy. Buy it right and you can't lose. Overpay and you cannot recoup.

How About Your Area?

How much thought have you given to the area where you currently live? Has the area appreciated in sync with your general economic area in the past ten years? Has the appreciation of housing values in your immediate area exceeded that of other homes and other neighborhoods in your region? If not, why not? If your neighborhood has outperformed other comparable neighborhoods, why has it? What does your Realtor® think about the short-term future in your area vs. other areas in your municipality or region? More importantly, what do you think and why do you think what you think? Have you taken a good look at the market, discussed it with your Realtor®, your banker, or the local appraiser?

Comparables

Home valuation, aka appraisal, is done in two separate ways: by comparable sales price and by replacement cost. In addition, the land is and can be valued as a separate item. When the land size exceeds that of your neighbors' lands and/or the location is better, the land can be given a premium value that adds to its overall value. Your local Realtor® and the local appraiser utilize recent sales of comparable homes as a basis for establishing value for a specific home. In today's industry, the Multiple Listing Service® (MLS®) in most areas is electronic, and data retrieval and analysis of data are more sophisticated than ever before. Both Realtor® and appraiser have at their fingertips all current property listings, past sales, and county tax records. Over the last several years, computerization of the MLS database has made data correlation and analysis almost instantaneous.

Are Appraisals Accurate?

One of the logical questions that people ask is "Are houses truly comparable?" The answer is twofold: for tract homes, yes, but for custom homes, not exactly. Appraisals for tract housing are relatively simple, due to the repetitive nature of tract home construction. The average tract composed of one to 300 homes generally has less than eight models. Even with the variations of trim and finish that are available, appraisals for this type of home are relatively straightforward. Even extra features that are available, such as additional garages, exercise rooms, swimming pools, additional bedrooms, etc., are all priced in a standard way by the builder and these items appreciate in a uniform manner over the years.

Custom homes, however, are a different proposition. A rule-of-thumb comparison can be done based on square-footage values. For example, in my neck of the woods, in 2004, custom homes are selling for about $200 per square foot. Using this as a starting point, most appraisers will then add to or subtract from the average valuation distinctive features such as additional bedrooms, swimming pools, oversize lots, exceptional views, and anything else they believe adds to or detracts from the value of the average home within that area. I refer to this as "tweaking the value," to make it more accurate.

Resales vs. New

There is also a value differential between new and resale homes. There does not seem to be a consistent price or value differential from region to region. In some places in the country, new homes carry a premium, but in others, comparing feature for feature and size for size, new homes sell for less money than more established homes. When you are evaluating your market, you need to research and factor in the new-vs.-used value. Hopefully, in your area there will be a premium for the resale home.

What's New?

A component of value that you should be aware of is the "bells and whistles" incorporated into new housing. Way back in the dark ages, we remember when wet bars were introduced to the then standard ranch-style home. This was followed by sunken living room, sunken tubs, walk-in closets, indirect lighting, wall-to-wall carpeting, and other features that are now standard in any new home. In recent years we have seen the addition of pot shelves, microwaves, double ovens, Corian® and marble counters, and a wide variety of upgraded flooring materials. If and when you consider modernizing, upgrading, or expanding your current home prior to selling it, you should look into and "value engineer" all of the new "gee whiz" desirable upgrades. In the Appendix you'll find some charts on this type of renovation. You'll see that it is very easy to overspend the value of this type of improvement. Leave a little upgrading potential for your prospective buyer.

Housing Costs

I'd like to spend a little time here analyzing the components of cost related to homes when you are contemplating a purchase, as well as looking at the different types of leverage available for home purchases. The purchase of housing today includes components of cost that didn't exist ten years ago. The list below is an attempt to bring you up to speed, but is not expected to be the final word on the subject. Your local Realtor® would be able to fill in any gaps or add items that I have left unaddressed.

- The purchase price
- The closing costs
- Loan points
- Termite inspection
- Home inspection
- Roof warranties
- Appliance warranties
- Insurance costs, including insured loss history on the home known as the CLUE report (Comprehensive Loss Underwriting Exchange)

Every individual item listed above has a very real dollar value attached to it. It's amazing how they add up. What is important is making sure that you include all of your costs associated with the purchase as part of your investment in the house. It is traditional that most lenders will include these costs in the total package when considering a mortgage loan application. A conventional loan today will allow you to borrow up to 80 percent of the total costs.

Leverage

There are many forms of leverage available to the perspective homebuyer, the most common of which is the mortgage. Mortgages come in an infinite variety of choices. Let's look at some of the potential loan choices available to you when you buy a home. They include the following:

- Purchase money loan or seller carry-back financing
- A contract for sale
- A wrap loan, aka an all-inclusive deed of trust
- A conventional 80-percent loan
- An adjustable-rate mortgage
- An interest-only loan

- Second mortgages
- A combination first and second loan
- Hard money loans

A little confusing, isn't it? We'll take a quick look at each of these loan types so that you have a good understanding of what is available. I do not necessarily recommend any particular type of loan. It is important, however, to be aware of them in case an opportunity arises in which any one of these might make good sense for your particular situation.

DEFINITION

All mortgage loan payments have two components, principal (P) and interest (I), and some mortgages have two additional components required by the lender, tax impounds (T) and insurance impounds (I). So a mortgage loan that does not require impounds has a ***PI payment*** and one that does require impounds is referred to as a ***PITI payment***.

Purchase Money Loans

A *purchase money loan* is financing provided by the seller of the property. It is often found in raw land transactions. It becomes common in the housing market in times of tight money or high interest rates. It is also quite common in a transaction where the buyer's credit is less than stellar. Terms for this type of the loan are totally negotiable, but, in general, interest rates and points are higher and more onerous than those found in more conventional bank financing.

Contracts for Sale

A *contract for sale* is exactly what the title states. Buyer and seller enter into an agreement for the buyer to make payments to the seller, which accrue toward the purchase price. In most instances, the seller retains title to the home with a contract for sale recorded as a lien against the property. A portion of the payment will accrue to the purchase price; the balance of the payment is interest to the seller. When the contract is fully paid or paid down to an agreed-upon amount, the deed is then recorded in the buyer's name and the balance of the contract, if any, is then converted into a mortgage loan.

Wrap Loans

A *wrap loan* is a loan granted by the seller to the buyer, leaving the seller's current financing in place. The incremental part of the loan (that amount over and above the seller's existing loan) is deemed to be "wrapped" around the existing loan. In most instances, the new total loan is at an interest rate higher than that of the existing loan. Table 8-2 shows the effect of this type of a loan on both buyer and seller. The virtue of this loan, from a buyer's point of view, is that this financing is available in times when financing is hard to get. From the seller's point of view, the advantage is a higher-than-face-rate effective rate of interest on the incremental part of the loan.

You can see why it's a good deal for the seller. While the buyer is paying a relatively conventional 8.5 percent interest rate on his home loan, the seller is receiving a whopping 21 percent interest on his incremental part of the loan. These types of loans proliferate during times of tight money and high interest rates.

Conventional Loans

The most common loan in use within the United States has been, since WW II, a conventional 80-percent loan. This is typically a bank loan and it carries a preferred rate of interest due to the substantial down payment required by the terms of the loan. Other relatively widespread loans made by the banking industry are *FHA* and *VA* loans. The FHA loan can be obtained with down payments as low as three

Item	Value
Existing mortgage value	$150,000
Existing interest rate	7% on 30-year payout
Existing loan payment (7.2% APR)	$10,800/year or $900/month (PI)
New loan amount increment	$25,000
New wrap loan total of the existing loan and increment	$175,000
New loan interest rate	8.5% on 30-year payout
New loan payment (9.23% APR)	$16,152/year or $1,346/month (PI)
Yield to seller: new payment for existing payment	$5,352/year or $446/month
ROI to seller on $25,000 loan	21%/year

TABLE 8-2. WRAP LOAN ANALYSIS

percent and a VA loan requires zero percent down. These loans generally carry a higher rate of interest and most of them require mortgage insurance. Mortgage insurance covers the difference between the 80-percent loan and the FHA 97-percent loan or 100-percent VA loan. Almost all conventional mortgage loans today require tax and interest impounds.

Adjustable-Rate Mortgages

Increasingly popular today, and introduced over two decades ago, is the *adjustable-rate mortgage*. This loan came into being due to the increased value of the average home in today's housing market. To make homes more affordable, builders needed to lower the monthly payments so that their potential buyers could qualify for the loan. The typical adjustable-rate mortgage starts out at a nominal low rate of interest for a period of years and increases or decreases based on a predetermined index, such as the *cost of living* or the *federal funds discount rate*. In many of the loans, a clause allows the loan to float up or down and most lenders set a "floor" rate below which the rate cannot go. The middle-of-the-road compromise seems to be an adjustable-rate mortgage with both a "floor" and a "ceiling" rate of interest. As housing prices rise higher and higher, this loan becomes increasingly popular.

Interest-Only Loans

Taking matters a step further, today lenders are allowing *interest-only loans* as mortgages. Unheard of in the past, these are becoming very common, especially in areas where the appreciation rate of housing is equal to or greater than the rate of inflation. In the past, lenders used to rely on the 20-percent down payment in the case of the conventional loan and mortgage insurance in the case of the VA and FHA loans. The lenders now look to home appreciation as protection against loss in case of foreclosure.

Second Mortgages

Since our country's economy seems to be fueled by consumer debt, a new type of loan has become very popular. The universal use of credit cards has led many people into debt and interest charged on credit card debt is at least 100 percent higher than interest rates charged on mortgage loans. Inflation and rapid appreciation in housing values have prompted lenders to loan against the equity in the home, over and above the first mortgage. This is known as the *home equity loan* or *second mortgage*. It has become a popular way to pay off credit card debt, and it has the added advantage that the interest on this type of loan is tax-deductible. Interest on personal loans, automobile loans, credit card loans, or any other form of loan is, for the homeowner, not tax-deductible. Mortgage loans are the only exception. Today it makes more sense to take a second on your home to buy a car than it does to buy a car with a conventional auto loan.

A Combination First-and-Second Loan

Carrying this concept a step even further, there are companies such as ditech.com that advertise 100- to 125-percent financing. The concept here is that the appreciation will provide protection for the lender against a potential recovery shortfall (deficiency) in the event of a foreclosure. These types of loans typically require better-than-average credit. There are even loans now offered by conventional bank financing, using a combination of first and second mortgages, offering a buyer 100-percent financing on a purchase. These loans, however, carry a premium interest rate commensurate with the risk.

Hard Money Loans

The lender of last resort is a group of private lenders known as the *hard money lenders*. These lenders charge 500 percent more in points and front-end costs, and, as much as 5 to 8 percent more per year in interest. In addition, unlike the conventional financing offered by banks and other finance companies, these lenders require personal guarantees by the borrower for any recovery shortfall in the event of foreclosure.

Lenders

Lenders are broken down into four major groups:

- Banks, REITs, and insurance companies
- Mortgage companies
- Other lenders: GMAC, ditech.com, e-loan.com
- Portfolio lenders

Banks and Insurance Companies

By far the most common and prevailing lenders are banks and insurance companies. These two groups have been traditionally the largest and most consistent lenders in both the housing and commercial building industries.

Mortgage Companies

Between the borrower and the lender is a group of companies known as *mortgage brokers* or *mortgage bankers*. The difference between a broker and a banker is relatively simple.

The mortgage banker represents a very limited and specific list of lenders and the mortgage broker shops his or her potential loans to any lender in the market. In addition to making loans, the mortgage banker normally services the loans on behalf of the lenders represented by that company. *Loan servicing* generally means collecting the payments, distributing the funds to the lender, and making payments from impound accounts. The mortgage bankers collect a fee, usually equal to or less than 1/10 of one percent of the funds collected. The mortgage banker's first allegiance—his or her *fiduciary duty*—is to the lender; the mortgage bankers is referred to as the lender's *correspondent*.

The mortgage broker, representing the prospective borrower, takes a loan application from the borrower, collects the borrower's credit history and other information, and shops the loan to any lender in the marketplace. Mortgage brokers do not service loans; they earn their living from *origination fees*. Origination fees are points charged as fees for making and/or arranging the loan. Not uncommonly, the mortgage broker can be compensated by both borrower and lender. By law, mortgage broker should disclose these dual fees to both borrower and lender.

An additional function of both mortgage bankers and mortgage brokers is what is known as *warehousing* loans. This is the compiling of closed home loans in bundles of $1,000,000 or more. These bundled loans, generally in amounts of tens of millions of dollars, are then sold to investors in what is known as the *secondary mortgage market* or *secondary loan market*. These bundles of loans are securities backed by a large numbers of mortgages on individual pieces of real estate, sometimes guaranteed by an agency of the federal government such as *Fannie Mae*, *Freddie Mac*, or *Ginny Mae*.

The secondary market is populated by entities with funny names. Fannie Mae (otherwise known as the Federal National Mortgage Association, FNMA) is a federal agency that guarantees repayment of home loans sold to investors with a Fannie Mae guarantee. Other agencies known as Ginny Mae (Government National Mortgage Association, GNMA) and Freddie Mac (Federal Home Loan Mortgage Corporation, FHLMC) fulfill basically the same function. Unless you have a large amount of money to invest, you will probably never come into contact with any of these federal agencies.

Other Lenders

Periods of high inflation and tight money have caused the rise of alternative lenders for real estate products. Commercial lending companies like GMAC, which was originally formed to loan money on automobile purchases, have moved into equipment loans and real estate loans. Their first foray into real estate loans was usually the second loan or equity line of credit loan, but increasingly these companies and new companies like ditech.com are becoming more and more mainstream lenders.

Portfolio Lenders

Portfolio lenders are, from the point of view of commercial loans, my all-time favorite lenders. Up until the early 1980s, most life insurance companies and commercial real estate lenders were portfolio lenders; that is to say they made the loans, serviced the loans, and kept them until they were paid in full. Starting in the 1980s, commercial lenders, mostly local banks, started making commercial loans and bundling them for sale in the secondary market. To make these loans easier to sell, the borrower was "locked" into the loan for a minimum period of time; that is to say that the borrower could not pay off the loan before the expiration of the term.

In lieu of absolutely forbidding prepayment, the lenders instituted a fee roughly equivalent to the amount of interest that would be due and payable if the loan went to the full term. An alternative to this has been what is called a *yield maintenance*, which edged its way into the loan market. It states that a borrower who wants to pay off a loan early must pay a fee equivalent to the difference between the projected interest yield on the loan and the yield possible at the prevailing market rate at the time the loan is paid off.

These two types of clauses enabled these bundled loans to be sold in the secondary market, because the investor had the confidence that, whether the loans were held to term or prepaid, the lender would make the promised yield on the loan dollars. From the borrower's standpoint, if interest rates were high when the loan was committed, it was very expensive to prepay the loan as rates began to fall. Conversely, on a loan made during a period of low interest rates, the yield maintenance provision made it very easy for the borrower to prepay as the penalties became nonexistent.

Unfortunately, many lenders, including traditional banks and insurance companies, found that they could make good income from origination fees and commercial loans and an additional markup or "discount" on the bundled loans when sold in the secondary market. The result is that the prevailing loan in the commercial market today is the bundled loan with lock-ins varying from five to ten years. The lock-in or yield maintenance provision generally comes with a clause specifying that, in the last year of the loan, the borrower has a penalty-free window in which to refinance the property.

The portfolio lender generally allowed prepayment without penalty. This was of great benefit to the borrower, as he or she did not have to wait nine years to refinance the property. In addition, if the property involved multiple phases, it allowed the borrower and lender alike to roll the new phases into the old loan as they were constructed and put into service. From the lender's point of view, especially with a good loan, it keeps the relationship between borrower and lender close, allowing the lender an opportunity to make additional loans to a good borrower.

All things considered, I like portfolio lenders very much. There are still some around, but they are so conservative that their loans make little or no sense to anyone but a real estate investment trust (REIT).

WHICH LOAN SHOULD YOU USE?

When you're buying a house or any other form of real estate, your rates of return on your investment are going to be better if you leverage the transaction. Having said that, I believe that there is no specific loan that fits every occasion. The best you can do is to familiarize yourself with what potential loans are out there, keep updating yourself annually, and make sure that you and your projects are as creditworthy as possible. In addition to your talent, your next best asset is your creditworthiness!

Financial Analysis

In Table 8-1 we took a hypothetical look at the financial impact of your current home. In this section of the chapter, I would like to walk you through the analysis of other pieces of personal real estate that you might consider owning, specifically a second (vacation) home and a rental property. When we get into investment and development tools later on in the book, we will expand on these financial analysis charts in greater detail. For now a quick look at the potential of different types of investment will get you thinking about what you might like to consider, at least in the residential arena.

THE VACATION HOME

Table 8-3 is relatively similar to Table 8-1. Let's keep the assumptions the same as in the original table to make it consistent.

The only difference between Table 8-1 and Table 8-3 is in the bottom of the chart, where you have incurred a taxable gain. If you are an investor, you can argue that this house was a long-term investment and, therefore, is eligible for capital gains treatment. I'm not at all sure that a profit on a vacation home would ordinarily be treated as a capital gain and I'm not an accountant, so I would defer to your accountant's opinion on any subject regarding taxation.

THE RENTAL PROPERTY

If we take the same look at a rental property, using the same assumptions, the results will look like Table 8-4.

Item		Dollar Value
Purchase price		$160,000
Down payment (20%)	conventional loan	$32,000
Closing costs	estimate	$3,500
Mortgage amount	80%	$128,000
Mortgage (PI) 8%/30 years (APR = 8.81%)	PI = principal and interest on $128K	$11,276.80/year $939.73/month
Appreciation (10% x 5 years)	compounded year 1	$176,000
	compounded year 2	$193,600
	compounded year 3	$212,960
	compounded year 4	$234,256
	compounded year 5	$257,682
Initial investment	down + closing costs	$35,500
Gross appreciation/ profit	end of year 5 new value less cost	$94,182
ROI	on $35,500	265% or 53%/year
Annual benefit during ownership	estimated tax write-off	$10,240
Taxable gain		$94,182
Tax rate	capital gain	15%

TABLE 8-3. THE VACATION HOME

As you can see, the bottom of Table 8-4 looks completely different. What you have accomplished with this rental property is that you have made a capital gain of $94,182 and rental income over a five-year year period of $4,200—but the best part of it is that your tenant has made the interest and principal payments over the five-year period. You lost your annual interest write-off of $10,000, but the trade-off is that you did not have to pay the $10,000 in interest every year; your tenant did that for you. The potential problems are in selecting a decent tenant, maintaining the property in a competitive condition, and keeping it leased throughout the five-year period. In a hypothetical situation where you are in a 30-percent tax bracket, you lose the interest write-off, costing you $3,000 in after-tax gain, but you pick up $10,000 in rental income to offset it. That's a $7,000 tax-sheltered gain.

Multifamily Rentals

A multifamily spreadsheet, while similar to Table 8-4, is necessarily more complex from the point of view of cost and income analysis.

Item		Dollar Value
Purchase price		$160,000
Down payment (20%)	conventional loan	$32,000
Closing costs	estimate	$3,500
Mortgage amount	80%	$128,000
Mortgage (PI) 8%/30 years (APR = 8.81%)	PI = principal and interest on $128K	$11,276.80/year $939.73/month
Appreciation (10% x 5 years)	compounded year 1	$176,000
	compounded year 2	$193,600
	compounded year 3	$212,960
	compounded year 4	$234,256
	compounded year 5	$257,682
Initial investment	down + closing costs	$35,500
Gross appreciation/ profit	end of year 5 new value less cost	$94,182
Rental income $1,000/ month/5 years	$1,000 x 12 x 5	$60,000
Less maintenance	$720/year	($3,600)
Net rental income	5 years	$56,400
Less interest	5 years	($51,200)
Net taxable profit	ordinary income 5 yrs	$4,200
ROI	on $35,000	265% or 53%/year
Taxable gain		$94,182
Tax rate	capital gain	15%

TABLE 8-4. THE RENTAL PROPERTY

Therefore, we shall deal with this in greater detail in Chapter 12.

How to Shop for Your Next Home

The final section of this chapter outlines steps you need to take when looking for your next home. You need to perform a two-part analysis, to locate a property that satisfies your needs for a home as well as a house.

A House as a Home

What to look for in a home will not be very much different from what you have looked for during past purchases. You will have to consider at least the following items:

- Amenities required in the house itself: number of bedrooms, baths, and garage space
- Transportation corridors (commuting): how close is it to your work, your spouse's work, and your children's schools?
- The area: does it meet your needs for raising a family, your current station in life, your ego needs?
- The neighborhood: Is it consistent in value? Are housing values uniform in the immediate neighborhood or all over the block? All over the block is not necessarily bad. It may provide opportunities for expansion and upgrading.
- Are all essential services, shopping, schools, medical, and recreation available nearby or close enough so as not to be inconvenient for day-to-day living?

Investment Considerations

Now that you are a savvy investor, you need to contemplate additional considerations:

- How much are you willing to pay for shelter and how much are you willing to pay in addition for a good investment?
- Are you willing to pay anything extra for the investment potential of this property?
- What is the property's potential for upgrading, for expansion? Do you have the time to devote to anything other than normal maintenance? Will the neighborhood in the area support an upgrade or an expansion?

A Financial Projection

Before "pulling the trigger" on your decision on a new place to live, consider the following potential of the proposed property from an investment point of view:

- Is it a quick turnaround possibility? If so, do you want to go to the trouble and expense of moving in and out in a short period of time?
- Is this an area that you can live in and move from within the two-year tax-free window or are you going to want to stay longer because of your family situation?
- If you are looking for a property where you need to spend more than two years living, you should very seriously look at the potential of a house that can be upgraded and/or expanded, as this will allow you to maximize your capital gain during the longer period of time you're likely to hold the property. To do this you must confine your search to areas containing custom homes with as large a spread in value as possible.

When you find such an area, you want to buy a house that is at the low end of the value spectrum, with adequate extra land and potential value so that you can, while living in this house, expand it as you can afford the time and money.

The Silent Bonus—Added Value Without Cost

After having plowed through this book, you might decide that the entire process is beyond you or you don't want the hassles. Does this mean that you can't make money on your home? Absolutely not! There are strategies you can use to make money, perhaps not on your current home, except by doing the lipstick approach, but you can apply these strategies when buying future homes. In fact, you can accumulate a surprising amount of money in a relatively short period of time.

Rank	City	1999 Population	1990 Population	Numerical Change	US Rank 1999	US Rank 1990	Percent Change
1	Henderson, NV	166,399	65,109	101,290	123	223	155.6%
2	North Las Vegas, NV	101,841	47,956	53,885	217	224	112.4%
3	Chandler, AZ	169,053	90,703	78,350	117	210	86.4%
4	Pembroke Pines, FL	121,279	65,454	55,825	174	222	85.3%
5	Plano, TX	232,904	128,507	104,397	71	144	81.2%
6	Las Vegas, NV	418,658	259,834	158,824	37	63	61.1%
7	Corona, CA	119,594	76,181	43,413	175	221	57.0%
8	Scottsdale, AZ	199,943	130,086	69,857	85	142	53.7%
9	Coral Springs, FL	116,136	79,137	36,999	185	218	46.8%
10	Laredo, TX	183,160	125,029	58,131	102	149	46.5%

TABLE 8-5. TOP TEN GROWTH MSAS IN THE USA

Strategies for Profit

How is this possible? The answer to this question is you must live in an area with constantly rising demand, where housing is appreciating consistently. Today jobs are portable and, as long as you're going to work, you might as well live in an area that will also produce a profit for you in housing. Table 8-5 lists the areas of the country that are constantly experiencing growth. If you live in one of these areas, this strategy will work for you.

I'm not suggesting that you immediately pull up stakes and move, only that you consider the consequences of doing so. Recently, a friend of mine's daughter and her husband moved from the San Francisco area to Phoenix because they were starting a family and wanted to own a home. The cost of housing in San Francisco MSA was too high for two well-paid middle-management people to afford a decent-size home. In Scottsdale, they could purchase a 2,400-square-foot home with four bedrooms for just over $300,000. The same home in the San Francisco MSA, within a reasonable commute to their employment, would have cost them $850,000 to $1,000,000. Neither one had any trouble in locating comparable if not better employment.

Why move to an MSA like Phoenix? The answer is relatively simple. Housing here appreciates reliably every year. We have a net in-migration in excess of 250,000 people every year. The *Arizona Republic* publishes annually a chart showing the Phoenix SMSA historical housing appreciation.

You can find a comparable chart for any area you are interested in. In general, the local newspaper is the best source for this type of information. Failing that, ask your local Realtor®. The National Association of Realtors® routinely publishes data like this for its members. Many articles in our local paper routinely update us on the rising values of homes in our MSA. Assuming that you live in a

Item	Cost
Home purchase	$160,000
Closing and loan costs	$2,300
Total investment	$162,300
Cash investment	$16,230
Value after two years	$183,184
Net gain in value	$20,884
ROI on case invested	128%
Annual ROI	**64%**

TABLE 8-6. APPRECIATION ANALYSIS

reasonably prosperous MSA and you find these types of articles in your local paper, you will see that merely owning and maintaining a home in your MSA is profitable. If you assume that you could conservatively expect an appreciation of seven percent over the next ten years, you could easily expect to make some money. If you upgrade your home every two years, you can make more. Why upgrade? The answer is simple: seven percent of $400,000 is more money than seven percent of $200,000.

What does this mean and how can it affect you? If we take an example of a couple purchasing a home for $160,000 with seven percent down and a loan at today's rate of 5.5 percent, what can we expect?

This simple analysis indicates that just owning a home in an area of constantly growing demand can be profitable. If the home is rotated every two years, the cash profit, acquired tax-free, can be reinvested in another home, keeping the debt constant or escalating the mortgage payments to keep pace with your job growth. This will result in ever-increasing profits that can in turn be reinvested. If you are able to work your way up to a home worth $400,000, you will be earning $28,000 per year tax-free. I'll bet you can't make that much and save it on your day job.

Planning Ahead

All this sounds great, doesn't it? Well, to take advantage of this, you need to plan ahead and be willing to move every two years. The single best ploy when doing this is to move up from one economic level to another. You can begin in a starter home, which, with today's financing, can be acquired for little or no down payment, and then work your way up from that to an upper-middle-class home within ten to 12 years. To do this, you need to do at least the following:

- Commit a fixed percentage of your net income to mortgage payments. These payments will escalate every time you move.
- Commit to selling every two years. You might have to live in the first home three or more years to have the appreciation accumulate enough to offset the sales commission, but once you are over that hurdle, you can start moving every two years.
- Select areas in your MSA where price escalation is the highest.
- When you roll into a new home, use all of the profit to make the down payment. This, coupled with your fixed percentage of income dedicated to mortgage payments, should guarantee you a significant upgrade in house price every time you move. Remember: the more expensive the home, the more dollars you're grossing each year.
- Keep in good touch with the real estate

community, because you want to confine your activity to home prices where sales velocity is the highest.

> **HEADS UP**
>
> Do not exceed this price point.

There are many statistics available in each area to guide you on your choice. Find the area in your MSA where price escalation is the most reliable and highest and check the price point where this starts to peter out.

If, like everyone else, your funds are limited, you might have to start your march toward riches in a lesser neighborhood. Do not despair; you can move up as soon as you have accumulated enough of a down payment. Each MSA has different grades of housing and most MSAs are predictable. The most exclusive homes will be found in the NE part of town, the middle value in the SE, and the lower-cost homes in the NW. The industrial area and low-cost housing will be found in the SW part of town. This holds true throughout the country, unless there is a geographical limitation like a mountain, lake, or other natural barrier to limit access to that part of town.

> **HEADS UP**
>
> You can count on it; wealthy people do not like driving to and from work with the sun in their eyes.

Maximizing Your Yield

How do you make this program really sing? In areas of constant growth, there are always new housing developments. In our area, these are tract homes for which the cost ranges from $110,000 to $850,000. I'm sure that will be the same in any area you choose.

When you start out, try to buy one of the first homes in the tract. Choose the one that is going to be the most popular, not the one you like the best. There is always one obvious choice, but if you cannot decide, get help choosing from an experienced Realtor®. By buying one of the first units, you will enjoy an extra boost, as the builder always raises the price on the most popular units as they start to sell out. This cost escalation will be an added bonus above and beyond the usual seven-percent appreciation. Certain builders are more popular than others; pick a good one and follow him or her around. Most builders today build in a variety of price ranges to protect themselves from market swings. Take the time to study the new communities; you should be able to spot those that will be hugely popular. Again, if you need help, ask your Realtor®; he or she is getting paid to know what's going on.

> **HEADS UP**
>
> Most tract home sales pavilions are set up to sell without the benefit of you having a Realtor® as they can save the commission. However, if you show up with a Realtor® or register your Realtor® the first time you visit the new home sales pavilion, the sales rep will pay him or her a commission. Your Realtor® will appreciate this and go the extra distance for you.

CHAPTER

9

Maximizing Your Investment

As we progress through this section on housing, we will be looking at strategies for the short term in an attempt to cover all the bases that may pertain to your current situation. The short-term approach will deal with periods from now to six months from now, the medium term will cover periods of up to two years, and long-term strategies will deal with upgrade and renovation projects that can be implemented over periods of two to five years or more. There are many strategies for improving your home, but all will be based on the market potential of your particular house. We have covered how to assess the market potential of your house. Once you have done this, you should be prepared to create your battle plan. A realistic strategy to maximize the value of your home prior to resale should incorporate examining everything from the lipstick approach to a teardown and rebuild. Where your home fits within these two extremes will depend largely on your estimate of the market potential, your available resources, and the advice of your professional real estate broker.

It is essential during this process that you do not overreach yourself or overestimate the potential sale price of your home. With your first attempt, you should be conservative and rigorously realistic. While this may result in less potential profit than a more aggressive approach, it should ensure that you have a rewarding experience with your first attempt.

HEADS UP

This is the crucial part of the entire process. I strongly recommend that you take as much time as you need to do your research and analysis of the market, your neighborhood, and your general area. The decision on what to do is the hard part; executing your plan is the easy part. Just remember the old adage that "you make your money when you buy." If you didn't buy the house right, the potential for profit may be less than ideal.

With your next home, if you have studied the buyer's approach in this book, you should be able to make a much better buy and therefore set yourself up for a larger profit when you sell that home. Let's explore the range of potential improvement for your current home.

The Lipstick Approach

The lipstick approach is your basic fix-up, paint, and re-carpet job. Most of this work you can do yourself, in this minimum-cost and maximum-result approach that yields such good results. You would employ this approach if you have limited resources or if you live in a tract home where major variation from the models is not a viable option.

The basic part of any facelift is to make the house as presentable as possible. This includes not only the house itself, but the front and back yards as well. Think of sprucing up your yard and landscaping as grooming the house to make it more presentable. The exterior of the house should look sharp; fresh paint and detailed trim are a must. Inside the home each room should be either completely repainted or refreshed so that it looks demonstrably clean. Ask your Realtor® to take a long look at the home to suggest what clutter should be removed from the rooms to make them appear larger and more elegant. You should gather up this clutter and put it into storage (other than your garage) until you move. All of your rooms should be simply decorated, free of clutter, and very presentable. It is strongly suggested that you make your garage as presentable as the rest of the home. While women tend to select a home for the family to buy, the man of the house will want to put his blessing on areas of the home that are important to him. Traditionally, the garage and potential workshop are large items for the male buyer.

Timing and Leverage

As with most things in life, timing is one of the most important factors contributing to success or failure. Earlier we discussed the condition of the national and local economies and their relation to the current and potential value of your home. I recommend that you time your decision and execution to coincide with a rising market or, at the very least, a stable or growing market, unless you're forced to make a decision that does not seem compatible with what is going on in your area. Again this is not rocket science, simply keeping an eye on what's happening from day to day should give you ample understanding of this aspect of your project.

Leverage will play a vital role in your percentage return on dollars invested. Let's take a

HEADS UP

If you become comfortable with the idea of buying and selling every two years, you should pay close attention to the traditional three-year business cycle. By buying at the bottom of the cycle and selling at or near the peak of the cycle, you should maximize your potential return on investment in a spectacular fashion.

brief recap at the role of leverage in your transaction. If you purchased a home for $100,000 and sold it two years later for $120,000, your profit would be $20,000, or $10,000 per year on an investment of $100,000. If you paid cash for the home, your rate of return (ROR) would be a total of 20 percent or 10 percent per year. If you took out a conventional 80-percent loan, your initial investment would have been $20,000. Using the same gross sales price at the end of two years, your rate of return on cash invested would be 100 percent on dollars invested, or 50 percent per year. The difference between the all-cash transaction and the transaction using borrowed money is known as *leverage*. As you can see by the above example, your use of leverage has made your money work harder for you, increasing your ROI from 20 percent gross to 100 percent gross and your annual ROI from ten percent to 50 percent. The same holds true when you go to fix up your house.

DEFINITION

ROI is an acronym for ***return on investment***. It is synonymous with ***rate of return*** (ROR), ***cash on cash return***, and ***percentage profit***. It should always be annualized to reflect your ROI per year on your investment.

Let's keep the same example, but in this case we believe that if we spend a few dollars to fix up the house, we might be able to sell it for $130,000. We determine that it will cost $2,000 to improve the house for resale. If you put the cash up yourself and you are able to obtain the increased sale price, your rate of return on this $2,000 will be 500 percent during the six-month fix-up and resale. This is an annualized rate of return of 1,000 percent. If, however, you borrow the money as a home improvement loan, your rate of return at the time of sale becomes infinite. This is the effect of leveraging the additional $2,000.

Given the above, does it ever make good business sense to pay off a home? From a strictly business point of view, it does not. However, if you are retired or nearing retirement, having a paid-for home can be a great comfort. So, once you are finished with buying and selling and are satisfied with the results, you should consider a paid-for home as a retirement gift for yourself.

How Far Can You Go?

How far can you push the value of your home? This is a very difficult question to answer. This is what separates the amateur from the professional house remodeler. For your first attempt at maximizing your home value, as I mentioned earlier, I would recommend that you not push the sales price too high. Once you have gained experience and pushed it a little bit higher each time, you will be better prepared for taking the additional risk.

In a situation like this, what is the real risk? If you have lived in a home for a period of time and you do not live in an area where population and employment are stagnant or decreasing annually, your home will already have accumulated some appreciation. If your home is in decent condition, you do not need to do anything to pocket this appreciation when you sell, other than to make your property as presentable as possible. Once you start spending money to increase the value of the house, you will incur two separate potential risks: one, that you might not recoup your investment after the fix-up, thereby lowering your net profit from the normal appreciation, and two, that you might do the wrong thing and lower the value or potential value of your home. If you have done your homework on your area as well as the potential market value, you should totally eliminate the potential of the second risk. The first risk, that you do not fully recover the cost of the fix-up, would be a pretty acceptable risk to most people, unless their resources are so strained that they cannot afford to pay for the fix-up. If you are in this category, just make your home as presentable as possible and put it on the market; save your fix-up for your next opportunity.

Realtors® are always making recommendations. Figure 9-1 is an excerpt from a Century 21 local Realtor® flyer reprinted with permission of C21 Kern Realty, Fountain Hills, AZ, copyright 2003.

Knowing Where to Stop

Knowing how far to push your enhancement of the house is a delicate matter. The more research you do, the more confidence you will have in your ability to make this decision. As a rule of thumb, in my business, I spend twice the amount of time researching and planning as I do in executing the plan. I've found that preparation and study are a major contributor to profit. It has been a long time since I have failed to recoup or make a return on my investments. I'm not blowing my own horn as a genius in this matter, merely testifying to the fact that I have proven to myself that the work of research and planning is the largest single contributor to the profits I have made. I believe that if you study the lives of successful business people, you'll find this approach to be a common thread in most if not all of their success.

> **HEADS UP**
>
> Shooting from the hip is for gunslingers. Real estate investors must avoid hasty decisions and do the homework.

The Quick Turnaround and Taxes

In any given situation where profit is taken, there are tax implications.

Disclaimer—What I'm about to say here does not constitute tax advice, as I am not qualified to advise anyone on taxes.

I can however pass on the benefit of the guidelines given to me by my tax accountant. For investments for a period of time of less than one year, you can count on these profits being

REMODELING: *How Much is Too Much?*

Many homeowners choose to remodel existing rooms, or add on to their current plan, in an attempt to increase their home's value. But, what projects should you choose? And how much rehab is too much, in terms of recovering costs when you decide to sell?

First, always protect the character of your home. Nothing sticks out more than a new addition that is at odds with the architectural style. Recognize your home's character and stay within its framework.

The most financially rewarding areas to remodel are usually the kitchen and bath. Newly re-done cooking spaces, cabinetry and additional storage areas can attract more buyers and may command a higher price for the home than a comparable one on the market.

Enlarged bathrooms are very popular attraction for home buyers, according to the National Kitchen and Bath Association. Today, the most popular additions for younger buyers are sunken whirlpool baths and larger showers.

Replacing worn carpeting, tiles and wood floors can give your home an immediate advantage over similar properties.

Updating paint colors in all areas of your home can also prove beneficial. It's important that you use neutral colors, when adding new floor and wall coverings.

Replacing outdated drawer-pulls and door knobs and some light fixtures is another relatively easy project that can add a lot of appeal.

Try to stay simple when remodeling, and look at your home as though you were the buyer. If you find the upstairs bedroom could be brightened by a new coat of paint or a more modern light fixture, potential buyers will probably feel the same.

Concentrate on improving two or three areas in your home. More than likely, the time and money you spend adding quality to your home will be rewarded with greater profit when you sell.

Smart Home Tip:
Make a paste of lemon juice and salt to remove rust stains in the kitchen or bathroom areas, without scratching.

FIGURE 9-1. CENTURY 21 FLYER ABOUT REMODELING

taxed as ordinary income. That is to say these profits will be added to your normal gross income. For investments in excess of 12 months, these qualified for capital gain treatment. The current federal tax rate on capital gain is 15 percent. For housing used as a primary residence for a period *not less than* 24 months, these profits are totally tax-free.

Does this mean that if you purchased a home only a few months ago you should not sell it for profit? Not at all. It simply means that if you do sell it within a period of less than one year, you will pay taxes at the same rate as the rest of your ordinary income. As a quick rule of thumb, look at your last year's tax rate and multiply it by your potential profit to see how much of that profit will be paid to Uncle Sam in taxes. To put this into dollars and cents, let's assume that you purchased the home for $100,000 and you can sell it for $120,000 without too much work. This will yield you a profit of $20,000. If you were in the 25-percent tax bracket last year and assuming that this additional income does not boost you into a higher tax bracket, you would pay $20,000 times 25 percent or $5,000 in taxes on this profit. That would mean that your net profit would be $15,000 on an investment of $100,000 or 15-percent return on investment. With the ability to evaluate the tax impact of potential short-term profit, you should then be able to make an intelligent decision about whether it is worth it to you to proceed with your project.

If you will have held the house for more than one year but less than two, you will be in a capital gain situation and paying a 15-percent federal tax on your profit. Using the same example above, your $20,000 profit will be reduced by 15 percent, or $3,000. Your net yield on this investment will then be $17,000 or a 17-percent rate of return. Again, you should evaluate the profit potential rather than its taxable impact. You'll find that if you use leverage in either situation, your ROI should make the tax impact very easy to accept.

HEADS UP

Over the years I have found that an opportunity to profit should never be overlooked. Having to pay taxes on a profit is better than not making any profit and all. When you are evaluating any potential project, focus on the positive aspects of the plan, plan for the potential negatives, and work hard to produce the best results.

Finally, let's look at the tax-free transaction to see what its potential impact would be, not only on your initial home, but if you continue to buy and sell on a regular basis. Let's assume that you took advantage of leverage and invested $20,000 to purchase your current home and then, at the end of two years with a little fix-up, your net profit was $17,000 after subtracting the cost to fix up. You now have in your hand a total of $37,000, none of which is taxable. If you take this $37,000 and purchase a $150,000 home, live in it for two years, improving it as you live there, and then sell it for a net profit of $30,000, this means that in less than four years you have increased your cash nest egg from $20,000 to $67,000.

All of this income is tax-free!

If you are employed, you have to ask yourself how long it would take you to save $47,000 out of your current salary. If you're like most people in this country, it would take you a long time and you would have to pay taxes on every dollar saved. That means that if you're in the 25-percent tax bracket, you have to make $1.25 for every dollar you save, a dollar you can save only after you pay all of your bills.

By using the capital invested in your home, rolling in every two years, you are able to accumulate in a relatively short time a fairly large tax-free pile of cash. If you assume that you continue with the above scenario three more times with the same predictable results, that would mean that in ten years you will have parlayed your initial $20,000 into $150,000 tax-free.

The price for this profit is moving every two years. Most people consider moving to be a traumatic event; however, if you have made a game plan and stick to it, you should be more than compensated for the inconvenience. If you are looking to your day-to-day employment as a source for long-term retirement savings, you need to be in a situation where you can dramatically increase your income without substantially increasing your cost of living. If this is the case, then you will have several choices when planning to salt away money for your retirement. Most people, however, are not in the situation described above. Their income, even with steady raises and progression within the ranks, is relatively predictable and serves only to keep pace with their increased cost of living.

Capital Items

The primary purpose of this section is to address the investment opportunity represented by the potential of maximizing the value of your current home. Under normal circumstances, whether you are dealing with this home or another home that you would be living in, you would be expected to maintain the home properly so that the value of the home would not deteriorate. Maintenance itself does not produce profit; it does, however, produce some profit indirectly. Annually, through inflation and increasing scarcity of homes in your area, the price of housing rises. The value of a properly maintained home should rise with the rest of the homes in the area. While some of the increase in value can be attributed to inflation, there's also a component that is profit. In a normal situation, you would expect that your home should increase in value by the cost of routine maintenance plus inflation. In essence, that recapture of the maintenance cost can be construed as a profit. You are essentially recapturing your cost of living in the home. Think of it, combined with your tax savings in interest paid, as free rent.

Maintenance vs. Capital Items

Maintenance is defined as keeping your home in good repair. In general, maintaining a home in good repair should at the very least include the following items of maintenance:

- Paint
- Wallpaper
- Floors
- Exterior paint and trim
- Landscaping
- Mechanical maintenance
  - HVAC
  - Plumbing
  - Septic systems
  - Electrical
- Built-in appliances
- Common areas (in condo situations)

Taking care of these items is normal maintenance. Anything beyond this work, such as upgrading any of these items, can be considered a *capital* item.

When you are attempting to elevate the value of your home and you are contemplating something in excess of the lipstick approach, you will be dealing with capital expenditures. These costs must be added to the original cost of your home to determine your new basis for

DEFINITION

A ***capital*** item is an expenditure not to maintain but to raise the value of a home. Examples of this are better flooring, lighting, mechanical systems, or alterations of any kind.

evaluating your potential profit from the sale. The spreadsheet below is a tool for analyzing the process. To start with, let's put together a spreadsheet to determine your actual cost to date. A typical spreadsheet would look something like Table 9-1.

Item	Cost
Purchase price	$100,000
Closing costs	$1,500
Loan costs	$1,600
Title insurance	$300
Termite inspections	$300
Building inspection	$300
Home appliance warranty	$300
Total costs at closing	**$104,300**

TABLE 9-1. BASIC SPREADSHEET

As you can see, the home you thought you paid $100,000 for actually cost you $104,300. This is a relatively typical situation. In some cases, like the situation involving FHA and VA home purchases, some of these costs were paid by the seller; these should not be added to your cost basis. We will use this basic spreadsheet as a tool as we go along, to illustrate how to analyze your actual investment and return on investment.

Cost and Leverage

As discussed earlier, leverage is a basic concept when dealing with any form of investment. You use other people's money (OPM) to make your money work harder. We discussed a simple example of this when we compared the ROIs for several ways of buying a home for $100,000 that is sold after two years for $120,000. If you paid all cash, the profit is 20-percent profit. If you used a conventional 80-percent loan, the ROI is 100 percent. If you have had any experience with investments of any kind, you know that a return like this would be impressive.

HEADS UP

Returns on investment in real estate can be quite spectacular when they are planned properly. You might even come to the conclusion that you can make a career out of this type of transaction. At the very least, real estate investing can provide you with a low-risk, high-yield, tax-free nest egg.

To take this a step further, we should take our initial spreadsheet a step further by using the leverage of an 80-percent loan. It will look something like Table 9-2.

At this point, we have documented your house purchase and shown that you have invested $23,300 in cash. As we follow the transaction through, you will be able to track your investment accurately. If you are the true bean counter type, you can add your annual principal repayment to your cash investment. For the sake of this book, I'm going to assume that your annual tax savings will more than offset your annual principal payments and we will not allude to this refinement in the rest of this book.

Item	Cost	Cash Invested
Purchase price	$100,000	
Closing costs	$1,500	
Loan costs	$1,600	
Title insurance	$300	
Termite inspections	$300	
Building inspection	$300	
Home appliance warranty	$300	
Total costs at closing	$104,300	
Loan dollars	–$81,000	
Equity		**$23,300**

TABLE 9-2. COST BASIS

Spreadsheets and Planning

Now that we have some basic tools, how do we use them to analyze your project? It's quite simple: we simply add to them as you formulate your plan. Let assume the following as part of your battle plan:

- The neighborhood is sold out: the original builder has no more new homes for sale.
- The homes in the neighborhood are at least five years old.
- Your home is a three-bedroom, two-bath house with a two-car garage on a quarter-acre lot (an average suburban home).
- You have made no capital improvements to your home as yet.
- Prices for your model home are now at $115,000 to $120,000, depending on condition.
- Some of the homes in the neighborhood have been improved with capital additions and are worth more than the average.

What's your battle plan to be? If you've done your homework, you have found out that several homes have upgraded appliances, some have upgraded carpet and flooring, and some have added space, bedrooms, family rooms, playrooms, and workrooms. What should you do?

Your research should show exactly how much these modifications have affected the selling price of these particular homes. If none of them has yet sold, there may be no reliable way to guess what they might sell for. For some guidance in this area, you can consult your local Realtor® and your local residential appraiser. If there is no definitive answer, you might be better off not taking a chance on the additions; just play it safe on this move and make a better purchase next time. If, on the other hand, you find out that the homes that have made some capital improvements have sold for significantly more money, then you can consider not only a good lipstick approach, but perhaps an addition. If the upgraded homes have been selling the extra square footage at the same price as the basis home, say $80 per square foot, then you know that if you can add some space at a cost less than $80 per square foot, you can make a profit. If construction costs in your area are around $50 per square foot for additions and they raise the selling price by $80 per square foot, your profit potential is $30 per square foot.

For the sake of this example, let's determine that you have found out that the best sales included a modest kitchen upgrade and an added family room of 250 square feet and that you can make a profit at this. Let's look at the potential deal and put it into perspective. We will use the following assumptions:

- A complete lipstick job on your place will cost $1,000.
- The kitchen upgrade will cost $1,500.
- The 250-square-foot family room addition will cost $50 per square foot or a total of $12,500.
- The basic house will be worth at least $120,000 and, with the addition, no less than $140,000 ($80 per square foot for the additional 250-square-foot family room).
- Brokerage commissions are six percent in your area.
- Fully improved, you house should sell for a worst-case $140,000 less the six percent commission or a net of $131,600 to you. How does this stack up? Let's put it to the spreadsheet (Table 9-3).

If you could sell the home for $120,000, without the additional expenditure of $12,500, your yield would be as shown in Table 9-4.

From Table 9-4 you can see that the addition costing $12,500 will add $18,800 to your gross cash yield, for an additional net profit of $6,300. This addition alone will yield a 50-percent profit over the short time you will have the additional money invested. Annualized, this

Item	Cost	Cash Invested
Purchase price	$100,000	
Closing costs	$1,500	
Loan costs	$1,600	
Title insurance	$300	
Termite inspections	$300	
Building inspection	$300	
Home appliance warranty	$300	
Total costs at closing	$104,300	
Loan dollars	–$81,000	
Equity		**$23,300**
Lipstick job	$1,000	$1,000
Kitchen addition	$1,500	$1,500
Family room addition	$12,500	$12,500
Total investment		**$38,500**
Sales price	$140,000	
Less commission	–$8,400	
Net yield/cash after loan paid off	**$131,600**	**$50,600**

TABLE 9-3. GROSS PROFIT WITH ADDITION

Item	Cost	Cash Invested
Purchase price	$100,000	
Closing costs	$1,500	
Loan costs	$1,600	
Title insurance	$300	
Termite inspections	$300	
Building inspection	$300	
Home appliance warranty	$300	
Total costs at closing	$104,300	
Loan dollars	–$81,000	
Equity		**$23,300**
Lipstick job	$1,000	$1,000
Kitchen addition	$1,500	$1,500
Total investment		**$25,800**
Sales price	$120,000	
Less commission	–$7,200	
Net yield/cash after loan paid off	**$112,800**	**$31,800**

TABLE 9-4. GROSS PROFIT WITHOUT ADDITION

component of your project produces a 100-percent per annum yield.

Potential Profit and ROI

So then, now that your plan looks pretty good, how should you proceed? In case you have not noticed, we have assumed that you will pay for the costs of preparing your home for sale in cash. Do you have that amount of cash to invest? If you do, do you really want to invest it in this project? What are the alternatives? You can take out a home improvement loan. For the sake of this example, let's assume that the interest rate will be eight percent and it will take four months to do the work and an additional three months to sell the house, for a total project duration of seven months. How does this affect the deal? Let's go back to our spreadsheet to find out (Table 9-5).

With the family room addition included, we can see that you will yield $50,600. Subtracting your total investment of $38,300, you will make a net profit of $12,300 or a 32-percent ROI. Remember: the addition yielded a 50-percent ROI, so your total yield went up substantially by doing the addition. Realistically, I believe that we could expect that you could borrow 100 percent of the home improvement loan.

By leveraging the costs, you added $700 in interest, but the bottom line went up by $3,800.

Item	Cost	Cash Invested
Purchase price	$100,000	
Closing costs	$1,500	
Loan costs	$1,600	
Title insurance	$300	
Termite inspections	$300	
Building inspection	$300	
Home appliance warranty	$300	
Total costs at closing	$104,300	
Loan dollars	–$81,000	
Equity		**$23,300**
Lipstick job	$1,000	
Kitchen addition	$1,500	
Family room addition	$12,500	
Loan dollars	$15,000	
Loan cost interest	$700	$700
Total investment		**$24,000**
Sales price	$140,000	
Less commission	–$8,400	
Net yield/cash after loan paid off	**$131,600**	**$36,400**

TABLE 9-5. LEVERAGE ANALYSIS

This is the effect of leverage. Your gross yield on dollars invested is now calculated by taking your net profit of $36,400 and deducting your investment of $24,000 for a total dollar yield of $11,400 or an ROI of 47 percent.

Almost without exception, you can leverage your plan by doing the research and backing it up with proper cost analysis. Your lender understands the process, and that is how lenders earn their money. Let their money work for you.

HEADS UP

Leverage has increased your yield from 32 percent to 49 percent in just seven months.

CHAPTER

10

Nuts *and* Bolts—Inside

This subject is a monster, so I have broken it into two parts, inside and outside. The following chapter is the outside. It's everything I know about housing and how to modify it. There are many authoritative sources for home renovation; I suggest you seek out more sources than these two chapters. However, these two chapters will get you launched.

I can find no documented proof that specific remodeling of your home will add value specific to your home. While it is necessary to keep your home well maintained and groomed, modifying it beyond that point may not necessarily line your pockets with additional profits. The key to profitable renovation of your home is to do enough to keep the home current within the context of the home's design and the general neighborhood. This will guarantee that you will get the maximum possible yield from your house and ensure a prompt sale when the time comes to sell. Major renovations and additions are covered in Chapters 12-17.

HEADS UP

The single most profitable thing you can do to a home is to add square footage. Hand in hand with adding space is revamping the existing spaces, making them work with the addition for a totally improved and upgraded look and livability.

Interiors

American homes have evolved in recent years and have added features and rooms that are today considered essential. Thirty years ago, the American dream home was a three-bedroom, two-bath ranch house, on a quarter-acre lot with a two-car garage. Today the most popular home that attracts buyers is a four-bedroom, two-and-a-half-bath house with a three-car garage. The lot size varies all over the country, from a quarter acre down to 7,000 square feet. The internal configuration of houses has also changed. Older homes have smaller rooms with fewer amenities. The art of remodeling or redecoration now includes modernizing and adding to older homes to make them more competitive in the marketplace, to compete with new homes under construction. In this chapter we will cover and describe briefly the ideal configuration of the modern home. Within each type of room, innovation and design have created features that are now considered essential to modern living.

These features are not really essential. They are, however, very desirable to potential buyers. Our society has become more materialistic and we have more choices in housing. Because of the money available for mortgage loans, it is easier for home buyers to satisfy their desires. In some areas, it is now possible to borrow 100 percent or more of the cost of a new home. The rule of thumb for most mortgage underwriters is to allow borrowers to allocate one third of their income for mortgage payments. The net effect of this is that people are able to buy more expensive homes at a younger age. With this kind of buying power, Americans can exercise complete discretion when buying a home. This has forced the sellers of older homes to modernize and, in some cases, expand their homes before placing them on the market.

A renovated home can compete effectively with new housing. By modernizing and renovating your home, you can actually show a decent profit. There are some people who do this for a living. The big trick is to know what to do and how to do it at the least possible cost. For in-depth detail on the art of renovating and remodeling, please refer to *The Complete Idiot's Guide to Investing in Fixer-Uppers* by Stuart Leland Rider (Penguin/Alpha Books, 2003, ISBN 0-02-864465-4). It provides great detail on how to approach a large fixer-upper project.

Rooms

One of the fundamental differences between the older home and the new home is room size. One hundred years ago, people in this country were considerably smaller than people are today. In addition, incomes were more uniform than they are today. This resulted in smaller homes with smaller windows and considerably fewer amenities. Typical room sizes today are shown in Table 10-1.

Room dimensions represent net usable space and assume allowance for traffic areas within the rooms. To the extent that spaces are combined, traffic zones can be overlapped.

The dimensions are guidelines for modest and mid-priced, contemporary production homes. Dimensions may vary considerably from market to market. In competitive areas, rooms that are significantly smaller or larger than in other homes may affect value.

The perceived value of the arrangement and emphasis of the rooms will vary based on the stage of life of the potential buyer. For example, young families emphasize the public areas and their separation from the private areas, while couples without children are less concerned with the separation of public areas from the private areas.

	Minimum	Optimum
Public Areas		
entries	Placement to provide joining public spaces is more important than square feet. Dimension and separation vary with floor plan configuration. They should be large enough to allow entry without hindrance from front door. Review sight lines from entry for views of unsuitable areas (bathrooms, kitchen, and other private spaces).	
living room	12 x 12	14 x 16
family room	12 x 12	14 x 16
great/living/dining rooms	12 x 20	14 x 24
dining room	12 x 12	12 or 14 x 14
kitchen	8 x 8 (galley)/ 8 x 9 (U- shape)	12 x 12 (island), work triangle 16' to 20'
breakfast area	6 x 6 (built-in nook) 8 x 8 (table—no circulation) 10 x 10	12 x 12
pantries	18" wide x 24" deep (cabinet)	6′ x 8′ (walk-in)
washroom/laundry room	6 x 6 (room), 3 x 6 (laundry closet)	7 x 12 (mud room)
guest closet	3 lineal foot rod and shelf	4 lineal foot rod and shelf
powder bath	3 x 5 / 4 x 4	3 x 6 / 5 x 5
Privacy Areas		
master bedroom	12 x 15	16 x 18
master bath	6 x 6 - 3' vanity, 1 sink / 6 x 8 - 5' vanity, 2 sinks	9 x 12 - 6' vanity, 2 sinks / 10 x 12 - 8' vanity, 2 sinks + sit-down. Includes separate tub and shower
master closet	linear – 8'/walk-in – 4' 6" x 8 (L-shape)	walk-in 6 x 8 (18 lineal foot)
secondary bedrooms	10 x 10	12 x 12
office	10 x 10	12 x 12
guest bath	5 x 5 – single sink	5 x 10 – dual sink, compartmentalized
stairways	4' tread	6' tread
Exterior Spaces		
covered patios	10 x 10	12-14 x 16-24
garages	12 x 20 (1 car) / 20 x 20 (2 car)	24 x 30 (3 car)

TABLE 10-1. TYPICAL ROOM SIZES

You need to roughly compare the room sizes in the above list with the room sizes in your current home before you embark on any significant renovation project. Once you go beyond the standard lipstick approach, you start entering the realm of the legitimate renovation project. When you get into this type of project, you need to determine what exactly are your goals and how do you plan to compete with other homes for sale in this economic bracket. I'm not trying to suggest that you turn your home into a carbon copy of some of the newer homes. What I am suggesting is that you should determine what you're competing against, so that you are more able to come up with a strategy to compete effectively. Sometimes it is not necessary to rebuild your rooms, but merely to add to them the amenities that have become expected in new housing. Here are some of the items that you will encounter in these new rooms:

- Plant shelves
- Generous dual-pane windows
- Maintenance-free flooring
- Enhanced lighting
- Ceiling fans
- Electrical outlets every eight feet
- Minimum ceiling height of eight to ten feet
- Vaulted ceilings
- Varied wall textures
- Light-colored walls
- Enhanced communication options, such as cable TV, computer wiring, and high-speed telephone lines

The above items are relatively easy to incorporate into an older home. They just require some planning and some expenditure.

We will look at individual rooms and discuss what would be an ideal situation to create before selling your home. Do not look upon these ideas as necessarily goals, but merely as guidelines if you plan to make more than fundamental changes in your home. What we are discussing here is not only the ideal for each room, but ideas that can be incorporated into your existing rooms without any dramatic changes to the room itself. When you approach your project, you want to do it in the most economical manner rather than attempting to match the ideal. The entire thrust of this exercise is to make a profit, not just to spend your money.

> **HEADS UP**
>
> I strongly recommend that before you put your home on the market you go to see the homes that are already on the market. Try to look at homes that are in the economic bracket you wish to target based on the research you have already done. Every time you see something that appeals to you, make a note of it. You may use that list when putting together your battle plan for your property. At the very least, you will have a list of things that you deem desirable.

Entries

Unless the homes are in an upper economic bracket, a separate entry is not a large item. Most middle-of-the-road housing incorporates the entry into the family dining room area. In homes that sell above the average price, entries tend to get larger and more elegant. If you do not have an entry in your home, it is relatively easy to create one by adding onto the front of the house. (This is possible only if your setback requirements will permit it.)

Living Rooms

Unlike other rooms in the modern home, the living room has become smaller. The American way of living has become less formal and, therefore, the family room has replaced the living room as a place to gather and entertain. On a daily basis, Americans use the family room to gather around a television set. A living room needs to accommodate, comfortably, at least a three-person couch and two easy chairs. Beyond that, you get into the realm of the above-average home.

Family Rooms

Today's family room has become rather elaborate; it is not only larger, but also can incorporate things such as a wet bar, a media room, an office, and an eating area. It is most often adjacent to or part of an extended kitchen, separated only by a counter. This room has become the focal point of family living and is usually the largest room in the downstairs portion of the home. If you have an older home that has a standard living room, a standard family room, or, in the case of a really old home, a parlor and a living room, you might want to restructure the dividing wall to make the room closest to the kitchen more like today's family room. Adding that required television wiring for a TV hook-up is easy.

Great Rooms

Very popular in current housing construction is the great room. This room is a combination of living room and family room. It is usually built in conjunction with an expanded kitchen and dining area. The use of the great room allows the space generally allocated to the formal living room to be allocated to additional bedrooms, storage, and other amenities.

Dining Rooms

Most modern homes do not have a formal dining room. The current custom is to incorporate a dining area in the formal living room. Other than for entertaining, the dining room gets little use by the modern American family. More popular today is the eat-in kitchen between the kitchen and the family room. If your home can be reconfigured to accommodate this, you'll find that this will become an attractive feature when you sell.

Kitchens

The up-to-date kitchen tends to be fairly spacious, with a central island for food preparation and eating. Areas usually found in new kitchens include a generous pantry and sometimes a laundry room. Expanded amenities include the following items: dishwasher, double oven, microwave oven, four-burner cook top, garbage compactor, refrigerator/freezer, telephone, TV, computer outlets, and pantry.

Master Bedroom Suites

The master bedroom and bath have become a major focal point of current housing design. Marketing people have determined that the kitchen and the master suite are two rooms that are essential to get right to entice discriminating buyers. Items commonly included in the minimum master bath are his-and-her sinks, separate tub and shower, and generous walk-in closets. The bedroom itself absolutely must be able to contain a king-size bed and several large chests of drawers. If your home does not incorporate these items, as a minimum, this would be an ideal place to consider expanding. You may not have to build additional space; you might be able to demolish and reconfigure. To attract the attention required to sell your home, you will have to have a very attractive kitchen and master suite.

MASTER CLOSET

The master closet is essential to the modern home. Today's women look for an eight-by-twelve walk-in, with men being accommodated in separate and smaller walk-ins or traditional straight closets.

The Guest Bath

Today, the guest bath comes in an infinite variety of styles and sizes, from the standard combination tub and shower, toilet, and sink to the more elaborate separate tub, shower, and toilet room. Other variations include the Jack-and-Jill bathroom, which is shared between two bedrooms but not the rest of the house, and the combination guest bathroom and powder room.

Other Bedrooms

Other bedrooms are not as vital as the master bedroom, but it is essential that new homes have at least three additional bedrooms. You might not be able to compete with this, but do not despair; you will be in the majority at the moment, as most homes are this way. The reason for the fourth bedroom is that people today deem a home office to be an essential part of any new home.

Guest Closet

The guest closet has been completely overlooked as an area of emphasis in modern housing. A standard five- or six-foot-long closet will suffice. The modern touch would be to have bifold doors rather than sliding doors, but that is generally overlooked by buyers when they are looking for a home.

The Den

The den is another popular room. If you do not have four bedrooms, but you have an area that you can create or designate as a den or office, that space will serve as an office. Some older homes have a library; this is ideal for today's office requirements. Make sure that the requisite electrical and communication wiring is in place.

The Office/Media Room

As mentioned above, the home office has become a desirable feature of the new American home. Few houses built today lack this amenity; it is provided as a fourth bedroom, a separate den or office, or a media room.

Washrooms

Today's utility room is typically placed between the garage and the kitchen and it is as spacious as possible. At the very least, this room must be able to contain separate washer and dryer and a sorting table. If you have an old-fashioned home with a generous garage, you might be able to incorporate a portion of the garage to accommodate this function.

Stairways

If you have a two-story home, the stairway may be a fairly important feature. The modern stairway has at least one landing, sometimes two. The older homes usually have a fairly steep, narrow, and rather utilitarian stairway. If this is the case and you do not have the room to renovate your stairway, you have to make it as attractive as you can. If possible, you should try to incorporate at least one landing with as much width and depth of stair tread as possible.

Pantries

Pantries are very desirable areas; you should make the effort to have one incorporated into your kitchen or at least accessible to the kitchen. When attempting to accommodate this amenity, consider the washroom and the coat closet or linen closet. A pantry would be a more desirable feature than a large utility room or coat closet. When tackling this, "the larger the better" is the general rule of thumb.

Patios

While patios are probably more properly dealt with as part of the backyard, it is essential for the modern house to have a covered area for outside seating that runs off either the family room or the living room, preferably both.

Garages

In a large part of the country, the garage has become a vital area of the house. In the East and Midwest, most homes have basements, but in the West a large garage is essential. In the past the size of garages has varied considerably from East to West and state to state; however, the minimum size today for a two-car garage is 24 feet by 24 feet. Some older garages were built 20 feet by 20 feet, which can cause a problem. Whether a home has a two- or three-car garage is less important than the dimension of the garage in front of the parking space. The additional four feet not only allows people to move around the garage, but provides an area for storage essential to a home without a basement. It was the lack of a basement that was the impetus for adding the third-car space to the garage. Most people in the West use the third-car space for storage.

Basements

If you live in a part of the country where basements are the norm, a basement is obviously essential. The modern basement has more headroom than older ones; this provides room to utilize the basement as additional living space. If you have an older home that has a basement with very restrictive headroom, there isn't much you can do about it. You simply need to make your basement as presentable as possible so that it can be used for storage. It is also an ideal area for a utility room or a playroom for the children.

To be counted as part of the living space of a home, any area must be heated and/or air-conditioned. This rule of thumb includes any spaces and add-ons that were converted in any other areas of the house. If you convert an old porch into a dining room or an expanded living area, you must extend the heating and cooling into this room to include it as part of the living space of the home.

Kitchens and Baths

What is an older home? I think the answer depends on where you live. In New England, homes can be over 100 years old and still be desirable. In fact, restoring these old homes has proven to be profitable. Out West, a 25-year-old home is considered old and in need of modernization.

What's the case where you live? The easy way to find out what is old in your neck of the woods is to talk with an appraiser or a realtor. While you will not get a guaranteed answer, you should get a pretty good idea where your home stands. In my mind, a house that qualifies as old has definite possibilities. The old homes tend to have advantages that the new ones do not have.

Old Houses

What sets the older home apart from new housing? The old home usually has the following advantages:

- It sits on a bigger lot.
- It is larger than the newer homes.
- It has more rooms.
- It has washrooms and pantries.
- It was built better than the new homes.

While this might not be true of all older homes, it most likely is the case. What are the disadvantages of the older homes? They likely have the following problems: inadequate wiring, antiquated plumbing, basements with low headroom, smaller rooms, detached garages, and antiquated kitchens. While some of these problems are potentially expensive, all have a solution; those solutions could very well improve your older home within your housing market. In many areas of the country, for the last 20 years, people have been buying up older homes, Victorians, Brownstones, and cottages and renovating and expanding them at a profit.

SIZE

One big advantage of the older home is that the kitchens were always large and sometimes had walk-in pantries and washrooms. Size has again become fashionable in new homes as people invest more time and money in their residences. Renovating a kitchen can be expensive and taking an old kitchen all the way to the latest and greatest will most likely not pay back all of your investment. If you have an older home, I suggest you modernize it enough so that it meets the minimum requirements for the modern kitchen. It must have the following appliances:

- Garbage disposal
- Double sink
- Microwave oven
- Family-size refrigerator (23 cubic feet minimum)
- Four-burner cook-top and oven

The counters should be in good condition and, at the least, covered with a good grade of Formica™. The kitchen cabinets should be freshly painted or stained. The floor should be tiled or covered with a good vinyl. To go beyond this could take a great deal of money and you won't necessarily get it back. If the layout works well and all the basics are there, the buyers can upgrade whatever they deem necessary. If they are going to be there for a while, they can recoup the upgrade better than you can in the short term.

EXPENSE

When dealing with an older home, the focus should be to make sure that the basic systems—electric, plumbing, and HVAC—are brought up to code and are functioning properly. Unless you are going for a total remodel, demolition, and addition, you should concentrate on these items and not get into glitz and glamour. If you look at the potential of any older home, you should view it as a project to be broken down into stages, wherein each stage has a risk/reward ratio. Depending on the level of upgrade you are contemplating, your project can be limited in scope in the last stage. Your project, broken down into phases, would look something like this:

1. Research your market.
2. Determine how far you want to go.
3. Make a plan and do the numbers.
4. Draw the plans, line up the money, and get the permits.
5. Demolish and upgrade the power, plumbing, and HVAC.
6. Build it out, installing the basic amenities.
7. Finish out the interior based upon the market potential (basic, if it's skinny, and all the way if you can push it to the top).

COSMETIC VS. FUNCTIONAL

Step seven above crosses the line between general upgrades and true renovation and refinishing. Beyond upgrading the infrastructure, power, plumbing, and HVAC, the refinishing can take on a very broad range of upgrading. New Formica™ counters are about ten percent of the cost of stone counters. Formica™ will do the job, but stone is needed when you are shooting for the top of the market. Chances are that, if your home is average, you should go for the functional and let the buyers provide more if they feel they need it. If you remodel to fancy, you will most likely not recapture your investment. In the Appendix, you will find a chart that shows the cost recovery of different renovations in different markets. You should be guided by its warning.

> **HEADS UP**
>
> The infrastructure is functional; everything else is cosmetic. Functional renovation is necessary; cosmetic renovation must be discretional. Do not overdo the cosmetic, as you might not get your money back.

APPLIANCES

Appliances are an extension of the kitchen. They must cover the basics and be functional. Unless you are going for the gold, they need not be top-of-the-line. Items like built-in refrigerators, double ovens, and other refinements should be saved for the top-of-the-line market. The only real way to recover the cost of these items is to live with them long enough for the market to catch up. If you live in a dilapidated mansion in the Hamptons, Palm Beach, or Beverly Hills, you can take the remodel all the way, at once. However, if you are upgrading an older home in a neighborhood that has started to improve, but still contains unrenovated properties, you would be wise to limit your remodel to adding space and basic amenities. Let the serious upgrade wait until all homes catch up with modernization requirements.

BATHROOMS

Bathrooms are a bit like kitchens: they need to be modernized, but not necessarily state-of-the-art. In new housing, the master bath has become a component of the master suite, which includes bedroom, sitting room, baths, and closets. The ultimate setup contains his-and-her sinks, his-and-her closets, a separate toilet room, perhaps a bidet, a separate shower, and a Jacuzzi™ tub. Also, the floor should be tiled with granite or marble, there should be counters around the sinks, and the fixtures should be top-of-the-line, very fashionable.

MASTER BATHS

Do you need to go all the way with the master bath? Certainly not, unless you are shooting for the top of the market. You do, however, need to incorporate as many of these basics as possible in the master bathroom:

- At least one sizeable walk-in closet
- Separate toilet room
- Separate tub and shower
- Two sinks and generous counter space

In older homes, where the master bedroom and bath were traditionally pretty basic, you might need to cannibalize an adjacent bedroom to gain the additional space needed. In my home, we added a room off the bath to contain the walk-in closet and expand the bathroom space.

Some of the tricks to adding class can be found in decorating books. One of my favorites is to make one sink a pedestal with a medicine cabinet over it. This is the man's sink. The other should have ample counter space and, perhaps, a place to sit. The pedestal sink gives the bath a classier look and men can handle the lack of counter space. Tub enclosures should be sliding glass instead of curtained or, better yet, if you can have separate shower and tub, make the tub a Jacuzzi™ and use the glass door on the shower. Jacuzzi™ tubs come in all sizes and are not that expensive. People like the idea of the Jacuzzi™ tub, but seldom use it. It does, however, make a good selling point. Finally, if you have the space, adding a bidet gives the master bath cachet.

The Second Bath

Traditionally, the second bath opens to the hallway, to be used by the occupants of bedrooms two, three, and four. It should have two sinks, a separate toilet room, and a combination bath-and-shower. If you create anything fancier than this, you might not get your money back. I recommend a tiled floor, but carpeting is acceptable.

The Jack-and-Jill Bath

The second bathroom is another spot for innovation. These baths today can take on a whole new dimension. They can be made to open only into two bedrooms, as Jack-and-Jill baths, used exclusively by the occupants of the bedrooms. Another variation is a bath that opens to the hall for guests, as well as to the guest room as an attached bath for the guest "suite." The extra door to the hall can be closed and locked when guests are staying.

The Powder Room

The extra bath, known as a half-bath because of the lack of tub and/or shower, is traditionally known as the powder room or guest bath. If you have the room for it, it can add real value to the home. If not, the setup allowing guests to use the second bath will suffice. It should be modern and well lit and have a decent mirror, so people can use it to put on cosmetics, etc.

Fixtures

The bathroom fixtures should be modern. The toilets should be the new low-flow-flush models, with elongated bowls and comfortable seats. Sinks, tub, and shower should have combination hot-and-cold faucets. Chrome or polished brass accessories are the most popular and easy to get. All fixtures should have matching accessories (handles) and be clearly from the same pattern. This will appeal to the buyer and not be very costly. If you cannot upgrade the fixtures, at least upgrade the accessories and trim.

CHAPTER

11

Nuts *and* Bolts— Outside

Exteriors

Housing exteriors deal with everything from architecture to configuration. As we discussed briefly earlier in the book, architecture varies from area to area and within each area. The difference between a Cape Cod and a Victorian should be understood by anybody who's looking to improve an existing home. Unless you are simply doing a lipstick approach type of renovation, you will probably be making some modifications to your home. Exterior modifications must be planned and executed within the context of the architectural style of your house. In some instances, with a little help from an architect, you might even be able to transform one architectural style into another.

Why would you want to do this? Quite simply, it may be very profitable to turn a Cape Cod into a stately Victorian. If, however, you do not have the proper guidance when you attempt this, you might accomplish nothing but butchering an architectural style. If this occurs, you will have likely lessened the value of your home rather than enhanced it. It is necessary to have at least a basic understanding of architectural styles and their differences.

Architectural Styles

Here is a brief rundown on the most common styles used coast to coast. Most likely you will easily recognize those architectural styles that are in use within your community and geographical area.

The National Association of Realtors® has online graphics and descriptions of some architectural styles:

Art Deco (www.realtor.org/rmomag.nsf/pages/arch1)—Homes built in this style feature geometric elements and a vertically oriented design.

California Bungalow (www.realtor.org/rmomag.nsf/pages/arch3)—A forerunner of the Craftsman style, California bungalows offer rustic exteriors, sheltered-feeling interiors, and spacious front porches.

Cape Cod (www.realtor.org/rmomag.nsf/pages/arch4)—A true classic, Cape Cod homes—square or rectangular one-story structures with gabled roofs and unornamented fronts—were among America's first houses.

Colonial (www.realtor.org/rmomag.nsf/pages/arch4.1)—An offshoot of the Cape Cod style, Colonial homes feature a rectangular, symmetric design, second-floor bedrooms, clapboard siding, and gabled roofs.

Contemporary (www.realtor.org/rmomag.nsf/pages/arch5)—Unmistakably modern in feel, contemporary-style homes are identifiable by their odd-sized windows, lack of ornamentation, and unusual mix of wall materials.

Dutch Colonial (www.realtor.org/rmomag.nsf/pages/arch8)—German ("Deutsch") settlers in Pennsylvania originated the Dutch Colonial style, dominated by a barn-like broad gambrel roof with flaring eaves.

French Provincial (www.realtor.org/rmomag.nsf/pages/arch10)—Balance and symmetry define the French Provincial style, which includes a steep hip roof, balcony and porch balustrades, and rectangular doors set in arched openings.

Georgian (www.realtor.org/rmomag.nsf/pages/arch11)—Two- to three-story brick structures crowned with multiple chimneys, roof balustrades, and pedimented doors and windows.

Italianate (www.realtor.org/rmomag.nsf/pages/arch15)—Italianate houses are typified by symmetrical bay windows in front, small chimneys set in irregular locations, tall, narrow windows, and in some cases towers.

Monterey (www.realtor.org/rmomag.nsf/pages/arch16)—The Monterey style updates the New England Colonial style with an Adobe brick exterior and a second floor with a balcony.

Neoclassical (www.realtor.org/rmomag.nsf/pages/arch18)—Recognize Neoclassical homes, which exist in incarnations from one-story cottages to multilevel manses, by their porches with Ionic or Corinthian columns.

Pueblo (www.realtor.org/rmomag.nsf/pages/arch20)—Flat roofs, parapet walls with round edges, straight-edge window frames, earth-colored stucco or adobe-brick walls, and projecting roof beams typify Pueblos.

Queen Anne (www.realtor.org/rmomag.nsf/pages/arch21)—Emerging in the late Victorian era, the style employs inventive, multistory floor plans that often include projecting wings, several porches and balconies, and multiple chimneys with decorative chimney pots.

Ranch (www.realtor.org/mromag.nsf/pages/arch22)—Similar to the Spanish Colonial, Prairie, and Craftsman styles, Ranch homes are set apart by pitched-roof construction, built-in garages, wood or brick exterior walls, sliding and picture windows.

Saltbox (www.realtor.org/rmomag.nsf/pages/ arch23.1) —This New England Colonial style gained the Saltbox nickname because its sharply sloping gable roof resembled boxes used for storing salt.

Shotgun (www.realtor.org/rmomag.nsf/pages/arch)—Tradition says that a shotgun blast can trace a straight path from the front to back door of this long, narrow home. The style is characterized by a single story with a gabled roof.

Split Level (www.realtor.org/rmomag.nsf/pages/arch28)—A modern style, split-level design sequesters certain living activities, such as sleeping or socializing.

Tudor (www.realtor.org/rmomag.nsf/pages/arch30)—Half-timbering on bay windows and upper floors and facades that are dominated by one or more steeply pitched cross gables typify Tudor homes.

Victorian (www.realtor.org/rmomag.nsf/pages/arch31)—A popular housing style, Victorian architecture, which dates from the second half of the 19th century, has two main styles: Second Empire and Queen Anne.

CONFIGURATION

Architecture is primarily concerned with vertical design. Configuration deals with things like layout of the home on the lot, how many stories, and the design of rooms within the home. Configuration may also be extended to deal with lot layout and additional buildings. If extensive renovation is contemplated, configuration must be taken into account along with architecture, to ensure that the final result will be harmonious within the context of the overall architectural design.

The primary thrust of configuration is to provide a harmonious group of living spaces that flow one into the other. The size and shape of individual rooms are as important as their relationship to each other. You would not want to have a pantry and washroom immediately adjacent to formal living room or a children's playroom next to a formal dining room. The sizes and shapes of these rooms and their interrelationship are what constitutes a livable home layout. These types of considerations matter only in the event of a substantial renovation or remodel. They are of no concern at all to a standard lipstick job.

PAINT AND TRIM

Whether dealing with a quick and dirty lipstick job or a complete renovation, exterior paint and trim are essential to create a pleasing first impression. Routine home maintenance requires periodic painting of the exterior; obviously, if you're getting your home ready to sell, it is absolutely essential that the exterior have a clean and fresh appearance. A new paint job, in itself, does not guarantee any increase in value of the house; rather, it is essential to maintaining the basic value of the house. All things being equal, a freshly painted home will sell more quickly and most likely for more money.

BASIC

A basic paint job is generally two-tone. Typically, the bulk of the house is painted one color and the door jams, roof trim, and window frames are painted with a contrasting and complementing color. The reason for the differing color on the trims is to "frame" the basic paint job of the house.

REVITALIZED

Depending upon the architectural style, variations on the above could include several different paint colors and several different trim colors. Other decorative items, such as millwork, awnings, and decorative trim, can be added in contrasting colors.

Landscaping

Landscaping is very important for most housing. Depending upon where you live, the prevailing tastes in landscaping range from broad expanses of lawn and stately trees to rock and cactus. The basic purpose of landscaping is to decorate the home and the site around the home. Other uses of landscaping are to provide shade and privacy for the occupants of the home. Most homes are landscaped in a fairly haphazard manner or in a basic way by the original builder. To really maximize the impact of landscaping, I suggest the use of a landscape architect to help you with the design and plant selection. In the short term, if you're preparing a home for sale, cleaning up and adding some color here and there is probably all you can manage for a quick sale. If, however, you are taking a longer view, you might employ the services of the landscape designer to come up with a long-range plan for your home. Then, over a period of time, you can expand your landscaping with this design as the ultimate goal.

Trees

Trees are major features of landscaping; it takes some thinking before planting them. You can purchase trees for planting in sizes starting at one to five gallons and going up to 48-inch box size and larger. You can even pay to have mature specimen trees transplanted to your home for an instant result.

Trees are either deciduous or evergreen. The deciduous ones shed their leaves in the fall and the evergreens are fully leafed year round. There are also other considerations, as some trees are more densely leafed than others. The densely leafed trees will screen the home from view; others, such as the willow or Palo Verde, will allow the home to be seen while providing some shade. The type of tree you pick will alter the effect of the curb view to the public. In the end, it is a matter of individual choice and personal maintenance considerations.

> **DEFINITION**
>
> A ***one-*** or ***five-gallon*** tree is so-called because it is planted and raised in a one- or five-gallon container. A 48-inch box tree is a tree whose roots are confined to a 48-inch-by-48-inch box, 48 inches deep. The general rule is the larger the container, the larger the tree and the higher the price for that tree.

Shrubs and Ground Cover

Shrubs and ground cover are used to cover up the dirt and to keep the dust down. Most communities require that residential property be landscaped and all of the bare dirt covered with grass, ground cover, or some form of decorative rock. While the practical effect of this is to control dust and erosion, the economic results of good landscaping are that the home with upgraded landscaping will sell for more money and more quickly than a haphazardly landscaped property.

Ornamental Features

Other features that can be found within the definition of landscaping are both ornamental and practical. Items such as a fishpond or aviary can be wonderful additions to a landscape plan. Common items found as ornamental additions to landscaping are columns, arches, sundials, gazebos, greenhouses, fishponds, swimming pools, spas, and arbors.

Exterior Remodeling

Modification of the exterior of a home can either be simple, such as adding or modifying trim details, or major, such as adding additional rooms, porches, and overhangs. Major modifications are considered major due to their structural requirements rather than because of their cost or function. Most, if not all, of these types of modification require both architectural design and a building permit. Unlike interior modifications, which can be done with little or no permitting process, exterior and structural renovations always require plans, building permits, and inspections.

Awnings and Patio Covers

Some items that can be used to dress up a home are awnings and patio covers. These are relatively light structures and will require little or no prior modification of the house itself. Awnings are built and installed by specialists, and I strongly recommend that if you're considering this type of an addition you start out by talking to the specialists. Patio covers can be designed and constructed by anybody who's handy with a hammer and saw. They need not even be attached to the house itself. In fact, if you're doing it yourself, I recommend that you consider building it freestanding. The most important consideration when adding something like an awnings or a patio cover to your house is to make sure that it fits in with the architectural style.

Siding

If you live in an area where homes are sided with wood or other similar materials, it is relatively easy to change the siding on your home. In most cases this will require modifying and/or changing the design of the trim that frames the siding. This is a fairly costly step, and you must be convinced that this will add significant value to the house before you consider this type of change. Again, I strongly suggest that you consult with a house designer or architect to see if the change you are contemplating fits with the architecture of the home. Another easy change is to replace your wood siding with stucco. This can be done easily, but should only be done in areas where stucco is a recognized exterior housing finish material.

Additions

The granddaddy of all home renovations is the addition of space, by demolishing and replacing major components of the home. It is not uncommon to see someone add a second floor to a home or a new room or a series of rooms. Another common major modification is demolishing interior walls and reconfiguring the living space. Both of these types of renovations are considered major and potentially structural and will require the services of a home designer, structural engineer, or architect.

Other Structures

Other major exterior renovations would be the addition of freestanding structures to the lot on which the house sits. These could be garages, guest quarters, or decorative structures such as gazebos. These will require design engineering and permits. This type of renovation or remodel would be tackled only if the home is considered to be eligible to take it up a class or two. In areas of estate housing, there may be situations where a smaller home on a large lot could be elevated to the class of the surrounding estate home neighborhood. This smaller home would be a prime candidate for this type of renovation.

All About Roofs and Roofing Materials

You have probably noticed that there are many different types of roofs and roofing materials. Certain types of roofs go with certain styles of architecture. In Chapter 13, I include some pictures of different architectural styles. In this chapter, I'd like to walk you through the variety of roof styles and discuss the alternative materials that you can use to alter the look of the home to complement the shape of your roof.

In certain instances, you can change the roof style completely, giving the home a totally different character and potential value. One of the most effective modifications to the exterior of the home is to change the roof design.

The most common remodel is to transform a flat roof into a sloped roof. This is considered to be a major structural and architectural alteration and will always require approved plans and inspections during construction. It is one of the few things that you can do that will change the design of the house significantly. For example, it can transform a simple ranch style into a Southwestern style. By adding or modifying a specific style of roof, you can transform a mediocre home into a fairly spectacular-looking one. On homes where the roof is already sloped, you can also change the design by adding things like dormers, cupolas, and overhangs.

Most of the roof modifications you will see will require some form of structural modification of the house. Therefore, I recommend strongly that when you're considering this option you deal with a house planner or architect in deciding whether this type of remodel might be a viable option for your renovation. Some modifications, such as dormers and cupolas, may be made without serious structural modification so long as they are cosmetic rather than being integrated into the roof itself.

> **HEADS UP**
>
> An architect uses the roof in the same manner as a woman uses her hair. It is a major style statement. In the case of the roof, it is the most prominent feature of the architectural style.

Roof Design

All roofs are sloped, even the so-called flat roofs. The reason for this is simple: weather. Most places around the country have rain; some places have snow. This condition drives the roof design. Both snow and rain can cause damage from intrusion and weight. In some areas where snow is prevalent, the freeze/thaw cycle compounds the potential damage. In most designs the roof overhangs the exterior walls, protecting them from water and other intrusions. Flat roof designs are treated in a different manner and flat roofs are generally used in geographical areas with less-than-average rainfall and less-than-severe freeze/thaw cycles.

Snow, Rain, and Roof Loads

In addition to the potential of water incursion into the home, water and snow are heavy. Water weighs over eight pounds per gallon. Snow, while less dense, is also heavy, as eight inches of snow are equivalent to one inch of water.

All buildings are designed to carry certain loads; these design criteria are applied to floors and roofs. The load design criteria differ in various parts of the country, to address the local weather conditions. In addition to accommodating the weight of the roofing material, the roofs are designed to carry live loads (people working on the roof), dead loads (the weight of snow, ice, and water), and wind loads.

The most common roof design and the simplest structure is the shed roof or one-slope roof. It is high on one side of the structure and slopes to the other side. More common is the two-slope roof, which slopes from a center ridge to the two eaves. These are the simplest form of pitched roofs. Pitched roofs come in a variety of shapes and materials. The basic component of any pitched roof is the roof slope or the amount of *pitch* required to meet the design criteria. The most common slope is the "3 in 12" roof. The designation of "3 in 12" means that the roof has three feet of fall from the ridge for

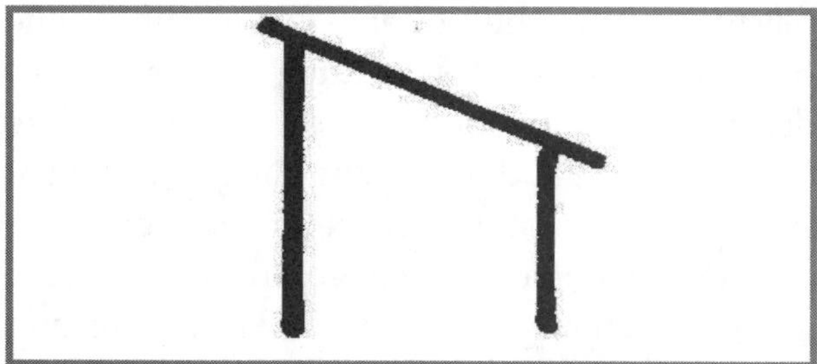

FIGURE 11-1. THE SHED ROOF

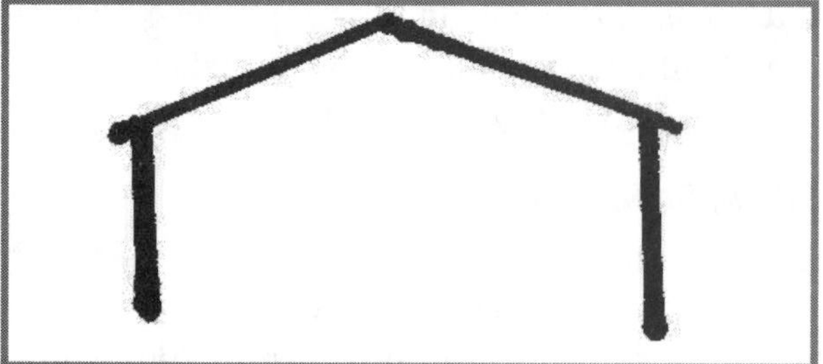

FIGURE 11-2. THE TWO-SLOPE ROOF

every 12 feet of width of the slope from the ridge to the eave.

DIFFERENT SLOPES

As architects exercise their design skills, roofs take on many different and complicated shapes. In general, the more complicated the roof, the more expensive to build and, with more shapes, the more opportunities are created for leaks. Where two roof slopes come together, valleys are formed to transition from one slope to another. These valleys are places where leaks can occur and the changing temperatures in all climates affect these transition areas more than any other part of the roof.

These compound slopes require specialized construction techniques to make the junction areas waterproof. These junction areas also slow down the roof's ability to shed water and snow. Snow and ice can jam up these valleys and cause a damming effect. When this happens, more water (weight) is retained on the roof, requiring the entire structure to carry more weight. In winter climates this is compounded by the daily freeze/thaw cycles. This combination of water, snow, and ice expands as it freezes, tearing at the roofing material. Improper designs fail and roof leaks can occur.

ROOF CONSTRUCTION

How a roof is constructed is as important as the materials it is constructed with. To perform properly, the roof must be structurally independent from the rest of the house. Above the ceiling, the roof structure is insulated for two reasons: one, to protect the interior of the home from the outside temperature, and two, to keep the roof structure at the same temperature throughout. If there is a temperature difference,

FIGURE 11-3. SIMPLE SLOPE ROOF AND COMPOUND ROOF SLOPES

the snow and ice on the roof will thaw and freeze at different times, causing more damage than if the cycle were consistent. Even without the snow and ice, daily changes in temperature cause the roofing materials to expand and contract at different rates. This causes wear and tear on the materials, causing roofs to fail over time. Most roof designs are rated as to their expected useful lives. In the industry we refer to roofs as being ten-, 20-, or 30-year roofs. This designation means that the manufacturer of the roofing materials and the builder putting the roof together guarantee the performance of the roof for the designated period of time. To avail yourself of a manufacturer's warranty, you simply pay for it. The manufacturer of the roofing then inspects the job during construction and issues you the warranty.

> **HEADS UP**
>
> The roof warranty is widespread in the commercial building industry, but is available to all. Just ask your builder.

Curves

Less common than the pitched roof is the curved roof. It is seen fairly often in commercial work, but can be seen occasionally in residential construction. Even though the roof surfaces are not flat, they follow the same design criteria for load and wearing.

FIGURE 11-4. A RARE ROOF—CURVED, POURED CONCRETE WITH A WIDOW'S WALK

Flat Roofs

Very common in commercial construction is the flat roof. This is a misnomer, as there is never a truly flat roof. These roofs seem flat, because the exterior walls of the building seem all the same height. In fact, the flat roof is constructed inside these perimeter walls with several slopes to channel the rain and snow to various points of discharge. This avoids damming water on the roof, which might cause the structure to fail when the weight exceeds the design loads.

When you hear of a roof collapse, it is most likely a flat roof design where the drains have become clogged and water has ponded on the roof, exceeding the structure's load capacity. These interior slopes of the so-called flat roofs are called *crickets* and can be any shape and

FIGURE 11-5. THE FLAT-ROOFED HOME

slope required to rid the roof of water as reliably as possible. The water is drained over the side of the roof by scuppers (openings in the walls) and downspouts or internally within the building by piping it down through and out of the building. Proper insulation is even more critical for this type of roof, because the aim is to keep the water load consistent throughout the roof structure. If water or snow builds up unevenly, the eccentric loading stresses the structure and the roof can fail.

Roofing Materials

All roofs are framed and then covered with wood or metal to support the roofing. The three components of the roof are insulation (either on the roof or under the roof), the impervious membrane, and the wearing surface. This construction holds true whether the roof is pitched or flat. There are many types of materials in use today and the industry is changing rapidly. Your home most likely has a pitched roof composed of felts covered with some kind of shingle or tile. Older flat roofs were composed of felts and sand and gravel wearing surfaces.

The material for membranes was originally felts sold in a variety of weights. Today this membrane can be very high-tech, lighter, and better than the old felt rolls. Manufacturers are also able to guarantee the new roof for longer periods for less money. The wearing surface for sloped roofs will remain fairly constant and provide ample choices to decorate the house, including the following:

- Asphalt shingle
- Wood shake
- Clay tile
- Concrete tile
- Metal
- Concrete

Each of these materials has advocates and critics. They have been used successfully all over the country.

Perhaps the most common and widespread and least expensive is the asphalt shingle. It comes in a variety of weights, colors, and textures and provides a good ten- to 20-year roof, depending on the climate and the shingle installed.

The wood shake is popular in California. It has a great look. It weathers well, but is affected by severe heat. Untreated, it can have a limited useful life. It is also more costly than the asphalt shingle and can attract critters to live in the roof material.

A better choice is the clay tile roof. It lends itself particularly to Western architecture and has a long useful life. The disadvantage of the clay tile is its fragility. It breaks easily when walked on and requires much skill to be used properly.

Rapidly replacing the clay tile and the wood shake roofs is the concrete tile roof. These tiles come in a variety of colors, weights, and textures and are available all around the country. Their disadvantage is their weight. They weigh at least 10 pounds per square foot, so the roof structure must be designed to accommodate this extra weight.

Metal roofs are used almost exclusively in commercial buildings and on homes in areas where a lot of snow is the norm. It is very expensive, but one of the best roofs you can buy. It is very long-lived and comes in a variety of colors and materials.

Poured-in-place concrete roofs are rare, except in high-rise urban buildings. More common are poured concrete porches over living areas. These can be a maintenance problem, they are expensive to build, and they are generally avoided except in very expensive homes. Refer back to Figure 11-4 for a rare look at one.

FLAT ROOFS: BUILT-UP AND SPRAY-ON

Flat roofs come in two varieties, the built-up roof and the spray-on roof. Both need to be properly sloped. The built-up roof is the traditional felt-and-sand-and-gravel roof. The spray-on roof is composed of a sponge-like material, coated with a waterproof membrane. The new spray-on roof seems to be gaining in popularity despite its greater cost. If you are contemplating a flat roof project, I suggest you consult the architect and the manufacturer to determine what guarantees are available and the expected lifespan of the material you want to use.

POTENTIAL CHANGES

When looking at a renovation or upgrade project for dramatically altering the appearance of your home, the roof is an obvious choice of an area where you can have some very real impact. The roof crowns the house; changing it will alter the architecture of the home forever.

The most dramatic change would be taking a flat-roofed home and putting on a pitched roof. By adding the appropriate trim and exterior finish, you can achieve almost any architectural style. The converse is also true. You can take off a pitched roof and install a flat roof for all or a part of the home. The most effective and modern approach is to have a combination of pitched and flat roofs with a collection of masses with various elevations. This sounds complicated, but it just takes time and money.

Perhaps the easiest way to dress up a home with a simple two-slope pitched roof is to add some other roof structure at right angles to the roof. This gives the roof multiple slopes and provides a lot of curb appeal. You could use the roof to add a new entrance to the home or cover a new porch or an added garage. This type of renovation is not too costly and relatively easy to do.

Sometimes people use a garage for new rooms for the home. This renovation is relatively simple, as the structure is already in place; you need only add plumbing, walls, and electrical work without disturbing the exterior. You might need to add a window or two to make the new rooms more habitable and appealing. Now that you have used the old garage, assuming that you have the space on your lot, you can add a new garage with a roof profile that contrasts and complements the older part of the home. It is quite common to see a garage with a flat roof attached to a home with a pitched roof. They tie together nicely, forming a new harmonious whole with architecture that is more interesting than the old house.

One variation for urban dwellers is the addition of roof gardens to their homes. Urban homes very often have flat roofs or roofs of poured concrete. If this is the case, you can modify the roof to include an area for seating and a garden. It would require construction of a covered stairway and exit to the roof, but can provide you with an

FIGURE 11-6. THE COMBINATION ROOF STYLE

exceptional new outdoor area. If you are fortunate to have a view, it can be a very valuable addition to the amenities of the home.

Very popular in New England waterfront towns is the widow's walk. This is an area built into the roof and accessible from within the home that allows people to sit or stand on the roof with a railing. It was popularized by sea captains' wives in harbor towns, since the structure allowed the wives to go out to watch for ships entering the harbor. Refer back to Figure 11-4 for a look at one.

A minor change that can have a tremendous impact on your home is changing the roofing materials only. Asphalt shingles can be replaced with shake, concrete tile, or metal roofing. The results can be dramatic. When contemplating concrete tile, you will need a structural engineer to determine whether your roof framing can support the added weight. This does not cost much and can be done quickly. Most structures are over-engineered so that these changes can be made without any problems. I would be concerned only with buildings that are more than 20 years old.

To achieve the modern look despite the architectural style, you need to add certain touches to your home. As these relate to roofing, you need to update the wearing surface to what is now fashionable in your area; you can find out what is selling by simply touring some of the new subdivisions. Another must is to finish the building eaves. Typically, older homes had unfinished overhangs. These should be boxed and refinished, with the appropriate touches added, such as gutters and/or venting. You should look at the roof slope to see if the addition of some simple new shapes can accent the home more dramatically.

Building masses are interesting when the roof line is varied. Look at your home to see if a simple change in the roof line over one area of the home could make a more dramatic statement. These types of changes are not necessary; they only provide additional choices when you contemplate upgrading your home. By doing the research and consulting with Realtors® and architects, you can develop a better feel for the potential value of this type of alteration. Tearing the roof off of a home is not cheap, but it might move your home up several categories in value. If the neighborhood and the area can support the new value, you just might hit a home run.

If you live in an area where it rains or snows a lot, you will find that gutters are a mixed blessing. They control the water cascading off the roof, but they are a maintenance nightmare, especially if you have many trees around the home. In addition, the freeze/thaw cycle tends to dam up the water at the eave and gutter line, forcing water back up the roof and under the

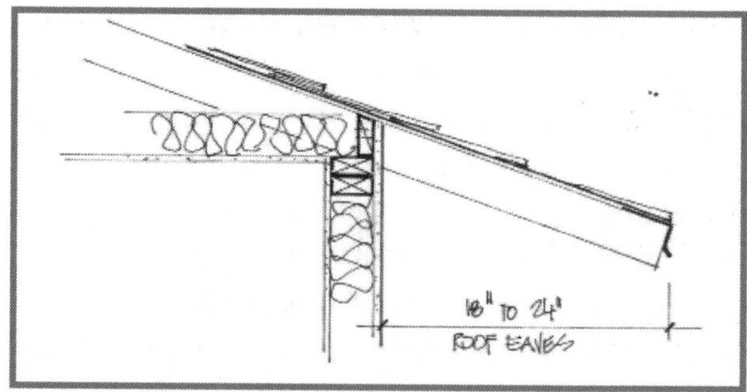

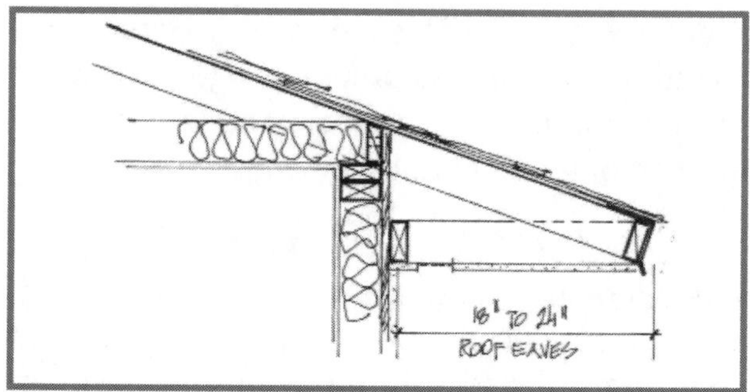

FIGURE 11-7. OLD OVERHANG AND FINISHED OVERHANG

roofing material, causing roof leaks. The only solution is to keep the gutters free of debris and install a heating system to melt the ice and snow from your roof.

Landscaping and Irrigation

In the beginning, all is raw land. When developers subdivide property, their first step is to gather information about the land itself. This is done by a surveyor; the two basic types of information provided are a boundary survey and a topographic map. Every residential subdivision starts with this basic picture. From there, the planners are able to lay out the lots and start the project design. Once a subdivision is built, all the houses have been placed within envelopes established by the original subdivision design. Outside these envelopes, but inside your property lines, are no-build zones known as *setbacks* and *easements*. You might wonder what use these areas are to your home and why you should have to purchase and maintain them. These easements enable the utility companies to serve not only your home, but all the homes in your area. The setbacks are part of the zoning regulations designed to enhance the area, in general, and provide a uniform, quality-oriented approach to the development process. In certain instances, you may apply for and be granted a variance to deviate from setback, coverage, and height restrictions as long as your neighbors do not object. The variance, once granted, is part of the land until removed, even after you sell your home. You cannot build on these "dead" areas, but you may landscape them. The only dead area that I recommend not spending a lot of money on is the right-of-way portion of your front yard. It is there so that the city can widen the road in the future; if that happens, you will not be compensated for your loss of investment in landscaping.

EASEMENTS

Easements are granted for many reasons, not the least of which is to provide utilities to each house. Normally, these easements run along the front of the lots alongside the streets. With projects with varied terrain, it is quite common to have situations where there are easements cutting across the sides and rear of some lots to transition from one grade to another. Most lots will have the PUE in the front, but when you buy any real estate, you must review the title report to see where your lot's easements occur.

> **DEFINITION**
>
> ***PUE*** is an acronym for the public utility easement.

If you look at a typical plat map of a residential lot (Figure 11-8), you will see the easements shown as part of the overall picture of the lot.

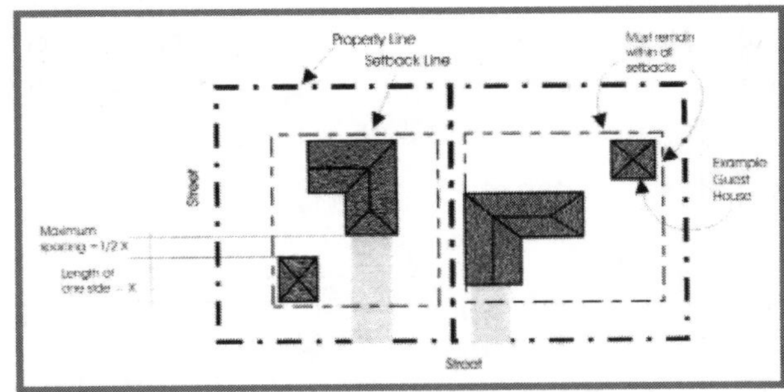

FIGURE 11-8. RESIDENTIAL PLAT MAP

The restrictions imposed by easements are simple: you cannot build over an easement, as the utility company must be able to access the utility lines for service. It is never a good idea to plant a tree or a large shrub in the PUE, as the maintenance crew might have to remove it to maintain service to the neighborhood. Other types of easements may exist for other purposes. It is quite common for one person to have an access easement over another person's property. Sometimes these easements are very specific and they are treated the same way as the PUEs: you cannot build on them or restrict access to them. Other easements are nonspecific and allow general passage through the property. This means that you must allow passage, however it is accomplished.

SETBACKS

Setbacks are another matter, as their purpose is different. Setbacks are designed to provide uniformity to a development and are used to control encroachment of one dwelling or building on another. Typical setbacks required in a residential subdivision are 20 feet from the street lot line, ten feet from the side lot lines, and five or ten feet from the back lot line. The effect of this regulation is to confine your improvements to your lot. No building can come closer to any of these lot lines than the setback allows. What is allowed in these areas is landscaping.

When you look at the effect of both easement and setback, you will find that your ability to improve your lot is quite restricted, especially on a small lot. What's left is for building your house, garage, outbuildings, and amenities such as a swimming pool or a tennis court. With renovation and expansion projects, you will have to work around these restrictions, as well as the existing improvements, buildings, and amenities, when you make your plan. If you are planning an extensive renovation or remodel, you must have a survey done to show where the existing improvements are and where you can place any additional improvements that you are planning.

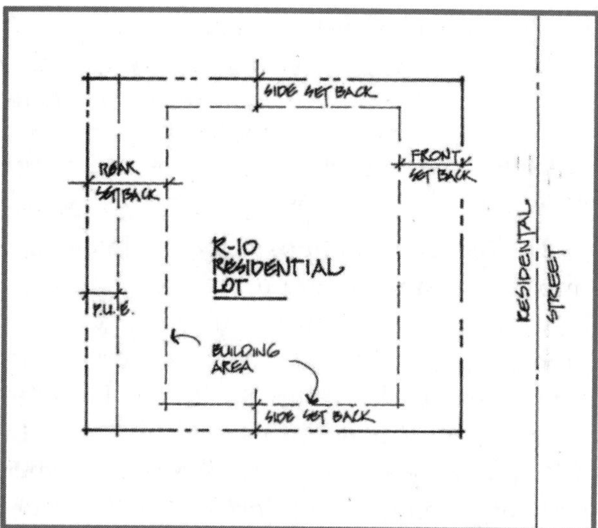

FIGURE 11-9. RESIDENTIAL LOT WITH SETBACKS AND EASEMENTS

THE FIRST IMPRESSION

If you remember the old adage that "you never get a second chance to make a first impression," then you will understand the importance of curb appeal. What lies between the house and the street is an opportunity to dress up your home. It can be used to show off the house, hide its bad features, and ensure privacy for the occupants. Landscaping is an important amenity on any property, as it provides the dressing for the building—curb appeal—as well as privacy, wind breaks, and a sense of shelter.

Lot Size and Amenities

What you can accomplish with a building lot depends largely on the size of the lot. Multifamily lots are so small, you are lucky to have a private patio and a bush out front, but your average residential lot of a quarter acre will provide ample opportunity for the buildings, as well as recreational amenities and extensive landscaping. When you take on a remodel, it is important to realize that a little well-placed landscaping can really make an impression. In general, planting is less expensive than building modification. Hiding less-than-desirable features on any building with plantings is very cost-effective.

Small Lots

When you have very little to work with, it is necessary to use the space carefully. In small lots, usually the front yard is regulated and maintained by the condominium association, but the back plot is all yours. If you are working with a small patio or a balcony space, the use of potted plants on the floor and hanging plants can give the impression of a pleasantly cool and shaded space.

The Normal, Quarter-Acre Lot

The average lot is about 10,000 square feet, or approximately 100 feet wide and 100 feet long. Most subdivisions will have the street frontage dimension a bit smaller and the depth a little larger.

For the sake of illustration, use a lot that's 80 feet wide by 125 feet deep. With ten-foot side yard setbacks, a 20-foot front setback, and a 20-foot wide driveway, you have left a patch of land 40 feet wide for large landscaping in the front. The depth will be a minimum of 20 feet and possibly more if the house is pushed back on the lot. Most home builders push the house as close to the street as possible to maximize the back yard, but for aesthetic appeal the customary dimension is 40 feet. This leaves a good planting area, but remember that the utility easement must be accessible, so you had better not plant any trees in it. The side yard setbacks are OK for planting large trees. Shrubs and lawn can go anywhere. I'll have more on the back yard later.

These generous lots can be a little more difficult, as it takes more of everything to fill them up and then it takes more time and effort to maintain the landscaping. A good ploy is to cluster the plantings around areas of lawn or decorative rock. The clustering will give the impression of masses of green and set off the defined open spaces, maximizing the effect. You can use rock and other features to good effect as well. In regions of the country that enjoy more rainfall, landscaping must be planted to ensure that there is space to enjoy each plant or tree, avoiding overgrowth. Where there is less rain, to achieve an overgrown look, you must have copious amounts of irrigation.

Basic Planting

When a developer builds a home, the landscaping will be minimal. A front yard starter package looks something like this:

- two 24-inch box trees
- three 15-gallon trees
- eight five-gallon shrubs

Most nurseries have weekly specials on this type of planting package. Our local one is offering one this week, at $699 planted and guaranteed. If you are doing a rebuild, you can take advantage of these weekly specials to spruce up your project with a small expenditure. Most nurseries will allow you to substitute and mix and match. New homes seldom have any planting in the back yard and it is not uncommon to encounter a newer renovation prospect with a back yard where there has never been any planting. When a newer home becomes a renovation candidate, it is because the owners did not have the money to maintain the mortgage, far less the house and yards. It then falls to you to provide a suitable back yard for the resale.

Landscaping to Increase Street Appeal

The most eloquent argument for landscaping in a fixer-upper project is curb appeal. You want people to notice your project and stop to see it. You can't sell it if they haven't seen it. Good landscaping in the front yard will have them pulling over to write down the number on the sign. An astute landscaping package can dress up an ordinary house very nicely. It is much more effective than architectural decoration of the building and much more cost-effective. If the house has a feature that you want to hide, plant something in front of it. If you want to emphasize some feature, frame it with landscaping. Look at the effect of landscaping on the house below (Figure 11-10). This is my own remodeling and expansion job.

FIGURE 11-10. A HOUSE BEFORE AND AFTER LANDSCAPING

CREATING AN OASIS

With the current trend of cocooning, you may want to consider a more elaborate approach to landscaping on your more ambitious projects. Families today are spending more and more time at home and their dwellings are starting to reflect this. Additions of media rooms, swimming pools, and other amenities allow people to recreate right in their own homes. In the old days, formal gardens and mazes were very popular; today a private and secluded atmosphere is very desirable. I'm not suggesting that you install a pool, as it is not cost-effective, but if you can transform the back yard into a private oasis, you will score with the average buyer.

HEADS UP

What is needed is lush landscaping, privacy, and low maintenance. Remember the irrigation system.

THE NEED FOR PRIVACY

Privacy is a big factor in modern living. In the western part of the country, fences and walls are accepted as part of a normal subdivision, so most of the houses have a private back yard. In the eastern part of the country, fences are not as common, so privacy must be achieved with planting hedges, etc. With the rainfall in the East, rows of trees and shrubs grow quickly and achieve the same effect as fences and walls.

Front yards are another matter. Many subdivisions preclude heavy planting in front so that homes are visible from the street. This is a safety issue. You can achieve privacy by planting trees and shrubs in front of windows to screen views into the home from the street. They can also block views from the house. Most lots situate the house so that the views are from the back of the house rather than the front, so that is not generally an issue. Judicious planting can achieve a great deal of privacy and provide a good selling point, as shown in Figure 11-11.

PLANTING—DECIDUOUS VS. EVERGREEN

Remember when planting, depending on your location, to choose plants and trees that hold

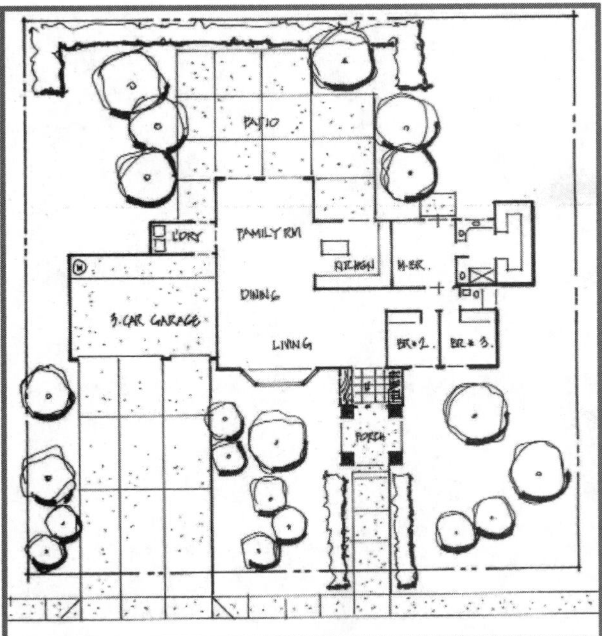

FIGURE 11-11. LANDSCAPE PLAN EMPHASIZING PRIVACY

their leaves year round. Obviously, for color and seasonal variety, you can sprinkle in a few items that are deciduous, but not too many or your house will look naked during the winter, which will dramatically affect its curb appeal. Be sure to plant your trees and shrubs as far ahead of your anticipated sale date as possible. The more mature your landscaping is, the better it will be for you.

Maintenance and Salability

For your own sake, while you own the home, and for the long term, choose plants, trees, and irrigation materials that will hold up well. In four-season climates, be sure that your irrigation system can be drained and made freeze-proof. Winterizing irrigation will ensure a long service life. Quality materials and planting techniques are the least inexpensive in the long run. If you have a limited budget, install a quality piping system, along with wiring for future automation, and run your system manually for a few years. Then add electronic controls and better dispersion when you can afford it.

SECTION III

RENOVATION *aka* REDEVELOPMENT

CHAPTER

12

Homes *with* Appreciation Potential

Market Research

In this chapter we examine the acquisition of a new personal home, plan for its investment potential, and examine the purchase of an additional house for investment only. Working with housing is a bit of a specialty; if you're going to be working with housing, you need to pay attention to those things peculiar to housing that give value to the houses. As with any investment, your project should start with market research. I know I've mentioned this before and I will mention it again. Researching your target market is probably the single most important aspect of any investment, whether it's in real estate or any other type of investment.

What to Look For

Working with your Realtor®, market research company, or whomever you elect to deal with regarding the real estate market, look for trends in values and absorption (velocity) rates. For any segment of the market that you're interested in, factor in the historical trends, what's going on today, and what your realtor thinks will happen tomorrow. Calculate the per-year value rise and average it over a five-, 10-, and even 15-year period. Find out how many homes sold in a given year and in what price categories. You're looking for the hot seller, the most popular segment of the target market. Check at least the following characteristics:

- Size
- Number of bedrooms and baths
- Garage size
- Land size
- Living room and family room vs. great room
- Formal dining room
- Kitchen size and type
- Age and design (Victorian, Cape Cod, Contemporary, etc.)
- Condition

These facts should give you a fairly good basis for projecting your thoughts onto tomorrow's market. Research, as it relates to housing, is relatively accurate today. The computerized MLS systems in use around the country make compiling statistical trends relatively easy. Just remember: the key component of market research is you; you must make the call based on the facts you gather.

Market research is largely a matter of gathering data and then interpreting it. My experience over the last 25 years has been that data can be manufactured as well as researched. Fortunately, in the housing industry, the accurate data is universally available to all who are in the industry. You'll find that this is not the case when dealing with commercial properties, so I would strongly suggest that, when you're dealing with commercial property, you spot-check your data periodically to verify its accuracy.

Where to Look

Where to look for a new home is always an issue. In addition to your personal considerations for housing, you have now added an extra layer of analysis because you are, from here on out, also going to look at your own personal housing as an investment. This approach will quickly change your thinking as investment considerations may come into direct conflict with your personal housing preferences. You might find, for instance, that you really enjoy the homes in a certain area, but, upon doing the research, you find that homes in this particular area have appreciated only two percent per year while the overall market in your immediate region is enjoying an average appreciation of eight to 12 percent per year. While this might prove to be a wonderful place to live, it will also be a lousy investment. You need to pass on this one and come back to the neighborhood after you have made your pile.

Your Home and the Market

If you run across this situation, what do you do? The choice is simple:, you can buy the house anyway and look elsewhere for an investment or you can bypass this house and keep looking. This is a time when you and your spouse need to be in total agreement on your investment plan. There is no such thing as the one and only perfect house for you and your family. Like most things in life, sound decisions are based on compromise, and housing is no different.

When you are looking for a home, what are some good areas to look in? Here are some of my pet areas:

- Custom home developments in the path of growth
- Established areas where older homes (30 years old or more) are being acquired and renovated by young families
- Rural locations and housing that may have excess land
- Urban areas in locations where the trend to downtown living has once again become a factor in the marketplace
- Light industrial areas between the suburbs and downtown (areas becoming increasingly popular for lofts and possible development opportunities)

This is only a partial list of potentially profitable locations where you can look for a place to live. I'm sure that you, knowing your area, can come up with a list of additional, potentially profitable locations. One of my favorite areas can be found in regions fortunate enough to have a lake, an ocean, or a mountain. These types of areas have the added cachet of having potential recreational and vacation draws. In Chapter 15, one of our case studies will take a look at a long-term renovation project of a property with a lifestyle, vacation, or second home location. Another aspect of your search will deal with your investment strategy.

If you recall, we mentioned earlier that one consideration will be how long you intend to occupy the home you're about to buy. I think it's unlikely that anybody is going to consider purchasing a home to live in for a quick turnaround. Moving is expensive: you need to make enough money to not only pay for the move, but also provide a profit on your investment. Most people who are looking at a home for investment consider a home that will be an investment for the medium or long term. This limits your choice to two categories of houses: ones that can be upgraded or ones that can be totally renovated and/or expanded.

The upgradeable home would be a home that has medium-term potential; this is an ideal choice if you are looking to move every couple of years. Upgrading a home is a relatively simple and not too disruptive process that will allow you a harmonious occupancy while you are doing the upgrades. A home that can be renovated and/or expanded is a major undertaking; you should know what to expect before you even embark on the project. In some instances, during a major home rebuild, the house may become temporarily uninhabitable. Chapter 13 will be the start of our section on renovatable properties. If you are considering this type of project, you should pay close attention to that section of the book.

Quick Results vs. Long-Term Strategies

When you're approaching a project involving a house, you must look at the entire spectrum, from the quick and easy lipstick process through the upgrade to the demolish-and-renovate approach. All three of these approaches have occupancy, financial, and living implications, not the least of which is a return on the cash invested. When looking at any form of investment, you need to consider the cash-on-cash rate of return and the time frame in which the return can be realized. This is similar to a cost-benefit analysis. I recommend "running the numbers" on any project you undertake before you launch.

As you saw in Chapter 8, it is relatively simple to take a quick look at the potential for any project's appreciation only. To make it relevant for improving the home, you need only add the cost of improvements to the analysis. If we stick with the home we were looking at in Chapter 8, using the same initial assumptions, then our new cost-benefit analysis would look something like you see in Table 12-1.

As you can see by going through the project analyzed in Table 12-1, in addition to the home's appreciation during the time you owned it, your upgrade of the home resulted in additional profits. Inasmuch as you lived in the home for 24 months or more, your capital gain profits were tax-free. This is the type of project that you can do again and again, reinvesting your profits as you go. By reinvesting your profits, you can either purchase increasingly larger homes or take some of the cash generated from this

Item	Notes	Dollar/% Value
Purchase price		$160,000
Down payment (20%)	conventional loan	$32,000
Closing costs	Estimate	$3,500
Mortgage amount	80%	$128,000
Mortgage (PI) 8%/30 years (APR = 8.81%)	PI = principal + interest on $128K	$11,276.80/year $939.73/month
Appreciation 10% x 5 years	compounded—year 1	$176,000
	compounded—year 2	$193,600
Convert garage to office		$15,000
Expand kitchen		$18,000
Paint, carpet, and landscape		$20,000
Initial investment	Down + closing cost	$35,500
Upgrade costs		$53,000
New home value		$305,000
Sales commission (6%)	$18,300	$286,700
Profit on sale	sale price – cost – renovation cost	$70,200
ROI	$35,500 + $53,000 renovation cost = $88,500 total investment	79% or 39%/year
Annual tax benefit during ownership	estimated tax write-off	$10,240/year
Captal gain taxes		$0

TABLE 12-1. COST-BENEFIT ANALYSIS

process and invest in a project that is separate and apart from the home you live in.

SHORT-TERM CASH GENERATION

The project outlined above can be classified as a short- or medium-term project. A large-scale demolition-and-renovation project would be a long-term project, if you occupied the home during the process. Once you have several generations of the above project under your belt, you will have generated enough cash to consider a separate house as an additional investment. There are several different ways that you can go about adding the second project to your investment plan. You can:

1. Tackle a project that is a quick lipstick-type project, turning over two or more per year.
2. Purchase a rental property, lease it out, and sell it later for a capital gain.
3. Purchase a rental property and upgrade it with the cooperation of the tenant.

4. Purchase a renovation property and go for the big one.

The first option will generate ordinary income, unless you hold the property in excess of 12 months. Typically, the lipstick approach is a quick turnaround, one to four months, and yields a relatively small, but quick profit on your investment. The only drawback with this quick turnaround project is the fact that the real estate commission at the time of resale represents a large percentage of your potential profit. I therefore recommend that if you are going to look at these types of projects, you become a licensed real estate salesperson. This will save you at least half of the real estate commission. The remaining three items on the list all generate capital gains: as long as you hold the property for a year and a day, you can claim a long-term capital gain.

Combine Home and House

An ideal plan of attack for residential properties is a combination of two homes. Live in and upgrade one; renovate and expand the other. Every two years, you'll have a nontaxable profit on your own home and, if your renovation project takes 12 months or more, you will have a capital gain on the second house. If you look into financial analysis of this type of approach over a ten-year period, you'll see that your net worth should have a dramatic increase. We will cover the renovation and expansion process starting in Chapter 13.

Planning and Financial Analysis

The prospects for profit when purchasing a home are relatively certain if you do the research. All that remains prior to purchase is coming up with a plan. Any plan involving a house purchase should be responsive to two considerations, time and investment. Time relates to how long you plan to live there and investment relates to how much cash you intend to put into the transaction, both at the beginning and while you are executing your plan.

In Chapter 8 we looked at the financial impact of simply buying and holding a piece of property, and, in Table 12-1 above, we can see the impact of upgrading a home while you live there. If we assume that:

- You started with the original investment of $35,500.
- You borrowed the $53,000 for the upgrades.
- At the time of sale, you now have $105,700.

This represents three times the working capital you started with a little over two years before. In addition, the $70,000 increase is tax-free. Part of your forward planning will be to decide whether to take most of this money and buy a new home or to split it up and buy two houses. If we assume that you wish to be a little aggressive with your financial planning, you would most likely split the investment and purchase either a rental property or an upgradeable property with part of the money. Using some of the assumptions from Chapter 8 about a rental property and the same assumption used in Table 12-1 for your personal home, then at the end of two years, you should have accomplished the following:

1. By living in and upgrading your home, you should have produced an additional $70,000 of profit.
2. By purchasing, leasing, and reselling a comparable rental property, you should have accomplished what you see in Table 12-2.
3. By extrapolating the results and adding the $25,585 to the $70,000 you made on

Item	Notes	Dollar/% Value
Purchase price		$160,000
Down payment (20%)	conventional loan	$32,000
Closing costs	estimate	$3,500
Mortgage amount	80%	$128,000
Mortgage (PI) 8%/30 years (APR = 8.81%)	PI = principal + interest on $128K	$11,276.80/year $939.73/month
Appreciation 10% x 5 years	compounded—year 1	$176,000
	compounded—year 2	$193,600
Initial investment	down + closing cost	$35,500
Gross appreciation/profit	end of year 2 new value less cost	$30,100
Rental income $1,000/ month/2 years	$1,000 x 12 x 2	$24,000
Less maintenance	$600/year	($1,200)
Net rental income	2 years	$22,800
Less interest	2 years	($22,552)
Net taxable profit	ordinary income 2 years	$248
ROI	on $35,500	84% or 42%/year
Taxable gain		$30,100
Tax rate	capital gain	15%
After-tax gain		$25,585

TABLE 12-2. RENTAL PROPERTY INVESTMENT ANALYSIS

your own home above, you realize that in this second round of investment, you've taken your original $35,000 in capital and increased it by an additional $95,585 over and above the $70,000 you made on your first home rotation. You now have $201,285 of available, after-tax capital.

Another thing you need to consider is that this rental property yielded only $25,000 in gain on $35,000 invested because you held the property for only 24 months. Since this investment property is not going to be tax-free, there is no reason for you to sell out after 24 months. Referring back to Chapter 8, Table 8-4, you can see the results of holding this property for five years. You should, therefore, consider modifying your plan to do the following:

- Rotate your own home ownership every 24 months.
- Split the cash yield generated by rotating your home each time, for purchasing a rental property every two years.

Item	Year	Cost	Invested	Appreciation
Rental 1	1-11	$160,000	$35,500	$176,000
Rental 2	3-11	$160,000	$35,500	$128,000
Rental 3	5-11	$160,000	$35,500	$96,000
Rental 4	7-11	$160,000	$35,500	$64,000
Rental 5	9-11	$160,000	$35,500	$32,000
Total Appreciation	Year 11		$177,500	$496,000
ROI	Average		279% or 28%/year	

TABLE 12-3. TEN-YEAR INVESTMENT PROPERTY SCHEDULE

- Hold all the rental properties until you decide to consolidate your investment portfolio.

Continuing to use our assumptions and using Table 12-3 for income property profit generation, we can see that, after the ten-year period, assuming no compounding of price escalation, your financial situation should look something like that shown in Table 12-3.

If we assume that prices escalate ten percent per year and we compound the yields as shown in Table 12-4, then the escalation per unit would be greater than the straight percentage of the purchase price in Table 12-3. Annual value escalation would be more like that shown in Table 12-4.

The effect of compounding yields the returns shown in Table 12-5.

In addition to profiting on your five rental properties, you will have turned your home over five times for a total tax-free profit on your home of $350,000. Adding these two investment returns together, you will now have $948,133 of capital to work with after liquidating all your properties. This total is composed of your profits plus your original $35,500 investment.

Obviously, there are many variables that will occur during a ten-year investment period, but you get the general idea. Before you say to me that compounding distorts the potential appreciation of a home, let me cite you three examples from my own experience.

1. In 1974, I purchased a duplex (half of a two-family house) for $38,000. In 2003 it sold for $620,000.
2. In 1977, I purchased a single-family home on 1.5 acres for $160,000 and renovated it for an additional $40,000. It is currently appraised at $4.2 million.
3. In 1979, I purchased a single-family home on 2.5 acres for $280,000 and renovated it for an additional $200,000. It is currently appraised at $2.8 million.

Here's a fourth experience that's the exception that proves the rule:

4. In 1984 I built a home at a cost of $285,000 and sold it four years later for $290,000. The market for that home was totally flat, as it was at the top end of the market. I had overbuilt the market.

The only thing that may differ from my experience with the above properties and your potential investment experience is the location of the homes. The first three of the above homes were purchased in California and Arizona, where we have a built-in growth factor due to migration and normal population growth. The forth house was built in a small town with a very dollar-conscious buying public. By researching the historical appreciation in your market, you should get a pretty good idea what to expect from your potential investments.

Item		Dollar Value
Purchase price		$160,000
Down payment (20%)	conventional loan	$32,000
Closing costs	estimate	$3,500
Mortgage amount	80%	$128,000
Mortgage (PI) 8%/30 years (APR = 8.81%)	PI = principal + interest	$11,276.80/year $939.73/month
Appreciation 10% x 5 years	compounded—year 1	$176,000
	compounded—year 2	$193,600
	compounded—year 3	$212,960
	compounded—year 4	$234,256
	compounded—year 5	$257,682
	compounded—year 6	$283,450
	compounded—year 7	$311,795
	compounded—year 8	$342,974
	compounded—year 9	$399,282
	compounded—year 10	$415,000
	compounded—year 11	$456,500

TABLE 12-4. RENTAL HOUSE 10-YEAR PROJECTION

Multiple Property Investment

In the investment scenario above, you will find that you would probably be quite busy buying and upgrading your own homes as well as purchasing and managing your five rental properties. In general, you'll find that after ten years of this, you will probably want to consolidate your investments into something more manageable. Once you have made a good start on long-term capital accumulation, you will probably back off from rotating your personal home every two years and, instead, buy bigger homes, expand them, and, periodically rotate them for additional tax-free capital gains.

Most people grow tired of dealing with multiple residential rentals, as they are a 24/7 proposition. Once you go beyond the realm of multiple properties, you will have to look into multifamily investment properties. Any property with more than one dwelling could be classified as a multifamily property, but in the investment game, multifamily rental properties are usually eight units or more. It is quite common to see duplexes, triplexes, and fourplexes. These units are usually purchased and lived in by retired investors who want not only a place to live, but some handily managed investment property for income purposes. It seems that the efficiency of managing apartment rental units demands a size of approximately 150 units or larger, because most properties of this type are professionally managed and you need a certain

Item	Year	Cost	Invested	Appreciation
Rental 1	1-11	$160,000	$35,500	$293,000
Rental 2	3-11	$160,000	$35,500	$148,295
Rental 3	5-11	$160,000	$35,500	$119,950
Rental 4	7-11	$160,000	$35,500	$70,576
Rental 5	9-11	$160,000	$35,500	$30,100
Total Appreciation	Year 11		$177,500	$661,921
Taxes: 15% capital gain				($99,288)
Net cash gain after taxes				$562,633
ROI	Average		Pre-tax gain 372% or 37%/year	
			After-tax gain 316% or 31.6%/year	

TABLE 12-5. TEN-YEAR PROFIT RECAP, RENTAL UNIT INVESTMENT

minimum size complex to support the cost of professional management. Besides the day-to-day operation of the complex, leasing units, and collecting rent, there is always a sizable maintenance responsibility that demands day-to-day, full-time professionals. In addition to the efficiencies of operation, there is a different financial analysis that pertains to this size of investment property. Properties of this type are sold and priced based on capitalization rates typical for that industry and that part of the world. In Table 12-6 you'll find an income and expense analysis for a typical multifamily property of approximately 150 units.

Average expense percentages were given to me by my friends at S-101 Management in Sunnyvale, California. They own and operate apartment rental projects for a living. As you can see, the property is a little more complex and its value is calculated, not by comparable sales, but by capitalizing the net income before debt service (NIBDS). We will have more on *capitalization rates* (cap rates) later in the book. The calculation is simple: merely take the NIBDS ($886,293) and divide it by the cap rate, in this instance 8.5 percent or 0.085, and the result is $10,426,986, the market value of the complex. Typically, you can borrow up to 75 to 80 percent of this value when purchasing this type of investment.

When you have tapped out your patience with managing six separate properties, you might want to consider cashing out your equities and investing them in one larger property, such as an apartment complex or a commercial property. Life will be a little easier and, depending on the market trend, more or less profitable. One thing for sure, your time will be freed up to look around at some new possibilities.

Item	Notes	Subtotals	Totals
Income			
50 studios	$550/month	$330,000/year	
40 one-bedrooms	$700/month	$336,000/year	
60 two-bedrooms	$900/month	$648,000/year	
Gross potential income (GPI)			$1,314,000
Less vacancy allowance of 5%		($65,700)	
Effective gross income (EGI)			$1,248,300
Expenses			
Operations	Average 25-40%	($312,075)	
Management	4% of EGI	($49,932)	
Total operating expenses		($362,007)	
Net operation income or NIBDS			$886,293
Capitalized value	@ 8.5 cap rate		$10,426,986
Loan value	Generally 75% of capitalized value		$7,820,232

TABLE 12-6. INCOME AND EXPENSE ANALYSIS, 150-UNIT APARTMENT COMPLEX

CHAPTER

13

Renovation Projects

Renovation projects run the gamut from quick décor jobs to major reconstruction. Regardless of the type of renovation you're contemplating, the key part of any of these types of projects is locating a suitable property. Where do you look? How do you know whether you have found a suitable one? The true answer is that renovations are where you find them, but there are some obvious places to look. In any given region, most of the neighborhoods, residential and commercial alike, are in a state of transition. It is this transitional state that may provide opportunities for people who are on the lookout. These properties, and the potential that they represent, will vary greatly in scope and potential from urban to rural locations and from city to city.

Locating a Property with Potential

When I'm looking for a piece of property, residential or commercial, with renovation potential, I start with the fringe areas. I define a fringe area as a gray area between two distinct neighborhoods or zoning uses. Modern general plans and a zoning that pertains to specific portions of the general plans generally seek to create buffer zones between specific uses. In the average city, on a scale of the lowest to highest best use, the lowest use is allocated to industrial development. Adjacent to industrial development, we will find the urban core, transitioning into commercial "retail" districts and segueing into residential areas. In suburban areas, we find old commercial districts, with town or city offices, some retail, surrounded by older residential areas. In the new-growth part of the suburban area, we see that zoning surrounding the major traffic arterials is laid out with commercial on either side of the major street, transitioning into multifamily zones and then to single-family.

In older cities and towns, this type of stylized or organized zoning did not take place. The adoption of master planning techniques and specific zoning categories is a relatively recent development. In urban and suburban areas that grew up prior to adoption of the modern master plan, we will find areas that we would describe as relatively disorganized when viewed in the light of our current master planning techniques. It is in these older, "disorganized" areas that we find a proliferation of custom housing, "spot zoned" commercial, light industrial, and any number of other odd situations. It is precisely in this type of neighborhood and in this mix of uses that we can find some sparkling opportunities for redevelopment.

DEFINITION

Spot zoning occurs when a nonconforming use is interspersed within an otherwise uniformly zoned area. For example, a commercial lot within a residential subdivision would be deemed spot zoned. Conversely, a single-family home on a busy commercial street would be spot zoned.

Residential Targets of Opportunity

This is a very common phenomenon that exists in every major city in the United States. A lot of this property is still viable from a business point of view, but from a residential point of view it lacks the cachet and appeal of newer and more stylized developments. When we look at it like this, what do we see? In most instances, we see run-down residential freely mixed with small, mostly run-down or obsolete commercial buildings. There are two ways to attack this type of area.

You can start adjacent to the last stylishly developed area along that arterial, taking your cue from whatever is currently there, commercial or residential, and look at the potential of expanding that use or style along the arterial into this mixed-use area.

HEADS UP

The two houses in Figures 13-1 and 13-2 sit side by side on the same street. The home on the top has not been upgraded or modernized and the one on the bottom has been and it sold for about $325,000. Older homes like the one on the top, in this neighborhood, sell for about $185,000. This is definitely a potential project, clearly visible from the street.

You can look at this mixed-use area and pick an area that, due to the volume of traffic on the arterial, is an obvious choice for assembling parcels of land for developing new commercial property.

Whichever approach you take, you need a critical mass to pull it off. By working on projects along major arterials, you will primarily be committing yourself to commercial development, whether converting old houses to commercial use or assembling land and demolishing old buildings to create new developments.

Within this same mixed area and away from a major arterial, you'll get into neighborhoods of older housing. As a general rule, the farther you get from the major arterial, the better the quality of the older houses and the

FIGURE 13-1. POTENTIAL PROJECT

FIGURE 13-2. ALREADY DONE

greater the potential for upgrading and/or renovation and expansion. Many of these older homes have incredibly appealing features that are no longer included in the new homes built today. They are generally larger, with more generous rooms, and represent good upgrade and renovation possibilities.

Neglect

Another fertile field for potential upgrades involves homes whose maintenance has been neglected. It is not uncommon in these relatively volatile and economic times for homeowners to fall into a situation of financial disadvantage. Unfortunately, someone's misfortune is potentially someone else's opportunity. As they say, "It's an ill wind that blows nobody some good."

This type of an opportunity can exist anywhere in any neighborhood in any economic bracket. The only sure way to find something like this is to have your Realtor® be on the lookout for properties that fit this profile or for you to be constantly on the alert for such properties as you drive around in your day-to-day activities.

These types of homes lend themselves to the quick turnaround or lipstick approach. If you're going to deal with this type of property, as I mentioned before, you will do well to have your own real estate sales license. In addition to that, having some fundamental skills with a paintbrush, wallpaper, and carpeting will serve you, too. The quick turnaround opportunity does not lend itself to hiring others to do the work. You'll find that this remains true unless the home you're dealing with is a very large and potentially very expensive property.

Physical Obsolescence

Other potential project opportunities involve buildings, whether residential or commercial, that have achieved some measure of physical obsolescence. Physical obsolescence comes in many forms.

Residential obsolescence can come through low ceiling heights, single bathrooms, small living areas, and carports. Other problems can involve lack of insulation, noncompliance with building codes, old plumbing, wiring, and general dilapidation. This is relatively common in vacation-type properties or in areas that evidenced extreme home construction expansion after World War II. Commercial properties suffer from many of the same limitations. What most effectively limits economic opportunities in both residential and commercial is ceiling heights. The modern office building generally requires heights between nine and ten feet, plus enough room above the ceiling to accommodate air conditioning, wiring, and plumbing. Typical older office buildings have ceiling heights of approximately eight feet. Buildings built before the 1960s and '70s lack air conditioning and, consequently, the plenum area (the area between the ceiling and the floor above) was very limited, because there was no need to accommodate ductwork for heating, ventilation, and air conditioning (HVAC). Similarly, retail buildings suffered some of the same limitations. Without exception, all of the old buildings, residential and commercial alike, were never constructed for modern adaptations required by the Americans with Disabilities Act (ADA). Any and all of these limitations present both problems and opportunities for properties that are falling into decay and/or neglect.

Small Lots

Yet another form of physical obsolescence involves lot size. In residential construction, older homes generally had larger lots than found in today's new subdivisions. Probably the most pervasive single-family lot across the United States is the quarter-acre lot. Counting the streets and other required public dedications, these lots would average approximately 10,000 square feet. As population grows and the cost of land rises, developers, in an effort to keep housing costs competitive, are putting the same homes and often even larger homes onto smaller and smaller lots. As a result, the older homes with larger lots represent significant rehabilitation and expansion possibilities, as these older lots have the room to add square footage to the homes. To give you an idea of the effect of adding square footage, all you need to do is subtract from the potential per-square-foot sales price of the rehab or expanded home the per-square-foot cost of building the addition. In my neighborhood, homes sell for approximately $180-$200 per square foot and the cost of adding space varies from $80 to $120 a square foot. You do the math.

MARKET SHIFT

We have all seen the effect of changing markets on our homes and businesses around us. As Americans transitioned from cities to suburbs, the character of the cities and the character of the suburbs changed dramatically. The cities became shabbier, less densely populated, and generally run down. The explosive growth in the suburbs gave birth to the phrase "urban sprawl." The result of all these changes is that nobody is truly satisfied with either of the two extremes. While the suburbs are new and more vehicle-oriented, the people who have moved to the suburbs to be able to afford a home must commute long distances to work. It is highly disruptive to the commerce of the city. Retail must follow the homeowner and industrial and office work needs to remain consolidated in a central location. This is somewhat less true today due to telecommuting, but by and large it remains true in most metropolitan areas around the country. What is the result of this flight from the inner cities to suburbia to rural communities? It leaves several conditions, all of which present potential opportunities for the entrepreneur:

- Inner city properties become underutilized, neglected, and ripe for development.
- As the suburbs expanded rapidly and construction boomed, developers bought up land that was cheaper and passed over land that the owners had priced too high. The resulting "gaposis" leaves property that is ripe with in-fill opportunities. Time has a way of making landowners more realistic about pricing and values rise as time passes. Sooner or later these passed-over properties become viable parcels for development.

Reversing the trend is a popular and profitable preoccupation these days. People are getting tired of long and expensive commutes from the suburbs and are, in droves, pursuing the possibility of moving back to the urban core. Cities coast-to-coast are actively condemning old run-down properties and offering the resulting "cleaned up" properties to developers.

Older, once stylish homes in the inner city now represent incredible opportunities for refurbishment and reoccupation. Often these properties are richly traditional in architecture. Cities coast to coast have enjoyed a rejuvenation of old Victorian and brownstone residences. As people consider moving back to the city, so do businesses. All commercial development, whether retail or office, follows the population. The more people move into a rejuvenated area, the greater the demand for all the services that support residential occupancy.

FIGURE 13-3. INNER-CITY NEIGHBORHOOD SHOPPING CENTER BEFORE AND AFTER

Commercial Possibilities

The rehabilitation of commercial properties is not much more mysterious than the rehabilitation of residential properties; it simply involves a different set of skills and a different cast of characters. Population changes in cities are a growing force in the commercial life of the city, forcing business to accommodate the shift in population. Retail tends to move with the population, office properties both stay put and migrate to the suburbs, and industrial, both light and heavy, tends to stay put. So how do you examine the possibilities in the potential of commercial rehabilitation? The answer is twofold.

As the population shifts to the suburbs, it leaves behind older commercial buildings. They start to immediately become locationally and functionally obsolete. These buildings represent opportunities as well as problems.

The market shift leaves a vacuum of jobs and opportunities in the urban core. This vacuum is generally offset by the in-migration of poor people. As the inner-city areas decay, they become much more affordable for people needing a cheap place to live. Typically these people do not have the wherewithal to maintain the properties they occupy and the downward spiral continues. The key to all this is timing. You need to keep your eye peeled for the reverse trend from suburb to city. When this occurs, there are incredible opportunities for rehabilitating old residential properties, followed swiftly and surely by the need for new commercial infrastructure. Typically, in the downtown areas, you will need to work with existing structures, as even in disadvantaged urban areas land prices tend to be quite high. The only people who seem to be able to afford to buy, demolish, and rebuild are people who are involved in the redevelopment of large urban properties.

INDUSTRIAL

Industrial properties can also represent some potential for redevelopment. Cities grow, shrink, decay, and are reborn: all phases of this transition will require the support of the sound industrial base. Whether a city is populated with industrial, residential, office, or other commercial development, it needs goods for support. These goods arrive by highway, by rail, and by water. They are processed through warehouses and small manufacturing facilities before entering into the city's urban commerce. The old warehouse buildings can be refurbished and reused; old manufacturing facilities can be retooled and revitalized. Old buildings that are seemingly useless are now becoming very popular as they are converted to loft apartments. In fact, a variety of properties today are being converted to loft-style residential neighborhoods, including the following:

- Old office buildings
- Old hotels
- Old industrial buildings, both warehouses and manufacturing
- Old multistory retail buildings

There are various novel uses for these old buildings. For instance, old retail buildings have, over the past ten years, been put to use as office facilities for people in the dotcom industries. As it turns out, many of these old buildings in the inner city were built on or near fiber-optic trunk lines. These locations are highly desirable for people in the dotcom or data industries. As luck would have it, the availability of these fiber-optic locations seems to be very limited. I have an acquaintance who made a killing over a four-year period by acquiring and redeveloping old retail buildings for people in the dotcom business. Happily, he was able to get higher-than-average rents for this type of space with little or no expenditure for tenant improvements. This particular micro market has cooled off considerably since the demise of the dotcom boom.

HEADS UP

Timing *is* everything!

Other interesting transformations are old hotels converted to loft space or apartments. This is a fairly easy transition, as hotels have adequate plumbing for modern residential units. Old office buildings have several potential approaches.

An old office building with low ceilings can be modernized by removing every other floor, thus creating more-than-ample height and very luxurious office space. In Houston, Texas, an old office building was gutted and refurbished into a high-rise mini-warehouse. The largest expenditure involved replacing the passenger elevators with freight elevators. By the time this renovation was complete, the owner had leased most, if not all, of the space to inner-city companies for paper storage.

Other than the retail conversion above, the renovation of retail space is relatively straightforward. To revitalize a shopping center, refurbish and attract new tenants. If this is not a viable option, then demolition and redevelopment is the most likely, if not the only answer.

Neighborhoods in Transition

If you have plowed through the discussion above, it must be apparent to you that a neighborhood in transition may represent a very profitable opportunity. How do you find these types of neighborhoods and how do you know that they're going to represent an opportunity for you? The answers will rely primarily on your common sense, but there are other sources of information about this type of phenomenon. If you're going to get into this business seriously, you need to make some reliable friends in the business. You'll need a good Realtor®, a good appraiser, and an honest contractor. There are a lot of other people you'll need, but the Realtor® will help you find the opportunities, the appraiser will help you verify that the opportunity is real, and the contractor will help you bring your plan to fruition. Few people come into this type of business with all of these skills. If you have one or more of these skills, you are way ahead of the curve, but even if you lack the skills, you can have them for an affordable price.

You most likely pass through areas of potential opportunity daily. In the eastern United

States and the Midwest, you'll find a host of old well-established communities. Each of these communities will have neighborhoods in transition. Take the initiative, drive around, and see if you can spot some potential areas. If you see areas completely run down and neglected, these areas are going to soon become pockets of opportunity. If you find run-down neighborhoods with one or two newly refurbished homes and/or businesses, you can bet that these areas have been discovered and are in the process of rejuvenation. I would suggest that, for your first venture, you seek out the latter neighborhood.

Urban, Suburban, or Rural

Where should you choose your first renovation project—in the city, in the suburbs, or in a rural setting? Most likely you'll probably want to kick it off in the area that is most familiar to you. You should, however, give some thought to other potential areas that may be readily accessible to you. Urban areas have some advantages and disadvantages that you should be aware of. First, there is a plethora of old buildings and, therefore, no end of buildings with renovation potential. The following are some of the drawbacks:

- City bureaucracies are large and slow moving.
- City building codes are more complex than rural codes and the infrastructure can be very complicated.
- Construction projects require a lot of space for material storage and construction staging; this is in short supply in the average city. Because of this, one of the most important people on inner-city construction jobs is the expediter, whose job is to make sure that the materials are scheduled to be used as they are delivered.
- Urban real estate tends to cost more than suburban real estate due to the density, actual or potential, of city properties.

Do these disadvantages mean that you should forget about the city? Not really, but for your first effort, unless you live in the city and are familiar with this bureaucracy, I would suggest you take a more low-key approach, either in the suburbs or in a rural setting.

The most common suburban areas in which to explore the possibilities for renovation are locations close to the city (the fringes). Older commercial properties are ideal to examine for commercial renovations. The immediate residential transition area, adjacent to these fringe commercial properties, should be fertile field for residential property renovation. Both of these areas should feed off each other and complement each other, as there will always be transition areas between suburbs and city, allowing for convenient commercial and closer residential.

The final place to look for potential renovations is in the country surrounding your target market. Rural areas have limited commercial and industrial possibilities, but unlimited potential residential possibilities. Residential properties in rural areas typically start at one unit to the half-acre and are as large as the typical family farm. As I mentioned earlier, this excess land has a development potential of its own and most truly rural housing is more mature than the average suburban housing. The older homes have great upgrading and redevelopment potential. We will cover this in some detail in Chapters 14 through 17.

Renovation Potential

To recap this chapter briefly, let's take a look at what you can do with various types of renovatable property. What you can do is truly limited only by your imagination and the market potential for the area in which you are choosing to work.

Housing

Relative to housing, the choices include the following:

- Subdivide the property and sell off or develop the excess land.
- Refurbish the house and resell it.
- Remodel and modernize the house, working with the existing structure, without adding on.
- Remodel and modernize the house and expand it to its potential without significant demolition.
- Tear down and rebuild, utilizing at least a significant portion of the old structure.

There are endless permutations and combinations of the above, but these are the basic choices for housing renovation. We will tackle the nuts and bolts of this process in Chapters 14, 15, and 16.

Rural Settings

With rural housing, some of the best potential lies with the land. At the very least, a large lot may be split into two lots if the configuration allows it. Earlier in the discussion regarding land, we covered lot splits, so the procedure should be familiar to you.

If you are fortunate enough to find a home on a large parcel of land, in excess of 40 acres, you may consider what we call a *lifestyle subdivision*. A lifestyle subdivision is one that is built around a common theme. Around the country, you will find subdivisions built around an airport where residents can taxi their airplanes down the street into their own hangars. Other subdivisions are built around waterways where residents can park their boats in the water in their own garages. A recent arrival in the lifestyle subdivision business is built around the wine business. Very common around the country are properties built around a central equestrian area, complete with riding trails, stables, and veterinary facilities. Whatever the theme, the process is quite simple. In Figures 13-4 and 13-5, you see a typical family farm layout and the transformation into a lifestyle subdivision.

Obviously, layout and lot sizes will vary with the type of subdivision, but the principle remains the same for all forms of subdivision: the layout becomes a designer's or engineer's work.

Tract Home Limitations

When dealing with potentially renovatable property, you must pay particular attention with tract homes. The potential of a tract home for profitable rehabilitation/remodeling is directly related to the minimum and maximum values within the tract itself. You cannot, for instance, go into a tract containing only single-story houses and add a second floor to one of the homes. This would be an over-improve-

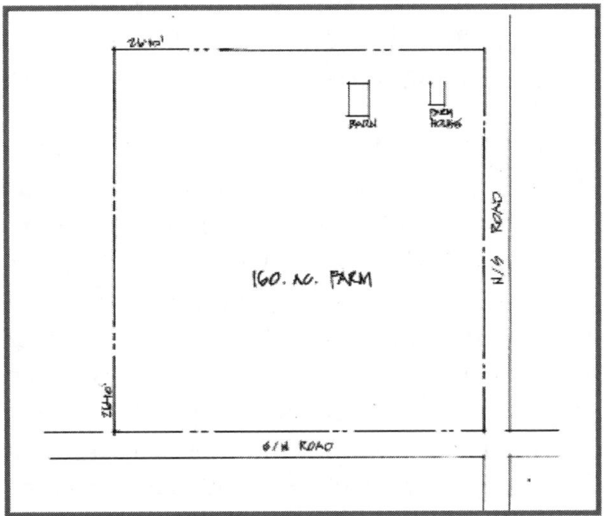

FIGURE 13-4. TYPICAL FAMILY FARM

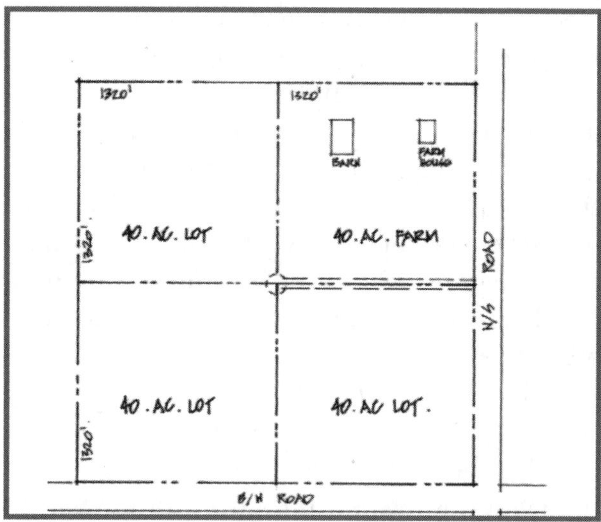

FIGURE 13-5. LIFESTYLE SUBDIVISION

ment: the value, or perceived value, could not be substantiated by comparable housing. The best approach with tract homes is upgrading and minor additions. Some other things you can do with impunity is to add a room, a bathroom, an extra garage or convert carports into garages or add amenities such as a swimming pool or extra landscaping. Do the research carefully within your target tract and see what, if anything has been done before to upgrade and/or expand. I would recommend confining your activity to tracts that have already experienced some modification.

Apartments and Condos

Other types of housing with built-in limitations are the multifamily units, apartments, and condominiums. These dwellings are even more uniform than tract homes. Therefore, you must exercise extreme caution when considering upgrades for these types of units. I have seen situations where someone has purchased two condominiums side by side, broken through the common wall, and created one very large unit. This ultra-size unit always proves to be very difficult to sell. However, it is not uncommon in urban areas for people to purchase two floors in a co-op building and create a two-story living unit with a gracious stairway connecting the two floors. Due to the scope, size, and cost of this type of living unit, it seems to have a decent resale potential among the wealthy buyers. I do not recommend this type of approach for your first project.

Converting apartments into condominiums is always potentially profitable. For such a project to be successful, certain design characteristics are necessary. The design must provide a moderate or high degree of privacy. It is handy if the units' utilities have been individually metered. This is not necessarily crucial, as retrofitting is possible, but it's expensive. Another thing to look for is the potential of converting carports into individual garages. Private, secure parking is a big asset when dealing with potential condominium conversion. Most people in this type of business tend to be experienced and well-capitalized, so I think this would not be an ideal choice for your first project.

Commercial Renovation

Similar to housing, the ability to renovate commercial property is limited only by your imagination. I have a list of strange approaches to redevelopment and, no doubt, you can give me a list twice as long. In general, the approach to commercial rehabilitation projects is similar to the approach to housing rehabs. It includes the following approaches.

For industrial, refurbish and refit or convert to a new use. With light industrial, there is a potential for conversion to residential lofts. With industrial property adjacent to water, there may be opportunities to convert to water-oriented commercial or tourist-oriented endeavors.

Urban residential such as apartments and hotels can be converted to loft residential or traditional apartments. Demolish smaller living units to create more luxurious and spacious units.

Selectively demolish portions of the building and change the use to such things as mini-storage or parking if the structure can handle it.

For urban office properties, demolish and reconfigure, selectively demolish and change the use, or completely demolish and redevelop.

For urban retail buildings, demolish and rebuild or demolish, change the use, and redevelop or vacate, refurbish, and re-lease.

One of the overriding possibilities, especially with urban properties, is to assemble a multitude of contiguous parcels, demolish all the buildings, and build a brand new development. In most urban areas this is a very costly proposition. The people in this business like Donald Trump, who are entrenched in the city, have a leg up on everybody else. I don't think this would be much of a concern to you on your first project; however, that may be something to aspire to in the distant future. While you're working on your own projects, you should keep an eye on what's going on with the big boys and girls, because their moves typically spearhead significant changes in and around the urban landscape.

CHAPTER

14

Renovation Is a Team Effort

In this chapter, I'd like to take you through the components of a building, any building, whether residential or commercial. In addition, we'll review the potential players and look at source material for your ideas. It is vital to any renovation effort that you understand the nuts and bolts. Once you go beyond the lipstick/new décor approach, you will need to understand what you are dealing with physically. For people who do not work with buildings for a living, the physical interrelationships among the components of a building may be somewhat mysterious. Once you have been through the nuts and bolts, then we'll discuss the people who can help you with demolishing, rearranging, and/or rebuilding these components and sources of information on what to do and where to buy your materials.

Putting the Pieces Together

In general, I like to take people through the component parts of a building in the order in which it would be constructed so that it makes sense logically. When creating a building, the architect/designer has to go through the same steps, in the same order, to "build" it on paper. The only difference between doing it on paper and doing it on the ground is that the architect first designs it from an exterior perspective and a floor plan so that he or she knows how to construct it on paper, starting with the structural design and foundations, while the contractor starts with site preparation, utilities, and then foundations.

Information Gathering

Before starting on any building, a designer needs information about the ground on which the building is to be built. This is gathered through a survey, a topographic map, and a soil test. The survey contains data showing the size and shape of the land parcel, the utilities that are available to the site, and their location. The topographic map shows the contours of the land. In addition, a soils engineer has tested the ground and designed the soil compaction requirements for the foundations. From that starting point, the project can be designed and built.

Site Preparation and Utilities

The site for any building must be prepared for it. This means grading and compacting the ground to receive it and bringing the necessary utilities to the building pad.

> DEFINITION
>
> A ***pad*** is a piece of land, prepared and ready to build on. The soil has been graded and compacted for the foundation and the utilities have been brought to the building perimeter, ready for distribution within the building.

This process is known as rough grading. Once the building is completed, the site will be fine graded prior to receiving curbs, gutters, landscaping, and paving.

Foundations

Foundations are composed of compacted soil, footings, and foundation walls. This is a rather simplistic explanation, as footings and foundations come in a variety of shapes and configurations, depending on the soil bearing capacity and the requirements of the building. It is enough that you know the basics, as the experts will determine what you need to hold the building up.

Another component of the foundation is the *on-grade slab*. "On-grade" means that the slab is resting on prepared ground rather than suspended over a basement. The slab serves two purposes: it pulls the footings and structural components together and it serves as the underlying floor for the ground floor of the building.

Structure

Attached to the footings and other foundation elements is the building's structure. A structure can be of many different types. In housing, there are two basic types of structure: perimeter load-bearing walls and post and beam. Commercial structures, due to their size, are generally a combination of the two or, in the case of mid- and high-rise structures, a steel skeleton on which the rest of the building is hung.

POST AND BEAM

Post-and-beam construction is a system that uses walls and columns tied together to form the structure of a building. The side-to-side bracing that protects a building from wind or seismic events is provided by the material that connects the structural components. This element provides the *shear* component of the structure. In post-and-beam structures, you need to consult the architect or engineer before removing any walls.

LOAD-BEARING OUTER WALLS

Perimeter load-bearing walls are used to provide the ultimate flexibility for the building's interior. With this structural system, you can demolish all the interior walls with impunity, as they do not contribute to the structural integrity of the building. Most homes today are constructed with load-bearing outer walls. In commercial buildings designed to accommodate a changing mix of tenants, this is also a popular approach. They are said to be "clear span" buildings. The roof and any upper floors are held up by prefabricated trusses that span from one load-bearing wall to another.

Roof Design and Construction

Roofs may take many shapes, from flat to peaked and everything in between. They can be angular, rounded, or, in fact, almost any shape imaginable. The support component is generally trusses, but may be as exotic as cables. It all depends on the designer and the shape. The roof is composed of the underlying structure of trusses and wood or steel panels to support the roofing material. The roof itself is then constructed of traditional shingles or built-up roofing, composed of felts, tar, and a wearing surface. Modern flat roofs are now also offered in sprayed-on foam with a watertight membrane over the foam. Shingles vary from the traditional asphalt to wood, concrete, clay, and slate. Another alternate for peaked roofs is a metal roof, as simple as the old corrugated roofing to prefinished standing-seam metal roofs, constructed of interlocking panels that run vertically from the ridge to the eave, with the seam where two panels interlock raised to channel water away without seeping between panels.

Interiors

Interiors are generally divided by non-load-bearing walls. In post-and-beam structures, some of the walls are permanent and load bearing and the rest can be moved around at your pleasure. There are different types of walls in commercial structures, serving different purposes, such as tenant separation and interior design. All walls are constructed from two components: studs (uprights, either wood or steel) and sheetrock or other wallboards. Insulation within the wall is optional. The finish is then applied to the surface of the wallboard.

Demising Walls

Demising walls are so-called because they separate the demised (transferred temporarily, leased) premises of adjacent tenants. These walls usually go from the floor to the underside of the roof or the floor above. This serves three purposes: security, HVAC separation, and acoustical separation. There are several different designs for demising walls, but the staggered stud seems to be the most popular; when insulated, it provides good acoustical separation.

Acoustic Walls

In areas within a tenant's premises, there is sometimes a need for acoustical privacy. The wall that is generally used, other than a demising wall, is one that penetrates the ceiling. Most simple interior walls stop at the ceiling. In fact, the ceiling grid is customarily installed prior to installing these simple partition walls. The acoustical wall extends above the ceiling, is fully insulated, and has a sound blanket draped over the top of the wall, extending at least four feet on either side of the wall. The resulting sound dampening is not as good as that obtained by a demising wall, but it is generally enough for the tenant's uses.

Room-Dividing Walls

These walls are merely partitions that divide up the work space. They can be moved around at will.

Mechanical Systems

A building's services are provided by its mechanical systems, composed of electricity, water, sewer, gas, telephone, cable TV, data distribution, and HVAC (heating, ventilation, and air-conditioning). These systems are installed in a building before the walls are finished, so that these systems are concealed. In renovation projects, you will need to demolish the wall surface to modify or remove any of them.

Electricity

Electricity is distributed throughout a building by a system that consists of a main power distribution panel, perhaps some subpanels, and then individual circuits designed to handle the anticipated loads take the electricity wherever it is needed. In a home, there is usually a 100-amp panel; if the house is large, the panel may be sized at 200 amps. Before attempting an extensive add-on project with a home, check with your electrical contractor or electrical engineer to determine whether the existing electrical service can accommodate the additional circuits needed for the addition. Commercial buildings generally have a large main panel and subpanels for each tenant. Most new buildings provide for individual metering of power for each tenant to control the operating costs of the building.

Plumbing

The plumbing is very straightforward: water in and sewer out. Modern structures are using new materials for the waste lines, but most incoming water lines are still built with copper pipe. In the older buildings, hot water was provided by a central boiler or water heater, but now builders can choose point-of-use water heaters, greatly simplifying the water distribution process. The utility distribution within a building is installed before the walls are finished so that these mechanical services are concealed from sight. In renovation projects, you will need to demolish the wall surface to move any of these service lines.

HVAC

Modern commercial structures are climate-controlled. Housing in most parts of the country is also climate-controlled. The building codes establish criteria for this, defined in number of air changes per hour to ranges of acceptable temperature differential between the inside and the outside of the structure. These mechanical systems can be separated, so that one heats and another cools, and some systems combine both. They all use electricity and gas or heating oil or a combination of all three. In some climates, primarily those with winter weather, boilers are still in use, but in parts of the country where the temperatures are more moderate, a combination unit known as a *heat exchanger* or *heat pump* is used. The air is heated and/or cooled in an air-handling unit and distributed throughout the building by ducts within the walls, floors, and ceilings.

Windows, Doors, Hardware, and Finishes

Once the interior and exterior walls are completed and the utilities are covered up, windows and doors are installed. There is an infinite variety of choices for these units, limited only by your imagination and budget.

The last touch is provided by applying the finishes, paint, wallpaper, etc., inside and outside the structure. Then, the building is complete.

Landscaping and Site Work

The finishing touch to any building is the site landscaping. There are many elements to the site, such as driveways, parking, walks, and vegetation. These can be done by you or your landscaper or designed and executed by a landscape architect. Essentially, you must think of landscaping as dressing up the building. Obviously, high-rise buildings are only peripherally impacted by landscaping, once you rise above the street level, but a combination of *softscape* and *hardscape* can sell any building.

DEFINITION

Softscape is the elements of landscaping that consist of living plants. ***Hardscape*** consists of inanimate elements, such as wood, concrete, brick, and stone.

Consultants and Contractors

It takes many people to put it all together, starting with the consultants who collect information and design and ending with the tradespeople who do the physical work. Each specialized professional has a specific function in any project. You will get to know them if you are going to be in the remodeling business.

Consultants

The consultants who gather information and design the buildings are engineers, architects, planners, and designers.

ENGINEERS

The engineering professionals are broken down into the following categories: civil, structural, mechanical, and electrical.

CIVIL ENGINEERS

Civil engineers are concerned with land development and utilities. Part of that function involves gathering information; that specialty is surveying. This profession has become very sophisticated since the advent of the Global Positioning System (GPS), which allows more accuracy and speed in producing surveys and topographic maps (topos). Another specialty of civil and structural engineering is soil analysis and compaction design. A soils engineer tests the ground and makes recommendations for soil compaction and engineering for the structural engineer. Once the data is gathered, the civil engineer prepares a grading plan, a parking plan, a soil preparation plan, and a utility plan based on the desired location and proposed elevation of the new building. This plan is then forwarded to the structural engineer.

STRUCTURAL ENGINEERS

The structural engineer takes from the architect/designer the building's floor plan, size, shape, and location and combines it with the civil engineer's grading plan and soils report and produces the foundation plan and the structural design.

ARCHITECTS AND DESIGNERS

The people who actually design the building are the architects. In the case of houses, there are professional *house designers* who are allowed to design homes. All other buildings are designed by architects and engineers. A house designer must have the structure designed by an engineer licensed in that state. The architect prepares the detailed building plans and sends them to the mechanical engineers to add the required utilities.

PLANNERS

A cross between the architect and the civil engineer called a *land planner* has evolved into a specialty for large projects. Rather than taking the strictly numerical approach of the civil engineer, the land planner strives to design the site so that it maximizes not only the building but also the aesthetics and sales appeal. Personally, I like to start with a land planner and then move on to the architect and engineer; I find that I get better projects by doing it this way.

Mechanical Engineers

These engineers handle water plumbing, waste lines, elevators and people movers, and HVAC design. They take the architectural drawings and the civil drawings and distribute the required services throughout the project. Often, they advise the architect and the structural and civil engineers of special requirements, such as floor loads and stress counteraction requirements necessary for these building components. It is common that, in home design, the licensed subcontractors get involved in this process, as their day-to-day familiarity with the installation and operation of these components make them a logical choice for a design-build option.

Electrical Engineers

The electrical engineer ensures the supply and distribution of electricity to all other building systems as well as the tenants. He or she must gather all the requirements of the other professionals to make sure that the power supply is both adequate and efficient.

Contractors and Builders

The building profession is loosely divided into residential and commercial companies. In general, the residential contractors are non-union and the commercial contractors are union. This is somewhat confusing in right-to-work states like Arizona, where there are no laws requiring union labor. In these states, the breakdown in housing is non-union labor, small commercial is generally also non-union labor, and high-rise and municipal projects are union labor. Within each category, there are two types of contractors—general contractors and subcontractors. Whether residential or commercial, union or non-union, all contractors are required to be licensed.

General Contractors

The general contractor is licensed to oversee the construction of the projects. He or she may or may not provide labor for one or more of the subtrades. Typically, the general contractor provides a construction superintendent or foreman and hires specialty subcontractors to do the specific work. The licensing procedure is the same for union and non-union companies. Each company must have a *qualifying party* to have a license for the company's use. That party must take a test and meet the practical experience requirements to become licensed.

Subcontractors

These companies represent many specialties, such as earth moving, underground, gas, steam fitting, plumbing, electrical, drywall, structural steel, framing, roofers, glazers, and equipment operators. All companies must have a qualifying party in order to be licensed.

Licensed vs. Unlicensed, Laws and Liens

The licensed contractor must post a bond to be placed into a recovery fund for the customers so that shoddy work or substandard materials can be replaced. There is a limit to what the recovery fund can pay on a single claim, so it is vital that you choose contractors, general and subcontractors alike, who are financially solvent, experienced, and clearly qualified to do the work.

A licensed contractor with a signed contract can enforce payment for completed work through the lien process. If the contractor has not been paid in a timely fashion, he or she is allowed to record a *mechanic's and materialman's lien* on the property. This class of lien provides for people working on the property or supplying materials to the project. To perfect a lien, several things must happen.

First, the contractor must have a contract directly with the owner of the project or the contractor or supplier must send a pre-lien notice to the owner prior to starting the work stating that he or she is providing labor or materials to the project under a subcontract with the general contractor. Then, if the contractor or supplier is not paid on time, he or she may file the lien and, with the two notices, the lien is deemed "perfected." Just because the lien has been filed and perfected does not mean that payment is automatically owed or will be paid. The owner may dispute the lien in court and, if successful, the lien may be voided. This lien must be paid before the property can be sold with a clean title. We will have more on the lien process in Chapter 24 on dealing with contractors and budget control.

Resources

In addition to the people outlined above, you will be able to draw on others to guide you in the remodeling process. There are many professions involved, and you are free to use or not to use any or all of the potential sources of talent, skill, and advice.

Front Line and Back Office

We have talked about most of these people before, so by now you should be familiar with most of them. They include marketing consultants, real estate brokers, title companies and lawyers, advertisers, interior decorators, handymen and -women, mortgage brokers and bankers, lenders, accountants, bookkeepers, and property managers.

Information

The other resource you need is information not provided by anyone with a potential profit motive. There is an almost infinite amount of material available to you for this type of project. There are remodeling industry publications, building design information, product design and installation manuals, and web sites galore.

These are some of those specific sources:

- How-to books such as the *Time-Life Series* on home remodeling and construction and the following publications:
  - *Family Handyman*
  - *Home*
  - *Old-House Journal*
  - *This Old House Magazine*
  - *Workbench*
- Trade publications such as *American Homebuilder*
- Manufacturers' brochures
- Online information

All manufacturers publish specifications and installation manuals on their home building products and they are readily available wherever these items are sold. All retailers are broken down into four basic categories: local neighborhood hardware stores like Paul's True Value Hardware and Ace Hardware, local lumberyards, large discount hardware stores like Lowe's and Home Depot, and specialty stores such as Color Tile, Dunn-Edwards Paint, Pella® Windows, etc. All of the lumber stores will cut your lumber to fit and sell it as a package right from your plans and the larger stores will entice you with a full package.

Online Information

By far the most up-to-date information is available from the internet. In fact, it can be overwhelming. Recently, I typed "home remodeling" into my search engine and received over 35,000 hits. I suggest that you try to narrow down your searches and select things like "how-to reference books," "financing," "building plans," and "contractors." This will give you a better selection of sites and potential contractors in your area. If you are taking a modest step into renovation, a little more aggressive than paint and wallpaper, you can attend free seminars given monthly by Home Depot and Lowe's. They have seasoned professionals teach the basics of the skills, like sheetrock, plumbing, ceramic tile, etc. These will allow you to tackle the modest projects without the necessity of dealing with contractors. Homeowners are legally allowed to do their own work as long as it is inspected at the proper progress points. It's a great way to get started.

CHAPTER

15

Regulations

We touched on zoning regulations briefly in Chapter 3, but this chapter will provide you with more detail so that you know what regulations govern any prospective project or acquisition you are contemplating. Once again, if you are only tackling a redecoration project, you can skip this chapter and come back to it when you have decided to undertake something more challenging. If you are into remodeling, purchasing investment property, or development, this chapter is vital to your understanding of the environment in which you seek to invest your hard-earned cash.

Zoning and Building Codes

We live in a free society, fortunately, but it's a highly regulated free society. By and large, the regulations are there for everyone's benefit and, while they are restrictive, they tend to create cohesive master plans, uniformity of value, and proper methods of construction. That is their function. In isolated cases, such as in California, land use regulations are used to control growth and, in some cases, halt it completely. No matter what type of project you are contemplating, you will need permits for anything beyond a change of décor. Can you do the work without a permit? The answer is yes; many people add on to their homes without permits, but if you decide to do so, you may run the risk of getting into trouble. Even a home addition can cause problems. When you sell the home, you are legally required to disclose any work done on the home and whether the work was done legally with a permit. If you fail to disclose that information and it comes to light at a later date, you might be liable to the municipality and to the buyer, long after the closing of the sale. You will most certainly be liable for any latent defects. What is permitted in any area is governed first by the general plan and then specifically by the zoning for the particular parcel of land.

The General Plan

In our computerized world, most of these regulations are available on the internet and are readily accessible. If you call your local planning department, they will give you the address for the web site. For example, I have just completed work on a project in Mesa, Arizona, and the web site is accessed by the following address: www.cityofmesa.org/planning/.

A typical master plan, shown in Figure 15-1, can be found on most city web sites.

Most municipalities have put these services and information on the internet to save money. Having staff available to meet with people to answer basic questions costs a great deal of money and budgets are stretched thin. Most if not all of the forms for making applications are also available online, together with checklists of requirements and a schedule of fees for each process. The online Mesa General Plan is over 180 pages long and provides more information than you will ever need. Always start with your planning department when you are doing research for property acquisition and improvements.

Zoning Classifications

Table 15-1 shows a typical municipal or county zoning classification breakdown. This will vary from state to state and county to municipality. Rest assured, however, that your area will be represented, unless you live in Houston where there is no zoning and you can build what you want where you want.

The breakdown in Table 15-1 is not overly significant, as it will change from jurisdiction to jurisdiction. What is important is that you realize that every piece of land or building you work with will be governed by these regulations.

We'll pick a category in this breakdown and follow it to the logical end so that you can see exactly what these regulations encompass. That way, you'll know how to analyze a project, whether it's a house you want to rebuild, a project you might want to acquire, or a new development you might want to undertake. Since most people will want to start their investment career with a house, let's follow along with the typical single-family home designation, R1-9. This effectively produces three or four homes to the acre and coast to coast is the most prevalent single-family home.

Residential Zoning

Let's start with the governing parameters for this zoning classification. The city's rationale behind these low-density districts is stated as follows: "This zoning category identifies locations where detached, moderate-sized lot, single-family residential housing is desirable. The target density for these areas is 3.0 du/ac."

DEFINITION

du/ac is shorthand for dwelling units per acre.

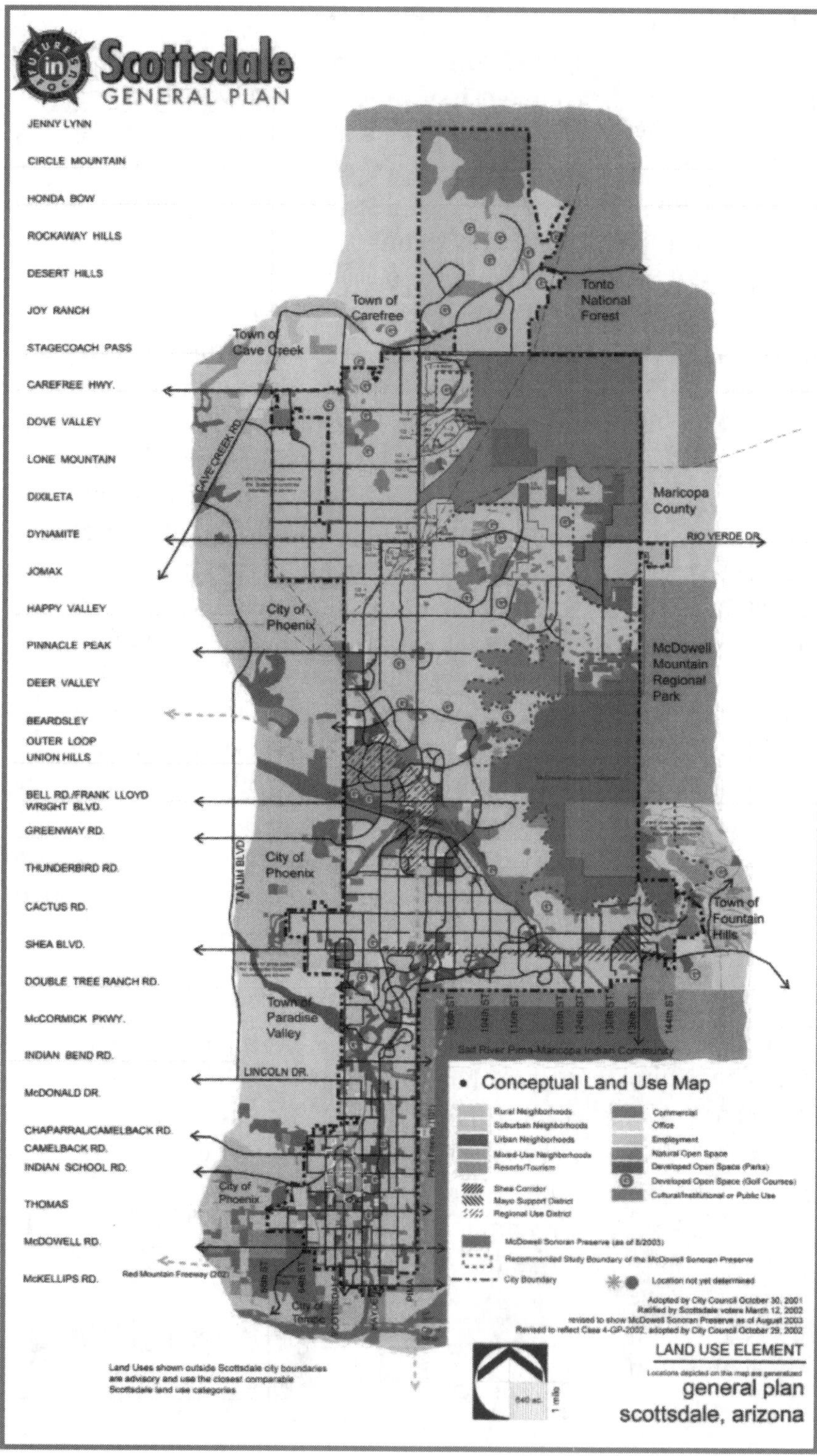

FIGURE 15-1. TYPICAL GENERAL PLAN (SCOTTSDALE, AZ)

Appropriate locations offer collector road access, connections to potable water and sanitary sewer, and proximity to public safety services. The provision of park and open space (15 percent of net area, excluding street system) is encouraged to provide opportunities for recreation and nonvehicular connections like pathways, trails, etc. Other uses permitted in this category may include office and neighborhood commercial of less than ten acres where deemed appropriate by the city. With this as a given, then, how do they regulate what you can do within this district? This specific regulation is contained in the guidelines for the R1-9 zoning category in the building department's regulations. Table 15-2 provides the general guidelines.

In this table, you can see that for the R1-9 zoning district the following restrictions apply:

- The minimum lot size must be 9,000 square feet per home.
- The lot frontage must be at least 80 feet.
- The minimum lot depth must be 100 feet.
- The maximum units per acre cannot exceed 3.3 for conventional design and 4.84 with a PAD overlay.

Agricultural District	
AG	Agricultural activities, minimum 10-acre lot
Single-Residence Districts	
R1-90	Rural low-density housing, minimum 90,000-SF lot
R1-43	Rural low-density housing, minimum 43,560-SF lot
R1-35	Suburban low-density housing, minimum 35,000-SF lot
R1-15	Suburban low-density housing, minimum 15,000-SF lot
R1-9	Urban density housing, minimum 9,000-SF lot
R1-7	Urban density housing, minimum 7,000-SF lot
R1-6	Urban density housing, minimum 6,000-SF lot
Multiple-Residence Districts	
R-2	Transition from Single-Residence Districts, maximum 12 DU/acre
R-3	Medium Density, maximum 17 DU/acre
R-4	High Density, maximum 25 DU/acre
Commercial Districts	
O-S	Office-Service: non-retail, small-scale offices, residential services on minimum 6,000-SF lot
C-1	Neighborhood Commercial: large-scale offices, small-scale retail
C-2	Limited Commercial: indoor retail, shopping centers, group commercial developments
C-3	General Commercial: variety of outdoor and indoor commercial activities
Industrial, Manufacturing, and Employment Districts	
M-1, M-2, PEP	Limited Industrial, General Industrial, Planned Employment Park: regional
Town Center Districts	
TCR-1	Low-density residential within Town Center Boundary, minimum 6,000-SF lot
TCR-2	Medium-density residential within Town Center Boundary, maximum 12 DU/acre
TCR-3	High-density residential within Town Center Boundary, maximum 40 DU/acre
TCB-1	Business district within Town Center Boundary, medium-density residential, professional offices
TCB-2	Business district within Town Center Boundary, intensive commercial, light manufacturing, access to arterial and rail
TCC	Town Center Core: highest-intensity land use with development incentives
Public Facilities District	
PF	Public Facilities: large-scale governmental, public utility, recreational, and educational facilities on minimum 10-acre lot

DU = dwelling unit, SF = square foot

TABLE 15-1. ZONING CLASSIFICATIONS

Zone Dist R1-	Max Lot Size			Max du/ac		Max Height/ Stories	Min Yard Setbacks					Max Roof Area
								Side				
	Area	Width	Depth	Conv.	PAD		Front	Min	Total	Street Side	Rear	
90	90,000 sf	150'	–	0.5	0.48	30'/2	30'	20'	40'	20'	30'	20%
43	45,560 sf	130'	–	1.0	1.0	30'/2	30'	10'	30'	30'	30'	20%
35	35,000 sf	130'	150'	1.0	1.24	30'/2	30'	10'	30'	10'	30'	30%
15	15,000 sf	115'	120'	2.1	2.9	30'/2	30'	7'	20'	10'	30'	35%
9	**9,000 sf**	**80'**	**100'**	**3.3**	**4.84**	**30'/2**	**25'**	**7'**	**17'**	**10'**	**25'**	**40%**
7	7,000 sf	70'	94'	4.0	6.22	30'/2	20'	5'	15'	10'	20'	40%
6	5,000 sf	60'	94'	4.7	7.26	30'/2	20'	5'	15'	10'	20'	40%

Conv. = Conventional Design, PAD = Planned Area Development

TABLE 15-2. TYPICAL ZONING TABLE

- The buildings cannot exceed 30 feet in height and two stories.
- Minimum building setbacks are:
  - Front: 25 feet
  - Side: seven feet and no less than 17 feet for both side yards.
  - Street: 10 feet
  - Rear: 25 feet
- The total roof area cannot exceed 40 percent of the lot size. For example, if the lot is 9,000 square feet, then the maximum allowable roof area is 3,600 square feet, including all structures.

DEFINITION

A PAD zoning overlay is a Planned Area Development. This allows for specific project designs approved by the city council or county board of commissioners. It allows the developer to exceed certain minimums in exchange for other concessions or amenities.

"What does all this have to do with me?" you ask. Unless you are the original developer, you are interested only in the restrictions on what you might add to the home. For instance, if you wish to add a room or another garage, the maximum roof coverage or the mandatory setbacks might affect your ability to do so. You might be forced to go up rather than out with your addition. The roof restriction allows a single-story home and garage combination of 3,600 square feet, but you can have 7,200 square feet in a two-story configuration and 10,800 square feet with two stories and a full basement configuration. These restrictions, together with market restrictions, completely govern what you can build or rebuild.

There are also other zoning and building regulations that you must abide by. They cover such things as:

- On- and off-street parking
- Types of vehicles that may park outside the garage or on the street
- Whether you can work on your car or truck in the driveway
- Restrictions on recreational vehicle storage in the driveway, such as RVs, motorcycles, personal watercraft (e.g., WaveRunners®, Jet Skis®, Sea Doos®), boats, and snowmobiles
- Number and type of animals permitted
- Number of occupants, if unrelated
- Paint colors
- Roof shapes, etc.

You get the idea. All these restrictions and regulations are spelled out in the zoning and building codes. You should check them all before you start planning any significant renovation project.

Commercial Zoning

Commercial buildings are similarly regulated. In Table 15-3, you can see a typical breakdown of zoning districts.

You will notice that the setback criteria are the same for all zoning categories. *The key to commercial zoning is not the* physical *constraints, but the* use *restraints.* The intent of these regulations are as follows (Mesa City, AZ, City Code, Chapter 6): "The Commercial Districts are designed to provide for a wide range of office and commercial uses, including personal services, professional businesses, retail stores, and entertainment establishments. The intent of these Districts is to allow for a variety of business intensities from personal services to regional retailing. These Districts are categorized in the following classifications:

"**A. Office-Service District, O-S:** The purpose of this District is to allow small-scale offices and residential service businesses without retailing. The intent of this District is to accommodate low-intensity business usage which satisfies the daily needs of local residential neighborhoods while maintaining compatibility with them.

"**B. Neighborhood Commercial District, C-1:** The purpose of this District is to provide for large-scale office complexes and small indoor retailing centers. The intent of this District is to ensure compatibility with adjoining residential neighborhoods while satisfying their daily commercial and service business needs.

"**C. Limited Commercial District, C-2:** The purpose of this District is to provide for a broad range of indoor retail businesses. The intent of this District is to allow commercial uses to satisfy the needs of the community with emphasis on shopping center and group commercial developments.

"**D. General Commercial District, C-3:** The purpose of this District is to provide for a diversity of general business and commercial uses. The intent of this District is to allow for a variety of outdoor and indoor commercial activities."

The city then follows up the policy statements with specific language, as in the list below, on what is and what is not permitted within these zoning categories (Mesa City, AZ, City Code, Chapter 6).

PERMITTED USES

"A. Permitted Uses in All Commercial Districts, O-S, C-1, C-2, and C-3, provided that all activities are conducted entirely within an enclosed

Dist	Min Lot Area (SF)	Max Roof Area	Max Height/ Stories	Minimum Yard Setbacks						
				Front		Side	Street Side		Rear	
				Abuts Arterial Street	Abuts Nonarterial Street		Abuts Arterial Street	Abuts Nonarterial Street	Abuts Arterial Street	Abuts Nonarterial Street
O-S	6,000	50%	30'/2	10'	20'	20'	10'	20'	10'	20'
C-1	6,000	50%	30'/2	10'	20'	20'	10'	20'	10'	20'
C-2	6,000	50%	30'/2	10'	20'	20'	10'	20'	10'	20'
C-3	6,000	50%	30'/2	10'	20'	20'	10'	20'	10'	20'

TABLE 15-3. TYPICAL COMMERCIAL ZONING

building with no outside storage or display except as specified below:

1. Bank and financial institutions, excluding drive-through windows and outdoor teller facilities.
2. Offices.
3. Medical offices and clinics, including physical therapy and massage, and chiropractic treatment. The preparation and sale of pharmaceutical, ophthalmic, prosthetic, and similar medical supplies are permitted in conjunction with a medical office or clinic provided such activity is dependent upon, and clearly subordinate to, the primary use and is not identified from a public street by signage, display, building orientation, or other visual means.
4. Studios for the practice of fine arts, excluding shops and galleries for retail sales.
5. Small animal hospitals or clinics, confined to completely enclosed sound-attenuated facilities.
6. Nursing and convalescent homes, philanthropic and charitable institutions, residential and out-patient care and rehabilitation centers, hospices.
7. Churches. Refer to Section 11-13-2(L).
8. Day care centers with accessory outdoor play yards.
9. Wedding and reception centers. Refer to Section 11-6-4 (A) and (D) regarding outdoor activities.

"B. Additional Permitted Uses in the C-1, C-2, and C-3 Districts, provided that all activities are conducted entirely within an enclosed building with no outside storage or display except as specified below:

1. Fraternal organizations, service and social clubs, lodges, fraternities and sororities.
2. Retail stores and group commercial developments, provided:
   a. No individual store shall exceed an area of ten thousand (10,000) square feet.
   b. No group commercial development shall exceed an aggregate area of fifty thousand (50,000) square feet.
   c. No drive-through facilities are provided."

   Etc., etc.

These regulations go on and on, addressing anything you can think of and a few things that would never occur to you. As you can see, these use restrictions are specific and very well delineated. You should note that, if you read carefully the character and intent of these zoning rules and regulations, they are designed to produce a well-thought-out and cohesive area plan with compatible uses and consistent standards intended to preserve quality and value. I have been developing commercial real estate according to these and other standards since 1973 and, once you get used to them, you can easily work within the guidelines. You need to know where to look and how to apply these rules to your proposed projects.

Overlay Districts

Not too common, but out there nonetheless, is the zoning overlay district. These districts are formed and put into effect for specific purposes. They can exist to preserve a historic neighborhood, to ensure consistency of architectural design, to allow a city's overall height limit to be exceeded for a downtown high-rise district, or to permit gambling within a specific city area. In short, a jurisdiction can impose any legal additional zoning requirements and/or restrictions to further the jurisdiction's goals for that purpose. This imposes yet another layer of compliance on projects within these districts.

Building Codes

An adjunct to zoning regulations is the local

building code. These additional regulations tell exactly how to construct any type of building or other structure. The master code is the national Uniform Building Code (UBC). This code sets minimum standards for design and construction and is overseen by OSHA, which regulates how the jobsites are to be managed to preserve minimum safety standards for the workplace. Specific additional regulations cover both mobile and modular home construction. There are additional regulations and standards that cover the following items:

- Soils and bearing capacity
- Design loading of roofs and floors
- Special zones
- Hurricane, seismic, and snow loads

There are also local standards applied to the UBC to accommodate special areas of the country affected by potential natural disasters such as floods, earthquakes, and excessive snow. These are supplemental codes applied to the UBC for local areas.

HEADS UP

Now you know why you need all these consultants and specialists when you start designing and building anything. It's not as tough as it sounds. All these people know their specific areas of responsibility and coordinating the design and building effort to meet all the requirements is "all in a day's work" to them.

Working with the Regulations

What you need to know as a homeowner, renovator, and/or developer is how to work with these laws and regulations. They will come into play when you want to:

- Split a parcel of land into two or more lots and sell the land to the public
- Renovate or add on to your home
- Build a house or a commercial building
- Change the use for a parcel of land
- Put an existing or proposed property to a nonpermitted use
- Create a residential or commercial subdivision

If you are changing the décor of your own home or of an investment property, chances are that you will not require any permits unless you are contemplating some major changes to the building exterior. The town will not care whether you add trim or change the outside color unless there is an ordinance regarding exterior paint colors, but your local committee of architecture or homeowners association may have something to say about it. (See below under "Other Constraints.")

Some of the major items that you may be called on to handle in connection with a renovation/remodel/development project are the following:

- Changing the general plan
- Changing zoning
- Variances
- Special use permits
- Building permits

Changing the General Plan

This is a major undertaking, but from the municipality's or county's perspective, a rather routine one, as a general plan is considered to be a work in progress. Most states require that jurisdictions routinely revisit and revise their general plans and also provide for citizen- or developer-initiated changes between the mandated revision periods. The process is simple and routine, but takes planning and research and, in all cases, the change in master plan is also accompanied by a rezoning request. Depending on your local jurisdiction, your requirements may include the following items of work:

- A signed application (by the current owner of the land and the applicant, if they are not the same)
- Payment of fees
- A narrative outlining the proposed request and your justification for the request as well as the anticipated impacts of the change in plan and zoning
- Site plans and proposed architectural drawings and renderings
- Traffic studies
- Environmental impact report (EIR) or environmental impact statement (EIS) (California)

The jurisdiction's planning staff will review the application and request a dialogue with you and suggest some changes that would make the application more palatable to the planning staff, as well as the planning commission, city council, or county board of supervisors. In some cases, you may need to get an OK for the proposed changes from the state highway department, the Army Corps of Engineers, or some other governing body. In California they have some doozies: the California Coastal Commission and, in San Francisco, the Bay Area Development Commission.

In all, it is generally an exhaustive, lengthy, and expensive process. Timing from the date of the completed submittal varies from a brisk nine months to two or three years, depending on your area. As a general rule, if you are successful and your zoning change is approved, the value of the land should be substantially enhanced and you can make some good returns on your investment.

CHANGING ZONING

Changing the zoning for a specific parcel of land is much the same process. If the use is permitted by the general plan, you may proceed without having to modify the general plan. You can refer to the same list above for the requirements, as they will all apply to a rezoning as well as the general plan amendment.

VARIANCES

Variances were mentioned earlier in the book. These pertain to requests to waive specific zoning or building code requirements such as setbacks to accommodate one-of-a-kind existing conditions or special requirements. These follow the same approval process from staff, to planning commission, and on to the city council or county board of supervisors. Once granted, these variances are a permanent part of the entitlements for that specific parcel of land. Requests for variances generally require the following:

- A signed application by land owner and applicant
- Fees
- Site plans and architectural layout
- Written consent or rejection of the request from the neighbors
- A narrative of what you want and why you need the variance, as well as an assessment of the impact on your land and on your adjacent neighbors' land

SPECIAL USE PERMITS

These permits allow for the right to use a property for something not allowed by the zoning code. For instance, while restaurants are permitted in most C-1 zones, you need a special use permit for the restaurant to serve liquor by the drink. The alternative is a rezoning to C-2 that permits that type of restaurant. These petitions and permits, if granted, expire when the use is terminated. This permit does not run with the land.

The application process is similar to that of the variance. The timing on the variance and the use permit is usually only a matter of months.

BUILDING PERMITS

To construct anything within a municipal jurisdiction, you need a building permit. Some rural counties do not require a building permit; this may cause you some trouble when you are dealing in a rural area. I once built myself a home in the country and the only permits I needed were a permit to drill a well and a septic system permit. These were also the only items inspected during the entire construction process. This is wonderful when you are building, but may give you pause when you are buying the product of someone else's energy and entrepreneurship. Most people build to code whether required to or not, but some people just dig a hole and start banging boards together. The results can be spectacularly bad and sometimes dangerous. If you are going to buy something in the country, hire a good inspector and make sure you know what you are getting.

Other Constraints

There are other regulations that I call civil restraints, imposed voluntarily by landowners to help the parcels of land within a specific development. They include the following:

- Covenants, conditions, and restrictions (CC&Rs)
- Neighborhood architectural committees
- Homeowners associations

Here's a quick look at these requirements.

COVENANTS, CONDITIONS, AND RESTRICTIONS

Documents known as covenants, conditions, and restrictions (CC&Rs) set out guidelines for construction and operation of a specific development or subdivision and are recorded against all the parcels within a defined development. In doing so, they become a deed restriction or a voluntary restriction by deed. Buyers of these parcels have these restrictions fully disclosed to them in the preliminary title report or abstract of title. They buy the property knowing full well the restrictions that apply to their land or home. CC&Rs are designed to preserve uniformity of design, quality of construction, and ease of administration for the project. In the beginning, the management of the CC&Rs is done by the developer; then, when the occupancy of the project reaches a certain percentage, generally 50-75 percent of the total houses, the neighborhood homeowners association takes over. In a tract home subdivision, all design and construction is controlled by the developer, but in a custom home subdivision, it can be controlled by the developer and a separate and independent architectural committee, ensuring that the developer's initial design guidelines spelled out in the CC&Rs are followed. This committee is responsible initially to the developer, but once occupancy has reached a certain percentage, the committee then reports to the homeowners organization.

HEADS UP

In recent times, abuses by homeowners associations have prompted the courts to intervene to prevent abuse and hardship imposed on individual homeowners by capricious boards of directors. It is increasingly common for homeowners associations to be run, by contract, by professional property management companies. This is an effort to forestall abuse and provide prompt and uniform service to the homeowners.

CHAPTER

16

Demolition *and* Expansion Case Studies

In relation to housing, and single family housing in particular, the most profitable investment will be found in expanding a home to its maximum value within the marketplace. There will always be a differential between the cost of construction and the completed value of housing and commercial buildings. That's what keeps developers and contractors gainfully employed. You too can capitalize on that fact. In this chapter, we will look at three typical projects that serve as examples of this type of project.

The first deals with a typical ranch-style home that can be found anywhere in the country. However, the potential is not found in a tract, because tracts, unless they are quite old, impose limitations on value that make profiting from an expansion project difficult.

The second project is a complete rebuild of a custom home in a custom home neighborhood. It is intended to capitalize on the expanding upper-middle market catering to the baby boomers.

The final look is at the conversion of an old single-family home found on Main Street, anywhere in the country, to a commercial use, in this case, a restaurant. As people move to larger homes in the suburbs, more and more towns are being revitalized by small business expansion into the older homes along the main drag.

To create this series of examples, I sat down with my architect of 30 years, Bozidar Rajkovski,

AIA, and created these projects from scratch. Although I commissioned the drawings, Bo outdid himself, taking much more time and putting in much more thought and detail than he was being paid for. The result is a very realistic and plausible step-by-step transformation of three very ordinary buildings into creations much more valuable and immensely more appealing in the marketplace. I would wager that your Realtor® could find you buildings exactly like the ones we started with.

The Ubiquitous Three-Bedroom Ranch

In this series of drawings below, you will see a typical three-bedroom, one-bath, two-car-garage, single-family home transformed step by step into a larger and more upscale version of itself. It is done in stages so that you can see how it can be done while you are living in the home. Of course, you can always move into a rental and do it all at once. The two sketches (Figures 16-1 and 16-2) are what we started with.

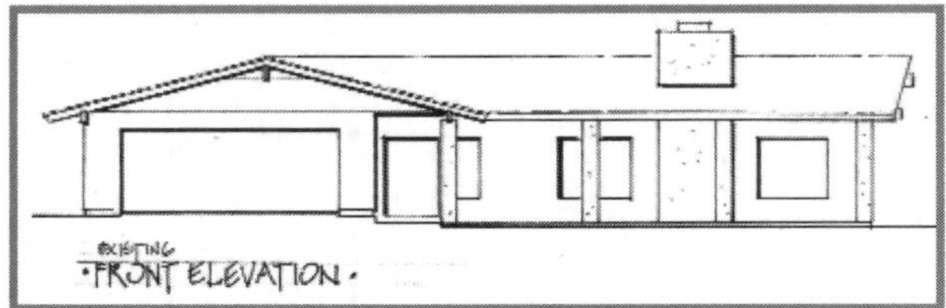

FIGURE 16-1. TYPICAL RANCH, SITE PLAN

In these figures you have the raw material. It's a house you can find anywhere, usually on a quarter-acre lot. It has three bedrooms, two baths, and a two-car garage. For years this was the average home in America, built with minor variations from coast to coast. The following drawing (Figure 16-3) is its first transformation.

In Figure 16-3 you can see the start of the transformation. An entry area and a porch have

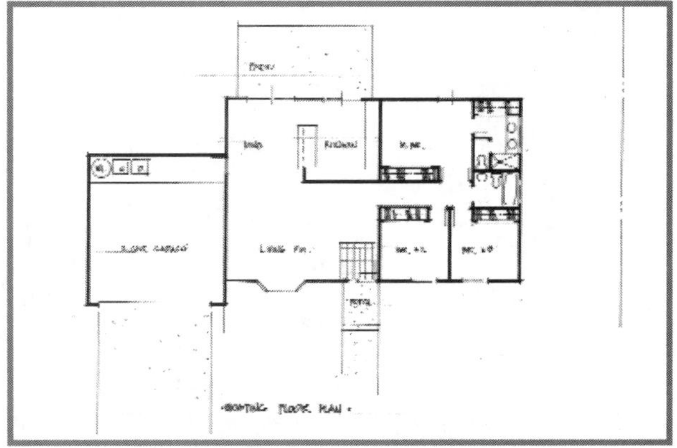

FIGURE 16-2. TYPICAL RANCH, ELEVATION

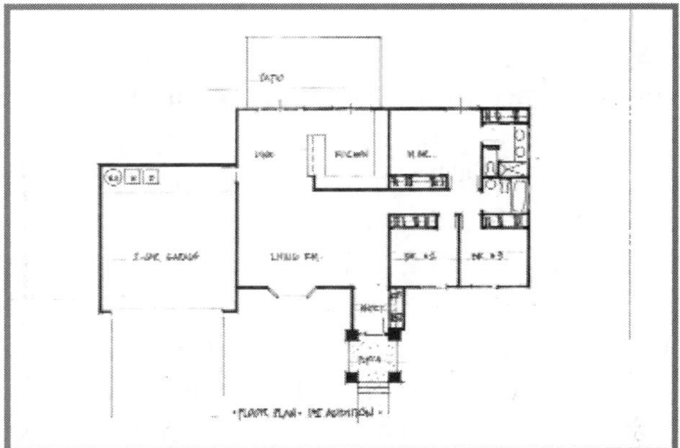

FIGURE 16-3. STEP ONE, SITE PLAN

been added. This accomplishes two purposes. It adds to the architectural character of the home by breaking up the roofline along the front of the house and it takes the foyer out of the living room, leaving more living space while providing an entry that can also double as a mud room in inclement weather. You will note that the new foyer has a closet for coats and boots as well.

In Figure 16-4, you can see the beginning of the expansion. The garage has been expanded to three cars and a laundry room has been shoehorned into the back of the original garage. The kitchen area has been expanded to the rear of the home, modifying the kitchen layout and creating a dining area off the kitchen and a family room. The home, in its present configuration, is

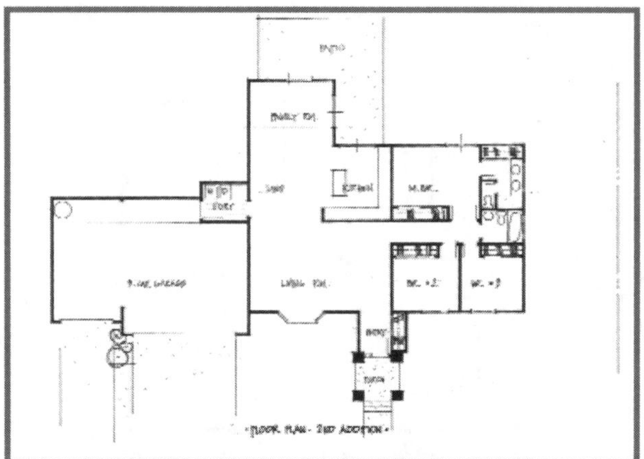

FIGURE 16-4. STEP TWO, SITE PLAN

definitely a more desirable family home. You could, in fact, just stop there. We, however, did not. Read on.

In Figure 16-5 you can see that we have expanded the living room by pulling the living room's front wall toward the street and adding a bay window. At the same time, we have added a center counter in the kitchen (Figure 16-4) to make it more workable and "with it." You might have noticed that we have, as yet, not touched the sleeping areas or the baths. Guess what's next.

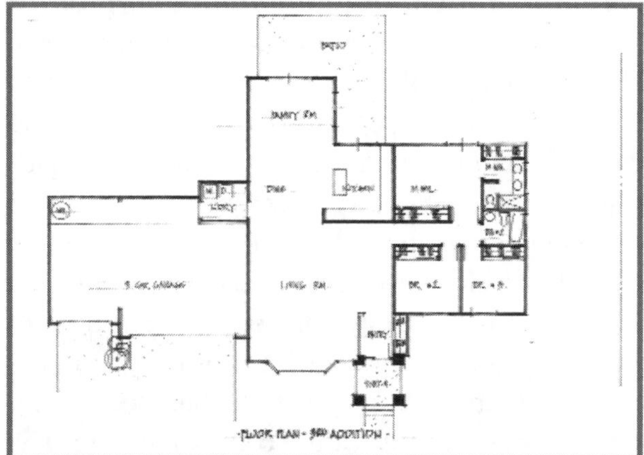

FIGURE 16-5. STEP THREE, SITE PLAN

In step four, we have taken the master bath and expanded it to incorporate a more spacious

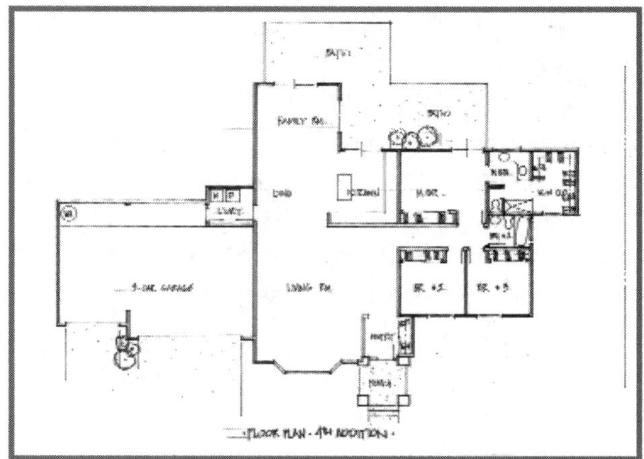

FIGURE 16-6. STEP FOUR, SITE PLAN

bathroom and a walk-in closet dedicated to the master only. It's not truly elegant, as the tub and shower are still combined, but there is room for his-and-her sinks. This step could be more dramatic if there is more room in the side yard for a larger expansion. The only limit is the space and your pocketbook. In addition, we could consider expanding the other bedrooms and adding more.

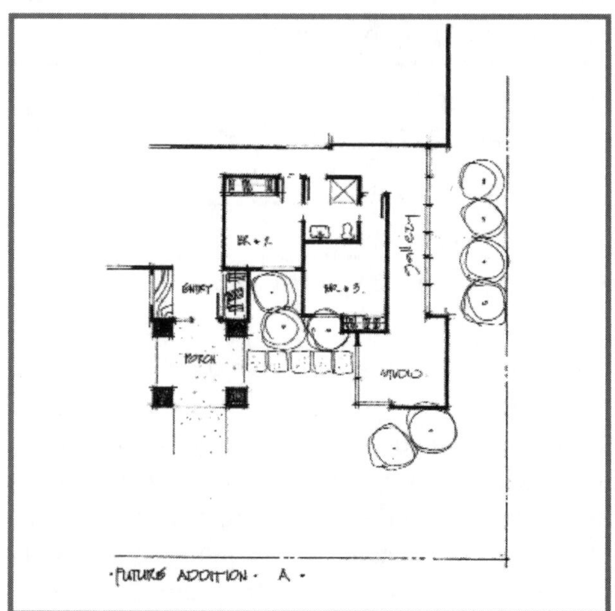

FIGURE 16-7. POTENTIAL FUTURE ADDITION, SITE PLAN

As you can see from Figure 16-7, we can go on and on, including a slight variation in the closet addition shown below. The two sketches (Figures 16-8 and 16-9) show a completed project, both site plan and elevation.

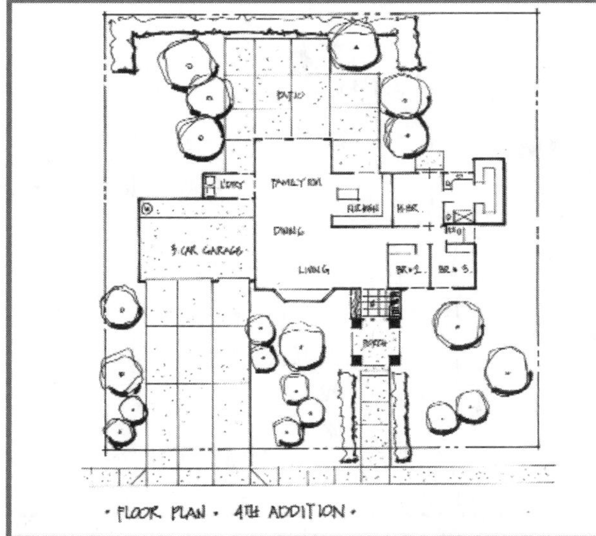

FIGURE 16-8. NEW RANCH, ELEVATION

FIGURE 16-9. NEW RANCH, SITE PLAN, WITH VARIATIONS

Evidently, with the site plan, we could not stop playing with this house, because it is so common and constructed everywhere. We felt that it was worth spending some extra time. This is not a very complicated project and the demolition and structural modifications were relatively straightforward.

In Figure 16-10 we used dotted lines where the walls were removed; the rear kitchen wall, the left garage wall, the living room wall, and part of the original master bath. While you can't

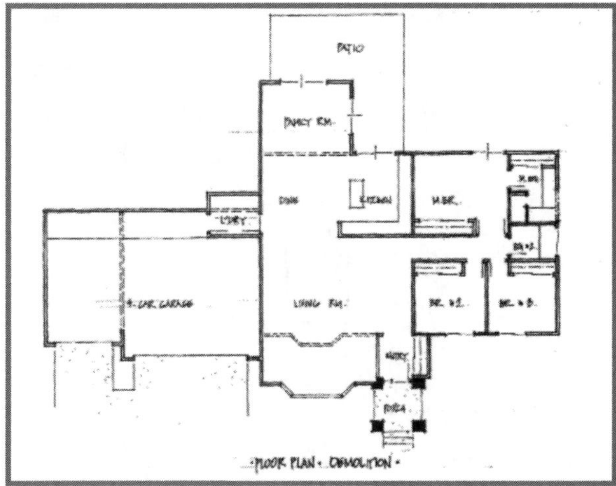

FIGURE 16-10. DEMOLITION PLAN

simply tear these down without bracing and structural modification, all these modifications are relatively routine.

Seasonal Home to Primary Residence

Throughout the country, on lakes, seashores, rivers, and mountains, there are vacation cottages. These structures were generally built for summer occupancy, uninsulated, and completely without frills. As our country grew from the post-World War II era, our cities and towns have expanded, gradually encroaching into these heretofore outlying areas. These buildings are now within modern commute times of employment centers. Those that are not are most likely now integrated into locations that have been transformed into lifestyle communities or retirement communities.

This project is another step-by-step approach so that you can envision the process over time and perhaps tackle it while living in the home. It also can accommodate newlyweds and track the expansion of their family, transforming the home as the family expands.

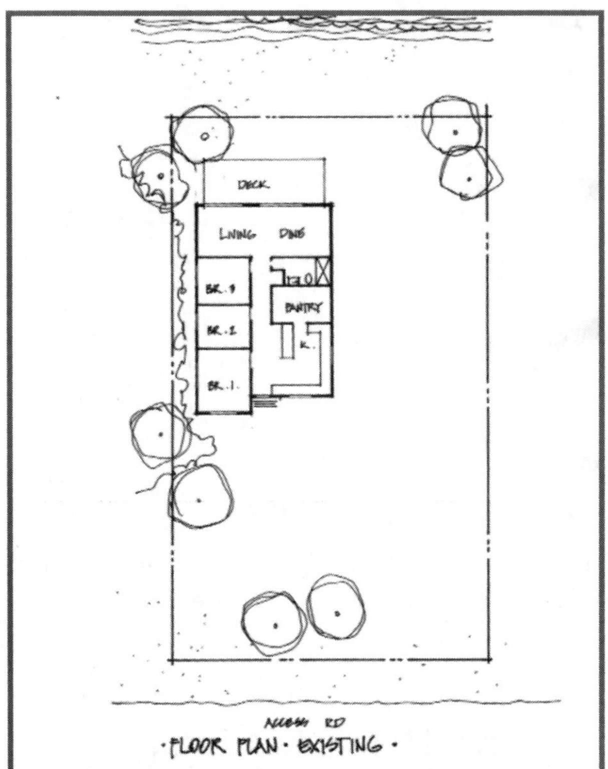

FIGURE 16-11. THE VACATION COTTAGE

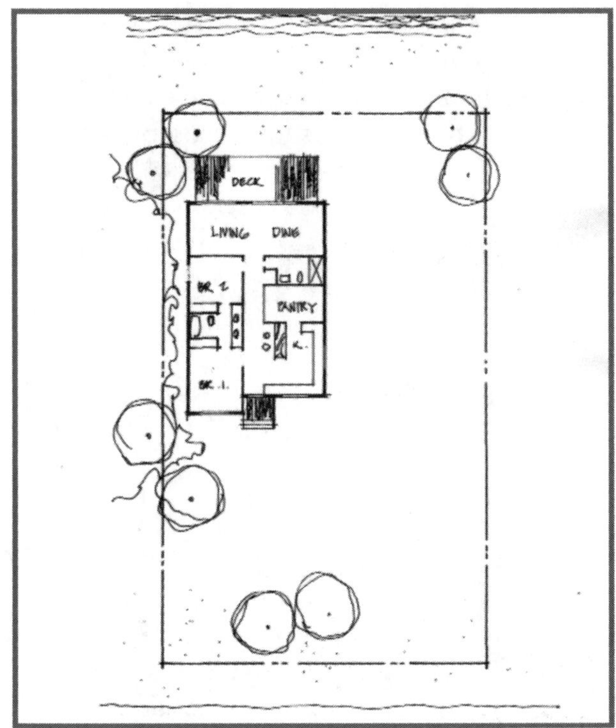

FIGURE 16-12. FIRST STEP

From the above sketch, you can see that we have a typical cottage, very basic and uninsulated. We will start the project by insulating the roof and all the outside walls. As we progress from area to area, we will replace all the windows with modern dual-pane windows for increased insulation. You will note that the home sits to one side of the property; that is typical of many vacation home layouts, so that the lot can accommodate the parking necessary for a vacation property. The changes to this building are designed to accommodate that layout, but you can adapt to any site configuration so long as there is room to expand.

In this adaptation, as shown in Figure 16-12, we complete the insulation, demolish the middle bedroom, and create a Jack-and-Jill bathroom between the two remaining bedrooms. In addition, we have added an enclosed entry off the kitchen to free up room in the kitchen area for our next step. This provides a permanent all-weather entry to the home. We also start replacing the windows in the rooms that will remain in the finished home.

Step two shows a major overhaul of the kitchen to accommodate a growing family and to set the stage for the first major changes in the home's configuration.

In step three you can see where we are headed with this project. The right side of the home is expanded, the rear entry is eliminated, a garage is added, and the old living and dining room is reconfigured to accommodate a den, a new dining area, and a living area. The new space creates two more bedrooms and a second bath. We now have a fairly livable single-family home. There's more on the way!

In Figures 16-15 and 16-16 you can see the final touch. The porch has been expanded and

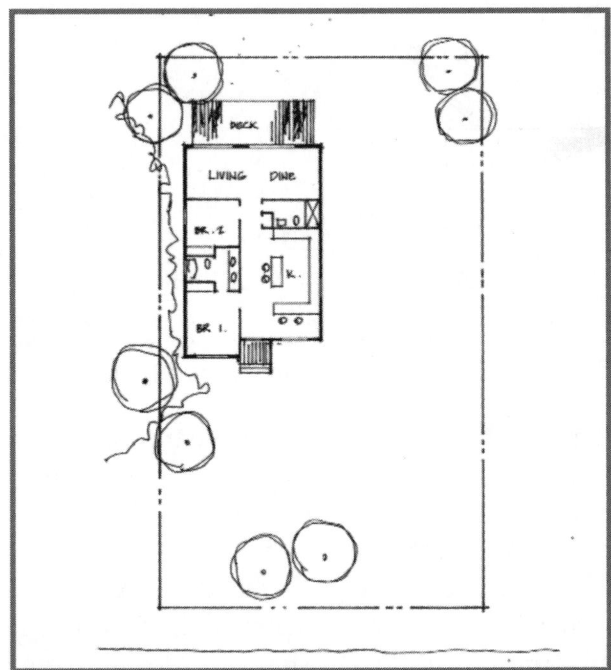

FIGURE 16-13. STEP TWO

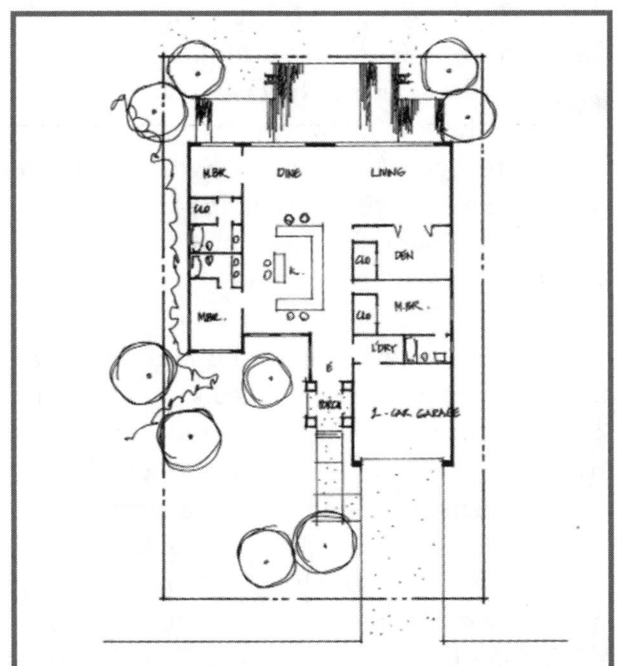

FIGURE 16-14. STEP THREE

fully enclosed to provide more all-weather living space. The new porch roof has been added

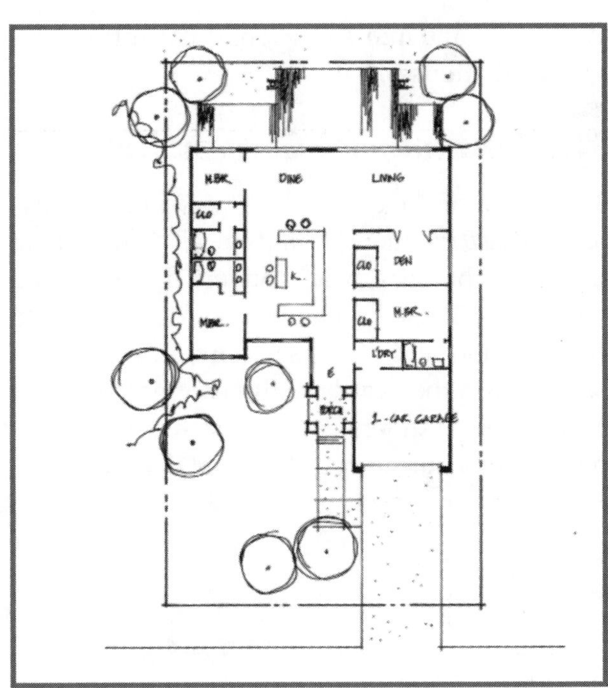

FIGURE 16-15. STEP FOUR, SITE PLAN

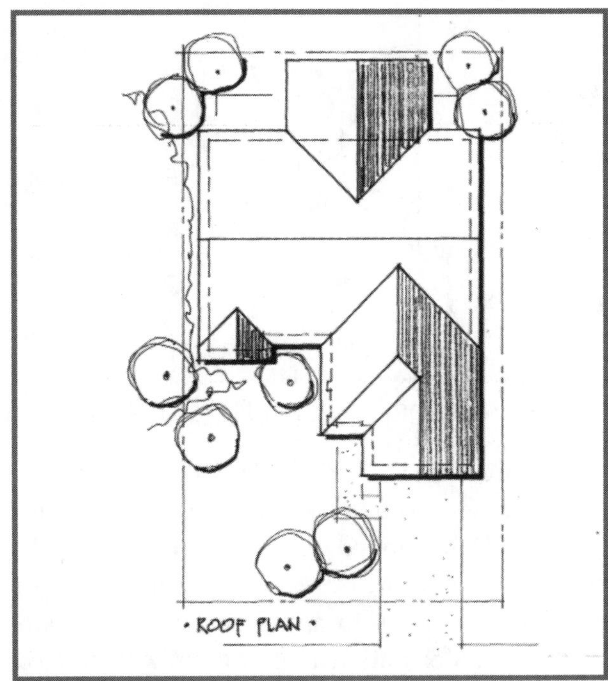

FIGURE 16-16. STEP FOUR, ROOF PLAN

to pull the entire project together. We have, over a period of time, transformed a small, basic vacation home into a spacious, year-round, single-family house.

The Commercial Conversion

This series of sketches will show you a step-by-step transformation of a typical Main Street dwelling that has been converted to a small restaurant. These houses can be found coast to coast, inland and at the seashore, in the mountains and in the heartland. It is a great use for a home that has suffered the encroachment of commerce. Let's start with the original dwelling.

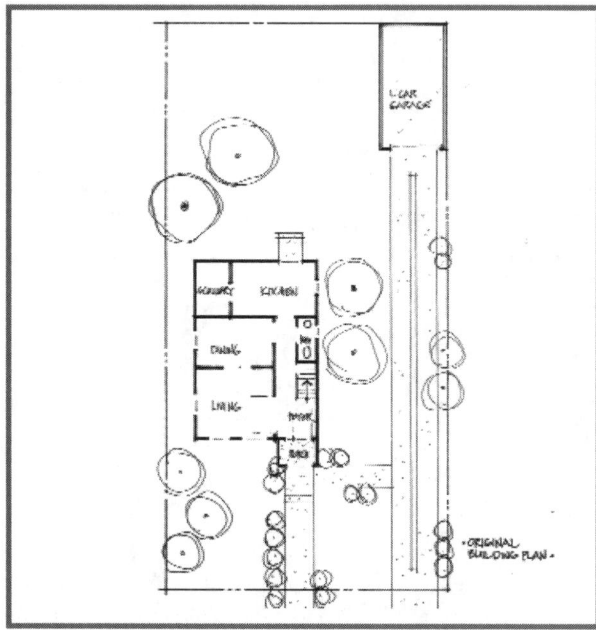

FIGURE 16-17. ORIGINAL HOUSE, SITE PLAN

Figures 16-17 and 16-18 depict a rather plain, contemporary two-story home on a lot with an old-fashioned detached garage. I would bet that you could track down quite a few of these in your own stomping grounds. This particular transformation is going to be modeled after an actual renovation project in my old town of Danville, California. This renovation is not intended to be what actually happened to

FIGURE 16-18. ORIGINAL HOUSE ELEVATION

that particular building, only what might have happened. The site layout is surprisingly similar and the results are designed to emulate the actual building in use today.

Since no one is living in the home and since it is to be transformed into a new use, we will do it all at once, albeit step by step. It cannot be accomplished all at once, as we need to use the site to stage materials and workers. First, we will demolish walls in the main building. Next, we will finish the exterior. Then we will move on to the rest of the site. The dotted lines on the demolition plan (Figure 16-19) indicate where walls are being removed prior to rebuilding the building.

With the demolition complete, the original building is closed in and the new space is added and finished. You can see in Figure 16-20 a new dining room in front, with the kitchen, stairs, and restroom in the rear. A walkway from the street has been created and a reception area built inside the front door. There is also a path connecting the main building to the old garage.

Here you can see in some detail the finished product. What is not shown are more dining areas and restrooms on the second floor. The old garage is now an additional dining area, connected to an open-air patio. The landscaping adds the final dressing. You now have a charming turn-of-the-century restaurant. In

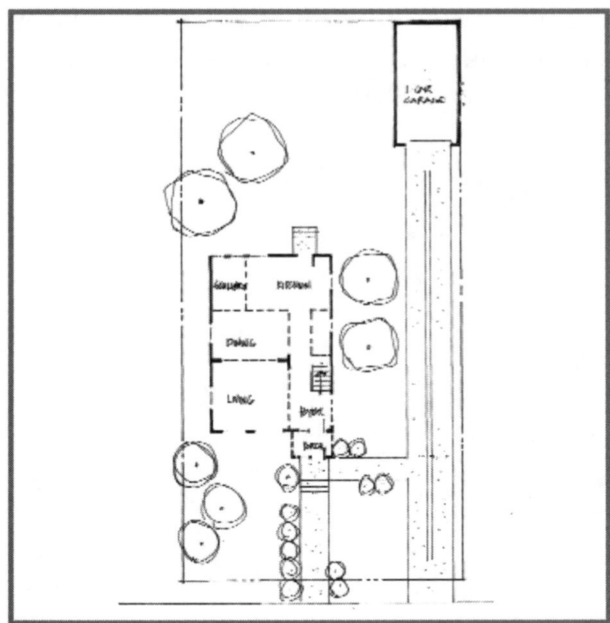

FIGURE 16-19. DEMOLITION PLAN

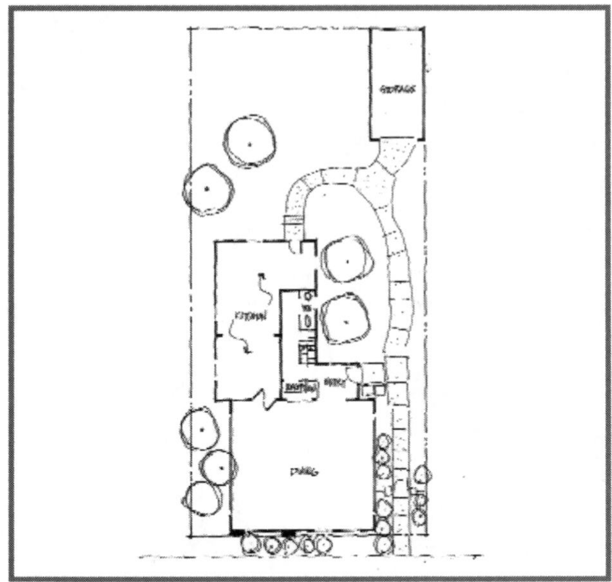

FIGURE 16-20. STEP TWO

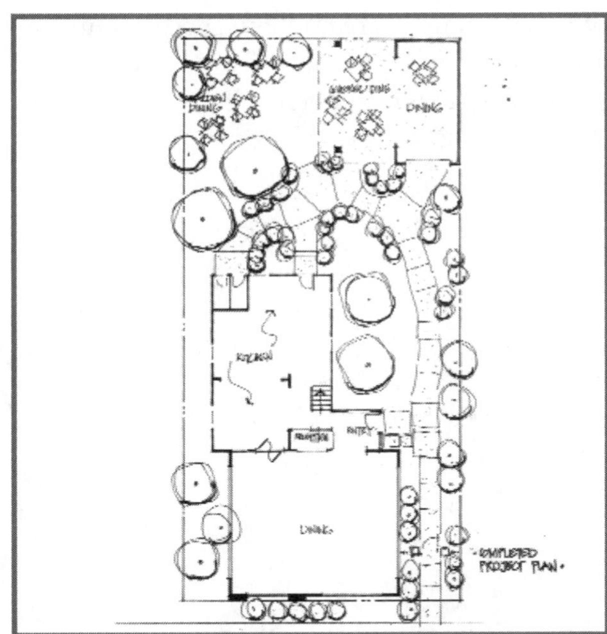

FIGURE 16-21. FINISHED RESTAURANT SITE PLAN

FIGURE 16-22. FINISHED RESTAURANT, ELEVATION

Figure 16-22, you can see the finished elevation.

The three examples in this chapter illustrate what is possible starting with relatively modest dwellings. I must reiterate that the physical transformations shown here are not the single most crucial part of making money on renovation, although you will have to be canny and cost-conscious. The crucial ingredient for success is the marketplace that can absorb this type of project. You need to look for opportunities in an organized fashion, weeding out the marginal and going for your projects in areas that can clearly stand the upgrade. Fertile areas to look at are along the old tree-studded main streets in small towns where people are moving to get out of the cities and in areas where good architecture abounds. Converting old Victorians or brownstones is great fun and generally very profitable. Older housing areas with the three-bedroom ranch homes of the ’50s and ’60s just cry out for a good rebuild. Have at it!

CHAPTER

17

Commercial Properties Case Study

The origin of commercial renovations is a murky topic. Commercial property in need of renovation and restoration is referred to as *distressed* real estate. The most typical occurrence happens when a tenant goes broke and vacates the premises. This happens every day and often results in a routine renovation, common to all forms of commercial property, from industrial to regional shopping centers. This loss of a tenant generally does not cause the property to be distressed and so these situations will not be discussed in detail until the chapter dealing with continuous redevelopment.

Despite the fact that commercial dislocations occur, not all distressed property is the result of losing a key tenant. Sometimes it is the result of fraud, lack of interest, and/or ineptitude. I helped turn a property around once that was a result of all three.

War Stories

A certain insurance company, which shall remain nameless, made a mortgage loan on a newly constructed 100-plus unit apartment complex in a major eastern city. At the time the loan was closed, the insurance company's representative inspected the property and declared it complete and ready for occupancy. The owner never made a mortgage payment. After a few months, the company sent someone to inspect the property; the inspector reported back that the property was locked up and there was no one in residence. The company instituted foreclosure proceedings and received permission to enter and inspect the development. What they found was interesting. Two apartments near the main entrance and rental office were completely finished with model furniture in them. The laundry room, once inspected and found complete, was stripped of all the machines. The rest of the complex was never finished. In several apartments carpet was stretched over joists to give the impression that they were finished, but flooring had never been laid. In the basement apartments, where sump pumps were supposedly installed to forestall potential flooding during a heavy rain, there were no pumps installed and the basement units were flooded. The original inspector had been fooled by the builder. When the loan closed, the builder pocketed the cash and split.

This did not result in a renovation project, but a simple "let's finish the construction and get on with it" project. After the foreclosure, the construction was completed, the project was rented out, and the complex was finally sold to a new investor for a modest profit. The effort produced a profit and a good new mortgage.

Distressed Property

Major causes of distressed property requiring extensive rehabilitation and remodeling work are the following:

- Neighborhood demise
- Deferred maintenance
- Transportation shifts
- Market shift

Neighborhood demise and deferred maintenance seem to go hand in hand. As the neighborhood slips, rental rates decline and disposable income is squeezed, so maintenance is deferred to a potentially happier time. It seems that the happier time seldom comes around for the landlord experiencing the slippage. It is generally the people who purchase the property after the foreclosure who make the profit. Why? It's simple. They are starting from a substantially lower cost basis.

A classic case of shift in transportation corridors occurred on a massive scale when Interstate 40 relocated the old east-west Route 66. Most, if not all, of the businesses that thrived on the heavy Route 66 traffic died off within months when the traffic was rerouted to the new Interstate 40.

Atlanta Apartments

Another project that I was active in was an apartment complex in the inner city of Atlanta, Georgia. During the 1960s, the life insurance industry committed to investing billions of dollars in disadvantaged inner-city areas throughout the country. Many of these projects, lacking the fundamentals of supply and demand at that economic bracket, fell on hard times and were foreclosed. Most of them were not successful in redevelopment. This particular project was a little different.

It had been taken over by a group of militants who intimidated the rest of the residents and who encouraged narcotic traffic out of the complex. People were moving out and property damage was severe. The owners were powerless to correct the situation and were physically threatened when they went onto the property. The lender eventually foreclosed and I was asked to see what could be done. After a cautious reconnoiter, I came up with a plan, which we subsequently implemented.

The first step involved a visit to the building department. With the cooperation of the department, I was successful in getting the property condemned. It was declared unsafe to inhabit. By hiring some off-duty police officers, we served notice to the residents to vacate. In some cases, the evictions were rather physical. Soon the property was vacant and we promptly fenced it off with a high-security emphasis.

The next step was to plan a complete facelift and interior renovation, with new landscaping and revitalized amenities, a pool, a recreation hall, saunas, tennis courts, and a gym. During this time, I sought out a local property manager with good ties to the community, who agreed to take on the project, pitching it as the new "place to be" in that area of town. Due to the stature of the company, they were able to attract new residents who were the cream of the crop, so to speak, within that area. The subsequent occupancy and new rent structure quickly reestablished a healthy cash flow. It proved to be so successful that the management company subsequently purchased it from us.

Again, with a little out-of-the-box thinking, we were able to produce a profit and a new mortgage loan. The simple key to this redevelopment was getting the property condemned. Without this, we would have been unable to legally evict the tenants in a timely manner.

Tulsa Apartment Conversion

During the 1970s, apartment construction boomed. Built-in tax advantages and too much money in the savings and loan industry combined to produce an abundance of apartments coast to coast. This is a lethal combination.

Our company had loaned money on a high-end apartment complex in Tulsa, Oklahoma. When the loan went into default after three months of operation, we went to see what the trouble was. Driving to the project, on one street, I counted 17 new apartment complexes in various stages of construction. The problem was obvious. There was a dramatic oversupply. After looking at the property and at the potential competition, it was obvious that our property was the nicest and, therefore, most expensive property in the area. The borrower had given up and deeded the property to us rather than go through foreclosure.

After extensive research, we decided to convert the new property into condominiums. Fortunately, the conversion was simple, requiring only a electrical refit to accommodate separate meters for each unit and the creation of a legal condominium. The documentation took about one month and the public hearings about three months. The local government was as eager as we were to solve the problem. Once the renovation and refurbishing was complete, we offered the units for sale and sold 100 percent of them within four months. The sale of condominiums was very lucrative, producing for us a profit of over 100 percent on our original loan.

Office Building in Downtown Norfolk

A relatively typical redevelopment project occurred about the same time in Norfolk, Virginia. A vintage office building in the downtown area went into default and subsequent foreclosure. I was sent in to see what could be accomplished.

I toured the area extensively with a local property manager and determined that, while the building was not in the prime area, it was on the fringes in an area considered to be quite viable in terms of the downtown office property. The problem seemed to be with the ten-story building itself. It had suffered a classic case of physical obsolescence. There was no parking, the floors were trashed, the ceilings were too low, the décor was hopelessly out of date, the elevators were inadequate, the mechanical systems were shot, the windows were broken and leaking, the roof was riddled with leaks, and the exterior brick was falling off. In all, it was in very sad shape.

I investigated two plans of attack: demolish and sell the land to a developer or evaluate and plan a complete reconstruction. Due to the size of our remaining investment, the demolition idea was not too favorable, as we would have to spend money and take a loss. No one was interested in the building, as it was, at a price that would let us come close to breaking even on our investment. With the help of a good structural engineer, a mechanical engineer, and an interior designer, we came up with a renovation plan that seemed plausible.

The plan was to remove every other floor, widen the hallways, rework and replace the windows, replace the elevators, and install a new roof and a completely new HVAC system. Once this was done, we sandblasted and repointed the brick exterior and completely redecorated the entire building. The final touch was to purchase a nearby vacant lot to use as dedicated parking for the new tenants. The result was a building with one half of the original leasable space, completely refurbished, with its own parking, its original art deco décor restored, and elegant new office space for rent. On the ground floor, off the lobby, we were able to attract a small café, which added to the cachet of the building. The space proved to be so appealing we were soon fully occupied with rents that provided an excellent rate of return on our total investment. Once again, the property was sold for a profit and the company was able to take back a good mortgage loan.

Retail Rehabilitations

The classic retail project is renovation of the exterior, resurfacing the parking lot, relandscaping, and re-leasing. Sometimes it involves subdividing a large space into two or more tenant spaces, but, in general, retail rehabilitation is pretty straightforward. The rehabilitation and rejuvenation of major enclosed malls is very expensive and time-consuming; it requires deep pockets, years of experience, and solid relationships with all the national tenants. Unless you inherit a fortune, you will never have to deal with a project this size.

SOUTH SCOTTSDALE

There are, occasionally, projects with a new wrinkle. Since I have been living in Arizona, I have witnessed several successful retail rehabilitation projects. One is in South Scottsdale, in a mature part of town. The new construction has moved north and this area was in the throes of a cycle of decline and rehabilitation. Figure 17-1 is before a renovation of Papago Plaza, completed several years ago. Since then, a nearby regional center has been demolished and is being rebuilt as a high-tech adjunct to the local university. The photos were generously donated by the owners, with permission to use them. The photos are old and, therefore, not

FIGURE 17-1. PAPAGO PLAZA, BEFORE

FIGURE 17-2. PAPAGO PLAZA, REVITALIZED

FIGURE 17-3. PAPAGO PLAZA, REVITALIZED

very good quality, but you'll get the idea.

In Figures 17-2 and 17-3 you see the new Papago Plaza as it exists today. It has given a shot in the arm to the entire area.

You can see that the new building does not resemble the old one in any way. It was a great effort.

Brownsville Strip Center

During the same period of my life, I was charged with finding a solution to a downtown strip center in Brownsville, Texas. Once again we had acquired it through foreclosure. We had

FIGURE 17-4. PAPAGO PLAZA, REVITALIZED

FIGURE 17-5. PAPAGO PLAZA, REVITALIZED

had the property for some years and it had been boarded up and completely ignored. It seemed to me like the town was in the process of fighting back against the population's move to the suburbs, but we could find no one to buy the property.

The central problem was that the property had no parking. It was a classic building with decent architecture. Our past project people had run into a local regulation that said an insurance company could not buy investment property in that area. It seemed odd, but that was, in fact, the case. I looked into it and determined that if we could solve the parking problem, we might have a chance to rehabilitate the building. On both sides of the building were structures in a similar state. I approached the owner of the property that was boarded up adjacent to ours and made him a proposition. We would make him a loan on his property equal to the value of it, as it was, and then foreclose on it, thus acquiring the property legally, surreptitiously for sure, but legally. When the foreclosure was completed, we demolished the building and created a parking lot. This gave us a viable base from which to operate. Since we now had surplus parking, I approached the property owner on the other side of the new parking lot and discussed the possibility of a joint renovation and re-leasing plan. He agreed, we started, and within nine months both buildings were fully tenanted and we were showing a decent return on the total costs. The adjacent property owner was pleased enough to buy our building from us. He arranged his financing locally and we recovered our costs. Although we did not make a profit, we were able to recover most, if not all of our investment and move on.

Box Stores

If you are out and about these days, you are probably familiar with the landlord's newest retail problem, the moving discounter. It seems that in the retail wars position is the key, so "box" retail stores have been vacated, not due to bad business, but to the desire of retail chains to improve their positions in the market or to redesign their stores to improve sales.

These abandoned stores are everywhere. In the Phoenix area, where we live, there are about 1.5 million square feet of empty box stores. Most of these are owned by the retail chains themselves, but sometimes, as is the case with the abandoned KMart stores, they have become problems for the landlord. In most states, the zoning laws are such that these buildings can be used only by another retailer, so the owner has to wait for a new tenant or break the buildings up into smaller stores. This can be costly in terms of lost revenue. Some jurisdictions allow them to be converted into different uses. In Houston, Texas, there is no zoning to speak of. Therefore, the empty store can be converted into any viable use. This makes it a little easier, but not much, as these buildings are gigantic and useful for very little else than their original intended use.

I have heard of successful adaptations: small stores in the front and storage or back office operations in the rear. Innovation and out-of-the-box thinking is the order of the day when faced with this type of problem.

Palo Alto Retail Center

Before you get the impression that I have a solution for everything, I'd like to tell you about one rehab that I couldn't make work. Another inner-city billion-dollar program loan was made to build a neighborhood shopping center in East Palo Alto, California. The one-of-a-kind grocery store failed and dragged all the other stores down with it. The only open store that remained was a bar and that paid little rent.

After discussing the location with every viable grocery chain in the country, I determined that no one would be willing to go there at that time. Without a grocer, there would be no neighborhood center. The only solution I came up with was to bulldoze the center, purchase some liability insurance, plant grass, and wait for the neighborhood to change. That's what we did and, to this day, I have not had any better ideas for that site.

The Common Thread

What is there about all of these examples that tie them together? They were, except for Papago Plaza, all foreclosed properties. Most were both economically obsolete and physically obsolete. Why were they able to be redeveloped successfully? The answer is bone simple.

We found a market for them—and the market is the key to everything in real estate. It affects supply and demand. Sometimes, with a little creative thinking and entrepreneurship, new markets can be found or created. The common thread running through these projects, allowing them to succeed, is *entrepreneurship*. After being involved in these projects in the early 1970s, I became convinced that I had that gift and I have not looked back since. I think of it as the knack of seeing around corners.

SECTION IV

DEAL STRUCTURES, MONEY, *and* PAPERWORK

CHAPTER

18

The Cost *of* Money

This chapter is devoted to the cost of equity money, i.e., that portion of the project's cost over and above that which can be borrowed by conventional means. Since we are discussing the entire spectrum of real estate in this book, this chapter will deal with housing and commercial property equity funding sources. Obviously, your cash is the first primary source for any deal, but often ready cash is not enough to accomplish what you want to do at any given moment.

> **HEADS UP**
>
> Think of interest, points, and forms of participation as rental rates for the use of the money you need.

Coming Up with the Necessary

Sometimes you may not have the necessary ready cash; this has been the case for the duration of my career. I started into the commercial development business with $6,000 in the bank and my first two deals cost over three million dollars each. Since then, I have raised money for every transaction I have undertaken. I'm not

Note—Chapters 18 through 24 and 26 through 34 are revisited versions of chapters from my book *From Dirt to Dollars: An Entrepreneur's Guide to Commercial Real Estate Development,* self-published in 1998. I have added some depth here and there and edited out some parts to avoid undue repetition on topics previously covered in this book. I could see no sense in rewriting these topics in their entirety.

suggesting that you take the approach that I did, merely that you become aware of the resources that are potentially at your command. The day will come when you will need to reach out to these resources, and then you'll know where to find them. The two basic places to look for cash are loans and partners.

Where to Look

Where you look will depend on what you are up to. Since this book starts with housing and moves on from there, let's first look at funding sources for home-oriented deals.

HOUSING

Housing, especially your primary residence, is the easiest asset to raise money on because the lenders and investors correctly believe that this is the sole asset that you would not be likely to walk away from in a disaster. On the average, this has proven to be so true that today you can actually borrow more than the home is worth, using the home as collateral. The first place to look at for ready cash is the equity built up in the home.

Since there is always an inflation factor in this country, however modest it might be, there will always be a time when your home is increasing in value due to overall inflation. In addition, if you live in an area where the homeowners maintain their homes and keep them in good repair and style, your home's value will rise with the neighborhood. That means that no matter what you borrowed on the home when you bought it, your home is worth more than you paid for it. This is your equity and you have the right to use it for investment purposes. To tap into this equity source is a simple matter of borrowing. You can borrow against your home's equity up to and even above 100 percent of value. There are several ways to do this:

> **DEFINITION**
>
> ***Equity*** is that portion of value over the debt on any asset. It is also described as the net value of the asset.

- You can refinance the home with a new first mortgage.
- You can take a second mortgage, known as a home equity loan or second mortgage.
- You can take a personal loan using your combined assets as security.
- You can take on a partner.

Partners in housing are nothing new in real estate; they have, however, in recent years, become more popular as people have started to realize the potential profit in real estate deals. Probably the most common form of partnership is the one where one person (the investor) puts up the down payment, and the other one, usually the occupant of the home, pays the mortgage. When the property is sold, the mortgage is paid off, the investor gets the down payment back, and the investor and the occupant split the profits on a previously agreed-upon basis. A variation of this can be used on an existing home with an existing loan just as easily. Let's say that you want to expand the home, but are not able to find enough cash from your own sources; it is feasible that you could offer someone a partnership deal to put up the necessary funds in exchange for a percentage of the profits when the enlarged home is sold.

COMMERCIAL

Commercial property works much the same way, except that the increases in value of the properties are due to the increase in net income rather than inflation. Raw land increases in value based on inflation, growth, and, ultimately, supply and demand. The built-up equity can be tapped, but due to the nature of commercial property, the percentage that lenders are willing to lend peters out at about 80 percent for income property and 50 percent for raw land.

In addition, the cash required in a commercial transaction is most likely to be around 25 percent of actual cost. This is true whether you are buying an existing income property or developing a new one. The most common loan in raw land is the purchase money mortgage. This occurs when the seller agrees to carry back a portion of the purchase price as a short-term loan. These loans vary from one to ten years in length (term) and usually command interest rates of one or two points (percent) above the commercial rate for land loans.

PARTICIPATING LOANS

Another popular form of borrowing is called a *participating* loan. This loan is usually a higher-percentage-of-value loan that "participates" in the cash flow and the long-term profits of a project. This type of loan is just another form of partnership or joint venture. The main difference between this type of financing and a joint venture is that the investor's money is secured against the property by a mortgage or deed of trust, whereas a joint venture partner is in an unsecured position.

Ownership Structures

When you step outside the realm of loans and enter into partnerships, you need to understand that there are many forms of agreements between the parties, resulting in many legal forms of ownership. Each arrangement has a different set of rules and regulations.

RESIDENTIAL

When it comes to housing, there are some traditional forms of ownership, usually used by husband and wife. They can also be used by any other two owners without the necessity of forming a formal partnership. These relations are governed by law and do not require anything other than a declaration on the deed of ownership. They are *joint tenancy with the right of survivorship* (JTWROS) and *tenancy in common*. These rights and relationships are spelled out in law, but can be modified by written agreement between the parties. If they are modified, it is usually a smart move to adopt a form of partnership rather than either of these two ownership types. Partnerships for residential ownership are the same as partnerships for commercial projects and are covered below in the section on partnerships. I define a partnership loosely as an arrangement between the parties to pool funding and work responsibilities for mutual profit. The actual legal arrangement can take many forms.

> **DEFINITION**
>
> ***Joint tenancy with the right of survivorship*** *(JTWROS)* is a form of ownership in which the property is shared equally by all owners. If an owner dies, his or her share transfers automatically to the surviving owners. *Tenancy in common* is a form of ownership in which the owners each own a stated percentage of the property and are free to do with it as they wish—to sell it, to mortgage it, to give it away, to bequeath. If an owner dies, his or her share becomes part of his or her estate.

THE TRUE COST OF PARTNERSHIP

Let us examine the cost of partnership, whatever the legal arrangement might be. (We shall look at the possible legal arrangements later on in the chapter.) There are many reasons to form a partnership, including the following:

- To acquire more money for the deal

- To bolster the group's borrowing power (credit)
- To acquire additional skills
- To spread the risk
- To eliminate potential competition
- To acquire the best land (site)

The results of this "coming together" of individuals or companies are tangible factors for each party to the agreement. They include the following:

- The acquisition of a new profit opportunity
- The loss of autonomy
- Potential differing priorities of return on equity or net profits

The net result for everyone is compromise. The deal starts out with a series of written rules and ends up being an endless series of discussions and compromises. It is rather like a successful marriage without the potential of divorce. To split up a joint venture, the asset must be liquidated, which can be disastrous for both parties. Compromise becomes the order of the day.

Commercial Joint Ventures

A joint venture (JV) is exactly what its name implies—a venture involving two or more entities. The legal arrangements can vary dramatically. Commercial partnership-type arrangements can take many forms:

- The pure joint venture
- Partnership
- Corporations
- Limited liability companies

Each of these forms of operation represents a legal entity that can take ownership of real property. For the purpose of the law, they are artificial persons and, with the exception of the corporation, have finite lives. Usually they are formed for the express purpose of undertaking one specific project. There are exceptions to this, but from a deal-making perspective, it is always a good idea to avoid comingling assets in one legal entity. This having been said, there may be compelling reasons for pooling deals into one entity. The overriding commonality among all these separate forms of ownership is that they are governed by a written, legal document, an operating agreement. The relationship between the parties is consensual and totally negotiable so long as it is legal. There are no hard-and-fast rules regarding who does what and who pays for what. The agreements can be whatever the parties agree to.

> **DEFINITION**
>
> For discussion purposes, as it relates to a real estate deal, I use the word ***partners*** to include fellow partners, fellow members, or fellow stockholders in a specific project. I use the word ***deal*** as synonymous with the words "property," "transaction," "project," "investment," etc.

The success of the venture, however, generally hangs on the fact that the agreements must be equitable and fair. If this is not the case, most ill-conceived deals soon unravel. That having been said, let's look at each of these potential arrangements to show you how they fit together.

THE PURE JOINT VENTURE

This arrangement is truly a joint venture. The agreement is by contract rather than an operating agreement and can be evidenced by ownership of the property by tenants in common. This is quite common in large international construction ventures, where firms combine their talents and resources to pull off a project that neither or none of them can handle alone. In real estate it is fairly common for a builder to join with a landowner. In that case, the builder may not take title to any of the land until it becomes time for the builder to actually start construction of the individual buildings. No matter what the legal arrangements, they are governed by the joint venture agreement.

The other forms of joint venture contain the common thread that the venture—whether partnership, corporation, or limited liability company—takes title to the property. As with any rule, there must be exceptions to this, but I have never happened upon one. Each joint venturer is charged with taxes directly related to his or her income or losses. The venture is not a legal entity and, therefore, files no tax return.

PARTNERSHIPS

A partnership is one of the oldest forms of property ownership. It is evidenced by a partnership agreement and a statement of partnership that is filed by the owners with the state office of partnerships or corporations commission. The reason for filing this and any other form of ownership document is to provide the public with information on the owners of the partnership, corporation, or other business entity.

Partnerships are either general or limited.

A *general* partnership is one where all partners take an active role in the operation and management of the venture. All general partners are liable for all of the unsecured debts of the partnership. Any partner may commit the partnership to any legal venture. Even if, between or among the partners in the operating agreement, only one partner may commit, the public, due to the legal nature of a general partnership, has the right to rely on the ostensible authority of any general partner.

A *limited* partnership has two classes of partners: *general* partners who are charged with the operation of the partnerships and the rewards and liabilities that go with it and *limited* partners whose liability is limited to their investment in the partnership. The limited partners have no say in the operation of the partnership. That is what preserves their limited liability. If a limited partner starts to take a hand in the management of a partnership, for any reason, he or she becomes legally a general partner and assumes all the liabilities of a general partner. The limited partner's only operational direction can be that the original terms of the partnership are followed. Partnerships file tax returns, but do not pay taxes. Each partner is given a K-1 return for his or her prorated percentage gain or loss from the partnership, and each partner must pay the taxes on his or her own portion of the partnership's gain or loss.

CORPORATIONS

The corporation is another traditional form of agreement between or among two or more people or entities for a venture. They are not too popular in real estate, as corporations pay taxes on their gain each year. Then, when proceeds are distributed to the owners (stockholders), the stockholders pay taxes on that distribution. In effect, profits are doubly taxed. The few instances of corporations in the real estate business are found in the home-building industry. This industry is a cash flow business, rather than an income-producing asset management business, and the sheer volume of business prompts the raising of large sums of capital without liability to the stockholders. As with limited partners, the stockholders are liable only for their investment. In the case of the corporation, only the officers of the corporation can be held liable, and then, only for fraud or malfeasance.

Corporations come in several different forms: close, subchapter S, and public.

A *close* corporation is a corporation with fewer than ten stockholders. When borrowing funds, most lenders insist that these companies' stockholders guarantee any loans granted. The logic is that these few stockholders have 100 percent of the say in the disposition of any of the company's assets. Most banks view this type of a corporation like a partnership.

The *subchapter S* corporation is a hybrid, usually but not always closely held, that is taxed like a partnership. This corporation is found where large sums of capital are raised for investment in income-producing assets.

The *public* corporation rates its own paragraph later in this chapter.

Limited Liability Company (LLC)

This form of ownership did not exist before the 1990s and it is now the single most popular way to own real property. It combines the tax structure of the partnership with the limitations of liability of the corporation. Its owners are called *members* and can run the LLC by consensus or entrust operations to a managing member. In my opinion, this is the single best way to own real property. The only drawback that I can find is the lack of historical case law pertaining to problems that can occur in any venture. Time will cure that. The members are not liable for unsecured debts unless they voluntarily guarantee the obligations individually.

Public Corporation

Public corporations are companies formed when large sums are needed for capital. These companies form the bulk of the operation companies in the U.S. The raising of capital for corporations is governed by the Securities and Exchange Commission (SEC) and is known as a *public offering*. To raise money from the public, the sponsors are required to produce a prospectus and a disclosure statement, outlining in detail how much money is being raised, the cost thereof, and how the money is to be spent, as well as the risks and potential rewards of the venture. Full disclosure is required. This is a very expensive process and is reserved for raising very large sums of money.

Private Placements

For smaller ventures, such as real estate projects, there are alternatives to a public offering, to wit, the *private placement*. This is permitted under SEC rules for presentation to a limited number of sophisticated investors with whom the sponsors have pre-existing relationships. The private placement (also known as a *regulation D offering*) can be used for partnerships, corporations, and LLCs alike.

I have never used a private placement for raising capital, so I'm not familiar with the details, but a friend of mine has used it several times. He states that you can present the deal to no more than 35 people and take no more than ten investors, total, to qualify as a private placement offering. You must also file SEC Form D. If you want to use this type of capital-raising technique, I suggest that you consult an attorney and a tax specialist.

Once a corporation, partnership, or LLC is formed, it can raise capital by using debt instruments such as notes, bonds, and debentures. Large corporations use these and the sale of additional stock to raise unsecured funds. Real property loans are secured by the real estate. Equipment loans are secured by the *chattel*, or the equipment itself, through the use of specific chattels or recorded liens.

Joint Ventures

Real estate partnerships or LLCs seem to be broken down into two major categories: the *working* partnership and the *investor* partnership. A variation on either category would be the investor partnership with more than one active partner.

The first type of company/partnership, the *working partnership*, is generally a marriage of skills and money, with the participants taking responsibility for various chores within the transaction. An obvious popular partnership could be a developer and a manager or "bean counter." One is a professional entrepreneur and the other is a professional manager. These are two separate and distinct skills. Many of my partnerships and LLCs over the years have included, in addition to the investor and me, key members of the project team, including the broker, the architect, the engineer, and the contractor. These projects have been among my most successful projects, as everyone or almost everyone involved in the profitability of the project had a stake in the outcome and had personally guaranteed the construction loan. That's a focused project team: the members have a stake in both the downside and the upside of the transaction. I'll cover the origin of this transaction in the chapter entitled "Development and the Zero-Dollar Deal."

The second type of company/partnership is the *investor partnership*, with a passive investor. This is one that I call "your money, my time."

Defining the role in any partnership depends on who is bringing what to the table and also heavily on when the parties are going to join in the project. Loosely, a project goes through the following phases:

- Identifying a need waiting to be fulfilled
- Locating a specific property
- Vetting the property
- Conducting the feasibility study
- Preliminary design and entitlements
- Preleasing
- Working drawings and financing
- Constructing and moving in
- Managing the finished asset

Every developer/investor/owner has his or her list of priorities and phases. This one is mine. It does not change much whether I'm looking to develop or build. If I'm investing, there is no construction phase unless it is a redevelopment project. Most working partners come into the deal at the early stage, when the work is heaviest and the risks are minimal. Once you hit the preleasing and working drawing stages, the project is established as feasible and the work starts in earnest.

The key point in the deal for the partnership or LLC is at what stage in the development process the investor comes into the deal and at what price. The consulting partners are all contributing skills and time to earn a piece of the action and all will join in the *joint and several guarantee* of the construction loan, but the investor can take several postures. In the early stages, the project has not yet passed into the relatively risk-free state of breakeven leasing; therefore, early participation by an investor is riskier and, by definition, worth a fairly large percentage of the deal. When the project is leased to breakeven, the construction loan is booked and ready to fund, and the construction contract is executed, the transaction is relatively risk-free. The only risk left is the contractor's ability to deliver the building on time and within budget. This is the most risk-free time to bring an investor into the deal, so money at this stage of the game cannot command as big a share of the deal as it could during the riskier stages of the project. It all boils down to negotiation.

What are these skills worth? What is the money worth and at what time? What kinds of fees are the working partners going to be able to charge and when are they going to be collected? These questions are for you, the developer/

owner/buyer to answer, as each slice of the ownership comes out of your action.

Formula for Joint Ventures

In 1975, I started my development business. Since I lacked the financial resources to get into the business, I took on a partner. Together, we had enough cash and experience to pull a deal together, but not enough money for the equity required to start construction on a sizeable project. Therefore, we sought out and found a joint venture partner, who elected to be a passive limited partner. In structuring that transaction, I came up with the formula that I have stuck with for almost all of my transactions since. The deal points were as follows:

- I put the project into the deal without any markup.
- The investor was responsible for all costs above the construction/permanent loan (i.e., the permanent equity).
- As developer, I would collect a predetermined overhead fee from the construction loan proceeds.
- The investor would receive from the cash flow an eight percent preferred return against one half of the cash flow.
- Upon sale or refinance, the investor's funds were to be returned first and then the profits would be split 50/50.

With some innovative wrinkles, I have stuck with this formula ever since. Every deal my company has done since 1975 has been a joint venture and we have always succeeded in raising the required equity. Some deals have brought the investor into the picture before the project was ready for construction; in those deals, the investor has received in excess of a 50-percent interest. By and large, this has proven to be a fair arrangement for all parties and we have had many profitable deals with this structure.

The Lender's Role

In addition to the above partners, the lenders have a role to play. Sometimes they like to make commitments contingent on occupancy levels, specific tenant deals, or percentage occupancy. Lenders can impose conditions during the negotiation stages of a loan, prior to the written commitment that you may have to live with. Your potential partners have to be aware of these conditions so that there is no possibility of misunderstanding and/or default down the line.

One of the great parts of real estate partnerships is that all relationships are negotiable. You can make the deal into any arrangement that all partners can agree upon. My take on it is that to make a deal work, the relationships and the profit-and-loss agreements must be fair and equitable or the deal may become unglued in the middle of the deal. No amount of legalese can force someone to do something that is onerous and contrary to his or her self-interest. Anything that lands in litigation is a disaster; litigation usually results in only the attorneys making money from a deal.

Job Assignments

To make sense of consultants and proposed partnerships, you should review what the people involved in a project actually do so that you can decide what their participation would be worth to you in the transaction. Most consultant participations are granted in exchange for the deferral of fees due at the front end of a deal. For a consultant to waive the upfront fees, it is reasonable to expect to either pay more later, once the project passes the go-or-no-go stage, or to pay the normal fee plus a kicker or a percentage of the profits down the line. It's up to you to decide how much is reasonable. Table 18-1 is a project responsibility chart for a typical development project; and you can use this, plus

Function	Job Description	Supervisor
Owner/developer/ buyer	Select the deal and make it happen	Self and/or investors
Architect	Project design	Owner, developer
Engineer	Site design	Owner, architect
Contractor	Pricing and construction	Owner, city, and architect
Leasing broker	Fill the building with tenants	Owner, investors, and lender
Mortgage banker/broker	Locate a viable construction and permanent loan	Owner and investors
Lender	Provide the cash needed above the equity provided	Owner and investors
Investors	Provide the equity over the loan needed to build/buy	Owner, lender

TABLE 18-1. PROJECT RESPONSIBILITY CHART

a specific fee quote from your consultant, to make up your mind. Sometimes, any percentage is too much for the service contemplated; you will then elect to pay the fees up front.

In addition to the above, there are the interrelated responsibilities of the entire project team to consider, as shown in Table 18-2.

I know it sounds somewhat complex, but you will find, as you progress through any deal, that all will become clear. Good projects acquire a life of their own; they evolve right along with the players. In the chapter, "Development and the Zero-Dollar Deal," I describe in detail a joint venture process that brings all the major players into a deal so that the front-end costs are kept to a minimum. You can use that as a guideline when starting out. It has served me well over the years.

Borrowing

Most real estate purchases or development projects involve the use of leverage, so up to 80 percent of the costs are customarily borrowed from an experienced real estate lender. These lenders include the following organizations:

- Banks
- Savings and loans (S&Ls)
- Insurance companies
- Pension funds
- Real estate investment trusts (REITS)
- Finance companies

These companies are considered to be traditional, conventional lenders in our industry. Banks, S&Ls, and finance companies make loans on houses; banks, insurance companies, pension funds, and REITs make loans on commercial property.

Whether you are dealing with homes or commercial property, there are two classes of loans: *interim* and *permanent*. Interim loans generally carry the projects through the completion of construction and permanent loans are put into place when the projects are completed.

Work Item	Who Is Responsible?	Prerequisites	Time Frame	Notes
establish escrow	developer	finding the site	none specified	
vet the title	developer and attorney	escrow	seller 4 weeks, buyer 4 weeks	crucial—get it right
preliminary site assessment	geotechnical engineer, architect, and engineer, marketing team, and developer	start as soon as the title looks OK	60 days from the time the seller delivers the prelim	this is the "free look" time: make the most of it
the go/no-go decision	developer	the site checks out all the way	should be done within the "free look" period	after this it gets expensive if the site must be abandoned
execute preliminary design	developer, architect, marketing, property manager, and contractor	the go decision	90 days	this is the major entitlement and leasing tool
flesh out the pro forma	developer, marketing team, and contractor	need design and market survey results	within the 90 days above	get it right, as the leasing will be based on the numbers
apply for the entitlements, zoning, and site plan approval	developer and attorney, if necessary	a completed preliminary plan	60 days to two years, depending on the request	always add 90 days to your time plan for the unexpected
preleasing	marketing team	a design and a firm rental figure	90 days to start of construction	normally 75% to close loan
working drawings	architect, engineer, marketing team, contractor, and developer	an idea of what will be approved for construction	six months and three to six months for building permit	big-dollar do or die: must meet lender's leasing requirement
loan commitments	developer and mortgage banker	firm design, some preleasing final numbers, and ownership	accomplish during the above time frame	the ownership must be OK to lender
close the land escrow and construction loan	developer and lender—escrow	building permits, preleasing, and loan commitment	should be done as soon as the permit is issued	the clock is ticking on the leases: complete construction and open
construction	contractor, developer, lender	money, leases to lender's requirement	six months to two years	tenant plans and meet occupancy dates
permanent financing	owner/mortgage banker/lender	the building must be leased to lender's specs	be completed within specified time frame	once complete, turn the project over to the property manager and go on vacation!

TABLE 18-2. REPORTING AND WORK FLOW CHART

Interim Loans

Interim loans run the gamut from land loans to construction loans. They are designed to aid in the development of land and the construction of buildings.

When a developer picks out a parcel of land to develop, he or she has to prepare the land for construction of buildings. In the case of housing, the infrastructure—streets, utilities, and services—must be in place before houses can be built. The loans that are taken out for this process run from the traditional seller-carry-back land loan to gap (bridge) financing and acquisition-and-development (A&D) loans. An A&D loan is taken for the express purpose of funding the infrastructure prior to house construction. In some cases, there may be a short period between the A&D loan and the construction financing that can be covered by a gap loan. This is known as *bridge financing*.

Once the infrastructure is in place, then the conventional construction loan takes place. The process for commercial development is then the same for individual homes. A loan is funded to cover all costs of construction that pertain to that parcel of land dedicated to that specific building. All interim financing is interest-only or non-amortizing. All of the principal and interest are due in full at maturity.

For commercial projects, there is a type of loan currently available, which I first came across in the 1990s, called a *mini-perm*. This loan is a conventional construction loan with a term of 12-24 months that can be converted at the completion of construction into a short-term permanent or amortizing loan. The lender charges a fee for the conversion. The mini-perm loan is used to bridge the gap between the completion of construction and the funding of a permanent loan. Why is this handy? It covers a multitude of sins, but in a nutshell it buys the developer time to get the project in order to get the most favorable permanent financing. Not all mini-perms are converted. It depends on many factors, not the least of which is timing. Sometimes the financing market is going through a period of high interest rates; this mini-perm allows you to weather that period without the necessity of taking a permanent loan that would lock in a high rate for a long time.

Permanent Loans

This brings us to the subject of permanent financing. Permanent loans are, traditionally, loans that are amortizing over a specific period of time. The most common term of amortization has been 30 years, but since the 1980s, it is common to see loans that are amortized over 20 and 25 years.

In the past, before the advent of the mini-perm, a developer had to arrange for and buy a permanent loan and a construction loan at the same time. Unless the developer was very large or extremely well heeled, the construction lender wanted assurance that the construction loan would be retired or paid in full at the end of the term. In fact, many construction lenders required the borrower to have a permanent loan locked in before they would fund for construction. The three parties then entered into an agreement whereby the permanent lender, with the consent of the borrower, agreed to "buy" the loan from the construction lender and the construction lender agreed to "sell" the loan to the permanent lender. This contract was called a *tri-party agreement* or a *buy-sell agreement*. It was the customary way to get a construction loan before the mini-perm came along. The disadvantage of this type of arrangement for the borrower was that the rate could be onerous and he or she was locked in because of the buy-sell agreement. You could get out of it, but it was expensive.

Modern Loans

In today's lending community, all loans start out as *terms sheets*. A terms sheet is generally a one- or two-page summary of the lender's loan offering. It provides a basis for negotiating the salient points of the proposed loan. Once the lender and the borrower agree on the terms, the lender issues an application for the borrower to sign and fees are exchanged. Then the lender does the required due diligence on the loan, doing the following, among other things:

- Purchases a third-party appraisal
- Verifies the title conditions of the property
- Checks the site for hazardous materials
- Verifies the ALTA survey
- Reviews the plans and specifications
- Reviews the leases
- Reviews the construction contract
- Reviews the credit of the borrower and the contractor

Once the lender does these things and approves the results, the loan is considered to be *underwritten* and a written loan commitment is issued. This process is identical for interim and permanent loans.

There is a new wrinkle in the permanent loan market today that has come about from the growth of the secondary market for loans. This market is made by bundling groups of permanent loans into a package for sale to investors. To maintain the yield on investment to make these attractive to investors, permanent lenders have added new provisions to permanent loans. These conditions are designed to lock in the borrower for a minimum period of time so that the buyer of the loan is assured the promised rate of return for the term of the loan. The method of providing this lock-in is to compel the borrower to agree to pay penalties for the right to retire the loan before the term expires. These penalties are very costly and virtually assure the loan buyer of his or her yield. The vehicle for these penalties is known as a *yield maintenance agreement*. The penalty clause says, basically, that the borrower agrees to pay the lender, as a cancellation fee, a percentage of the outstanding balance of the loan and a fee equal to the yield on the loan that the lender would get over the remaining life of the loan, less the yield that is readily available in the market at the time of the payoff. When the prevailing interest rates have fallen since a loan was made, these sums can add up to millions of dollars. During periods of rising interest rates, lenders are anxious to get their money back so that they can reinvest it at higher rates, so these fees shrink down to the cancellation fee.

The language of these clauses truly requires an attorney's review, as the clauses are very technical and complex. Below you will see an example of the language from a recent application letter. It is confusing enough in isolation here; imagine what it's like in the actual loan document.

> ***Prepayment:*** Prepayment is prohibited during period ending two years after the securitization of the note or three years after loan closing, whichever is later ("Lockout Period"). If prepaid after lockout period but prior to last 3 months of term, lender will charge prepayment fee equal to greater of (a) result of yield maintenance formula or (b) 1 percent of prepaid principal. No prepayment fee if prepaid during last 3 months. Instead of prepaying, borrower may defease the loan, at any time after the Lockout Period, by substituting a first priority security interest in qualified U.S. govern-

ment obligations (payable at times and in amounts sufficient to cover all note installments) for the mortgage on the property. Borrower shall pay all costs of defeasance including a 1 percent defeasance fee.

As you can see, this is confusing—even more so on your first time through. Lean on your mortgage banker and your real estate attorney and you'll get through it. It's painful only if you think about it. The bright side is that most yield maintenance loans have an assumption clause that allows you to sell the property without having to pay off the loan. There's always a bright side.

> **DEFINITION**
>
> To ***defease*** a contract is to comply with a condition permitting the annulment of that contract. Pure legalese!

PORTFOLIO LENDERS

Lenders that make loans and keep them in their own portfolios are known as *portfolio lenders*. Today they are few and far between—and they are so conservative that you need a fat wallet to purchase or develop property using this type of lender.

CHAPTER

19

Contracts *and* Consultants

The Contracts

Contracts, in all their various forms, more than any other documents involved in the development process, determine the cash value of the investment. While all documents, plans, specs, and contracts are vital in one way or another, the final executed leases will become the primary determination of present and future value. The other documents are what provide the owner/developer control over the development and ownership process.

All project documents should be drafted with the express purpose of being enforceable, interrelated, and self-referencing and to avoid potential conflicts within the overall documentation structure. If this is accomplished, the owner/developer will have a complete, necessary, and vital set of tools with which to create the final investment.

At a minimum, the set of documents required for the average commercial development project should include the following:

- The land purchase agreement and joint escrow instructions
- Ownership documents such as articles of incorporation, organization, or partnership agreements
- Exclusive leasing agreement
- The project lease

- All governmental approval documents, including the entitlement documentation applications and approvals
- Building permits and occupancy permits
- Construction loan documents
- Permanent loan documents
- General construction contracts and site improvement contracts
- Architectural and engineering contracts
- Utility agreements
- Any required environmental documentation
- The property management agreement

It sounds like a tall order and probably expensive. The truth of the matter is that these documents can vary all over the lot, from simple one-page agreements for leasing out an apartment to a 200-page government lease for the Department of Energy (DOE). Depending on the project, the documentation will find its own level of complexity. Generally, the smaller and more rural the project, the more basic the required documentation. Large sophisticated projects require complex and sophisticated documentation. There are common guidelines that run through all documents to make them both legal and enforceable.

The statute of frauds, a federal law, states in essence that real property contracts, to be enforceable, must be in writing, be of lawful intent, and be executed by competent parties and that consideration must have passed between the parties.

That is the starting point from which all real property contracts come into being. The parent is the owner/developer and the doctors/midwives are the attorneys. It is the very proliferation of attorneys that will often dictate the level of documentation. If neither party to an agreement can afford an attorney, the document will be very simple and easily understood. As more attorneys are introduced into the mix, the document starts to grow. The big trick for the developer is to have a sufficient level of documentation and no more. Too much or too little documentation can cause real problems.

The Purchase Agreement and Joint Escrow Instructions

The practical aspects of the purchase agreement will be covered in Chapter 26, "The Purchase Contract"; however, there are basic areas that need to be addressed in most situations. When dealing with small parcels of land or unsophisticated sellers, it may be prudent to use a local Realtor's® standard preprinted purchase form, with an addendum addressing specific concerns for the site. In most instances, I recommend that a developer create a purchase agreement that can be used in all situations. That way, you, as developer/buyer, will know the document well. Understanding a document and its cross-references will enable you to more effectively negotiate the final document. The attorney's favorite trick for creating tools with which to manage a document is to create cross-referenced, linked conditions. This enables the insertion of conditions that are interlocked and, therefore, less obvious to the seller. This sounds devious, but it is accepted practice for most

HEADS UP

Personally, I favor a document that tells the seller in plain English what I'm up to and lays out the schedule, the contingencies, and the price and terms I'm willing to pay for his or her accommodation. Without the wholehearted cooperation of the seller, it is very difficult to accomplish the entitlement process. Slipping one over on him or her in the document negotiation process will not go over well in the long run.

legal documentation.

The basic information needed to be included in the document is as follows:

- The legal description of the land
- The size of the land and how it will be determined
- The price
- Schedule of payments and close of escrow
- Seller's and buyer's representatives
- The designated escrow holder or title company
- Seller's scope of work and the permitted time frames
- Buyer's scope of work and related time frames
- Contingencies and how the deposits are treated (refundable or not)
- Buyer's and seller's representations
- Buyer's and seller's recourse
- Default provisions
- Governing law and miscellaneous provisions

Any attorney worth his or her salt can flesh out an agreement to include many more items, but the above outlined provisions should get the job done.

Ownership Documents for Nonpublic Entities

If you, the buyer/owner/developer, have decided to go it alone, then you can skip this section. If, however, there will be two or more people involved in the ownership entity, then the decision as to type of ownership has to be made. The popular choices have been covered previously. Each form of ownership has a different set of required documents.

The first set of documents is the detailed agreements of the parties and is a private document between or among the parties: stockholder agreements, partnership agreements, or operating agreements. These documents amount to the same thing, regardless of the form of ownership. They spell out why the venture was formed, its intent, who is involved, how it is capitalized, who is authorized to do what, how control is exercised, who gets what and when, how to resolve disputes, and, finally, how to terminate the agreement. Only the corporation has an indeterminate age. The longevity of both the partnership and the LLC is finite, but extendable, at the election of the partners or members.

The second set of documents is public and they must be filed with the state and recorded in the public record, so that the public knows who is involved and who is empowered to act on behalf of the ownership entity.

Articles of Incorporation

These articles are a short form of a corporation's stockholders' agreement and simply put the public on notice that a corporation has been formed. They provide the basic facts, such as the name of the corporation, its date of formation, its principal place of business, its incorporators and their addresses, and, in the event of legal notice being required, the name of the *agent for service*. They must list the corporate officers so that the public knows who is empowered to act on behalf of the corporation. They must also include other specific information as required by individual states. If the corporation is going to be doing business in other states, it must file *foreign corporation* operating notices in each state where it intends to do business.

Partnership Agreements

Partnerships, whether general or limited, must file a statement of partnership. Like articles of incorporation, the statement outlines who the general partners are, their addresses, the partnership's principal place of business, and all of the same information required of the corporation. A limited partnership is not required to identify the limited partners.

Articles of Organization

Articles of organization are filed for limited liability companies, providing the same information required of corporations and partnerships, as well as the method of management elected by the members and the identity of the managing member(s). Legally, in terms of public liability, LLCs are treated like corporations and for tax purposes they are treated like partnerships.

The Exclusive Leasing Agreement

This document employs the leasing agent (broker) to act on behalf of the owners to represent the property to prospective tenants. Always remember that without tenants there is no project and that without a good marketing agent there will be no tenants.

The contract should outline the duration of the agreement, the compensation, and when it is paid, generally one half when the lease is executed and one half when the tenant begins paying the rent. It should also spell out the duties and obligations of both agent and owner and remedies upon default by either party. If there are incentives offered, they should be spelled out here, with statements regarding how and when they are earned and paid. As with all contracts, the general provisions or "boilerplate" regarding governing law, genders, severability, lawful intent, and more must be included. It is the attorney's job to make sure the agreements are sufficient to enforce the developer's intent and spell out the leasing agent's obligations.

The Project Lease

This document, above all, must be done properly. It is the entire embodiment of the financial purpose of the project.

> **HEADS UP**
>
> Get it right! The executed leases will be the single most important factor in determining the cash value of the project, both initially and in the future!

In the past, most leases fell into four classes: gross, modified gross, modified net, and net, aka NNN. There were so many variations that it became confusing. The truly gross leases include all the operating costs of the building and the truly net leases include none of the operating costs. Many of these old confusing leases are still in force. If an investor is buying existing real property, the leases need to be carefully examined for their true economic impact on the cash flow.

A sample commercial lease is included in Appendix C.* A working copy of the lease, along with the other sample contracts, is contained on a CD-ROM available from the author on www.riderland.com. It is a lease I have developed over 25 years and the current form is set up for use for both retail and office projects.

For today's developments, the choice should be either a gross or an NNN lease. The terms of the lease should be clearly defined so that the gross lease rent includes all costs of

***Disclaimer**—The sample lease included in Appendix C is not intended to be used without the approval of your attorney. The sample commercial lease document is furnished to be used only as a guide to suggested topics for inclusion in a commercial real estate lease. No representation is made as to its sufficiency or legality in your state or its appropriateness for your proposed project.*

building operation except personal property taxes, for which the tenant may be responsible. The NNN lease, which includes none of the operating costs of the building, requires the tenant to pay, as "additional rent," its pro rata share of the building's *common area maintenance* (CAM) charges, taxes, and insurance. Typical CAM charges include the following items, prorated over the number of square feet of leasable space:

- Water
- Power for the common areas
- Landscape maintenance
- Window washing
- Parking lot sweeping
- Janitorial
- HVAC (heating, ventilation, and air-conditioning) maintenance
- Reasonable reserves for replacements
- General repairs except structural
- Management costs, typically ten percent of CAM costs

Which form of lease document is chosen depends on the owner/landlord and his or her level of experience, the type of building involved, the custom of the industry within the building's market, and the ability of the leasing broker to sell the chosen document. Arguments can be made for and against both types of lease. Personally, I use the net lease exclusively. No exceptions! The reasons for this choice are, rightfully, totally subjective, but I will share them with you.

First of all, I feel the concept is easier to sell and harder for the tenant to take issue with over the life of the lease. The basic difference between the two types of leases lies in the concept of cost control. If the landlord is paying all the costs of operation, the tenant is less likely to care about cost control and, subsequently, expense management is a never-ending battle between the tenant who leaves his or her lights on all night and the landlord. Over the years, I have found this to be futile and a complete waste of my time. The NNN lease puts cost management squarely on the shoulders of the tenant, where it belongs. It doesn't matter if the tenant wants to leave his or her lights on or run the air-conditioning over the weekend, because he or she pays the bill.

My concept for building maintenance is to set minimum standards for maintenance and let the individual tenants add more service if they find it necessary to their operation and are willing to pay for it. An example of this is daily janitorial service. Office spaces are vacuumed daily and trash is collected and dumped daily, while dusting is scheduled only once a week, and then only if the desks are cleared and ready for dusting. If the tenant wants dusting done more often, the tenant arranges this separately with the janitor and pays for it directly. Similarly, windows are washed a minimum of four times a year; if a tenant requests more frequent washing, it is billed directly to the tenant. In general, utilities are separately metered to each tenant and paid directly by the tenants. Water is part of the common area charge. Sometimes heating and air-conditioning are also part of the common area and are managed for extra service by sub-metering to the individual tenants.

Business Intent of the Lease

A good lease document must be easy to negotiate. An overly long or complicated document will tend to generate large legal fees due to the necessity of excessive negotiation. In the case of small, unsophisticated tenants, these cumbersome leases can become a "deal breaker." In the past, my commercial leases have been as lengthy as 60 pages long, complicated, and hard to read. In recent years, I have streamlined the document and found that the altered document made it easier to negotiate and less expensive (attorney's fees). The lease document contained in the companion CD-ROM is substantially the same document, but now it is in three separate parts.

The first part, the main body of the lease, contains all the "business points" of the lease. These are all the items within any lease that are generally negotiable between landlord and tenant and contain, with the exception of some of the exhibits, the entire business deal.

The second part, the general provisions (the boilerplate), contains all the clauses that are required by the landlord, the lender, and the insurer to cover themselves for actions by the tenant that may cause them loss. This portion of the lease, with few exceptions, is totally nonnegotiable. This fact makes that part easy, as it becomes a "take it or leave it" proposition for the tenant. Should the tenant insist on negotiating the general provisions, I refer him or her to the lender's attorney and say that I will live with any modifications agreed to by the lender. Lenders do not negotiate boilerplate with tenants.

The final part is the exhibit section. It contains the following:

- The property description
- A site plan
- A floor plan
- A tenant improvement plan
- A construction cost breakdown of who is paying for what, as well as how and when it is to be built, and by whom
- A list of rules and regulations
- A sample "Notice of Commencement of Rent and Acceptance of Premises"
- A sample "Estoppel Certificate" (acknowledgment of lease obligation)
- A "Special Provisions" exhibit, which spells out exclusives, specific restrictions, and options to renew

Special care should be given to the creation of the project lease as this not only sets the value of the premises, but also is the only tool the manager has to enforce the terms of the agreement. There are traditional areas of dispute between landlord and tenant that should be carefully addressed in the lease document; the owner/landlord must include clauses to address them or risk long-term management problems and diminished value.

Special thought should be given to carefully defining the following items:

- Actual operation expenses
- Capital costs and taxes
- A tenant's right of offset
- Late fees
- Default and remedies upon default
- Parking
- Signs (permanent and temporary)
- Exclusives
- Arbitration (binding and nonbinding)
- Hours of operation
- Assignment and subletting
- "Going dark"
- Insurance
- Legal notice and addresses

Special attention should be given to the permitted timing of, and compulsion to execute, documents such as estoppel certificates.

There are many other areas of concern in a well-written lease, but if care is given to these basics, the value of the lease and, by extrapolation, the project should stand firm and the management headaches should be rare. Each attorney has a "pet peeve" generated by experience. Do not let him or her create a dealbreaker clause to protect the landlord or the tenant. A detailed article-by-article explanation of the project lease is included in Chapter 22.

Architectural and Engineering Contracts

This area of contract negotiation is a classic area of negotiation, centering on responsibility and cost. The architectural and engineering professions have created a standard document called the AIA (American Institute of Architecture) contract. The consultants will tell you that it is the industry standard and, unfortunately, due to its acceptance by many unsophisticated owner/developers, it is. Do not execute it without specific modifications.

Most areas of contention center on the price of services and the scope of work. I always take the position that a consultant should be an expert in his or her field or should not be hired. An expert should be able to assess the scope of work and quote a fixed price. Only if the owner makes a substantial and easily defined significant change in the scope of work should there be an extra charge. Avoid all hourly fees. Get firm written prices for all proposed extras, *before* authorizing the work. Make sure the contract states that you will not pay for any changes not authorized, in writing, in advance.

Make each consultant financially responsible for all mistakes in design, for both the cost of correcting the design and the cost of any remedial construction work involved. If the consultant is inspecting work in progress during construction, make him or her jointly responsible with the contractor for the cost of any remedial work required to correct shoddy, unspecified, or unsafe construction, as well as any losses due to the delay in the project's scheduled completion date. Remember: if the tenants are delayed when moving in, so is the rental payment.

HEADS UP

Interest goes on eternally.

Governmental Approval Documents

This is both a tricky and an ever-expanding area of project documentation. It all started with a building permit and now encompasses an entire body of entitlements. Without painting a horror story of possible areas of concern, I need to elaborate only on basic areas of concern common to all parts of the country. They center around four concepts:

- Zoning controls
- Project limitations (height, setbacks, parking, landscaping, signs, and coverage)
- Civic and county requirements
- Environmental controls

Zoning is controlled by adoption of a general plan for the development and expansion of the town, city, or county. If the proposed project's use conforms, then usually only the site plan and elevations need be approved. California and Washington require the environmental impact report (EIR) process mentioned earlier in this book. If there are deviations in uses, shape, and/or encroachments, sometimes use permits or special use permits are required. Negotiate the wording of these permits, making sure they work for the project and its specific design requirements. In the event of a large or complicated project or one requiring extensive off-site improvements, often a *development agreement* is executed between the developer and the municipality. This agreement sets out the off-site improvements required, who will construct them, who will pay for them, and what is required to be completed before the main project can proceed. A typical example occurs in housing development, where homes cannot be sold before streets and utilities are completed. Sometimes these agreements specify that impact fees are to be paid when securing building permits, so that the municipality can afford to make the improvements to support the project. Examples of this are expansion of the sewer or water treatment facilities or construction of public schools.

Building Permits and Occupancy Permits

Building permits involve filling out forms and paying the required fees, which vary from reasonable, in a pro-development municipality, to confiscatory in a "no-growth" municipality. The permit is issued after the municipality's building department has examined and approved the project's working drawings. This is a costly and exhaustive experience, often involving redesign and changing the project's design characteristics to fit the department's interpretation of the governing ordinances. Fighting the building department's interpretations can be disastrous. Serious delays and increased costs will surely follow. Bureaucracy is no joke: its practitioners have been perfecting the art of frustrating people's desires for many thousands of years. Give them what they want!

Similarly, when construction is completed in accordance with the approved plans and specs, the municipality's building inspection department issues a certificate of occupancy for each demised premises. These must be kept in the building on file for verification.

Construction Loan Documents

The construction loan starts out as a commitment, to be converted into actual loan documents prior to funding. The loan commitment and acceptance by the owner/developer is an agreement by a lending institution to lend money for construction based upon some criteria. The criteria usually enumerate a certain percentage of preleasing from acceptable tenants, receipt of a building permit, and approval by the lender of not only the financial well being of the borrower and its component parts (the individuals involved) and the proposed tenants, but also of all of the documentation involved in the project. All this must occur within the time frame specified in the commitment or it will expire, leaving the borrower with a project in default.

When all this has been accomplished at the borrower's sole expense, including legal fees, appraisals, construction loan, administrative costs, etc., the lender will issue at least two documents for the borrower to execute prior to disbursing the funds. They are the *note* and the *deed of trust*. The note spells out the loan terms, amount, disbursals, interest rate, late fees, events of default, joint and several guarantees, payment schedules and due dates, and anything else the lender can think of. The deed of trust, sometimes referred to as the mortgage, is the recordable document that, when recorded, places a lien on the security (the land) and anything else agreed upon, such as additional collateral. This document usually spells out the security, the lender's rights, and the borrower's requirements, as well as the terms of its release, usually the full satisfaction of the note within the prescribed time.

Permanent Loan Documents

Similarly, the permanent loan documents start out with a commitment and end in a note and deed of trust. In the case of the permanent or take-out loan, the closing costs are higher and the number of inspections and warranties is greater. Usually, however, once the project is complete and fully occupied, personal joint and several guarantees are no longer required of the borrower.

General Construction Contracts and Site Improvement Contracts

This set of contracts will determine the cost, the schedule, and the quality of the improvements. Selection of a reputable general contractor is the key to achieving a quality project. Good general contractors charge a profitable fee for their work and expect to earn that fee. The owner's role in this process is to find a good one, treat him or her fairly, pay on time, and enforce the terms of the contract, the plans, and the specifications. Key items in the contract to be negotiated are:

- Price
- Contingencies
- Payment terms—draws and terms of the draw
- Withholding
- Subcontractors
- Work rules
- Bonding for performance and completion
- Schedules
- Completion date
- Penalties and incentives
- Quality control
- Independent inspection

Here again the ubiquitous AIA document rears its ugly head. Try not to use one, but if you must, modify it to be responsible and performance-oriented. Make sure the responsible party pays for the mistakes, including loss of time, interest, and rental income. To have an enforceable penalty clause, there must be a corresponding incentive clause. It is a good idea. Do not begrudge the payment of incentive fees. Remember: the rent will start early and compensate the owners for the additional fees to be paid and interest will be saved to offset the incentive pay. The penalties, if assessed, should offset the additional interest incurred by the delay.

Utility Agreements

These documents are customarily executed during the planning and working-drawing stages of the project. They enumerate the source of utilities and how they will be extended to the property line, who will pay for the work, and any easements and preconditions that must be satisfied for the work to be completed on time. These chores and their corresponding time frames can be costly in both money and time. Start them early and get them completed ASAP.

The time to contact the utility companies is when the architect and engineer are hired. Make them part of the design team. Make sure that the architect and engineer continually interface with the utility company's engineering staff to avoid any conflicts between the project's concept and the capability of the existing or proposed infrastructure. Pay attention throughout the process and attend all the meetings. *Do not delegate this chore.*

A completed building without power, water, and sewer cannot be occupied. The good news is that the utility companies are reasonable, publicly regulated bodies used to doing the work. They do not overpower the situation with legalese. They are one of the developer's natural allies, kindred spirits, interested in progress and more customers. Be nice to them!

Environmental Documentation

This subject could necessitate a book in itself. There is no way to cover the subject thoroughly without taking it one state and one municipality at a time. Suffice it to say that California is the most regulated geographical region on the planet. Study the situation there, learn to work within it, and you can work anywhere. Most environmental regulation is both necessary and fairly applied. As with most good things, environmental regulation has been perverted and abused to serve various political agendas. In California, there are state laws, local county overlays, the municipal overlays, the coastal commission, and, in certain areas, other special jurisdictions, like the Bay Area Development Commission. The net effect of all this regulation is to curtail growth, but it is also making any and all growth hideously expensive while promoting suburban sprawl. It is as if Californians took a look at New York City and said, "Anything but that."

The real effect of environmental concerns has evolved into personal and corporate liability for actions that result in contaminating the environment with hazardous waste. In the past, before these laws, many abuses occurred, resulting in land that is terminally polluted and unfit for use by any living beings. The worst of these examples are the nuclear test and fabrication sites created and administered by the United States Department of Energy (the DOE). Many of these abuses are environmental holocausts waiting to happen. The result of all this abuse is, in most cases, overregulation.

Contemporary loan documents now require the borrower to indemnify the lender against all past and future contamination of the site. This makes the developer responsible for prior problems as well as problems caused now and in the future by the tenants of the project. This assumption of liability now runs like a thread throughout all the documentation, hopefully back to the source of the problem. Here again, a good attorney can be worth his or her weight in gold.

The Property Management Agreement

This final document, properly drafted, charges the management agent with a *fiduciary responsibility* to both the landlord and the tenant. The manager's duty is to maintain the property in a condition that will honor the provisions of the lease documents and produce a profit for the landlord, minimizing potential traumas along the way.

The terms of this type of document vary, but a good one should include incentives for the manager to achieve better results and happy tenants and penalties for substandard performance. Since an agent acts on behalf of the owner, the agent must be carefully selected. Mistakes in representation can have far-reaching consequences. Often owners are tempted to manage, but in general, it is better to have a third party separating owner and tenant. This buffer allows for debate without rancor and gives everyone a chance to think things through without having to make a decision face to face. Important issues in this document are:

- Rent collection
- Maintenance
- Performance fees
- Leasing fees
- Lease renewal fees
- Trust accounts
- Cash handling
- Payment of expenses

The Exclusive Right to Sell Agreement

The culmination of the project is the sale. When it occurs will depend on the project objectives, the quality of its execution, and the desires of the owners. If the marketing team members have done a credible job and met their performance goals, they might have earned the right to sell the project. Most often, there are firms that specialize in investment sales. These companies will have the best chance to meet the owners' expectations at the time of sale. *There are no standard commissions for this type of contract.*

Consultant agreements differ, depending upon which side of the contract you happen to be on. As a consultant, I want to draft a "best efforts" contract, but as an employer, I want to draft a "specific performance" agreement. The main difference between the two approaches is the ability to demand certain results. If the consultant is in an advisory position or if the contract calls for a recommendation, the employer is in a better position when specific performance is required. A "best efforts" contract is just that. It calls for only the consultant's best efforts, not a specific result.

This may not seem like a big deal, but picture yourself asking a market analyst to find you an unsatisfied niche for your building or imagine hiring a broker who says that he or she can fill your new building within a 12-month period. Would you like to be able to lean on the specific performance clause? It is not the possibility that you could force the consultant to guarantee the results; it is merely that you might be able to force him or her to add more people to the effort if the work is falling behind schedule. Another way to ensure success may entail reduced fees or increased scope of the work. Most consultants specify their own scope of work, so it is your job to make them be as specific as possible. Build in deadlines and perhaps incentive and penalty clauses to enhance performance.

BROKERS

Leasing brokers always want to have you sign an exclusive agency agreement. They will tell you that they intend to invest considerable time and expense in representing you and they want to be assured that someone else will not be cashing in on all their hard work. This reasoning is true to a point, but take it with a grain of salt. Have them spell out exactly what they propose to do for your project, how much it will cost, and when it will be complete. Ask them about their reporting procedures; then, put those procedures into the contract, insisting on no less than a written, monthly report addressing all the issues that were included in their proposal. The report should include, at a minimum, the personnel assigned to the job, the advertising for the month, the companies contacted, their relative level of interest, and the status of any negotiations.

THE GOOD POINTS

If you can get the brokerage company to commit to all of the above, then you should be assured that it will perform for you. If you have pinned them down and if you have performance clauses in the contract, then you have the right to cancel if they do not perform. That is about all you can do to protect yourself. The best way to ensure a good performance is to find a broker who is enthusiastically recommended by other building owners.

Another consideration for the exclusivity issue is competing buildings. If you are giving the broker an exclusive, you can insist that the broker reciprocate by not handling buildings that will directly compete with your own. *This is an important issue. Do not back down on this point.*

The reason for this clause is that a large percentage of leasing brokers are tenant brokers: they represent a certain tenant or tenants exclusively in a certain area. This practice does not necessarily conflict with your building, but they have a conflict of interest with respect to the tenant. If you ask the broker to list as part of the contract all the projects and tenants that he or she represents exclusively, this will clarify the issue. You might find that he or she may be very reluctant to do so. Make up your own mind.

THE BASIC AGREEMENT

In addition to the above considerations and any resulting clauses, the exclusive leasing contract should cover the following, at a minimum:

- Start with the recitals (a brief statement of facts that provide the context for the agreement and state the purpose of the agreement), identifying the owner and the broker, explaining the purpose of the contract, and giving the location and a description of the project.
- Specify the term of the agreement.
- Outline the mutual rights of cancellation. Reference the performance clauses, if any. There should be strict guidelines relating to residual commission rights in the event of cancellation. It is not unreasonable to insist that all pending potential tenants be signed within 30 days of cancellation for the broker to have earned a commission.
- Include the marketing plan or a specific date for the broker to submit one. Specify that it must be approved by the owner. Spell out the reporting requirements and the details to be addressed in the reports.
- Specify the personnel assigned to the project and delineate the exclusivity on their part.
- List the services to be provided by the owner, tenant layouts, pricing, etc. Commit to turnaround times agreed to by your architect. Specify any sales materials that you will provide, such as renderings and brochures.
- Address the publicity and press release policy.

HEADS UP

You want to keep a tight rein on this one, as careless press releases can hurt your project.

- Address the sign issue. Include the project sign and any "for lease" signs. Make sure that the agent complies with all laws regarding signs.
- Address the issue of lease preparation. The typical agent wants a standard lease so that he or she can fill in the blanks. Do not use your agent's lease. Develop your own project lease. Refer to "The Project Lease" earlier in this chapter for guidelines.

HEADS UP

This is important, as all your profit and future value are tied up in this document. Do it well, take the time, and spend the money to create a good lease.

- Have the broker bring you a letter of intent from the tenant, prepare the lease, and meet face to face with the tenant if possible.
- Spell out the commission schedule, as well as when the commission is payable. In a development deal, it is customary to pay the first half when construction starts and the second half when the tenant occupies and starts paying rent. In an existing building, the first half will be paid upon execution of the lease.
- Insist that the agent cooperate with other brokerage companies. Look for proof that he or she is actively marketing your building to other brokerage firms.
- Specify the initial rental rate and give yourself the right to raise the rate with 30 days' notice. Set down clear terms that you want to include in the lease. Set a minimum term lease that you will accept. I recommend no less than three to five years.
- Specify the dates by which leasing goals have to be met and reference the broker's marketing plan. Insist that the broker must meet these goals in order to retain the listing.

- Address the issue of commissions if and when the tenant renews the lease or exercises any options. This should not be a commission to the broker. Renewals are due to your good management.
- Insert the boilerplate, including notices, change of addresses, owner's representative, attorney's fees, governing law, successors and assigns, severability, and miscellaneous.
- Finally, sign and date the agreement. Include as Exhibit A the legal description of the property and as Exhibit B the marketing plan when you approve it.

Architects and Engineers

These individuals are the most technical of any consultants you are going to hire. In view of this, you must research their backgrounds and verify their expertise. Get recommendations from people you trust. Then, get references and check with the references. Look into their financial standing and make sure that they will be able to back up any professional liability incurred during your project. Insist on *errors and omissions insurance*.

When Do You Need Them?

If you are developing a building, the architect and engineer will be on board as soon as you tie up the property. If you are acquiring a building, you should hire them to inspect the building during the "free look" period. In either case, they are some of the first people to work on your investment. You should do your research and selection during the time you are completing your market analysis.

> **HEADS UP**
>
> Try to get someone local, as code compliance, zoning regulations, and so forth are administered by each municipality. The consultant's specialized local knowledge and reputation will save you both time and money in the end.

How to Contract with Them

As mentioned earlier in this chapter, the average architect will want you to execute a preprinted AIA contract. I do not recommend this, but you will have to use it as a place to start. My normal practice is to amend a document by crossing out and initialing the offending language and adding an addendum to the agreement with my desired language. I have, over the years, developed a version of my own that few architects will sign. You will most likely have to use the AIA document. The areas that you will need to amend include the following:

- The scope of work. This is usually an exhibit. Plan this very carefully. Be specific about the work expected.
- Reproductions and other expenses. Include a basic list of the number of progress prints required, as well as a sufficient number of working drawing sets for permit submittal and for the general contract. Insist that the architect provide you with a sepia (reproducible drawing) of each finished drawing, so that you can order your own sets when necessary. It is considerably cheaper.
- Payment should be a flat fee. You should

> **HEADS UP**
>
> The architect's right to approve *anything* must be subject to your express, written approval—especially changes! This is especially important when dealing with the contractor. You want your architect to be responsible for compliance, with you approving any changes in material or specification.

agree in writing on any extras or changes in scope *before* the work is done. If not, do not pay for them.

- Insist on errors and omission insurance and liability insurance. This item is crucial, and it includes you, as well, if you have employees. If you deal with consultants only, make sure you have the certificates on file before they enter the site to do work. Include it in all the contracts.

HEADS UP

Any consultant who goes onto your building site or into your building *must* have the proper liability and workers' compensation insurance. If he or she does not and something happens, *you* will pay for it!

Consultants

There are a variety of other consultants that you will be encountering in real estate investment and who will require different arrangements. Some do not work with contracts, customarily attorneys and accountants. Research and feasibility consultants, site research consultants such as surveyors, environmental consultants, and soils consultants like to work from short, memo-type agreements written as loosely as possible. There are ways to work with these people that will be to your advantage when disputes arise. Make sure that the scope of the work is broadly stated, that agreements meet your requirements, and that payment is subject to the successful conclusion of the work.

Attorneys and Accountants

These people have customarily worked on an hourly rate. There are ways to change that and you need to explore these avenues.

With attorneys, you can clearly define some tasks, such as creating a lease document, a reciprocal easement agreement, or any other definitive contract. An attorney worth hiring should be familiar enough with these documents to be able to quote you a flat fee for preparing them. If not, then you need another attorney. Other chores, such as negotiating leases with anchor tenants and other agreements will, by the nature of the task, be open-ended. You can, however, control these costs as well. Do your own negotiating and use your attorney only for advice when you need clarification or when you require some specific language drafted.

Accountants do a variety of chores. If you permit an accountant to study your operation, he or she should be in a position to quote you annual fees for chores such as bookkeeping, monthly accounting reviews, and annual statements and tax preparation. Other chores can be handled with an open-ended arrangement.

HEADS UP

Whenever possible, get a fixed price from a consultant, put it in writing, and allow no extra charges unless you approve the change order in advance, in writing.

Research

Research work involving the land and the market can also cause you some sleepless nights. These consultants work on informal letter-type agreements; if they draft them, they tend to be very loose and prone to extras at a later date. Here are two rules that I always follow:

- Write the scope of work as broadly as possible and make sure that you tie the final payment to your satisfied review of the work.
- Include enough copies of the finished product (plans or reports) for your use. Add a few extra just in case; you will need

them. Make sure that you can order more copies at a fixed price, pegged in the original agreement. Insist on the computer file so that you can print your own originals.

These people are not out to get you, but they are human and they want to make a profit. If you neglect to negotiate a tight deal at the beginning, the extras will all become legitimate at a later date.

HEADS UP

You only get one chance to make a deal. Then you live with it. Do it right the first time!

MANAGERS

Managers work off contracts, and they are always "best efforts" agreements. They should contain some clauses that leave you clearly in control. At a minimum, the contract should provide for the following:

- Either party can cancel, with a mutual cancellation clause.
- The manager collects the rents and deposits them into your account.
- The manager receives the bills, approves them, and forwards them to you for payment.
- The manager never handles cash. The tenants should be required to pay by check or money order.
- Give the manager an emergency fund to be replenished when receipts are presented.
- Require detailed, monthly, written reports on rent collection, arrearages, bills and operating expenses, and any maintenance or management issues that come up.

Contractors

Since there is so much money involved in the construction process, the contracts must be drafted and administered carefully. These documents can make or break a project. In general, the industry tries to use the AIA documents, but I strongly recommend against them. My reason is, as usual, that they are drafted by architects and, therefore, put the architect strongly in the driver's seat as the owner's representative. Even if you are a novice, you do not want to abdicate your owner's prerogatives to the architect. His or her expertise is supposed to be in building design, not real estate investment. Make your own decisions, always! The architect should oversee and report to you, and you should make the decision. This is true whether you are developing a property from scratch or rebuilding tenant spaces in an existing structure. Detailed procedures for dealing with contractors and cost control are contained in Chapter 24.

GENERAL CONTRACTORS

Most people who invest in real estate use a general contractor to build anything. The general is the contractor with overall responsibility and financial accountability. He or she will give you a price and you must make him or her build it as planned for that price. There are ways to accomplish this, whether using the traditional bid method or the design-build method.

First of all, ask the general to state in the contract that he or she has reviewed the plans and specifications in detail and that he or she did not find any design deficiencies. Further, have him or her acknowledge that he or she is expert in the construction method contemplated in the plans and is competent to review the plans and construct the building according to the plans and specs. Offer the contractor the opportunity to put any deficiencies in writing before the contract is executed, stating that this is the sole opportunity to change the scope of work and alter the price. Discrepancies discovered during the course of construction will be corrected at the expense of the contractor.

Once the stage is set, the balance of the contract should contain, minimally, the following:

- Name of the owner, contractor, and engineer or architect
- The location and description of the site, also shown in detail in Exhibit A
- A list of the contract documents and a detailed scope of work, as further detailed in Exhibit B
- The project schedule, including start and end dates, referencing a detailed schedule in Exhibit C, and including incentive and penalty clauses
- The contract price, referencing a detailed cost breakdown shown in Exhibit D
- The progress payment procedures, including samples of the required paperwork required by the lender, attached as Exhibit E
- Specific time for the final payment and the conditions for payment
- Specific performance and completion bonds required, if any
- The need for temporary facilities such as power, storage, and security, the party responsible for paying for them, and the party responsible for stored materials
- Insurance requirements for both owner and contractor—and do not permit any work to start until all certificates of insurance are in your hand
- Work rules to comply with safety and drug laws, with the general contractor responsible for enforcing them and any expense resulting from delays due to shutdowns or noncompliance
- The rights of assignment and owners' and contractors' responsibilities to each other
- Payment and lien procedures. Insist that there will be no progress payment until all lien waivers for the previous payment are attached to the new invoice. Include material suppliers as well as all suppliers and subcontractors who have filed a preliminary lien notice at the start of the work.

HEADS UP

You must keep track of this or you will end up paying twice if there is a dispute.

- Decide whether you will arbitrate a dispute or settle things in court. I recommend binding arbitration: it's faster and cheaper for all concerned.
- Provide for termination of the contract for cause. You will also have to allow the contractor to terminate in the event of nonpayment of contracted work.
- Add the usual boilerplate clauses.
- Sign and date the agreement.

SUBCONTRACTORS

If you choose to use a general contractor as a construction manager, instead of as a general contractor, you will have to sign contracts with all the subcontractors ("subs") and suppliers. This is a good way to go, as it gives you more control and reduces the contractor's fees. It is a lot more paperwork, but you will find that you can learn a great deal about the construction process if you go through this exercise at least once. I prefer it to the general contract.

A thought to live with: "The job's not over 'til the paperwork's done!"

CHAPTER

20

Plans *and* Specifications

Paperwork, Paperwork, Paperwork

The reality of real estate investment and development is paperwork and more paperwork. The sad truth is that, no matter what the buildings look like, no matter what the financial state of the tenant, no matter what the background and financial capability of the owner, the value and desirability of any project will be determined by the paperwork.

Paperwork falls into two categories: one, plans and specifications, and two, contracts. Both types are legal documents. I consider governmental agreements and entitlements as contracts, because they are treated as legal documents and may, with one exception, be administered like contracts. The fact that the government can change the rules at any time and require the developer to accommodate new changes does not change the fact that the developer must keep the original agreements. Most changes by the government will be to make criteria more stringent and costly, rather than to relax the rules.

> **HEADS UP**
>
> It is imperative that the paperwork be as correct, free of conflicts, and clear and concise as possible. For this portion of the work, the KISS principle should be your operating mantra: "Keep it simple, stupid!"

All paperwork involved in a project is crucial to its success. Each document must be created with an eye for detail and enforceability. An investor/developer must look at the plans and legal documents with an eye not only to long-term enforceability, but also to cost control, schedule, and occupancy by the tenants, because each aspect of the paperwork is necessary in establishing and maintaining the value of the investment. The ongoing health and value of the investment depends on the clarity and enforceability of the leases and related ongoing contracts. The tools built into the leases will make it possible to grow the project into an ever more valuable investment as it matures.

Plans and Specifications

While the plans and specifications are considered legal documents, the graphic rather than written nature of their form has traditionally forced them to be handled separately from all the other legal documents and contracts. The plans and specifications for a project evolve in stages and each stage serves a crucial function. This section will follow a typical set of plans as they evolve into the final construction document phase.

Phase One—Schematic Design

This set of plans is the first step in defining the scope of the work, the quality thereof, and the character of the project. It is essential in establishing the financial feasibility of the project. At a minimum it should include, from the civil engineer, a boundary survey and a topographic map (topo). The architect will then use these tools to create the schematic design set of plans that will include the following:

- A preliminary grading plan
- A site plan
- An elevation
- A section
- A floor plate for each floor
- An outline specification
- A rendering

These tools will be used to establish the feasibility, obtain required governmental approvals, and entice prospective tenants to execute leases in the proposed development. These will be crucial to selling the project to all parties.

Site Plans

The preliminary grading plan and the site plan are the first two plans to be created. The preliminary grading plan takes the existing grades shown on the topo and reworks them into finished grades to establish the building pad, the required parking layout, and the landscaped areas on the site. The site plan then uses these newly established grades to locate the buildings, the parking, and show the location and extent of landscaping on the site. In addition to the above, the site plan is usually extended to show any required "off site" requirements such as street access, stop lights, and utility access.

The site plan will determine the "coverage" available on the site and establish the land cost per square foot (cost/SF) of leasable space. For example, if the site is 100,000 square feet in total size, most developers would want to build no less than 25,000 square feet of leasable space in a low-rise configuration. For most suburban low-rise developments, the land cost should end up somewhere around 20 percent or less of the total cost per leasable square foot of the project. The impact of this is that if a parcel of land costs $5 per square foot, it translates into $20 per leasable square foot of building. The impact on the cost side of the equation is obvious.

FIGURE 20-1. SITE PLAN

Elevations

The building's elevation plan will show preliminary details about the look of the project, the number of floors, the roofline, the window heights, and the detail of the finish work and will establish the character of the building. This establishes the architectural portion of the plans. The interior of the building is primarily engineering, while the outside provides the only statement that the building will make to the public passing by and to the prospective tenants. For a tenant to relocate to a new building, he or she must feel that the building will enhance the image of the company and provide a good address and suitable quarters for its staff. The exterior of the building sets the image, the interior provides the livability, and the finish establishes the quality. In addition, the elevations will enable the governmental agencies that have jurisdiction over the project to determine the compatibility of the project with the surrounding area.

From the site plan and the elevation, an artist can produce a *rendering* of the building depicting the artist's view of the future project. The intent of this is to show the public how the building will look from the outside when completed.

FIGURE 20-2. ELEVATION

SECTIONS

The *section* will depict a slice through the building, exposing the proposed structural system, the access (stairs and elevators), the utility accesses, the floor elevations, and preliminary details for exterior finish work. In addition it will show how the entry floor relates to new elevations of the site. The relationship of the building's floor elevations and windows to the site will establish views and potential view corridors for the tenant spaces within. This particular plan will be a combination of three inputs: the architect for aesthetics, the engineer for structural design, and the contractor for cost analysis. The developer will be the final judge of what is planned.

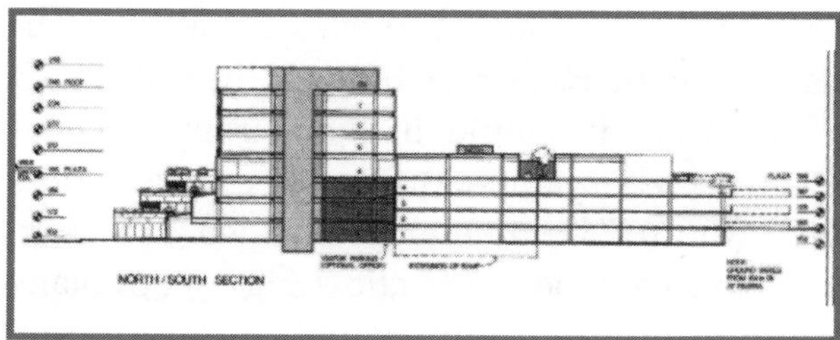

FIGURE 20-3. SECTION

The number of floors will influence the building materials as well as the choice of structural framing method, which in turn will determine the space required above the finished ceilings for utility access. The combination of finished ceiling height, utility requirements, and the dimension required to accommodate the proposed structural system will determine the building's overall height. Most communities have height restrictions in their zoning categories and each structure must be tailored to meet those requirements. The number of floors will directly impact the coverage achieved, which in turn reflects on the land cost per leasable square foot of building.

Floor Plates

A floor plate (Figures 20-4 A and B) is intended to show everything on a particular floor—tenant space, common areas, stairs, elevators, and mechanical rooms, etc. Floor plans, shown in Figure 20-5, are components of the floor plate dedicated to a specific tenant.

Floor Plans

The floor plan depicts the floor space (the leasable space) on each floor of the building.

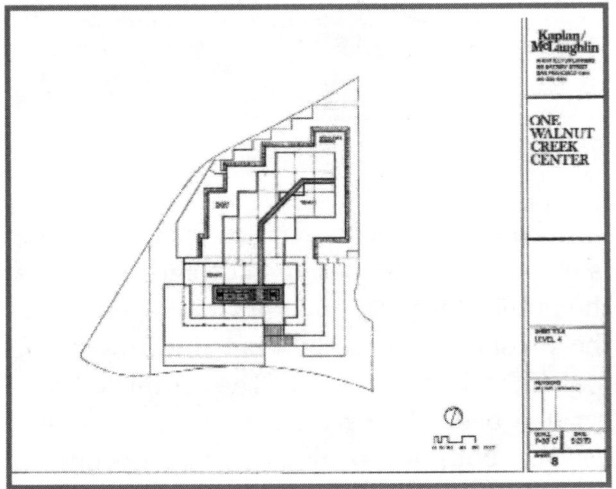

FIGURE 20-4A. FLOOR PLATES

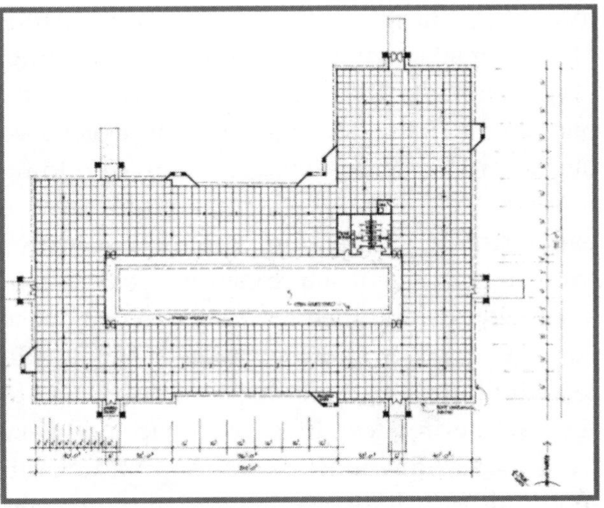

FIGURE 20-4B. FLOOR PLATES

This plan is sometimes referred to as the *floor plate* or *leasing plan* of the building.

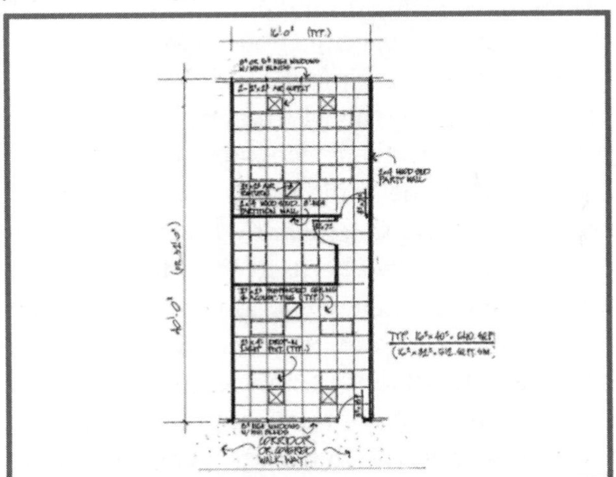

FIGURE 20-5. FLOOR PLAN

Different floor plates work for different types of tenants. Small tenants require shallow depths for their tenant space and large tenants require larger depths for their floor plans. The key to establishing the character and the feasibility of any project is to correctly identify the target market for the tenant space. Most commercial projects—regardless of whether they are industrial, office, retail, or residential—are multitenant facilities. Therefore, assume multiple tenant spaces when designing the building, even if, initially, the space is to be occupied by one tenant. Tenants can go bankrupt or move out when the lease expires and the building must be released. Multitenant buildings are better risks and, therefore, more conservative from an investment standpoint than single-tenant buildings. In office buildings, tenant space varies in depth from 32 feet to over 100 feet. In retail buildings, the space varies from 50 feet to several hundred feet. Industrial space will vary from 25 feet for mini-warehouse buildings to hundreds of feet for manufacturing plants and public warehouse buildings.

Outline Specifications

When the building design has been established, the preliminary specifications (specs) are written to establish the quality and detail expected of the building. This document is the key to establishing, early in the life of the project, exactly what the project will cost when constructed. This spec, together with the other preliminary plans, can be used to bid the project. Any competent general contractor (GC), given these documents, can, together with competent subcontractors (subs), establish a fair price for building the proposed project.

It is for this reason that the general contractor should be brought into the design team at the earliest possible time. This process is called *value engineering* and, without exception, results in more and better building for the money spent. No amount of retrofitting can make up for the lack of this process.

Outline specifications cover the gamut of topics from soil compaction to any and all components of the building. Often, rather than specify a make or model of component, a performance specification is proposed, so that competent subcontractors can propose proprietary packages such as air handling or other mechanical systems. In this event this type of bid becomes a bid as well as a design/build proposal. The onus then falls upon the architect and the engineers to evaluate the proposals to ensure that they fall within the design criteria specified.

Renderings

The rendering is the most important piece of advertising and promotional material that will ever be created to represent the proposed project. It should fairly represent the developer's vision of the project as well as faithfully represent the preliminary plans and specifications. Overdoing the rendering is a common failing of developers and planners alike. Sometimes the rendering will depict what developers want rather than what they can afford to build.

FIGURE 20-6. THE RENDERING

The problem with overdoing the rendering is obvious. The rendering is designed to show the public, the local governmental agency, and the prospective tenants what the project will look like when completed. The completed project had better be very close to the rendering, because both approvals and lease documents are going to be based upon the representations made in the plans and specs. Variations are permitted, but a complete redesign necessitates a fresh start with both the governmental body and the tenants. They will hold the developer to the approved plans.

Sometimes a more dramatic tool is needed. When necessary, developers have turned to a three-dimensional rendering known as a *model*. Models are very expensive, so developers used them as sparingly as possible. The most common use seems to be during the entitlement process for large or more far-reaching projects such as urban high-rise buildings or large master-planned community developments. Some expensive housing communities require models of homes to be built for their architectural committee approval process.

Phase Two—Working Drawings and Construction Documents

The working drawings, also known as the final plans and specifications, are produced to serve multiple functions. Primarily, they define the exact nature, size, shape, and texture of the building to be constructed. The building department must examine and approve these documents (plans) before issuing a building permit. The approved plans will serve as a basis for the issuance of the building permit and a guideline for the inspection and certification of the structure and civil engineering work to be performed. Strict adherence to the approved plans is necessary for the building department to allow occupancy of the completed project. If the project is completed in accordance with the approved plans, an occupancy permit is issued and the tenant may occupy the premises.

Plans and specs cover many areas; they can be simple, uncomplicated plans that contain all the data on several sheets or they can run into hundreds of sheets of plans and volumes of specifications. In general, the necessary information must contain details for the site work, civil engineering, grading and paving, utility supply and distribution, and detailed landscaping and irrigation plan.

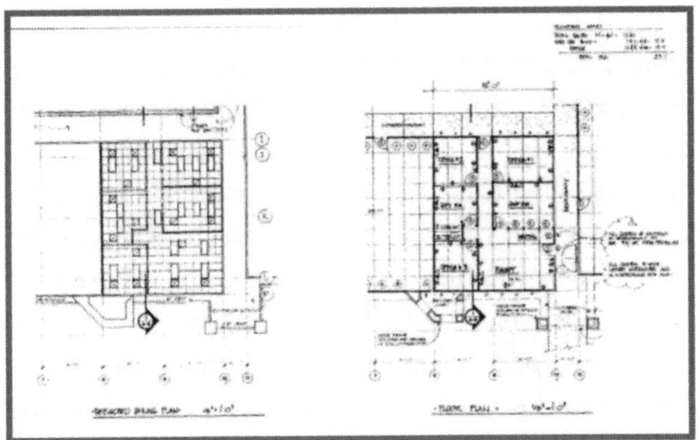

FIGURE 20-7. TENANT IMPROVEMENT PLANS

For the structures the minimum divisions of both plans and specifications must include the following:

- Foundation and soil preparation
- Structural design and details
- Floor plans for each floor
- Cross sections and connection details
- Finish schedules
- Detailed mechanical, electrical, and plumbing plans
- Any specialty trade details, such as elevators or escalators, etc.

The total cost of these documents, from preliminary plans through the completion of the working drawings, can vary from five to ten percent of the total cost of construction.

TENANT SPACE PLANS

Separate from the building plans and specs, but under the same umbrella of review, approval, and inspection, are the individual *tenant space plans*. These documents are created when the floor plate or leasing plan is subdivided into smaller spaces and allocated to specific tenants.

Each tenant's "demised premises," or leased space, as defined in the executed lease, requires a separate and complete set of building plans and approval thereof. Each must be built according to the approved plans before an individual occupancy permit for the tenant can be issued. Timing here is crucial and the creation of these plans is sometimes referred to a specialist called a *space planner*. In practice, the finish details and specs for these tenant spaces use the building standard finishes and the finish schedules on these plans refer to the building's master set already approved. Floor plans for walls, utility distribution, lighting, and special items such as built-in amenities and custom finish schedules vary widely from tenant to tenant.

The Critical Path Schedule

The development plan or business plan for the project is most often embodied in two important documents: the *project schedule* and the *pro forma financial plan*. The project schedule is a critical document. As everyone knows, "Time is money." The modern schedule is called a *critical path schedule* and is constructed of absolutes. It delineates a hierarchy of events that build one upon another. Each scheduled event cannot go forward until the critical item designed to precede it is completed. For example, the foundations cannot be poured until the rough grading is completed and the structure cannot be erected or framed until the foundations are completed. Thus, the schedule, from concept through final occupancy, becomes one completely integrated critical path. Deviation from this will spell disaster: the failure of any one component can bring a halt to the entire process. Part of a typical simple critical path schedule is shown in Table 20-1 in bar chart format.

Financial Plans—"The Numbers"

Over the last 25 years, I have had the best results with documents designed to serve the

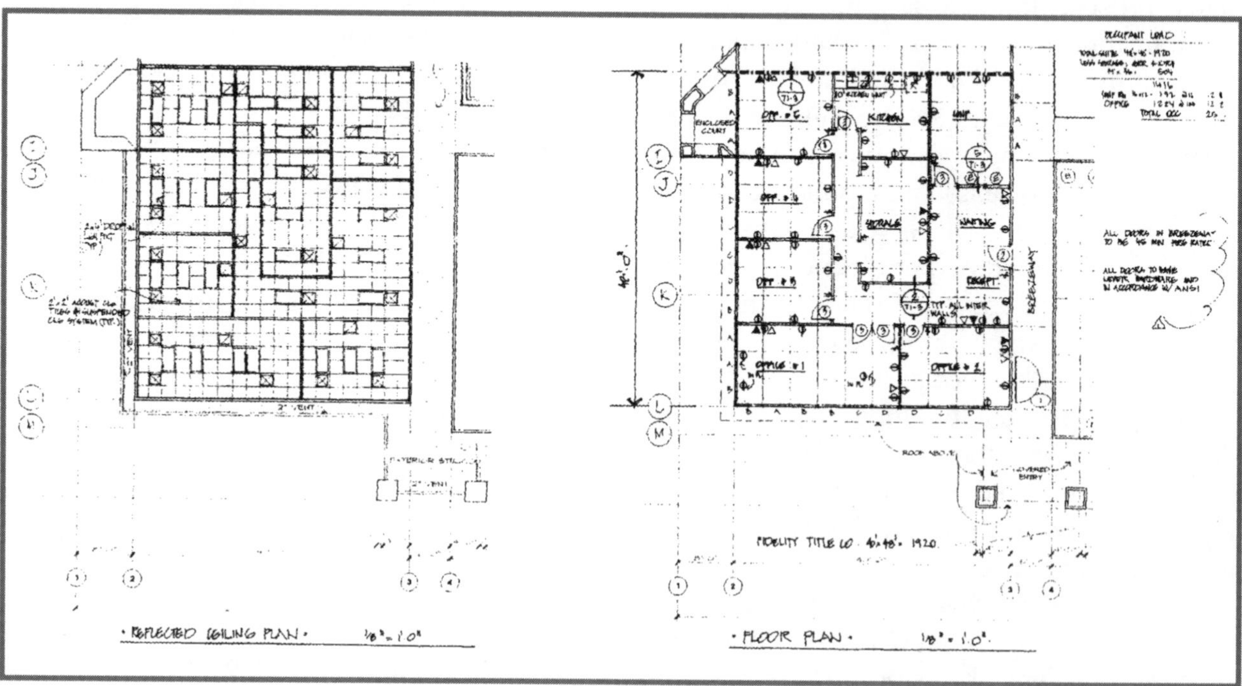

FIGURE 20-8. TENANT SPACE PLANS

Shell Week #	1	2	03/17 3	03/24 4	03/31 5	04/07 6	04/14 7	04/21 8	04/28 9	05/05 10	05/12 11	05/19 12	05/26 13	06/02 14	06/09 15	CO Issued 06/16 16	06/23 17	06/30 18	07/07 19	07/14 20	07/21 21	07/28 22	08/04 23
Footers			Done																				
UG inside (sewer & water)			Done																				
UG outside (sewer & water)			Done																				
Form & pour slabs						Done																	
Irrigation mains						Done																	
Set steel columns						Done																	
Set beams																							
Paving			Rough	Done																			
Set trusses									On skd														
Deck roof									On skd														
Soffits & trim									On skd														
Carts & slabs onsite									Slabs done														
Tile roof									Deliver		Load		Lay tile										
Pour column bases																							
Roofing																							
Set AC units									Early														
Glass wall										Start of tenant partitions													
Interior partitions																							
Rough electric										Done													
Rough plumbing									Early														
Rough mechanical																							
Phones																							
Stucco																							
Insulate																							
Drywall & texture																							
Pour sidewalks																							
Paint																							
Electric trim																							
Plumbing trim																							
Bath accessories																							
Hang doors																							
Punch list																							
Landscape											Early												
Final cleanup																							

Shell Week #	1	2	03/17 3	03/24 4	03/31 5	04/07 6	04/14 7	04/21 8	04/28 9	05/05 10	05/12 11	05/19 12	05/26 13	06/02 14	06/09 15	06/16 16	06/23 17	06/30 18	07/07 19	07/14 20	07/21 21	07/28 22	08/04 23
Priority							**Start**																
Tenant #1	3										**Set**												
Tenant #2	1								**Demise**					**Committed to Tenant**									
Tenant #3	2								**Walls**						**Committed to Tenant**								
Tenant #4	4							**S,W,N**				**Committed to Tenant**											
Tenant #5	6																						
Tenant #4	5																						

TABLE 20-1. CRITICAL PATH SCHEDULE

design/build-bid scenario, rather than the traditional fixed-bid process. One of the most prevalent problems in the development industry is maintaining a fixed budget. Operating for the last 25 years in a traditional joint venture format with all the capital paid in up front has forced me to ensure that all projects stay within budget. To date, this method of operation has not failed me. We will deal with the numbers, accounting, and management contracts in Chapter 21 and with contractors and cost control in Chapter 24.

CHAPTER

21

Numbers, Accounting, *and* Management Tools

As in any other endeavor, you are going to need tools to work with. In the real estate business, it is primarily information and its instant availability that will save your bacon. For this reason, I have separated the basic tools into three categories: plans and specs, contracts, and numbers. This chapter deals with numbers: how to create them, what you need, and how to use them. It also offers further and somewhat redundant comments on management-oriented contracts and ongoing leasing agreements.

The Logic of Accounting

Components

Since real estate investment is a money-oriented endeavor, you need to keep score. That is done in two ways: with traditional accounting (bookkeeping) and spreadsheets. Accounting systems are standardized the world over; everyone connected with business knows what a profit and loss statement and a balance sheet are and what they can tell you. The limitations of traditional accounting are that those reports contain so little information needed to actually manage a piece of investment real estate. It is for this reason that developers, investors, and property managers have created spreadsheets to augment the financial picture and manage the properties. The combination of the two systems creates a complete picture of the investment from a financial point of view.

TRADITIONAL ACCOUNTING

These systems are all based on the double-entry bookkeeping system. They are available from a variety of sources and are completely computerized and very user-friendly.

The double-entry system is simple. It is based on the fact that each component or transaction has two parts to it. The breakdown is *debits* and *credits*: debits are income and credits are payments. Each transaction has two components; e.g., rent received from a tenant is both cash in the bank (a debit) and rent (a credit). In this way, when the transaction is entered in tandem, the books are considered *balanced*.

This form of accounting is handy when summarizing all transactions into a snapshot in time. It allows also for instant comparisons with periods past and potential periods in the future. This system reliably results in reports like the balance sheet, the profit and loss statement, and year-to-date income and expense figures. Programs like QuickBooks Pro can also export data in spreadsheet form. From a management perspective, generalized and lumped-together numbers do not provide enough information to base management decisions on. For this we turn to spreadsheets.

SPREADSHEETS—DEAL TOOLS

These tools are what make the difference to a deal. They can provide information like the following:

- What suite is JP Butler, Inc. in, what are the address, phone number, fax number, e-mail address, square footage, move-in date, and lease expiration date, and when are the rent bumps scheduled?
- How do I calculate rent invoices for the month?
- Who paid rent this month, last month, last year?
- What was our income this time last year or what will our income be this time next year or in five years?
- How much can we bump rents and still stay within the market?
- Are our expenses on a per-square-foot basis competitive with the market?
- What maintenance contracts do we have and when do we need to renew them? Are they competitive?
- When is the next lease expiration going to occur? Whose space is it (suite number) and how much space will be available?

Generating These Numbers

This is one of your most important tasks and I believe that you need to set up these management tools yourself. That way, you'll know they're accurate and contain the information you and the manager need to make decisions. These spreadsheet tools will form the basis for all your management documents. There are two scenarios for developing these spreadsheets: one, when you buy the property, and two, when you build.

WHEN YOU BUY

These documents are created at the time you put the property into escrow. Up to now, all you have had was a rent and expense summary and some sketchy detail on some of the tenants. You now need to know it all and then put it to work.

We will construct the documents and then show you how they can evolve into meaningful tools.

First of all, you want to profile the leases and then insert them into some form of meaningful projection. You will create the following documents and cross-reference them:

1. The tenant summary
2. The detailed income and expense report (level 1)
3. The detailed projected income and expense report (level 2)
4. The expense breakdown, prorated by square footage and allocated tenant by tenant
5. A management agreement and maintenance spreadsheet, cross-referenced to number three above
6. Ten-year summary income and expense projections showing lease expirations with six-month lead-ins
7. An idealized five- and ten-year projected income and expense summary, showing your proposed income goals for the project

Starting with the basics, let's look at what we need to start with. Taking the existing tenant leases one by one, we start a list as shown in Table 21-1.

You get the idea: list all the tenants in the first column and sort them in any way you like. I prefer to sort them by building and suite number so that I can see any building's group of tenants at a glance, but some people like to sort them by last name or suite number. Whatever works for you! Once you have them listed, then, in the cells to the right of each tenant, you want at least the following information:

- Address
- Phone number
- Cell phone number
- Fax number
- E-mail address
- Web site (if applicable)
- Contact person in the case of a company tenant
- Billing address or corporate headquarter address, which should be the same as used for notices in the lease
- Suite number
- Square feet occupied
- Type of lease: gross, modified, or NNN
- Lease start date
- Initial rent and how calculated
- Percentage CAM charges, if applicable
- Expense stops, if any
- Per-square-foot rents
- Lease expiration date
- Optional renewal dates
- Rent bump dates
- Notice dates
- Type of notice required
- Any personal observations or notes that you need to remember

Graphically, these look like the column heads in Table 21-2.

Tenant	Last Name or Company Name	First Name of Contact		
Tenant #1				
Tenant #2				
Tenant #3				

TABLE 21-1. BEGINNING TENANT SPREADSHEET

Tenant	Last Name	First Name	Address	Phone	Cell	Fax	E-Mail	Etc.

TABLE 21-2. EXPANDED TENANT SPREADSHEET

From this, you can hide the columns and insert the rents and months. Excel and Lotus 123 both allow you to hide columns and rows not needed at all times. You can hide all of the above information you do not need on a day-to-day basis or simply link to another spreadsheet with only the tenant information you need every day. This is the financial spreadsheet. You will need, at the very least, the following information:

- Tenant name
- Suite number
- Suite size
- Basic rents
- CAM charges
- Taxes
- Total rent invoiced
- Total rent collected
- Month
- Quarter
- Year to date

The spreadsheet should look something like that shown in Table 21-3.

The row labeled "CAM charges" is imported from the detailed monthly expense breakdown sheet that looks something like that shown in Table 21-4. The expenses are listed against an annual budget with quarterly recaps, then allocated to the tenants on a pro-rata per-square-foot basis.

HEADS UP

Be sure to include all of your vacant space in your spreadsheet so that you have accounted for all of your square footage. You can fill in the tenant information as the vacancies are leased.

Alternatively, you can have a separate spreadsheet for rent invoiced and collected and link the summary to your master income and expense sheet. A basic rent calculation sheet

Item	Month 1	Month 2	Month 3	1st Quarter	Totals, etc.
Tenant name					
Suite number					
Suite size					
Basic rents					
CAM charges					
Taxes					
Total rent invoiced					

TABLE 21-3. INCOME AND EXPENSE DETAIL SHEET

Expenses	Monthly	January
Actual paid to date	Budget	$1,998.00
Real estate taxes	$2,000.00	$0
Maintenance/repair/HVAC	$150.00	$0
Insurance: fire/liability	$551.58	$3,120.00
Electricity	$300.00	$403.70
Water and sewer	$200.00	$0
Refuse	$51.00	$51.00
Janitorial	$1,300.00	$1,329.55
Window washing/parking lot sweeping	$200.00	$210.00
Security	$360.00	$0
Pest control on demand	$75.00	$0
Yard maintenance and common area	$200.00	$200.00
Subtotal	**$5,387.58**	**$ 5,314.25**
Management Fee	$538.76	$531.43
Total Common Area	**$5,926.34**	**$ 5,845.68**
Average Month/SF	**$0.36**	**$0.35**
Tenant Pro-Rata Shares	**% CAM**	**1st Quarter**
Tenant #1	8%	$461.81
Tenant #2	16%	$931.22
Tenant #3	12%	$720.19
Tenant #4	4%	$224.83
Etc.	24%	$1,402.96
Vacant	36%	$2,104.44
Totals	**100%**	**$5,845.45**

TABLE 21-4. MONTHLY EXPENSE BREAKDOWN

would look something like Table 21-5.

To link your numbers, you start with a workbook and put separate breakdowns on different sheets. Then, on the sheet you want to import the figure to, go to the correct cell and input "=" followed by the sheet and cell number. The shortcut is to go to that specific sheet and cell number after you input "="and put the cursor on that cell and hit "enter." Whenever that cell is updated, the updated data will transfer to the summary sheet.

As You Build

This same data is generated in a development deal, but in reverse order. You start with the simple one-page income and expense sheet and then flesh it out tenant by tenant. It will start with a simple one-page, quick-and-dirty income and expense sheet, like the one in Table 21-6, and progress to a more detailed effort, such as shown in Table 21-7.

Finally, in the third generation (Table 21-8), we can start inputting the tenant information as the building is leased out.

As the tenants are added, as shown in bold and italics in Table 21-8, the detailed information needed is compiled in a subledger, as shown in Table 21-2. From this you can go on to the necessary five- and ten-year income and expense projections like the one shown in Table 21-9.

By studying Table 21-9, you will see that this is an income projection for a development project with several assumptions shown in the Notes column. The income and expenses are escalated at five percent per year.

	From Tenant Sheet		From Expense Sheet			Month	
Tenant	**SF**	**Rent**	**% Occupancy**	**Expenses**	**Total Invoice**	**Invoiced**	**Collected**
Tenant #1	800	$800	8%	$461.81	$1,261.81	$1,261.81	$1,261.81
Tenant #2	1600	$1,600	16%	$931.22	$2,531.22	$2,531.22	$2,531.22
Tenant #3	1200	$1,200	12%	$720.19	$1920.19	$1920.19	$1920.19
Tenant #4	400	$400	4%	$224.83	$624.83	$624.83	
Etc.	2400	$2,400	24%	$1,402.96	$3,802.96	$3,802.96	$3,802.96
Vacant	3600		36%				
Totals	10000	$6,400	100%	$3,741.01	$10,141.01	$10,141.01	$9,516.18

TABLE 21-5. RENT AND INVOICING COLLECTION

Income	**Annual**
Rents	$225,400
Less 5% vacancy allowance	–$11,270
Gross potential income (GPI)	$214,130
Expenses	
At $4.75/SF x 16000 SF	$76,000
Less recapture from tenants	–$72,200
Net expenses	$3,800
NIBDS	**$210,330**
Value at 9% cap rate	**$2,337,000**

TABLE 21-6. ONE-PAGE INCOME AND EXPENSE ESTIMATE

This is acceptable when projecting a proposed cash flow. When you are dealing with actual leases, you will have to break down each year by month to show when the individual leases expire or escalate. This way your projection will accurately reflect the executed leases. The year-end totals are then transferred to a master sheet for five- and ten-year projections.

Purpose-Driven Tools

In looking at the list of questions in "Spreadsheets—Deal Tools" above, I'm sure you can see why this type of information is valuable to a building owner/manager. Imagine having to look in all the leases for the answers each time you have a question. Imagine having to go through the accounting reports to ferret out the data. These types of questions come up routinely, every day in the management business. You will need some or all of this data on a day-to-day basis. Believe me: I know from experience.

Management Tools

Additional management tools required are management contracts, maintenance agreements, and an ongoing leasing agreement. When you are dealing with a management situation, what are the tools of your trade? They are documents and accounting reports. Everything else is tenant relations. The management documents are tools. If they are properly designed and if you have the right tool for

Income	Current Year
Gross potential income [GPI]	$490,000
Vacancy allowance at 5%	–$24,500
Effective gross income [EGI]	$465,500
CAM Expenses	
Real estate taxes	$48,000
Maintenance/repair/HVAC	$3,600
Insurance: fire/liability	$14,400
Electricity	$7,200
Water and sewer	$4,800
Refuse	$1,200
Janitorial	$31,200
Windows/sweeping	$4,800
Security	$8,640
Pest control on demand	$1,800
Yard maintenance and common area	$4,800
Subtotal	**$130,440**
Management fee at 10% exp	$13,044
Total Common Area	**$143,484**
Tenant-reimbursed CAM	$136,310
Landlord's expense	–$7,174
Net Income Before Debt Service [NIBDS]	**$458,326**

TABLE 21-7. SECOND-GENERATION PRO FORMA INCOME AND EXPENSE TABLE

the job, then the battle is half over. Like any other profession, the tools are only just that—tools. You must provide the expertise and skill to be successful. We will cover the accounting tools later on in this book.

The documents start with the property management contract and the tenant leases. To that, as a base, you add contracts with various suppliers and contractors, such as utility companies, janitorial firms, maintenance companies, and other companies that will help you take care of your investment. The following is a list of services that you will need for most properties, with a few exceptions:

- Insurance
- Property management
- Leasing
- Janitorial
- Landscape maintenance
- Parking lot sweeping and snow removal
- General building maintenance
- Electric, gas, telephone, and water service
- HVAC maintenance and repair
- Window washing
- Security
- Legal and accounting

The Management Contract

The property management contract philosophy was covered in Chapter 19, but we need to address the details of the contract. If you are going to manage your own property, you will have no need of this agreement, but if you hire a manager or have partners in the investment, you will need this agreement. If you have partners and you are going to be the one who manages the property, you will especially need an agreement. The following is a list of items most often covered in a basic management agreement.

> **DEFINITION**
>
> A ***manager*** is the owner's agent with a clear, legal relationship that can bind the owner and a legal and enforceable fiduciary obligation to the owner.

TOPICS TO INCLUDE

1. The duties of the manager/agent:

Income	**Rents**	**Current Year**
Gross potential income [GPI]		$490,000
Tenant #1	***$15,255***	
Tenant #2	***$27,142***	
Tenant #3	***$16,555***	
Vacant space	***$27,850 SF***	***$0***
Total current rents		***$58,952***
Etc.		
Vacancy allowance at 5%		–$24,500
Effective gross income [EGI]		$465,500
CAM Expenses		
Real estate taxes		$48,000
Maintenance/repair/HVAC		$3,600
Insurance: fire/liability		$14,400
Electricity		$7,200
Water and sewer		$4,800
Refuse		$1,200
Janitorial		$31,200
Windows/sweeping		$4,800
Security		$8,640
Pest control on demand		$1,800
Yard maintenance and common area		$4,800
Subtotal		**$130,440**
Management fee at 10% exp		$13,044
Total Common Area		**$143,484**
Tenant-reimbursed CAM		$136,310
Landlord's expense		–$7,174
Net Income Before Debt Service [NIBDS]		**$458,326**

TABLE 21-8. EVOLVING RENTAL DETAIL SHEET (PRO FORMA INCOME AND EXPENSE BREAKDOWN OF NET LEASES)

- Collection of the rent, covering invoicing and the physical handling of the receipts, where and when they are to be deposited
- How to handle delinquency, notices, etc.
- Expenses: how they are incurred, how and when they are approved, and how they are to be paid
- Personnel, if any: the responsibilities and the authority to act and restrictions on responsibilities and authority
- Repairs and maintenance, casual and long-term arrangements
- Service contracts: who will negotiate and execute them and how they will be administered
- Supplies: who purchases, inventories and replacements, where they are stored, and who has access to them
- Taxes and insurance: who is responsible for what and how much insurance each party carries, coinsurance and additional insured(s)
- Leasing: who is responsible and who negotiates for the property owner
- Advertising: how much, how often, and how expensed

		Operating Period				
Income	**Notes**	**Year 1**	**Year 2**	**Year 3**	**Year 4**	**Year 5**
Gross potential income [GPI]	At 100% Occupancy @ $14 /sf	$224,000.00	$235,200.00	$246,960.00	$259,308.00	$272,273.40
Vacancy allowance at 5%	Per lender's allowance	–$11,200.00	–$11,760.00	–$12,348.00	–$12,965.40	–$13,613.67
Effective gross income [EGI]	Projected EGI	$212,800.00	$223,440.00	$234,612.00	$246,342.00	$258,659.73
CAM Expenses	All leases are NNN					
Real estate taxes	Projected until first assessment	$24,000.00	$25,200.00	$26,460.00	$27,783.00	$29,172.15
Maintenance/repair/HVAC	Budgeted	$1,800.00	$1,890.00	$1,984.50	$2,083.73	$2,187.91
Insurance: fire/liability	Bid	$6,612.00	$6,942.60	$7,289.73	$7654.22	$8,036.93
Electricity	Estimated	$3,600.00	$3,780.00	$3,969.00	$4,167.45	$4,375.82
Water and sewer	Estimated	$2,400.00	$2,520.00	$2,646.00	$2,778.30	$2,917.22
Refuse	Bid	$600.00	$630.00	$661.50	$694.58	$729.30
Janitorial	Bid	$15,600.00	$16,380.00	$17,199.00	$18,058.95	$18,961.90
Windows/sweeping	Bid	$2,400.00	$2,520.00	$2,646.00	$2,778.30	$2,917.22
Security	Bid	$4,320.00	$4,536.00	$4,762.80	$5,000.94	$5,250.99
Pest control on demand	Estimated	$900.00	$945.00	$992.25	$1,041.86	$1,093.96
Yard and common area maintenance	Bid	$2,400.00	$2,520.00	$2,646.00	$2,778.30	$2,917.22
Subtotal		**$64,632.00**	**$67,863.60**	**$71,256.78**	**$74,819.62**	**$78,560.60**
Management fee at 10% exp of CAM	Based upon actual expenses only	$6,463.20	$6,786.36	$7,125.68	$7,481.96	$7,856.06
Total Common Area		**$71,095.20**	**$74,649.96**	**$78,382.46**	**$82,301.50**	**$86,416.66**
Tenant-reimbursed CAM	Based on 95% occupancy	$67,540.44	$70,917.46	$74,463.34	$78,186.50	$82,095.83
Net landlord's expense	For vacant space	–$3,554.76	–$3,732.50	–$3,919.12	–$4,115.08	–$4,320.83
Net Income Before Debt Service [NIBDS]	Before debt service	**$209,245.24**	**$219,707.50**	**$230,692.88**	**$242,227.52**	**$254,338.90**
Less mortgage	Based on estimated loan					
	$1.3M @ 8%/30 yrs	–$103,311.00	–$103,311.00	–$103,311.00	–$103,311.00	–$103,311.00
Cash flow	Return on investor's equity	**$105,934.24**	**$116,396.50**	**$127,381.88**	**$138,916.52**	**$151,027.90**

TABLE 21-9. FIVE-YEAR INCOME AND EXPENSE PROJECTION (LEASABLE SPACE 16,000 SF WITH ANNUAL RENT ESCALATION OF 5%)

- Loan payments: who is responsible and how it is accounted for
- Monthly reports: what is to be covered
- Books and records: all accounting, who does what
- Other duties
- Mutual "hold harmless"

2. The owner's duties to the manager/agent
   - Compliance with laws

- Mutual "hold harmless"
- Furnish documents to agent so that the agent may correctly represent the owner
- Expenses incurred
- Good faith acts
- Insurance: who carries what, coinsurance and additional insured(s)
- Release of agent: to release the agent from the effects of his or her responsible acts in pursuit of his or her legal duties
- Signage: what is allowed, who approves, and how to administer the sign program
- Compensation of the manager: how much and how paid
- Miscellaneous provisions:
  - Severability of clauses
  - Hazardous substances indemnity, by both parties
  - Entire agreement
  - Successors bound in the event of an assignment
  - Independent contractor, to clearly establish that the manager is not an employee of the owner
  - Creditor or claims
  - Legal proceedings, arbitration vs. the courts in the event of a dispute
  - Equal employment compliance
  - Notices

3. The signature and date block
4. Exhibits
   - The property legal description
   - Miscellaneous charges
   - Leasing commissions and renewals, if applicable

WORKING WITH A PROPERTY MANAGER

Again, if you are managing your own property, you will not need this agreement, but you will need to know the correct procedures to follow as a routine. If you have partners, then you will be the manager (agent) in the contract, and if you hire someone else, then you will need to understand how it works and why.

The property manager plays an important role in building management. He or she is the face of management and speaks for the owners. Managers handle money, lots of it, and they have a legally enforceable fiduciary obligation to both owner and tenant. Managers are held accountable monthly and annually. They prepare budgets and rental projections. Often, they are the ones who negotiate with new and old tenants when leases are executed and renewed. It is crucial that this management function in your investment be handled properly. I highly recommend that you manage your first building.

There are two duties that I believe should always be performed by an owner: handling the money and negotiating the leases. These two items directly affect the investment and its long-term health. There are several reasons for this. First, you need to know how it is done so that you can properly manage the work of others at a later date when your portfolio becomes too large for you to handle alone. Second, you need an appreciation for the hands-on day-to-day problems of a good property manager. This will help you differentiate between chores you will reserve for yourself alone and those you will delegate to the manager.

Contracts with Subcontractors

The contracts with subcontractors, such as janitorial, can be handled in two ways. You can allow the manager to treat them as subcontractors or you can contract directly with them, while having the manager administer the agreements. I recommend that you contract for these services directly, with the manager's help and oversight. These contracts will have to be year-to-year and mutually severable with short notice. It is important that you be able to get rid of a contractor who is not performing adequately. Generally, one written warning is sufficient. When you have to warn a subcontractor about inadequate performance, you should start looking for a replacement immediately and then have the new company standing by.

These agreements should include, at the very least, the following, as briefly and as specifically as possible:

- The parties to the contract
- The scope of the work, adding an exhibit if it is lengthy or complicated
- The compensation and method of payment
- Notice provisions and severance arrangements, keys, etc.
- Liability and workers' compensation insurance—*absolutely mandatory before the subcontractor sets foot in the building*!
- Hours of operation and nondisturbance of the tenants
- Miscellaneous clauses
- Signature and date
- Exhibits, if any

Utility and Service Contracts

Without these agreements, you will not have any utilities or services for your building. In many cases, especially if you purchase a building, you might be totally unaware of these agreements that the original developer made with the utility companies. They cover the service to be provided, the date it is to be available, access to the building during and after hours, and any physical easements required to bring the utilities to the building. There will also be deposits required, initially. When you purchase the building, you should arrange in the purchase agreement for copies of all the agreements and the deposit schedule. The seller will also want to retrieve his or her deposits at the time of closing. Check these agreements for any obligations you might have to assume at the time of purchase.

Do You Need Them and, if So, When?

These agreements are almost moot if you are purchasing a building, because most of the arrangements will have already been made, such as the construction of the physical improvements, etc. There may be, however, residual, hidden expenses that you might have to assume. Most utilities are responsible for maintaining service up to the building meter. The owner is responsible for maintaining the service from the meter to the tenant. This might sound straightforward, but you should know where the meter is located and what any potential problems might be. If you are adding to a building, is the utility obligated to expand your service or will you have to pay for the increase on the utility's side of the meter? These questions are not necessarily handled in a standard manner and there may be exceptions. You must always check the location of the utility easements as well as any other easements that show up in the ALTA or as-built survey, because they might limit your ability to modify or expand your property in the future.

If you are the original developer, these utility agreements are among the first items that you need to address when designing your project. You will need to involve the utility companies in the design process and to have them committed to the construction of their work well in advance of your needing the service. You will need to draw up the agreements and the easements and execute and record them. The utility companies need lead time to schedule the work, as they have many demands on their time. Plan ahead and give them what they need when they need it. You will have little or no leverage over the utility companies, so you must have both your architect and your engineer on top of things if you want them to come out on time. If you do not start on this early, you might find yourself with a building full of tenants and no water, power, phones, or other utilities and services.

Enforcement

When it comes to enforcing the utility agreements, you have little leverage. The best approach is to give them what they want on time. If this does not get the job done, you will have to resort to some behind-the-scenes arm-twisting. All utility companies, with a few exceptions, are monopolies, regulated by the public utility commission. You can approach the commission for help; sometimes a word to the wise will help. Often, however, the situation is difficult. In areas of rapid growth and low unemployment, utility companies are stretched very thin. Their physical and personnel resources are struggling to keep up with the growth and maintain service to their current customers. There is only so much they can do. Throw in a bad storm or a natural disaster like an earthquake and schedules can unravel instantly.

HEADS UP

Give them what they want, when they want it, or you may live to regret it!

Your best bet is to be proactive. Start early, plan well, and leave yourself a generous margin of time for their work to be completed. Pay your fees early and allow them to get a jump on the schedule. You will find them very cooperative when you take this approach.

The Leasing Agreement

We've been over an exclusive leasing agreement in detail. However, you will have to decide who does the leasing—the property manager or an independent broker. When a property is under development, you need to have a broker to handle the leasing, but once the process is complete, you will have a choice. If the broker continues on, finding the occasional tenant when required, it allows the owner to maintain contact with the market as well as an outside source of talent. One distinct advantage is that if you maintain contact and a contract with the original leasing broker, he or she will be legally precluded from pirating your tenants for some new building project. Remember: the original broker has all of the information regarding your initial tenants. Once the relationship is severed, unless you have a specific agreement to the contrary, there is nothing to stop that broker from contacting your tenants around renewal time. An ethical broker will not do this, as word gets around and his or her reputation cannot long survive the breach of trust. A broker can, however, do considerable damage in a short time.

As Part of the Management Contract

An alternate to this arrangement is to have the property management company do the leasing. This opens up the question of paying for lease renewals. Most owners take the position that tenants will renew their leases if they are satisfied that they are getting good service in the building. Managers are paid to provide good service and should not necessarily be rewarded when tenants decide to stay on. In practical terms, I believe that the manager needs incentive to perform above average. It is the "going the extra mile" that impresses tenants. If your manager does not do that, he or she may still be doing a good job. There is no practical way to contract with someone for going the extra mile. The possibility of being rewarded when tenants choose to stay in the building is a great incentive. You do not have to pay the manager a full commission, as he or she has a "captive audience" and an advantage over other agents who might try to steal the tenant. You can pay one third to one half of a commission for renewals and most agents would be thrilled with the extra compensation.

As for giving the manager the exclusive right to lease the building, this is another question. The manager must have a full-service brokerage house affiliated with the management entity for you to consider this. Unless an agent is out in the market place, he or she is unlikely to have the contacts to keep up a steady steam of tenants. It is the day-to-day knowledge of the market and the constant contact with the potential tenants that keep a building full.

AN INDEPENDENT CONTRACTOR

How do you attempt to reconcile this dilemma? I think it depends on your goals. First of all, I believe that it is mandatory to maintain contact with the active leasing community, because you will, one day, want to expand your holdings or sell the building. Whether you're building or buying, you should ally yourself with a brokerage company that provides both leasing and investment services. This way you will have a healthy, ongoing agency relationship that offers you a good resource and protection from raids by the company's employees. Your exclusive arrangement is with the company and binds all its employees. In addition, you will have the most up-to-date information on market rents and trends in the rental industry. Your broker can keep you current on all movement in the marketplace. He or she will be in a position to advise you when the optimum time to sell comes.

At the same time, you need a harmonious arrangement with your management company. The solution, as I see it, is quite simple. Give the broker an exclusive on new tenants and give your manager a commission on renewals. Give your broker the right to resell the building when the time comes, as an incentive, and contingent with his or her keeping your building full and up to market rents. A good solution is one that benefits all parties. The broker will be placated for not having renewal commissions by being able to earn the right to resell and the manager will be happy with the commission on renewals. You will have ended up with the best of both.

Insurance

Insurance in any transaction is critical. There are two kinds of insurance that everyone must have when working on your property, including you: liability and workers' compensation insurance. There are other insurances necessary when dealing with specialized consultants, like errors and omission insurance, but everyone needs the two above to cover their potential liabilities.

Liability insurance insures you from injuries that happen to third parties. If someone trips and falls down your stairs, you're covered. Workers' compensation insurance covers you when anyone doing work on your building is hurt, whether your employees or not.

As an owner, you will need the following insurance to operate the building:

- If you are building, you will need course of construction, fire and extended coverage, workers' compensation, and a liability umbrella insurance policy.
- As an owner operating a building, you will need fire and extended coverage, rent replacement insurance with a workers' compensation rider. I also always recommend an umbrella override policy.

Rather than have everyone connected with the development or management of a building carry redundant coverage, you can buy and maintain the master policy, naming all the other entities as *additional insured(s)* to your policy. The other companies in question can then pass along the savings to you and lower your insurance costs. If you are building the building, you will find that this option will save you many thousands of dollars.

CHAPTER

22

Leases

Leases are a subject close to my heart because the leases determine the value of any income property. Income property, whether single-tenant or multitenant, sells for a multiple of the rents. The value of a property is calculated in terms of a capitalization (cap) rate. There may be differences in what cap rate is used to calculate value, but everyone in the business agrees that value is calculated by dividing the net income before debt service (NIBDS) by an agreed-upon cap rate. For example, if you have a property with $100,000 of NIBDS and an agreed-upon eight-percent cap rate, then the calculation is as follows:

$100,000 / .08 = $1,250.000

The calculation is simple and everyone can agree on the results. It makes valuation of any property a simple matter. Determine the NIBDS and agree on a cap rate and you're in business.

Net Income Before Debt Service

Determining the net income before debt service is a key issue in the valuation of income property; how it is derived directly relates to the leases and the expenses incurred in operating the project. Operating expenses are straightforward in the determination: anything above the line is an operating expense and can be substantiated by reviewing the building's expense history, and anything below the line is an ownership expense and is not considered an operating cost. Leases, however, are another story.

Historically, leases have come in many different forms: gross, modified gross, net, and triple net (NNN). In the beginning, all leases were gross leases; the favored lease is the NNN lease. The difference between gross and NNN is the cost of operating the building and who pays for what. If you look at a modern pro forma income and expense sheet, like the one in Table 22-1, you can see how the NIBDS is derived.

As you can readily see, this is a breakdown of a project in which the leases are all NNN. The landlord is responsible for all expenses pertaining to the vacancy; those expenses are deducted from the income before determining the NIBDS. It is appropriate to remember when you are buying a building that you may inherit leases that are not NNN leases; you will need to determine exactly what you, the landlord, must pay and what the tenant must pay. When you are doing your due diligence prior to purchase and creating the spreadsheets as outlined in Chapter 21, pay particular attention to the expense clauses and add to your list of items in the spreadsheet tenant reimbursements to CAM charges.

Income	**Current Year**
Gross potential income [GPI]	$490,000
Vacancy allowance at 5%	–$24,500
Effective gross income [EGI]	$465,500
CAM Expenses	
Real estate taxes	$48,000
Maintenance/repair/HVAC	$3,600
Insurance: fire/liability	$14,400
Electricity	$7,200
Water and sewer	$4,800
Refuse	$1,200
Janitorial	$31,200
Windows/sweeping	$4,800
Security	$8,640
Pest control on demand	$1,800
Yard and common area maintenance	$4,800
Subtotal	**$130,440**
Management fee at 10% exp	$13,044
Total Common Area	**$143,484**
Tenant-reimbursed CAM	$136,310
Landlord's expense	–$7,174
Net Income Before Debt Service [NIBDS]	**$458,326**

TABLE 22-1. PROFORMA INCOME AND EXPENSE

Potential Problems

The entire philosophy behind writing a lease is to create a document secure in its enforceability. You need to collect the rent on time, every time, and you need to be able to manage the building and the tenants in an orderly manner. This is the entire thrust of the lease. From the landlord's point of view, its terms are all aimed at that objective. From the tenant's perspective, he or she wants to be able to count on a reliable premises and uninterrupted use thereof. Tenants want the building properly maintained and utilities available 24/7. If they do not get what they're paying for, they want spelled out in the lease the right to enforce what they are entitled to.

The negotiation of the lease is very straightforward if both the parties are fair-minded, but if they are adversarial, they can burn up a lot of time and attorney's fees. The best lease is a fair lease, and if you write the lease that way in the beginning, you should be able to get it executed without too much trouble.

The lease document in the Appendix is the one I am currently using and it is the easiest lease I have worked with in my entire career. That does not mean that you cannot improve upon it, so if you see some areas that can be polished, please drop me an e-mail.

The other, unnamed party to the lease is your lender, who is deeply concerned about your lease. Most lenders take the position that they are the default owners of the property in the event of a foreclosure, so their legal department seeks to ensure that they have the right not only to step in and take over but to run the building and collect the rents. Most of the general provisions in the lease document are geared to enable them to do so. Any significant changes in the general provisions may cause your lender to disapprove the lease, which may cost you your loan.

Arguments for the NNN Lease

This form of lease is what I describe as a pure lease: it separates rent from operating expenses and it obligates both tenant and landlord to operate the building economically. One item that is not initially included in my lease is the *expense stop*. This is the landlord's guarantee to the tenant that the base year operating expenses will not exceed a certain figure. It is usually negotiated into the lease by the tenant, but not necessarily so. To address the issue, I have an estimate of operating expenses prepared in advance, so that we can deal with the matter and insert an expense stop if the tenant feels the need for it. In the last ten years, I have not had to insert the expense stop clause in one of my leases.

CAM charges are broken into several sections; it's important to understand them, as each has control issues attached to it. In Table 22-2 I have enumerated all the potential expenses that should be subject to negotiation and resolution between landlord and tenant. Some can be controlled and some cannot. CAM charges are composed of three broad categories of expense:

- Operating expenses
- Taxes
- Insurance

Most NNN leases list the three categories and account for them separately. Taxes and insurance are items beyond the landlord's control and, therefore, are not guaranteed by the landlord. The operating expenses are expected to be controlled, and the landlord and tenant must understand how they are projected and how they will be administered as it pertains to CAM charges. These are detailed in Table 22-2.

Lease Structure

My commercial lease is composed of three parts: the main body, general provisions, and exhibits. The following is a breakdown of that lease that explains why each article is in the lease and what it is supposed to do. This is the lease included in the Appendix.

Main Body

Article 1 is a quick reference summary containing the following topics:

- The date of execution
- The landlord's name
- The tenant's name
- The tenant's trade name
- The name of the guarantor, if any
- The lease term and any options
- The minimum rent

Expense Item	Comments	Guaranteed
Water and sewer	Routine; no surprises	Yes
Parking lot sweeping	Weekly at a minimum	Yes
Common areas utilities	Routine; no surprises	Yes
Security	Bid	Yes
Window washing	4 times/year minimum	Yes
Refuse collection	Weekly/bid	Yes
Janitorial	Minimum standards/bid	Yes
Repairs	Routine estimate	Yes
Reserves for replacements	Negotiable but routine	Yes
Landscape maintenance	Monthly/bid	Yes
Snow removal	Seasonal	No
Administration	10% on the above	Yes
Taxes	Uncontrolled	No
Insurance	Third party	No
Total CAM charge	Prorated to tenants by SF of premises divided by total net rentable SF	Partially; snow removal, taxes, and insurances excluded

TABLE 22-2. EXPENSE CHART

- The calculation of the additional rent
- Percentage rent if any (retail leases only)
- The size of the premises
- The intended use of the premises
- Addresses for legal notice
- A list of exhibits

Article 2 defines the tenant's premises, referencing the exhibits for clarification, and spells out the intended use of the premises.

Article 3 contains the term of the lease, defining how it is calculated and spelling out the definition of its *commencement date.* It references the exhibit wherein the tenant accepts the premises and acknowledges the commencement date of the lease term and rent payment.

Article 4 deals with the tenant's possession of the premises and spells out who is responsible for what. In this case, it is a developer's lease, wherein the developer has 24 months to deliver the premises to the tenant.

Article 5 deals with the rent: the amount, when it is due, and any local taxes pertaining to rent payment. It also details the rent and security deposits collected when the lease was executed. It further spells out the tenant's right to the use of the parking lot. It delineates the rent escalations after the base year of the lease, referencing the exhibit where the calculation is spelled out.

Article 6 deals with the additional rent, showing how the tenant's portion is calculated and defining which items are included in the additional rental calculation. It also shows how the landlord will account for these expenses and how the tenant can monitor the expense annually. It specifies reporting and adjustments. The important section here addresses the issue of late rental payment and the charges and penalties that the landlord may apply when rent is late. It is specific regarding the tenant's time to cure the late rent before the lease goes into formal default.

Article 7 deals with the tenant's right to assign or sublet the leased premises.

Article 8 obligates the tenant to provide the landlord with specific insurances covering the tenant's premises, including rent loss endorsement.

Article 9 spells out the landlord's obligation to provide and maintain utility services to the tenant's demised premises.

Article 10 deals with the tenant's right to hold over, to occupy the premises after the lease expires. It spells out the term of this right and the rent the tenant must pay when holding over. It provides for written notice of the tenant's intentions.

Article 11 is a crucial section dealing with the landlord's rights if and when a tenant defaults on the lease obligations. It should clearly define what constitutes default and spell out all of the landlord's options. It should be very specific about notices and times to cure the default.

Article 12 deals with the many remedies available to the landlord in the event of default as defined in article 11 above. Some of these provisions will be subject to the courts and their laws regarding eviction and bankruptcy proceedings.

Article 13 is the covenant to operate. This will appear in retail leases only and parts of it can be stricken when the lease is used for other applications. It also addresses trash and waste disposal, deliveries, and hours of operation. It may address the issue of competing stores within a certain radius of the site.

Article 14 This clause spells out the Americans with Disabilities Act (ADA) and how it affects the project and the requirement for the tenant to comply with the act.

Article 15 spells out who the brokers are in connection with this lease and who shall pay the commission. It provides for mutual indemnity by landlord and tenant regarding undisclosed third parties to the transaction. It further spells out that this entire transaction is contained in this lease document, with no other representations made by the parties, and that this is a binding and enforceable contract. It states that the tenant has been informed to consult with an attorney.

The section is then signed, dated, and notarized (optional) by both tenant and landlord.

General Provisions

This part of the lease contains the "boilerplate" that is dear to the hearts of all attorneys. It is required by the lenders and will not be the subject of much negotiation, except with very large national tenants. Your ability to alter these provisions is directly related to the lender's attorney's approval to do so.

Article G-1 deals with the use of the premises; it is here that you may insert any exclusives that you have granted to your tenant. These exclusives should be as specific and narrowly defined as possible. They prohibit the tenant from taking any action that will materially affect the project's insurance rates.

Article G-2 spells out the tenant's obligation to comply with all laws. It requires the tenant to indemnify and hold the landlord harmless against the results of failing to do so.

Article G-3 delineates the tenant's rights to make alterations within the demised premises. It spells out procedures for the landlord's approval and specifies who shall pay the costs. It requires the tenant to prevent liens on the premises. It further details when and how the work may be done so that none of the other tenants are disrupted.

Article G-4 recounts the landlord's rights to enter and make repairs in the event of the tenant's failure to do so.

Article G-5 deals with liens: who is responsible for them and how and when they must be removed. (This clause should be as onerous as possible. You do not want liens!)

Article G-6 is the hold harmless clause. To be effective, this clause must be mutually obligating. It simply states that the landlord and tenant will hold each other harmless from actions resulting from their conduct or that of their employees and representatives.

Article G-7 deals with the waiver of rights to collect on insured losses so long as the required insurances are in force.

Article G-8 deals with the collection and payment of real estate taxes and taxes on the tenant's specific improvements and personal property.

Article G-9 spells out the tenant's obligation to abide by the rules and regulations of the project as delineated in an exhibit entitled "Rules and Regulations."

Article G-10 is the hazardous materials clause. This is an area of ever-increasing concern for landlord and lender alike. This clause should be as detailed as possible to protect both landlord and tenant from careless or negligent actions of the other. It must mandate absolute compliance with laws and regulations regarding hazardous materials.

Article G-11 deals with the landlord's continuous right to enter the premises to inspect and protect the project and the tenant's premises. It should provide for any actions by the landlord to safeguard and preserve the premises.

Article G-12 provides for reconstruction of the building in the event of a fire or flood or other catastrophic damage. It should spell out who should do what and who will pay for it. It normally addresses who controls the insurance proceeds until the building is restored. In practical terms, the lender will control the proceeds.

Article G-13 deals with the public's right of eminent domain and the potential results to a commercial project in the event of the public exercising its right of condemnation. It offers relief to both landlord and tenant if business is sufficiently disrupted. The lender will not waive this clause under any circumstances.

Article G-14 deals with the infamous estoppel certificate referred to in Chapter 20. It will be an exhibit to the lease. This clause must compel the tenant to execute this document, whenever required, in a timely manner.

Article G-15 is a catchall clause which includes miscellaneous provisions such as:

- Riders, plats, and exhibits
- Waiver
- Notices
- Joint obligations
- Marginal headings
- Time is of the essence
- Successors and assigns
- Recordation
- Quiet possession
- Late charges (*very important!*)
- Prior agreements

- Inability to perform
- Attorney's fees
- Sale by landlord
- Subordination and attornment
- Use of the building name restrictions
- Severability
- Cumulative remedies
- Choice of law
- Signs and auctions
- Gender and number
- Consents. It is not necessary to dwell on this article. Your attorney will explain the items, in general, and the lender will insist on this article.

Article G-16 provides for the landlord to expand the project and move parking and materials around so long as the tenant's ability to do business is maintained. It also contains strict guidelines for tenant parking and the landlord's ability to enforce the rules.

Article G-17 prevents discrimination, as mandated by the government.

This section of the lease is then signed and dated.

The Exhibits

Each lease will require a different set of exhibits, but, in general, they will include the following:

- The property description, which will include a legal description, a site plan, a floor plan, and a tenant layout
- The construction specifications, plans, and costs delineating both landlord's and tenant's work and the method of payment
- The cost-of-living adjustment or specific rent adjustment and how calculated
- Tenant's Acknowledgment of Commencement, which the tenant must sign to gain occupancy and which triggers the start of the lease term and the payment of rent
- Sign regulations, as detailed as possible, to avoid disputes. These regulations are subject to the permits issued by the municipality.
- Estoppel certificate
- Rules and regulations
- Special conditions that spell out any specific, nonstandard agreement between landlord and tenant, including exclusives, options, and additional rights granted as consideration for the lease

Finally, the exhibit section will be signed and dated. Modern leases generally require that all parties initial each page to acknowledge that each party to the lease has read and understood the entire lease. All of the above will be the subject of negotiation, as was the main body of the lease. The exceptions are the rules, the rent commencement document, and the estoppel certificate. Hold firm here.

HEADS UP

No one can dictate the terms of a contract to another party. Contracts are enforceable agreements that the parties enter into voluntarily and should, therefore, be negotiated in good faith and administered with a spirit of fair play. Adhere to this principle and you will get along well with your tenants and prosper.

CHAPTER

23

Loan Documents

Origination

Most real property carries a mortgage, due to the fact that leverage allows an owner to dramatically improve the yield on invested capital. No matter how much you borrow, all real property loans start out the same way: application, commitment, and funding. There are some fundamental differences between residential mortgages and commercial loans, so we will address them here. Residential loans are relatively simple, tend to be handled informally, and are pretty much on a take-it-or-leave-it basis, whereas commercial loans are negotiated at the beginning and then granted or not.

Residential

Residential loans tend to be less structured until it is time to actually execute the loan documents; then, at the last minute, you might find out that the lender has changed the terms on you. Usually you start out with a mortgage broker who gets a handwritten, signed application from you and collects a check for the appraisal. This gets the ball rolling. To protect yourself from the usual practice of both lenders and mortgage brokers, always do the following:

- Make sure that you add language to the application that makes any fees and expenses contingent on the loan being "granted as applied for."

- Keep a legible copy of the signed application.
- When you are notified that the loan has been granted, request a letter from the lender stating that the loan was "granted as applied for." This will serve as a commitment when attached to your original mortgage application.

Many times I have experienced a last-minute change in the terms and rates at the loan closing. At that time you are stuck; you have to close on the home and the mortgage loan or you are homeless. If you have in your possession a copy of the original application and the commitment letter you requested, you will have the lender and the mortgage broker over a barrel. They will have to amend the papers to reflect the original application.

HEADS UP

Do not stand for last-minute changes. If you have done as I instructed above, you will prevail. I have done it several times.

The Bait and Switch

A popular change that the lender may pull at the closing is to require insurance and tax impounds. This is normal when you have a loan that is 70-80 percent of value. If, however, you are applying for a low-percentage loan, you can request in your application that the lender waive the tax and insurance impounds. Most lenders ignore this request and, at closing, require you to re-execute the loan application, now typed—and altered. Do not be persuaded that you have to accept this. At a loan closing four years ago, I picked up a change on a 40-percent loan-to-value (LTV) mortgage and made them change the documents on the spot. I merely pointed out that they made the commitment as applied for, I had paid the fees as requested, and if they changed the commitment at the last minute they would be liable for breach of contract and damages. The upshot of this lesson is, make your application carefully and legibly at the outset, request the exact terms that you would like to have, and if the loan is committed, make sure you have a commitment letter for the loan "as applied for." You will avoid any last-minute crisis.

Commercial Loans

Commercial real estate loans fall into two categories: new loans and refinancing. New loans are construction loans and first-time permanent loans. Everything else is a refinancing.

All commercial loans begin with a written request to a mortgage banker or mortgage broker. When a lender expresses an interest in making the loan, the lender usually issues a "terms sheet" whose detailed terms are subject to the lender satisfying himself or herself that your representations regarding leases, financial condition, and income and expense are accurate. Construction loans are often applied for directly with the lender, especially if you are an established borrower in the market.

The Terms Sheet

A terms sheet will be similar to the one shown in Table 23-1.

Let's walk through this document (Table 23-1) and interpret exactly what the lender is offering.

- Lines 1-6 are self-explanatory.
- Line 7 says that the loan is to be a 75-percent loan-to-value (LTV) with a debt service coverage ratio (DSC) of 1.25. That means that the NIBDS must equal 125

1.	Mortgage Banker:	XYZ Mortgage, Ltd.
2.	Loan Type:	Fixed Rate
3.	Property:	The Shopping Center
4.	City, State:	Podunk, RI
5.	Quote Date:	9/14/2004
6.	Loan Amount:	$16,200,000
7.	LTV, Debt Service Coverage:	75% LTV / 1.25 DSC
8.	Term:	10 years
9.	Amortization:	30 years
10.	Margin:	1.61%
11.	Treasury Issue:	10-year treasury
12.	Current Index Rate:	4.13%
13.	Current Interest Rate:	5.74%
14.	Interest Rate Floor:	5.40%
15.	Loan Fee:	None
16.	Interest Calculation:	Actual/360
17.	Liability:	Nonrecourse, with standard carve-out liability
18.	Assumable:	Yes, with a 1% assumption fee
19.	Prepayment Penalty:	Yield Maintenance/Flexpay
20.	Lock-in Period:	3 years
21.	Upfront Standby Deposit:	.5% of the loan amount (refundable at closing)
22.	Rate Lock Available:	Yes, additional 1.5% deposit w/ remargining rights, 100% refundable at closing
23.	Rate Lock Cost:	Included in the spread until 9/1/2005
24.	Tax and Insurance Impound:	Required
25.	Retenanting Reserves:	Required
26.	Structural Reserves:	Required
27.	Single Purpose Entity:	Required—SPE Level III
28.	Lock-Box:	Not Required
29.	Legal Opinion Letter:	Not Required
30.	3rd-Party Report Deposit:	$12,000—includes items with *
31.	Physical Condition Report:	Required*
32.	Appraisal:	Required*
33.	Environmental Phase I:	Required*
34.	PML or Seismic Study:	Required*
35.	ALTA Survey:	Not required, unless required by title company
36.	Legal Fees:	None required, unless borrower changes standard CMO loan documents
37.	Processing / Closing Fee:	$8,500
38.	Other:	

* Preliminary quote subject to credit/underwriting review and site inspection. Spreads are held on quotes converted to completed applications within one business day.

TABLE 23-1. LENDER'S TERMS SHEET

percent of the proposed mortgage payment.

- Lines 8 and 9 are self-explanatory.
- The margin refers to the percentage over the ten-year treasury notes' daily rate of interest at the time the rate is fixed.
- In lines 12 and 13 we see that the current treasury rate is 4.13 percent and, adding the margin, if the rate is fixed today, the loan rate of interest will be 5.74 percent.
- Line 14—The lowest rate the lender is willing to consider at the time of fixing the rate is 5.4 percent.
- Line 15—There is no commitment fee.
- Line 16—Interest is calculated on a daily basis, on the unpaid balance of the loan, on the basis of a 360-day year and a 30-day month.
- Line 17—No personal guarantees are required except on the "carve-outs" (fraud and misrepresentation by the borrower).
- Line 18 states that the loan is assumable by a buyer with the payment of a one-percent fee.
- Line 19 spells out the prepayment penalty, if any; in this case there will be a yield-maintenance clause and a loan cancellation fee. You will get the details on this in the loan application document.
- Line 20—There is no prepayment allowed during the first three years of the loan.
- Line 21—To book the loan, the borrower must pay a refundable fee of .5 percent.
- Line 22 indicates that to lock the rate the borrower must put up, on the day the rate is locked, a fee of 1.5 percent that, together with the standby fee, is refundable at closing.
- Lines 23-29 are self-explanatory.
- Line 30 indicates that the borrower must tender, with the application, a $12,000 fee for the appraisal and any other third-party reports required by the lender.
- Lines 31-37 are self-explanatory.
- Line 38 is lender boilerplate.

Now you know how to read a terms sheet. You should find that almost any lender's terms sheet will be similar. You are free to negotiate any of the points up to the execution of the formal application. That's when the paperwork really starts.

The Application

Construction loans used to have a permanent loan to "take out" the construction lender, which required a forward commitment (approximately 24 months out) at the time the construction loan was granted. In addition, the two lenders used to require a "tri-party agreement," aka a buy-sell agreement. All parties agreed that, with all conditions met, the permanent lender, with the consent of the borrower, would buy out the construction lender at the agreed-upon point in time. This virtually locked the borrower into the forward commitment. Sometimes this was not a good thing, as the forward could be granted with onerous terms. It was costly to substitute a new take-out and buy off the first lender.

The industry finally came to the rescue with the advent of the *mini-perm loan*. This was a construction loan that, for an additional fee (usually one point), could be converted into a fully amortizing short-term permanent loan. This new arrangement allowed a borrower more time to shop for a more sympathetic permanent loan.

Loan applications differ. A loan application will include, at the least, the following items:

- The loan request, with specific conditions

- The plans and specifications of the project
- Financial projections
- A leasing exhibit showing current and projected leases
- Copies of all executed leases
- Financial statements of the borrower(s)

This application will, in general, contain the following clauses in letter form, addressed specifically to the lender:

- A specific file number and project reference
- A deadline date for the application
- Name and legal identity of the borrower
- The specifics on the proposed security and proposed document (deed of trust, mortgage, etc.)
- Application data sheet, including information regarding the principals of the borrowing entity, the financial condition of the principals, management of the property, additional information on the property, existing debt on the property, and authorization for credit inquiries by the lender, included on Exhibit A, attached hereto
- A statement regarding any loan guarantees offered, if any, or a statement regarding the borrower's desire for a nonrecourse loan
- The terms and conditions of the proposed loan, including the following:
    1. loan amount
    2. interest rate
    3. payment terms
    4. impound accounts for taxes and insurance
    5. annual financials
    6. prepayment terms
    7. yield-maintenance clause, if any
    8. assignment and transferability clauses
    9. secondary financing provisions
    10. lender's rights to approval of leases, fees, and costs
- The proposed application fee
- The commitment fee
- A condition precedent to closing, such as appraisal, environmental report, architect's and engineer's certification, seismic reports, etc.
- Broker's role and fees
- Breakdown of costs and who pays for what
- Proposed closing conditions, such as:
    - Lender's inspection
    - Required leases
    - Documentation list
    - Appraisal
    - Change in interest based on prime at the time
    - Environmental documentation
    - Architectural and engineering report requirement
    - Tenant estoppel certificates
    - Miscellaneous provisions
    - Boilerplate clauses
- Receipt by lender
- Borrower's representations
- Additional requirements
- The date and the borrower's signature

Commitment

Once you have signed this application and included all the exhibits requested, you can attach the check and sit back and wait. Loan underwriting usually takes many weeks and is followed by formal approval by the lender's loan committee. After that, you will get a commitment letter reiterating the terms of the loan approved. Once the loan is granted, the commitment letter will contain, in addition to the terms spelled out in the executed application, at least the following:

- Acceptance language and a restatement of the terms granted
- The date by which the borrower must accept and pay for the loan commitment
- Enumeration of fees, charges, and closing costs: who pays what and when
- The closing date, usually stated as "on or before"
- Conditions of funding, such as lender's approval of leases, physical inspection of the buildings, collection of estoppel certificates, proof of taxes having been paid, and a minimum percentage occupancy at the time of closing
- A date and time of acceptance signature block

Aspects of the Commitment

You would think that, with all this paper, you would be OK to go. The truth is, maybe not. In the case of a forward commitment, it has happened that, at the time of closing, the lender has declined to fund. Sometimes lenders simply run into trouble and do not have the funds to close. They are liable, but it can be a nightmare trying to sue and collect. If there is an exculpatory clause in the commitment that frees the lender, you are out of luck. I have not heard of lenders running short of money in recent times, but be aware that this is a remote possibility and keep track of your lender during that period up to closing. Be in contact with your mortgage banker. The banker is also liable, as he or she has brokered the deal. Generally, if trouble surfaces, the mortgage banker can find you a substitute loan at no further cost.

HEADS UP

In the old days the construction lender was concerned about the "bankabilty" of the take-out lender and insisted on specific language to ensure the take-out. The mini-perm has put a stop to most of this nonsense.

Funding and Documentation

When a loan funds, there are mounds of documents and procedures to be followed. In the case of the construction loan, the lender is aware of the contractor's lien rights and wants to be assured that the loan will have priority of payment over any contractor's liens. So, the site is inspected prior to closing to assure the lender and the title company that work has not yet started. Then, the title company issues the lender a lender's policy of title insurance, in this case the aforementioned ALTA extended coverage policy, and all is well. The loan is then recorded. The loan documents are in two parts: the note and the security agreement, either a deed of trust or a mortgage, which will be recorded against the property at closing.

Note

The note is a relatively simple document that will contain the following items of information:

- Principal sum
- Date
- Maker and entity identification
- Address of the maker
- Holder
- Holder's address
- Interest rate
- Term
- Payments
- Definition of late payments and charges
- Default interest rate

- The promise to pay
- Partial payment provision
- Acceleration and pre-payment provisions
- The security description (deed of trust or mortgage) attached as an exhibit
- Boilerplate regarding attorney's fees, governing law, venue, etc.
- The signature of the maker and the date

There may be more on your note, but these basics will surely be in any note.

Deed of Trust or Mortgage

This security agreement puts the world on notice that the owner of this property owes money to a specific lender and loosely outlines the terms. It is intended to keep the owner from selling the property and ignoring the note obligation. The deed of trust or mortgage document will contain at least the following information:

- A cover sheet containing the recording information
- The documents, entitled Deed of Trust or Mortgage
- The account number
- The borrower's name and mailing address
- The beneficiary's name and mailing address
- The trustee's name and mailing address
- The date
- The property's description: location (town, county, and state), address, and legal description attached as an exhibit
- The original loan amount on the note
- Recitals
- The terms and conditions, legal defense, attorney's fees, liens, payments, etc.
- Mutual agreements: damages, trespass, rights of assignment, partial reconveyance, personal guarantees (if any), surrender and satisfaction, and reconveyance
- Additional security, if any
- Default provisions and remedies in default
- Recording authority
- Successors in interest
- Rights of assignment by the beneficiary
- The borrower's signature and date of execution

The reassuring thing about these documents is that they are universal. Unless you are very wealthy, you will have little latitude in negotiating changes in your lender's documents. Be comforted that everyone else is in the same boat. Remember: it is their money and you are trying to rent it. The terms are theirs, not yours. After all, you are the supplicant. Close your eyes and sign. Then go out and make some money to repay the loan. Try to make enough so that you can keep some for yourself!

CHAPTER

24

Dealing *with* Contractors

It matters little what you are doing with real estate; whether you're remodeling your home, expanding it, retenanting a commercial property, or developing a new property, sooner or later you will be dealing with contractors. Licensed contractors are only one group of people who build buildings. It is legal for other people to build buildings as well. For instance, a homeowner can build his or her own home so long as it meets code and it is inspected by the building department. Handymen and handywomen can work on your property as well.

This chapter leans heavily on controlling costs for new construction in a development deal, but it applies just as meaningfully to a renovation or tenant improvement situation.

Licensing, Bonding, and Payment Enforcement

With all that is going on in the building industry, there are people regulating the people doing the work. Each state has a licensing agency that is state-operated and regulated by state laws.

The way it works is that individual companies are licensed to do the work. This involves an individual who qualifies for the license, having passed the test and posted a bond against faulty work or fraudulent practices. It is the companies that are licensed, not the individuals doing the work. Individuals running their own companies are usually licensed as well. One of the primary reasons for using licensed contractors is that they have been tested to determine that they have a minimum experience to do the work and they are bonded at the time of licensing. To become licensed, each contractor—general and subcontractor alike—has to put up a bond or a cash payment to the recovery fund. If a contractor does not do a professional job, he or she can be made to correct the work or lose his or her licenses. In addition, to a limited extent, the owner may recover damages against the licensing agency's recovery fund. This is of use only to homeowners for small amounts of money; commercial contracts have to rely on specific bonds purchased for a particular job. This system protects the owner and the contractor; it assures the homeowner or commercial owner that the people who are doing the work are regulated and meet minimum standards for competency, and it protects the contractor because he or she has the right to enforce payment for work performed. Only licensed contractors may lien a property for nonpayment for work performed. As mentioned earlier, contractors fall into two major categories: general and subcontractors. Basically, general contractors are licensed generalists who deal with an entire project and subcontractors are specialists who deal with only one part of the work. However, some subcontractors may act as general contractors if the job falls primarily under their specialty.

General Contractors

To serve as a general contractor, these companies must be licensed as general contractors. In addition, general contractors may do some of the subcontractor work, such as framing or concrete placement. As a rule, however, the general contractor earns his or her keep by overseeing the entire job and taking responsibility for budget, scheduling, and completion. His or her compensation is generally twofold: overhead (general conditions) and profit. The general conditions may include the following items:

- Mobilization (moving onto and off of the job site)
- Demolition
- Site supervision
- Layout
- Insurance
- Site security
- General cleanup
- Providing an on-site office and communications
- Temporary power

Subcontractors

Subcontractors (subs) provide all the specialty labor. They include the following specialties:

- Earth movers and heavy equipment operators
- Carpenters
- Electricians
- Plumbers
- Mechanical contractors
  - HVAV contractors
  - Elevator and escalator installers
- Painters and finishers

As mentioned above, some subcontractors may act as general contractors if the job at hand falls primarily under their specialty. For instance, a power plant project may be correctly generaled by the electrical contractor and a dam project may be generaled by an earthmoving contractor.

Heavy Equipment Operators

These folks drive the big machines—the diggers, compactors, haulers, and lifters. They are also, quite frequently, general contractors on large land improvement projects. They also tend to be uniformly the most unionized of the trades.

CARPENTERS

This trade has the following specialties within it:

- *Framers:* They work as a team and they are responsible for erecting the structure of a new building and putting on the rough roofing and siding. They then move on to a new building. You will need a framer only if you are developing a building from scratch or adding space to an existing building.
- *Finish carpenters:* They take over from the framers and apply the finished siding and the interior. There are even specialists within this specialty who deal only with doors and windows. Within this specialty are the people who do hardwood floors and decorative millwork.
- *Cabinetmakers and millwork specialists:* They install the cabinets and add the fancy trim throughout the house that establishes the basic décor. There are even specialists within this grouping that make the cabinets and specialty items such as stair railings and trim.

PLUMBERS

Plumbers range from steamfitters to general plumbers. They are most often broken down as follows:

- *Steamfitters:* They work in heavy industry and shipping. They handle heavy pressure piping, boilers, and steam generators as well.
- *Site and underground pipe fitters:* They install sewers and water systems up to the buildings.
- *General plumbers:* They install the plumbing for the buildings and install plumbing fixtures.

ELECTRICIANS

Electrical work is also broken down into subspecialties.

- High-voltage transmission and power plant work is a specialty that is in the "heavy construction" category.
- Site electrical work, distributing power within subdivisions, is a further specialty involving underground installation and working with transformers and distribution systems.
- General electricians deal with installing the basic electrical services in a building and distributing power throughout the buildings.
- The final specialty, which is a subspecialty of the general electrician, is the trim man or woman. He or she installs all the light fixtures and appliances in the finished building.

PAINTERS AND FINISHERS

These people apply décor to the finished structures. There are several specialties that overlap with other trades, but deserve their own mention:

- Painters and wallpaper hangers
- Bath accessory installers
- Glass and mirror suppliers
- Cabinet shops making cultured marble walls and vanity tops
- Kitchen countertop makers, who work in Formica®, Corian®, granite, and other stone
- Carpet layers
- Flooring installers, who use tongue-in-groove hardwood, vinyl tiles, ceramic tile, and stone
- Hardware specialists and locksmiths who furnish locks and decorative hardware

Mechanical Contractors

These people deal with specific mechanical systems, such as heating and cooling systems, elevators, and escalators.

Unlicensed Workers

Some construction workers are unlicensed. Over 95 percent of people who work in the new construction industry are licensed, bonded, and insured, but in the remodeling end of the business, the overwhelming majority are unlicensed, not bonded, and not necessarily insured. Why this disparity in practice? In general, it boils down to contract law, state regulation, and industry practice. It is accepted in the contracting business that unlicensed contractors seldom or never work on a commercial structure or new housing project. However, the inverse is true in the housing industry. Most work done for homeowners involves remodeling and repair jobs and is done by unlicensed contractors or handymen and handywomen. The exceptions to this rule seem to be the plumber and the electrician; consumers are not comfortable with unlicensed plumbers and electricians. Consequently, these two trades are the highest paid in the remodeling industry. You can hire a carpenter for $15 to $25 per hour, but you will pay $50 an hour or more for an electrician and over $60 an hour for a plumber.

Construction and Cost Control

By the start of construction of any project, the die is cast. If it is going to succeed, the right moves will already have been made. It can, however, still run afoul of problems if the construction process is not carefully monitored. The work to date sets the stage for the construction phase.

Prerequisites for Construction

For the project to succeed, the following elements must have been successfully completed:

- The land has been properly selected for price, location, physical characteristics, and proper condition of title.
- The market has been clearly established for the intended use and the numbers show sufficient upside to warrant the investment and potential risks.
- The preleasing has progressed to the point of breakeven and the lender has given the go-ahead.
- The consultants, including the general contractor, have been retained with proper accountability and integrated into the design process.
- Sufficient money has been raised through equity and loans to assure the owners that the project can be completed without problems.
- The documentation is in place through the completion and management phases.
- The construction loan is ready to fund and the owner and the lender have agreed upon the draw system.
- All utilities are available at the site or at least scheduled to be available well in advance of the scheduled completion date.
- The necessary permits have been issued and the project is 100 percent in compliance with the governing regulations.

If all of the above have been successfully completed, then the project is ready to start the construction phase. At this point, the meter starts ticking on the borrowed funds—and time truly is money.

Let's examine the players at this point and monitor their responsibilities and backup. Who are they and exactly what are they being paid to do? To whom do they report and in what way are they accountable? Any project, to be successful, must control the costs and timing at this point. The process has now come to the final phase, delivering the finished premises.

Control

How are all of these entities tied together and how do they function so that the owner/developer retains control? The answer is in the documentation. The key to the enforceability of the documents is in the expertise, financial strength, and responsibilities spelled out in the contracts. If the consultants have been properly selected, they will have sufficient credentials, net worth, and liquidity to back up their professional expertise with cash, should the need arise. If this is not the case, then they should not be retained. Most consultants also carry errors and omissions insurance (E&O) to cover them in the event of professional liability or malpractice. It is a good idea to select only those consultants who have this type of coverage, because their ability to procure and pay for this coverage speaks well for their financial condition and volume of work.

Budgets and Fat

The owner's primary tool in controlling costs is in his or her budgeting for the project. Everyone needs some "Kentucky windage" or leeway built into the budgeting system. Everyone knows that something always goes wrong and, generally, it is something that has fallen through the cracks, not necessarily attributable to anyone's incompetence or negligence.

How do developers plan for this? It is best budgeted for when preparing the quick and dirty pro forma. When this analysis is made, certain "fat" can be built into the projection for use at a later date. This is not necessarily an easy job, because the lender not only insists that there be a healthy contingency in the budget, but also demands control over what you pay out in each budget category. Every owner/developer has a favorite spot to stash extra money in case of a rainy day. In Table 24-1 you will see a typical development budget for one of my current projects with specific areas of "fat" identified for my future use. To actually use these amounts of money you will need to convince the lender that these monies are not needed within most specific cost allocations. By the time you need these funds, you should have established the maximum cost within these categories by contract, prior expenditure, or lack of need.

How to Bury the Fat and Fight Murphy's Law

Obvious cost categories in which to squirrel away money are the contingency and miscellaneous line items, as well as insurance and interest budgets. Once complete cost for these line items is established, lenders will allow the extra money budgeted to be moved into the miscellaneous budget and used as part of it.

Within the construction contract itself, there should be a line item for contingencies. This line item can be a godsend to the owner and the general contractor. If this line item is incorporated into the contract amount by prearrangement, it can be used to correct oversights that are no one's fault. In addition, it can be used to improve the quality of the building or add to the tenant improvement (TI) allowance. Once the building shell is complete, these unused funds can be used to add incentive for the leasing process. The fatter the tenant improvement budget, the easier the leasing. It gives the broker an edge over the competition and lowers a prospective tenant's cost of occupancy. Tenants really respond to this type of incentive and it can add

Budget Fat	Item	Notes		Budget
	Land			
$113,500	Lot 5	61420	16	$982,720
	Lot 6	52272	16	$836,352
	Closing costs	WAG*		$7,500
	Total Land			**$1,826,572**
	Soft Costs			
	Civil engineering	Contract		$20,000
$20,000	Architecture and landscape architecture	Estmate	4	$101,440
	Insurance during construction	Estmate		$45,000
	Soils and materials testing	WAG*		$7,500
	Miscellaneous blueprints, etc.			$5,000
$25,000	Miscellaneous and contingency			$25,000
	Building permits and hookup fees	In hard costs		
	Project management	6% of costs less land		$150,000
$6,000	Appraisal and loan closing costs	Estimate		$12,500
	Legal—Finance			$5,000
$5,000	Legal—Leasing and REA**			$5,000
	Construction loan fee			$30,000
	Permanent loan fee			$40,000
	Interest and lease-up reserve	$2.5 M @ 8%		$100,000
	Leasing commissions	$5 per SF	22,000	$110,000
$50,000	Contingency reserve	WAG*		$50,000
	Total Soft Costs			**$706,440**
	Hard Costs			
	Off sites	Included in land cost		
	Site preparation	$3.50 per SF		$244,372
	Building shell			
	Anchor tenant—vanilla shell	$56 per SF	12,000	$672,000
	Retail building—grey shell	$47 per SF	10,000	$460,000
	Tenant improvement allowance	$22 per SF	10,000	$220,000
	Nail salon	Bid	1,200	$33,600
	Super cleaners	Bid	1,800	$64,600
	Tenant improvements lot 6 only	$22 per SF		$220,000
	Sales tax	x .65 x Cost x .07		$62,625
	Total Hard Costs			**$1,997,197**
$224,500	**Total Project**	**$205.01**		**$4,510,209**

TABLE 24-1. BUDGET WITH "FAT" EXPOSED *WAG = Wild Ass Guess
**REA = Reciprocal Easement Agreement

real value to the finished product by financing the tenant's over-standard improvements above the base term of the lease, adding the payment to the lease as additional "rent." This is capitalized as extra value for the building.

Representation, Expertise, and Accountability

A key factor in drafting the documents should be spelling out the consultants' advertised backgrounds and their representations regarding their capabilities, experience, financial condition, and expertise. The owner has the right to rely on these representations. Clearly state the responsibilities and the fiduciary nature of the consultants' relationship to the owner. It is this unifying thread that should link all of the consultants, making them responsible to the owner and requiring them to look over each other's shoulders on the owner's behalf.

The architect's job assignment is, in reality, the most responsible of all the consultants in the process. He or she is charged with the responsibility of producing a quality building of sound design that meets the requirements of the intended use and complies with all applicable codes and governmental regulations. He or she is responsible for the compliance of the project's design, up to the time the building permit is issued. Once the project construction gets under way, the architect then becomes responsible for seeing that the general contractor does the job properly within the design parameters and the applicable building codes. If new regulations are promulgated after the design has been finalized and the building permit issued or if new legislation is passed after the date the permit is issued, then the cost of compliance with these new requirements becomes the responsibility of the owner. However, implementation of rules or laws passed, but not yet in force, prior to or during the design process, such as the Americans with Disabilities Act (ADA), are the responsibility of the architect.

Construction inspection for compliance with specifications and the quality of work also falls under the architect's responsibility. Lenders require certification monthly that the construction is on time and in accordance with the approved plans and the applicable codes. If the design is in error and correction is called for, the architect should be responsible for paying for the redesign and the remedial work. If the general contractor was part of the design team in a design-build contract, then the GC should share these costs in some prearranged manner with the architect.

The GC is presumed not only to be financially responsible, but also to be an expert in building construction and the current building codes. However, the GC is not presumed to be an architect or a structural, mechanical, or civil engineer.

The GC is responsible, within the scope of the plans and specifications, for execution of the required work within the code, as well as for the quality and timing of all work under the construction contract. Late or shoddy work should be remedied at the contractor's expense. Timing is always a critical and costly issue in construction. The realistic approach dictates that events of *force majeure*, aka acts of God, such as natural disasters, severe weather, and strikes, beyond the contractor's control, are the risk of the owner. All else is the responsibility of the GC; the financial consequences attributed to this delay should be laid at his or her door.

Since the meter is running on the interest clock, this cost of money can be tied directly to the schedule. To be enforceable, the contract clause must include a reward as well as a penalty. If the work is completed in advance of schedule, a bonus must be paid. If the work is delayed, a penalty can be enforced. The penalty is customarily assessed against the final payment of the traditional ten-percent holdback from the monthly construction draws.

The Monthly Draw and Interest

Every month during the life of a commercial construction project there is a construction draw. Customarily, this draw is for a percentage of the total project and is estimated by the contractor and approved by the architect, the lender's inspector, and the owner before being paid out by the lender.

There are compelling arguments against this method of payment. First, it does not accurately reflect work in place. Second, it never reflects the cash value of the work previously paid for by the GC. Third, it allows the GC to get ahead of the subs and the owner, costing the owner too much interest on outstanding construction loan money.

A more precise method of payment, fair to all (the owner, the lender, the GC, and the subs) is payment by the invoice method. This method of payment requires that each sub, supplier, or consultant invoice for work completed during the current month.

Once the sub costs are tallied, the GC adds his or her work, overhead charges, and specific costs incurred, suitably backed by invoices from suppliers or payroll records, and the total cost of construction for the month is tallied. The owner then adds the soft costs invoiced for the current month and the total is forwarded to the lender for payment. If this method is followed, the owner's expenditure for interest during construction, prior to the tenants' occupancy, should drop by approximately half. This is a significant savings, and once the tenants have occupied and the rents are paying the interest, this savings becomes permanent and money budgeted for this purpose may now be diverted to some other area to good effect.

> **HEADS UP**
>
> Be sure to exclude any materials stored on or off site, as these are properly the responsibility of the suppliers or the subs. They become the owner's property only when they are incorporated into the project. The owner's insurance will be lower if this distinction is made and there will be less "shrinkage" of stored materials as a result.

Another point about payments is tied to the monthly lien releases.

> **HEADS UP**
>
> Each sub and supplier is required to submit, with the current invoice, a lien release for all prior work paid for by the owner. No further payment should be made until this is submitted.

This check-and-balance procedure assures the owner and lender that suppliers and subs have been paid, thus lessening the possibility of liens resulting from nonpayment by the GC. Any supplier or sub not contracted directly by the owner is required by lien law to notify the owner and lender that he or she is doing work on the project. This "Preliminary Notice" is required by law to protect the lien rights of the supplier and the sub. At the same time, it puts the owner and lender on notice that this person is working on the project, thus enabling the owner and lender to track payments to avoid possible liens. The invoice method provides an excellent method of tracking these obligations. If there is any question as to whether suppliers or subs are being paid, payments to the GC may be made jointly to include the supplier or sub in question.

Other Resources

Several third-party agents are usually employed to oversee the process on behalf of the owner and the lender, in particular the testing engineer and the lender's construction draw certification agent.

The testing engineer, usually required by both the lender and the building department, is an excellent consultant to check on various aspects of the construction. His or her role is primarily one of quality control. Timely reporting of compliance or noncompliance can have a profound effect on the schedule and, by extension, the total project cost. Once a quality control test is taken, the project is presumed to be in compliance unless reported otherwise. Therefore, timely notice of noncompliance is essential for keeping the work on schedule. Having to backtrack to remove and replace work can cause severe delay, not to mention increasing costs. The testing engineer should always work for the owner, at the direction of the owner and the architect. The building department and the lender will have some minimum requirements for inspection, but the owner's and architect's best interests are served when inspections are thorough, random, and timely.

The lender's construction draw certification agent, increasingly likely to be an outside consultant, is responsible only to the lender. The owner, however, can make this agent an ally by requiring that he or she be detailed and timely with the reports. Since the owner is paying for this service performed on behalf of the lender, he or she has the right to insist on having detailed inspections reported promptly. This way the owner can more accurately pay for the construction and, if these reports are completed in a timely manner, can make this payment in time to maximize any potential discounts from subcontractors and suppliers. If the GC knows that payment will be rendered promptly, he or she will not have to build into the budget the cost of interest on the payments that they are required to make to suppliers, to keep the work on schedule. This minimizes the impact of construction interest on all parties.

Best Building for the Buck

A common mistake made by developers is to try to save money on the budget. This can become a very shortsighted and ill-advised approach, depending on the project and the project's concept and goals. Obviously, if one is building a project for sale, such as a house, then reducing costs for subs and materials that do not affect quality will have little effect on the project. These savings will, in fact, raise the profits. In a project where rentals are the determining factor in establishing value and profit, money saved can be used to improve the project's final value by increased rent payments. If additional money is available from savings in certain areas, these funds may be used to improve the project's quality, to reduce long-term operating costs, or to allow tenants over-standard improvements.

Typically, these over-standard improvements are, in reality, loaned to the tenant and repaid with interest, fully amortized, over the base year period. They are not flagged anywhere as secondary income, but customarily are evidenced by an increased rental rate. How does this improve value? Take, for example, over-standard tenant improvements of $20,000 installed for a tenant with a five-year lease. If the tenant agrees to pay for this at 12 percent, which is not unreasonable, the result is an additional annual rental payment of $5,340. This amount of money, capitalized at eight percent, will yield a value of $66,750 that can be sold with the building. You will note that the net gain between cost and value is $46,750. This is a good deal by anyone's standard. The increase in cash flow, by extrapolation, is real. It is not hard to visualize how some significant "fat" can be turned into gold by an astute owner/developer.

SECTION

V

BUYING INVESTMENT-GRADE PROPERTIES

CHAPTER

25

Seeking a Suitable Investment Property

The process of selecting an investment property for purchase is one of the crucial steps in the investment game.

> **HEADS UP**
>
> The reality is that *you make your money when you buy.* This is absolutely true, so do not lose sight of this fact in the process.

The Selection Process

There are a few basic steps that may seem obvious to you, but most of the material contained in this book is intended to organize the obvious, apply a modicum of common sense, and formulate a step-by-step approach to the real estate investing process. It does not hurt to repeat it from time to time either. Going back to the beginning, you will:

- Select the real estate market that you wish to invest in. Hopefully, this market will be a geographic area that is readily accessible to your home area.
- Review the different products available within your chosen market and select a type of property that you can be comfortable with and whose product and market you understand, from the general choices of multifamily, industrial, office, or retail projects.
- Select three final properties presented by

your investment broker and re-examine the specific market segment for each property.

- Finally, draft an offer and get the property into escrow so that you can go to work on it. We will deal with the specifics of the purchase agreement in Chapter 26.

PICKING A MARKET

Real estate markets comprise the entire spectrum of real property within a defined geographic or economic area such as an SMSA or MSA. Picking the MSA itself is a very subjective exercise.

While I was working for a life insurance company in the early 1970s, I was involved in investing the company's money in diverse real estate markets. I became curious about these markets and how we came to be interested in them. I found that there was no formal criterion for our involvement in the areas where we were doing business; we were in markets because of our correspondent relationships with local mortgage bankers. I then decided to do my own analysis of the top 100 MSAs in the country. To do that, I needed statistics that I thought might be meaningful economic indicators, readily available for the top 100 MSAs. I found a surprising number of available statistics. While I cannot remember them all, I will list a few that I can remember:

- Population size
- Population growth (ten-year average)
- Unemployment rates (ten-year average)
- Disposable income
- Per capita income
- Vacancy rates in all categories of property (ten-year averages)
- Absorption rates for new construction in all property types

In all, I remember using about 25 statistics with reliable historical data. The results were surprisingly consistent using a combination of only 20 of the criteria as well as all 25. Chicago always came out on top. It makes sense: Chicago is the hub of the country's commerce; all goods must travel through Chicago. However, when I dropped out MSA size, Minneapolis/Saint Paul rose to the top. Not surprising, the top ten MSAs, with the exception of Minneapolis/Saint Paul, were consistently comprised of the Sunbelt states' major MSAs. These are areas of the country that historically attract net in-migration due to the weather and the lifestyle. I, therefore, headed west as fast as I could go. I have never had cause to contradict my initial analysis. Today, the top 10-15 list has expanded to include the Carolinas and Georgia. This is an exercise you should go through to satisfy yourself that you have selected a real estate market that will be reliable for you for the foreseeable future.

It is your job to sort through your chosen market and decide which segment of the market

> **HEADS UP**
>
> While I have been writing this book, Florida, a historically impressive state for real estate investment, enjoying significant annual net in-migration, has been flattened by four hurricanes in less than six weeks. The property damage losses are estimated to be in excess of $20 billion. More importantly, the state will suffer massive out-migration as a result of this calamity. Do not despair: it will be short-lived and Florida will rise again. Over one half of the country's population lives less than one day's drive from Florida and the weather makes it the only viable mecca for the winter-weary Northeasterners. *Actually, it might be a great time to buy some of the distressed properties.*

appeals to you. Each market is composed of submarkets for each type of real estate and each submarket is broken down into specific geographic locations. This is where you must go back to the economic breakdown of your chosen target market and diagram the area in more detail. You should choose the general market because it has healthy characteristics of growth and historical stability. Boom-and-bust areas should be avoided until you become more sophisticated in your ability to analyze a market.

While it is important that you be comfortable with the type of product you choose, it is more important that you choose a type of property that has maintained, for a number of years, good historical demand and reliable historical appreciation. You might find, for instance, that your chosen MSA has overall vacancies in retail space of eight percent, in office space of six percent, in industrial space of three percent, and in multifamily properties of 12 percent. This is only part of the picture. How long have these vacancy rates been at those levels and how are they broken down within the product categories? For instance, you might find that apartment vacancy, currently at 12 percent, was only three percent 18 months ago and 15 percent 24 months before that. This will tell you that there is a pattern to this market that indicates going from tight demand to overbuilt supply in two- to three-year cycles. Further examination might reveal that the boom-or-bust syndrome applies only to the middle market and that luxury units are historically in short supply, having held steady over the last ten years at a three-percent vacancy rate. You might find much the same scenario in office space, where downtown class "A" space has gone from scarce to overbuilt, but suburban class "B" space in the NE corridor has been historically in short supply.

HEADS UP

There are conclusions to be drawn here—and that's your job. That's what this game is all about: using your best judgment, based on the best facts you can gather about the market. Your success or lack of it will depend completely on your own judgment. That suggests two imperatives: one, gather the facts in a systematic manner and check them for their veracity, and two, get the best advice you can pay for before making your decision. *Do not abdicate your decision to anyone else. It's going to be your money on the line, so, good or bad, make your own decisions.*

SELECTING A PROPERTY TYPE

Selecting a good property type is a bit like looking for a mate. You can only select from the available inventory; that will always be a limiting factor. If you do not like the available inventory, either you are being too choosy or you have selected the wrong MSA to play in. Property types will seldom vary from MSA to MSA, but you might stumble on one that is unique to a particular geographical area, such as second-floor retail in Hawaii. I would recommend that you take a hard look at any type of property that is in constant demand with a steady rise in rental rates. You can become familiar enough to get comfortable with any property type that is destined to be or has proven to be a sure winner. Another possible approach is to look at submarkets for trends in all types of property, such as a fringe area enjoying a renaissance. It stands to reason that if the residential market is being rejuvenated and elevated, the commercial space within that area cannot be too far behind.

KEEP IN MIND WHAT YOU'RE BUYING

Another key element of astute real estate investment is to focus on what you are buying. In residential real estate, you are looking at areas that will enjoy an increase in value due to inflation, great maintenance, and increased scarcity. In commercial, you are buying an income stream, and the long-term health and growth of that income stream will depend on your ability to select a good property in the right location and manage that property to increased prosperity. When property is presented for sale, there are several elements that you will be called upon to evaluate: the income and expenses and the physical plant (building). The single most important element of the deal is the economic picture represented by the leases and the historical expenses. The physical condition of the building is also important, but the value rests with the economic prospects rather than the building condition.

Evaluate the Seller's Representations

The seller's package will include a bunch of photos, a list of tenants with their rents, and a list of operating expenses. It is your job to verify all these expenses during your "free look" or due diligence period. The emphasis must be on the area of financial analysis; for detail on that procedure, refer to Chapters 18 and 19 for ways to catalog and analyze the pertinent data.

Put It in Escrow

The first step in actually buying a property is getting it under control. Until it is under control, you do not have the right to buy it. Until it is under contract, do not waste any time on that specific property. To get control, it must be the subject of an enforceable contract. Remember the statute of frauds: the contract must be in writing, it must be executed by competent parties, it must be lawful, and consideration must have passed (i.e., you must have put down a deposit). Once this is accomplished, you can go to work on the property secure in the knowledge that you actually have the right to buy the property at the stated price. The Agreement of Purchase and Sale and Joint Escrow Instructions is the subject of Chapter 26.

> **HEADS UP**
>
> Getting a property under control is the act of legally acquiring a *beneficial interest* in the property. This is a legal right with tangible value and may be legally assigned, bought, or sold.

USE THE "FREE LOOK" PERIOD

Any good purchase contract will have built-in time frames for you to accomplish all the necessary investigations, negotiate the appropriate new loans, and examine the documents and the building itself. Exactly how to do all this is covered in detail in Chapter 26.

EVALUATE THE PAPERWORK

In Chapter 21, I covered in detail how to create a spreadsheet on each tenant and to project the building's future income stream over a ten-year period. It will become readily apparent when you see the lease expiration dates that you have only a certain amount of time to work with the tenants before you need to replace them or renew their leases. This will give you a feel for the building's potential. If, for instance, you feel that, due to your market analysis, the building's rents are under the average for the area, then you can extrapolate the impact of re-leasing and exchanging the existing tenants for better ones or renewing the existing tenants at a better lease rate. You will have to balance the cost of temporary vacancy with a lower increase for the current tenants with no interim vacancies. Obviously, if the lease rates are severely under market, the current tenants will balk at a large increase and it will be better to swallow temporary vacancy to significantly lift the rental rates. This will also require capital investment; budget for it.

This analysis process will also furnish you with a vital management tool for your month-to-month operating plan for the building after the close of escrow.

INSPECT THE BUILDING(S)

While it is not as important as the paper, the building's condition will also have a direct effect on your bottom line. If the building has been properly maintained, then the historical cash flow on which you are basing your purchase price will be reliable. If, however, maintenance has been deferred significantly, the cash flow projections will not provide an accurate picture of operations. You will need to come up with an accurate financial estimate to put the building back in shape and factor that expense into your financial projections. You might be able to negotiate a reduction in the purchase price to accommodate the required renovations or make the landlord bring the building up to snuff prior to the close of escrow. If you are not an experienced builder, architect, or engineer, I suggest hiring some professionals to inspect and rate the building. Have a roofer look at the roof, a structural engineer eyeball the building, and a mechanical engineer or HVAC contractor give the mechanical systems the once-over. Examine the maintenance agreements, talk with the maintenance contractors, and attempt to verify the maintenance history as represented by the seller. If one of the maintenance contractors has been contracted with only recently, insist on meeting with the prior contractor. He or she may have been let go for doing a good job and being unwilling to overlook the deferred maintenance items.

BEFORE YOU CAN CLOSE THE DEAL

Before you start thinking that closing escrow on an investment property is a simple transaction, let's look at it in detail. You might think that you are buying a building, but in reality you are buying a pile of paper about two feet high. You should have a pretty good idea what must happen, but we should review the closing process in detail so that you are ready for the experience.

Documentation

If we break down the documents into three categories, you can see the logic of this. When you understand the process, it ceases to be mysterious.

BUYER

The paper trail goes back to the originator. Your pile is relatively small. It consists of at least the following:

- The initial purchase agreement
- A loan assumption application or new loan documents
- Any approvals you must grant or contingencies you must waive in writing
- Cash—the purchase price in full!
- The closing documents, which you must sign, and in some states the deed, which you must also sign to accept its conveyance

SELLER

The seller's documents are more involved. They include, at the least, the following, shown in order of appearance:

- Leases
- Original loan documents
- Warranties and representations
- A complete accounting
- Hazardous material report, if appropriate (require it when you are buying a property that contains beauty salons, dry cleaning establishments, or any tenant that stores, uses, or sells hazardous materials)
- Copies of contracts that will survive escrow closing
- Maintenance agreements that will survive escrow closing
- Estoppel agreements
- A general warranty deed
- A formal written assignment of the leases and other contracts to remain in force after escrow closes

Third-Party Documents

The most common third-party documents originate from the title company, the lender, and the tenants. They are:

- The preliminary title commitment and the title insurance policy after closing
- The loan documents, originated by the lender
- Acknowledgement of assignment of leases from the tenants (not a common document, but one I'd recommend any time, as it puts tenants on record that there is a new landlord and reaffirms their rental obligations to the new owner)

Seller's Chores

All of this takes time and costs money. The biggest problem is making sure that the submittals are complete. There is so much paper involved in the development and ownership process that the parties have to make sure that it is all accounted for. *Make check lists and use them in conjunction with your acquisition bar chart schedule!* Most leases have subsequent agreements that have to be approved, not the least of which is the parties' acceptance of the plans and specifications and of the completed construction. These executed acknowledgments are, by reference, made a part of the lease along with the plans and specs. There may also be other agreements, made informally, through the exchange of letters that need to be disclosed to and accepted by the buyer.

Estoppel Certificates

Every landlord's nightmare is the estoppel agreement. This document must be executed whenever there is a sale or a new loan. In fact, most loan documents provide that the lender may request that it be executed whenever the lender deems it necessary. It is a relatively simple document that becomes a formidable chore when it is required. Tenants delight in making it difficult for landlords, and lenders and buyers will not consummate any transaction without them. For an example of an estoppel certificate, see Figure 25-1.

Warranties and Assignments

By comparison with estoppel certificates, the assignment of leases and warranties is simple; almost any language will satisfy the parties as long as it is simple and unequivocal. If the assignment of the documents is accepted or acknowledged by the third parties in question, then the assignments are considered to be perfected.

Tenant Security Deposits, Utility Deposits, and Reserves for Replacement Accounts

All lease deposits and utility deposits must be assigned to the buyer; in the case of the utility deposits, adjustment in the purchase price must

TENANT OFFSET AND ESTOPPEL CERTIFICATE

To:

RE: Lease dated ________, 20 _____, by and between ______________________________ [insert landlord's name] as "Landlord" and: ______________________________ [insert tenant's name] as Tenant, on Premises located in ______________________________ [insert premises address]

Gentlemen:

The undersigned tenant (the "Tenant") certifies and represents unto the addressee hereof (hereinafter referred to as the "Addressee") and its attorneys and representatives, with respect to the above-described lease, a true and correct copy of which is attached as ***Exhibit* A** hereto (the "Lease"), as follows:

1. All space and improvements covered by the Lease have been completed and furnished to the satisfaction of Tenant, all conditions required under the Lease have been met, and Tenant has accepted and taken possession of and presently occupies the Premises covered by the Lease.
2. The Lease is for the total term of _______ (________) years, ____ (_______) months commencing ________, 20___, has not been modified, altered, or amended in any respect and contains the entire agreement between Landlord and Tenant, except as _________ [list amendments and modifications other than those, if any, attached to and forming a part of the attached Lease as well as any verbal agreements, or write "None").
3. As of the date hereof, the Minimum Rent under the Lease, payable in equal monthly installments during the term, is $ __________, subject to the CPI Adjustment escalation and Percentage Rent, in accordance with the terms and provisions of the Lease.
4. No rent has been paid by Tenant in advance under the Lease except for $ ______, which amount represents rent for the period ________, 20___ and ending ________, 20___ and Tenant has no charge or claim of offset under said Lease or otherwise, against rents or other amounts due or to become due thereunder. No "discounts," "free rent," or "discounted rent" have been agreed to or are in effect except for _________.
5. A Security Deposit of $ ______ has been made and is currently being held by Landlord.
6. Tenant has no claim against Landlord for any deposit or prepaid rent except as provided in Paragraphs 4 and 5 above.
7. Landlord has satisfied all commitments, arrangements, or understandings made to induce Tenant to enter into the Lease, and Landlord is not in any respect in default in the performance of the terms and provisions of the Lease, nor is there now any fact or condition which, with notice or lapse of time or both, would become such a default.
8. Tenant is not in any respect in default under the terms and provisions of the Lease (nor is there now any fact or condition which, with notice, or lapse of time or both, would become such a default) and has not assigned, transferred, or hypothecated its interest under the Lease, except as follows:
9. Except as expressly provided in the Lease or in any amendment or supplement to the Lease, Tenant:

FIGURE 25-1. ESTOPPEL CERTIFICATE (CONTINUED ON NEXT PAGE)

(i) does not have any right to renew or extend the term of the Lease,
(ii) does not have any option or preferential right to purchase all or any part of the Premises or all or any part of the building or premises of which the Premises are a part, and
(iii) does not have any right, title, or interest with respect to the Premises other than as Tenant under the Lease.

There are no understandings, contracts, agreements, subleases, assignments, or commitments of any kind whatsoever with respect to the Lease of the Premises covered thereby except as expressly provided in the Lease or in any amendment or supplement to the Lease set forth in Paragraph 2 above, copies of which are attached hereto.

10. The Lease is in full force and effect and Tenant has no defenses, setoffs, or counterclaims against Landlord arising out of the Lease or in any way relating thereto or arising out of any other transaction between Tenant and Landlord.

11. The Tenant has not received any notice, directly or indirectly, of a prior assignment, hypothecation, or pledge by Landlord of the rents of the Lease to a person or entity.

12. The current address to which all notices to Tenant as required under the Lease should be sent is:

13. Addressee's rights hereunder shall inure to its successors and assigns.

14. With respect to the Merchant's Promotional Association and/or the Promotional Service, if any, Tenant has no claims, liens, or offsets with regard to any amounts due or to become due thereunder except for______. [If the Addressee is a purchaser or prospective purchaser of the Premises and/or the Building, Tenant shall also include the following.]

15. Tenant acknowledges that Addressee is acquiring ownership of the building in which the Premises are located. Tenant agrees that upon Addressee acquiring ownership, Tenant will attorn and does attorn and agrees to recognize and does recognize Addressee as Landlord on the condition that Addressee agrees to recognize the Lease referred to in this document as long as Tenant is not in default thereunder; provided, however, that Addressee shall have no liability or responsibility under or pursuant to the terms of the Lease for any cause of action or matter not disclosed herein or that accrues after Addressee ceases to own a fee interest in the property covered by the Lease.

16. The Tenant agrees to execute such documents as Addressee may request for the purpose of subordinating the Lease to any mortgage or deed of trust to be placed upon the property by Addressee from time to time and any estoppel certificates requested by Addressee from time to time in connection with the sale or encumbrance of the Premises.

17. Tenant makes this certificate with the understanding that the Addressee is contemplating acquiring the Premises and that if Addressee acquires the Premises, it will do so in material reliance on this certificate and Tenant agrees that the certifications and representations made herein shall survive such acquisition.

Executed on this ____________________ (date)

TENANT: ____________________________

By: ___________________________, Title _________________

FIGURE 25-1. ESTOPPEL CERTIFICATE (CONTINUED)

be made. The cash on deposit with utility companies is the property of the seller and not part of the purchase price. Lease deposits are the property of the tenants and the seller must give them to you to hold in trust for the tenants. The "reserve for replacement" account is funded by the tenants and therefore goes with the building. The seller must pass it along to you at close of escrow.

YOUR JOB

Your job is relatively straightforward. You originate the purchase agreement, then you approve all the paper piled in front of you, and, finally, you pay the money. Sounds simple, doesn't it? The long-term viability of the investment will depend 100 percent on two factors: the effectiveness of your evaluation of the documents and your ability to manage and improve the property.

EVALUATION

We have covered the evaluation process in detail and you have seen the spreadsheets wherein you can analyze the leases at a glance, but it is the projection of the data, your assumptions, and your game plan that will play a pivotal role in the future operation and potential increase in value of your investment. You must determine whether to keep or rotate tenants, how much to raise the rents, and how to insert your lease into the equation. You will have to balance the difficulty of changing the lease with current tenants against the cost of bringing in new tenants. You will have to evaluate the necessity of downsizing an individual tenant's space against the reality of periods of vacancy to implement that strategy. These decisions are all trade-offs. You will be trading periodic cash flow for a stronger, more diverse, and more valuable income stream down the line. In essence, it will be a trade-off of cash flow for capital gain—a difficult, but not too unpleasant chore.

OWNERSHIP, STRUCTURE, AND CAPITAL

One of the biggest decisions in the process will involve the money and the ownership. Are you going to go it alone? Will you bring in partners? If so, why? There are as many compelling reasons for bringing in partners as there are for going it alone. This decision is intensely personal.

Most of us, however, defer to the practical when making this decision. If you have sufficient capital and all of the requisite skills, then you will most likely decide to go it alone. If, however, you are like the rest of us, you never have enough of either. The most likely scenario is that you will recruit some people with cash to invest or the skills to complement your own. If you recruit people with both, you can save money managing the enterprise, but most important of all, two heads are generally better than one and splitting the financial risk is always a sensible and conservative way to go. Not only that, having a partner to back you up may allow you to occasionally take a vacation.

The Money

The largest part of the equation is always the money. Without many exceptions, the purchase price must be paid in cash, retiring the old loans. The exceptions to this rule tend to be very new buildings where the developer has just closed some assumable financing. The reality we face is that most new loans will be limited to 75 percent of the purchase price, necessitating cash equity for the remaining 25 percent. Couple this with the necessity of also having reserves and you have a substantial equity requirement. You may, of course, put the cash up yourself or you may become innovative and see what the other possibilities might be.

EQUITY

Equity may be raised in a number of ways. The governing body for this process is the Securities and Exchange Commission (SEC). The SEC sets the rules governing raising capital through solicitation. Most of the process is exempt from these regulations if you keep the process well within its rules for what is known as "private placements." These rules state that if you solicit no more than 35 people with whom you have a pre-existing relationship and if you form an investor group with ten or fewer of these people, then you are exempt from the formal disclosure laws that the SEC requires for public solicitation. The individuals must meet certain net worth criteria and must qualify as sophisticated investors. These regulations are designed to protect the people who are not able to evaluate a complicated long-term investment or to risk their money in the investment.

Disclaimer—*It has been some time since I actively solicited an investor. Rules and regulations change frequently, so I suggest that you consult a securities attorney to check on the current regulations before presenting any data to a prospective financial partner.*

Another way to raise the equity is to find one investor who will put up all the money required and allow you to earn a share of the incremental increase in value realized through management and subsequent sale. Most investors of this type will make a deal wherein their equity is paid a preferred, minimum rate of return from day one and a percentage of any increase in cash flow as the property increases in value. Upon sale, the investor recaptures his or her equity prior to the agreed-upon split of the profits. You might notice that I said "split of the profits" rather than "capital gain." Profit is defined as the increase in sales price over the original purchase price, whereas taxable gain is defined as profit, plus the recapture of any depreciation taken during the period of ownership.

LOANS

The balance of the purchase price may be in the form of a loan. The elements of any loan that determine the viability of the loan are the amount, the term, the interest rate, and the debt service constant or the amortization rate.

Obviously, the amount of the loan must be sufficient to meet your needs, but what about the rest? The interest rate of the loan is the interest charged annually to borrow the money—the cost of funds. Most loans today are simple interest loans that calculate interest monthly based on the unpaid balance of the loan. The payment is determined by the *amortization schedule* or the *debt service constant*. This is defined as a constant percentage multiplied by the principal amount, sufficient to yield a payment that includes the required annual interest and provides for the complete retirement of the principal balance over the term of the loan. The resulting constant is expressed as a percentage, known as a *loan constant*. These constants are contained in tables or calculated as needed. From the loan constant tables I have used for years, the constant required to pay a loan at an eight-percent interest rate over a 30-year term is 8.81 percent. The annual payment is calculated by multiplying the principal of the loan by the constant .0881.

FOR EXAMPLE

A million-dollar loan would yield an annual mortgage payment of $1,000,000 x 0.0881 = $88,100. This is then translated into monthly mortgage payments by dividing by 12, yielding monthly payments of $7,416.67.

The final factor in any loan is the term of the loan. A typical loan today would entail a 25-year amortization rate and a ten-year term. This means that the payments are based on an amortization rate of 25 years, but the principal balance is due at the end of ten years. This *balloon payment* is set up for several reasons. Lenders have learned over the years that income property can deteriorate under poor management, as well as improve under good management. The early due date does not necessarily mean that the lender wants the loan paid off; rather, the early due date provides the lender with the opportunity to re-examine the security to ascertain its continued viability at the ten-year mark. If the loan looks good, the lender will most likely offer to extend the term with or without changes in the interest rate and amortization schedule. This also provides the borrower with the opportunity to increase the loan dollars, recapturing cash equity, in the event the borrower has been successful in substantially increasing the NIBDS. This could provide the capital to take on another property while keeping the current one.

RESERVES

The final part of the investment equation lies in setting aside and maintaining proper reserves. How much is enough? How is it determined? The answer is that every investor must make his or her own determination. I can share with you my philosophy, but you must make your own determination.

There are four factors that I evaluate when constructing a reserve:

- Cash flow
- The relative size of the tenants
- The tenants' financial condition and business
- Lease expiration dates

If the cash flow is at 100 percent of GPI, I will always set aside the imputed five-percent vacancy factor as a cash flow reserve. I will let it accumulate at least until such time as I have built up a six-month mortgage payment balance. This reserve will see me through the period of releasing, if and when it happens.

The size of the tenants will determine whether I will need to replace large tenants with smaller ones. I will, at least, tie the large tenants into a long-term lease. At renewal time, I want them to extend well beyond my projected sale date or I will replace them. The cash flow fund will see me through this period of reduced cash flow.

The next consideration is the tenants' financial condition and the state of their businesses. If some of the tenants look flaky, I will set aside a month or two of their rent, to allow me time to replace them. I will also set aside sufficient funds for recapitalizing the required tenant spaces.

The final significant factor is the expiration date of the leases. I would generally provide for rent and recapitalization of any leases expiring within 24 months of the purchase date.

Finally, there is Murphy's Law. Pick your own number; you will most likely need it. Finding additional capital during a crisis is always expensive. Plan ahead and beat the odds.

Add these factors together and you will find that it's a big number. More than likely, you will not need that much, but if you do, you will be glad you have it.

CHAPTER

26

The Purchase Agreement

The purchase agreement is, in my world, the pivotal element of a successful real estate venture. You have heard me say over and over that "you make your money when you buy." My business lives and dies by those words—and *the purchase agreement is the single most important tool in the deal. (No exceptions!)*

In the Appendix of this book is a document entitled "Agreement of Purchase and Sale and Joint Escrow Instructions." This agreement with specific variations is the one I have used for over 25 years in the real estate investment and development business. It is not perfect and I do not recommend that you copy it and start using it. Rather, I do recommend that you read it carefully and understand it as a tool to help you craft a deal that you would like to pursue.

This chapter is all about that contract and how to use it. The agreement that I use starts out with 35 clauses plus a paragraph entitled "Effective Date." This is a three-party contract: buyer, seller, and escrow agent. We will cover all parts of the contract as well as the construction of it.

Draft Around Your Schedule

The first thing you need to do in preparing a purchase agreement is to create a critical path schedule for your preclosing chores. This is not exactly rocket science. It should be simple.

Item	Time Frame in Weeks														
	1	2	3	4	5	6	7	8	9	10	11	12	13	14	15
Check title															
Review leases															
Inspect building															
Arrange financing															
Prepare closing															

TABLE 26-1. CRITICAL PATH, SCHEDULE 1

The Critical Path Schedule

The finished product should look something like Table 26-1.

This schedule is obviously for purchasing a building. Table 26-2 shows the same approach, but for purchasing a parcel of land to build on.

As you can see from the two schedules, there are different chores to be done, but the principle remains the same. You need to know how long it is going to take you to get ready to close the escrow. With this chore out of the way, you can start drafting your purchase agreement.

Development Projects

Development projects proceed in a very logical way. The order of chores is generally as follows:

- Place the land in escrow.
- Examine and approve the title and zoning.
- Contract for a survey and topo.
- Hire an architect and an engineer.
- Start the preliminary design.

Item	Time Frame in Months															
	1	2	3	4	5	6	7	8	9	10	11	12	13	14	14	16
Check title																
Survey and topo																
Preliminary design																
Schematic design																
Preleasing																
Financing																
Working drawings																
Bid construction																
Close construction loan																
Start construction																

TABLE 26-2. CRITICAL PATH, SCHEDULE 2

- Initiate any governmental zoning requirements.
- Finalize design and start leasing process.
- Create schematic design for preliminary bidding.
- Select your contractor.
- Start the financing process.
- Initiate working drawings.
- Complete any zoning work.
- Submit the plans for a building permit.
- Commit to your construction loan.
- Close escrow on the land and the construction loan simultaneously and start building.

Income Property Purchases

Purchasing an investment property is much the same as purchasing a parcel of land for development, without all the design and construction considerations. The chore list looks something like this:

- Open the escrow.
- Check the title report.
- Examine the leases and create your tenant spreadsheets.
- Review and weed out the maintenance contracts.
- Make a decision on property management and maintenance agreements.
- Review your financing options and apply for financing.
- Inspect the building and have the seller correct any glaring problems. (Do not forget the potential of hazardous material liability.)
- Formalize your management plan.
- Close the escrow and the new loan.
- Initiate your management program.

From the above list of chores and the ones listed for the development project, you must have surmised that there will be several contingencies to the closing of the escrow of your target project. In the case of the development project, your contingencies should be at least the following items:

- An acceptable title report
- An acceptable survey and topo
- Contract for and approval of the level-one environmental assessment
- Completion of any necessary governmental approvals, like zoning or master plan changes
- Completion of working drawings and affordable bid prices
- Preleasing to an anchor tenant or breakeven, whichever triggers your financing
- Arranging suitable financing
- Receipt of a building permit

For a purchase of investment property, your contingencies to closing should be as follows:

- An acceptable title report and hazardous material survey
- Approval of the lease documents and maintenance contracts
- An acceptable building inspection and remediation agreement
- Completion of any required maintenance issues and resolution of any title defects
- Receipt of acceptable new financing or assumption of the existing financing

These items will become part of your purchase agreement and they will be built into the time frame outlined in your critical path schedules shown above for the two projects.

The Contract

How many of us have purchased a home or another piece of real estate and signed a contract prepared by someone else? Did you actually read it from start to finish? Did you understand the entire contract? If you are going to become an intelligent buyer, you need to know what you are signing and why each clause is included in the contract. A quick review of the contract is in order:

The preamble is standard; it sets out the parties and their intentions and identifies the property.

Article 1 identifies the escrow holder and sets the conditions of the escrow.

Article 2 states the intent of the parties, buying and selling a specific parcel of property.

Article 3 spells out the purchase price and how it is to be paid into escrow. It is specifically tied into the successful resolution of specific contingency items by references to articles 4, 6, 7, and 10, etc. It also goes on to reference conditions and options spelled out in articles 4, 5, and 3. This effectively ties the buyer's payments to specific events and approvals. It also says that if these events are not successfully completed on time, the buyer is entitled to his or her money back.

Article 4 lays out the first contingency, the title report, and delineates the time frames within which the title is to be presented, examined, and approved. It also ties this operation into the survey. This is a key element, because a survey acceptable to the title company can take six to eight weeks. The type of title commitment is also a key issue. You want an ALTA extended coverage title policy and the lender will require it. This covers the buyer and the lender from all items of record *and* any problems observed on the land itself, as well as any unrecorded potential title problems. The survey should be specified to be an ALTA survey so that the title company can cross-check any items in the title report with those physical items found in the field. The title company will also be required to physically review the survey in the field to determine whether anything was overlooked before committing to issue an ALTA insurance policy. This combination of title report and survey requirement should buy you at least 60-90 days at the front end of a development project and 45-60 days in an investment property purchase. This paragraph should be cross-referenced to article 6, "Right of inspection," and article 7, "Survey."

HEADS UP

You must have wondered why this contract is designed to be a three-party agreement. It is for the control of the monies and conditions. By accepting this contract and executing the effective date paragraph, the escrow holder has become a party to the agreement and must abide by the terms of this agreement. It further states that if a separate escrow agreement is drafted and executed, the terms of this agreement govern. As a buyer, you must have control of your cash deposits at all times; if you decide to opt out of the contract within the specified time frame, you want the escrow company to be obligated to return your cash if you are entitled to it, with complete disregard of the sentiments of the seller. This point is reiterated in several places in the contract. In fact, you can get back your earnest money deposit until you instruct the escrow agent to release the cash to the seller in article 8.

Article 5 starts to spell out your right to cancel this agreement and get your deposit back by referencing other articles in the contract, specifically 4, 6, 7, and 10. Remember: the title company is bound to execute the return of cash upon receipt of notice from you.

Article 6 delineates your right to inspect the property and have your consultants go onto the property for examination and testing. On a cautionary note, you must verify that all your consultants have insurance *before* you authorize them to invade the property.

Article 7 discusses the time frame for the survey. I always try to get 30 days from the time I approve the title report because I do not want to waste money on a survey if the title is unacceptable to me. The bonus is that this additional 30 days gives you a total free look of 60 days. After that, you invariably have to risk some nonrefundable money. You can maintain contingencies, but the results after this period almost always reflect your efforts rather than the seller's.

Article 8 is a key money control paragraph. It states that once you have removed the agreed-upon contingencies specified in articles 3, 4, 5, and 7 you will release the nonrefundable earnest money to the seller. The seller, simultaneously with the release, has to place an executed deed into escrow. This is for your protection. Should anything happen to the seller before the close of escrow, the closing becomes automatic when you place the balance of the purchase price into escrow. This protects you from having the property tied up in a probate situation or some other time-consuming problem centered on the seller.

Article 9 deals with you placing the purchase price in escrow according to the terms of article 3. It is somewhat redundant.

Article 10 is a detailed list of *conditions precedent* to closing, primarily the responsibility of the seller. It reiterates the buyer's option to pass in the event of nonperformance by the seller.

Article 11 is a detailed instruction to the escrow holder specifying under what conditions the escrow company is permitted to close the escrow. It references all the contingencies (articles 3, 4, 7, 8, and 9), the documents, the money, and the title policy. It also alludes to potential extension of the closing date as specified in article 23.

Article 12 spells out the closing costs and who pays for what.

Article 13 deals with the seller providing the buyer with all substantive existing information on the subject property within 48 hours of the opening of escrow.

Article 14 spells out the seller's specific representations. This paragraph is tailored to each specific property and will vary considerably from an investment purchase to a land purchase.

Article 15 discusses documentation pertaining to the tax code and the legal status of the seller.

Article 16 is a clause about hazardous waste and who is responsible. This clause seems to grow with each use. The one contained in the sample purchase agreement is mercifully brief, but any attorney worth his or her salt can improve on it. It is very important to protect you from any liability attached to an event or condition that precedes your taking title to the property.

Article 17 reiterates that this escrow is a cooperative venture between buyer and seller and compels cooperation between the parties to get the contingencies met and the deal closed. It specifically compels the parties to execute the required documents in a timely manner.

Article 18 is the liquidated damages clause. It is designed to specifically protect you, the buyer, in the event you default on the purchase of the property. It limits the damages due the seller to the nonrefundable deposit you released to the seller. It specifically precludes any suit for "specific performance." You want to avoid at all costs a clause that allows the seller to sue for specific performance. This way, your financial risk is limited solely to your deposit.

Article 19 allows you to place "for lease" and "for sale" signs on the property.

Article 20 specifies that the title company will distribute the title policy ASAP.

Article 21 delineates when the buyer may take possession. This clause is drafted to suit each specific project. Sometimes the seller needs time to vacate the premises.

Article 22 This clause allows buyer and seller to agree on changes in the deal and to modify the contract and the escrow instructions.

Article 23 spells out that the entire agreement is contained in this contract and there is no agreement outside the scope of this executed agreement. This is a boilerplate clause.

Article 24 is another boilerplate clause.

Article 25 spells out who receives any real estate commission and what amount(s).

Article 26 allows the agreement to be executed in counterparts. This is a boilerplate clause.

Article 27 puts the onus on the parties to perform in a timely manner. This is a boilerplate clause.

Article 28 is also boilerplate.

Article 29 spells out where to send the notices and how they must be sent to be enforceable. This is also boilerplate.

Article 30 allows for litigation rather than arbitration and allows the prevailing party to recover attorney's fees. This is a negotiable point because there are compelling arguments in favor of both arbitration and litigation. This is a boilerplate clause. Amend this article to suit your preferences.

Article 31 allows the buyer to assign this contract to a successor or, if so stated, precludes any assignment. The right to assign is vital if you wish to flip the property or put it into a partnership.

HEADS UP

If you have a contract for purchase for over 12 months and assign it at a profit to a third party, your gain is taxable as long-term capital gain rather than ordinary income because you have sold an asset held for 12 months or more. If you have no rights of assignment and are forced to double-escrow the property, taking title and selling it simultaneously, you have lost your capital gain because what you will be selling is not your contract, but the land you held title to for an instant.

Article 32 spells out the conditions and stipulations regarding the possible recordation of this agreement. You may want to record the contract to put any third parties on notice that you own a beneficial interest in the property that cannot be circumvented by the seller. In other words, he or she cannot sell it twice.

Article 33 compels the parties to cooperate in the executions of required documents in a timely manner.

Article 34 is a clause saying that this offer is null and void unless accepted by a certain date and time. This is a boilerplate clause.

Article 35 gives the buyer a one-time right to extend the closing by an agreed-upon number of days at an agreed-upon amount of money. Whether the additional money accrues to the purchase price or not is also the subject of negotiation with the seller. I recommend having an extension clause in any purchase agreement, as there is invariably some form of last minute detail to iron out. Remember Murphy's Law.

Signature blocks are self-explanatory.

Effective date marries the title company to the deal and compels it to act in compliance with the terms of the agreement.

Notary blocks are mandatory if you want to record the agreement. Each jurisdiction has specific rules for the recordation of documents. In my area, the documents must have a cover page, be on 8½-by-11 paper, be written in 12-point type with a minimum 1-inch margin, and have a full legal description attached. *This document must be notarized to be recordable.*

Exhibit A is the property description.

Exhibit B spells out any personal property or leases that go with the real estate.

Now that you fully understand the purchase document, you are ready to draft your first deal.

Writing the Contingencies

When drafting a purchase agreement, you need to decide how it is to be presented. To be successfully executed, it must be palatable to the seller. That implies that it should be a fair agreement, with both parties satisfied with the executed document. Whenever someone feels that he or she has been had, the deal never goes smoothly. A successful deal is one that satisfies both parties.

The Seller's Point of View

Any seller wants the same thing: the asking price paid as quickly and as easily as possible. Most sellers and sellers' agents are swift enough to realize that this is not likely to happen. First of all, most people price their property a little higher than they will settle for so that they can come down on the price to give the buyer the impression that he or she is getting a bargain. This is generally the situation that you will be addressing when you put an agreement together.

The Buyer's Mindset

When you are buying a piece of investment property, your mindset is different than if you are buying a parcel of land to build on. So, let's address both philosophies to establish a mindset for drafting a workable agreement.

The Investment Property Offer

What you want is the best possible income stream for the best cap rate, coupled with the best-maintained building for the dollars invested. This is a tall order, but in reality, to accomplish this, the seller and the seller's representations are your best ally. Most likely, the easiest thing to establish is the price, but what you want to establish is a price based on a cap rate of verifiable NNN income. You need to create language that establishes that this is the way the final purchase price will be established, without alarming the seller at the time of negotiation. The way to do that goes something like this:

> *The purchase price shall be $1,300,000, plus or minus, determined by multiplying the verified net income before debt service (NIBDS) by a cap rate of 8.5 percent.*

Sounds innocuous, doesn't it? The mention of a cap rate is merely acknowledging how the purchase price has been established between buyer and seller. The other side of the coin is to build into the agreement an exhibit B that delineates the leases, in both rate and duration, and in the representations clause, article 14, allude to an *actual* operating expense represented by the seller. Having an expense exhibit is also very helpful. The time frame that will be built into the agreement will coincide with your critical path schedule and will be spelled out in the contingency clauses, the conditions precedent clause, or both.

The Land Offer

Your objective in making a land offer is to put off the purchase date as far as possible so that you have the opportunity to get as many front-end chores completed as possible prior to having to purchase the land. Again, the seller's objective is your best ally. I never want to own a parcel of land without the following items in hand:

- The building permit
- A construction loan ready to close
- Preleasing to breakeven
- All the required equity

If you have been paying close attention so far, you will have deduced that this will take a considerable amount of time to accomplish, about 18-24 months on the average. The big trick is to come up with a way to get that time. I have been successful by offering the seller three things in the offer:

1. I am upfront about not purchasing the land until the above contingencies are accomplished.
2. I always, within reason, offer full price.
3. I offer a reasonable nonrefundable deposit, with the amount varying on the type of chores to be done. In the case of a rezoning, the deposit will be minimal until the rezoning is granted, then stepped up during the period between the rezoning and the receipt of a building permit.

Basic Contingencies

There are certain clauses in any agreement that are out-and-out contingencies that the seller must live with, including the following items:

- A clean and marketable title and ALTA commitment
- An acceptable survey and topo for a development property or an as-built survey for an income property
- Verifiable representations, i.e. document review, including zoning, entitlements, leases, and contracts

These are basic contingencies; until you, as the buyer, have had an adequate time to evaluate these documents, there is no deal. Your earnest money is not or should not yet be at risk.

Specific Contingencies

In a development project, you may have a list of chores that you need to accomplish before you are able to build the project. In an investment purchase, the same holds true, but the list is generally confined to finding and closing new financing, which is usually accomplished in 60-120 days. Once the basic contingencies are accomplished, it is customary for the buyer's deposits to "go hard." This means that a specified sum of money is now nonrefundable and is set aside in escrow or released to the seller as liquidated damages in the event that the buyer does not close escrow. It is not the seller's fault that the buyer cannot complete the rest of the conditions precedent to the closing.

In a very real sense, you, the buyer, must pay for the time needed to do your work. That is the subject of the last topic in this chapter, working with the executed contract.

Behind "Outs" Clauses

Why are the above items so important that the seller has to sit still until they are verified? The answers are simple, but, unless you have been through this, you might not understand the significance.

- In the case of the title, you have to have an absolutely clear title, subject only to routine items such as taxes and agreed-upon assessments, or your investment may be in jeopardy and your lender will not make the loan.

- The survey and topo are germane to what can be built on the site and to the availability of the necessary utilities and street frontage. If it's not all there, you may have to spend a fortune getting the utilities to the buildings. In the case of an as-built survey, this is essential to verify that the builder did not encroach on any required setbacks or rights of way. This is imperative to new financing and will prevent losing a strategic piece of property in any future condemnation or expansion of existing rights of way.
- The document, zoning, and entitlement review work for investment and development projects alike in that you have to have time to assess the legal rights and obligations that govern the property you are purchasing. They must be appropriate to your uses to make the property developable or profitable.

Working with the Executed Agreement

Once you are past the basic contingencies and your deposit has "gone hard," you are embarked on your part of the deal. Theoretically, you have now paid the seller for the time necessary for you to accomplish your tasks. In an investment deal, the only real contingency is, generally, financing: if you do not have a likely lender before you open the escrow, then you might be in trouble. You should prequalify yourself with a reputable mortgage banker so that the only real contingency to the deal is the appraisal and the loan commitment.

In a development deal, you may have the following chores, broken into two different levels:

- Entitlements
  - Modifying the master plan
  - Rezoning
  - Use permits
  - Variances
- Permits, leases, and financing
  - Building permits
  - Leasing to anchor tenants or breakeven
  - Construction and permanent financing commitments

The entitlements level is one that you can expect the seller to ride out with you, because if these conditions precedent cannot be met, then the property is useless for your intended project. During this stage, the seller will be eager to cooperate and work on your behalf.

HEADS UP

It is during this period that you have all the leverage on your side, because the land does not yet have the required entitlements to be useful as a development project. You will not have to pay for extensions during this period if it runs over. The seller has to cooperate with your request for more time or go back to square one with another buyer.

Once this phase is completed, you can expect the seller to want a vastly increased deposit to compensate him or her for sitting still while you do your thing. The fact is that if you cannot accomplish the last few chores, it's not the seller's fault. The property is now entitled and is, therefore, more valuable than when the deal started and he or she will not have to go back to square one with a new buyer. If you need extensions now, you'll have to pay through the nose. That's the rationale for building potential late-term extensions into the deal upfront, in an article within the original purchase agreement. The seller will always be more reasonable at the front end of the deal when he or she is eager to make a sale. After the fact, it is invariably more costly to negotiate an extension.

Once you have been through a development deal from start to finish, you will have acquired a real appreciation for the role of both buyer and seller and a genuine respect for the cash value of time.

The Other Side of the Coin

All of the preceding points in this chapter have been geared to make you a better informed and more organized buyer. Once you have purchased your investment property or developed your new project, you might realize that someday you will be a seller; at that point, the shoe will be on the other foot. In Chapter 35, we will cover the best way to sell your property; in either situation, a fair and enforceable agreement is the best way to go.

SECTION

VI

DEVELOPMENT: ACQUIRING AT WHOLESALE

CHAPTER

27

How *to* Buy a Development Site

It matters not whether you are buying a house, an income-producing property, raw land for investment, or a parcel of land for development, the prudent approach is the best approach. Most of the following is intended for use when dealing with commercial property; however, if you tone it down a little, apply some common sense, and use the Realtor's® preprinted forms with a few contingencies thrown in, the principles outlined in this chapter will also work for you when you are buying houses. The steps outlined in this chapter are used by my companies and have been developed over a 25-year period. They have served me well. Every step has a purpose and a risk-limiting value. Skip these steps at your own peril.

The Step-by-Step Approach

Start with Site Selection

Site/building/project selection may be initiated in many ways: looking for a site for a specific use, looking for a viable use for property already owned, or simply looking to maximize the value of a parcel of land by converting it to its "highest and best use." The practical approach to site selection must incorporate many factors that influence the decision to acquire or prepare a site for subsequent development. How do the developers pick their sites? While there are no rules as such, there are some factors that are common to all developers when looking for a site.

First of all, the site should be in the path of growth or along a highly used traffic arterial. Most cities or SMSAs grow in fairly predictable directions unless there are physical limitations such as rivers, lakes, or mountains.

LOCATION

The old commercial real estate's adage of "location, location, and location" is in reality now redefined as "traffic count and accessibility." In the old days, location was defined in the old downtown in terms of visibility and volume of foot traffic. In general, the closer the department store, the better the location. This rule holds true today for location selection within a regional mall in the same way that it did in the old downtown of the '40s and '50s.

For a site to be viable today for commercial development, it must have visibility to automobile traffic and be accessible to the automobile. The single best location characteristic for suburban developments is to locate along traffic corridors between the residential sections and the traditional downtown. The more vehicles that pass a given site in a day, the more valuable the site will be.

One key element in any development is to pass along information about the site. This is accomplished by signs; the ability to use signs is heavily regulated by all governmental bodies. Signage rights will determine how to get these vehicles onto the subject site. The ideal site or "100% location" is a site that sits at the intersection of two major arterials with a traffic light. Accessibility for automobiles is the reality and the ability to place signs where the motorists can read them is essential for a site to be considered truly viable.

There are other factors that also influence the selection, such as curb cuts and traffic flow, but these can usually be worked out with the planning staff and the developer's design team. These secondary considerations are part of the evaluation of the configuration of the site and generally fall within the preliminary design phase of the project.

Limiting Financial Exposure

The purpose of this approach is to limit your financial exposure as you progress through the deal. In Chapter 34, we will go over a joint venture transaction that I call the "zero-dollar deal." That chapter will tie all the steps together and demonstrate to you how you can own a piece of investment-grade real estate without a cent of your own money left in the deal. If you think this does not work, know that I have done this successfully over 40 times in my career. It is the only way I develop income-producing property and it is a proven good deal for all concerned. As you review the steps below, keep in mind why you are doing it this way. See how each step allows you to remove obstacles before you commit your funds.

SITE ACQUISITION

Once the prospective site is identified, it becomes the "subject site." The next assignment is to get control of it. Having control of the site is, by definition, acquiring a *beneficial interest* in the site. Beneficial interest means having de facto rights of ownership, the unequivocal right to acquire the site. This can be accomplished in various ways, the least prudent of which is immediate noncontingent purchase. The best possible way is to option the site for future purchase. The most common method of acquisition is the execution of a *purchase agreement* between the developer/buyer and the seller, spelling out the terms of purchase and any contingencies thereto, with an escrow period sufficiently long to enable the developer to evaluate the potential risks.

This is the definitive tool for site acquisition in the commercial development business. When drafting this document, there are some conservative rules that I recommend using as a fail-safe mechanism so that you as the buyer/developer are able to limit your financial exposure at the front end of any project.

The Land Purchase Agreement

The purchase agreement is the most vital tool in the early stages of any project, as it lays out the project schedule and spells out to both buyer and seller who is responsible for what and when it is to be completed. This agreement will determine the lead time and cost of establishing the feasibility of the proposed development. At least, it should provide the developer with a period of time to perform what is known as *due diligence.* The period in which this is scheduled is known as the "free look" period, so called because the buyer may cancel the purchase contract anytime within this period and receive his or her money back. During this time a buyer can test, evaluate, and analyze the site to determine its viability as a potential commercial real estate investment. Appendix B is a sample "Agreement of Purchase and Sale and Joint Escrow Instructions" and a companion CD-ROM is available from the author with working copies of the contracts and spreadsheets used in the development and management process.

Basic Clauses to Be Included

The purchase agreement should incorporate all the representations of the seller and the buyer, as well as the steps required to vet (evaluate) the project and the general business terms and schedule of the proposed land purchase. The various approvals and evaluations necessary to successfully complete a commercial development project can be used as contingencies to preserve the buyer's earnest money deposit in the event that the site does not shape up during the evaluation process. By listing the *conditions precedent* necessary for development of the proposed site as contingencies to the buyer's completion of the site purchase, the buyer can effectively limit the earnest money deposit that is nonrefundable. The buyer should disclose to the seller what he or she intends to do with the land, stating that if that is not possible or feasible based on his or her market and site feasibility studies, then the purchase agreement will become voidable. It is important to have the option to void the transaction belong exclusively to the buyer, as the buyer may elect to proceed for some reason other than that initially intended for the transaction.

It is vital for the buyer to represent to the seller that the purchase agreement is the beginning of the development process, not the beginning of a potential land speculation. The purchase agreement should be clearly the first step in a serious commercial development project. Most sellers will agree to contingencies if the buyer actively works to remove these contingencies. They take great comfort in the fact that a principal/developer is willing to spend his or her own money on someone else's land.

Contingencies

Some specific types of contingencies common to purchase agreements in the commercial development industry are:

- Approval by the buyer of the preliminary title report
- The geotechnical investigation
- The zoning
- The boundary survey and topographic map
- The traffic impact study

- In California, the environmental impact report (EIR or EIS)
- Approval by the appropriate governmental jurisdiction of the level-one environmental assessment
- The lender's preliminary leasing requirements
- The archeological evaluation
- An endangered species survey
- The development plan
- Use permits, if required
- Finally, if possible, the actual building permits

This sounds like the seller is willing to be overaccommodating to the developer, but depending on the seller and the buyer's experience and reputation, any or all of these conditions, and more, can be inserted into a contract as conditions precedent to the earnest money becoming nonrefundable or at least the final closing of the site purchase. The price for this accommodation is, generally, that the buyer must pay top dollar for the site.

Most often, the seller will permit an examination of title, geotechnical investigation, and zoning to be accomplished during the "free look" or due diligence period, but after that he or she usually wants to see some "hard cash" (nonrefundable money) at risk for delaying the closing any further. The customary method of converting the earnest money deposit into "hard cash" is to render the earnest money forfeitable after the expiration of the "free look" period in the event that the buyer does not close the escrow. It is common practice for the buyer to put up additional sums of money to delay the closing, as it enables the buyer to complete his or her laundry list prior to committing the large amount of capital necessary to purchase, develop, lease, and sell the land with or without the proposed development in place.

There are some realities that you need to take on board during this process. Remember them well.

This agreement is the most important risk-limiting document in the entire development process!

Set your goals down in the agreement.

- Do not close escrow until you are ready to break ground if you are building.
- Do not close the escrow until all contingencies such as permits and financing are obtained.

This sounds simple, but it is not always possible. If this is not possible, then, at the very least:

- Do not close the escrow until acquiring the legal right (the entitlement) to build the project as conceived and evaluated.

This right consists of having not less than the required zoning, site plan, and architectural approval, and, if pertinent, special use permits or, in the case of residential and/or commercial subdivisions, preliminary plat approval.

How to Evaluate the Site

These general rules of acquisition aside, the factors that influence the buying decision include the following:

- Market and economic demand for the proposed project
- Price per leasable square foot of the proposed project
- The specific zoning
- The specific stipulations (stips) of the governing body (county or city)
- Geotechnical considerations, topography
- Exposure to the public (site configuration)
- Coverage available for development, i.e., how many square feet can be built on the site?

How do developers evaluate or vet the sites they chose? Using the new location criterion as a given, there is the gut instinct of the true developer, as most sites cry out for a particular treatment. The technical or practical analysis is also vital and is generally performed by the developer during the "free look" period contained within the purchase agreement.

HEADS UP

Until sufficient experience is accumulated, newcomers to the development business are strongly encouraged to hire experts to perform market demand and economic analysis of potential sites.

Finally, the clinical, "by the numbers" analysis must also pass muster. Ultimately, the numbers will govern. If the property passes all other tests, the total land cost per square foot of buildable leasable space will be the real deciding factor in the numbers analysis, as the cost must be low enough or there is no hope of producing buildings at competitive rents. Most often, the price of the land will determine the feasibility of the project. You cannot overcome a purchase price that is too high. To determine the land price per leasable square foot, simply divide the land price by the number of net rentable square feet in the proposed project. Accomplish as much front-end work as possible, the ultimate goal being a workable budget and enough preleasing to enable the project to be built.

In the 1970s, most lenders' preleasing requirements were about 25 percent of the *gross leasable area* (GLA). Today their requirement is, generally, at least 75 percent for conventional construction financing and 95 percent leased and occupied for permanent nonrecourse financing. This is a tall order, so developers should try to eliminate most of the contingencies prior to investing a great deal of irretrievable capital. These front-end costs cannot be recaptured if the project has to be scrapped and the land resold. So keep these front-end expenditures to a minimum. Most principals are comfortable with the market risks of leasing and financing, but almost uniformly, developers want to see all the governmental approvals, except, perhaps, the final plats and building permits, prior to closing on the land. Be sure that the purchase price is determined by a specific cost per square foot or per buildable unit as determined by an accurate ALTA survey! If possible, try to have the final purchase price determined by the total number of usable square feet or number of buildable units.

Obviously, as with all rules, there are exceptions. Large public housing developers break them all for large-scale new community development. While they are usually assured by strong political commitments that they will not be left holding the bag, they too get stung occasionally.

Usable and buildable square feet are determined by subtracting all areas that do not permit building, by easement, deed restrictions, or topographical limitations. During the "free look" phase of the project, the feasibility must be established to justify the purchase of the site. This all costs money and, minimally, the following items need to be done to evaluate the site:

- Survey and topo
- Geotechnical evaluation
- Market survey and competition analysis
- Schematic design
- Pro forma evaluation

First, the Preliminary Title Report or Abstract

When referring to this precondition in the purchase agreement, there are some good ideas that can be incorporated into the language.

Legal points should be supplied by the project's attorney.

Disclaimer: *Nothing contained in this book or the companion CD-ROM constitutes the author's attempt to render legal advice, except "Trade honestly with all parties!"*

The title should be conveyed in as broad a manner as possible. Ask your attorney for guidance in this matter. The exceptions noted in schedule B of the preliminary title report (the prelim) should reference certain recorded documents. Stipulate that the seller has not delivered a complete prelim for your evaluation unless the prelim is accompanied by legible copies of all documents referenced in the preliminary title report. Seek to have as much as a month to evaluate and approve the prelim. In no case agree to less than two weeks for the process. For states that do not use the title process, the prelim will be known as an *abstract of title*. Make sure that the title attorney evaluates each and every document in terms of the developer's intended use, understanding all the limitations and benefits that each document conveys.

HEADS UP

Always purchase the extended coverage title insurance; it insures the buyer against all defects of title not appearing in the recorded documents. Tie this into the ALTA project boundary survey and topo and insist on written approval of the survey and topographic map by the title company as part of the extended coverage title policy.

The Well Driller Legend

The old urban legend of the driller appearing in the lobby of the high-rise building and stating that he has purchased the subsurface rights and wants the lobby cleared so that he can drill for oil is not necessarily a myth. These things happen and are always financially ruinous!

Do the homework and do not approve the document until your attorney is 100-percent satisfied that the title will be sufficiently beneficial for the intended use. If not, back out and find another site.

The site should always be inspected for conformance with the boundary survey and approved by the title company so that the buyer can get the extended coverage title policy at the close of escrow *(COE)*, i.e., coverage for those problems that do not appear in the recorded documents. The boundary survey and the topographic map will be used by the project engineer and architect to determine the suitability of the land for the proposed use as well as the potential site plan and coverage (achievable density). Once again, if the site does not shape up, pass and find another. Throwing good money after bad is never a good idea.

Second, Physical Evaluation of the Site

During the "free look" period, it is necessary to determine whether the geotechnical characteristics, topography, and survey are adequate to support the proposed project. Most likely, there will be many government-imposed evaluations required. Geotechnical evaluations should be exhaustive, including, as a minimum:

- Seismic evaluation
- Topo or drainage impact
- Archeological evaluation
- Environmental and endangered species evaluation—flora and fauna
- Potential vehicle emissions
- Traffic impact
- Visual impact
- Lighting and sound emissions

- Soil testing for load-bearing capacity
- All of these considerations must be taken into account in a development.

The Environmental Impact Report (EIR or EIS)

In California, the EIR process includes, among other items, an environmental assessment, a seismic evaluation, prior-uses research (including actual and potential hazardous material contamination), soil condition (including load-bearing capacity), storm drainage characteristics before and after development, an examination of flora and fauna (including the potential presence of endangered species on-site), traffic impact before and after, visual impact, economic impact to the area, visual or architectural impact, impact on existing "view corridors," and anything else the city or county planning staff can come up with.

In Arizona the required evaluation is only prior uses and possible past contamination. Most states fall somewhere between the two extremes and some states have no environmental evaluation at all. In reality, all states will soon have some form of environmental impact analysis, as it is the only responsible way to determine the actual impact of a proposed development. In the case of California, Washington, and Arizona, it has been escalated beyond a legitimate tool of evaluation. It is now frequently used to limit growth and to generate revenue for the governing authority.

The Boundary Survey

The boundary survey will verify the size and configuration of the land and should show all existing improvements or remnants thereof, recorded easements or restrictions, and anything that will show up on visual inspection and unrecorded documents. It will also provide buyer and seller with an exact square foot total to determine the final purchase price. The boundary survey, if done to ALTA or extended-coverage criteria, will determine not only the exact size of the site, but also any restrictions, such as easements, that affect the buildability of the site.

The Topographic Map

The topographic map (topo) will determine the extent of potential site development (grading, cuts, and fills) needed for the intended use. For the most part, the analysis will boil down to the amount of buildable square footage or coverage available on-site. Coverage is dictated by zoning as well as physical limitations on the site. It is also determined by decisions about the proposed building, such as the shape and the number of stories. The buildable square footage and the required parking and landscaping will set the stage for the economic analysis. Each of these decisions will affect the feasibility of the site.

One-, two-, and three-story buildings are the most common in suburbia. Two-story buildings are considered to be less expensive per square foot, providing more room for on-site parking and landscaping. Even with the ADA requirements, the two-story building, while not any less expensive, still may afford better building coverage. Three-story buildings are considered to be the least cost-effective for suburban development and are used only as a last resort when the market will support the increased cost.

Buildings of four to seven stories are considered to be low-rise and appropriate for more dense suburban developments, usually accompanied by parking structures. In buildings over seven stories high, effective exterior access fire fighting vanishes and built-in, automated fire fighting capability is required, forcing the taller

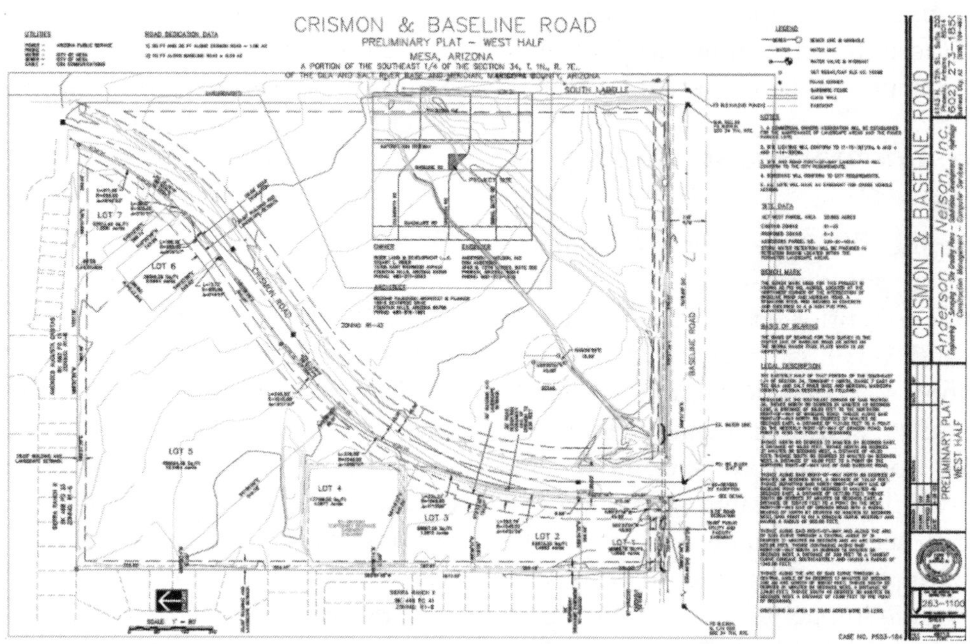

FIGURE 27-1. BOUNDARY SURVEY AND TOPOGRAPHIC MAP

building to become even taller to amortize the additional costs of this fire-fighting capability.

Parking requirements are most economically met by surface parking at a year 2000 cost of approximately $5,000 per car. When a car is stored in a structure, it adds a minimum of $15,000 per car to the cost of parking. If the car is moved underground, it adds a minimum of $25,000 per car to the cost of parking.

Zoning, Entitlements, and Environmental Approvals

One of the trickiest areas of commercial development today is project entitlement—the right to proceed with the development of any site. This process starts with the zoning and ends with the issuance of a building permit. Some states are simple; if the site is correctly zoned for a certain use, then the developer needs only to apply for a building permit and then, when it is approved, construction starts. Most states, however, starting with California, Washington, and now Arizona, are using land use regulations to effectively limit growth and to raise a lot of money for the affected community.

In California, if a site is zoned correctly, the developer must also submit an environmental impact report or statement (EIR/EIS), as the case may be. This document usually costs from $250,000 to as much as several million dollars per site. If it is not approved by the regulating body, city, county, or state, then the project cannot proceed. The contingency of an approved EIR is imperative when purchasing land in states that require the EIR process.

This is a very real and substantial front-end cost, one that has driven many developers away from California and other states using these statutes. It is not uncommon that a developer purchases a site zoned for the use and then the EIR is rejected. What then? These costs are not refundable. Most developers are actively pursuing political agendas to keep close ties to the various political bodies in their area so that they do not run afoul of this process. It is, however, a very real risk.

In the normal course of events, the potential for zoning or EIR approval can be ascertained by extensive conversation and negotiation with planning and zoning officials. Rare is the problem that cannot be resolved, unless the government is bent on limiting growth at all costs. This is usually evidenced by the extensive use of inordinate *impact fees*. Normal zoning contingencies involve a master plan change to accommodate a proposed project and a zoning change, as well as site plan and architectural approvals. Sometimes a special use permit may be required as well. Normally a seller will agree to delay closing, with suitable nonrefundable deposits, until these approvals are received. This process is not perceived by the seller as particularly risky, as these approvals enhance the value of the seller's land at the buyer's expense.

The Market Study

Probably the most vital feasibility tool is the market survey, including, at a minimum, the following criteria:

- Demographics
- Size, net in- or out-migration; population education levels
- Financial makeup and average wages, future health of the marketplace, and competing geographical areas and their relative impact on the subject market
- Limits to growth, land and water, physical barriers, etc.
- Reasons for growth, general political climate (California vs. Arizona), and inevitable change (the "Washington factor"—when residents say, "We're here, now everyone else stay away!")
- Shopping patterns, i.e. supply and demand of potential users within the defined "trade zone"
- Market segments and locations, residential growth, transportation corridors, airports, industrial base, office and retail markets, submarkets, and peripheral influences
- The target market and its needs: identifying scarce or high economic use potentials
- Development resources, such as commercial brokers, title companies, contractors, architects, engineers, and designers

At minimum, within a three- to five-mile radius of the proposed site, you must know the following:

- Supply and demand, absorption, and vacancy of the potential use
- Your competitors: visit all of them, by category of use, and determine which are successful and why
- High and low vacancy, by type of building (between the highest absorption rate and the lowest supply lies the best opportunity)
- Any category of competition that's nearing obsolescence
- Any projects that are planned (check with the planning department)
- Any potential uses not being addressed within the "trade zone"
- Any of these uses that are economically viable for building

You must examine the MSA's market to determine the basic characteristics of the market—i.e., static, shrinking, or expanding—and how it relates to the specific site in question. This will determine the most prudent type of project: urban high-rise, low-rise, suburban space, or mixed-use development. Specific project design can be tailored for any target market.

In the absence of a clearly expanding market place such as occurred nationwide in the 1970s, I tend to look for the vacant niche in the market place, specialized submarkets, medical, legal, intercept sites, or small towns, etc.

The basic tools for financial evaluation of a specific site with a specific proposed use—the pro forma income and expense and the cost breakdown—should be prepared on a cash-on-cash basis first. Any other benefits will only enhance the transaction. This document should be as realistic as possible, leaning, if at all, to the side of pessimism.

Preliminary Design

At this stage of the game, most developers will have commissioned an engineer or architect or both to do a preliminary or schematic project design to determine the usability of the site. This tool will determine the overall building and site configuration, showing total leasable and buildable square feet or units, the parking and landscaping required, and any governmental stipulations attached to their approval of the development plan. The results of this preliminary design will enable the developer to do a "quick and dirty" set of numbers to see if the proposed project will be financially feasible.

The Pro Forma

The pro forma, defined as the financial objective of the venture, is usually a two-part document.

Part one is dedicated to the projected income and expense, usually resulting in a net cash flow projection. The form of this set of numbers varies from a one-page look at the assumed stabilized cash flow of a rental income-generating project to a year-by-year analysis of the project's cash flow.

In Tables 27-1 and 27-2, I am using the following constants:

- Land size 1.67 acres or 72,745.2 square feet
- Building size 20,000 square feet

Part two, the cost breakdown, is just that, but it also includes an analysis of the cash-on-cash rate of return (net income before debt service [NIBDS] divided by total project cost) generated by the income-and-expense projections.

What does this exercise tell you? It says that, on the first pass through the numbers, the project is not only feasible, but that it may likely finance out. This term implies that you will have no residual investment in the building if you achieve your pro forma rents and if you control your costs to be less than the potential permanent loan.

The cost breakdown can also be expanded to include any other form of analysis deemed relevant to the transaction, including *after-tax yield analysis* and *discounted rate of return analysis*, which are not covered here.

Sum It All Up

The site selection process is like a merry-go-round: you can get on anywhere in the process.

- Legal limitations—What may be done on the site?
- Physical constraints—What can be placed economically on the site?
- Market constraints—What is feasible?
- What do the numbers say?

Boil it all down and add your best guess. In the end, the numbers will determine the viability of the proposed venture. Remember the old adage, "Figures never lie, but liars can figure." Do not lie to yourself when putting numbers on paper. Use the best numbers you can find. Consult the most authoritative sources you can locate and double-check all the projections. Finally, build into the budget some fat so that

Item	Notes	Preliminary Budget
Income		
Gross potential income (GPI)	20,000 SF @ $ 16.00/SF/ year NNN	$320,000
Less assumed vacancy	5% assumed	($16,000)
Effective gross income (EGI)		$304,000
Expenses		
Operating expenses		
CAM charges	Estimated @ $5/SF	($100,000)
Less recapture from tenants	95%	$95,000
Net operating expenses		$5,000
Net income before debt service (NIBDS)		$299,000
Project Valuation		
At 7.5 cap rate	NIBDS/0.75	$3,986,666
Mortgage value at completion of lease-up		
Project valuation x .75 = $2,990,000		
Construction loan estimate: $2,500,000		

TABLE 27-1. THE ONE-PAGE INCOME-AND-EXPENSE PROJECTION

you are prepared for the unexpected or unforeseen. It always comes up. Murphy's law is alive and well in the real estate development industry. My corollary to Murphy's law is O'Reilly's law, which promulgates the position that Murphy was an optimist.

The Go-or-No-Go Decision

If the site evaluation process has passed the muster, the numbers look reasonable, and the project still looks feasible, then the developer/principal has to make the decision to commit nonrefundable capital to take the project forward. The capital expenditures include, at the very least, the now nonrefundable earnest money deposit, architecture, engineering, leasing commissions, financing costs, zoning approvals, building permits, and construction commitments.

It is at this stage that the "Lone Ranger decision" is made. If the investor/developer goes ahead on his or her own, then both the reward and the risk are his or hers alone. If the decision

> **HEADS UP**
>
> In my opinion, all other forms of evaluation, such as after-tax analysis, discounted rates of return, etc., only serve to make the proposed project look better. The pro forma must show a sound investment and stand up on a cash-on-cash basis, meeting the investment criteria of the proposed investors.

Item	Notes	Budget
Land		
Land cost	1.67 acres @ $8/SF	$581,960
Closing costs	Estimate	$9,500
Total Land		**$591,460**
Soft Costs		
Architect and engineering	Budgeted at $4/SF	$80,000
Survey/staking/testing	Budgeted—Estimate	$7,800
Leasing commissions	By contract $4/SF	$80,000
Insurance/taxes/legal/ accounting	Estimated	$10,500
Permits and fees	Budgeted	$55,000
Construction loan points	1% on $4M	$25,000
Permanent loan points	1% on	$29,000
Interest during construction	8% on $2.5M six months	$100,000
Miscellaneous and contingencies	Estimate (WAG)	$25,000
Total Soft Costs		**$412,300**
Hard Costs		
Paving, curbs, and gutters	Inc. site work, 31,700 SF @ $4/SF	$126,800
Landscaping	19,000 SF @ $2.50/SF	$38,000
Building shell	20,000 SF @ $48/SF	$960,000
Tenant Work (TI)	20,000 SF @ $30/SF	$600,000
Taxes	.075 x 65% on TI + shell costs	$76,050
Total Hard Costs		**$1,800,850**
Total Project Costs		**$2,587,290**
Valuation and ROI		
Valuation at completion from Exhibit 2 above [Table 27-1]		$3,986,666
Less project total cost		($2,587,290)
Gross profit		$1,399,370
Residual equity required	Permanent loan—costs	($402,630)
ROI		Infinite

TABLE 27-2. THE ONE-PAGE COST BREAKDOWN

is made to attract partners to help with expertise and/or capital investment, then the ability to attract an investor/risk taker/partner is also another valuable check on the feasibility of the project.

There are always other points of view. Select yours and live with it. No matter what the decision at this point, if the project goes ahead, serious nonrefundable money is committed.

Who and What Are Available to Help You?

Before you get all upset and think that you cannot do this because you do not have the knowledge or training, read on and see who can help and what they can do for your deal. The cost of the professionals' help can always be built into the cost of the project or purchase investment. Even seasoned professionals rely on these specialists; they are worth the price of their time and effort.

The Players

> **HEADS UP**
>
> I have always had investors involved in my projects on the assumption that if I could not attract an investor or get the project financed, I should strongly consider abandoning it.

The subject of this section is consultants and how they help in controlling your front-end costs. The astute use of selected professionals can save you time and money and can, properly guided, improve your project/purchase.

Since fees amount to approximately 23-25 percent of the total cost of a project, select the consultants carefully. Insist that they give some relief on the front-end costs prior to the go-or-no-go decision. Often consultants will do this in exchange for getting *market rate* fees rather than a negotiated fee. Try for it all. Boom times will not last forever and most consultants would prefer long-term relationships with a developer rather than a one-time project.

Almost without exception, a commercial development project will require the services of a marketing consultant, an architect or planner, an engineer, a broker, an attorney, a contractor (not strictly a consultant but to be treated like one), and a property manager. Remember: if you do not ask, you will not receive.

When I was starting out, I did not have the luxury of a capital pool. Therefore, I was forced to put together my first project in an innovative manner. In the process I acquired an attitude about the process that has stayed with me for 25 years.

In an effort to develop my first project, I decided to give away some of the ownership in exchange for services rendered to the project. The net result of that was that I was able to "front end" the project with little or no cash. In the process, I evolved a work pattern and ownership format that has served me well over the years.

> **HEADS UP**
>
> I believe it is better to have part of a number of good deals, than 100 percent of any one deal.

Brokerage

The first step in the development process is finding a site. Typically, a commercial broker will present a prospective site to the developer. It is at this point that the potential project begins. Since brokers can earn up to ten percent of the purchase price on a land purchase, they are usually eager to help establish the bona fides of the subject parcel to make it easier for their developer/buyer to make the decision to purchase. Most brokers specialize in specific areas such as residential land, office, retail, or industrial projects. As a general rule, the land specialist works hand in hand with the leasing specialist as a team.

There are many things a developer needs to know about a site and the broker is uniquely situated to produce authoritative knowledge for the feasibility process. Most commercial brokers work in large companies that cover many bases within the brokerage community. Typically, a good commercial brokerage firm will have departments that specialize in land sales, leasing, investment sales, and property management.

Since the most vital aspect of any development process is the delivery of a fully occupied building, the market survey becomes perhaps the crucial element in the feasibility analysis. Nothing has yet transpired on the project, no money has been spent; therefore, this is the perfect time to establish this parcel as a viable project by using the information stored within the broker's own company. While this does not constitute a formal market survey, it will suffice for most experienced developers.

How do you motivate the broker who already stands to make a solid ten percent on the sale? He or she wants you to purchase the site, of course, but does not get paid until you close the escrow. My approach is to make the project more profitable to the broker by offering the brokerage company's team the opportunity to increase their fee income and to participate in the ownership of the project, should it proceed. This added factor on the ownership side will put the broker's knowledge and experience to work for the project at the beginning of the project, where the design and marketing decisions will be made. This approach evolves into a ten percent ownership, full leasing commissions, and the right to list the property for sale if the brokerage group meets the leasing criteria and schedule over the lifespan of the project.

Remember: at this point the broker has been given nothing other than an opportunity to make more money and the developer has spent no money to date. The land broker immediately recruits a leasing specialist from the company and, together, they become the initial project brokerage team or marketing team. Later, if the team is successful in meeting the project's absorption goals, they may add an investment property specialist to market the completed project.

Between the developer and the brokers, they establish the market feasibility by finding out the following market characteristics:

- Net annual absorption of product categories (housing, retail space, office, or industrial space)
- Direction of growth
- Current rents achieved by new buildings and existing rental building stock
- Location and effectiveness of competing projects
- Location of this subject parcel in relation to the potential market
- Potential sites that can compete with the subject parcel and the price for each potential competitor

At this point, the investor/developer has all the tools to make the decision regarding the subject parcel's potential to compete successfully within the market. He or she must determine:

- If the site is located properly and priced competitively in relation to the potential competition
- If the site is configured to have the

required frontage for signage and exposure
- If the site is accessible to traffic
- If the potential rents are enough to justify a new building
- If the projected absorption of new space indicates that there is a need for new space

Then the developer can feel comfortable placing the site in play by executing a purchase agreement with the seller.

The net result of this is that the developer has accomplished three things at the start of the process, prior to spending anything. The developer has:

- Found a viable site
- Acquired a partner who can help make the project a success
- Retained 90-percent ownership of the project

The Architect

For the sake of this discussion, I will specify that the subject site is essentially a building project, rather than a land development project, when placed into escrow. This will necessitate the services of an architect rather than a planner or engineer. Sometimes, all three are used, but for the sake of this discussion we can assume that only an architect is needed. Within the profession, most companies specialize in certain types of buildings. If the developer is inexperienced in a particular type of building, it is vital that he or she choose an architect experienced in the building type required of the subject parcel.

Most architectural contracts are based upon the cost of the building. This is dangerous for a developer, because it runs counter to the developer's interest if a building cost exceeds its budget. A typical developer negotiates a per-square-foot price for the project, with an additional price for tenant improvement (TI) design. Sometimes a *space planner* is assigned this task, as it is an architectural specialty and not always found in an architect's practice. Once the price is established, the payment schedule is worked out.

It is in the developer's best interest to keep the front-end expenditures to a minimum, so, where possible, the architectural contract should always include the civil engineering. Once this is established and the price is set, then the last chore becomes the payment schedule. Often a developer can persuade an architect to limit the early costs incurred prior to the go-or-no-go decision, to out-of-pocket items. Sometimes a piece of the action will be required to sweeten the pot. I have frequently given a ten-percent ownership position in a project to the architect. This keeps the early and usually risky financial exposure to a minimum for the developer and costs nothing at this point. The resulting project ownership would now reflect this addition: broker ten percent, architect ten percent, and developer 80 percent.

The Engineer

Almost any commercial project will need engineers:

- For buildings, a structural and a mechanical engineer
- For site work, a civil engineer and a soils engineer
- For quality control, a testing engineer

Most of these functions do not represent a significant early dollar expense and, with the exception of the soils engineer, they can be added to the architect's contract for budgeting purposes. This is generally the case with the structural and mechanical engineers, except in the case of the design/build scenario. In the event that the project is a master-planned community or large subdivision, the civil engineer should not be under the umbrella of the architect.

For large land projects, the civil engineer replaces the architect in the example outlined in the last paragraph and should be handled accordingly. The testing engineer and soils engineer at the front end of the project, as well as the compaction and concrete testing during construction, should always be under the control of the developer. This is a vital part of the quality control process for the project. Contracts for large land projects can be negotiated on a per-unit basis, akin to a flat-fee approach and, if necessary, participation should be considered as a sweetener to keep the preliminary costs to a minimum.

HEADS UP

Remember: until the project is a reality, participation costs nothing, and when a project becomes a reality, all parties with a participation in the project will have their net worth on the line and their attention fully focused.

Everyone has so much to gain and so much to lose that the net result is a very focused project team. This ownership structure will ensure that the project will take precedence with the individual consultant/partners over any other project where fees alone are at stake.

The Attorney

First of all, choose a firm that specializes in real estate law or, at least, one that has an experienced real estate department. Brokers are often a good source of information on attorneys who are "deal makers" rather than "deal breakers." When planning a project, documentation will be a vital part of the developer's working tools. Their proper design and format will make the difference between success and failure if problems occur. Contract documents are the developer's major tools and enable him or her to control the team, the consultants, and the tenants. The key documents are:

- The purchase agreement
- The project lease
- The exclusive leasing agreement
- The architectural and/or engineering contract
- The construction contract
- The property management agreement

Traditionally, attorneys have worked by the hour only. This is no longer the case. There are a great many attorneys, approximately one for every 350 people in the country, so a developer can afford to be choosey. Attorneys will negotiate flat fees for various documents. Put your agreement with the attorney in writing; keep it simple, one page or less. Specify that until the developer approves the final documents, there are to be no extra charges.

Contract with your attorney for documentation only, not negotiation services; do your own negotiating! Remember: you are retaining an attorney for legal knowledge, not for business acumen. Do not let the attorney make your business decisions for you. Seek advice, but make your own decisions. Never hire an attorney known to be a "deal breaker." When retaining an attorney, do not skimp on quality. Even an attorney who is or is not an expert in this field should have no trouble quoting a flat fee for each document. After all, attorneys, above all other consultants, should know what is needed to properly document a project. They are not reinventing the wheel.

The Property Manager

The management role, while the last to be utilized, should be negotiated at the beginning of the project so that the manager's experience can be called upon during the preliminary design phase of the project. Above all, this person, who has experienced all of the problems built into projects by developers, will provide some insightful input. If given the chance, the manager should make an effective contribution to help prevent obvious, long-term management problems. The manager's experience can be a major source of innovation for the project.

> **HEADS UP**
>
> Do not pay a management fee on the collection of operating expenses.

In any case, managers must live with reality and should have the opportunity to provide input wherever possible. Negotiate a flat percentage-of-net-income (NIBDS) fee for property management, making sure that lease renewals are included in the basic fee. Replacing departed tenants with new tenants should always justify a leasing commission, but lease renewals for current tenants should not. Any owner/developer should always handle renewal negotiations with current tenants personally. Experience shows that this minimizes tenant turnover.

The Contractor

The construction contract and the process of using a general contractor will be covered later in great detail, but suffice it to say that a developer wants the most building for the money budgeted. Having the contractor on board at the outset, after having him or her bid for a fixed profit, will ensure that there is another experienced team member available for the design process. It may also make sense to add the general contractor to the partners list for an ownership interest, as the general contractor is a major factor in the project's cost and quality control. Once the contractor is a partner, you can rest assured that the prices will remain fixed. The resulting project ownership would now reflect this addition: broker ten percent, architect ten percent, contractor ten percent, and the developer 70 percent. This leaves the developer with ample ownership interest remaining to attract an investor at a later date.

The Accountant

Since we are dealing with money and making a profit, we must always be in a position to know what is going on. The numbers are the primary tools of evaluation, just as the contract documents are the primary tools of control. From the first one-page "quick and dirty" pro forma through the management and resale of the project, the numbers should follow with an ever-increasing detail from one stage to the next. All spreadsheets should be integrated into the accounting system, so that no matter what information is required, it can be accessed in both formats. This is very easily accomplished today, as most accounting systems allow import and export of data. Until you become proficient with this tool, it is highly recommended that you have a consulting accountant set up the system. Even though I have been doing this for years, I still have my accountant do a monthly check on the books and systems so that there are no errors. Working with investors' capital demands the highest level of fiduciary care.

Since you will need an accountant for tax purposes anyway, it should not be a significant cost to have one set up your system initially. The spreadsheets contained in the companion CD-ROM are all designed for direct importation into the QuickBooks Pro accounting system.

Team Efforts

The whole purpose of involving other professionals in your project/purchase is to enhance the deal. Job assignments must be specific, interlocking, and enforceable. This issue is covered in Chapter 19. Always be aware that there is a difference between responsibility and authority. We will deal with this matter in greater detail in the chapter on contracts.

CHAPTER

28

The Development Process

Once the site has been deemed worthy and the land has been placed in escrow or "under control" in some manner, the whole feasibility and development process must be set in motion. The first task is to define the *scope of work* and set some sort of preliminary schedule as shown in Chapter 27. Since it is impossible to foresee all the problems or chores in advance, it is necessary to build in some flexibility. The chores should be structured around the time frame of the escrow.

If it were a perfect world, the purchase agreement would have a minimum of 12 months for the due diligence period and provisions for extending the close of escrow for another 12 months, in three-month increments.

In most instances this time frame would enable all chores to be accomplished, including the financing and the building permit, so that the escrow could be closed simultaneously with the closing of the construction loan. In any event, the road to the close of escrow generally follows a prescribed set of procedures, with little emergencies thrown in along the way for some added excitement. The time progression goes something like that outlined in Table 28-1. It may seem a little daunting to the inexperienced, but a typical suburban building can be started and completed within two years if the tenants are receptive and the governmental agencies are friendly. Most low-rise, low-impact projects are welcomed in any community and are generally expedited where possible. The public needs the space and the services and the municipalities need the increase in the tax base.

The crucial chores center around making sure the site is properly located, has no insurmountable problems, and is eagerly received by prospective tenants. Most developers' leases have a built-in two-year window within which to deliver the finished tenant spaces. This is crucial, as the first few leases will have been signed early in the game. These govern the schedule, for if they are lost, then the financing will probably fall apart. Meet the schedules and all will be well.

Expanding on the Team Assignments

Once the escrow is open, you (the owner/ developer/principal) must decide to do the work all alone or to bring in the experts. During this process, the developer must remember that he or she is the sole responsible party and ultimate decision maker. "The risk follows the money." The relative importance of the steps previously outlined above are expanded upon in Table 28-1.

The Due Diligence Period

During the first 30, 60, or 90 days of any project there is a due diligence period, aka the "free look" period. This is a time wherein the developer may cancel the escrow for any reason whatsoever. It is this period of time that is customarily used to check and approve the following items relating to the proposed development project:

- The title report and commitment
- The survey and topo
- The zoning and designated uses

Once the land has passed the muster, the onus is on the developer to make his or her project a reality. The time frame for this process must be built into the purchase agreement. If not, the developer may have to purchase the land without knowing whether he or she can pull off a successful project on that site.

The Preliminary Design

The preliminary design is the next crucial step, as it will determine whether the potential tenants choose the project for their new home and whether the community likes the project and wants it to be built. These plans are often referred to as "eyewash," because of their elaborate nature and color, and will be used to form the basis for the leasing package as well as the approval process. The relative success of these two chores will make or break the investment. The community's reception will determine the costs and time frame within which the developer must operate to construct the project, the tenants will dictate the actual rental rate achieved, and, by extrapolation, the ultimate profitability of the project. Good input is vital to the success of the project.

Most importantly, the marketing team and those brokers charged with filling the building will have the most sway. The *projected absorption rate* will dictate the amount of space likely to be absorbed within the project's allotted time and the *competition analysis* will dictate what the tenants must have as inducements to commit to leasing the space. The developer must decide which amenities can be included in the tenant improvement budget. The architect, the engineer, the contractor, and the management agent should all have input into what must be included, what can be omitted, and what it should all cost. Sometimes all of these skills are embodied solely in the developer, but, if not, then it is plain to see that the additional partners or consultants necessary to the development process should be on board at this stage.

Work Item	Who Is Responsible	Prerequisites	Time Frame	Notes
Establish escrow	Developer	Finding the site	None specified	
Vet the title	Developer and attorney	Escrow	Seller: 4 weeks Buyer: 4 weeks	Crucial, get it right
Preliminary site assessment	Geotech engineer, architect, engineer, marketing team, developer	Start as soon as title looks OK	60 days from the time the seller delivers the prelim	"Free look" time, make the most of it
Go/no-go decision	Developer	Site checks out all the way	Done within the "free look" period	Gets expensive after this if site must be abandoned
Execute preliminary design	Developer, architect, marketing, property manager, contractor	The go decision	90 days	Crucial as this is major entitlement and leasing tool
Flesh out the pro forma	Developer, marketing team, contractor	Need design and market survey results	Within the 90 days above	Get it right; the leasing will be based on the numbers
Apply for entitlements, zoning, and site plan approval	Developer and attorney, if necessary	Completed preliminary plan	60 days to 2 years, depending on the request	Always add 90 days to your time; plan on the unexpected
Preleasing	The marketing team	A design and a firm rental figure	90 days to start of contruction	Normally 75% to close loan
Working drawings	Architect, engineer, marketing team, developer, contractor	An idea of what will be approved for construction	6 months and 3-6 months for building permit	Big $$, do or die, must meet the lender's leasing agreement
Loan commitments	Developer and mortgage banker	Firm design, some preleasing final numbers and ownership	Accomplish during the above time frame	Ownership must be OK to lender
Close the land escrow and construction loan	Developer and lender, escrow	Building permits, preleasing, and loan commitment	Should be done as soon as the permit is issued	Clock ticking on the leases; complete construction and open
Construction	Contractor, developer, lender	Money, leases to lender's requirement	6 months to 2 years	Tenant plans and meet occupancy dates
Permanent financing	Property manager	Leased to lender's specs	Completed within specified time frame	Manage well and relax!

TABLE 28-1. WORK DISTRIBUTION AND TIME FRAMES

The Pro Forma

As part of the preliminary design process, the pro forma becomes the project's financial blueprint. It will set the parameters and cost considerations involved in every facet of the project. Changes in timing will ultimately impact the pro forma and, hence, the profitability of the project. It is at this juncture that the "quick and dirty" pro forma must be expanded to reflect the project's schedule during the development process, as well as at least the first five-year operating period. The pro forma shown in Tables 28-2, 28-3, and 28-4 is constructed for a suburban office building with costs frozen in the 1997 period. The details of how each item is assembled follow the table. The constants or assumptions for the calculation are listed in Table 28-2.

Applying for Entitlements

Term	Rate/Value Assigned
Construction Loan	10% [0.1]
Permanent Loan	8% [0.08] interest
Capitalization Rate	9% [0.09]
Rental Rate	14.00/SF/Year
Total Leasable SF	16,064 SF
Rent Escalations	5%/Year [0.05]
Annual Operating Cost Increase	5%/Year [0.05]

TABLE 28-2. PRO FORMA CONSTANTS

Since the late 1960s, most states have enacted planning and zoning ordinances to ensure orderly and quality growth in the communities. These controls dictate that any proposed development projects be approved prior to construction. The forms of approval range from obtaining a simple building permit to the long, drawn-out EIR process. In Florida and on the West Coast, where growth has been constant since the 1950s, most communities have enacted ordinances that result in approval processes that slow down the growth, raise land prices, and extract impact fees from the proposed projects. The most common approvals for projects to be built on land zoned for the particular use are the *site plan approval* and the *architectural approval*. This assures the community of standard coverage and buildings that fit the community's image.

In some cases, the land is zoned for a different use than the one contemplated by the developer and must be rezoned to conform to the developer's planned use. This chore may dictate altering the community's approved master plan as well as the parcel's specific zoning. Requirements for this process vary, but if the proposed project is well thought out, most communities will eventually approve the project with stipulations. These "stips" generally take the form of impact fees and/or improvements that the community feels will offset the potential negatives that the project will bring upon completion.

> **DEFINITION**
>
> An ***impact fee*** is a fee charged to a developer based on the jurisdiction's assessment of the development's impact on a particular infrastructure. For example, sewer impact fees are charged to developers of new housing, based on the number of units and the number of baths in those units. The fees are designed to allow the particular jurisdiction to afford to build and expand infrastructure to support the increased load.

Some states (notably California, Oregon, and Washington) have used the approval process to substantially halt or drastically slow development or to make the process so expensive that all but the wealthy are completely deterred. The most blatant examples of this are the areas around San Francisco, Los Angeles, Portland, and Seattle. The net result is urban sprawl, freeways, and pollution. Developments spread out to contiguous communities where development is easier and more inexpensive. As communities insist on low-rise, low-impact development, the community must spread out. Affordable housing is always on the periphery, so most workers are doomed to a long commute.

Pundits have for many years predicted one

Land	Estimated Budget	Pre-construction	To Date	Current Month	At Closing	Totals	% of Cost
Land 1.67 Acres , 72,745 SF	$364,640	$14,000	$14,000		$350,640	$378,640	21%
Closing Costs	$9,500				$3,500	$3,500	0%
Assessments	$7,500				$7,500		
Total Land	$381,640	$14,000	$14,000		$361,640	$382,140	21%
Soft Costs							
A&E	$60,000	$44,000	$571		$16,000	$60,571	3%
Engineering	Inc. Above						0%
Survey/Staking/Testing	$7,500	$2,500			$5,000	$7,500	0%
Leasing Commissions @ $3/SF	$48,000	$18,072	$1,197		$29,928	$49,197	3%
Insurance/Taxes/Legal/Acctg	$7,000	$2,000			$5,000	$7,000	0%
Governmental Permits	$10,000	$3,500	$85		$6,500	$10,085	1%
Development Overhead	$40,000						
Loan Points $1,300,000 @ 3 pts	$39,000	$28,000			$11,000	$39,000	2%
Interest @ 10% (1/2 out-standing for 6 mos.)	$35,000				$35,000	$35,000	2%
Misc and Contingencies	$10,000	$3,500	$1,434		$6,500	$11,434	1%
Total Soft Costs	$256,500	$101,572	$3,287		$114,928	$219,787	12%
Hard Costs							
Landscape Area 19,025 SF @ $2	$38,000				$38,000	$38,000	2%
Paved Areas 31,710 SF @ $2.25	$72,000				$72,000	$72,000	4%
Building Shell @ $32/SF, 20,000 SF	$630,000		$19,530		$630,000	$649,530	36%
Tenant allowance @ $25/SF, 16,064 SF	$400,000				$400,000	$400,000	22%
Taxes	$33,430				$33,430	$33,430	2%
Total Hard Costs	$1,173,430		$19,530		$1,173,430	$1,192,960	66%
Total Project	$1,811,570	$115,572	$36,817		$1,649,998	$1,794,887	100%
Notes		**A**			**B**		**Cost**
Funding analysis after lease-up	During construction	Pre-construction cash requirement			Maximum construction loan @ 80% of cost		Maximum takeout loan @ 75% of value
Construction loan @ 80% of cost maximum conservative estimate	$1,300,000				$1,449,256	$1,300,000	
Investor's initial equity requirement	$511,570	$115,572	$152,389		$362,314	$511,570	
Total available dollars	$1,811,570				$1,811,570	$1,811,570	

TABLE 28-3. DETAILED COST BREAKDOWN

Leasable space 16,000 sf with annual rent escalation of 5%

		Operating Period				
Income	**Notes**	**Year 1**	**Year 2**	**Year 3**	**Year 4**	**Year 5**
Gross potential income [GPI]	At 100% occupancy @ $14 /sf	$224,000.00	$235,200.00	$246,960.00	$259,308.00	$272,273.40
Vacancy allowance at 5 %	Per lender's allowance	–$11,200.00	–$11,760.00	–$12,348.00	–$12,965.40	–$13,613.67
Effective gross income [EGI]	Projected net	$212,800.00	$223,440.00	$234,612.00	$246,342.00	$258,659.73
CAM Expenses	All expenses are NNN					
Real estate taxes	Projected until first assessment	$24,000.00	$25,200.00	$26,460.00	$27,783.00	$29,172.15
Maintenance/repair/HVAC	Budgeted	$1,800.00	$1,890.00	$1,984.50	$2,083.73	$2,187.91
Insurance: fire/liability	Bid	$6,612.00	$6,942.60	$7,289.73	$7,654.22	$8,036.93
Electricity	Estimated	$3,600.00	$3,780.00	$3,969.00	$4,167.45	$4,375.82
Water and sewer	Estimated	$2,400.00	$2,520.00	$2,646.00	$2,778.30	$2,917.22
Refuse	Bid	$600.00	$630.00	$661.50	$694.58	$729.30
Janitorial	Bid	$15,600.00	$16,380.00	$17,199.00	$18,058.95	$18,961.90
Windows/sweeping	Bid	$2,400.00	$2,520.00	$2,646.00	$2,778.30	$2,917.22
Security	Bid	$4,320.00	$4,536.00	$4,762.80	$5,000.94	$5,250.99
Pest control on demand	Estimated	$900.00	$945.00	$992.25	$1,041.86	$1,093.96
Yard maintenance and common area	Bid	$2,400.00	$2,520.00	$2,646.00	$2,778.30	$2,917.22
Subtotal		**$64,632.00**	**$67,863.60**	**$71,256.78**	**$74,819.62**	**$78,560.60**
Management fee at 10% exp of CAM	Based upon expenses only per lease	$6,463.20	$6,786.36	$7,125.68	$7,481.96	$7,856.06
Total Common Area		**$71,095.20**	**$74,649.96**	**$78,382.46**	**$82,302.00**	**$86,416.66**
Tenant-reimbursed CAM	Based on 95% occupancy	$67,540.44	$70,917.46	$74,463.34	$78,186.50	$82,095.83
Landlord's expense	For vacant space	–$3,554.76	–$3,732.50	–$3,919.12	–$4,115.08	–$4,320.83
Net Income Before Debt Service [NIBDS]	Before debt service	**$209,245.24**	**$219,707.50**	**$230,692.88**	**$242,227.52**	**$254,338.90**
Less mortgage	Based on estimated loan					
	$1.3M @ 8%/30 years	–$103,311.00	–$103,311.00	–$103,311.00	–$103,311.00	–$103,311.00
Cash flow	Return on investor's equity	**$105,934.24**	**$116,396.50**	**$127,381.88**	**$138,916.52**	**$151,027.90**

TABLE 28-4. FIVE-YEAR PROJECTED INCOME AND EXPENSE

continuous city from the Mexican border to the Canadian border. The only gaps currently remaining on the West Coast are due to natural barriers and governmental restrictions.

What this means to the developer is that each must concentrate his or her efforts in areas where he or she is comfortable with the size of the front-end risk. The process can take as little as 90 days and as long as three years, with the cost varying from a few thousand dollars to several millions of dollars. In general, reward balances risk so long as the market holds up.

Preleasing

While the project is being entitled, the working drawings processed, and the loan commitments sought, the marketing team is busy trying to fill the proposed project by soliciting signed leases from prospective tenants. This is no mean feat. The leasing team has only a preliminary plan, a list of proposed amenities and improvements, a target rental rate, and the reputation of the developer to offer. The lease document, when executed, usually gives the developer 24 months from the date of execution to deliver the premises, aka the proposed tenant's space.

While signing a lease well in advance of construction is a common practice among tenants of some size and sophistication, it can become an awesome accomplishment when dealing with small-town "mom-and-pop"-type tenants. They all seem to be from the "Show Me" state. This is why the bulk of projects in small towns are built by local people who are known to the community. While they might not have done this particular type of thing in the past, they have an established local reputation for business acumen and honesty. This gives the local entrepreneur an edge over the outside competition and opens up the game to both newcomers and small investors/principals. Today's newcomer can become tomorrow's established development company.

Working Drawings

When the approval process looks favorable and the project is leasing according to schedule, the time arrives to finalize the design by creating the *working drawings,* the final plans and specifications for the proposed development. This process details all the design elements so that the developer may obtain a building permit.

This process, like many other elements in the project, can make or break the investment. The building's design and finish schedule must be matched up with the target market. While on the surface this may sound simple, many projects go over budget, squeezing profits along the way. Value-added items such as continuous glass, marble entries, and other amenities must be evaluated in terms of cost vs. market value to the target market.

This part of the project may be made easier by having expert input from the architect, broker, contractor, and building manager during both the preliminary design stage and the working drawing stage. The leasing agent and property manager will push for what they need to do their jobs and the contractor will put a price tag on each item. Ultimately, the developer will decide on the final package, since it must meet his or her investment objectives.

The Appraisal

The appraisal is intended to be an independent third party's expert opinion as to the projected value of the completed project and a statement regarding its economic viability as an investment and as collateral for a loan. In the past (during the 1970s) it was not uncommon for an apartment builder to borrow 110-125 percent of the total cost of a project. During the late 1980s, loans were being made by institutions such as savings and loans (S&L) and commercial banks without any thought to demand. A certified appraiser carries the industry's certification, MAI (Member, Appraisal Institute). Appraisals during this irresponsible era were jokingly referred to as MAI—"made as instructed." As a consequence, the appraisal industry suffered a big hit in its credibility department as a result of the Great Recession of 1988-92. Consequently, whereas then appraisers were inclined to be generous with their view of feasibility and market, they are now niggardly with their projections of value. They err on the side of caution to avoid criticism.

Today, the lender's exposure, except to fraud, is or should be little or nothing. Generally, the loan is limited to 75 percent of the actual cost of land and building, plus some soft costs. The salvage value of the property, sold at a distressed price, will most often be sufficient to make the lender whole. If the property is completed and occupied, the salvage value should exceed the lender's exposure. The borrower, therefore, should have little or no real exposure. The joint and several guarantees are there to assure the lender that all is on the up-and-up and that the developer will finish the project as contemplated. If these two items are not successfully accomplished, the borrower's exposure can be very real and very costly.

HEADS UP

The real risk of loss and the borrower's exposure should be in completing the building on time and within budget.

Loan Commitments

The most common commercial development project utilizes some form of other people's money (OPM), usually construction and permanent loans. This use of conventional financing leverages the investor's equity dollars to increase the rate of return to the owners. This type of financing is the most common. Other forms of financing such as bond issues, special and general improvement districts, and public syndication are less common and tend to be used only in specific instances.

The financing climate today has been tempered by the Great Recession of 1988-1992, when almost half to two thirds of the value of commercial real estate in the United States was wiped out. It has been estimated that in the Phoenix SMSA alone, some *eight billion dollars* of real property value vanished within a year. The lessons learned in that process are dictating the terms of today's financial markets. The object of the new lending patterns and requirements is to prevent another situation where the industry could go wild with speculation and suffer another meltdown. Most lenders require preleasing of 75 percent of the total leasable space for conventional, 75-percent-of-cost, construction financing. In the past, lenders would lend 80 percent of projected value, not cost, sometimes creating a situation where the developer had little or no cash investment in the project at all. After some hard lessons, the current formulas evolved. They seem to be working, at least through 1999.

Likewise, permanent or take-out loans used primarily to pay off the construction loans provide a more permanent mortgage loan. These loans were previously funded when a project reached approximately 85 percent leased and occupied, or breakeven. This assured the lender that, at a minimum, the debt service (the mortgage payment) was covered. In today's market the most common take-out, nonrecourse permanent financing occurs only when the project reaches 95 percent leased and occupied. This nonrecourse form of financing is secured only by the value of the project, with no guarantees by the owners.

For projects of lesser absorption or where tenants are not deemed satisfactory to the lender, the permanent or take-out loan must be guaranteed by the borrowers jointly and severally. As additional checks on the continued health and value of the project, most lenders commit the financing for only a ten-year period, with the right to review and renew at that time.

The most effective way to secure any loan is to start the process at the beginning of the project. Contact prospective lenders or lenders' representatives, known as *mortgage bankers*, early. Give them all the preliminary information on the project and the borrower. This will enable you to locate a lender that is in the market for your type of project. If the lender is kept in the loop during the lease-up and permit period, it will be much easier for him or her to issue a commitment when it is needed. Refer back to Table 28-2 for typical loan types and costs in the late 1990s.

Loan Closings

The two most exciting periods in the life of any successful project occur when the loans are closed. The first, closing the construction loan, enables the project to be built. The second, closing the permanent loan, signals the successful culmination of the risk period of the project and the start of the reward period. When the permanent loan is funded, cash flow actually starts coming to the owners/investors and makes all the trials and travails worth while. In some instances, if the pro forma has been significantly surpassed, the permanent financing may yield more dollars than predicted in the pro forma, thus making some cash available to pay down the investor's equity. It sounds trite, but it is truly a moment to be treasured.

HEADS UP

A typical project takes between five to ten years to achieve its most profitable and saleable state. It is the consistent achievement of these two goals on all projects that establishes the commercial real estate developer as a career professional.

Ongoing Management

Once the excitement is over, the project settles into the day-to-day management mode; this requires a totally different skill than that of the risk-taking entrepreneurial development process. The management process requires the accountant's "bean counter" mentality coupled with the skills of the diplomat. The care and feeding of the tenants is the lifeblood of the investment. It is these skills that will enable the investment to mature and ripen into a truly profitable asset over time. The process of "debugging" the project during the first five years involves correcting any defects in the building and allowing the landscaping to mature, thus creating an "established" look to the project. The maturing of the leases allows the first five-year period of rental increases to take effect, thus "seasoning the leases." The resulting building with its stable of tenants and their seasoned income stream becomes a very valuable commodity.

CHAPTER

29

Design Ramifications

This chapter discusses, in a general way, the philosophy and considerations that are part of the design process. It is not an attempt to suggest specific design criteria or design elements, only to serve as a guide to your thinking when you and the architect tackle the design of a specific project. Most of the criteria used within this section are subjective and the constraints that govern the decision process are both economic and aesthetic. The decisions made during this phase of the work could make the difference between disaster and spectacular success.

There are many considerations that can and should affect the actual design of any building. Key among these is based upon the target tenant. Tenants are defined arbitrarily as small (1,000-2,000 SF), medium (3,000-5,000 SF), or large (6,000 SF and up). Another vital part of determining the target tenant is to determine the desired market level (low end, middle market, or class "A" market). These constraints establish the framework within which buildings are designed. A single-purpose building like a factory, restaurant, bank, or supermarket is designed around the specific operations of the occupant, but buildings constructed for multiple-tenant occupancy have to be designed in a generic manner, to accommodate a wide variety of tenant sizes.

The key element to all design is function. Warehouses are designed around access, egress, and cubic footage of storage space. Multitenant residential units offer various sizes and configurations based upon market demand and local taste. Retail stores stress signage, exposure to the passing motorist, a featured display area (window), and some form of stockroom in back of the merchandise display areas. Office buildings attempt to accommodate employees and their necessary interrelation within various sizes of companies.

Land Yield vs. Marketability

As you may well imagine, all design starts with a land plan. For subdivision projects such as large master-planned communities, the land plan will deal with many diverse uses of the land, but for most projects, the overriding land plan is the jurisdiction's general plan. It is within this framework that most projects are conceived and executed.

Due to the ever-increasing cost of land, one of the overriding concerns to developers is the yield on land. It makes sense, because, as with low-rise office buildings, you can only get 10,000-14,000 square feet of building per acre, an effective 25-percent coverage on that land parcel. That translates directly to project cost. If you are getting only 25-percent yield, that means that for every dollar per square foot you pay for land, the cost per buildable and/or rentable square foot of building is $4. This translates directly to rent. If you are leasing to your tenants at the rate of 12 percent on cost, then each rentable square foot is costing your tenants $0.48 per dollar paid for the land. Typical prices for low-rise office building land in my neck of the woods, in 2004, are running between $6 and $10 per square foot. That means, at the $10 figure, that the land cost for my office project is $40 per net rentable square foot and the tenant must pay $4.80 per square foot per year just for the land cost. That is not necessarily significant, because most projects in this area will be paying roughly equivalent amounts. It means, however, that the first concern for a developer in planning any project is yield on the land coverage. Whatever the product, to stay competitive, you must design your project within the competitive coverage range or drastically reduce your land costs.

Enhancing Value Through Design

The residential subdivider's mantra is "number of units per acre." If you look at the average tract housing development, you can see that it was designed by the civil engineer with a view to cramming as many units onto the land as possible. This is very common at the low end of the market, but from the upper middle of the market to the luxury end, developers have to take aesthetics into consideration. Sometimes, less is more.

I was involved in the planning of a large residential tract some years ago and, because of the available views, it was decided to orient the house lots toward the views wherever possible. The result was 25 percent fewer building lots, but over 90 percent of the lots had what the developer called a "view premium." In this particular case, the view premiums almost matched the basic lot prices, so with 25 percent fewer lots we were able to command 100 percent higher sales prices for the lots, more than compensating the developer for the reduced density.

Commercial Land

Commercial subdivisions are completely different. The overriding concern is visibility and accessibility, more than coverage. Without the first two, you cannot fill the development with tenants. For retail centers it is absolutely vital, and it is not at all uncommon to take less square footage for a better exposure. Coverage for retail centers varies from 10 percent to 12 percent.

For office projects, visibility is also a consideration, but less so than with retail projects. In office design, efficiency and amenities govern the design criteria. Most, if not all, project designs start with the *floor plate*—the layout of the building floor prior to tenant improvements.

- *Warehouse* design generally is set up for large, full truckload or rail shipments at one side of the building, storage in the middle, and less-than-truckload lot shipping on the other side of the building.
- *Apartment or condominium* projects generally offer units varying from efficiency units to one-, two-, and sometimes, three-bedroom units.
- *Large tenant retail stores,* over 10,000 square feet, are generally custom designed. *Smaller stores* usually are housed in buildings with display windows in the front and shipping docks in the back. The buildings tend to vary from 40 to 75 feet deep.
- *Office space*, except for very large tenants, tends to be no more than 40 feet deep.

Ideally, both the entry side and rear walls of the space have windows, but most medium and large buildings are built around cores of elevators, corridors, and stairs, with only the perimeter of the buildings having windows. These core areas must somehow be amortized into the rent and can place an undue burden on the cost of the net usable space. Extreme care and consideration must be given to this wasted or common area. A building, to be competitive in the modern marketplace, must be no less than 85 percent efficient.

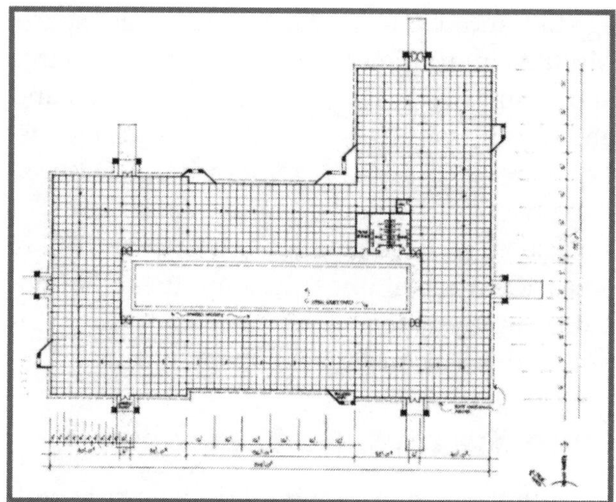

FIGURE 29-1. FLOOR PLATE

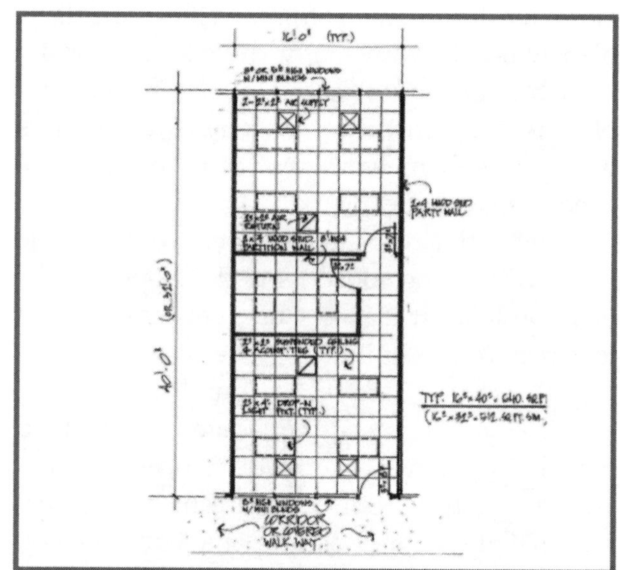

FIGURE 29-2. FLOOR PLAN

The *floor plate* (Figure 29-1) shows the entire floor while the *floor plan* (Figure 29-2) shows a tenant's layout with improvements. In floor plates, shaded areas must be deducted from the total square footage of the footprint to determine net leasable area. The net result is then divided by the total square footage to determine efficiency.

Other design criteria involve a variety of items, including:

- Environmental constraints
- Zoning restrictions
- Parking and landscaping requirements
- Numbers of buildings
- Numbers of stories
- Elevators, stairs, and escalators
- Cost considerations regarding construction method
- Aesthetic choices
- Material selection
- Suitability for the community

In general, most of these items have hard-dollar cost considerations assessed against marketing considerations. The goal of creating a successful design is to balance expenditures and practical considerations with the most aesthetic and effective design package for marketing, while remaining within the budget constraints. If you can pull this off, the building design can be considered successful.

Environmental Constraints

Most environmental constraints are a product of the design review and approval process, whether generated in an elaborate EIR process or a simple site plan and architectural review. Some restrictions are due to the lay of the land, washes, hills, or vegetation, protected or regulated by the federal, state, or local government. The federal government regulates groundwater, drainage, and wetlands, with states adding another layer of regulation and control. The local government generally adds site configuration, height restrictions, slope, grading restrictions, and landscaping requirements.

The thrust of these guidelines is to curtail the potential damage or to minimize the environmental impact of the development on the surrounding environment. The most potentially damaging of these is housing, as it eats up the land and requires large, inefficient amounts of public utilities spread over a large area. The concentrated developments tend to be more easily controlled, but less aesthetically pleasing and acceptable to the majority of communities.

Since the 1960s, the concept of more concentrated housing development surrounded by greenbelt has been popular with ecologists, economists, and developers. Referred to as *cluster housing*, it has generally been a flop with the public at large. Most people want their own private yard rather than an untouched greenbelt to be shared and enjoyed by all. This sentiment results in urban sprawl.

Interestingly enough, the public looks upon developers as the bad guys, blaming them for the proliferating sprawl. Given the choice, the American public prefers single-family housing 10-to-1 over cluster development. The only environment where cluster housing is well received is in the urban setting, where all buildings are vertical.

Zoning Restrictions

Most communities in the United Stares have adopted zoning codes. These rules and regulations, *ordinances*, are detailed uses permitted within a community's master plan. Generally, a master plan is adopted to locate certain defined uses within the community, regulating the physical characteristics of the specific buildings permitted. A master plan is not designed to be absolute, but to give a community a general guideline on how to expand in an organized and harmonious manner. An example of the commercial uses permitted is shown in the breakdown in Table 29-1.

Most cities within the U.S. have centered around a decaying urban or village core four

Classification	Symbol	General Uses
Commercial office	C-0	Professional office
Neighborhood commercial	C-1	Neighborhood retail and office
Intermediate commercial	C-2	C-1 plus larger users and limited recreational uses
General commercial	C-3	C-1, C-2, and wholesale, distribution, and entertainment

TABLE 29-1. COMMERCIAL ZONING CLASSIFICATIONS

areas: industrial uses in the SW quadrant, high-end housing in the NE quadrant, middle-income housing in the SE quadrant, and blue-collar housing in the NW quadrant. Most exceptions to this rule occur due to geographical constraints, such as mountains or rivers, or political constraints, such as government reservations or public preserves.

Most community master plans are updated every five to ten years and are constantly modified due to rezoning, special use permits, and the like. Each local community guides its future by having the right to monitor all new development projects. Each community's population is represented on planning commissions, city councils, and school boards and has a hands-on influence on all new growth.

Within the zoning ordinances, codes delineate the maximum amount of building that is allowed per acre, the maximum height, setbacks, parking, and landscaping requirements, and, in some cases, the type of architecture permitted in a specific area or within the community as a whole. As communities become more popular and start to grow, these codes seem to multiply as established residents scurry to place roadblocks in the way of change. While this concept seemed to start and proliferate in California, it has spread like wildfire throughout the Sunbelt states.

Economic Choices

Economic choices are the ones that revolve around the numbers and are determined by the choice of target tenant. They include the following considerations and all affect the economics of the building:

- Suitability for the community
- Number of buildings
- Number of stories
- Floor plates
- Elevators, stairs, and escalators
- Lobbies, corridors, and rest rooms
- Parking requirements
- Landscaping requirements
- Cost considerations regarding construction method
- Aesthetic choices and material selection
- Type of leases

The impact of all choices relating to the above items becomes cumulative, as each stage of design shapes not only a project's aesthetics and marketability, but its potential success as an investment. Starting with finding an overall design concept that will fit into a community, the architect and the developer must build into the design the aesthetic, according to the "gut instincts" of the developer. What I mean by this is that each developer must decide how to play the hand. It is not dissimilar to a hand of poker. Do you play the cards dealt or do you trust your instincts?

You pay your money, and you take your choice.

A good example of this would be placing a traditional colonial building in a New England town setting, rather than opting for a modern glass office building, gambling that the potential tenants want to be seen as "with it" and modern. Both approaches work, but the choice remains unique to the developer. Both choices have cost implications: colonial buildings have fewer and smaller windows and therefore cost less and are more efficient to heat, but provide a less pleasing atmosphere for the tenants inside. People working indoors love to look out windows and thrive on light spaces. Studies of office environments have shown conclusively that access to natural light and the ability to look out result in increased productivity in the workforce as well as a significant reduction in employee turnover.

Similarly, the number of buildings will determine the coverage, the land cost/square foot of building and the cost per square foot of construction. The more square feet under one roof, the lower the cost per square foot. The effect of a high-rise, which is fairly cost-efficient, over multiple-, single-, or two-story buildings (a campus effect) has definite marketing and cost impacts. With the number of square feet necessary to build the project as a constant, the number of buildings, the number of stories, and the floor plate become totally interrelated. These constraints will determine the safety items such as the size and shape of lobbies and the number of stairs, elevators, and escalators. These choices will then force the necessity of dedicating a certain amount of the building's gross square footage to corridors and rest rooms. These choices will determine the efficiency of the building and will therefore finally translate into the rent that needs to be charged in order to reach the desired investment yield. See Figure 29-3 for floor plate analysis.

An example of this can be stated simply. If a building project's desired yield is one dollar per square foot NNN ($1.00/SF NNN) to the investor and the type of design that dedicates 15 percent of the gross building for common areas, then the necessary rent is calculated as follows:

square feet of gross building x
$1.00/net rentable square feet of building =
necessary rent

10,000(SF) x $1.00/8,500(SF) =
$1.18 /SF of net rentable SF

The resulting building is considered to have an 18 percent *load factor*. The tenants have to pay 18 percent more rent to carry the inefficiency of the common areas; the resulting surcharge is commonly referred to as the *load*. Obviously, buildings that do not carry this load factor can more effectively compete with those that do. The elimination of load factors will justify higher than normal construction costs.

Parking and landscape requirements are seldom a matter of choice. In most instances,

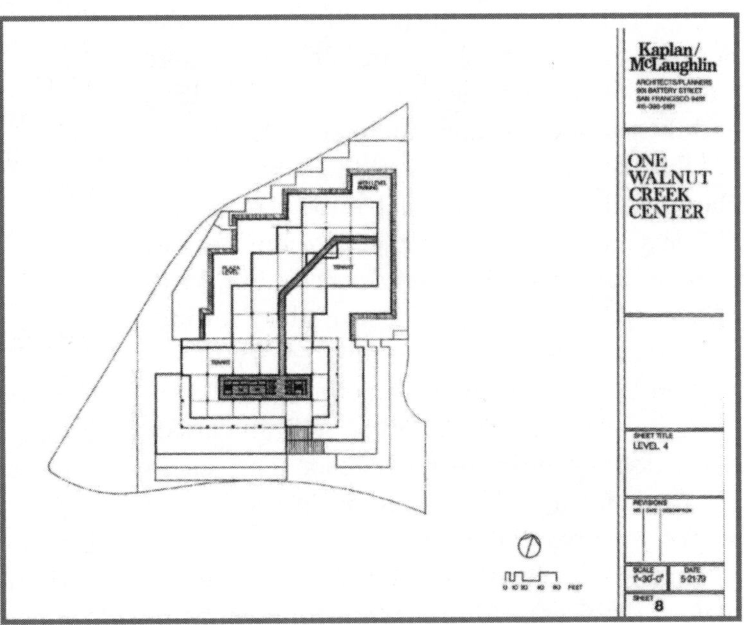

FIGURE 29-3. FLOOR PLATES AND EFFICIENCY

the zoning code will dictate the number of parking spaces required for specific uses and the minimum area required for landscaping. Beyond the codes, however, the developer may want to add additional parking for certain target tenants. For example, federal and state government office space requires one third to one half more parking than conventional office space due to the density of workers per square foot of rentable space, which exceeds that of the private sector. Similarly, the mandated landscaping may not be enough to give the desired aesthetic impact that the project requires to attract the target market.

Building Detail

Some design choices boil down to dollars and cents vs. marketing realities. The number of buildings, floors per building, stairs, escalators, elevators, and even building materials have economic and marketing impacts. Floor plate design will determine the amount of window wall per leasable square foot. The number of stories will determine the lineal foot of foundation per gross leasable square foot, the square feet of roof per leasable square foot of building, and the number of stairs and elevators.

For most commercial buildings, the choices above will have a very real impact upon the public's reception of the project. When it comes to retail, one floor is the most accepted. With office space, it depends on the setting. Suburban areas like one- and two-story buildings and peripheral areas sometimes will tolerate up to seven floors, but urban settings call for many floors—the more, the merrier, it seems. In an urban setting, the farther up in the air the tenant, the greater the prestige.

In low-rise buildings, one to three stories, material choices need to be made for both framing and finish. Construction method, aesthetic choices, and material selection will definitely affect cost and absorption of the finished space. Sometimes this is a matter of local custom, but increasingly it has become a race to establish new standards for new buildings. Once eight-foot ceilings were the norm; now ten feet is considered modern. In the past, wood-framed buildings were the "in thing." Today steel, concrete, and glass have overtaken the low-rise market. The increase in cost and, by deduction, the rents of new buildings have pushed older buildings to modernize and stay competitive. The marketplace has become one in which no building can rest on its laurels; no neighborhood, either, for that matter. It has become a question of keeping up or losing out in almost all markets.

Over time, all buildings suffer from both economic obsolescence and physical limitations. This is the concept behind the depreciation of investment property. The theory is that by writing off part of the building each year, the government allows an investor to put away some money to replace the building when its economic obsolescence has reached a point where tenants will no longer be willing to occupy the building. In reality, however, by that time the land has appreciated to the point where it becomes economical to demolish the obsolete building and build a new one that can compete in the evolved marketplace.

Types of Leases

For years there has been confusion about *net* leases and *gross* leases. A gross lease was always understood to include all operating expenses, but net leases have varied all over the block, depending on who wrote them. To end the confusion, a truly net lease is now defined as a NNN or triple net lease. This designation assures everyone that the lease is, in fact, net of all operating expenses and is a true net lease.

The type of lease used for a project, gross vs. NNN, will dictate the arrangement, type, and flexibility of utility distribution within the building. If the leases are gross leases, then economy will be greater by choosing central metering and distribution for sewer, water, power, gas, and telephone. Sewer and water are, almost without exception in all types of buildings, centrally metered and distributed at a cost to the common area. Power and gas, when centrally metered, may call for submetering for weekend or off-hour occupancy. Today, state of the art submetering systems allow a landlord to accurately charge tenants for off-hour and weekend occupancy. In larger buildings, a sophisticated version of this system may be used to individually meter tenants for all consumption. Some states restrict the resale of power and other utilities without a license, so landlords' choices for management of the utility systems may vary from state to state.

Buildings utilizing NNN leases call for as much individual metering as possible. The logic that the tenant may control his or her total rent by monitoring his or her power and gas consumption is a compelling marketing tool. In these cases, it is wise to minimize common areas so that these areas do not become a burden on the monthly common area maintenance (CAM) charge.

Telephone service has evolved into a more flexible utility. With the advent of satellite uplinks and digital switches, super large buildings or a large group of buildings can gain considerable savings and flexibility by installing a proprietary switch, with or without a satellite uplink, for its tenants. In effect, the building owner/operator may become a local phone company, purchasing telephone services (local and long distance) in bulk and reselling phone service to the tenants, thus establishing another profit center for the building. Today this has become common practice in very large projects.

CHAPTER

30

Project Staffing *and* Philosophy

Who does what in a development deal is as important to the success of your venture as what is done. The makeup of your team is a major consideration. This short chapter will serve as a reminder to collect your group with considerable forethought.

Partners

For the sake of realism in this section, assume that you will be the motivating force in the development process and that you will be the one in charge of locating, selecting, and creating the project. In essence, construct a transaction around you in your head, as if it were an actual project. This will personalize the exercise and start you thinking in the direction of practical solutions.

In any development or investment project, there are two essential skills required to create and enhance a successful income project. They are the skills of the entrepreneur and those of the manager, or bean counter.

These skills are not necessarily compatible, but often you will be required to serve both functions. Let's look at the ingredients of both so that you can see where you can fit into the picture. The characteristics of each personality type are evidenced by what they do and how they go about it. If you are fortunate, you might be someone who possesses enough of each type to really shine in this business. As you read this section, be honest with yourself when comparing yourself against the profiles outlined. If you approach the exercise honestly, you will have a better chance of pulling together a successful team when the time comes for your first deal.

Who Gets to Be the Entrepreneur?

What does an entrepreneur really do and how does he or she do it? Not an easy question. I have been making a living as a full-time entrepreneur for over 25 years and I'm not sure whether I am typical or not.

HEADS UP

Entrepreneurs see things other people do not. What they see is opportunity. They see it because they are always looking for it.

Why are entrepreneurs looking for opportunity? They are naturally curious and restless, generally unsatisfied with the status quo. In another era, they would most likely be the explorers and the immigrants. They populated the West and expanded the country. They wanted more out of life and were willing to work hard and take risks to get it. Entrepreneurs generally do not shrink from hard work and they seldom, if ever, give up on something once they have set it in motion.

HEADS UP

Persistence and hard work are 90 percent of entrepreneurship. The rest is vision and a little luck.

You might think back on the need for research and fact-finding and feel that this does not sound like entrepreneurship; rather it sounds "beancounterish." Not so! Research and fact-finding go hand in hand with curiosity and seeking. By unearthing the facts, something most people are too lazy to do, an entrepreneur will uncover patterns that are not apparent in the market place. Most people assume certain things, taking the opinions of others as truth. The entrepreneur wants to find out the real facts for himself or herself.

HEADS UP

By placing your judgment ahead of others, you will find that you are taking the road less traveled and doing something original.

If the above describes you to a T, then you are most likely emotionally qualified for this endeavor. The other ingredient for the job of entrepreneur is common sense. Realism and pragmatism are the cornerstone of the entrepreneur's role. Vision, insight, and desire amount to nothing if the goal is neither realistic nor practical. You must be an individual who can see intuitively if something makes sense and understand how it will work. For example, most people who ride a motorcycle do not know that to turn left, you turn the front wheel slightly to the right, and vice versa. If you doubt me, look at any photograph of a motorcycle in a high-speed turn. A true pragmatist can look at that photo and recognize the dynamics of the action. My generation was always amused by the antics of a character known as Rube Goldberg who was famous for creating impossibly large and complicated machines to do very simple things. He was inventive, but impractical. Entrepreneurship thrives on the KISS principle: Keep It Simple, Stupid!

The Bean Counter

Who then is the bean counter? People for years have poked fun at the bean counter, describing him or her as being excessively anal. Some of this is true. The reality of the bean counters is that they do a great job with what they are given. Most accountants seem to fit this description, but a true practitioner is much more than a figure juggler. Most people charged with this responsibility shine when given a game plan to follow. One of their principal delights is finding holes in the plan and making improvements in it. Sound a bit like an entrepreneur? Maybe, but the entrepreneur is the one who created the game plan for the bean counter to follow.

The bean counter is innovative in his or her own right. The constant search for improvement is, most often, coupled with a fervent dedication to detail. Bean counters make great accountants and stewards of complex mechanisms. To be effective in the income property management business, they must also have the skills of the diplomat. They will be dealing with tenants who think that their payment of rent entitles them to more than just a place to do business. The inspired bean counter must point out that they are entitled to what is in the lease and no more. They must do this with diplomacy and tact. By finessing the situation, the effective manager will get the tenants to see that they are part of a community whose members need to work together to ensure that everyone gets what they need and are entitled to, not necessarily what they want.

Both the entrepreneur and the bean counter should be in a position of ownership when dealing with income property. Rarely are these talents housed in one body; in the practical world of investment real estate, you will see many two-person partnerships. Together, two talented individuals can make a formidable team. The talents are complementary and incredibly synergistic.

Consultants

You need to regard consultants as hired guns. They should be experts in their field, hired to perform specific tasks, when needed. When you contract with a consultant, you are purchasing knowledge and experience.

HEADS UP

Do yourself a favor: verify their expertise. Talk with their customers. Examine their work. See firsthand how they do their jobs.

Make a critical judgment as to the effectiveness of their work product. After all, it's your money; you have a right to get your money's worth. More importantly, you must evaluate the probability of that person's work being compatible with your game plan. You know where you're headed and, therefore, you are in the best position to evaluate their effectiveness in helping you get where you want to go.

Managers

Managers are apprentice bean counters. Property management needs people who are in the field, overseeing maintenance and talking to tenants on-site. Most good real estate bean counter types made their start in the field. The hands-on experience is necessary to properly set up and administer a true management program.

There is a lot more to property management than just collecting rents. The proper care and feeding of tenants is an art form. Remember: you are not dealing with a finite commodity.

New rental space comes on the market every year and all of the new buildings need tenants. Your tenants are fair game for the brokers charged with filling the newer buildings. Remember also that's how you got your tenants in the first place. Some were most likely new businesses, but most came out of someone else's building.

Tenants move for a variety of reasons, not the least of which are:

- They need to expand and their landlord cannot accommodate them.
- They feel that the building's location no longer meets their needs.
- They feel that they are not getting prompt service.
- They feel that the building is not properly maintained.
- They are mad at the landlord.

It does not matter why they move. Despite all your expertise, some will always move. The trick is anticipation and accommodation. Figure out what they have to have and give it to them, and you will keep your tenants. When a manager becomes effective at this, he or she is well on the way to becoming a first-class bean counter.

Accounting and Legal Services

Both accounting and legal advice are needed functions in any transaction. The accounting is a day-to-day function with monthly reports, whereas the legal function is required sporadically.

The key to the accounting functions lies not in the bookkeeping, but in the setup and presentation of data. The bookkeeping function is performed for the banks and the IRS. The owners require spreadsheets and other data so that they can see at a glance what they need to know.

The legal function tends to be front-end loaded. Most of the work is performed before and immediately after the purchase. In a development deal, most of the legal work occurs before the close of escrow. After that, unless there is a crisis, the legal function is confined to the odd lease or loan closing. Both of these functions should be hired and paid for rather giving up partnership interest for these services. While their contributions are necessary, they are relatively routine and require little or no innovation.

Brokers

Brokers are not only necessary, but vital in all real estate transactions. They are involved in all three crucial aspects of the investment, whether purchased or built.

- They are involved in the purchase of the land or the income property.
- They are crucial in leasing the property.
- They will be involved in the sale of the asset.

There is no way to be involved in real property as an investment without the services of one or more brokers. Of course, you can be your own broker, but even if you have the experience, chances are that you will be involved with other brokers as well. The practice of cooperation, started in the residential industry, is slowly filtering through the commercial industry. More and more transactions involve two or more brokers who cooperate by bringing buyer and seller together. In the not-too-distant past, commercial brokers seldom exposed their listings to other brokers. Today, most owners insist that commercial brokers cooperate with all other brokers to afford their properties greater exposure in the market. This is essential, and it is good business for the brokers as well.

HEADS UP

Making a broker one of your partners can provide a powerful incentive to the individual to perform beyond the call of duty. You should consider it.

Architects and Engineers

Most of the work of architects and engineers occurs at the beginning of a development project. Sometimes an investor will purchase a property for renovation and the process becomes similar to that of a building project, with these two consultants involved at the beginning of the project. Most common of all, however, is the instance where an investor purchases a building full of tenants. The architect, sometimes aided by an engineer, is involved only sporadically when tenants are replaced. Rarely have I seen either of these two consultants involved in the ownership of an investment property unless they have been brought into the deal by the original developer. Their services at the front end are a valuable contribution to the development effort, and often I have asked the architect to speculate along with me on some early plans to keep my front-end costs down. In exchange for this favor, I have offered a piece of the action and the full fee when the project proceeds. If money is tight, I recommend that you consider this strategy.

Employees

When dealing with this array of consultants, from market research through property managers, you will be tempted to add up the fees to be paid and conclude that you might be better off hiring these people as employees. This is a big step and has some long-range implications. The largest consideration is cost. If you hire these people by the job, then your exposure is limited to payment as needed; however, if you hire them, you are taking on serious, continuous overhead. The only reason to justify this group as employees would be if you were embarking on a full-time program of acquiring and owning multiple properties. This could require the services of the consultants involved on a full-time basis. I would still be inclined to hire them as consultants, however, because I believe that the experienced professional who is not available for hire will do a better job. If, however, you are a generalist who wants to hire and train your own staff, then you might be correct in hiring them as employees.

Authority and Responsibility

One of the major considerations, beyond the cost of employees vs. consultants, lies in their authority to act. When representing you with third parties, consultants are almost exclusively hired in an advisory capacity, whereas employees are considered to be the "owner's representatives" and, therefore, are perceived by third parties to "speak for the owner." If this is what you want, fine, but one of the most useful functions of a consultant is that of a buffer between you and any third party. The consultant's inability, or apparent inability, to commit you buys you time to consider all your options.

HEADS UP

If someone is empowered to act, or perceived to be in a position to act, he or she may inadvertently find himself or herself in a position where there is no way out of making a decision. If the consultant cannot act for you, the problem is rendered moot and the pressure is off.

You will find that this will become one of your most useful tools in negotiation. Besides finding property and tenants, the most valuable service provided by a broker is to provide this buffer, leaving you free to think about the negotiations. The only time I like to be face to face with the other party is during lease negotiations. Most owners, however, prefer the arm's-length approach.

Handling the Cash

Another function served by both consultants and employees is to collect and disburse money. Collecting the income is why you made the investment. It is also where you can be most vulnerable to fraud. There is no problem with having either the consultant or the employee collect the money, as long as you follow three simple rules:

- Never allow them to accept cash. Make sure your tenants know that cash payments will not be credited as rent.
- All funds are to be deposited in an account controlled only by the owner.
- Handle all disbursements personally. Sign all the checks yourself or have one of your partners sign the checks. Do not delegate check-signing authority to an employee or a consultant.

Follow these three simple rules and you will never get hurt.

There are obviously circumstances where these rules will be cumbersome or become impossible to implement.

The first instance is emergencies. Set up a special account for the use of your property manager with a balance sufficient to pay for small emergencies. Seldom, if ever, will an emergency exceed a few thousand dollars. Most will require between $100 and $500. When the receipts are presented to you, replenish the fund. Your exposure is then limited to the original deposit.

The second instance where this may become impossible is when the size of your investments and the sheer volume of the rents collected require a formal accounting department. When this happens, you will need to set up one group to do the accounting and issue the checks and a second group to check the results and sign the checks. At this point, you may find that you will have to start paying close attention to your monthly reports, cross-checking them against your bank statements—a happy problem indeed!

Tenants

While all this is going on, what are your tenants doing and what should you be expecting in terms of their performance? In the development phase, you should be primarily concerned with financial health, experience, and business plan. During the management phase of your project, the two most important aspects of the tenants' role are the conduct of their business, in general, and the timely payment of your rent. You must, in a general way, keep an eye on your tenants to determine that they are prospering. This is crucial with retail tenants, and one of the important clauses in a retail lease is the quarterly reporting on gross sales. There may be little you can do to help, but if you can spot a downtrend early, you will be in a better position to replace a tenant who is going broke. Their conduct in the building, their treatment of their fellow tenants, their adherence to the rules and regulations, their respect for the parking rules, and their business hours are all areas that the property manager needs to monitor. You should instruct the property manager to inform you before taking any action so that you may provide some guidance in the matter, as you might be privy to information that is not available to the manager.

Their Business

There are things that you can do to help your tenants. Why should you bother? The answer is simple. A prosperous tenant can pay the rent and a bankrupt one is a complication you do not need. If, for example, you have a small tenant that sells goods similar to those sold by one of the anchor tenants in your shopping center, you might consider intervening on behalf of the little business. You can request that the larger store not emphasize this particular part of its business. If this fails, you might allow the smaller store to diversify, changing its line so that the little tenant does not directly compete with the major tenant. Today, with stores like Wal-Mart, Best Buy, and Home Depot, the small stores are scrambling to stay out of their way.

HEADS UP

Ignore this advice at your peril.

Paying Rent

Prompt payment of rent is crucial to your cash flow. You will, most likely, have a mortgage to pay; if you do not receive the rent, taxes, and common area expenses on time, you will find that you can be in a cash flow bind.

HEADS UP

Sloppy rent collection is fatal for your investment future.

The major problem in income property management is late rental payments. The solution to this lies in the lease document. There must be a series of steps built into the lease that make late payment of rent very unpleasant and costly to your tenants. Major tenants always object to this, as their credit is deemed to be superior. My response to this is that these rules are not a problem to anyone intending to pay their rent on time. If they do not intend to do so, I have second thoughts about allowing them into my building. The only response to this I have ever heard is "It is our corporate policy." My response is always "My policy is not to do business with people who will not commit to paying their rent on time."

HEADS UP

Stand firm on this point, or you will live to regret it!

The tools you need incorporated in your project lease are, at the very least:

- A clear definition of the rent and how it is calculated
- A specific rent due date, together with a clearly defined place where the rent must be received (not in the mail)
- A specific date on which the rent is late
- A specific financial penalty when the rent is late
- Clearly defined remedies for nonpayment: over 30 days, specifically, the right to declare the tenant in default
- The right in the default remedy to accelerate the rent and evict the tenant within the shortest possible time allowed by the statutes of the state having jurisdiction

HEADS UP

The threat of financial penalties is not enough. You must enforce them the first time and every time.

You must be able to evict the bad apples as fast as possible.

Do not be intimidated by the large companies. They are subject to the same law as any other tenant. Make them pay the penalty and your rent will start to arrive on time. The deliberate, slow payment of rent is a cash management tool used by many companies. They can get away with it only if you let them do so.

This is one of the most common management problems that you will encounter in owning income property. You must develop effective tools for keeping this problem under control, as the consequences of failure can dramatically damage your investment program.

SECTION

VII

CONTINUOUS REDEVELOPMENT

CHAPTER

31

Project Completion—Collecting Rent

The culmination of the discussion of real estate development is the completion of the build-out and lease-up phases of a project. For this to be accomplished, the tenants have to be in place, paying rent, and occupancy permits have to be issued. The minimum prerequisite for this is to have completed the building and off-site improvements and to have all safety systems turned on and operational. Then, the tenants may occupy their premises as their own tenant improvements are complete and occupancy permits are issued. Timing for tenant space design and approval is, therefore, critical during the construction phase. If the critical path schedule in Chapter 26, Tables 26-1 and 26-2, is followed carefully, the preleased tenants should occupy their tenant spaces at roughly the same time, soon after the building has been approved for occupancy.

Start-Up

Closing out the construction phase and making the transition into the operating phase is tricky, because usually there is a period during which the first tenants are in occupancy and the final tenants are in the build-out process. This period must be kept to a minimum and building out must be as inconspicuous to the tenants in occupancy as possible. It will vary in time depending upon the strength of the preleasing effort and the size of the project. Shoddy work, late delivery of the premises, and poor follow-through can raise untold havoc with the tenants and the landlord's relationships with them. A smooth transition from construction to operation will separate the amateur from the professional. This phase will always have a profound effect on the bottom line if it is not handled properly.

To avoid problems during the move and to complete the lender's required documentation, the developer should use the situation to his or her advantage. Do not allow occupancy of the premises until all the construction and take-out lender's required paperwork is fully executed. These items are, customarily:

- The acknowledgment of commencement
- The estoppel certificate
- The punch list, also required at move-in, a list of items that have to be corrected or completed at the end of the tenant improvement construction

The execution and presentation of the punch list can be flexible, as some things remain undiscovered until the tenant has actually moved in. The first two documents are critical. The acknowledgment allows the landlord to start charging rent for the premises from the specified date in the document. The estoppel certificate is required by the lenders for funding and it may have to be re-executed for the closing of the permanent loan.

Once the tenant is occupying the premises, the first order of business becomes the completion of the punch list. Insist that the tenant take several weeks to prepare it so that it is as complete as possible. This way, the work can be accomplished all at once, with minimal disruption of the tenant and his or her business. If there are items critical to the opening of the tenant's business, make sure they are handled before the tenant opens for business. Access to the tenants is critical for the tenant's customers, so particular attention must be given during this opening time to contractors and their vehicles in the parking areas. Wherever possible, there must not be any parking in the designated visitor parking areas. This is always a problem, as the visitor parking is customarily the most convenient to the tenant's premises.

The initial period of property management's relationship with the tenants is crucial, as it will set the tone for their relationship during the entire duration of the lease. Be as cooperative and helpful as possible, while at the same time establishing the rules for the duration of the lease. Typical problem areas are:

- Tenants' employees parking in the visitor areas
- People cutting through the landscaping
- Litter
- Smoking areas
- General maintenance

The key to relationships with the tenants is having realistic expectations. Tenants are people, and people are going to do things that the landlord would wish they did not.

- Don't fight with tenants over their cutting through the landscaping.
- Wait to see where it is happening and establish a paved path for their use, rather than allow the landscaping to look abused.
- Confine the smoking areas to any other location than the main building entrance. Nothing looks or smells worse than a cluster of people grouped around an ashtray at the entrance to the building. The smoke is offensive to visitors who do not smoke.

HEADS UP

Enforce this rule or live to regret it!

- The parking issue is the easiest to resolve. Insist that the tenants police their own employees and those of their co-tenants.
- Do not become the parking police, as it will offend the tenants. The easiest method is to point out that visitors and clients are the source of revenue to all the businesses in the building and, therefore, their access to the building should be facilitated, not made less convenient.

The tenants will see the wisdom of these actions eventually and will act accordingly. They tend to sort things out among themselves. Intervene only if there is a serious problem between or among tenants.

Who Should Manage and Why

This is traditionally an area of much debate. The reality of the situation is that the skills required of a good developer are not necessarily compatible with or often coexistent with the skills required of a good manager.

> **HEADS UP**
>
> It takes entrepreneurial skills to create a development and it takes a bean counter mentality to maximize the return on investment; seldom are both talents found in the same individual.

If you are not going to be a developer and you have made your decision to purchase a specific piece of real estate, who is going to manage it? Is this a difficult decision? The answer depends upon your circumstances and the size and complexity of your purchase. If you are starting out with a second home rental or a small fourplex of apartments, the time required for management is minimal. I would always recommend that you manage the property yourself. If, however, you and your partners have pooled your resources and purchased a 50,000-square-foot office building, then the management is going to entail some more work and you will need to evaluate the time necessary and the nature of the management chores.

A good developer generally has a separate property management department or hires an outside firm to do the chore. The job calls for diplomacy, attention to detail, and a great deal of paperwork. Seldom are these the skills of the entrepreneur.

To maximize the cash flow, it is important to understand exactly what the costs are and why they are what they are. These costs also need to be examined and tested to see if they can be reduced. Invariably, the initial tax assessment should be questioned and appealed to minimize that hit. Fortunately, in today's NNN leases, all operating expenses are the responsibility of the tenants. This also is a challenge, as tenants are very sensitive to costs. The building must be managed with the attitude that it is going to be operated at a cost competitive with the competition. The goal is to have a beautifully maintained building at a lower cost per square foot than the competition. The tenants will rightly scrutinize monthly, quarterly, and annual expense breakdowns. Make sure the costs are defensible. The best tactic is for the landlord to establish minimum criteria for maintenance, such as janitorial, window washing, landscape maintenance, common area cleanup, and parking lot sweeping and let the tenants increase the scope and frequency if they so desire. So long as the landlord's standards are high enough to have the building compare favorably with the competition, then all will be well.

This approach puts cost control squarely on the shoulders of the tenants, where it belongs. After all, they are the landlord's clients and they do pay the bill.

Collecting Rents and Paying Bills

This section of the chapter is as relevant to a developer as it is to someone who has purchased a building. While the manager is charged with the paperwork, it is generally a good idea for the developer/landlord to handle the money. The manager should invoice for, receive, and deposit the rents, so that he or she may keep track of the payment or nonpayment, as the case may be. However, the rent should be deposited in a bank account controlled by the landlord. Similarly, the manager should receive and approve all bills, forwarding them to the landlord for payment. The whole effort of creating this investment has been to achieve the desired cash flow, so logic dictates that control of the cash flow should rightly rest with the owner/developer.

If the reporting is accurate and timely, it can provide important information required for management decisions. Specific and timely monthly reports should be available for:

- Rent: when due, when invoiced, when paid, late fees and any other pertinent items (see Table 31-1)
- Expenses: fully itemized monthly, when due, and when paid, also broken down by tenant and per square foot for analysis (see Table 31-2)
- Rental projections: showing escalations, lease expiration dates, and dates of options, etc. (see Table 31-3)
- Continuously updated cash flow projections showing the projected increase in values due to scheduled rent increases and re-leasing (see Table 31-4)

These basic tools will tell any landlord what is transpiring with the project and allow him or her to monitor the progress of the investment. They also serve to alert the landlord to the need for new tenants or the need to renew leases with current tenants. It also reminds everyone when mortgages are due and when might be an optimum time to refinance or place the project up for sale.

HEADS UP

Remember: this is not brain surgery! Do not fear. Take a deep breath and think. Go back and review the process you went through to get to this point. Remember all you have learned about the market and your property in particular. This will start the blood flowing again to the brain.

By now, you have created some of your management tools, specifically, the tenant spreadsheet. At a glance you can see how many tenants you have and how soon leases will be renewing. You will have evaluated the leases and decided how much you can escalate the leases over the period of your planned ownership. The fact is that you only have two choices anyway. It's going to be you or a hired gun.

Owner-Managed

Unless you have made the decision to be a full-time developer/investor, you might have a job that requires your attention 60 to 80 hours per week. It is not in the cards for you to manage the property from day to day. Perhaps one of your partners can do it. Owner-managed property seems to run more smoothly, simply because owners spend the extra time and care more about the results. Employees have a different threshold of care than entrepreneurs.

Square Footage	Tenant Name	Suite No.	Security Deposit	Rent Init.	Rent Bump	% Bump	Comm. Date	Exp. Date	Renewal Option
35,000	Office Bldg								
2,560	Tenant #1	100	$2,987	$12	7/1/2004	5%	7/1/2003	2/28/2010	1x5
6,600	Tenant #2	300	$7,700	$12	8/1/2004	5%	8/1/2003	7/31/2010	1x5
5,120	Tenant #3	120	$5,973	$12	7/1/2004	5%	8/1/2003	7/31/2010	1x5
4,000	Tenant #4	200	$4,667	$12	7/1/2004	5%	8/1/2003	3/31/2008	1x5
1,280	Tenant #5	220	$1,493	$14	8/1/2004	5%	8/1/2003	5/31/2008	None
4,000	Tenant #6	400	$4,667	$13	8/8/2004	5%	8/1/2003	7/31/2008	1x5
1,280	Tenant #7	240	$1,493	$14	10/1/2004	5%	10/1/2003	9/31/2008	None
2,560	Tenant #8	450	$2,987	$14	12/1/2004	4%	12/1/2003	11/30/2010	1x5
1,280	Tenant #9	250	$1,493	$14	9/1/2004	3%	9/1/2003	8/31/2008	1x5
1,280	Tenant #10	230	$1,493	$14	12/15/2004	3%	1/1/2004	12/31/2008	1x2
5,040	Tenant #11	420	$5,880	$14	5/1/2004	5%	4/1/2004	3/31/2009	1x5
50	Covered Parking Spaces	1-50							
35,000	Total Security Deposits		$40,833						

TABLE 31-1. RENTAL SUMMARY

If you are part of a group that made the purchase, you might consider splitting up the chores, appointing one member to be the "face," or the contact person with the tenants, and another to do the bookkeeping, invoicing, and rent collection. A third might be the handy type who could become the one to oversee the maintenance and upkeep of the property and to supervise the tenant improvement renovations required to keep the investment going. This is an ideal solution, as you will be learning the ins and outs of the business, hands on.

Third-Party Managers

If you and your partners are 70-hour-a-week people, then you will have to turn to a third-party manager. How do you select the perfect candidate? You might start out by conferring with the broker who helped you buy the property, as well as talking with any of the other professionals that you encountered in the process. If you are going to hire a manager, I recommend that you start the selection process during the purchase evaluation or development process. A manager should be involved in the evaluation and selection decision early on. An experienced manager is in a position to point out some flaws and pitfalls in the investment and to suggest some long-term management strategies for improving the property. If you used an investment broker, you might ask him or her for a recommendation. Ask which properties he or she thinks are the best of their kind and find out who manages them. A seasoned professional manager is a known quantity and should be able to manage almost as

Tenant Pro Rata	% CAM	1st Quarter	Paid to Date	Adjustment	2nd Quarter	Paid to Date	Adjustment
Tenant #1	7.3%	$928	0	$928			
Tenant #2	18.86%	$2,394	0	$2,394			
Tenant #3	14.63%	$1,857	0	$1,857			
Tenant #4	11.43%	$1,451	0	$1,451			
Tenant #5	3.66%	$465	0	$465			
Tenant #6	11.43%	$1,451	0	$1,451			
Tenant #7	3.66%	$465	0	$465			
Tenant #8	7.3%	$928	0	$928			
Tenant #9	3.66%	$465	0	$465			
Tenant #10	3.66%	$465	0	$465			
Tenant #11	14.44%	$1,828	0	$1,828			
Totals	100%	$12,695	0	$12,695			
Cost/SF/Qtr		0		Refunds			Extra Billed

TABLE 31-2. EXPENSE BREAKDOWN

well as a motivated owner. You should consider all the incentives that can be made available to the manager as a sweetener. The more motivated you can make the manager, the better the potential results. It is not uncommon to have a manager participate in the increase in value of the property during his or her tenure. If the management company has a stake in the building, you will get better management.

In any case, if you can find a good manager, you will get good management. Take your time, do the research, and find the right person. Even within a good company, there are outstanding performers. Often they are looking to start their own business. You might get lucky and find someone who is ready to launch and is looking for his or her first property. If you sign up with a new company in the early days, you can take advantage of the hard work required to build a solid reputation. Do not underestimate the rewards coupled to ambition.

HEADS UP

Look around: the possibilities are everywhere. Sift through them and find someone who will fit into your plan.

Management Tools

Once you have selected the manager, it is up to you to provide the tools. Take your lease spreadsheet and review it with the manager or, better still, have him or her do a spreadsheet from the leases and compare the two.

Leases

The leases are the main concern in the management plan. You must preserve them, improve their quality, and make the tenants happy.

Tenant Name	Suite No.	Square Footage	August Invoiced	Collected	Sept. Invoiced	Collected	Total This Quarter
Rent							
Tenant #1	100	1,280	$1,280.00	$1,280.00	$1,280.00	$1,280.00	$2,560.00
Tenant #2	120	2,560	$2,560.00	$2,560.00	$2,560.00	$2,560.00	$5,120.00
Tenant #3	200	1,920	$1,060.00	$1,040.00	$1,520.00	$1,500.00	$2,540.00
Tenant #4	220	640	$748.00	$748.00	$746.67	$746.67	$1,494.67
Tenant #5	230	640	$1,493.00				
Tenant #6	240	640					
Tenant #7	250	640			$746.67	$746.67	$746.67
Tenant #8	300	2,260			$3,360.00	$3,360.00	$3,360.00
Tenant #9	440	1,280					
Tenant #10	420	1,280					
Tenant #11	400	1,920	$1,493.00		$2,080.00	$2,080.00	$2,080.00
Subtotal			$7,141.00	$5,628.00	$12,293.34	$12,273.34	$17,901.24
Common Area Charges							
Tenant #1	100	1,280	$380.00	$380.00	$462.00	$462.00	$842.00
Tenant #2	120	2,560	$880.80	$880.80	$924.00	$924.00	$1,812.80
Tenant #3	200	1,920	$293.00	$293.00	$693.00	$693.00	$986.00
Tenant #4	220	640	$231.00	$231.00	$231.00	$231.00	$462.00
Tenant #5	230	640					
Tenant #6	240	640					
Tenant #7	250	640			$231.00	$231.00	$231.00
Tenant #8	300	2,260			$1,051.05	$1,051.05	$1,051.05
Tenant #9	440	1,280					
Tenant #10	420	1,280					
Tenant #11	400	1,920	$462.00	$442.00	$693.00	$693.00	$1,135.00
Subtotal			$2,254.80	$2,234.80	$4,285.05	$4,285.05	$6,519.85

FIGURE 31-3. MONTHLY CASH FLOW PROJECTIONS (CONTINUED ON NEXT PAGE)

Tenant Name	Suite No.	Square Footage	August Invoiced	Collected	Sept. Invoiced	Collected	Total This Quarter
Sales Tax (2%)							
Tenant #1	100	1,280	$67.00	$67.00	$33.97	$33.97	$100.97
Tenant #2	120	2,560	$67.25	$67.25	$67.94	$67.94	$135.19
Tenant #3	200	1,920	$83.21	$83.21	$43.15	$43.15	$126.36
Tenant #4	220	640	$38.70	$38.70	$19.06	$19.06	$57.76
Tenant #5	230	640					
Tenant #6	240	640					
Tenant #7	250	640			$19.06	$19.06	$19.06
Tenant #8	300	2,260			$86.02	$86.02	$86.02
Tenant #9	440	1,280					
Tenant #10	420	1,280					
Tenant #11	400	1,920	$38.12	$38.12	$92.20	$92.20	$130.32
Subtotal			$294.28	$294.28	$361.41	$361.40	$655.68
Mo. Totals			$9,960.08	$8,157.08	$16,939.80	$16,919.79	$25,076.87
Mgt. Fee Calc.			$375.83	$314.51	$663.14	$662.34	$976.85

TABLE 31-3. MONTHLY CASH FLOW PROJECTIONS (CONTINUED)

The first step is to have a game plan that your manager can support and that he or she thinks is doable. The two primary areas of concern in the leases are the rent and the lease itself. You have examined the lease and determined the ideal lease for you. The rent is a function of the marketplace. You and your manager can look at the schedule of lease expirations and compare your rent levels with those projected in the marketplace. You can, and you must, devise a strategy to maximize the cash flow during the time you are going to own the property.

There are two ways to justify the rental increases. Normal cost of living increases are easy to justify, but if you want to make your building better than the average, you will need to justify better-than-average increases when the time comes. There are two ways to do that: increased service and a better building.

> **HEADS UP**
>
> Merchant developers tend to sell their properties within 24 months of completion, contenting themselves with the "developer's profit." Those who retain ownership for longer periods reap the additional rewards of good management and "continuous redevelopment"—managing the property and maximizing the cash flow.

Service

Whether you are operating an existing building or working with one you have just completed,

Income	Year 1	Year 2	Year 3	Year 4	Year 5
Rents	$225,400	$236,670	$248,504	$260,929	$273,975
Less 5% Vacancy Rate	–$11,270	–$11,834	–$12,425	–$13,046	–$13,699
Gross Potential Income	$214,130	$224,837	$236,078	$247,882	$260,276
Expenses					
$4.75/SF x 16,000 SF	$76,000	$79,800	$83,790	$87,980	$92,378
Less Recapture from Tenants	–$72,200	–$75,810	–$79,601	–$83,581	–$87,760
Net Expenses	$3,800	$3,990	$4,190	$4,399	$4,619
NIBDS	**$210,330**	**$220,847**	**$231,889**	**$243,483**	**$255,657**
Value @ 9% Cap Rate	**$2,337,000**	**$2,453,850**	**$2,576,543**	**$2,705,370**	**$2,840,638**
ROI on Cash $460,000	**21%**	**23%**	**26%**	**28%**	**31%**
Add'l Annual Capital Gain	**$576,087**	**$692,937**	**$815,630**	**$944,457**	**$1,079,725**
ROI on Gain if Sold	**125%**	**151%**	**177%**	**205%**	**235%**

Income	Year 6	Year 7	Year 8	Year 9	Year 10
Rents	$287,674	$302,058	$317,160	$333,018	$349,669
Less 5% Vacancy Rate	–$14,384	–$15,103	–$15,858	–$16,651	–$17,483
Gross Potential Income	$273,290	$286,955	$301,302	$316,368	$332,186
Expenses					
$4.75/SF x 16,000 SF	$96,997	$101,847	$106,940	$112,287	$117,901
Less Recapture from Tenants	–$92,148	–$96,755	–$101,593	–$106,672	–$112,006
Net Expenses	$4,850	$5,092	$5,347	$5,614	$5,895
NIBDS	**$268,440**	**$281,862**	**$295,955**	**$310,753**	**$326,291**
Value @ 9% Cap Rate	**$2,982,670**	**$3,131,804**	**$3,288,394**	**$3,452,813**	**$3,625,454**
ROI on Cash $460,000	**33%**	**36%**	**39%**	**43%**	**46%**
Add'l Annual Capital Gain	**$1,221,757**	**$1,370,891**	**$1,527,481**	**$1,452,613**	**$1,864,541**
ROI on Gain if Sold	**266%**	**298%**	**332%**	**368%**	**405%**

TABLE 31-4. TEN-YEAR CASH FLOW PROJECTION

how can you improve services? You must ask yourself, "What do the tenants need?" There are many services that business owners require in the course of the day. Can you work with the phone company to bring better and more flexible telephone service to the building? Can you bring in high-speed internet and cable access? Can you arrange for better FedEx, UPS, or postal service? Can you find restaurants that will deliver food for lunches? What about starting a concierge service for your tenants? You might even find a concierge who will service the building. Can you arrange with a local dry cleaner to pick up and deliver? Can you arrange with a mobile car washing service to take care of your tenants' cars? It will only take two spaces in the worst location in the parking lot.

There are so many innovations that you can seek out and offer that you should be able to improve the level of service significantly. Most building owners think in terms of bricks and mortar. Use your brain to think globally and proactively. Think of what you would like to have for services and act on those ideas. Most of these services will not cost you a dime. Businesses are always looking to expand and will jump at the chance to add a bunch of new customers all in one place.

Renovation

The other side of the upgrade coin is the building. This concept can be applied to newly developed buildings as well as those purchased as an investment. What can you do to take it up a notch? All buildings have limitations imposed by the design of the structure. Hopefully, you will have built or chosen one with good ceiling heights and ample parking. The first thing you can do is beef up the landscaping. Periodic redecoration to maintain the most modern look is always a good strategy. The latest look is generally cosmetic in nature and can be done over time as you allocate a budget for these capital expenses. If you purchased a building, you might want to budget a lump sum and do it all at once when you take over, to signal to the tenants that you are a better property owner and that they are in for a treat under your tenure.

Accounting

Remember the numbers. These are your most important tools. They will tell you whether you are gaining or losing. If you have a professional manager, you will have to review the accounting documents carefully. The manager will have his or her own system and you cannot expect him or her to change a system that works. Whatever the system, it should use computers. You should require the manager to submit reports both in written form and electronically. This will enable you to access the data directly and manipulate it into the form you have chosen to keep track of the building's progress. Modern spreadsheet programs will enable you to set up a conversion process to input the new monthly data automatically.

Traditional Bookkeeping

You will use traditional accounting methods to handle the books of your partnership or LLC; these will reflect income and taxable income, as well as provide data to establish your rate of return before and after taxes. You will find, however, that your manager will be providing you with data in spreadsheet form, because that is more useful for management than traditional accounting methods. Modern accounting programs such as QuickBooks Pro are designed to export spreadsheets from the accounting data, but you are better off designing your own format so that it is meaningful to you.

Spreadsheets

No matter what you are doing with spreadsheets, you are going to have to do one that reflects your long-term game plan. It is against this one that you will compare the actual results of your management plan. Remember: you and the manager are the management team and you cannot abdicate the implementation of your plan to the manager. You must work together, so that even if you have a manager, you will be involved in the process. You should negotiate your own leases unless the manager has a flair for the process and your tenants should get acquainted with you even though your manager is running the day-to-day business of the building.

All spreadsheets today allow you to plot numbers as a graphic, so it is easy to compare the projected and actual, both numerically and visually. Sometimes a visual display will be more meaningful than just the numbers. It is especially dramatic when you are projecting rapid change. Table 31-5 is a good example.

Integration

In its final form, your financial package will be an integration of traditional accounting methods and spreadsheet analysis. You should seek out systems that allow you to cross the line between the two, so that you can minimize the amount of input required. Again, research. By the time this book is published, there will be more software packages on the market, so it would be pointless to recommend one. Talk with your accountant and have him or her set you up with whatever you think you will need. It is a good investment so get it set up properly, as it makes the accountant's job easier to do and, therefore, less costly to you.

Above and Below the Line

No, this does not refer to keeping two sets of books. The line simply separates the building's operating expenses from those of the partnership or LLC. Why is this important? The reason is that when you sell, you will be selling the NIBDS for the building, not that of the partnership or LLC. The building requires the expense of a manager, but the partnership or LLC will require the cost of an accountant to file the taxes. This tax preparation is not a building expense and, therefore, will be shown "below the line."

Operating Costs

You must clearly define operating costs. In an NNN-leased building, these costs are paid for by the tenants. If you cannot convince a tenant that a cost is directly related to the operation of the building, then it is not an operating cost. If it is not an operating cost, then it will become an ownership cost. Operating costs include the following types of expenses:

- Utilities
- Refuse collection
- Janitorial
- Maintenance and repair
- Window washing
- Parking lot sweeping
- Snow removal
- Landscape maintenance
- Taxes
- Insurance
- Management

Ownership Costs

There can be many costs that are paid by the cash flow of a partnership or LLC before cash is distributed to the owners. The magnitude of these expenses is limited only by the agreement of the partners or the members. What expenses can there be?

Would you believe an airplane? Obviously, this is not possible when you and your cohorts own a 50,000-square-foot office building, but

Item	Year 1	Year 2	Year 3	Year 4	Year 5
Projected NIBDS	$250,000	$262,500	$275,000	$287,500	$300,000
Actual NIBDS	$250,000	$262,500	$275,625	$289,406	$303,877
Projected Cash Flow	$100,000	$112,500	$125,000	$137,500	$150,000
Actual Cash Flow	$100,000	$112,500	$125,625	$139,406	$153,877
Percent Difference	8.00%	9.00%	10.05%	11.15%	12.31%
ROI Projected	8.00%	9.00%	10.00%	11.00%	12.00%
ROI Actual	8.00%	9.00%	10.05%	11.15%	12.31%

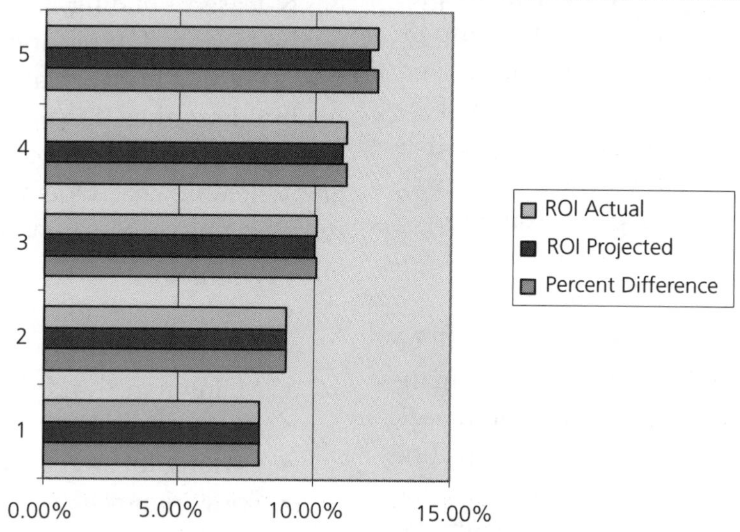

TABLE 31-5. PROJECTED VS. ACTUAL ROI (TABLE AND CHART)

picture your group owning 20 properties scattered all over the place. Might it be reasonable to have a plane available for monthly inspections? It saves time and is very efficient for reaching smaller cities and towns.

By extrapolating between the two extremes, you can imagine all sorts of other expenses. When you have multiple properties, you might start your own management company or your own maintenance company. These can all be owned by the original partnership or LLC.

Why is this a good idea? Having employees creates liabilities. In this world, the liabilities are increasing daily. Most liabilities are insured against, but the courts have shown that no one is invulnerable. If people are employed by the property owner, then your ownership interest in the investment itself is vulnerable to litigation. If, however, people are employed by a separate

> **HEADS UP**
>
> If you are going to start hiring employees, do not make them employees of the entity that owns the property. Start a separate corporation or LLC and make that the employer of all.

corporation or LLC, the owners can lose only their initial start-up capital. This approach assumes that there is no deliberate fraud or gross negligence on behalf of the corporate officers and shareholders.

Maximize the Salability

The above-and below-the-line costs are significant solely at the time you are ready to sell. You will sell the cash flow, not the ownership entity. It is crucial, therefore, that you keep ownership costs separate from the operating costs of the asset. Sloppy bookkeeping will come back to hurt you later.

> **HEADS UP**
>
> One dollar, on the bottom line, capitalized at nine percent, is worth $11.11 at the time of sale. Keep the airplane and the yacht separate!

The way to do this is to keep ownership expenses out of the spreadsheets completely. Account for these costs only in your accounting system. If you create a management company or a maintenance company, keep the ownership of these entities separate within your accounting system. They will be line items only, with a note that they are wholly owned subsidiaries. When you sell the building, the buyer is entitled to examine the income and expense history and, if these expenses are isolated, there will be no question of their legitimacy.

The Documents

In review, what are the management documents that you will need for managing the building? The obvious one is a contract between you and the manager. You should draft this, perhaps using the manager's document as a place to start. Build in whatever incentives you can afford. In addition, you will need to originate or inherit the following documents, at a minimum:

- The ownership document
- Leases
- Utility agreements
- Maintenance contracts
- Construction contracts for tenant improvements
- Leasing agreement
- Consultant agreements: accountant, attorney, etc.

If you are inheriting these documents because you purchased a building instead of building your own, there is nothing in your purchase agreement that obligates you to accept a document that you feel is inadequate. You can make it a condition of closing that a glaring inadequacy be corrected. It matters not whether the document is a consulting contract or a lease. If there is a fatal flaw, correct it before you accept assignment of it.

You will have to accept assignment of leases, so scrutinize them carefully. It might be impossible for the current owner to negotiate a change in the lease to accommodate your concern, but it may be better to pass than accept a serious known problem. The other contracts, except for utility agreements, can be canceled and renegotiated after the purchase. This is generally a good idea anyway, as it allows you to create your own contracts. If you create them, you will know and understand them better. This allows you to be more effective when administering the agreements.

The Cash Flow

The final purpose of this whole exercise is to get your hands on the cash flow.

This is the reason why you have made the

HEADS UP

Cash flow is what you have left after you have paid the mortgage. It's also called *distributable funds* or *net spendable cash.*

investment. Unlike stocks, income-producing real estate is designed to pay monthly returns on invested capital. It is most likely true that there is not as much potential upside in appreciation as there might be in the stock market, but there is little or no possibility of the dramatic downswing in value that exists in the stock market. It takes years of overbuilding to wreck the value of real estate. It also takes years of a city's expansion to alter the desirability of any location. If you are alert to the market and if you see vacancies cropping up or increasing throughout the market, you can react proactively to protect your investment.

CHAPTER

32

Long-Term Investment Management Strategies

The Care and Feeding of Tenants

While you own the project, the type, size, and occupation of your tenants will have a major effect on your ROI. It matters little whether you have purchased or developed apartments, a retail building, an industrial building, or an office building, your tenants, and their relationships with you and with each other, will affect the project, positively or negatively.

Imagine going to your doctor. Upon entering the building, you have to wade through a large crowd of office workers taking a smoke break at the front door. This is not a desirable event. What is the problem? It is twofold. First, the building designer does not provide smoking space away from the front entrance of the building, so people entering the building have to wade through a cloud of smoke. Second, you are experiencing incompatible office uses. You might have noticed that different buildings have different orientations. There is no Costco in a regional mall and you will not find an orthopedic surgeon in a suburban office building surrounded by real estate companies. How then are tenants distributed? They are housed, ideally, in groups differentiated by industry, size, and public visibility.

Tenants and Investment Types

First of all, tenants are separated by industry types:

- Residential
- Industrial
- Retail
- Office
- Recreation
- Special uses

You may find instances where the uses are mingled, but, in general, most developments tend to specialize in one type of tenant. You will find mingled uses in business parks and regional mall developments, as these afford large concentrations of development spread over large areas.

RETAIL

Retail developments break down into the following general categories:

- Strip centers
- Neighborhood centers
- Community centers
- Power centers
- Regional malls

These different types of centers attract different types of tenants and each has its own set of economics.

The strip center is usually a small development, under 30,000 square feet, and is geared to highway traffic. Because it is small and generally lacks credit tenants, the development is considered risky by most lenders. The combination of high land price due to the very visible location, smaller land size, and the higher-than-average interest rate of the available loans creates higher rents. This attracts tenants who need the high degree of visibility and who do not necessarily have the greatest credit. The landlord is compensated for the increased risk by the higher rents and the tenants, in exchange for the higher rents, get greater exposure to the buying public.

Neighborhood centers are built around the grocery store. They have evolved from the local supermarket and bank into complexes that take up to 150,000 square feet on 15 to 16 acres. They contain all the convenience services needed by the surrounding residential community, including grocery stores, drug stores, banks, dry cleaners, sandwich shops, fast food restaurants, and limited offices.

Community shopping centers are expanded neighborhood centers often containing the smaller, junior department stores as well as the standard neighborhood mix of tenants. These centers can reach a quarter of a million square feet. They are not too common, but can be found in the larger suburban cities.

The power center, aka discount center, is a recent arrival on the development scene. Started in the 1980s, this center grew up around the growing discount retailer. Starting with the advent of Wal-Mart, Costco, Home Depot, and similar retailers, these centers soon grew to be a very popular venue for America's shopping public. These centers have now grown in size to exceed 1,000,000 square feet each. They tend to cluster in areas near regional centers or heavily traveled suburban arterials. They account for a significant part of America's retail sales. The late 1990s saw explosive growth in this type of development, as retailers staked out territory in the growing communities.

Finally, there is the regional shopping mall, the traditional new downtown of American retailing. As the population moved to the suburbs following the World War II residential building boom, the regional mall became established as the new downtown for the new communities. These centers house the traditional department store and an ever-changing array of specialty retailers. These centers are also evolving into major centers for entertainment and leisure activities.

> **HEADS UP**
>
> The regional shopping center defines the "mega buck deal." It takes hundreds of millions of dollars and ten or more years to create this type of development.

INDUSTRIAL

Industrial tenants, by their very nature, naturally segregate into manufacturing, warehouse, and distribution facilities. There seems to be little co-mingling of uses. In general, however, they all seem to mix well in an industrial park setting, as all uses are generally compatible. Industrial buildings that cater to smaller users tend to be grouped in similar industry types. Industrial buildings are one type of investment that lends itself well to the single-tenant, build-to-suit project.

RESIDENTIAL

Residential tenants are found in apartment buildings; even there, they tend to be segregated by lifestyle. There are singles complexes, family units, and adult complexes.

This is no accident. The senior tenants do not want to have to put up with the noise and activity associated with the singles complex and families want to cluster together for social and recreational opportunities. Sometimes, in smaller apartment developments, you will find a comfortable mix of all three, but, as the size of the developments has grown, so has the segregation of the various tenant types. This manifested itself in all forms of residential development, not only the rental market. Housing projects tend to segregate along the same lines. In new communities you will find different areas of the community catering to different markets. Today, there are whole communities that cater to retirees, excluding all other occupants; they are age-restricted, limiting residents to age 55 and older.

Office

In the office building category, you will find that the product is even more diverse, separating tenants by occupation and size. Tenant size restricts where the tenant can find space to occupy. Very large tenants are relegated to the large, midsized, and high-rise office buildings and smaller tenants can find a home only in the smaller, suburban low-rise buildings. I have made a career out of catering to small office tenants: my buildings can accommodate tenants as small as 640 square feet and the average tenant is 1,280 square feet.

SIZE

Tenant sizes dictate which type of project is built. If you purchase a particular type of building, you might find yourself having to cull the tenants and massage the leases to create a more compatible tenant mix. It is true that a large tenant may occupy a building designed for smaller tenants; in this case, this tenant becomes a liability as well as a blessing.

If you have a building with this type of tenant, you must budget enough money to carry you through the transition period when this tenant is replaced. Sometimes this tenant will not want to move, because the location is such that it is vital to the tenant's business. When this occurs, you must raise the rents to a point where the extra rent compensates you for the risk of

> **HEADS UP**
>
> If you have any tenant occupying more than 20 percent of a project, you will find that this one tenant represents 100 percent of your cash flow. Avoid or change this situation at all costs!

eventually losing the tenant. Often in this situation the tenant purchases the building in order to stay on. You can look at this potential problem as an opportunity as well. Most large tenants have negotiated concessions from the developer that are not available to the average tenant, but when their leases expire they are not necessarily in as favorable a position. It is very expensive to move: the larger the tenant, the greater the expense. If you can find a building for sale with this type of situation, in a great location, you can look at it as an opportunity to greatly increase the rental revenue. If this tenant wants to stay, he or she will most likely be willing to pay market rate rents to do so. If there is no serious newer competition nearby, you are relatively assured that the tenant will stay put. The trouble with large tenants in suburbia is that most developments cannot accommodate them unless they are under construction. Once a building is built and occupied, the remnant spaces tend to be too small and scattered for the larger tenants. If the tenant is well-heeled and you are able to keep the building at market rate, chances are that the tenant will be interested in purchasing the project when you are done with it. By buying the building, the tenant can use the cash flow from other tenants to lower his or her cost of occupancy.

Occupation

Further differentiation occurs in the office building category based upon tenant occupation. Tenants tend to stratify into several well-known categories: medical, general, and back-office uses. Within these categories, there are subcategories, such as real estate, government, and legal.

Some buildings are deliberately built to attract specific tenants. If you built or bought a building near the courthouse, you might expect to attract lawyers as tenants. Similarly, if you have an office building near the hospital, you will find that medical uses are a natural. You can design a building to attract specific tenants by adding specific improvements that cater to these tenants. Buildings designed to attract attorneys now offer a built-in legal library and communication system. Medical buildings require extensive plumbing and cabinetry modifications, as well as specialty areas for X-ray and other testing facilities, medical libraries, medical transcription services, and accounting and billing services.

In suburban areas where there are no obvious specialty requirements, your building must be adapted to be usable by a variety of tenants. This can be accomplished by providing utility access throughout the building and custom designing the office suites for each tenant. In the future, any office building will require state-of-the-art communication facilities; therefore, it is best to design them in at the development stage. If you are purchasing a building, you would be well advised to find out how to modify the building in the future, as fiber-optic communication capability becomes the norm. This does not have to be done immediately, but you should include this modification in your planning and budgeting.

Government Tenants

Government tenants can be a real problem for the rest of the building. For many years, government has been building its own buildings, but it never keeps up with the growth of the bureaucracy. Both state and federal governmental agencies rent privately owned office space and often you must bid for them as tenants. Their requirements are spelled out in the RFP (request for proposal) and your bid, if successful, will require you to meet the government's specifications.

These specifications require you to meet all federal and state standards for access for people with physical disabilities and some of the new energy requirements. The main problem with government tenants is the number of employees. In most buildings, parking is required in the ratio of four cars per one thousand square feet of occupied space. Government tenants have a greater employee density, around one person for every 150 square feet. This means that these tenants will fill your parking lots. In an effort to forestall this problem, you must specify that the government employees must occupy specific parking spaces and no more. This is quite common; in fact, most government agencies offer incentives to their employees to carpool and use public transit. Forewarned is forearmed. Do not ignore this if you are considering any form of government tenant.

HEADS UP

One of the first things a prospective tenant looks for is available parking. If a prospect looking at your building sees that the building is 50-percent occupied, but the parking lot is 80-percent full, he or she will think that you will run out of parking before the building is full. This is the kiss of death for a building.

How do you avoid this problem? You must monitor your prospective tenants carefully, specifying that if they have an inordinate number of employees, they must make off-site parking arrangements for the overflow. The types of tenants to be wary of, in addition to government tenants, are schools, telephone solicitation companies, and the back-office operations. Back-office operations are companies that have a large number of telephone operators, such as airline reservation offices. These companies must be handled differently than normal tenants. There are no rules about these uses. You just have to find your own solutions. Luckily, these tenants are not attracted to class A or even suburban office space. They like converted industrial space or old shopping center properties. They require a low level of tenant improvement and extra parking; these secondary locations work well for them.

The Number of Tenants

We have looked at tenant size and diversity, but what are the implications of size? If you have your cash flow tied up in one or two tenants, you are vulnerable to the tenant's or tenants' plans. I recommend that you plan for replacing these larger tenants with smaller ones. This is a good strategy, especially if you are planning to own the building for a long time. If you are building a portfolio of properties and you want to keep them for the long pull, then this is a necessary strategy. Set up some reserve capital, and start prospecting for new tenants well in advance of any large tenant's lease expiration date. If you have things arranged in advance, then your vacancy period will be confined to the time it takes you to remodel the tenant space. In very few cases will it exceed 60 days. Once you have accomplished this, you will have a better building in terms of cash flow and diversity. You should look for this when you are purchasing a building. While it is not necessarily recognized, I believe that many smaller tenants make for a more stable and, therefore, more valuable property.

At the Beginning

When you are purchasing a property and you find that several of the tenants are too large for your comfort, how do you react to this situation? How should it affect your offer?

Most buildings will be offered for sale with no details on the tenancy, so it is not until the seller accepts your offer that you will have a chance to examine the leases and discover the details of the tenancy. When you encounter this problem, you need to examine the tenants in great detail. What does each company do and is the company expanding or contracting? What is the company's financial standing? Could it be a likely candidate to purchase the building or is it rent-sensitive?

You must make your own determination. The key piece of information is the length of the lease. If the lease expires within five years of your proposed purchase, you need to discount that cash flow by whatever you believe it will cost you to replace the tenant. This is a task for your leasing agent and your contractor. Your cost of replacement will be brokerage fees, tenant improvements, and lost rent. On the plus side, you will, most likely, improve the rental income on the space in question.

THE GOAL

What are you shooting for? My take on an ideal tenancy for a suburban office building is a mix of tenants in different professions, with few, if any tenants occupying more than five percent of the building. Why do I want this? First, smaller tenants are easier to replace with little or no tenant improvement work. Second, they pay more rent than their larger cousins. The larger the tenants, the larger the bank accounts and, therefore, the more they feel they can demand when they are negotiating their leases. If you find yourself needing these tenants, you will find this to be quite true. If, however, you are in a position to pick and choose, you can still take them as tenants, but give this type of tenant less in the way of tenant improvements, keeping the unused portion of the TI allowance in a fund to replace this tenant when you can. If possible, I would recommend charging a large tenant more rent to offset the added risk of vacancy. Take the added rent and put it into a sinking fund for replacement. This will enable you to live with the large tenant on your own terms.

> **HEADS UP**
>
> Unless the market is in recession, remember: it's your building and you call the shots. If you act in haste, you will repent at leisure.

Fine-Tuning the Tenancy and Synergy

Your goal as a building owner is to have the best possible tenant mix and the most stable and reliable cash flow. The two components of this are a compatible tenant mix and optimum tenant size.

COMPATIBLE USES

Compatible tenant mix is defined as tenants who have a synergistic relationship. If, for instance, you have a real estate broker in your building, then an escrow agent, an insurance agent, and a mortgage banker would be compatible. All of these tenants can be involved in one transaction. It is the same if you have a family doctor and a dentist in the building. Adding an optometrist would be a natural thing to do.

LOCATING THE TENANTS WITHIN THE PROPERTY

You need not seek to make the entire building project into one great synergistic cabal. Rather, you can separate compatible uses in different areas of the building. In a multistory building, you can separate the categories by floor; in a single-story building, you can separate them in different wings. There are many ways to accomplish this. It is not life and death. It only requires some thought when you are leasing the building. If you have a vacancy next to a medical use, have the broker look for a tenant who will be compatible. The negotiations will be easier.

What you want to avoid is too many tenants competing with each other. This will cause you to have premature vacancies, as one tenant drives the other out of business or out of your building. Do not get into the habit of granting exclusives in your building, as it will tie your hands, but use your judgment. A shopping center cannot survive having two grocery stores. Your office building can survive having two real estate brokers, but you are better off with one broker and one title company. If you achieve a synergistic tenant mix, you will find that your turnover will decrease and your tenants will prosper. When this happens, you will have become a destination, effectively bettering your location. Eventually, this will show up in greater rents and a more stable cash flow.

> **HEADS UP**
>
> You cannot make any exceptions. This will cause a full-scale tenant revolt. If that happens, you will lose tenants. No exceptions—ever!

SIGNS

One of the real problems in managing an office building is sign control. Tenants want to put signs everywhere. You need to create a comprehensive sign policy and stick to it.

Things to know about signs are:

- All door information signs must be a standard size. You can allow the company logos and other distinctive features in the names.
- Signs on the building must be built the same way and all the electric signs are on your timer, so that they are all on or all off. There are no exceptions.
- No signs in the windows. It is very tacky.
- It is best if all the building signs are the same color, but this is a hard one to enforce, as most companies have distinctive logo colors.
- *Strive for uniformity.*

CHAPTER

33

Maintenance, Accounting, *and* Reserves

While you own a building, whether you built it or bought it, you must maintain it. If you developed the property and did your job correctly, all you will have to do is maintain it properly. If, however, you are like most of us and several mistakes have surfaced, then this chapter is for you. When you are buying a building, any building, you must find out what shape it's in. This process is reversed when you sell the building. If you approach each situation the same way, you will profit at both ends. At the front end, you can uncover the real condition and, at the same time, gain a thorough understanding of the building and how it is put together. This is the process of inspection, and there are no half measures.

If you are not particularly experienced in building ownership or if this is your first time investing, I recommend that you hire an experienced contractor, an architect, and specialists to help you evaluate the building. Third-party inspections have become routine in the single-family housing market, and they should become even more so in the investment real estate business.

The Building's Condition, When You Buy It or When You Own It

Any defects, minor or major, are known as *deferred maintenance* items. The big trick is to distinguish between the routine maintenance items that are normally scheduled and those items that have been completely neglected or inadvertently overlooked. It will be your job to inherit the tenants' repair and maintenance fund and to take over the routine maintenance chores. The rest of the items are the responsibility of the seller. You would be surprised to know that fewer than 15 percent of buyers go through this exercise. Many do not want to hire the experts and many rely on a cursory inspection. They all regret it later.

> **HEADS UP**
>
> Do not skip this step it will cost you a lot of money during your ownership.

How to Make the Seller Pay for It

If you buy a building rather than develop it, you should look for ways to save money. One of the easiest ways is to look to the seller. When you write your purchase agreement, simply include a clause that states that you, the buyer, have the right to inspect the building for defects and that the seller agrees to repair them before the close of escrow or to adjust the price at the close of escrow, so that you may do the repairs. This will guarantee that you will be inheriting a building that is up to snuff from the beginning. Personally, I favor adjusting the price and doing my own repairs. This gives my contractor a chance to get better acquainted with the building.

When you are inspecting the building, what specifically do you look for? If there are elevators or escalators, you should talk directly to the company servicing the equipment; if you are not satisfied, find another company to inspect the equipment. The same holds true for all of the mechanical equipment, from HVAC to boilers, exhaust systems, etc. Personally, I would have them all inspected. Do not forget the fire safety systems. The law requires regular maintenance. Check the logs and talk with the company doing the maintenance. Definitely inspect the roof. A leaky roof can be costly, as water damages electronic equipment. The rest of the items are not critical, just costly. They need to be checked anyway. At a minimum, look at the following:

- Inspect the ceiling. Broken tiles and stains indicate roof leaks.
- Check the walls for cracks. They might indicate differential settlement in the foundations.
- Look at the floors; you can tell if there is a problem even if they are carpeted.
- Check the restrooms for functioning fixtures, fans, etc.
- Look at all the door hardware, including closers.
- Check all security equipment and door locks, exit signs, stairways, etc.
- Walk the entire parking lot looking for cracks and pavement failures.
- Check all the curbs and parking lot lights.
- Inspect the landscaping and turn on and check the irrigation system.
- Check all the paint, noting locations in the common areas of the building that need immediate attention.
- Walk through the tenant spaces looking for inordinate wear. The tenants will want this modernized at renewal time.
- Make a list of all the items above and get a bid from your contractor to fix all but the wear and tear in the tenant spaces.

> **HEADS UP**
>
> Sounds like a lot of work, doesn't it? On the positive side, it is not brain surgery. Do it right and prosper. Do it wrong and pay.

A Strategy for the Future

Having done all that, the building should be in good condition when you take it over. Together with your maintenance people and your contractor, make a list of all the routine items that will be regularly checked during your tenure. Set up your schedules and a budget for maintenance.

Routine Maintenance

What constitutes regular maintenance and who does it? Your front line in the maintenance campaign is the janitorial staff. Their daily routine in the building should include chores that are in addition to the daily janitorial work. In addition to cleaning, they should check the lights, replacing burned-out bulbs daily. They do not charge extra for this if you furnish the bulbs. They should do a weekly inspection of the premises and furnish you with a written report of its condition. You should make this as easy as possible for the janitors. Create a checklist of items to be inspected weekly and monthly, with a column for comments. This makes inspection easier for the janitors and will ensure that they do it. Check it monthly yourself.

Janitorial services exist only in office buildings; therefore, for industrial buildings and shopping centers and any other buildings, you must have your manager do the inspections. Check up on the manager from time to time. The maintenance will have to be contracted out. I recommend finding a company that specializes in building maintenance. They are generally jacks-of-all-trades and can handle almost anything that does not require heavy equipment.

What's Needed?

Specific services to be included in routine maintenance depend on the type of building you have invested in. If you purchased a single-tenant building with an NNN lease, the maintenance is 100 percent up to the tenant. You must still inspect the building routinely to be sure that the tenant is maintaining it properly. The lease should give you the right to give the tenant notice of any deficiencies and, if they remain uncorrected, allow you to do the maintenance and charge the tenant. The same holds true for all buildings. The multitenant buildings are the easiest, as you will be doing the maintenance anyway and are therefore in a position to be sure it is done. After your purchase inspection, you will have created a list of chores and a schedule. Stick to it and you will avoid having to pay for these items when you sell the building.

How to Pay for It

Sounds expensive, doesn't it? It is, but it is cheaper than letting the building get run down. When that happens, the costs go up and you run the real risk of losing your tenants. The lease gives them the right to expect a well-maintained building and it also provides that they will pay for it. Whether it is a gross lease or a NNN lease, there should be provisions in the lease for maintenance and repairs as well as reserves for replacement. If the previous landlord has been lax, you must persuade the tenants that the increase in this monthly expense item will be for the building's welfare. To help

HEADS UP

This is the hard part, but you must be able to make this transition. Take it slowly. Do not lump all the increases into the first month. If the maintenance program is going to mean a significant increase in operating expense, phase it in over a year. You should budget for this expense when you buy the building.

sell it, do something visible at the start. Add some amenity that will be a one-time cost to you, but will be a long-term benefit to the tenants.

Accounting

In Chapter 31 I discussed the accounting systems. Here is where they are implemented. You will have two sets of accounting tools, bookkeeping and spreadsheets. The spreadsheets are your management tools and the bookkeeping system allows you to report the overall progress of the investment and pay your taxes.

Billing and Money

Starting with the tenant information spreadsheet prepared when you purchased the building and then adding the monthly expense and tenant allocation spreadsheet, you can construct your monthly tenant rental invoice. It is necessary to be specific, because no matter what form of lease you use, the tenant will have the right to inspect your operating costs annually. Keep good records and keep them in a form that is easily understood. This is not a profit center. It is a pass-through-expense item, so you need to be 100 percent reimbursed. If your records are good and easy to understand, you will be able to recover. If, however, you cannot substantiate an expense, you will end up eating it. The monthly invoice should show the following breakdown:

- Rent
- Operating expense
- Special services ordered by the tenant
- The total rent
- Any rental tax required by the local government
- The total invoice

Again, your manager should collect the rents and deposit them into your bank account. From that account *you* will pay the bills.

Formats and Tools

In Chapter 31 I discussed the types of spreadsheets that I recommend, but you will have to take them apart and modify them so that you find them useful for your style of management. In general, you will need some basic information to base your management decisions on. These items are, at a minimum, the following:

- Which tenants have paid their rent and which have not?
- What are the expenses and how are they escalating? The rent should escalate at a rate greater than inflation, but the rate of increase in operating expenses should never exceed the rate of inflation.
- When are leases going to expire and how much space will be available?
- What is the market rate for new leases?
- What does the cash flow projection look like for five and ten years? Update it every time you have any specific change in rent or expense.

Accounting Packages

Accounting packages are getting more elaborate every day. I believe that you should seek out a package that will suit your specific needs. If you are operating only one property, you will most likely not require a very elaborate system. The problem with a simple system is that it is difficult to upgrade. If you are like most people who get into real estate investments, you will most likely expand your operation and you will eventually have a full-time bookkeeper. When this happens, whatever system your bookkeeper starts with will be with you for a long time. The bookkeeper is a creature of habit and loathes potential changes in his or her methods. Start your bookkeeper off with the best accounting system that you can afford. Try to pick one that can generate the spreadsheets you need. Be sure that the company writing the software has been around for a while. Get all the updates when they are issued and insist that your bookkeeper stay current on the system. You should know the system as well as your bookkeeper does, because you could lose that bookkeeper and have to hire a replacement. Someone on the ownership side should know and understand the system.

Establishing Value for Resale

Why are you going through all this work every month? The answer is simple: you will profit from it. A well-managed building will show a consistent monthly profit, which is why you got into this business. The payoff for this is twofold. First, you will have established a regular, ever-increasing cash flow that will pay a good return on your invested capital, and second, you will have created a capital gain upon sale. The increase in the monthly cash flow increases the annual NIBDS. This is what you sell when you sell.

What Do You Have for Sale?

The ultimate goal for any investment is the payoff. This can be accomplished by either selling or refinancing. If you have purchased a good property and managed it well, you will face the decision to sell with certain trepidation. If you sell, you will pay a federal capital gain tax of 15 percent on your profit, and then you will have a rather large sum of money in your hand. What will you do with it? If you remember, you were facing this question when you bought the building. If you do not sell the building, what is the future for your investment and how can you add to it? The answer is to keep the property and refinance it. If you have been clever at the time of purchase and selected a multitenant property and you have subsequently improved the tenancy to the point where all of your tenants have less than five percent of the occupied space and the building's location is holding up well against the market's changes, then you should strongly consider holding on to the building.

A good multitenant building with an established track record of increasing rents and a great location is very financeable. If you have owned it for ten years and your first loan is due to be retired, you stand a great chance of securing a bigger loan, based on your newly enhanced NIBDS. If you make the decision to keep it, go for a 30-year loan. You might have to agree that the lender will have the right to adjust the interest rate every ten years, but try to lock in the loan. You can finance out some, if not all, of your initial capital investment, using the proceeds to buy another building. This is how real estate empires are built.

The alternative to refinancing the building is selling it. You can still build your empire by selling. When you sell, you have two choices: sell and pay the tax or sell and reinvest the money in a like investment. This sell-and-reinvest option is called the right to exchange one investment for another, a Section 1031 exchange. The two properties must be of like kind.

Consult your attorney on this one. There is latitude in the definition, established by legal precedent, so that you may exchange a shopping center for an office building, but you will need to have a good attorney, experienced in exchanges, to advise you on the procedures and the latitude of the exchange possibilities. You may even exchange for more than one property. There are advantages in having more than one property, so long as you follow some simple guidelines. If you purchase multiple properties in the same market, make them different types of property. You do not want to become your own competitor. If you have become enamored of a particular type of property, acquire the same properties in different markets. This is geographical diversity. It might be nice to own the best of that type of property in several markets. You will have to do the same research and selection in each market, but the diversity is worth it. Some investors opt for a diverse property mix in one market. Whichever option you select, go through the acquisition process for each property exhaustively.

What Shape Is the Building In?

Finally, whether you are selling or refinancing, you must have your building up to snuff. It is not enough for you to know that the building is in good shape; you must have a paper trail to prove it. Starting with the reports you created when you purchased the building, create a file on building maintenance logs. This will be backed up by the expense ledgers. You can use these documents together to convince either buyer or lender that your building is in great shape.

Reserves

Reserves are cash accounts established for several reasons. You might need to refurbish your building when moving a new tenant, you might want to upgrade your building, or you might need to replace the air conditioning system. Whether you acquire an existing building and inherit the seller's reserves or impounds or you develop your property from scratch, you will need to establish reserve accounts.

Do You Really Need Reserves?

The need for reserves is a question with many answers. In general, I believe you need reserves for different reasons. If you own a building that uses gross leases, you should have a line item in your expense column that reads, "Reserves for replacements." This line item is designed to repair and replace building components that wear out. The most common use of reserves is for parking lot maintenance, HVAC repair and replacement, and painting. A parking lot of standard construction is designed to be failure-free for no less than two years. It is usually guaranteed by the contractor for one year, two at maximum. After ten years it is normal to see the wearing surface dry out and start to crack. In areas of the country with freeze/thaw cycles, it is quite common for the pavement to deteriorate completely, necessitating a repaving after 15 years or more. In the rest of the country, the paving will require resealing and restripping every eight to ten years. The average air conditioning system will operate trouble-free for about 15 years. Then it will require periodic repair. When the repairs get to be too expensive, you will have to replace the unit. Painting is an annual, ongoing problem.

If your building is an NNN-lease building, you will have to build this fund into your lease under the "additional rent" clause. It is a reasonable expense item and should be set at around ten percent of your budget before management expenses. This fund should be kept separate and held against the day when you will need it.

CAPITAL REQUIREMENTS

There is also the instance when you are purchasing an existing building and you plan for some upgrading of the building to keep it competitive in the market. For this purpose, you will need funds that cannot be generated by the expense portion of the lease. These funds are capital improvement funds and cannot be expensed against operations. The building improvements must be capitalized and depreciated along with the entire building.

That is also the case with new tenant improvements. The money to recapitalize a tenant space must come from your cash flow. This fund should be established at the beginning of your ownership and should be set at a size to pay for the first lease when it is due for renewal. This fund should grow until you are satisfied that you have enough reserves so that you do not have to borrow for the purpose.

SOURCES

Where do these funds come from? There are three major sources: your initial cash investment, lease deposits, and retained earnings. Your initial cash is just that, an additional cash investment set aside at the time of purchase. When you purchase the property, the seller will have to turn over the tenant lease deposits to you, as the owner holds them in guarantee of the tenants' performance. When a tenant vacates and you have to return the deposit, it will be replaced by the next tenant's even larger deposit. Some states require that these funds be kept in a separate interest-earning trust account, not co-mingled with your own funds. Some states, however, treat these deposits as a liability only and allow the funds to be co-mingled with your own. Retained earnings are funds that are part of your NIBDS. These funds are not operating expenses, but capital improvements, and are therefore accounted for "under the line." These are cash flow funds that you do not distribute, but retain in the owner's account. You will pay taxes on these funds along with the rest of your cash flow.

> **HEADS UP**
>
> You must set up reserves for all three contingencies. You will need them.

How Much Is Enough?

When you purchase a building, I recommend that you add approximately five percent of the building's purchase price to a fund for reserves and replacements, as well as capital improvements. This fund can be replenished monthly from your normal cash flow. The amount must be large enough to accomplish the upgrades you have selected in your game plan and to recapitalize the first lease premises to be renovated. Starting with the first month of operation, your cash flow fund will add to this reserve. The object is not to be caught short if you lose a tenant or if you need to replace a large item in the normal course of business. You should be able to handle anything that comes your way.

ROUTINE REQUIREMENTS

What can you expect? You can expect the following occurrences in the management of any form of income-producing real estate:

- Losing a tenant
- Mechanical breakdowns
- Occasional severe weather damage
- Late rents
- Tenant bankruptcy
- Parking lot repairs
- Roof leaks
- Refitting tenant space for a new tenant
- Constant painting
- Legal expenses
- Increased taxes

DISASTER FUNDS

There is no such thing as enough money when a disaster occurs. This is what insurance is for. However, you will still need to make the mortgage payment while the insurance company is sorting out the problem. If a disaster such as a flood or a tornado occurs, you will be able to collect, but in the meantime, keep your mortgage payments current!

WHO OWNS THEM?

When you are dealing with reserves and you are using funds collected from several sources, who owns the money and how are the funds treated? If your tenants are contributing to maintenance through a reasonable reserve for replacement fund in their monthly expense column, these funds belong to the building tenants and must be passed on to the new owners when you sell. This is important to know when you are buying, because the seller must also pass these funds along to you. If he or she does not, then any maintenance item that occurs before the fund is built up will be out of your pocket. This is not necessarily an enforceable item, either by you as the buyer or by any one buying from you. You must build it into the contract from the outset.

There is another very important item to build into your purchase contract, to deal with any vacancy at the time of purchase. When you buy, even if the building is 100 percent full, you will be buying with an assumed vacancy factor of at least five percent. If the building is full, then this is not a problem. If, however, there is a vacancy and you are paying for the income stream from this vacant space, you must have the seller credit your purchase price with sufficient money to improve that space for an incoming tenant. Without the tenant, there is no cash flow. Without the improvements, there is no tenant.

HEADS UP

You must insist on this when you buy and you should expect to pay for this when you sell. It is reasonable at both times.

TENANT SECURITY DEPOSITS

Tenant lease deposits are always the property of the individual tenant; regardless of whether you keep them separate or not, you are only holding these funds against the time when the lease is terminated. If the tenant leaves the premises in the condition specified in the lease, you must return the funds to the tenant. These funds are replaced by the next tenant. The only time you need worry about this is when you have co-mingled the funds and you are losing tenants without replacing them. You will need to have cash available for this purpose.

YOUR CASH—BELOW THE LINE

Any funds that you set aside, either in cash at the outset or from your NIBDS below the line, are your funds. You are not accountable for them to anyone else when you sell. You have paid taxes on these funds and you own them outright. Your reserves are no one's business but your own. You'd be surprised at the number of building owners who do not have reserves. They pay for it in the end. It is like any form of maintenance. You can pay for it a little at a time or in one lump sum when it comes up.

When You Sell

If you get into the habit of accounting for funds in one account, then you should be in great shape when the time comes to sell. You will know what is what and your accounting system will have the correct totals. It may be easier, however, if you keep the funds in separate bank accounts. You can open two or three additional bank accounts: one for the tenant lease deposits, one for the tenants' reserve account, and one for your own funds set up by a capital fund or funded from your cash flow after the NIBDS line. The accounting will still be the same in the general ledger, but you will know at a glance what is what and to whom the funds belong. Comingling funds is not a good habit to get into. State law permitting, the lease deposit account is a fund that you can use, so long as you know it will come off the purchase price when you sell. If you use it at all, use it to improve the building, not for the routine replacement of worn-out building components. Treat it as a fund that goes with the building, established by the tenants. It can be yours to use while you own the building, but you must replace it when you sell, sometimes with interest.

FORESTALL THE PROBLEMS

Use your fund for replacements and routine maintenance regularly. Remember the deferred maintenance you inherited. Do not let that happen to you. The reason for maintenance is not to have the building look good, although that is a result. It is to preserve and enhance your capital investment. This is the paramount goal of everything you do as the building manager. The details are only a means to get to the end. Do it properly and you will prosper.

BE PROACTIVE

There are two types of people in the world: those who wait for something to happen and then react to it and those who see what can happen and act before it occurs. The latter people are known as proactive.

HEADS UP

It is always cost-effective to be proactive rather than reactive. You will find, if you develop this trait, that it prevents all sorts of crises.

SECTION VIII

LONG-TERM STRATEGIES *for* WEALTH

CHAPTER

34

Development *and* the Zero-Dollar Deal

In any transaction, purchasing investment-grade real estate or development, there are certain risks. The owner/developer's mission is to eliminate or minimize as many risks as possible before the project is purchased or development starts. Earlier in the book, when discussing consultants, we looked at the potential of limiting front-end risks by asking some of the consultants to participate in the front end of the project.

I have done so on many occasions. As a general rule, I have offered a ten-percent participation, plus their standard fee, once the project started construction or passed the critical pre-leasing percentage. If the architect participated, I was left with a 90/10 split. If I included the engineer, the broker, and the general contractor, it turned out to be a 60/10/10/10/10 split.

My view of this is that while I was giving away potential profit, it was profit I did not yet have and the people I was offering it to were going to help me to create it. In addition, they were going to share in the construction period risks. I believe today as I did then that limiting front-end risk is important and that half a loaf is better than none. I do not need 100 percent of the profit in any transaction. I need a string of successful projects.

The upshot of this arrangement is that, when the joint venture with an investor was formed, the ownership was then cut in half for all parties. The result was a 50/30/5/5/5/5 split with the investor having 50 percent and me, the developer, with 30 percent

The Reward, the Money, and the Endgame

The ultimate practical reason for engaging in developing or investing in commercial real estate must be the potential for profit. There are other rewards, as well, such as the satisfaction of doing something useful that other people can use and enjoy for years, but the bottom line is still profit.

Earlier chapters dealt with the profits involved in taking a quarter section of agricultural land and rezoning it for residential development. Assume now that some corner of these 640 acres was, in the same or subsequent process, rezoned for commercial use and that you have secured an option to develop this corner into a commercial project. This example will consume only three acres and the project to be built will be a suburban office building of 35,000 square feet leasable, 40,000 gross building (88 percent) efficient. If we track this project through the entire process, we can identify the various profit centers.

First of all, the land must be purchased; that is a commissionable act. The land would typically be listed for sale with a commercial broker with a ten percent sales commission. Calculating the cost and, therefore, the commission available is as follows:

3 acres x 43,560 SF/acre x $4.50/SF =
$588,060 x 10% = $58,806

Customarily this sales commission is split 50/50 between the selling broker and the broker representing the developer, thus yielding the first return to the developer's team of $29,403.

The next step is to hire an architect and/or an engineer. A typical developer's price for architecture would be no less than $3.00/SF. Since the building will gross 40,000 SF, the fee would translate into a minimum of $120,000, with surveyors and testing engineers adding another $20,000. While this $140,000 is a cost to the project, it is also revenue to the consultants involved on the developer's team. Similarly, the broker hired to lease the project will charge at least $3.00/SF. This, multiplied by the leasable square footage of the project, will yield another $105,000 in brokerage commissions. Again, this is a cost as well as revenue to the project team. Another brokerage function is mortgage banking. This loan broker will earn a point, maybe two, for arranging the construction and permanent loans, thus producing another fee of no less than $26,000 (one point).

The developer responsible for doing all the work will generally ascribe an overhead cost to any project to attempt to defray specific overhead devoted to that project. Sometimes it is a percentage of the construction cost; sometimes it will be a flat dollar figure per square foot. The prevailing rate seems to be six percent of hard and soft costs. For the sake of this example, let's say that a fee of $3.00/SF will be assessed for this project. This produces a cost to the project and revenue to the developer of $105,000, the equivalent of the brokerage commission.

Finally, there is the general contractor who will guarantee to build the project for a set dollar amount. In this case, the total cost will be $2,379,000. A reasonable profit for this size transaction will vary between ten percent and 20 percent, depending upon the circumstances surrounding the project. If it is a negotiated contract set up as a design-build project, a reasonable profit after all costs should yield the general contractor 15 percent or $356,850.

If we refer to the pro forma (Table 34-1), we can see that even with these built-in costs, the

	Costs				Revenues					
Budget Item	**Risk Dollars**	**From Budget**	**Pre-construction**	**Start of Construction**	**Year 1**	**Year 2**	**Year 3**	**Year 4**	**Year 5**	**Sale Year**
Cash Flow					$229,265	$252,182	$276,244	$301,509	$328,037	$2,549,436
Developer	($158,500)	($158,500)	($158,500)	$158,500	$114,633	$126,091	$138,122	$150,755	$164,019	$1,274,718
Investor	$0	($1,040,531)	$0	($1,040,531)	$114,633	$126,091	$138,122	$150,755	$164,019	$1,274,718
Fee Income	Developer									
Acquisition		$29,403		$29,403						
Development Overhead		$105,000		$105,000						
Loan Brokerage		$26,000		$26,000						
Leasing Fees		$105,000		$105,000						
Gen. Contr. Fees		$356,850		$356,850						
Sales Commission		$185,750		$185,750						
Min. Totals					$114,633	$126,091	$138,122	$150,755	$164,019	$1,274,718
Developer			($158,500)	$292,903	$114,633	$126,091	$138,122	$150,755	$164,019	$2,315,249
Investor			$0	($1,040,531)						
Cum. Cash Flow										
Developer			($158,500)	$134,403	$249,036	$375,127	$513,249	$664,003	$828,022	$2,102,740
Investor			$0	($1,040,531)	($799,808)	($925,899)	($661,686)	($510,931)	($346,913)	$1,968,337
Annual ROI										
Developer ($158,500)					73.2%	79.55%	87.14%	95.11%	103.48%	804.24%
Investor ($1,040,531)					11.02%	12.12%	13.27%	14.49%	15.76%	122.51%
Average ROI										
Developer					221.11%					
Investor					59.13%					

TABLE 34-1. CASH YIELD ANALYSIS TO DEVELOPER/INVESTOR

project is able to yield a good return on the investment. In this case it is an annual return ranging from 22 percent the first year to 31.5 percent in year five of operation. If the project is sold at the end of year five, it could easily, in today's market, fetch a capitalization rate of nine percent, or a sales price calculated as follows:

NIBDS of $557,097 / .09 = $6,189,967

If we look at the project strictly from the investor's view, we need to calculate the average rate of return per year on the whole experience. We must assume that the investment lay dead for a year at the beginning while the construction was under way, so we are, in reality, looking at a rate of return over a six-year period rather than a five-year period.

There are several ways to examine this scenario. First of all, the equity here is arbitrarily set at $1,040,531. In reality, depending on the mortgage market at the time, a permanent loan is secured and given a NIBDS of $458,326, the potential permanent loan could have yielded a theoretical high of $3,820,000, calculated as follows:

Year	Cash Return	Notes
0	($1,040,531)	Investment year
1	$229,265	First operating year
2	$252,182	Second year
3	$276,244	Third year
4	$301,509	Fourth year
5	$328,037	Fifth year
Sale	$2,549,436	Gross profit on sale
Gross Profit	$3,936,672	For six years
Annual Rate of Return	63%	Gross $/6/Equity

TABLE 34-2. INVESTOR'S CASH-ON-CASH RETURN

$438,326 (NIBDS) / 9% (cap rate) =
$5,092,522 (value)
mortgage at 75% of value = $3,820,000

This approach to mortgage underwriting in the past effectively reduced a developer's cash equity to less than zero. In reality, lenders today insist on hard equity, so if one assumes that, as a worst case, the equity will be a high of $1,040,531, then whatever else transpires should only improve the situation.

Examine the Dollars

A breakdown of the project shown in the pro forma cost breakdown and income and expense spreadsheets, Tables 34-1 and 34-2, yields the information found in Table 34-3 on the next page.

What does this mean to the average potential entrepreneur/principal—you? It clearly indicates that there is money to be made in almost every facet of a good transaction. It also means that there seems to be enough potential profit to weather a few disasters along the way. A fledgling developer would be strongly advised to involve experts in all of the fields required to complete the project.

Over time, however, as a developer picks up experience and skills, his or her potential yield can increase dramatically. If one examines the above scenario, it looks as if the developer could garner a fee of $105,000 over two years for managing the development, from land acquisition through completion and start-up. This, coupled with the return on investment, only serves to enhance the deal. Over the years, however, most developers increase their income potential through additional fee income by becoming brokers and at least acquiring the commission on the land acquisition. The added skill of brokerage also serves to give a developer the license and experience needed to lease a project, should the need arise. Remember:

Item	Dollars	Notes
Land buy commission	$29,403	One half to team
Architect's fee	$120,000	Reasonable
Engineers' fees	$20,000	Reasonable
Loan initiation fee	$26,000	Average
Development overhead	$105,000	Low
Leasing fees	$105,000	Low
General contractor's profit	$356,850	Average
Gross yield, sales only	$2,549,436	Good return
Sales commission	$185,700	3% on $6,189,998

TABLE 34-3. DEVELOPER'S CASH-ON-CASH SPREADSHEET

wherever possible, use an outside broker, as it helps ensure the success of the project. Just make sure that the broker is handling the project as an exclusive.

While it is unreasonable to expect the successful developer to acquire the skills necessary to claim most or all of the sources of revenue entailed in a project, most developers, over the long run, seem to acquire some brokerage skills, generally assuming the chore of land selection and loan negotiation. Most often a developer is also able to sell his or her project when the time is right. Good developers seem to have a ready market for their finished product, as seasoned real estate is an attractive investment for individuals, small groups, pension funds, and REITs. A great many developers join the ranks after many years as general contractors, as they have seen over the years, firsthand, the potential profits of the projects they have built for others. For the general contractor, the investment risk is a logical extension of the risk inherent in the general contracting business.

For whatever the reason, from whatever the background, entrepreneurs continue to look at the development business as a long-term potential livelihood. The reality of the business is the more the merrier. If the industry becomes too consolidated, it becomes less competitive and less interesting. Large companies are, by their very nature, not as good at the development business as individuals and small partnerships. The type of person who is attracted to a large company is not an entrepreneur. The development business needs people who are willing to bet on themselves. Likewise, smaller projects offer better yields than larger, institutionalized projects. Small groups can be more flexible with lenders. Often lenders will recognize the forbearance of fees and overhead as real equity contributions, thus lowering the cash requirement for the developer/investor.

I have shown how the principle of leverage applies to an investment in real property by using borrowed funds to increase the rate of return. Expanding on that concept, extrapolate the idea of leveraging the developer's rate of return by using investors' dollars in the traditional joint venture.

Goals for the Conservative Developer/Investor

Since 1975, I have been developing commercial property using the principle of OPM (other people's money). Why? The answer is twofold. First, when I started, I had no money of my own to invest. Second, after I acquired some, I began to feel strongly, from experience with the first two projects, that the raising of both equity and loan dollars was an essential check and balance needed in any project.

What, for me, started as a necessity, has become my standard modus operandi. The basic risks I undertake in any deal are confined to the two most critical times during the project. The first phase, the acquisition and feasibility stage, is the riskier. This phase is pure developer's risk. Until the project is approved and the project is leased to breakeven, there really is no project. Once this is accomplished, I go to the marketplace and raise enough capital to enable me to extract my cash invested and insert the investor's money as the project's required equity. The standard cost for raising this capital is half the ownership of the project and a negotiated, preferred annual rate of return on the paid-in capital.

At this point, I own 50 percent of a project, often shared with the broker, architect, and general contractor, with only time invested. The investor has acquired half of a feasible, proven project at wholesale. The land, entitlements, contracts, and leases are signed over to the deal at cost. Even though a year has passed, the project is leased to breakeven and the construction lender is either in place or at least ready to commit to the project. With all of this work accomplished and all of the front risk eliminated, why is the investor admitted at no extra cost? What is the trade-off for the developer?

The answer is that, in addition to making a profit with no invested capital, I can sweeten the deal for myself by being paid a developer's overhead fee to do the work and collect the initial brokerage fee for the land purchase and any brokerage fees relating to leases that I negotiate.

The second developer's risk period in the zero-cash deal begins during the construction and lease-up period and ends at the completion of the project within budget, the achievement of the pro forma rentals projected at the start of the project, and the closing of the permanent loan. If the costs run over or if more cash is needed than that invested by the investor/partner, the developer must make up the shortfall. If that occurs, the developer's capital generally goes into the deal as an interest-bearing loan to be prepaid upon sale or refinance of the project, after the investor's capital is repaid.

HEADS UP

In reality, if the project is properly conceived, the land is purchased only when all contingencies are met, and construction is started only after the project is leased to breakeven, then the practical risk to a competent developer is minimal.

As further insurance against the vagaries of the process, the developer may negotiate a possible second call on the investor's capital at the beginning of the project. Joint ventures come in an endless variety, and a good project offered to an investor at wholesale is a good deal for both parties. Flexibility can be built into any deal. It is limited only by the imagination of the parties involved and their goals for the transaction.

By applying the approach to the project detailed in this chapter, the risk and the reward to the developer are as follows:

- The developer is out of pocket approximately $154,500 for the items shown in the expanded cost breakdown in Table 34-1, before the investor is brought into the picture.
- Once the developer recaptures his or her risk capital, the return on that initial risk capital becomes incredible.
- In a zero-cash deal, then, the developer can look forward to returns on the initial risk capital that vary. At minimum, the

developer gets the sum of the acquisition brokerage fee plus the development overhead fee plus half of the five-year cash flow plus half of the profit on the sale. At maximum, the "one-man band" can potentially earn it all, as shown in Table 34-4.

How, then, does this deal stack up for both parties? Let's look at it over the life of the project, from the inception to the sale, examining not only the cash outlays, but also the risks and rewards (Table 34-4). From this analysis, it is a good deal for all parties. The developer who takes the riskiest position and actually turns a piece of dirt into a viable project is rewarded with a great return. If the developer chooses to limit his or her out-of-pocket cash by bringing in an investor, his or her return goes wild: the investor is treated to a handsome cash-on-cash return, in this example, of 59.13 percent annually, over the life of the project.

The level at which these considerations are met will determine the fate of the project. In general, if the tenants are happy, they will stay and expand, rather than go to a newer project when their leases are up. If the investors are receiving their targeted returns on equity, they will probably want to maintain ownership for the economic life of the project. If the tenants are happy and the investors are happy, the odds are that the lender will be happy for the duration of the initial term of the loan and be willing to extend the loan until the cost of the building is amortized.

Additional Benefits

If this were the sum total of the remuneration involved in a real estate development project experience, then it would be a great deal by anyone's standard. However, it gets even better!

Item	Dollars	Notes
Initial capital at risk	($154,500)	Recovered at start of construction
Acquisition fee	$29,403	At land purchase
Developer's overhead	$105,000	Throughout construction
Leasing fees	$50,000	Available
General contractor's profit	$356,850	Available
Half of gross on profit on sale	$1,274,710	Developer's share
Sales commission	$185,700	Available
5 years' cash flow	$693,618	Half of cash flow
Minimum total yield for a "one-man band"	$2,012,730	Acquisition fee, developer's overhead, cash flow, and half of profit
Maximum total yield for a "one-man" band with $158,500 invested	$4,862,511	Maximum potential yield on initial risk capital

TABLE 34-4. DEVELOPER'S TOTAL POTENTIAL INCOME

During the cash flow period, the cash flow is tax-sheltered in part by depreciation. In the past, the tax implications of building ownership could shape the fate of a project by overshadowing the feasibility. Tax options for accelerated depreciation resulted in projects that were built regardless of the return on investment. The Tax Reform Act of 1986 put a stop to that consideration. Now all investment properties are depreciated on a straight-line basis over a period of approximately 27.5 years for residential rentals and up to 39 years for commercial projects. Some people will say that this was the death of the development profession, but I think of it as leveling the playing field. It helped eliminate the MBA development mills producing projects that had no real demand and thus enabled good developments to survive in an environment where only feasible projects are built.

Depreciation

This tax advantage is based on the assumption that each year the value of the project diminishes by a predetermined amount, currently based on a useful life of an arbitrary 30-plus years. This has been revised over the years, but simply put, if the building is theoretically wearing out over a 30-plus-year time frame, then the government allows an annual tax break. The government allows owners to take a *depreciation allowance*, calculated by taking the cost of the building and dividing it by the number of years allowed in the government's table of "useful life," which provides a valuable incentive to developers.

Simplistically, this project, taken as having a 30-year useful life, will generate a paper loss of $121,351:

$3,640,531 / 30 years = $121,351 per year

This means that the first $121,351 of cash flow each year is sheltered by the allowed, artificial "loss" of $121,351. This benefit of some tax-free or, realistically, tax-deferred income continues throughout ownership of the project. When the project is sold, the original investment is returned tax-free to the investor, then the amount of depreciation taken by each party is taxed at the prevailing capital gain rate. The balance of the profit is taxed at 15 percent, the maximum federal capital gain rate. The new owners are allowed to start all over, depreciating their new asset at their cost of acquisition.

The Developer's Endgame

Building owners, content with their investment, must consider many aspects of their situation before they consider selling the property. If the project is a bust or a mediocre investment, a sale is usually wise so that the owners may take their losses and move on to a better investment. Successful projects are always a dilemma. If they sell one, the owners must pay taxes on their gains.

> **HEADS UP**
>
> Pragmatically, at the end of a good return on investment in a known project, a sale results in and necessitates the reinvestment of the capital into something new, which may or may not be as good a deal.

What if the people involved do not want to pay taxes on the gain? Can they avoid it? No, but they can postpone it indefinitely! If a piece of property is disposed of, it can be exchanged tax-free for a "like property" of equal or greater value. The implications of this are infinite, limited only by your imagination.

This concept is what real estate empires are built on. By this mechanism, profits from one deal may be parlayed into one or more others, building over time into a veritable cash flow gold mine. The original owners may go their separate ways, each one trading his or her share of the profits into a new venture on his or her own.

The truly useful part of this exchange principle is that, while one must purchase a "like property" of equal or greater value, one does not have to invest all the cash proceeds in the purchase. This allows someone exchanging into a property to retain sufficient cash to develop the newly acquired property and, again, to maximize his or her return on investment. The unused cash retained is referred to as *boot* and will be taxable.

HEADS UP

Now that you have acquired the blueprint of how and why, just remember: none of this is rocket science. The best asset in your arsenal is common sense.

If something does not make sense to you, pass on it. The first deal is the hardest and the anxieties can be brutal, but once the baptism by fire is over, you should find the rewards worth the effort.

HEADS UP

The only valuable criticism is an empty building.

One of the greatest dividends of the business, seldom discussed, is that this is a useful trade. Your product is used daily by real people. Without it, people's lives would be severely diminished. It is a profession in which any practitioner may take pride.

CHAPTER

35

Selling Investment Property *and* Beyond

How do we wrap this up? We have discussed housing, purchasing, developing, and managing income property. The highlights are:

- How to make tax-free money on your own home
- Investing in houses for profit
- How to buy and renovate housing and commercial property
- How to develop real estate
- Managing income property for profit

The last point to go over is the disposition of assets when you are ready to sell, and then, what's beyond the sale. The thrust of this book is to guide you to accumulate some serious amounts of money and to minimize your downside. I will deal with the remaining points in this order:

- How to dispose of property in the best way
- How to minimize or defer the tax burden
- What to do over the long pull

If you remember what you went through when you were getting ready to purchase or develop a piece of property, housing or commercial, you must now realize that someone who has read this book may be looking at your property to buy. Fair's fair, after all. Since a fair deal is one that satisfies both parties, then you are charged with maximizing your sale price and, at the same time, giving the buyer a fair deal. The system for selling property differs depending on whether you are selling single-family housing or commercial property, so we will separate the two.

Common Elements

As we have seen in Section IV, Chapters 18-24, there are common elements to all real property deals. As for acquisition, disposition, and retention, it matters little whether you're dealing in houses or commercial properties. The common points include the following:

- Taxes
- Exchanges
- Leverage
- Portfolio building

Taxes

We have discussed taxes. Just as a reminder in capsule form, here's a reiteration of what I know based on my experience to date.

> **HEADS UP**
>
> The items below do not constitute tax advice. I am not qualified to give you tax advice. Consult your attorney or tax professional regarding these issues.

1. You can sell your personal residence after 24 months of occupation, tax-free. You can do it over and over again.
2. If you buy and sell real property, you will pay ordinary income tax on investment properties held for less than one year and capital gains tax on investment property held over 12 months.
3. If you build or refurbish houses or any other property specifically for resale, your profits will be classified as ordinary income.
4. If you refinance property, the proceeds are tax-free until the properties sell.
5. You can defer taxes on investment property sales by doing a 1031 tax-deferred exchange. The properties must be "like for like." Consult your attorney and tax professional for specific guidelines.

Leverage

With all that in mind, you can create an impressive portfolio by leveraging your profits with new loans, reinvesting the proceeds into new properties. This is how empires are built. One word of caution. Go to your local news library and look up the name of "Zekendorf." Read his story and remember it well. It is a classic case of how not to leverage your empire.

Portfolio Building

When you are using your profits to increase your holdings, here are some fail-safe rules to live by so that you do not put your entire pile in jeopardy.

1. Keep each property separate in ownership; create an LLC for each one.
2. Keep the monies from each property separate; make each deal pay its own way.
3. Do not cross-collateralize multiple properties.
4. Take advantage of insurance that can cover the whole portfolio, using common elements of ownership to make the insurance effective.
5. Pay attention to all of the properties, all of the time. Changing markets can sneak up on you; remember 1989-1990.

Residential Portfolio Growth

If you think that commercial income property is significantly better than residential property, consider this scenario. Buy two renovatable houses each year. Keep one and sell one. Live on what you make on the one you sell and keep the other one in your portfolio.

How does this work? Let's set up a scenario for the purpose of analyzing the possibilities. We will make the following assumptions:

- You have completed one live-in renovation project and have made $100,000 profit, tax-free.
- You will use the $100,000 to set up the business.
- You will tackle two projects at a time, in the $100,000-to-$300,000 price range.

To analyze this, we will need to make some reasonable assumptions about the market. You will be working in an older, established neighborhood that is experiencing a renaissance. The old homes are selling for $120,000 on large lots and the upper limit of the market is around $350,000. This is not a far-out scenario; you can find locations like this if you look.

The renovation budget might look something like Table 35-1.

If you assume for the sake of this scenario that both your projects during this particular year were approximately the same in size and profitability, then you will have a year in which you have made approximately $150,000 if you sell both houses. If we assume you are prudent and parsimonious and you desire to build a portfolio for your future, you sell one and keep one, renting out the keeper. You live on the $75,000 produced from the house you sold. Let's look at the impact of keeping the one house (Table 35-2).

By keeping this property, you are effectively letting someone else increase your equity. If you rent this house out for a net of $1,265 monthly, anything else is gravy. In a neighbor-

Item	Notes	Cost
Acquisition price	1,750 SF, 3 bedrooms, 2 baths, 2-car garage ($68/SF)	$120,000
Landscape	Minor planting and cleanup	$5,000
Painting	Inside and out	$5,000
Add rooms	600 SF @ $60/SF	$36,000
New carpet	210 yards @ $15/yard	$3,150
Appliances and fixtures	Kitchen and baths	$10,000
Loan fees	80% loan, 1 point, $100,000	$1,000
Interest	9% for 6 months	$4,500
Miscellaneous overhead		$5,000
Total costs		($189,650)
Proposed sale price	After commission and marketing costs	$265,000
Gross profit	Sale less costs	$75,350

TABLE 35-1. RENOVATION COST BREAKDOWN

Item	Notes	Cost
Appraised value	At completion	$265,000
Mortgage value	As an investment property, assume 75% of value	$198,750
Your cost	Look carefully	$189,650
New financing	$190,000, 30 years @ 7%, .0799 K*	
Monthly mortgage	Above at APR .0799	$1,265

*K = constant, the percentage necessary to fully amortize the principal of a loan over the term of the loan at a specific interest rate

TABLE 35-2. LEVERAGE ANALYSIS

hood where homes are valued at the above prices, it is not at all unreasonable to assume that you can achieve this level of rental income.

If we look at the effect of this game plan, selling one and keeping one, you have accomplished the following during your first year of operation:

- Made $75,000 cash
- Created $75,000 in capital gain
- Recovered your working capital from both houses
- Made good progress toward your long-term goal of financial independence

Going a step further, assume that you are able to keep doing this every year for ten years; what, then, have you accomplished? You have supported yourself for ten years and accumulated ten rental properties. Not too bad! If the value of these homes has not increased over the ten years and the tenants have repaid none of your principal, then Table 35-3 calculates your new net worth.

If these assumptions are accurate, you have accumulated $750,000 in net worth over the ten years. However, when you factor in a conservative, noncompounded, annual appreciation factor of five percent per year on the houses and the amortization of the original debt, the values look like Table 35-4.

Item	Value
Ten houses worth $265,000 each	$2,650,000
Less mortgage debt of 10 x $190,000	($1,900,000)
Net value	$750,000

TABLE 35-3. NEW NET WORTH

As you look at it, I bet you're impressed!

COMMERCIAL DEALS

If you contrast that residential scenario with only one commercial deal purchased and properly managed, you get a ten-year spreadsheet that looks something like Table 35-5.

You can plainly see that the capitalized value in year one is $2,337,000, and by year ten, it is up to $3,625,454. This is a net gain through ownership and good stewardship of $1,288,454.

This leads me to believe that housing does not have to take a back seat to commercial or vice versa. If you look at the potential of having developed a commercial property, then you have the added bonus of the initial developer's

House #	Original Value	5%/Year	Mortgage Balance	Net Value after Mortgage Balance
1	$265,000	$132,500	($163,020)	$234,480
2	$265,000	$119,250	($166,630)	$217,622
3	$265,000	$106,000	($170,050)	$200,953
4	$265,000	$92,750	($173,090)	$184,664
5	$265,000	$79,500	($176,130)	$168,375
6	$265,000	$66,250	($178,790)	$152,466
7	$265,000	$53,000	($181,450)	$136,557
8	$265,000	$39,750	($183,730)	$121,028
9	$265,000	$26,500	($186,010)	$105,499
10	$265,000	$13,250	($188,100)	$90,160
Total net worth and new net worth				**$1,611,804**
Total increase in value		$728,750	($1,767,000)	

TABLE 35-4. APPRECIATED VALUE

profit as well as the potential increase in value over a ten-year period.

Selling

Houses

Getting residential or commercial property ready to sell is roughly similar. You must target your potential buyer and sell to that buyer. Both residential and commercial require presentation and representation, but with commercial property there is added paperwork that has to do with the income portion of the real estate. Homes are sold as buildings, but income property is sold as an income stream with the building tossed in as a bonus.

Homes are set up for sale by targeting a specific buyer. Why is this important? The answer is relatively simple and logical. All selling boils down to presentation. If you have positioned the home correctly, or at least in the ballpark, there will be one specific buyer that you should appeal to more than others. I'm not referring to a specific person, rather a type of buyer, such as a young family, an empty-nester couple, or a single person. There are features in your home that might appeal to a variety of buyers, but the sum of all the features should appeal to one group more than to others. The size of the home and the proximity to schools and transportation are factors that appeal to families. The proximity to entertainment and shopping would appeal to single adults and empty nesters who have more time and discretionary money than young families. You need to push all the buttons, but your realtor can advise you how to "spin" your home's features to appeal to a specific target audience.

You should always offer a home warranty that includes all mechanical equipment and appliances. The average cost is somewhere around $350.

Income	Year 1	Year 2	Year 3	Year 4	Year 5
Rents	$225,400	$236,670	$248,504	$260,929	$273,975
Less 5% vacancy	–$11,270	–$11,834	–$12,425	–$13,046	–$13,699
Gross potential income	$214,130	$224,837	$236,078	$247,882	$260,276
Expenses					
$4.75/SF x 16,000 SF	$76,000	$79,800	$83,790	$87,980	$92,378
Less recapture from tenants	–$72,200	–$75,810	–$79,601	–$83,581	–$87,760
Net expenses	$3,890	$3,990	$4,190	$4,399	$4,619
NIBDS	**$210,330**	**$220,847**	**$231,889**	**$243,483**	**$255,657**
Value @ 9% cap rate	**$2,337,000**	**$2,453,850**	**$2,576,543**	**$2,705,370**	**$2,840,638**
ROI on cash $460,000	**21%**	**23%**	**26%**	**28%**	**31%**
Additional annual capital gain	**$576,087**	**$692,937**	**$815,630**	**$944,457**	**$1,079,725**
ROI on cap gain if sold	**125%**	**151%**	**177%**	**205%**	**235%**
Income	**Year 6**	**Year 7**	**Year 8**	**Year 9**	**Year 10**
Rents	$287,674	$302,058	$317,160	$333,018	$349,669
Less 5% vacancy	–$14,384	–$15,103	–$15,858	–$16,651	–$17,483
Gross potential income	$273,290	$286,955	$301,302	$316,368	$332,186
Expenses					
$4.75/SF x 16,000 SF	$96,997	$101,847	$106,940	$112,287	$117,901
Less recapture from tenants	–$92,148	–$96,755	–$101,593	–$106,672	–$112,006
Net expenses	$4,850	$5,092	$5,347	$5,614	$5,895
NIBDS	**$268,440**	**$281,862**	**$295,955**	**$310,753**	**$326,291**
Value @ 9% cap rate	**$2,982,670**	**$3,131,804**	**$3,288,394**	**$3,452,813**	**$3,625,454**
ROI on cash $460,000	**33%**	**36%**	**39%**	**43%**	**46%**
Additional annual capital gain	**$1,221,757**	**$1,370,891**	**$1,527,481**	**$1,691,900**	**$1,864,541**

TABLE 35-5. TEN-YEAR INCOME (CASH FLOW) PROJECTION

SELL THE NEIGHBORHOOD WITH THE HOME

What you also have to offer is your neighborhood and its features that can help attract the buyer. Lots of children make it a good place to raise kids and a place where the buyer's kids can find new friends and have a good time.

Similarly, a home in a community with recreational facilities like exercise rooms, tennis courts, and swimming pools will appeal to active single adults.

When you start to create the sales pitch, you will want to create a flier for the property. Your realtor will create a flier that is consistent with the standard in your area for handouts, but you might want to consider spending a few hundred dollars to create a better one with more pictures, a floor plan, and a list of newly remodeled features. The nicer the brochure, the better your home will hold up in the buyers' minds when they are doing their comparison shopping.

THE LISTING

An integral part of any sale is listing your home with a realtor. This is normally done by executing a *listing agreement*. These documents are relatively uniform in any area and can be executed without much concern. Your attention should, however, focus on the business points of the agreement and address the performance part in the agreement. Remember: to be enforceable, all agreements must be in writing and executed by both parties. Issues you should specifically address include the following items:

- Is this an agency listing or an exclusive right to sell?
- The broker's obligation to publish in the MLS directory and cooperate with other brokers in the system.
- Your broker's commitment to split the commission; you will pay 50/50 with any cooperating broker.
- How long will the listing be effective?
- Your right to cancel the listing any time if your broker fails to perform satisfactorily.
- Advertising and open house obligations.

PROMOTION

What value are open houses? They give your home exposure and they also provide the broker with a steady stream of potential clients for your home, as well as other listings for the broker. I encourage you to have open houses on weekends when there are a lot of people out looking, but don't overdo it. Most important is to have a box on the sign out front full of brochures on your home. People driving by who like what they see can take a brochure with them; if they like what they see on the brochure, they can arrange to see the home. This is more important than open houses. Make sure that you have the brochures under your control and that you keep the box full. The broker should supply the brochures, but you should make sure they do not run out.

SHOULD YOU HIRE AN AGENT?

Some people think that paying a brokerage commission to sell a home is too big an expense. In certain areas of high desirability, that might be the case. On the average, though, it is very difficult to sell your home on your own. The only people who are aware of the house are those who drive by. Homes for sale by owners (FSBOs) move very slowly unless they are in a very desirable area. If that is true of your home, you might want to try selling it yourself. If you decide to do that, you also need to consider the contract of sale and what you should do if a broker brings you an offer from one of his or her clients. You need to use a lawyer for the sales agreement. If a broker brings you a deal, you should consider paying a half commission to that broker.

Commercial Property

By now you can see where I'm going with this chapter. There is life after a sale. Selling a piece of commercial income property is a little more complicated than a residential property because of the documentation, but the philosophy is the same: make it easy for the buyer to decide to buy. The major thrust of preparing to sell an income property is to have all the homework done for the buyer so that the free look period is as short as possible. This leaves new financing as the only substantive contingency.

Meeting the Buyer's Objectives

This is a rather straightforward process and it includes the following:

- Prepare the background history of the property.
- Establish the investment scenario—the competition and how your building fits in.
- Run the numbers.
- Back them up.
- Separate the above- and below-the-line items.
- Prepare a tax history.
- Inspect and document the physical plant and do any needed maintenance.

I want to comment briefly on the above. You need to prepare the background history of the building, couching it in the context of the current market, delineating its niche within that market, and providing a positive narrative on how the building fits into that niche and how it got there (purchased and massaged into position or developed for that niche). This will provide the selling broker with a story to tell and, at the same time, position the building in the buyer's mind. It makes the job easier for the broker and the buyer.

You already have your spreadsheets prepared, so you have to pick a point in time, such as the beginning of the current year, and project the numbers forward five or ten years, depending on the type of property you are selling. Five years should be sufficient for most, unless you have some large tenants scheduled for some significant increases in rent between years five and ten. The rationale for creating the five- and ten-year income and expense projections is to demonstrate to a prospective buyer that his or her ROI will start to grow significantly in a short time. This demonstrates that the asking price is reasonable. Make sure your income and expense data sheets do not include any below-the-line items. The current ownership's income tax records are not relevant to the buyer and should not be exposed to the buyer.

You should have a current third-party physical inspection of the building and its major systems done and ready to show. Make sure that you take care of any identified deferred maintenance items.

Now you are ready to put the property on the market. Through this preparation for sale you have effectively shortened the buyer's review and approval time; it helps the process along and controls the time frame.

Setting the Price

The selling price is a function of two factors: the properly documented and proven NIBDS of the investment property and the market for real property investments. The NIBDS is a given if your numbers are in line and easy to substantiate. The market is a little harder to determine; your take on it may differ from the buyer's. The more empirical the data backing up your position, the easier time the buyer/investor will have meeting your asking price. Items to factor in include the following:

- The market, the MSA
- Cap rates and the competition
- Current investment alternatives

- Potential financing for the buyer
- Timing

How these items string together to become a reasonable pricing structure is as follows. The income property market is a function of rate of return, supply and demand, comparable sales data, and competing investments like REITS, stocks, and bonds. In addition, the big item is the actual anticipated cash-on-cash potential dictated by the current loan market. This will determine how much the buyer must invest and what his or her leveraged cash-on-cash ROI is likely to be.

Who Gets the Listing?

Another important item is who lists the property for sale. If you have become a broker, it is still unlikely that you have become an income property specialist. Selling income property is not like buying or leasing. It is a specialized field, and the broker's buyer contacts are a very real and important part of the process. Good investment property brokers have acquired a reputation with buyers coast to coast and their recommendation to a prospective buyer can go a long way to getting your property closed. This is not a good time to attempt to save on the commission.

You are responsible for providing the raw material for a proper sales package and the broker is responsible for assembling it and paying for the brochure or sales package. It should include at least the following items:

- Photos and graphics
- Floor plans and as-built surveys
- Short-form spreadsheet of income and expense, with major tenants featured *without any lease details*
- Comparables and market data

From this material the broker can assemble a viable sales package. Detailed information should be available to the buyer only after he or she has made an offer and you have accepted it and the buyer and buyer's broker have executed a nondisclosure agreement. You should have all the pertinent leases, contracts, spreadsheets, etc. duplicated and ready to turn over as soon as escrow has opened.

Documentation

The required documentation will be at least the following items:

- As-built surveys
- A set of building plans, including tenant improvements
- Any warranties still in force
- Hazardous materials report
- Level-one environmental report
- Tenant leases and floor plans
- Maintenance and management agreements
- Operating costs and income and expense data for at least one year prior
- Any pertinent business between the landlord and any of the tenants that might survive closing, such as ongoing lease renewal negotiations

Now What?

If you have done all this and someone steps up and buys your property, you are faced with the same dilemma as any income property owner. Do you pay the tax and shut down or do you exchange into another property and continue to build your portfolio?

Before You Put the Property for Sale

Rather than wait until the property sells, you must map out your future in detail prior to listing the property for sale. You have basically three options:

- Sell and pay the tax.
- Exchange into another property.
- Keep the property, refinance, and buy another.

These options were discussed earlier in the chapter. The options for commercial are the same as they are for residential. Your objectives will most likely be shaped by your experience with any particular deal. The aggressive approach is to sell and exchange into larger properties or multiple properties. I personally favor keeping a good property you know and have worked on, refinancing it to provide cash to buy or develop another property. The only caution I can give you on this approach is to make sure of your tenants. You must have tenants who will not wipe out your cash flow by moving on. If that is a potential problem down the road, then set up reserves to carry you through. Make sure that any property you keep will not fall prey to locational obsolescence.

Now you know everything I know about making money in real estate, so you are at least as well equipped as I am to make a living at it. All you need is practice, perseverance, and a little luck.

Have at it with my best wishes. Please feel free to drop me an e-mail (slrider@riderland.com) if you need to vent or if you have a question about what you have read in this book. In addition, since I am the typist and I am prone to typos, if you can identify one, gleefully it will be corrected in future editions.

While I get a great many e-mails, so far I have been able to keep up with them. If you need working copies of any of the documents and spreadsheets in this book, you can log onto my web site (riderland.com/cdrom.html) and purchase a CD-ROM with them on it.

SECTION

IX APPENDICES

APPENDIX A. GLOSSARY

APPENDIX B. AGREEMENT OF PURCHASE AND SALE AND JOINT ESCROW INSTRUCTIONS

APPENDIX C. COMMERCIAL LEASE

APPENDIX

A

Glossary

1031 exchange A transaction in which a person makes an agreement to transfer property held for business use or as an investment and then receives another property to be held for business use or as an investment, deferring any taxes. Section 1031 of the Internal Revenue Code of 1986, as amended, reads: "No gain or loss shall be recognized on the exchange of property held for productive use in a trade or business or for investment purposes if such property is exchanged solely for property of a like-kind which is to be held for either productive use in trade or business or for investment purposes."

A&E Architectural and engineering.

Absolute net Income with no expense deductions.

Absorption The rate at which available space is leased.

Accelerate To call a note early, to force a premature payoff.

Accessibility The ability of a person or vehicle to gain access to a property or a building.

Acknowledgment of commencement A document attesting to the fact that the tenant has taken possession, is occupying a premises, and is paying rent.

ADA See *Americans with Disabilities Act*.

Adjustable rate mortgage (ARM) A home loan for which the interest rate is changed periodically based on a standard financial index, such as the *cost of living* or *federal funds discount rate.* Most ARMs have caps that limit increases in the interest rate. ARMs typically start out at a low rate of interest for a period of years and increase or decrease based on the index.

Agency The legal representation of another party; it does not imply the ability to bind that party to a transaction.

Agent One who represents another.

Agent for service of process The person or entity authorized to receive legal papers on behalf of a corporation, as required by law. Also known as a *registered agent* or a *resident agent.*

Agreement A written contract between parties involving real property.

AIDT All-inclusive deed of trust, a recorder lien wrapping an existing *first deed of trust.*

ALTA survey A boundary survey prepared according to minimum standards prepared and adopted by the American Land Title Association and the American Congress on Surveying and Mapping, that includes the results of a physical inspection of the property.

ALTA title insurance An insurance against any and all documented or undocumented flaws in the title to a property, through the American Land Title Association, consisting of policies and endorsements that lenders usually require when making a loan, including unrecorded mechanic's liens and physical easements, facts not revealed by a physical survey, water and mineral rights, and the right of parties in possession such as tenants and buyers who have recorded claims.

Amateur One who is learning the trade, inexperienced.

Americans with Disabilities Act (ADA) Federal legislation enacted in 1990 that ensures access to all public and commercial buildings for all people with disabilities.

Amortization The retirement of the principal of a loan over the term of the loan, scheduled to level payments.

Amortization schedule See *debt service constant.*

Anchor tenant A tenant with sufficient net worth to enable financing for a project.

Annual percentage rate (APR) A figure that expresses the relationship of the total finance charge to the total amount of the loan, including all fees and expenses paid to acquire the loan, as required under the federal Truth-in-Lending Act; it must be calculated to the nearest one-eighth of one percent.

Apartments Multiple dwelling units for rent.

APN Assessor's parcel number. See *parcel number.*

Appraisal A formal document that gives an "expert's" opinion of value.

APR See *annual percentage rate.*

Arbitration The binding settlement of disputes between parties by a third party selected by the parties in dispute.

Architect A licensed designer of buildings.

ARM See *adjustable rate mortgage.*

Arterial A major road or highway.

Article A section in a legal contract.

As-built survey A survey performed when a project is completed to show the location of all the improvements and any modifications made to the plans during construction.

Assessment A special lien for a specific improvement benefiting two or more properties.

Assessment district A specific area of multiple properties included in a special assessment for the purpose of acquiring, constructing, or maintaining a public improvement.

Assessor's parcel number (APN) See *parcel number*.

Asset Something with a positive worth definable in currency.

Attorney A licensed lawyer, one approved to practice law.

Attornment An agreement by the tenant of a property to be a tenant to a new owner or landlord of the property.

Balloon payment A final payment of a loan that is considerably larger than the periodic payments, because the loan was not fully amortized.

Bank A public depository and lending institution.

Bankable A loan commitment that can be borrowed against, easily financed.

Bean counter An accountant, one who pays great attention to detail.

Bearing capacity The ability of a soil to support a given load distributed over a given surface area.

Bench appraisal An estimate of value informally given by an appraiser.

Beneficial interest The right to the use and benefit of property resulting from a contract, a legal right with tangible value and may be legally assigned, bought, or sold.

Beneficial title A document that is as good as ownership rights to real property, although it is not the *legal title*.

"Best efforts" contract An agreement that obligates a party to do a job as well as possible, with no legal obligation to achieve some specified result, in contrast with a *"specific performance" contract*.

Bid A binding commitment to build for a specific price.

Boilerplate Required clauses in a contract.

Bonds Publicly sold financial instruments, generally guaranteed by a municipality.

Boundary survey A map showing the boundaries and direction and geographical orientation of a parcel of land.

Box store See *discount store*.

Breakeven Point at which income equals expenses.

Bridge loan A loan to tide one over until another can be funded.

Broker A licensed real estate agent, one who can employ other agents.

Building department A city function to evaluate and approve proposed building projects within a community.

Build-to-suit A project designed and built for one tenant.

Buyer An entity purchasing a piece of real property.

Buy-sell agreement A contract between the interim and permanent lenders and the borrower to pay off the interim loan.

Call the loan To accelerate a loan's due date.

CAM Common area maintenance.

CAM charges Costs of *common area maintenance* (CAM) passed on to the tenants.

Campus A collection of buildings in a park-like setting.

Cap rate See *capitalization rate.*

Capital Cash, money, funds available for investment.

Capitalization rate A ratio used to estimate the value of income-producing properties: the net operating income divided by the sales price or value of a property, expressed as a percentage.

Carry-back financing Financing given by a seller to a buyer.

Carry-back loan A loan made by a seller to a buyer to finance part of the purchase price of real estate.

Carve-out Specific items for which a lender requires a personal guarantee from the borrower for the life of the loan, generally including fraud and misrepresentation.

Cash Money—the absolute required commodity in any real estate deal.

Cash flow Income less expenses.

Cash on cash Net income (net income before debt servicing is deducted, NIBDS) divided by total project cost.

Category A use designation for a piece of real property, a zoning definition.

CC&Rs See *covenants, conditions, and restrictions.*

C corporation See *public corporation.*

Ceiling height The height of the ceiling above the finished floor.

Chain store One of a series of stores under one ownership; if large, a chain store is also known as a *credit tenant.*

Chattel Any item of tangible property except real estate and things connected with real property, such as buildings.

City A large municipality.

City council The governing body of a city, always elected.

Class "A" building A high-rise of good-quality construction, an "institutional" building.

Clause An article in a contract dealing with a specific subject.

Close corporation A corporation with fewer than ten stockholders.

Co-housing Housing sharing common features or amenities.

Collateral Land or other saleable assets pledged against the timely repayment of a debt.

Commercial Nonresidential or residential on a large scale.

Commercial real estate Real estate not single-family-oriented, the practice of developing investment property.

Commitment A contract to lend money.

Common area maintenance Common expenses prorated to the tenants of a building.

Compaction The degree of compression of soil, expressed in terms of its *bearing capacity* or as a percentage of ideal requirements.

Complex Two or more buildings in one development.

Conditions precedent Premises that a party may establish in an agreement as necessary, without which the party is not obligated to the agreement.

Condominium Ownership of central facilities that benefit all owners.

Construction The building of buildings or other improvements to the land.

Contingency An event that will preclude consummation of a contract.

Continuing guarantee A guarantee that survives a closing event.

Contract A legal, binding agreement between or among two or more parties.

Contractor One who is licensed to build buildings and other improvements to the land.

Contribution A donation toward the whole, an offering.

Convertible A construction loan that may be converted to a permanent or mini-permanent loan.

Co-op Residential units in a high-rise building, individually owned, not including the building, which is held by a co-op association.

Core The original center of a city.

Corporation A form of company ownership where the stockholders' liability is limited to the loss of their investment. See *public corporation* and *S corporation*.

Corridor Land accessed by a traffic arterial, a linear description of a zone.

Costs The amount of money required to do something.

County board of supervisors The elected governing body of a county.

Course of construction insurance A policy that covers the owner of a property against any claims that may result from the construction, such as personal injury or damage to other property.

Covenants, conditions, and restrictions (CC&R) Limitations placed on the use of real property, usually intended to maintain a uniformity of appearances within a specific area, such as a subdivision, a condominium community, or a planned unit development.

Coverage The amount of building allowed on a given site area, generally defined as square feet per acre.

CPI The Consumer Price Index published by the Bureau of Labor Statistics of the U.S. Department of Labor.

Credit tenant The tenant in a shopping center or office building with a *bankable* financial statement, i.e., one that can easily allow a developer to obtain financing.

Cricket A drainage-diverting roof structure of single or double slope, to promote drainage of water.

Criteria A list of requirements for an event or item.

Critical path schedule A sequence of events, of which the execution of each depends on the successful completion of a prior event.

Cross-collateralization Assets liened as a result of a loan on other assets.

Cross-collateralize To use an asset that is securing one loan to secure another loan.

Debt coverage The amount of total net income before debt service (*NIBDS*) over the amount of a loan payment expressed as the percentage of total income, e.g., a 50-percent loan to value.

Debt coverage ratio The total net income before debt service (*NIBDS*) divided by the amount of the debt payment.

Debt service The mortgage payment.

Debt service constant Percentage of the principal of a loan that must be paid annually in order to fully repay the principal and pay the interest over the term of the loan. Also known as *debt constant*.

Deed of trust A recorded lien on real property, generally a mortgage.

Default When one party fails to live up to the terms of a contract.

Defease To render null and void an agreement specified in a document.

Deflation A contraction in the volume of money or credit, resulting in a general decline in prices and an increase in the value of money.

Demised (premises) A piece of real estate in which an interest has been transferred temporarily, such as conveyed in a lease; the legal definition of a *premises*.

Demising wall An interior wall that separates the premises of adjacent tenants and tenant premises from common area, such as hallways and bathrooms.

Demographics The statistical sampling of a population; information pertaining to a specific population.

Department store A chain store selling a varied selection of goods.

Depreciation The systematic accounting of building obsolescence through time.

Depreciation allowance The legal amount allowed for annual depreciation.

Depreciation schedule The unequal depreciation allowance over a period of time.

Depth The dimension of a premises measured from the front door to the rear windows.

Design The creation of a building's configuration.

Design-build A construction contract wherein a contractor agrees to deliver a finished building within a certain price range, without the benefit of final plans and specifications.

Design review The municipality's review of a project's proposed design.

Developable A piece of land that can be made suitable for commercial or residential purposes.

Developer One who creates commercial real estate for a living, principal, owner.

Developer's risk The period of time during which the developer's cash is at risk.

Development The production of income-producing real estate.

Dirt Land, project, subject parcel, site.

Disclosure The process of revealing all the pros and cons involved in a project.

Discount store A retailer that specializes in selling discounted merchandise at less than the manufacturers' suggested retail cost, in a warehouse-type setting, such as Costco, PETsMART, OfficeMax, or Ross Dress for Less. Also known as a *box store*.

Distressed A term used to describe property that is in poor physical or financial condition, whose value has decreased due to loss of tenants, economic obsolescence, or both.

DOE The U.S. Department of Energy.

Down payment Cash invested to buy something with a balance due; a percentage of the price.

Downsizing The reduction of a workforce or leased premises.

Draw The tenant that attracts people to a shopping center.

Due date The date on which a loan must be fully paid.

Due diligence The process of discovering all the pertinent facts about a piece of real property.

E&O insurance See *errors and omissions insurance.*

Early call An acceleration of a loan's due date, usually for cause.

Earnest money Money given as a deposit against the purchase price for real property.

Easements Portions of real property reserved for use by the public or third parties, generally restricted as to buildings thereon.

EIR *Environmental impact report.*

EIS *Environmental impact statement.*

Elevation Graphic depiction of a building's facade above ground.

Encumbered property Property with liens recorded against the title.

Endangered species A life form designated by the government as threatened with extinction and protected by law.

Endgame See *exit strategy.*

Engineer A licensed designer of structural components.

Entitlement A legal right to occupy, use, enjoy, and otherwise benefit from a piece of land for a specified period of time.

Entrepreneur One who seeks to profit through innovation and risk.

Environmental Pertaining to the physical surroundings of any given property.

Environmental impact report (EIR) A study conducted by specialists, of the effect of a project on the environment and infrastructure, generally required by state or federal law to be completed before a project can begin. Also known as *environmental impact statement* (EIS).

Equity The value of a property minus any mortgage balance and any claims or liens against it; the net value of the asset.

Errors and omissions insurance A policy designed to protect the clients of architects and engineers from damages or losses resulting from mistakes, negligence, and bad judgment of the architects and engineers.

Escrow A real estate sales and purchases facilitator.

Escrow instructions Executed instructions to the escrow agent from both buyer and seller in a real property transaction.

Estoppel certificate A document stating that the tenant is in possession and paying rent, that the lease is in force, and that the landlord is not in default.

Exchange The process of trading one piece of property for another to avoid immediate taxation of profits.

Exclusive The right to represent a property without worry about another agent's preemption of the listing position/commission.

Exculpatory clause A provision in a document intended to free a party from liability.

Execute Of a document, to sign.

Exhibits Documents attached to a contract detailing specific issues.

Exit strategy A plan for disposing of an investment, specifying time and means. Also known as *endgame.*

Expenses Costs of operation of a project.

Expense stop A dollar amount, generally stated as an amount per foot per year, that the landlord agrees to pay for building expenses, with the tenant agreeing to pay any expenses in excess of this amount.

Expert One paid to do a specific chore and acknowledged as competent and highly experienced in the field.

Fannie Mae See *Federal National Mortgage Association.*

Fat Budgetary surplus, contingency monies.

Fauna Animals, species, critters.

Feasibility The likelihood of successful execution of a planned action.

Feasibility study The process of evaluating a deal.

Federal funds discount rate The interest rate that an eligible depository institution pays to borrow funds for a short term directly from a Federal Reserve Bank.

Federal Home Loan Mortgage Corporation (FHLMC) A federal agency, usually known as *Freddie Mac,* that guarantees repayment of home loans sold to investors with a Freddie Mac guarantee. It is a *secondary market lender.*

Federal National Mortgage Association (FNMA) A federal agency, usually known as *Fannie Mae,* that guarantees repayment of home loans sold to investors with a Fannie Mae guarantee. It is a *secondary market lender.*

Fee The land; a charge for services rendered.

Fee simple The unequivocal, unencumbered ownership of a piece of land. Also known as *fee, fee absolute, fee simple absolute,* and *fee title.*

Fee title The land; clean ownership rights to land.

FHA Federal Housing Authority, source of loans to allow low-income families to own a home.

Fiduciary obligation An enforceable, legal responsibility undertaken by an agent or a partner to another person or entity, requiring the agent or partner to treat the interests of the other person or entity above his or her own interests.

Fire department A government agency charged with preventing and extinguishing fires.

First deed of trust A recorded, primary lien on real property, second in priority only to the local taxes assessed.

Flipping The practice of reselling land before having purchased it.

Floor A horizontal division of a building. Also known as a *story.*

Floor plan The layout of tenant improvements in a specific location.

Floor plate The layout of a building floor prior to tenant improvements.

Flora Plants, vegetation, naturally occurring growth.

Force majeure Events or circumstances that are beyond the control of the party affected and not the result of fault or negligence, such as natural disasters, strikes, riots, wars. Also known as *acts of God.*

Foreign corporation A corporation doing business in a state other than the state in which it was incorporated.

***Fortune* 500** A designation by *Fortune Magazine* of the 500 largest companies in the United States.

Freddie Mac See *Federal Home Loan Mortgage Corporation.*

Free look The time period in a real estate contract during which the buyer's deposit is fully refundable.

Free trade zone A legal tax-free zone for import, export, and manufacturing of goods.

Gap loan The loan that covers the gap between equity and financing, usually a land loan or seller carry-back loan.

General partner A partner who is *jointly and severally* liable for all debts of a partnership.

General partnership A business entity in which all partners take an active role in the operation and management of the venture, with each general partner liable for all of the unsecured debts of the partnership and able to commit the partnership to any legal venture.

General plan A map showing the distribution of zoning categories in a designated area, e.g., township, city, or county.

General provisions Boilerplate clauses in a legal document.

Geotechnical Pertaining to geology, seismology, and soil conditions.

Geotechnical engineer A civil engineer with expertise in soils and foundations who evaluates and stabilizes foundations for buildings, roads, and other structures.

Ginny Mae *See Government National Mortgage Association.*

GLA See *gross leasable area.*

Global Positioning System A system for locating any point precisely, based on data transmitted from a network of satellites.

Going dark Of a tenant store, ceasing operations while still paying rent.

Government National Mortgage Association (GNMA) A federal agency, usually known as *Ginnie Mae*, that guarantees repayment of home loans sold to investors with a Ginny Mae guarantee. It is a *secondary market lender*.

GPI See *gross potential income.*

GPS Global Positioning System, a system for locating any point precisely, based on data transmitted from a network of satellites.

Graphic A visual representation.

Gross leasable area (GLA) The total floor area, in square feet, of a building designed for leasing, generally the area available for the exclusive use of tenants.

Gross lease A lease that includes all costs of operation.

Gross potential income (GPI) Total income before deductions or offsets.

Guarantee A promise to pay if another does not.

Hard costs Construction costs.

Hard money loan Financing with private funds, at higher interest rates than charged by banks and requiring personal guarantees by the borrower.

Hardscape The inanimate elements of landscaping, such as wood, concrete, brick, and stone—in contrast with the *softscape*, living plants.

Hazardous material/waste Any substance that is considered by the government to pose a substantial or potential hazard to human health and safety, to property, and/or to the environment. The United States Environmental Protection Agency considers a substance hazardous if it can catch fire, can react or explode when mixed with other substances, is corrosive, or is toxic.

Hazardous waste Any substance to be disposed of that is considered by the government to pose a substantial or potential hazard to human health and safety, to property, and/or to the environment if disposed of improperly.

Health department A government agency charged with protecting the health of the citizens.

High-rise building A commercial or residential structure more than seven floors high.

Highway department A government agency in charge of roads and transportation.

Holding over The month-to-month extension of a tenant's occupancy after a lease expires.

Home A dwelling for a single family, generally synonymous with *house.*

Home equity loan A line of credit for which a homeowner uses his or her residence as collateral. Also known as a *second mortgage.*

Hotel A mid-rise to high-rise transient lodging facility.

House A dwelling for a single family, synonymous with *home.*

HVAC Heating, ventilation, and air-conditioning.

Improvement A publicly owned addition to land that provides a benefit, such as a street, a sewer, a sidewalk, or a curb, or a structure added to a site to improve the value of the property, such as a driveway or a fence.

Improvement bonds Interest-bearing certificates issued by a government to allow the public to invest in financing public projects to benefit real property.

Industrial building Single- or multitenant manufacturing or warehouse building.

Inflation A continuing rise in prices in general resulting from an increase in money and credit relative to goods and services, causing money to decrease in worth.

In-migration The movement of people into a region or community to live there.

Institution A financial entity, usually a bank, a savings bank, a life insurance company, or a trust.

Interest Rent paid on capital or money borrowed.

Interest-only loan An advance of money for which the payments cover only the interest accumulating on the balance, but not the principal. A period is usually set for interest-only payments, after which the payments increase to cover principal as well as interest.

Interim loan Temporary or construction financing.

Investment Capital, money devoted to equity or ownership of real property.

Investment grade Commercial property worthy of a financial commitment for the long term.

Investor One who risks capital in a venture.

Joint and several guarantee A legal contract that binds those who sign it to pay back a loan if the borrower fails to do so, with each guarantor of the loan assuming responsibility for the entire amount guaranteed.

Joint and several liability A situation in which two or more parties are liable for a debt or an obligation, together or individually or jointly.

Joint tenancy with the right of survivorship (JTWROS) A form of ownership in which the property is shared equally by all owners and, if an owner dies, his or her share transfers automatically to the surviving owners.

Joint venture A project undertaken by two or more entities.

Judgment An obligation to pay granted by the court in favor of a plaintiff against a defendant. Payment of this judgment may be ensured by recording it as a lien against property, such that it is paid out of funds from selling the property.

Junior department store A retailer similar to Mervyn's or a small Sears or J.C. Penney store.

K Constant, the percentage necessary to fully amortize the principal of a loan over the term at a specific interest rate; in residential parlance, the APR (annual percentage rate).

Kentucky windage A term dating back to Sergeant Alvin York, a World War I sharpshooter from Kentucky who would adjust his aim to compensate for any wind, roughly synonymous with terms such as guestimate, fudge factor, margin for error, and leeway.

KISS Keep It Simple, Stupid!

Land Real property, aka the *fee*, the site, the plot, the dirt.

Land lease A contract for the use of land without the transfer of ownership; it conveys a beneficial ownership.

Landlord The owner, the lessor.

Landscaping Plantings added to a piece of real property.

Late fee Penalty charged when a rent or a mortgage is paid later than specified in the contract.

Lawyer A licensed practitioner of the legal profession, an attorney.

Leasable Able to be leased (rented) for money.

Lease A written contract enabling the use of an item or premises for money.

Leasehold interest The legal right to occupy or possess real property, not ownership rights but enforceable and transferable.

Lease-up 95-percent occupancy of a building.

Legal notice Notice recognized by the courts as having been duly received by the party being notified.

Lender One who lends money for a fee.

Lessee Occupant of a building, evidenced by written or oral agreement.

Lessor Owner or landlord.

Leverage The principle of increasing one's yield through borrowing money.

Liability A legal obligation.

Lien A recorded legal obligation, a claim secured against a property, which is a flaw in the title to that property; a legal notice of an obligation of the owner.

Lifestyle subdivision A residential development built around a common theme, such as a gold course, an airport (with each unit having a hangar), waterways (with each unit having a boat garage), vineyards, or an equestrian area (with riding trails, stables, and veterinary facilities).

Like kind A piece of real property defined by the IRS as being equivalent to another for tax purposes. See *1031 exchange*.

Limited liability company A form of ownership with the limitation of liability of a corporation and the tax benefits of a partnership.

Limited partner A partner whose risk is limited to the loss of his or her investment.

Limited partnership A form of ownership where the general partner assumes the liabilities and manages the partnership and the limited partners do not participate in managing and can lose only their investment.

Lineal foot A measurement of one foot, in length only, as opposed to a *square foot*. Also known as a *linear foot*.

Lipstick A strictly cosmetic approach to fixing up a house—generally paint, wallpaper, and carpet.

Liquidity The relative speed of converting an asset to cash.

Listing agreement A contract between a property owner and a real estate broker by which the owner employs the broker to find a buyer for the property, which is described in the agreement, with the basic terms of the listing, including the price, the expiration date for the listing, and the sales commission.

LLC See *limited liability company*.

Load The surcharge to rent that distributes among the tenants the cost of common areas, such as restrooms, hallways, and lobbies.

Load factor The percentage of the building that is allocated to common areas (such as restrooms, hallways, and lobbies) and is used to increase tenants' usable area to rentable area. For example, a load factor of ten percent would mean that 1,000 usable square feet would be calculated as 1,100 rentable square feet.

Loan constant A composite of principal and interest on the principal, calculated so that each payment pays the interest on the outstanding balance of the loan and enough of the principal to amortize the loan over the term of the loan.

Loan package A collection of documents that constitutes a complete loan application: the loan request, collateral description and appraisal, financial statements and projections, and sample documentation.

Loan servicing Collecting loan payments, distributing the funds to the lender, and making payments from impound accounts. These are normally the responsibilities of a mortgage banker on behalf of the lenders represented by that company. For these services, the mortgage bankers collect a fee, usually equal to or less than one-tenth of one percent of the funds collected.

Location The relative position of a parcel of land within a designated zone (city, town, etc.).

Lot line Property boundary.

Main body The business deal part of a lease.

Majority in interest Ownership totaling over 50 percent.

Manufacturing plant An industrial building where goods are produced.

Maquilladora plant A plant on the U.S.-Mexico border employing Mexican labor and U.S. or imported parts.

Market The free, legal exchange of money, real property rights, and entitlements between or among parties.

Master plan A plan for a whole project.

Master planned development An approach to subdividing a piece of land that sets forth specific principles of design for use, usually a large residential community, often with recreational facilities.

MBA shop A company employing masters of business graduates in the 1980s, generally credited with causing the Great Recession of 1988-1991.

Mechanic's lien A notice, recorded against a building, that a contractor has done work on that building but has not been paid. When the property is sold, this lien will be paid before the seller receives any money.

Mediation A process of negotiating a nonbinding settlement between opposing parties.

Member A person or entity in a limited liability company.

Merchant builder One who builds and sells rather than building and holding his or her projects.

Metes and bounds A legal description of legal property using geographical coordinates.

Metropolitan statistical area (MSA) An entity consisting of a large population center and adjacent communities (usually counties) that have a high degree of economic and social connection with that center. MSAs sometimes contain more than one central city and/or cross state lines. Also known as a *standard metropolitan statistical area* (SMSA).

Mini-perm loan A combination of construction loan and permanent loan, providing temporary financing for a short time, usually five years or less, typically with a *balloon payment* at the end of the term consisting of all unpaid principal and accumulated interest.

Mini-storage An industrial multitenant storage building.

MLS See *Multiple Listing Service.*

Model A three-dimensional *rendering* of a proposed project.

Modified gross A lease that includes only some of the operating expenses.

Modified net A lease that includes at least one expense of operation.

Mom-and-pop stores Local retail stores with limited credit.

Mortgage A recorded loan on real property.

Mortgage banker An institution that represents a very limited, specific list of lenders. In addition to making loans, the mortgage banker normally services the loans on behalf of the lenders represented by that company. The mortgage bankers collect a fee, usually equal to or less than one tenth of one percent of the funds collected.

Mortgage broker A person or a firm that serves as an intermediary between borrower and lender; the broker, takes a loan application from the borrower, collects the borrower's credit history and other information, and shops the loan to lenders. Mortgage brokers are paid through *origination fees*. They can be compensated by both borrower and lender, in which case they are required by law to disclose these dual fees to both borrower and lender.

Mortgage insurance Money paid to insure a mortgage, usually required when the down payment is less than 20 percent of the purchase price, to pay the lender for the costs of foreclosing if the borrower stops making payments.

Mortgage payment One of a series of payments of principal and interest calculated to amortize the principal over the term of the loan.

Motel Low-rise transient lodging facility.

MSA See *metropolitan statistical area.*

Multifamily A residential building housing more than one family.

Multiple Listing Service A local or regional database of houses for sale by real estate professionals, typically owned and operated by a local information systems vendor, sometimes maintained by a large real estate company or local real estate trade association.

Multitenant building Building designed for occupancy by more than one tenant.

Multiuse complex Projects mixing two or more of the following uses: office, retail, and industrial.

Municipality An aggregation of population acting as one political entity.

Negative Below zero, in the minus column, in debt, without positive value.

Net income The receipt of money over a designated period of time, money left over after all bills are paid.

Net lease A lease that does not include all operating expenses: the tenant must pay certain costs associated with the operation of the property, such as utilities, property taxes, insurance, maintenance, and repairs.

Net net net (NNN) lease See *triple-net lease.*

NI See *net income.*

NIBDS Net income before debt servicing is deducted.

NNN See *triple-net lease.*

Note A contract for repayment of a loan.

Numbers Financial projections, accounting documents. Also known as the *pro forma.*

Obsolescence The process of rendering a building economically useless over time.

Occupancy permit A legal document entitling occupancy of a building.

Occupant A tenant occupying a demised premises.

Occupational Safety and Health Administration A government agency whose mission is "to assure the safety and health of America's workers by setting and enforcing standards; providing training, outreach, and education; establishing partnerships; and encouraging continual improvement in workplace safety and health."

Office building Single- and multitenant building housing offices only.

Offset The right to pay expenses and deduct the cost from rent or other monies due.

OPM Other people's money: equity capital or loans.

Option A right to purchase or a beneficial interest, generally transferable.

Ordinance A law passed by a community regulating land use.

Origination fees *Points* charged by mortgage brokers for making and/or arranging a loan.

OSHA See *Occupational Safety and Health Administration.*

Over standard Improvements other than those offered as standard.

Owner An entity that or who takes title to a piece of real estate.

Pad A piece of land, prepared and ready for building: the soil has been graded and compacted for the foundation and the utilities have been brought to the building perimeter, ready for distribution within the building.

Parcel A piece of land.

Parcel number An identification used in real property records, assigned by the county to identify and track a specific piece of property. Also known as *assessor's parcel number* (APN).

Parking space A temporary storage location for a motor vehicle.

Participating loan A loan that enables the lender to participate in the revenues from the property, calculated in terms of gross receipts, net operating income, net income, or net cash flows.

Pension fund An investment account set up to make payments to retired employees of a company, a government entity, or other organization.

Percent A portion of a whole divided by the whole.

Percentage A portion of a whole expressed in hundredths.

Permanent loan A loan for ten or more years, whose payments include principal and interest, calculated to amortize the principal.

Personalty Personal property, as distinct from *real property*.

Pitch Slope of a roof, usually expressed as a ratio, such as inches per foot.

PITI An acronym for principal, interest, taxes, and insurance—the four components of most mortgage payments.

Planning and zoning department A government agency charged with examining and evaluating building projects.

Planning commission A government body charged with the oversight and approval of building projects, generally elected.

Plenum, ceiling A totally enclosed area above the ceiling, used for HVAC ducts, electrical and electronic conduits, and water pipes.

Point One percent of the principal of a loan; plural, money paid to secure a loan, either interim or permanent.

Portfolio lender A lender that makes loans with its own funds and then keeps the loans on its books (i.e., in its *portfolio*), rather than selling the loans on the *secondary loan market*.

Preleasing Executing leases prior to the start of construction of a building.

Preliminary lien notice A legal notice that a supplier or contractor is starting work on a property that could result in a lien if unpaid.

Premises A specifically and legally defined, usually co-mingled, leasable space; a specific location within a building, designed for and occupied by one tenant.

Principal The owner of a business; the balance of a loan.

Private placement The limited solicitation of equity capital, the legal securing of investment capital from others without public solicitation.

Pro forma Projections of cost and income.

Pro rata A percentage share allotment.

Project A deal, a development, an investment, a building or a group of buildings, land, lots, a subdivision.

Project costs Costs involved in the creation of a project.

Property description A legal definition of a piece of real property.

Public corporation A corporation owned by members of the public, through shares of stock. Also known as a C *corporation* because it is taxed under subsection C of the IRS code.

Punch list A list of unfinished or defective work.

Purchase agreement A contract to buy and sell real property.

Purchase money loan Financing provided by the seller of the property, with terms that are negotiable, but in general less favorable than with conventional bank financing.

Quadrant A quarter of a legal subdivision, containing approximately ten acres and generally divided north to south and east to west.

Range and township A form of property description common to the western United States.

Rate of return (ROR) Dollars made on capital investment, cash back from an investment expressed as a percentage of the money invested. Also known as *return on investment.*

Real estate industry Inclusive term denoting all individuals and entities, all property, skills, disciplines and functions involved in the production of commercial real estate.

Real estate investment trust (REIT) A publicly traded company that owns, develops, or operates commercial properties.

Realtor® A licensed salesperson or broker engaged in the sale of houses.

Realty Real property, generally defined as a house and land, in contrast with *personalty.*

Recession A period of economic downturn.

Recitals A brief statement of facts that provide the context for the agreement and state the purpose of the agreement.

Recourse The ability to enforce payment of a loan or obligation.

Regional mall A very large shopping center usually anchored by three or more department stores.

REIT See *real estate investment trust.*

Remedy A negotiated or adjudicated compensation for a default.

Rendering A prospective graphic representation of a proposed project.

Rent Money paid for the temporary use of someone else's real property.

Restrictions A list of uses denied for a particular site.

Retail building Single- or multitenant buildings used for sale of merchandise to the public.

Return A positive return on capital or effort expended.

Return on investment (ROI) Dollars made on capital investment, cash back from an investment expressed as a percentage of the money invested. Also known as *rate of return.*

Right of offset The ability to offset expenses against monies owed.

Risk An estimate of the likelihood of an event not taking place, i.e., quantifying the potential of an investment.

Risk capital Money invested in a guaranteed venture that is not guaranteed.

ROI See *return on investment.*

Roll over To convert an interim loan to a permanent loan.

Rollover loan A loan that is amortized over a long term, such as 30 years, but with an interest rate that is fixed for a shorter term, such as three or five years, and terms that allow the borrower to extend it when the shorter term ends.

ROR See *rate of return.*

Salability Marketability of an item.

Schedule A timed sequence of events.

Schematic A preliminary, rough graphic representation of a project.

Scupper An opening in the wall of a building to allow water to drain from a flat roof.

SEC See *Securities and Exchange Commission.*

Second mortgage See *home equity loan.*

Secondary loan market The selling and buying of loans that are bundled and sold as securities to investors.

Secondary market lender A company or an agency that buys loans from mortgage bankers and mortgage brokers bundled in amounts of millions of dollars. (See *warehousing [loans].*) Examples are the *Federal National Mortgage Association* (FNMA or *Fannie Mae*), the *Government National Mortgage Association* (GNMA or *Ginny Mae*), and the *Federal Home Loan Mortgage Corporation* (FHLMC or *Freddie Mac*). Secondary lenders help the mortgage market nationally by allowing money to move easily from state to state, which helps ensure that mortgages are available in all areas.

Secondary mortgage market The selling and buying of home loans that are bundled and sold as securities to investors. Also known as *secondary loan market.*

Section A graphic "slice" through a building or a parcel of 640 acres.

Securities and Exchange Commission A federal agency whose primary mission is to protect investors and maintain the integrity of the securities markets, including regulating public offerings by corporations.

Seismic Pertaining to the earth's stability.

Sell To dispose of a property.

Seller An entity selling a property.

Service the debt To pay the mortgage or note.

Setback The distance from the property line defining an area in which nothing may be built.

Shear A condition or a force that causes two parts of a material that are in contact to slide in opposite directions parallel to their plane of contact.

Shell The outside of a building without tenant improvements.

Shoppers People who exchange credit or cash for goods or services.

Sign A graphic mode of advertising the occupant of a premises.

Signage A coordinated group of signs designed to work closely together.

Silicon Desert The area in Arizona where the computer industry flourishes or the area in Utah where the computer industry flourishes.

Silicon Valley The area in California where the computer industry was founded, i.e., Santa Clara County or San Jose.

Single-family A dwelling for one family unit.

Single-tenant building A building designed and built for a specific tenant, a building leased to one tenant.

Site Subject parcel, the land, the dirt, a location, the fee.

Slab, on-grade A concrete foundation that is supported entirely by the surface soils rather than suspended over a basement. The slab serves two purposes: it pulls the footings and structural components together and it serves as the underlying floor for the ground floor of the building.

SMSA Standard metropolitan statistical area. See *metropolitan statistical area.*

Soft costs Costs of a project other than land and construction.

Softscape The elements of landscaping that consist of living plants—in contrast with *hardscape,* which consists of inanimate elements, such as wood, concrete, brick, and stone.

Soils analysis The examination of soils for *bearing capacity* and consistency.

Special assessments Specific liens for specific benefits to real property.

Specifications The specific description of an item as to use, dimension, construction, and quality.

Specific density The relative *compaction* of soil.

"Specific performance" contract An agreement requiring a party to achieve specified results, in contrast with a *"best efforts" contract.*

Specs See *specifications.*

Speculation The risking of capital for potential inordinate gain due to possible increased demand for a commodity.

Speculator One who buys and resells unimproved land for a profit.

Spot zoning Applying to specific individual properties zoning ordinances that differ from the zoning ordinances applied to surrounding or adjacent areas, such as a commercial lot within a residential subdivision or a single-family home on a commercial street.

Square foot An area of 144 square inches.

Standard survey A survey showing the physical boundaries of a parcel of land showing any recorded easements.

Statute of frauds A generic term for the various statutory provisions in state laws that render unenforceable certain types of contracts unless they are in writing, applied most commonly to contracts that involve the sale or transfer of land and contracts that cannot be completed within one year.

Stipulations A list of items to be done prior to improving or entitling a piece of real property.

Stock One or more ownership shares of a corporation, represented by transferable certificates.

Stockholder One who owns *stock* in a corporation.

Story A horizontal division of a building. Also known as a *floor.*

Strip commercial A retail building, small and usually without an anchor tenant.

Structural Pertaining to a building's support skeleton.

Structure A building or constructed edifice, the skeletal support for a building.

Subchapter S corporation A corporation that is usually but not always closely held and is taxed like a partnership.

Subcontractor A contractor employed by another contractor or supplier rather than by the owner.

Subdivision The process of breaking up raw land into five or more separate and saleable parcels.

Subject site/parcel A specific piece of land, as a point of reference.

Sublet To lease or rent to another party, the subtenant, all or part of property leased or rented by a tenant, generally requiring the landlord's consent.

Subordinated Status of a lien junior in position to another lien.

Subordinated land lease A *land lease* that is junior to a loan in the event of default; that loan can foreclose out the land lease.

Suburban Pertaining to an area outside the core city, usually located in adjacent towns.

Supplier A company that supplies materials for a project.

Supply and demand A prime determination of price: the greater the demand, the higher the price and the less the demand, the lower the price.

Survey The act of gathering data for the graphic legal description of a piece of land.

Syndication The raising of capital pools by public solicitation.

Take-out loan A long-term, permanent loan provided to a builder or a developer upon completion of construction to pay off a short-term, interim construction loan.

Tax write-off The depreciation allowance.

Taxes The price of financial success, a contribution to the welfare of others in the state and the nation, the government's "pound of flesh."

Tenancy in common A form of ownership in which the owners each own a stated percentage of the property and are free to do with it as they wish—to sell it, to mortgage it, to give it away, to bequeath—and, if an owner dies, his or her share becomes part of his or her estate.

Tenant An entity occupying any premises.

Tenant broker One who represents the interests of the tenant rather than the interests of the landlord.

Tenant improvements Items constructed within a demised premises for the exclusive use of the tenant.

Term The length of the loan and/or the amortization period.

Terms The conditions of a transaction.

TI The taxes and interest included in mortgage payments. See *PITI.*

TI See *tenant improvements.*

Title Ownership rights to real property or a document outlining the condition of a property's legal encumbrances.

Title insurance Insurance issued to protect the buyer or lender in the event of flaws to the ownership of real property.

Title report A written report regarding liens and claims recorded and not recorded on real property.

Topo See *topographic map.*

Topographic map A graphic description of the grades (contours and elevation) of a piece of land.

Topography The shape of land, ups and downs, contours.

Total costs The all-inclusive number, excluding nothing, including *land*, *hard costs*, and *soft costs.*

Township A map section used to locate land.

Tract home One of numerous mass-produced houses constructed by one builder in a subdivision project. Also known as a *production home.*

Trade zone See *free trade zone.*

Traffic Vehicles or people or passing a specific point.

Traffic count The number of vehicles or people passing a specific point in an average 24-hour period.

Traffic study A report dealing with the extent and effects of vehicular activity within a given area.

Tri-party agreement A contract, a buy-sell agreement, among the construction lender, the permanent lender, and the borrower that assigns the mortgage to the permanent lender when the construction is completed.

Triple-net lease (NNN) A lease arrangement that excludes absolutely all operating expenses: the tenant must pay for any utilities, services, and maintenance associated with the leased space, such as electricity, insurance, janitorial, and repairs. Also known as a *net net net (NNN) lease.*

Unsubordinated land lease A land lease that has a higher lien priority than the loan.

Urban renewal A government-mandated land acquisition to promote the redevelopment of blighted areas of a city.

VA Veterans Affairs, known before 1989 as Veterans Administration, source of loans for veterans of military service.

Value engineering A systematic team approach to a project, consisting of breaking the project down into functional performance elements, assigning costs and benefits to each element, evaluating the costs and benefits, and seeking creative options if costs are disproportional to benefits.

Warehousing (loans) The compiling of closed home loans in bundles of $1,000,000 or more by mortgage bankers and mortgage brokers. They then sell these bundled loans, generally in amounts of tens of millions of dollars, to investors in what is known as the *secondary mortgage market* or *secondary loan market*. These bundles of loans are securities backed by a large numbers of mortgages on individual pieces of real estate, sometimes guaranteed by an agency of the federal government such as *Fannie Mae, Freddie Mac*, or *Ginny Mae*.

Wrap loan A method of financing by which a buyer assumes the seller's mortgage and secures a loan, which is considered to be "wrapped" around the current loan. This combined loan is usually at an interest rate higher than that of the assumed loan. Through a wrap loan, a buyer gets financing at a time when financing is hard to get and the seller gets an effective rate of interest on the additional loan that is higher than face rate (rate of interest as specified in the loan document). Also known as a *wraparound loan* and an *all-inclusive note.*

Yield maintenance A penalty for paying off a loan before the expiration of the term. It enables the lender to earn the same yield as if the borrower had made the mortgage payments as scheduled. The fee is calculated as the difference between the projected interest yield on the loan and the yield possible at the prevailing market rate at the time the loan is paid off.

Zero-lot line A term used to describe the right allowed by zoning and the deed, to position a structure on a lot so that one side is at the boundary, without any *setback*.

APPENDIX

B

Agreement of Purchase *and* Sale *and* Joint Escrow Instructions

WITNESSETH

1. Designation of Escrow Holder
2. Agreement to Sell
3. Purchase Price
4. Title Obligations
5. Right of Cancellation
6. Right of Inspection
7. Survey
8. Placing Deed in Escrow
9. Placing Purchase Price in Escrow
10. Conditions Precedent
11. Closing of Escrow
12. Closing Costs and Proration of Expenses
13. Existing Information

14. Representations
15. Documentation
16. Hazardous Waste
17. Cooperation
18. Liquidated Damages
19. Signs
20. Distribution of Title Policy
21. Possession
22. Amended Escrow Instructions
23. Entire Agreement
24. Waiver
25. Real Estate Commissions
26. Multiple Originals
27. Time Is of The Essence
28. Binding Effect
29. Notices
30. Attorney's Fees
31. Assignment
32. Recordation
33. Covenant to Sign Documents
34. Expiration
35. Extended Closing

Signatures
Effective Date
Notary Page
Exhibits

THIS AGREEMENT, made this ___ day of ____________, 20___ by and between [INSERT SELLER'S NAME] (hereinafter called "Seller"), and [INSERT BUYER'S NAME] (hereinafter called "Buyer").

WITNESSETH

WHEREAS, Buyer has offered to purchase from Seller that certain real property, hereinafter more particularly described, which property is located in the County of ________, State of ________________ (hereinafter referred to as the "Property"), for a purchase price equal to ________________________, for approximately ____ acres, subject to a complete and accurate survey to determine the precise number of acres contained in the property; and adjustment of the purchase price as provided in paragraph 3 hereof; and

WHEREAS, Seller is willing to sell the Property on the terms and conditions contained herein;

and

WHEREAS, the parties desire not only to enter into a formal detailed agreement of purchase and sale but also to establish an escrow through which the purchase and sale contemplated herein will be consummated.

NOW, THEREFORE, in consideration of the terms of this Agreement, the parties hereto agree as follows:

1. DESIGNATION OF ESCROW HOLDER

Buyer and Seller designate ________________________________, the escrow holder (hereinafter referred to as the "escrow holder"). This Agreement shall constitute Escrow Instructions for the sale of the Property and a copy hereof shall be deposited with escrow holder for this purpose. Should escrow holder require the execution of its standard form printed Escrow Instructions, the parties agree to execute same, provided, however, that such instructions shall be construed as applying only to escrow holder's employment and that if there are conflicts between the terms of this Agreement and the terms of the printed Escrow Instructions, the terms of this Agreement shall control.

2. AGREEMENT TO SELL

Seller hereby agrees to sell, and Buyer hereby agrees to buy from Seller, the Property located at __________ and described in Tax Assessor's Parcel #____________ which is attached hereto as Exhibit "A" and incorporated herein by reference, which exhibit shall subsequently be replaced by a complete and accurate survey as soon as the same is available.

3. PURCHASE PRICE

Buyer agrees to purchase the property for the sum equal of the product of the number of square feet times $______ (which sum is hereinafter called the "purchase price"). The purchase price shall be payable in the following manner:

a) Cash in the amount of _____________ ($______) shall be deposited with escrow holder in an account bearing a minimum of 5¼% interest to Buyer upon the execution of this Agreement and the designation by escrow holder of the "effective date." This payment shall constitute consideration for this contract. This payment shall be refundable except as noted hereinafter. This payment shall become nonrefundable and shall be released to Seller upon Buyer's completing to his satisfaction all items of work outlined in paragraphs 4, 6, 7, and 10. If the Buyer for any reason except as noted in paragraphs 4 and 5 does not release the above payments, this Agreement becomes null and void with no further obligation or liability by either party. Escrow agent shall not release any funds to Seller until Seller has delivered the executed deed as outlined in paragraph 8 herein.

b) The balance of the purchase price, approximately __________ ($_____) shall be deposited in escrow on or before the date of closing and together with the original deposit of ___________

($________) shall constitute 100% of the purchase price pursuant to paragraph 3 herein.

4. TITLE OBLIGATIONS

Within fifteen (15) days from the effective date of this Agreement, Seller shall cause to be delivered to the Buyer, at Seller's sole cost and expense, a current title commitment for an ALTA owner's extended policy of title insurance to be issued by escrow holder, showing the status of title of the Property and all exceptions, including leases, easements, restrictions, rights-of-way, covenants, reservations, and other conditions, if any, affecting the Property, which would appear in an owner's extended policy of title insurance, if issued, and committing to issue such policy of title insurance to Buyer in the full amount of the purchase price for the Property. Accompanying such title commitment, Seller shall also cause to be furnished to Buyer legible copies of all documents, operating agreements, utility agreements, maintenance and management contracts, and any other existing agreements in effect, affecting the Property referred to in such title commitment. Provided Seller has timely provided Buyer with the preliminary title report (and copies of the exceptions), Buyer shall notify Seller of any objections which Buyer may have to the status of title within thirty (30) days from the date Buyer receives such title report. Buyer, at Buyer's sole option, may extend the subsequent dates in this agreement by the amount of time Seller is late delivering this title commitment and accompanying documents to Buyer. If Buyer fails to give such notice of dissatisfactions as to any exception or other matter within such thirty (30)-day period, such exception(s) shall be deemed approved by Buyer. If Buyer disapproves of condition of title, the earnest money deposit shall be returned to Buyer, the Agreement shall terminate, and neither party shall have any liability or obligation to the other. Time is of the essence in this agreement. Should Seller not deliver title commitment within the time frame specified, then all dates in this agreement are automatically extended by the amount of the delay of Seller's submittal.

Seller shall convey marketable title to the property to Buyer by grant deed in fee simple absolute, subject to no exceptions other than those specifically set forth in this Agreement and those approved in writing by Buyer. Any exceptions to title approved in writing by Buyer in the aggregate are referred to herein as "permitted exceptions," and they shall not constitute a breach of Seller's duty to convey marketable title or of Seller's implied covenants of title arising from said deed. Buyer shall be provided, at Seller's cost, at close of escrow a policy of title insurance written by escrow holder on American Land Title Association (ALTA) Title Insurance Policy Standard Form with liability in the amount of the purchase price (hereinafter referred to as "title policy"). Such title policy shall show no exceptions other than the permitted exceptions: the usual printed exceptions and/or conditions and stipulations of the ALTA Standard Form policy.

5. RIGHT OF CANCELLATION

a) Anything to the contrary notwithstanding in this Agreement, including but not limited to paragraphs 3(a) and 4 hereof, Buyer may, for any reason, cancel this Agreement and the escrow provided for herein, at any time within the first thirty (30) days following receipt by Buyer of the preliminary title report to be furnished by Seller. Such cancellation shall be effected by Buyer providing Seller and escrow holder with written notice of election to terminate prior to the expiration of such thirty (30)-day period, in which event escrow holder shall pay to Buyer the initial ________________ ($______) earnest money deposit, at which time this Agreement shall terminate and be of no further force and effect and neither party shall have any further obligation or liability to the other. If Buyer does not cancel this Agreement within such thirty (30)-day period as provided for herein, the initial __________________ ($______) earnest money deposit shall be released to Seller, upon completion and approval by Buyer of items covered in paragraphs 4, 6, 7, and 10. Such cancellation shall be effected by Buyer providing Seller and escrow holder with written notice of election to terminate prior to the expiration of such ___ (__)-day period.

6. RIGHT OF INSPECTION

Buyer shall have ___ (__) days from the effective date of this Agreement at Buyer's sole cost to effect an inspection of the subject property. Buyer and Buyer's engineers, employees, and representatives have the right to enter upon the Property for the purpose of making the necessary investigations, including but not limited to, building inspection, surveying, soils tests, location of utilities, storm drainage, and any other tests Buyer deems necessary. If Buyer shall enter the subject property during the term of this Agreement for any reason whatsoever, Buyer hereby agrees to indemnify and hold Seller harmless from and against any and all claims, liabilities, causes of action, and damages which Seller may have filed against it or may suffer or incur, arising out of or attributable to the entry upon the subject property and the acts thereon of Buyer, its agents, employees, and representatives. Such indemnification shall extend to the costs of litigation incurred by Seller, if any, and to the reasonable attorney's fees which may be expended by Seller in connection therewith.

7. SURVEY

During the first thirty (30) days after the effective date of this Agreement, Seller shall furnish an ALTA As-Built Survey acceptable to escrow holder and Buyer. The contents of the survey and map shall be deemed approved by Buyer unless disapproved by Buyer in writing conveyed to Seller within ten (10) days of the receipt of the survey.

8. PLACING DEED IN ESCROW

On the ____ day after the effective date of this Agreement or Buyer's approval of the Title commitment and prior to escrow holder releasing to Seller, Seller shall execute and deliver to escrow holder the duly executed and acknowledged deed conveying the property to Buyer. Buyer then, subject to having approved all items in paragraphs 3, 4, 5, and 7 within ___ (__) days of the effective date of this Agreement, shall instruct escrow holder to release to Seller the ___________ ($______) earnest money deposit. Said deposit shall be nonrefundable and deemed earned by Seller subject to paragraphs 3, 4, 5, 7, and 23 herein.

9. PLACING PURCHASE PRICE IN ESCROW

Prior to the close of escrow, Buyer shall deliver or cause to be delivered to escrow holder, as set forth in paragraph 3(b) above, cash and all other documents in the amount of the balance of the purchase price inclusive of all deposits plus those closing costs to be paid by Buyer.

10. CONDITIONS PRECEDENT

The following conditions are conditions precedent to Buyer's obligation to consummate its purchase of the property:

a) Seller shall have performed each and every, all and singular, its obligations, and promises contained in this Agreement.

b) Bonds and assessments. Buyer understands that there are no outstanding assessments against the property. Seller shall deliver title to Buyer free of all liens and encumbrances at the close of escrow.

c) Buyer shall give written notice to Seller, through escrow agent, thirty (30) days prior to closing of escrow to vacate the property.

If any of the above conditions precedent shall fail to occur, Buyer's obligation under this Agreement shall terminate by Buyer's giving written notice thereof to Seller and escrow holder. Thereupon, Seller shall instruct escrow holder to return all payments to Buyer, unless forfeited as provided for hereinabove, and both Buyer and Seller agree to execute such documents, releases, and/or instructions as may be necessary to reflect fully the termination of Buyer's obligations hereunder.

The Conditions of Closing are exclusively for the benefit of Buyer, and Buyer may, in writing (at his option), at any time waive any such condition. In the event Buyer shall fail to notify Seller in writing prior to the end of such investigation period that all such Conditions of Closing have occurred or been waived, then this Agreement shall immediately terminate and neither party shall have any further obligation or liability hereunder, and Buyer's deposit of _________ shall be immediately returned to Buyer.

11. CLOSING OF ESCROW

Escrow holder shall not close escrow until it holds the following items in its file:

a) The moneys, documents, and instruments specified in paragraphs 3, 4, 7, 8, and 9 hereof.

b) The title policy insuring that Buyer holds title to the property as of the time of closing escrow and showing the following additional matters:

1) The permitted exceptions; and

2) The usual printed exceptions and/or conditions and stipulations of the title policy.

c) A duplicate original of this Agreement executed by Seller and Buyer.

This escrow shall close within fifteen (15) days of receipt of building permits for Buyer's contemplated project.

d) Notwithstanding anything to the contrary above, Buyer has the right at Buyer's discretion to extend the escrow two times for a period of ______ (__) days each upon payment by Buyer to Seller to escrow of ________________________________ (_________) for each ______ (__)-day extension. Said funds shall be paid into escrow and released to Seller at Buyer's option, and shall be subject to paragraph 23 as additional earnest moneys.

12. CLOSING COSTS AND PRORATION OF EXPENSES

Escrow holder shall pay immediately upon closing the required documentary transfer tax and recording fees on the conveyance charging the same to Buyer. Seller shall pay the title insurance premium for the title policy as set forth in paragraph 4 above. Property taxes shall be prorated as of the date of closing on the basis of the latest available information. The amount of any bond(s) or assessment(s) which is a lien against the property shall be paid in full by Seller as of the date of closing. Seller and Buyer shall share equally in paying the escrow fees of escrow holder. Other charges shall be allocated in the manner customary in _______ County.

13. EXISTING INFORMATION

Seller shall provide Buyer with all existing information in Seller's possession, including, but not limited to, Engineering, Civil and Geology, Land Plans, Architecture, Appraisals, Market Studies, and potential leases within 48 hours from opening of escrow. If Buyer fails to complete this purchase, all items delivered hereunder shall be immediately returned to Seller.

14. REPRESENTATIONS

All of Seller's representations stated in this Agreement and in any addendum attached hereto shall be true and correct as of the date of execution of this Agreement, and Seller shall notify Buyer immediately in writing if at any time prior to Close of Escrow, Seller believes that it would not be able to make any one or more of the representations provided herein. All of Seller's representations shall be true and correct as of the date of Close of Escrow and shall survive Close of Escrow. Seller hereby represents as follows:

a) Seller is the owner of and has full right, power, and authority to sell, convey, and transfer the Property to Buyer as provided in this Agreement and to carry out Seller's obligations under this Agreement and shall convey to Buyer at Close of Escrow marketable fee title to the Property, free and clear of all liens, assessments, covenants, conditions, restrictions, easements, encroachments, leases, rights of third parties, encumbrances, exceptions, and other title defects.

b) Until Close of Escrow, Seller shall maintain the Property in its present condition, and shall not enter into any lease of the Property or any contracts or agreements pertaining to the Property without first obtaining the prior written consent of Buyer.

c) Seller has not received any notice and has no knowledge of:

1) Any requirement by any governmental authority requiring that expenditures be made in connection with the Property;

2) The widening of the streets adjacent to the Property;

3) Any proceeding to change the zoning applicable to assessments upon all or any part of the Property. To the best of Seller's knowledge, the Property is in full compliance with all applicable building codes, environmental zoning, subdivision, and land use laws and any other applicable local, state, and federal laws and regulations.

d) To the best of Seller's knowledge, the Property does not contain and no activity upon the Property has produced any hazardous or toxic waste, deposit, or contamination which violates any federal, state, local, or other governmental law, regulation, or order or requires reporting to any governmental authority. See paragraph 16.

e) To the best of Seller's knowledge, there exists no management, maintenance, operating, service, or any other contract of similar nature, commitments, agreements, or obligations of any kind, written or oral, affecting the Property which would be binding upon Buyer after Close of Escrow except those enumerated in the title report and approved by buyer as permitted exceptions.

f) To the best of Seller's knowledge, there are no existing actions, suits, or proceedings pending or threatened against or involving the Property.

g) To the best of Seller's knowledge, Seller has not filed or been the subject of any filing of a petition under the Federal Bankruptcy Code or any insolvency laws, or any laws for composition of indebtedness or the reorganization of debtors.

h) To the best of Seller's knowledge, Seller has obtained all licenses, permits, easements, and rights-of-way requested for the normal use and operation of the Property and to ensure vehicular and pedestrian ingress and egress from the Property.

i) To the best of Seller's knowledge, all documents submitted to Buyer for Buyer's review shall be true, correct, complete, and not misleading, and Buyer shall be immediately notified if any documents are altered, amended, modified, terminated, or canceled.

j) At the Close of Escrow, there are no sums due, owing, or unpaid for labor or materials furnished to the Property at the request of Seller which might give rise to mechanics', material men's, or other liens attaching to the Property.

k) There exists no breach nor any state of facts which with the passage of time, the giving of notice, or both would constitute a default under any contract which relates to the Property and will be assumed by Buyer at Close of Escrow.

15. DOCUMENTATION

Prior to Close of Escrow, Seller shall furnish Buyer any and all documentation required by Internal Revenue Code 1445 ("1445"), including without limitation a Certificate of Non-Foreign Status. Seller further agrees that in the event that Seller does not furnish Buyer a

Certificate of Non-Foreign Status, Buyer is authorized to withhold and deduct from the Purchase Price any and all amounts required by 1445 and transfer said sum within ten (10) days to the Internal Revenue Service.

16. HAZARDOUS WASTE

Seller warrants that, to the best of Seller's knowledge, no toxic materials have been stored on or under the soil, used, or disposed of on the property; nor have toxic materials migrated on or into the subject property, including but not limited to asbestos, heavy metal, petroleum products, solvents, pesticides, or herbicides, unless otherwise disclosed in writing to Buyer. Seller agrees to indemnify, defend, and hold Buyer harmless from and against any claims, costs, liabilities, causes of action, and fees, including attorney's fees, arising from the storage use or disposal of existence of any toxic materials on the Property which result in contamination or deterioration of ground water or soil at a level of contamination greater than established by any governmental agency having appropriate jurisdiction.

In the event that the soil, subsoil, ground water, or other constituent parts of the Property are determined contaminated as provided above, Buyer shall have the option to either (a) require Seller to clean up and otherwise restore the soil, subsoil, ground water, or other constituent parts of the Property to a condition which would comply with the requirements of any governmental agency or body having any jurisdiction over the property, or (b) terminate this agreement without further liabilities on the part of either party. In the event of such termination, the Deposit shall be returned to Buyer. Buyer and Seller acknowledge that neither Broker nor its salespeople have made any representations regarding the absence of toxic materials on the property, and further warrant that neither Broker nor its salespeople are qualified to detect the presence of toxic materials on the property.

17. COOPERATION

Seller agrees to fully cooperate with Buyer and to use its best efforts in obtaining all governmental approvals, to execute all necessary applications and related documents in such form as may be required by such governmental authorities, all without cost to Seller.

18. LIQUIDATED DAMAGES

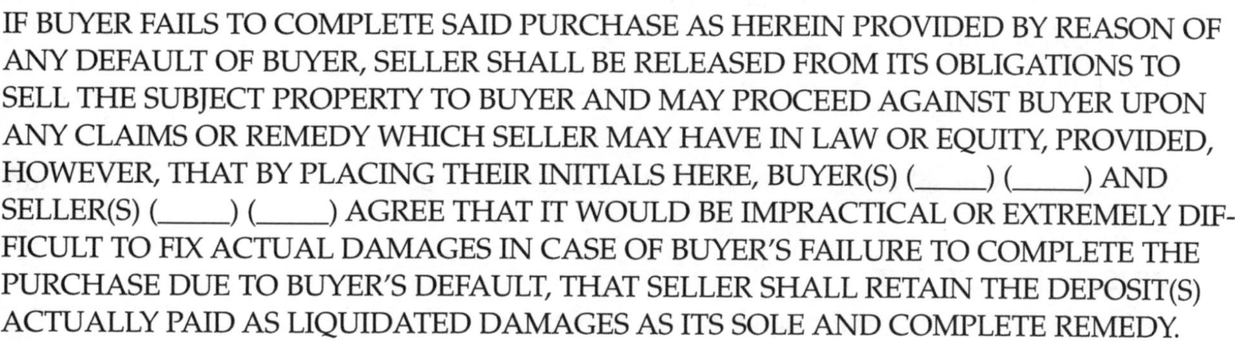

IF BUYER FAILS TO COMPLETE SAID PURCHASE AS HEREIN PROVIDED BY REASON OF ANY DEFAULT OF BUYER, SELLER SHALL BE RELEASED FROM ITS OBLIGATIONS TO SELL THE SUBJECT PROPERTY TO BUYER AND MAY PROCEED AGAINST BUYER UPON ANY CLAIMS OR REMEDY WHICH SELLER MAY HAVE IN LAW OR EQUITY, PROVIDED, HOWEVER, THAT BY PLACING THEIR INITIALS HERE, BUYER(S) (_____) (_____) AND SELLER(S) (_____) (_____) AGREE THAT IT WOULD BE IMPRACTICAL OR EXTREMELY DIFFICULT TO FIX ACTUAL DAMAGES IN CASE OF BUYER'S FAILURE TO COMPLETE THE PURCHASE DUE TO BUYER'S DEFAULT, THAT SELLER SHALL RETAIN THE DEPOSIT(S) ACTUALLY PAID AS LIQUIDATED DAMAGES AS ITS SOLE AND COMPLETE REMEDY.

19. SIGNS

Buyer shall be allowed to place marketing signs upon the property.

20. DISTRIBUTION OF TITLE POLICY

Escrow holder shall distribute to Buyer as immediately as possible after Close of Escrow the Buyer's policy of title insurance mentioned above.

21. POSSESSION

Possession of the property shall be delivered to Buyer at closing. Notwithstanding the foregoing, at any time or times prior to closing, Buyer, its agents, and its contractors shall have the right to enter upon and inspect the property, testing the physical properties thereof and evaluating the feasibility of development activity thereon as set forth in paragraph 6 above.

22. AMENDED ESCROW INSTRUCTIONS

Amended or additional instructions may be received into escrow at any time until escrow is ready to close. To be effective, such amended or additional instructions must be in writing and signed by both Buyer and Seller. Buyer and Seller agree to execute such other documents and papers consistent with the provisions of this Agreement as may be required by escrow holder to complete escrow.

23. ENTIRE AGREEMENT

The terms of this Agreement contain the entire agreement between the parties and supersede any and all previous agreements. No representation, covenant, agreement, or condition not included herein has been or is relied upon by either of the parties.

24. WAIVER

Any condition contained herein for the benefit of either one of the parties may be waived only by the party to be benefited.

25. REAL ESTATE COMMISSIONS

Commission shall be the sole obligation of the Seller. Buyer and Seller agree that they are as follows and shall be paid from proceeds of escrow:

Commission amount: ______________________________________

Paid as follows: ____

26. MULTIPLE ORIGINALS

This Agreement may be executed in one or more counterparts, each of which shall be deemed an original.

27. TIME IS OF THE ESSENCE

Time is of the essence in the performance of this Agreement.

28. BINDING EFFECT

This Agreement is binding upon the parties hereto and upon their successors and assigns.

29. NOTICES

Any notice or written direction required or designed to be given pursuant to this Agreement may be given personally or by United States mail, certified mail, return receipt requested, with postage thereon fully prepaid, addressed to Buyer at:

[INSERT BUYER'S NAME] ______________________

Address ________________________________

____

Phone Numbers ___________________________

Fax ____________________ E-mail ____________________

To Seller at:

[INSERT SELLER'S NAME] ______________________

Address ________________________________

____

Phone Numbers ___________________________

Fax ____________________ E-mail ____________________

To escrow holder at:
[INSERT ESCROW HOLDER'S NAME] ______________________

Address ________________________________

____

Phone Numbers ___________________________

Fax ____________________ E-mail ____________________

or to such other address as either party may designate from time to time by written notice to the other. The date of service of such notices, certificates, documents, statements, or requests required by this Agreement shall be the date such notices are received as evidenced by the return receipt or the date such notices are refused if such be the case.

30. ATTORNEY'S FEES

If either party to this Agreement resorts to legal action to enforce any of the terms or provisions hereof or to recover damages for the breach hereof, the prevailing party shall be entitled to recover reasonable attorneys' fees, court costs, and other expenses incurred from the unsuccessful party.

31. ASSIGNMENT

Seller agrees that Buyer may assign its rights under this Agreement to other persons or entities and it will deliver title to such nominee upon written notice prior to Close of Escrow of the identity of the nominee taking title. Seller agrees that this Agreement shall be binding on its heirs, assigns, and successors.

32. RECORDATION

If Buyer records this Agreement, Buyer shall simultaneously deliver an executed quitclaim deed to the escrow holder to be recorded by the escrow holder upon termination of this Agreement or default by Buyer.

33. COVENANT TO SIGN DOCUMENTS

Within five (5) days of presentation thereof, Buyer and Seller agree to execute such other documents as may be required.

34. EXPIRATION

This Agreement expires if Seller's written acceptance or response is not received by Buyer on or before ________________ at 5:00 p.m.

35. EXTENDED CLOSING

Buyer may, at Buyer's sole option, extend the closing date of this agreement by 90 days. To exercise this option, Buyer must notify escrow holder and Seller in writing no later than 30 days prior to the scheduled closing and pay into escrow an additional Fifty Thousand and no/00 Dollars ($50,000.00) earnest money. This additional earnest money deposit shall immediately be released by escrow holder to Seller as additional liquidated damages pursuant to article 18 herein. This additional deposit (shall/shall not) accrue to the purchase price at the close of escrow.

SIGNATURES

Buyer: [INSERT BUYER'S NAME] ________________________________

by ________________________________ Date ________________

Seller: [INSERT SELLER'S NAME] ________________________________

by ________________________________ Date ________________

EFFECTIVE DATE

This Agreement, fully executed by Seller and Buyer, together with the cash deposit, has been received by escrow holder on the date specified below. Such items, together with the deposits to be received within five (5) days of the effective date, will be held in escrow and handled by escrow holder pursuant to this Agreement by the undersigned escrow agent. Escrow agent accepts this Agreement as its escrow instructions without the necessity of executing its standard printed form of escrow instructions.

Effective Date: ____________________

Agreed and Accepted by: [INSERT TITLE COMPANY]

____

Escrow Officer

NOTARY PAGE

Insert Notary Blocks for all signatures

EXHIBITS

Attach the following exhibits:
A. Property Description
B. List of Leases

APPENDIX

C

Commercial Lease

For and in consideration of the rental and of the covenants and agreements hereinafter set forth to be kept and performed by the Lessee, Landlord hereby leases to Lessee and Lessee hereby leases from Landlord the Premises herein described for the term, at the rental, and subject to and upon all of the terms, covenants, and agreements hereinafter set forth.

ARTICLE 1. SUMMARY OF CERTAIN LEASE PROVISIONS

DATE OF EXECUTION: [INSERT DATE]

LANDLORD/LESSOR: [INSERT LANDLORD'S NAME]

TENANT/LESSEE: [INSERT TENANT/LESSEE'S NAME]

GUARANTOR(S): [INSERT GUARANTOR'S/GUARANTORS' NAME(S)]

TENANT'S TRADE NAME: [INSERT TENANT'S TRADE NAME]

LEASE TERM: Five [5] years. Provided Lessee has not defaulted under any terms and conditions of the lease, Landlord will extend for two [2] five [5]-year options.

If and in the event Lessee wishes to exercise an option to renew the lease, Lessee shall give written notice to Landlord one hundred twenty (120) days before the expiration of the then current term. Tenant's failure to provide timely notice to Landlord shall be interpreted by Landlord as Tenant's rejection of any and all remaining options and Landlord shall be free to seek other tenants or make other arrangements for the Premises without any liability or further obligation to Lessee. (*Use for leases with options only!*)

MINIMUM RENT: Minimum monthly rent on a triple net basis.

Years 1-5	$_____/SF/Year	[$____/SF/Month]
Years 6-10	$_____/SF/Year	[$____/SF/Month]
Years 11-15	$_____/SF/Year	[$____/SF/Month]

As additional rent, Lessee shall pay its pro rata share of real property taxes, insurance, and common area expenses on a pro rata basis per *Article 6* herein, subject to the CPI adjustment in *Exhibit "C."*

PERCENTAGE RENT: None

SECURITY DEPOSIT: First month's rent $________ plus a security deposit of $____________.

APPROXIMATE SIZE OF PREMISES: Tenant's premises shall contain approximately ______ square feet. The final square footage and layout will be determined by a mutually approved space plan.

USE OF PREMISES: The primary business shall be a ________________________________.

ADDRESSES FOR NOTICES:

To Landlord: [INSERT LANDLORD'S NAME]

[INSERT ADDRESS AND PHONE NUMBERS]

To Lessee(s): [INSERT LESSEE'S/LESSEES' NAME(S)]

[INSERT ADDRESS AND PHONE NUMBERS]

EXHIBITS:
A. Site Plan
B. Construction
C. CPI Adjustment and Acknowledgment of Commencement
D. Signs
E. Lessee Offset and Estoppel Certificate
F. Guarantor's Obligations
G. Special Conditions

Exhibits "A" through "G" are incorporated herein by this reference as if set forth at length.

The foregoing is a summary only and reference should always be made to the full Lease provisions. References have been provided for convenience and designate some, but not necessarily all, of the other Articles and/or Sections where references to the particular Summary of Certain Lease Provisions appear. Each reference in this Lease to any of the summarized lease provisions contained in this ***Article 1*** shall be construed to incorporate all of the terms provided under each summarized lease provision and in case of any conflict with the balance of the Lease, the latter shall control.

ARTICLE 2. PREMISES

a) Landlord hereby leases to Lessee and Lessee hereby leases from Landlord that certain space (the "Premises") indicated on *Exhibit "A"* hereto, the Premises being agreed, for the purpose of this Lease, to have an area of approximately _______ square feet and being situated in that Building (as hereinafter defined) known as _________________ [INSERT ADDRESS] located on the property described on *Exhibit "A"* hereto and depicted on the project site plan attached as *Exhibit "A"* hereto.

b) This Lease is subject to the terms, covenants, and conditions herein set forth and Lessee covenants as a material part of the consideration for this Lease to keep and perform each and all of said terms, covenants, and conditions by it to be kept and performed and that this Lease is made upon the condition of said performance.

c) The Premises shall be used solely for ___________

ARTICLE 3. TERM

The term of this Lease shall be for three years, commencing (except as provided in *Exhibit "C"* hereto) on ______________ (the date of commencement of the Lease term, sometimes herein called the "Commencement Date") and, unless sooner terminated in accordance with the terms hereof, ending on ______________, or if, under *Exhibit "C"* hereto, the Commencement Date is other than the date specified above, ending on the_______ anniversary of the Commencement Date of this Lease as determined under *Exhibit "C"* hereto.

ARTICLE 4. POSSESSION

a) If Landlord, for any reason whatsoever, cannot deliver possession of the Premises to Lessee on the Commencement Date of the term hereof, this Lease shall not be void or voidable, nor shall Landlord be liable to Lessee for any loss or damage resulting therefrom, and the expiration date of the above term shall be extended for an equal period so the term of the Lease shall be as indicated in *Article 3* above, but in that event, all rent shall be abated during the period between the Commencement Date of said term and the time when Landlord delivers possession. If within twenty-four (24) months from the date of execution hereof Landlord has not delivered the premises to Lessee this Lease shall be automatically terminated with no liability to Landlord or Lessee.

b) In the event Landlord shall permit Lessee to occupy the Premises prior to the

Commencement Date of the term, such occupancy shall be subject to all the provisions of this Lease and the term of the Lease shall expire, unless sooner terminated in accordance with the terms hereof, on the _______ anniversary of the date of occupancy by Lessee.

ARTICLE 5. RENT AND RENT ADJUSTMENT

a) Lessee agrees to pay Landlord at such place as Landlord may designate without deduction, offset, prior notice, or demand and Landlord agrees to accept as rent for the Premises the total sum of $____________ in lawful money of the United Stated in monthly installments of $____________ payable in advance on the first day of each month during the term of this Lease, except that the rent installment for the first full calendar month shall be paid upon execution of this Lease. The rent for any portion of any calendar month of the term preceding the first full calendar month shall be paid on the first day of the first full calendar month. The rent payable for any portion of a calendar month included in the term of the Lease shall be a pro rata portion of the rent payable for a full calendar month. The date for commencement of Lease rent shall be the Commencement Date except as provided to the contrary in *Article 4* hereof.

b) Lessee shall also pay Landlord a sum equal to the aggregate of any municipal, city, county, state, or federal excise, sales, use, gross receipts, or transaction privilege taxes now or hereafter levied or imposed, directly or indirectly, against or on account of the amounts payable hereunder or the receipt thereof by Landlord, which sum shall be paid with each installment of rent as hereinabove provided.

c) Lessee has deposited with Landlord the sum of $__________ as security for the full and faithful performance of each and every provision of this Lease. If at any time Lessee shall be in default with respect to any term, covenant, condition, or provision of this Lease, including without limitation any payment of rent or payment of any other sums due Landlord as and for any other purpose whatsoever, Landlord may, but shall be under no obligation to, use, apply, or retain all or part of the security deposit for payment of rent or any other sum in default, or for payment of any other amount which Landlord may spend or become obligated to spend because of Tenant's default, including without limitation the repair of damage, or to compensate Landlord for any other loss or damage which Landlord may suffer because of Tenant's default. In such event Lessee shall on demand pay to Landlord as additional security an amount sufficient to restore the security deposit to its original amount, and Tenant's failure to do so shall be a material breach of this Lease. If Lessee is not in default at the termination of this Lease, Landlord shall return the deposit to Lessee, except any portion used as a cleaning fee as hereafter provided. Landlord shall not be required to keep this security deposit separate from its general funds, and Lessee shall not be entitled to interest on such deposit. Landlord may use a reasonable portion of this deposit as a non-refundable cleaning fee [not to exceed $100.00] to clean the Premises upon any termination (by expiration of term, default, or otherwise) of this Lease.

d) Lessee shall be entitled to reasonable parking in common with other tenants of the Building. Lessee agrees not to overburden the parking facilities and agrees to cooperate with Landlord and other tenants in the use of parking facilities. Landlord reserves the right in its absolute discretion to determine whether parking facilities are becoming overcrowded and in such event to allocate parking spaces among Lessee and other tenants. Landlord may also require Lessee and its employees to obtain parking off the site of the Building and adjacent parking areas in the event Tenant's customers, clients, or invitees appear to be using for their own purposes the number of parking spaces that would otherwise be attributable to a reasonable number of spaces for Tenant's use. There will be no assigned parking.

e) If the term of this Lease is greater than one year, then the rent payable under subparagraph a. of this *Article 4* and *Exhibit "C"* shall be subject to adjustment as hereinafter provided for in *Exhibit "C"* herein.

ARTICLE 6. ADDITIONAL RENT: DIRECT OPERATING EXPENSE

a) Commencing with the first month of the term of this Lease, Lessee shall pay to Landlord monthly within three (3) days of demand as additional rent its pro rata share of any Direct Expenses (as hereinafter defined) for the operation and maintenance of the Building as such Direct Expenses are estimated by Landlord. Tenant's pro rata share of any such estimated expenses shall equal a sum obtained by multiplying the Direct Expenses as estimated by Landlord for the month for which the demand is made times a percentage obtained by dividing the total square footage contained in the Building into the total square footage contained in the Premises leased to Lessee herein.

b) The term "Direct Expenses" as used herein includes all direct costs of operation and maintenance of the buildings, real property, and improvements of which the Premises are a part, as determined by standard accounting practices, including without limitation the following costs by way of illustration: real property taxes and assessments; water and sewer charges; insurance premiums; utilities; security; window washing; trash removal; costs incurred in the management of the Building and property, if any, including administrative overhead or property management fees not exceeding ten percent (10%) of gross expenses; reserves for replacement of machinery and equipment; supplies; materials; equipment and tools; costs of maintenance and upkeep and replacement when required of all landscaping, parking, and common areas. ("Direct Expenses" shall not include depreciation on the Building or equipment therein, loan payments, executive salaries, or real estate brokers' commissions.)

Following the end of each calendar quarter, Landlord shall submit to Lessee a statement of the actual Direct Expenses for the preceding calendar quarter. If the payments made by Lessee, as provided hereinabove, for said preceding calendar quarter based upon Landlord's estimate of Direct Expenses were less than Tenant's share (based upon the formula provided hereinabove) of the actual Direct Expenses, Lessee shall pay the difference by the date the next regular monthly rent payment is due. If said payments made by Lessee were more than Tenant's share of the actual Direct Expenses, the overpayment by Lessee shall, so long as Lessee is not then in default and Landlord has no claim against Lessee for any prior default, be credited against the next monthly rent falling due. The estimates of Direct Expenses by Landlord as well as the quarterly statements of actual Direct Expenses may each contain, in the case of items such as, but not limited to, property taxes and insurance premiums which may be paid less frequently than monthly, an allocation for each month based on the actual cost (or if the actual amounts are not known, Landlord's estimate thereof) of such items. If an estimated amount for any such item is used in a quarterly statement of actual Direct Expenses, then, at such time as the actual amount is known, it shall be set forth in the next quarterly statement of actual Direct Expenses prepared by Landlord and shall be reflected in the adjustment described above. If the Lease commences on other than the first day of a calendar month or expires on other than the last day of a calendar month, any amount due under this *Article* shall be prorated based upon the number of days during the month which were included in the term of the Lease.

c) Lessee hereby acknowledges that late payment by Lessee to Landlord of Rent and other sums due hereunder will cause Landlord to incur costs not contemplated by this Lease, the exact amount of which are unknown and will be extremely difficult to ascertain other than such charges and late charges which may be imposed on Landlord by the terms of any mortgage or trust deed covering the Premises. Accordingly, if any installment of Rent or any other sums due from Lessee shall not be received by Landlord or Landlord's designee within ten (10) days after such amount shall be due, Lessee shall pay to Landlord, in addition to the late charges incurred by Landlord under any mortgage or deed of trust covering the Premises, a late charge equal to ten percent (10%) of the amount(s) past due and additionally all such installments of Rent or other sums due shall bear interest at the rate provided for on Past Due Obligations as provided in *Article 11* from the date the same became due and payable. The parties hereby agree that such late charge represents fair and reasonable estimate of the costs Landlord will incur by reason of late payment by Lessee. Acceptance of such late charge by Landlord shall in no event constitute a waiver of Tenant's default with respect to such overdue amount, nor prevent Landlord from exercising any of the rights and remedies granted hereunder.

d) Accordingly, if any installment of Rent or any other sums due from Lessee shall not be received by Landlord or Landlord's designee within ten (10) days after such amount shall be due, Landlord shall give Lessee written notice of Lessee's non-payment of rent. Lessee shall have three working days from the date of Landlord's written notice to cure the late payment. Upon failure of Lessee to cure, Landlord may declare Lessee to be in default under this lease pursuant to *Article 11* hereto.

ARTICLE 7. ASSIGNMENT AND SUBLETTING

Lessee shall not, either voluntarily or by operation of law, assign, transfer, mortgage, pledge, hypothecate, or encumber this Lease or any interest therein, and shall not sublet the Premises or any part thereof, or any right or privilege appurtenant thereto, or suffer any other person (the officers, employees, agents, servants, invitees, and guests of Lessee excepted) to occupy or use the Premises, or any portion thereof, without the written consent of Landlord first had and obtained, which consent shall not be unreasonably withheld. Any such assignment or subletting without such consent shall be void, and shall, at the option of the Landlord, constitute a default under this Lease. Regardless of Landlord's consent, no subletting or assignment shall release Lessee or Tenant's obligation to pay the rent and to perform all other obligations to be performed by Lessee hereunder for the term of this Lease. The acceptance of rent by Landlord from any other person shall not be deemed to be a waiver of any provision hereof. Without regard to whether Landlord consents to an assignment or a subletting, if Lessee or any assignee or sublessee assigns this Lease or sublets the Premises or any portion thereof for a rental rate greater than that paid to Landlord, such excess shall be paid to Landlord.

ARTICLE 8. INSURANCE

a) Lessee shall, at Tenant's expense, obtain and keep in force during the term of this Lease a policy of comprehensive general public liability insurance insuring Landlord and Lessee (naming Landlord as an additional named insured) against any liability arising out of the use, occupancy, maintenance, repair, or improvement of the Premises and all areas appurtenant thereto including without limitation coverage against "occurrences." Such insurance shall provide single limit liability coverage of not less than $1,000,000 per occurrence for bodily injury or death and property damage. The limits of said insurance shall not, however, limit the liability of the Lessee hereunder, and Lessee is responsible for ensuring that the amount of liability insurance carried by Lessee is sufficient for Tenant's purposes. Lessee may carry said insurance under a blanket policy, providing, however, said insurance by Lessee shall have a Landlord's protective liability endorsement attached thereto in form and substance satisfactory to Landlord. If Lessee shall fail to procure and maintain said insurance, Landlord may, but shall not be required to, procure and maintain same but at the expense of Lessee. Insurance required hereunder shall be in companies rated A+, AAA, or better in *Best's Insurance Guide*. Lessee shall deliver to Landlord prior to occupancy of the Premises copies of policies of liability insurance required herein or certificates evidencing the existence and amounts of such insurance with evidence satisfactory to Landlord of payment of premiums and thereafter within thirty (30) days after any demand therefore by Landlord. No policy shall be cancelable or subject to reduction of coverage except after thirty (30) days prior written notice to Landlord and Landlord's lender. Lessee acknowledges and agrees that insurance coverage carried by Landlord will not cover Tenant's property within the Premises or the Building and that Lessee shall be responsible, at Tenant's sole cost or expense, for providing insurance coverage for Tenant's movable equipment, furnishings, trade fixtures, and other personal property in or upon the Premises or the Building, and for any alterations, additions, or improvements to or of the Premises or any part thereof made by Lessee, in the event of damage or loss thereto from any cause whatsoever. Lessee shall furnish Landlord with renewals or "binders" of any such policy at least ten (10) days prior to the expiration thereof.

b) **Rent Loss Endorsement.** Landlord may at its option require that the above described policies of insurance shall be written with rent loss endorsements in favor of Landlord in amounts sufficient to pay Tenant's obligations hereunder including, without limitation, the Minimum Rent, Promotional Costs, insurance premiums, taxes, Common Area expenses and utility costs excluding only Tenant's and/or Landlord's avoided costs.

ARTICLE 9. SERVICES AND UTILITIES

Provided that Lessee is not in default hereunder, Landlord agrees to furnish to the Premises during reasonable hours of generally recognized business days, to be determined by Landlord in its sole discretion, and subject to the rules and regulations of the Building, the parking areas and common entries in the Building. Landlord shall not be liable for, and Lessee shall not be entitled to, any reduction or abatement of rental by reason of Landlord's failure to furnish any of the foregoing when such failure is caused by casualty, Act of God, accident, breakage, repairs, strikes, lockouts, or other labor disturbances or labor disputes of any character, or by any other cause, similar or dissimilar, beyond the reasonable control of Landlord. Landlord shall not be liable under any circumstances for injury to or death of or loss or damage to persons or property or damage to Tenant's business, however occurring, through or in connection with or incidental to failure to furnish any of the foregoing.

ARTICLE 10. HOLDING OVER

If Lessee remains in possession of the Premises or any part thereof after the expiration of the term hereof, with the express written consent of Landlord, such occupancy shall be a tenancy from month to month at a rental, payable monthly in advance, in double the amount of the last monthly rental, plus all other charges payable hereunder and upon all the terms hereof applicable to a month-to-month tenancy. In such case, either party may thereafter terminate this Lease at any time upon giving not less than thirty (30) days' written notice to the other party.

ARTICLE 11. DEFAULT

The occurrence of any one or more of the following events ("Events of Default") shall constitute a material default and breach of this Lease by Lessee.

a) The vacating or abandonment of the Premises by Lessee.

b) The failure by Lessee to make any payment of rent or any other payment required to be made by Lessee hereunder, as and when due, where such failure shall continue for a period of three (3) days after written notice thereof by Landlord to Lessee.

c) The failure by Lessee to observe or perform any of the covenants, conditions, or provisions of this Lease to be observed or performed by Lessee, other than as described in *paragraphs a, b, or d of this Article 11,* where such failure shall continue for a period of thirty (30) days are reasonably required for its cure, then Lessee shall not be deemed to be in default if Lessee commences such cure within said thirty (30) day period and thereafter diligently prosecutes such cure to completion, and if Lessee provides Landlord with such security as Landlord may require to fully compensate Landlord for any loss or liability to which Landlord might be exposed.

d) The making by Lessee of any general assignment or general arrangement for the benefit of creditors; or the filing by or against Lessee of a petition to have Lessee adjudged a bankrupt, or a petition for reorganization or arrangement under any law, now existing or hereafter amended or enacted, relating to bankruptcy or insolvency (unless, in the case of a petition filed against Lessee, Lessee has not consented to, or admitted the material allegation of said petition and said petition is dismissed within sixty [60] days); or the appointment of a trustee or a receiver (other than in a bankruptcy or insolvency proceeding) to take possession of substantially all of Tenant's assets located at the Premises or of Tenant's interest in this Lease, where possession is not restored to Lessee within thirty (30) days; or the attachment, execution, or other judicial seizure of substantially all of Tenant's assets located at the Premises or of Tenant's interest in this Lease, where such seizure is not discharged in thirty (30) days; or if Lessee becomes insolvent within the meaning of the federal bankruptcy code.

ARTICLE 12. REMEDIES UPON DEFAULT

a) In the event of any such Event of Default then, and in any such event (regardless of the pendency of any proceeding which has or might have the effect of preventing Lessee from curing such Default), Landlord, at any time thereafter, may invoke, simultaneously or successively, any one or more of the powers, rights, and remedies set forth in this Lease and/or which Landlord may now or hereafter have at law or in equity or by statute or otherwise. "Default" as used in this Lease shall mean any condition or event which constitutes or which, after notice or lapse of time, or both, as provided in *Article 11*, would constitute an Event of Default.

b) If an Event of Default shall have occurred, Landlord may, at any time thereafter, either:

1) Terminate this Lease by written notice to Lessee, or

2) Re-enter the Premises by summary proceedings or otherwise, with or without terminating this Lease, remove all persons and property from the Premises without liability to any person for damages sustained by reason of such removal and relet, in the name of Landlord or Lessee or otherwise, the Premises at such rental and upon such other terms and conditions (which may include, without limitation, concessions, or free rent) as Landlord in its sole discretion may deem advisable. In such event, Lessee shall remain liable for all rent, additional rent, and all other obligations hereunder plus the reasonable cost of obtaining possession of and reletting the Premises and of any repairs and alterations, including without limitation replacement of or changes in Lessee improvements, necessary to prepare them for reletting, less the rents received from such reletting, if any. Any and all monthly deficiencies so payable by Lessee shall be paid monthly on the date

herein provided for the payment of rent. Notwithstanding any such reletting without termination, Landlord may at any time thereafter elect to terminate this Lease for such previous breach.

Should Landlord at any time terminate this Lease for any breach, in addition to any other remedies it may have, it may recover from Lessee all damages it may incur by reason of such breach, including, without limitation, the cost of recovering the Premises (including without limitation reasonable attorneys' fees), the portion of the leasing commission paid by Landlord in connection with this Lease and applicable to the unexpired term of this Lease, and including the worth at the time of such termination of the excess, if any, of the amount of rent and charges equivalent to rent reserved in this Lease for the remainder of the term over the reasonable rental value of the Premises for the remainder of the term, all of which amounts shall be immediately due and payable from Lessee to Landlord. No re-entry of taking possession of the Premises by Landlord shall be construed as an election of its part to terminate this Lease unless a written notice of such intention be given to Lessee.

All amounts due Landlord under this *Article* shall bear interest at the rate of twelve percent (12%) per annum from the date due until paid. In addition to the foregoing remedies and so long as this Lease is not terminated, Landlord shall have the right but not the obligation to remedy any default of Lessee and to add to the rent payable hereunder all of Landlord's reasonable costs in so doing, with interest thereon until the same is repaid at the rate of the lower of twelve percent (12%) per annum or the maximum rate then allowed by law.

All remedies herein conferred upon Landlord shall be cumulative and not exclusive of any other remedy conferred herein or at law or in equity. If Lessee is in default, Landlord may prevent removal of property from the Premises by any lawful means it deems necessary to protect its interests.

ARTICLE 13. COVENANTS TO OPERATE

a) Lessee covenants and agrees that, continuously and uninterruptedly from and after the commencement of the term of this Lease, it will operate and conduct within the Premises the business which it is permitted to operate and conduct under the provisions hereof, except while the Premises are untenantable by reason of fire or other casualty, and that it will at all times keep and maintain within and upon the Premises an adequate stock of merchandise and trade fixtures to service and supply the usual and ordinary demands and requirements of its customers and to maximize sales volume upon the Premises and that it will keep its Premises in a neat, clean, and orderly condition.

b) Lessee shall refrain from dumping, disposal, reduction, incineration, or other burning of trash, papers, refuse, or garbage of any kind in or about the Premises. Lessee shall store all trash and garbage within the Premises or at a location designated by Landlord in covered metal containers so located as not to be visible to customers or business invitees in the Shopping Center. Lessee shall also arrange for and bear the expense of the prompt and regular removal of such trash and garbage from the Premises. Landlord may provide central trash removal facilities for Lessee and Lessee shall pay costs upon demand for such removal on a pro rata basis, providing such costs to Lessee are not more than if Lessee made its own arrangements for trash removal with a reputable firm. Landlord may include such costs and expenses thereof in the Common Area costs.

c) Lessee shall complete, or cause to be completed, all deliveries, loading, unloading, and services to the Premises, during times designated by Landlord, and in a manner that will not interfere with Landlord, other tenants, or employees or customers of Landlord or other tenants, nor shall Lessee permit delivery vehicles to park in front of the customer entrances to any shops, between the hours of 10:00 a.m. and 6:00 p.m. of each day. Landlord reserves the right to further regulate the activities of Lessee in regard to deliveries and servicing of the Premises, and Lessee further agrees to abide by such further nondiscriminatory regulations of Landlord.

d) Commencing with the opening for business by Lessee in the Premises and for the remainder of the term of this Lease, Lessee shall conduct its business in the leased Premises and will keep the leased Premises open for business not less than the following hours: 10:00 a.m. to 6:00 p.m. Monday through Saturday, except for Thanksgiving, Christmas, and January 1. In no event shall Lessee remain open for business longer hours than any anchor store without Landlord's written permission.

e) Lessee agrees that it will not, during the term of this Lease, directly or indirectly, operate or own any similar type of business within a radius of two (2) miles from the location of the Premises. The preceding sentence shall not apply to any such similar business which Lessee owns or operates on the execution date of this Lease, the existence of which was previously disclosed to Landlord. Without limiting Landlord's remedies in the event Lessee should violate this covenant, Landlord may, at its option, include the "net sales" of such other business in the "net sales" transacted from the Premises for the purpose of computing the Percentage Rent due hereunder.

ARTICLE 14. AMERICANS WITH DISABILITIES ACT

Lessee shall, at all times during the term of this Lease, and at Tenant's sole cost and expense, maintain and keep the Property in full compliance with the Americans with Disability Act of 1990, Public Law No. 101-336, 42 U.S.C. § 12101 et seq. (the "ADA"), for its intended use by Lessee as approved herein. Lessee shall indemnify, defend, and hold Landlord harmless from and against any and all claims arising from noncompliance or alleged noncompliance with the provisions of ADA in effect during the term hereof, including any extensions and renewals, and from and against all costs, attorneys' fees, expenses, and liabilities incurred in or from any such claim. Lessee, upon notice from Landlord, shall defend the same at Tenant's expense by counsel reasonably satisfactory to Landlord. Lessee, as a material part of the consideration to Landlord, hereby waives all claims in respect thereof against Landlord.

ARTICLE 15. BROKERS

Lessee warrants that it has had no dealings with any real estate broker or agents in connection with the negotiations of this Lease, excepting only Rider Land & Development LLC, and that it knows of no other real estate broker or agent who is entitled to a commission in connection with this Lease. Lessee agrees to indemnify and hold Landlord harmless from and against any and all claims, demands, losses, liabilities, lawsuits, judgments, and costs and expenses (including without limitation reasonable attorneys' fees) with respect to any alleged leasing commission or equivalent compensation alleged to be owing on account of Tenant's dealings with any real estate broker or agent other than the aforesaid broker.

The parties hereto have executed this Lease on the dates specified immediately adjacent to their respective signatures.

ARTICLE 16. ENTIRE AGREEMENT

THIS LEASE IS THE RESULT OF NEGOTIATIONS THAT OCCURRED OVER THE COURSE OF SEVERAL MONTHS, WHICH NEGOTIATIONS INVOLVED WRITTEN AND ORAL COMMUNICATIONS BY AND BETWEEN THE PARTIES, THEIR ACCOUNTANTS, AND ATTORNEYS. THE NEGOTIATIONS THAT PRECEDED THIS LEASE AT TIMES CONSIDERED ARRANGEMENTS THAT WERE AT VARIANCE WITH THE PROVISIONS OF THIS LEASE. ALL THE PRECEDING AND CONTEMPORANEOUS ORAL AND WRITTEN STATEMENTS, UNDERSTANDINGS, REPRESENTATIONS, WARRANTIES, AND PROMISES, WHETHER CONSISTENT OR INCONSISTENT HEREWITH, ARE AGREED TO BE OF NO FORCE OR EFFECT FOR ANY PURPOSE WHATSOEVER UNLESS EXPRESSLY OR EXPLICITLY STATED IN THIS LEASE. THIS LEASE, TOGETHER WITH ALL ATTACHMENTS, SCHEDULES, AND SPECIFIC REFERENCES, REPRESENTS THE COMPLETE AND FINAL AGREEMENT OF THE PARTIES AND IS INTENDED AS THE COMPLETE AND EXCLUSIVE STATEMENT OF THEIR INTENT, AND IT SUPERSEDES ALL PRIOR AND CONTEMPORANEOUS CONSISTENT AND INCONSISTENT STATEMENTS, REPRESENTATIONS, WARRANTIES, UNDERSTANDINGS, NEGOTIATIONS, AND AGREEMENTS, AND IT MAY NOT BE SUPPLEMENTED, MODIFIED, OR AMENDED BY EVIDENCE, EITHER ORAL OR WRITTEN, OF ANY SUCH MATTERS OR BY COURSE OF DEALING, BUT ONLY UPON THE WRITTEN AGREEMENT OF THE PARTIES. THE PARTIES HEREBY STIPULATE THAT EACH AND EVERY PROVISION CONTAINED IN THIS LEASE WAS BARGAINED FOR AND THE PLAIN MEANING OF SAID PROVISIONS MEMORIALIZES THE INTENT OF THE PARTIES HERETO.

ARTICLE 17. SCRUTINY

THIS LEASE HAS BEEN SUBMITTED TO THE SCRUTINY OF ALL PARTIES AND THEIR RESPECTIVE LEGAL COUNSEL AND SHALL BE GIVEN A FAIR AND REASONABLE INTERPRETATION IN ACCORDANCE WITH THE WORDS HEREOF WITHOUT CONSIDERATION OR WEIGHT BEING GIVEN TO ITS BEING DRAFTED BY OR FOR ONE OF THE

PARTIES. IF IN FACT ONE OF THE PARTIES HAS NOT SUBMITTED THIS LEASE TO THE SCRUTINY OF HIS OR HER LEGAL COUNSEL, SUCH PARTY STIPULATES THAT, DESPITE HAVING HAD THE OPPORTUNITY TO DO SO, HE OR SHE WAIVED THE SAME AND ELECTED TO PROCEED WITHOUT THE BENEFIT OF SUCH LEGAL REVIEW.

Initials ________ ________

Executed this ___________ [INSERT DAY AND DATE], at _________________

Landlord:

[INSERT LANDLORD'S NAME]____________________________

Address ___________________________________

____

____

By: Name of Signatory

ATTACH NOTARY PAGE (OPTIONAL)

NOTARY PAGE

STATE OF _________________________ ss.

COUNTY OF _______________________

On this __________ [INSERT DATE] day of ____________ [INSERT MONTH, YEAR], before me, the undersigned, a Notary Public in and for the State of ___________ [INSERT STATE], duly commissioned and sworn, personally appeared ______________ [NAME OF SIGNATORY], known to me to be a _________________ [INSERT TITLE], of _______________ [LANDLORD'S NAME], the limited liability company that executed the foregoing instrument, and acknowledged the said instrument to be the free and voluntary act and deed of said limited liability company, for the uses and purposes therein mentioned, and on oath stated that he is authorized to execute the said instrument.

Witness my hand and official seal hereto affixed the day and year first above written.

Notary Public in and for said state,

residing at ____

My commission expires _____________________________

Lessee: ________________________________

By: ________________________________ By: ________________________________

Print Name: Print Name:

Dated: ________________________________ Dated: ________________________________

STATE OF ________________________________ ss.

COUNTY OF ________________________________

On ______________ [INSERT DATE] before me, the undersigned, a Notary Public in and for the State of ________ [INSERT STATE], duly commissioned and sworn, personally appeared ________________, known to me to be the person that executed the foregoing instrument, and acknowledged the said instrument to be the free and voluntary act and deed of said limited liability company, for the uses and purposes therein mentioned, and on oath stated that he is authorized to execute the said instrument.

Witness my hand and official seal hereto affixed the day and year first above written.

Notary Public in and for said state,

residing at ________________________________

My commission expires ________________________________

General Provisions

ARTICLE G-1. USE

Lessee shall use the Premises for the purposes permitted in *paragraph c of Article G-2* hereof and shall not use or permit the Premises to be used for any other purpose without the prior written consent of Landlord.

Lessee shall not do or permit anything to be done in or about the Premises nor bring or keep anything therein which will in any way increase the existing rate of or affect any fire or other insurance upon the Building or any of its contents, or cause cancellation of any insurance policy covering the Building, or any part thereof, or any of its contents. Lessee shall not do, or permit anything to be done, in or about the Premises which will in any way obstruct or interfere with the rights of other tenants or occupants of the Building, or injure or annoy them, or use or allow the Premises to be used for any improper, immoral, unlawful, or objectionable purpose, nor shall Lessee cause, maintain, or permit any nuisance in, on, or about the Premises. Lessee shall not commit or suffer to be committed any waste in or on the Premises.

Lessee shall not do nor permit anything to be done in or about the Premises in violation of the covenants and restrictions governing the property. By signing this Lease Lessee assumes responsibility for making itself aware of all covenants and restrictions governing the property.

EXCLUSIVES. It is herewith agreed that this Lease contains no restrictive covenants, and Lessee shall have an *exclusive right to be* the ___________________ within the boundaries of the property described in *Exhibit "A."*

ARTICLE G-2. COMPLIANCE WITH LAW

Lessee shall not use the Premises or permit anything to be done in or about the Premises which will in any way conflict with any law, statute, ordinance, or governmental rule or regulation now in force or which may hereafter be enacted or promulgated. Lessee shall, at its sole cost and expense, promptly comply with all laws, statutes, ordinances, and governmental rules, regulations, or requirements now in force or which may hereafter be in force, and with the requirements of any board of fire insurance underwriters or other similar bodies now or hereafter constituted, relating to, or affecting the condition, use, or occupancy of the Premises. The judgment of any court of competent jurisdiction or the admission of Lessee in any action against Lessee, whether Landlord be a party thereto or not, that Lessee has violated any law, statute, ordinance, or governmental rule, regulation, or requirement, shall be conclusive of that fact as between Landlord and Lessee.

ARTICLE G-3. ALTERATIONS AND ADDITIONS, SURRENDER OF POSSESSION

Lessee shall not make or suffer to be made any alterations, additions, or improvements to or of the Premises or any part thereof without the written consent of Landlord first had and obtained and any alterations, additions, or improvements to or of the Premises, including, but not limited to, wall covering, paneling, and built-in cabinet work, but excepting movable furniture and trade fixtures, shall on the expiration of the term become a part of the realty and belong to Landlord and shall be surrendered with the Premises. In the event Landlord consents to the making of any alterations, additions, or improvements to the Premises by Lessee, the same shall be made by Lessee at Tenant's sole cost and expense, and any contractor or person selected by Lessee to make the same must first be approved in writing by Landlord, which approval shall not be unreasonably withheld. Any such alterations, additions, or improvements made by Lessee shall be performed in accordance with all applicable laws, ordinances, and codes, and in a first-class workmanlike manner, and shall not weaken or impair the structural strength or lessen the value of the Building. Prior to commencement of any alterations or additions, Lessee shall cause its contractors to provide Landlord with certificates of insurance from the insurer certifying that each contractor has in full force and effect insurance meeting all the requirements of *Article 8* hereof. In making any such alterations, additions, or improvements, Lessee shall, at Tenant's sole cost and expense:

a) File for and secure any necessary permits or approvals from all governmental departments or authorities having jurisdiction, and any utility company having an interest therein; and

b) Notify Landlord in writing at least fifteen (15) days prior to the commencement of work on any alteration, addition, or improvement so that Landlord can post and record appropriate notices of non-responsibility.

Upon the expiration or sooner termination of the term hereof, Lessee shall, upon written demand by Landlord given at least thirty (30) days prior to the end of the term, at Tenant's sole cost and expense, forthwith and with all due diligence remove any alterations, additions, or improvements made by Lessee, designated by Landlord to be removed; provided that Lessee shall, forthwith and with all due diligence at its sole cost and expense, repair any damage to the Premises caused by such removal. Lessee may also, upon the expiration or sooner termination of the term hereof, and provided that Lessee is not then in default hereunder, remove Tenant's movable equipment, furnishings, trade fixtures, and other personal property (excluding any alterations, additions, or improvements made by Lessee not specifically designated by Landlord to be removed), provided that Lessee shall, forthwith and with all due diligence at its sole cost and expense, repair any damages to the Premises caused by such removal. Upon the expiration or sooner termination of this Lease or upon the termination of Tenant's right of possession, Lessee shall immediately surrender possession of the Premises to Landlord and remove all of its property therefrom as permitted or required herein, and if such possession is not immediately surrendered, Landlord may reenter the Premises and remove all persons and property therefrom. If Lessee fails or refuses to remove any such property from the Premises, Lessee shall be conclusively presumed to have abandoned the same, and title thereto shall thereupon pass to Landlord without cost, setoff, credit allowance, or otherwise, and Landlord may accept title to such property or, at Tenant's expense, remove the same or any part thereof in any manner that Landlord shall choose and store the same without incurring liability to Lessee or any other person.

ARTICLE G-4. REPAIRS

a) By taking possession of the Premises, Lessee shall be deemed to have accepted the Premises as being in good, satisfactory, and sanitary order, condition and repair. Lessee shall, at Tenant's sole cost and expense, keep the Premises and every part thereof in good condition and repair, damage thereto from causes beyond the control of Lessee (and not caused by any act or omission of Tenant's agents, officers, employees, contractors, servants, invitees, licensees, or guests) and ordinary wear and tear excepted. If Lessee does not make such repairs, Landlord may make such repairs and replacements, and Lessee shall pay Landlord the cost thereof upon receipt of a statement therefore unless Landlord deducts the same from the security deposit pursuant to *Article 5 c* hereof and is entitled to reimbursement pursuant thereto. Lessee shall, upon the expiration or sooner termination of this Lease, surrender the Premises to Landlord in good condition, ordinary wear and tear and damage from causes beyond the control of Lessee (and not caused by any act or omission of Tenant's agents, officers, employees, contractors, servants, licensees, invitees, or guests) excepted. Except as specifically provided in an addendum, if any, to this Lease, Landlord shall have no obligation whatsoever to alter, remodel, improve, repair, decorate, or paint the Premises or any part thereof and the parties hereto affirm that Landlord has made no representations to Lessee respecting the condition of the Premises or the Building except as specifically herein set forth.

b) Notwithstanding the provisions of *Article G-4 a*, above, Landlord shall repair and maintain the structural portions of the Building, including the basic plumbing, air conditioning, heating, and electrical systems installed or furnished by Landlord, unless such maintenance or repairs are caused in part or in whole by the act, neglect, fault, or omission of any duty by the Lessee, its agents, officers, employees, contractors, servants, licensees, invitees, or guests, in which case Lessee shall pay to Landlord the reasonable cost of such maintenance or repairs. Landlord shall not be liable for any failure to make any such repairs or to perform any maintenance for which Landlord is responsible as provided above unless such failure shall persist for an unreasonable time after the written notice of the need of such repairs or maintenance is given to Landlord by Lessee and is due solely to causes within Landlord's reasonable control. Except as provided in *Article G-11* hereof, there shall be no abatement of rent, and in any event there shall be no liability of Landlord by reason of any injury to or interference with Tenant's business arising from the making of any repairs, alterations, or improvements in or to any portion of the Building or the Premises or in or to fixtures, appurtenances, and equipment therein. Lessee, to the extent permitted by law, waives the right to make repairs at Landlord's expense under any law, statute, or ordinance now or hereafter in effect. Landlord may enter the Premises at all reasonable times to make any repairs Landlord deems necessary or desirable, or as Landlord may be required to do by a government authority.

ARTICLE G-5. LIENS

Lessee shall keep the Premises, the Building, and the property in which the Premises are situated free from any and all mechanics', material men's, and other liens and claims thereof, arising out of any work performed, materials furnished, or obligations incurred by or for Lessee. Landlord may require, at Landlord's sole option, that Lessee shall provide to Landlord at Tenant's sole cost and expense a lien and completion bond, or its equivalent, in an amount equal to one and one-half times any and all estimated costs of any improvements, additions, or alterations of or to the Premises, to insure Landlord against any liability for mechanics' and material men's liens and to ensure completion of the work and Landlord's cost of defending against any such claims and liens.

ARTICLE G-6. HOLD HARMLESS

Lessee shall indemnify and hold Landlord harmless from and against any and all claims arising out of (i) Tenant's use of the Premises or any part thereof or the conduct of its business, or (ii) any activity, work, or other thing done, permitted, or suffered by Lessee in or about the Building or the Premises, or any part thereof, or (iii) any breach or default in the performance of any obligation on Tenant's part to be performed under the terms of this Lease, or (iv) any act or negligence of the Lessee, or any officer, agent, employee, contractor, servant, licensee, invitee, or guest of Lessee, and in each case from and against any and all damages, losses, liabilities, lawsuits, judgments, and costs and expenses (including without limitation expert witness fees and reasonable attorneys' fees) arising in connection with any such claim or claims as described in clauses (i) through (iv), above, or any action or proceeding brought thereon. If any such action or proceeding be brought against Landlord, Lessee upon notice from Landlord shall defend the same at Tenant's sole expense by counsel reasonably satisfactory to Landlord. Lessee as a material part of the consideration to Landlord hereby assumes all risk of damage or loss to property or injury or death to persons, in, on, or about the Premises, from any cause other than Landlord's sole negligence, and Lessee hereby waives all claims in respect thereof against Landlord.

Landlord or its agents shall not be liable for any damage or loss to property entrusted to employees of the Building, nor for loss or damage to any property by theft, or otherwise, nor for any injury to or death of or damage or loss to persons or property resulting from any accident, casualty or condition occurring in or about the Building or the Premises, or any part thereof, or any equipment, appliances or fixtures therein, or from any other cause whatsoever, unless caused solely by the negligence of Landlord, its agents, servants, or employees. Landlord or its agents shall not be liable for interference with the light or other incorporeal hereditaments or any loss of business by Lessee, nor shall Landlord be liable for any latent defect in the Premises or in the Building. Lessee shall give prompt written notice to Landlord in case of fire or accidents in the Premises or in the Building or of defects therein or in the fixtures or equipment.

ARTICLE G-7. SUBROGATION

As long as both of their respective insurers so permit, Landlord and Lessee hereby mutually waive their respective rights of recovery against each other for any damages and losses to the extent such damage or loss is reimbursed by insurance under fire, extended coverage, and other property insurance policies existing for the benefit of the respective parties. Each party shall obtain only special endorsements, if required by its insurer, to evidence compliance with the aforementioned waiver.

ARTICLE G-8. PROPERTY TAXES

Lessee shall pay, or cause to be paid, before delinquency, any and all taxes levied or assessed and which become payable during the term hereof upon all Tenant's leasehold improvements, equipment, furniture, fixtures, and personal property located in the Premises; except only that which has been paid for by Landlord and is the standard of the Building. In the event any or all of the Tenant's leasehold improvements, equipment, furniture, fixtures, or personal property shall be assessed and taxed with the Building, Lessee shall pay to Landlord its share of such taxes within ten (10) days after delivery to Lessee by Landlord of a statement in writing setting forth the amount of such taxes applicable to Tenant's property. If Tenant's leasehold improvements, equipment, furniture, fixtures, and personal property are not separately assessed on the tax statement or bill, Landlord's good faith determination of the amount of such taxes applicable to Tenant's property shall be a conclusive determination of Tenant's obligation to pay such amount as so determined by Landlord.

ARTICLE G-9. RULES AND REGULATIONS

Lessee shall faithfully observe and comply with the rules and regulations attached to this Lease as *Exhibit "E"* and such other reasonable rules and regulations as Landlord may from time to time promulgate. Landlord reserves the right from time to time to make all reasonable modifications to said rules. The additions and modifications to those rules shall be binding upon Lessee upon delivery of a copy of them to Lessee. Landlord shall not be liable to Lessee for the non-performance of any said rules and regulations by any other tenants or occupants of the Building.

ARTICLE G-10. HAZARDOUS SUBSTANCES

a) Compliance with Environmental Laws. Lessee shall conduct all operations or activities upon the Premises, or any portion thereof, in compliance with all Environmental Laws, as hereinafter defined. Lessee shall not engage in or permit any dumping, discharge, disposal, spillage, or leakage (whether legal or illegal, accidental or intentional) of such Hazardous Substances, as hereafter defined, at, on, in, or about the Premises or any portion thereof.

1) For purposes of this Lease, "Hazardous Substance Law" means any federal, state, or local statute, regulation, rule, ordinance, or common law principle concerning the presence, possession, handling, storage, treatment, transportation, disposal, or cleanup of, or liability for, a Hazardous Substance, as currently in effect and as hereafter enacted or modified, including but not limited to the Comprehensive Environmental Response, Compensation and Liability Act as amended by the Superfund Amendments and Reauthorization Act (42 U.S.C. § 9601 et seq.), the Safe Water Drinking Act (42 U.S.C. §

300F et seq.), the Toxic Substances Control Act (15 U.S.C. § 2601 et seq.), the Resource Conservation and Recovery Act (42 U.S.C. § 6901 et seq.), the Federal Water Pollution Control Act (33 U.S.C. § 1251 et seq.), the Hazardous Waste Management Act of 1983, and other applicable statutes passed and enacted by the __________ [INSERT STATE] Legislature, and common law principles of tort and strict liability.

2) For purposes of this Lease, "Hazardous Substance" means any chemical, compound, or material which is deemed a hazardous substance, hazardous waste, hazardous material, infectious waste, or toxic substance, or any combination or formulation of substances defined, listed, or classified by reasons of deleterious properties such as ignitability, corrosivity, reactivity, carcinogenicity, toxicity, reproductive carcinogenicity, extraction procedure toxicity, toxicity characteristic, leaching procedure toxicity, petroleum, including crude oil and any fractions thereof; "hazardous waste," "restricted hazardous waste," and "waste" with the above stated properties, as defined in __________ [INSERT STATE] code; and any other chemical material or substance to which, because of its quantity, concentration, physical, or chemical characteristics, exposure is limited or regulated for health, safety, and environmental reasons by any governmental authority with jurisdiction, or which poses significant present or potential hazard to human health and safety or to the environment if released to the work place or environment.

b) Indemnification. Lessee agrees to indemnify, protect, defend (with counsel reasonably approved by Lessor), and hold Lessor, any assignee of Lessor, the directors, officers, shareholders, employees, and agents of such entities and their respective heirs, executors, administrators, legal representatives, successors, and assigns, harmless from and against any claims (including, without limitation, third party claims for personal injury or real or personal property damage), actions, administrative or other proceedings (including informal proceedings), demands, liabilities, liens, judgments, damages (including punitive damages and all foreseeable and unforeseeable consequential damages), penalties, fines, suits, defenses, offsets, obligations, duties, costs (including all remedial, removal, responsive, abatement, cleanup, compliance, legal investigative, preventive, planning and monitoring costs and other related costs, expenses, and disbursements, such as attorneys', paralegals', consultants', and experts' costs and expenses, and also including, without limitation, any such fees and expenses incurred in enforcing the Lease or collecting any sums due hereunder), charges, expenses, interest, or losses (including, without limitation, diminution in the value of the Premises), together with all other costs and expenses of any kind or nature (collectively, "Costs"), which arise out of, are connected with, or are attributable to, directly or indirectly, the presence, suspected presence, release, or suspected release of any Hazardous Substance in or into the air, soil, surface water, groundwater, or soil vapor at, on, about, under, or within the Premises or any portion thereof. If Lessor shall suffer or incur any such Costs, Lessee shall pay Lessor the total of all such Costs suffered or incurred by Landlord upon demand therefore by Lessor. Without limiting the generality of the foregoing, the indemnification provided by this *Article*

G-10 shall specifically cover Costs, including capital, operating, and maintenance costs, incurred in connection with any investigation or monitoring of site conditions, any cleanup, containment, remedial, removal, or restoration work required or performed by any federal, state, or local government agency or political subdivision, or performed by any non-governmental entity or person because of the presence, suspected presence, release, or suspected release of any Hazardous Substance in or into the air, soil, groundwater, surface water, or solid vapor at, on, about, under, or within the Premises or any damage due to such Hazardous Substance.

ARTICLE G-11. ENTRY BY LANDLORD

Landlord reserves and shall at any and all times have the right to enter the Premises, inspect the same, supply janitorial service and any other service to be provided by Landlord to Lessee hereunder, submit the Premises to prospective purchasers, mortgagees, or tenants, post notices of non-responsibility, and alter, improve, or repair the Premises and any portion of the Building that Landlord may deem necessary or desirable, without any abatement of rent, and may for such purpose erect scaffolding and other necessary structures where reasonably required by the character of the work to be performed, always providing that the entrance to the Premises shall not be blocked thereby, and further providing that the business of the Lessee shall not be interfered with unreasonably. Lessee hereby waives any claim for damages or for any injury or inconvenience to or interference with Tenant's business, any loss of occupancy or quiet enjoyment of the Premises, and any other damage or loss occasioned thereby. For each of the aforesaid purposes, Landlord shall at all times have and retain a key with which to unlock all of the doors in, on, and about the Premises, excluding Tenant's vaults, safes, and files, and Landlord shall have the right to use any and all means which Landlord may deem proper to open said doors in an emergency in order to obtain entry to the Premises without liability to Lessee except for any failure to exercise due care for Tenant's property under the circumstances of each entry. Any entry to the Premises obtained by Landlord by any of said means or otherwise shall not under any circumstances be construed or deemed to be a forcible or unlawful entry into, or a detainer of, the Premises, or an eviction of Lessee from the Premises or any portion thereof.

ARTICLE G-12. RECONSTRUCTION

In the event the Premises or the Building are damaged by fire or other perils covered by the extended coverage insurance carried by Landlord for the Building, Landlord agrees to repair the same with reasonable promptness and this Lease shall remain in full force and effect, except that Lessee shall be entitled to a proportionate reduction of the rent while such repairs are being made, such proportionate reduction to be based upon the extent to which the making of such repairs shall materially interfere with the business carried on by the Lessee in the Premises. If the damage is due to the fault or neglect of Lessee, or its agents, officers, employees, contractors, servants, invitees, licensees, or guests, there shall be no reduction or abatement of rent.

In the event the Premises or the Building are damaged as a result of any cause other than the perils covered by the fire and extended coverage insurance carried by Landlord on the Building, then this Lease shall remain in full force without rent reduction and Landlord shall forthwith repair the same, provided the extent of the destruction be less than ten percent (10%) of the then full replacement cost of the Premises or the Building, as applicable. In the event the destruction of the Premises or the Building is to an extent greater than ten percent (10%) of the full replacement cost thereof, then Landlord shall have the option (i) to repair or restore such damage, this Lease continuing in full force and effect, but the rent to be proportionately reduced as hereinabove provided in this *Article* unless the damage is due to the fault or neglect of Lessee, or its agents, officers, employees, contractors, servants, invitees, licensees, or guests, or (ii) to give notice to Lessee at any time within sixty (60) days after such damage terminating this Lease as of the date specified in such notice, which date shall be no less than thirty (30) and not more than sixty (60) days after the giving of such notice. In the event of giving such notice, this Lease shall expire and all interest of the Lessee in the Premises shall terminate on the date so specified in such notice and the rent, reduced (if Lessee is entitled to a reduction under this *Article*) by a proportionate amount based upon the extent, if any, to which such damage has materially interfered with the business carried on by Lessee in the Premises, shall be paid up to the date of such termination.

Notwithstanding anything to the contrary in this *Article* or *Articles 10 b or 16*, Landlord shall not have any obligation whatsoever to repair, reconstruct, or restore the Premises when any damage thereto or to the Building occurs during the last twelve (12) months of the term of this Lease or any extension thereof. (However, this sentence does not relieve Landlord of the obligation to perform such routine maintenance as it is obligated to provide under this Lease.)

Landlord shall not be required to repair any injury or damage by fire or other cause, or to make any repairs or replacements, of any panels, decoration, office fixtures, furniture, or any other portable property installed in the Premises by Lessee.

Lessee shall not be entitled to any compensation or damages from Landlord for loss of the use of the whole or any part of the Premises, for damage to or loss of any of Tenant's fixtures or personal property, or for any damage to Tenant's business, or any inconvenience or annoyance occasioned by such damage, or by any repair, reconstruction, or restoration by Landlord, or by any failure of Landlord to make any repairs, reconstruction, or restoration under this *Article* or any other provision of this Lease.

ARTICLE G-13. EMINENT DOMAIN

If more than twenty-five percent (25%) of the area of the Premises shall be taken or appropriated for any public or quasi-public use under the power of eminent domain, or conveyed in lieu thereof, either party hereto shall have the right, at its option, to terminate this Lease by written notice to the other party given within ten (10) days of the date of such taking, appropriation, or conveyance, and Landlord shall be entitled to any and all income, rent, award, or any interest therein whatsoever which may be paid or made in connection with such public or quasi-public use or purpose, and Lessee shall have no claim against Landlord for the value of any unexpired term of this Lease. If any part of the Building other than the Premises may be so taken, appropriated, or conveyed, Landlord shall have the right at its option to terminate this Lease, and in any such event Landlord shall be entitled to the entire award as above provided whether or not this Lease is terminated. If less than twenty-five percent (25%) of the Premises is so taken, appropriated, or conveyed, or more than twenty-five percent (25%) thereof is so taken, appropriated, or conveyed and neither party elects to terminate as herein provided, the rental thereafter to be paid hereunder for the Premises shall be reduced in the same ratio that the percentage of the area of the Premises so taken, appropriated, or conveyed bears to the total area of the Premises immediately prior to the taking, appropriation, or conveyance, and in any such event Landlord shall be entitled to the entire award as above provided.

ARTICLE G-14. ESTOPPEL CERTIFICATE

Within ten (10) days of written request by Landlord at any time, or from time to time, Lessee shall execute, acknowledge, and deliver to Landlord a statement in writing, (a) certifying that this Lease is unmodified and in full force and effect (or, if modified, stating the nature of such modification and certifying that this Lease as so modified is in full force and effect), and the date to which the rental and other charges are paid in advance, if any, and (b) acknowledging that there are not, to Tenant's knowledge, any uncured defaults on the part of the Landlord hereunder, or specifying such defaults if any are claimed. Any such statement may be relied upon by any prospective purchaser or encumbrancer of all or any portion of the real property of which the Premises are a part or any interest therein. Tenant's failure to deliver such a statement within such time shall be conclusive against Lessee that (i) this Lease is in full force and effect, without modification except as may be represented by Landlord, (ii) there are no uncured defaults in Landlord's performance, and (iii) not more than one month's rent has been paid in advance.

ARTICLE G-15. GENERAL PROVISIONS

a) Plats, Riders, and Exhibits. Clauses, plats, and riders, if any, signed by Landlord and Lessee and endorsed on or affixed to this Lease are a part hereof. The Exhibits (including without limitation *Exhibits "A" through "G"*) hereto, including without limitation any agreements therein, constitute part of this Lease. Lessee acknowledges and agrees that the site plan shown on *Exhibit "A"* hereto is subject to such reasonable modifications as Landlord may desire to make prior to completion of construction of the Building.

b) Waiver. No waiver shall be binding unless executed in writing by the party making the waiver. The waiver by Landlord of any term, covenant, or condition herein contained shall not be deemed to be a waiver of such term, covenant, or condition on any subsequent breach of the same or any other term, covenant, or condition herein contained. The subsequent acceptance of rent hereunder by Landlord shall not be deemed to be a waiver of any preceding breach by Lessee of any term, covenant, or condition of this Lease, other than the failure of Lessee to pay the particular rental so accepted, regardless of Landlord's knowledge of such preceding breach at the time of the acceptance of such rent.

c) Notices. All notices or demands of any kind required or desired to be given by or to Landlord, Lessee, or Guarantor (s) hereunder shall be in writing. All notice between the parties shall be deemed received when personally delivered or when deposited in the United States mail postage prepaid, registered or certified, with return receipt requested, or sent by facsimile transmission, telegram, or mailogram, or by recognized courier delivery (e.g., Federal Express, Airborne, Burlington, etc.) addressed to the parties, as the case may be, at the address set forth in *Article 1* of this Lease or at such other addresses as the parties may subsequently designate by written notice given in the manner provided in this section.

Notice personally delivered will be effective upon delivery to an authorized representative of the party at the designated address. Notice sent by mail or courier in accordance with the above will be effective upon receipt or upon the date the party refuses to accept receipt, or the date upon which such notice is returned to sender as undeliverable. Notices sent by facsimile transmission, telegram, or mailogram will be effective upon transmission.

d) Joint Obligations. If there be more than one Lessee, the obligations hereunder imposed upon Tenants shall be joint and several.

e) Marginal Headings. The captions of paragraphs and *Article* titles of the Articles of this Lease are not a part of this Lease and shall have no effect upon the construction or interpretation of any part hereof.

f) Time. Time is of the essence of this Lease and each and all of its provisions in which performance is a factor.

g) Successors and Assigns. The covenants and conditions herein contained, subject to the provisions as to assignment, apply to and bind the heirs, successors, executors, administrators, legal representatives, and assigns of the parties hereto.

h) Recordation. Neither Landlord nor Lessee shall record this Lease or a short form or memorandum hereof without the prior written consent of the other party.

i) Quiet Possession. Upon Lessee paying the rent reserved hereunder and observing and performing all of the covenants, conditions, and provisions on Tenant's part to be observed and performed hereunder, Lessee shall have quiet possession of the Premises for the entire term hereof, subject to all the provisions of this Lease.

j) Late Charges. Lessee hereby acknowledges that late payment by Lessee to Landlord of rent or other sums due hereunder will cause Landlord to incur costs not contemplated by this Lease, the exact amount of which are impracticable or extremely difficult to ascertain. Such costs include, but are not limited to, processing and accounting charges and late charges which may be imposed upon Landlord by terms of any mortgage or trust deed covering the Premises or any part of the real property of which the Premises are a part. Accordingly, if any installment of rent or any other sum due from Lessee shall not be received by Landlord or

Landlord's designee within three (3) days after written notice that said amount is past due, then Lessee shall pay to Landlord, in each case, a late charge equal to ten percent (10%) of such overdue amount. The parties hereby agree that such late charge represents a fair and reasonable estimate of the cost that Landlord will incur by reason of late payment by Lessee. Acceptance of any late charges by Landlord shall in no event constitute a waiver of Tenant's default with respect to such overdue amount, nor prevent Landlord from exercising any of its other rights and remedies hereunder.

k) Prior Agreements. This Lease contains all of the agreements of the parties hereto with respect to any matter covered or mentioned in this Lease, and no prior agreements or understanding pertaining to any such matters shall be effective for any purpose. No provision of this Lease may be amended or added to except by an agreement in writing signed by the parties hereto or their respective successors in interest. This Lease shall not be effective or binding on any party until fully executed by both parties hereto.

l) Inability to Perform. This Lease and the obligations of Lessee hereunder shall not be affected or impaired because Landlord is unable to fulfill any of its obligations hereunder or is delayed in doing so, if such inability or delay is caused by reason of strike, labor troubles, Acts of God, or any other cause, similar or dissimilar, beyond the reasonable control of the Landlord.

m) Attorneys' Fees. In the event of any action or proceeding brought by either party against the other under this Lease, the prevailing party shall be entitled to recover all its costs and expenses, including without limitation expert witness fees and the fees of its attorneys in such action or proceeding in such amount as the court may adjudge reasonable as attorneys' fees.

n) Sale of Premises by Landlord. In the event of any sale of the Building, Landlord shall be and is hereby entirely freed and relieved of all liability under any and all of its covenants and obligations contained in or derived from this Lease arising out of any act, occurrence, or omission occurring after the consummation of such sale; and the parties or their successors in interest, or between the parties and any such purchaser, to have assumed and agreed to carry out each and every of the covenants and obligations of Landlord under this Lease, and Lessee will look solely to Landlord's successor in interest in and to this Lease. Landlord, upon notice to Lessee of any such sale, may transfer any security deposit to its successor in interest and Landlord will thereupon be discharged from further liability in reference thereto.

o) Subordination, Attornment. Landlord reserves the right to place liens and encumbrances on and against the Premises, the Building, and the property of which the Premises are part, superior in lien and effect to this Lease and the estate created hereby, and Lessee will execute and deliver, upon Landlord's demand, any instrument or instruments necessary to subordinate this Lease to such liens or encumbrances; provided, however, that any such subordination is conditioned upon the holders of any such lien or encumbrance agreeing not to disturb Tenant's possession of the Premises so long as Lessee remains in full and complete compliance with the terms hereof, notwithstanding any foreclosure of such lien or encumbrance. This Lease is and shall be subordinate to the lien of any deed of trust or mortgage placed upon the Premises, Building, and property of which the Premises are a part or any part thereof.

p) Name. Lessee shall not use the name of the Building or of the development in which the Building is situated for any purpose other than as an address of the business to be conducted by Lessee on the Premises.

q) Severability. Any provision of this Lease which shall prove to be invalid, void, or illegal shall in no way affect, impair, or invalidate any other provision hereof and all such other provisions shall remain in full force and effect.

r) Cumulative Remedies. No remedy or election hereunder shall be deemed exclusive but shall, wherever possible, be cumulative with all other remedies at law or in equity.

s) Choice of Law. This Lease shall be governed by the laws of the State of __________ [INSERT STATE].

t) Signs and Auctions. Lessee shall not place any sign in or upon the Premises, windows, or Building or conduct any auction thereon without Landlord's prior written consent.

u) Gender and Number. Wherever the context so requires herein, each gender shall include any other gender and the singular number shall include the plural and vice versa.

v) Consents. Whenever the consent of Landlord is required herein, the giving or withholding of such consent in any one or any number of instances shall not limit or waive the need for such consent in any other or future instances.

ARTICLE G-16. BUILDING PLANNING AND EMPLOYEE PARKING

a) In the event Landlord requires the premises to be used in conjunction with another suite or for other reasons related to the building planning program, upon notifying Lessee in writing, Landlord shall have the right to move Lessee to other space on the premises of which the Premises forms a part, at Landlord's sole cost and expense. The terms and conditions of the original Lease shall remain in full force and effect, save and excepting that a revised *Exhibit "A"* shall become a part of this Lease and shall reflect the location of the new space in *Article G-2* of this Lease, which shall be amended to include and state all correct data as to the new space. However, if the new space does not meet the Tenant's approval, Lessee shall have the right to cancel said Lease upon giving Landlord thirty (30) days' notice within ten (10) days of receipt of Landlord's notification.

b) It is understood that Lessee and employees of Lessee shall not be permitted to park their automobiles in the automobile parking areas which may from time to time be designated for patrons of the Shopping Center. Lessee and its employees shall park their cars only in those portions of the parking areas, if any, designated for that purpose by Landlord. Lessee shall furnish Landlord with its and its employees' license numbers within fifteen (15) days after taking possession of the Premises and Lessee shall thereafter notify Landlord of any changes within five (5) days after such change occurs. If Lessee or its employees fail to park their cars in designated parking areas, then Landlord may give notice of such violation. If Lessee does not cease such violation, or cause such violation by its employees to be ceased, as the case may be, within two (2) days after Landlord's said notice is given, Lessee shall pay to Landlord an amount equal to twenty-five dollars ($25.00) per day per violating vehicle calculated from and including the day on which Landlord's notice was given to and including the day when all violations by Lessee and its employees cease. If, from time to time, after such cessation, Lessee or any of its employees again violate this *Article*, Landlord need not give Lessee any further notice of violation and the said twenty-five dollar ($25.00) per day per violating vehicle charge shall commence against Lessee for each violating vehicle immediately upon such further violation and run until such violation ceases. All amounts due under the provisions of this *Article* shall be payable by Lessee as additional rent within ten (10) days after demand therefore. Lessee shall notify each of its employees of the provisions prior to their commencing any employment connected with the demised Premises and shall also inform them that their cars are subject to being towed away at such employees' expense in case of any violation.

ARTICLE G-17. DISCRIMINATION

The Lessee herein covenants by and for Lessee and Tenant's heirs, personal representatives, and assigns and all persons claiming under Lessee or through Lessee that this Lease is made subject to the condition that there shall be no discrimination against or segregation of any person or of a group of persons on account of race, color, religion, creed, sex, sexual orientation, or national origin in the leasing, subleasing, transferring, use, occupancy, tenure, or enjoyment of the land herein leased, nor shall Lessee or any person claiming under or through Lessee establish or permit any such practice or practices of discrimination or segregation with reference to the selection, location, number, use, or occupancy of tenants, lessees, sublessees, subtenants, or vendees in the land herein leased.

ARTICLE G-18. AUTHORITY OF PARTIES

a) Corporate Authority. If Lessee is a corporation, each individual executing this Lease on behalf of the corporation represents and warrants that he/she is duly authorized to execute and deliver this Lease on behalf of the corporation, in accordance with a duly adopted resolution of the board of directors of the corporation or in accordance with the bylaws of the corporation, and that this Lease is binding upon the corporation in accordance with its terms.

b) Limited Liability Company. Landlord is a(n) ______________ [INSERT STATE] Limited Liability Company, it is understood and agreed that any claim by Lessee on Landlord shall be limited to the assets of the Limited Liability Company and, furthermore, Lessee expressly waives any and all rights to proceed against the individual Members, except to the extent of their interest in the Limited Liability Company.

______________________________ ______________________________

[INSERT AUTHORIZED SIGNATORY] Date

____

[INSERT LANDLORD]

______________________________ and ______________________________

Name of Lessee Name of Lessee

Exhibits

EXHIBIT "A"

Insert the following drawings

- Site Plan
- Demised Premises Within Floor Plate
- Floor Plan

To be added when approved by Landlord and Tenant

Property Description

Insert legal description of site

EXHIBIT "B"

CONSTRUCTION

Landlord shall, at its own cost and expense, construct the Premises for occupancy by Tenant incorporating the items of work set forth in the "Description of Landlord's Work." Tenant shall, within thirty (30) days after the execution of this Lease, submit to Landlord complete architectural drawings at Tenant's sole cost and expense, prepared by Tenant's licensed architect, which drawings shall indicate the specific requirements of Tenant's space, including types of materials and color, interior partitions, reflective ceiling, plan, plumbing fixtures, and electrical plans prepared by a licensed engineer setting forth all electrical requirements of Tenant, all in conformity with the "Description of Landlord's Work" and "Description of Tenant's Work."

In the event Tenant does not have an architect to do the work herein described, then Tenant shall engage Landlord's architect and pay the cost thereof. In the event that said drawings are, in the sole judgment of Landlord, incomplete, inadequate, or inconsistent with the terms of this Lease, Landlord may elect to have them revised, corrected, and/or completed by Landlord's architect at Tenant's expense. Upon final approval by Landlord, the drawings shall be by this reference incorporated herein as part of the Lease. Any subsequent changes, modifications, or alterations requested by Tenant shall be processed by Landlord's architect, and any additional charges, expenses, or costs, including Landlord's architect's fees, shall be at the sole cost and expense of the Tenant and Landlord shall have the right to demand payment for such charges, modifications, or alterations prior to performance of any such work in the Premises. No such changes, modifications, or alterations in said approved drawings can be made without the written consent of the Landlord after written request therefore by Tenant.

DESCRIPTION OF LANDLORD'S WORK

The following is a description of the construction work which shall be provided by Landlord. The material specifications and layout shall be at Landlord's option.

I. STRUCTURE

1. **Floor.** Landlord shall provide a concrete slab floor troweled smooth to receive Tenant's floor covering.

2. **Roof.** Roof penetrations will be held to the absolute minimum. All required penetrations of the roofing system must be clearly shown on Tenant's plans and specifications and approved by Landlord and will be made at Tenant's sole cost and expense by Landlord's contractor and/or under Landlord's supervision.

3. **Walls.** Interior demising walls will consist of gypsum or similar board with joints taped and sealed on wood or metal studding, or exposed masonry, at Landlord's option.

4. **Ceiling.** Landlord shall provide a suspended T-bar acoustical ceiling having a height of approximately ten feet (10') to eleven feet (11') unless otherwise requested by Tenant and approved by Landlord.

5. **Storefront.** Landlord will provide basic straight-line storefront, glass and extruded aluminum framing, including one entrance door (at a location to be mutually agreed to).

6. **Service Door.** None, shops serviced through front entrance door.

II. ELECTRICAL/AND TELEPHONE

1. Landlord shall provide meter base for Tenant's meter, and a service line and 100-amp panel board. In the event Tenant requires greater electrical capacity, the cost shall be paid for such services in advance by Tenant including, without limitation, the cost of any modification of the main service facilities for the building, if required, and the cost of installation of electrical

service greater than 100 amp, and such additional service shall be installed by Landlord at the time of completion of Landlord's work. Tenant shall be required to submit all the necessary information as to its electrical power needs to Landlord.

2. Landlord shall provide one basic 2' x 4' four-tube fluorescent fixture per 125 square feet (approximate) of leased area plus one duplex convenience outlet on demising walls approximately 24 feet on center from rear of Premises.

3. Landlord shall provide one entry conduit for telephone service at location and discretion of Landlord.

III. MECHANICAL

1. The basic Premises will possess a heating and air conditioning unit ____________ [INSERT SPECIFICATIONS] equipped with its own thermostat. Any duct work and/or equipment required for distribution and returns, interior partitioning, fixturing, or other work by Tenant will be the responsibility of and at the expense of the Tenant. It shall be the Tenant's responsibility to operate and maintain this system in accordance with Landlord's instructions and manufacturer's requirements.

IV. PLUMBING AND SANITARY FACILITIES

1. Landlord shall provide one standard rest room (designed for use by people with disabilities) at location and discretion of Landlord.

V. SPRINKLER SYSTEM

1. Landlord may provide an automatic fire sprinkler system to accommodate Tenant's Premises. Any additions or changes to said system, other than any provided by Landlord, required as a result of interior Partitions fixturing, restrooms, etc., will be made at Tenant's sole cost and expense by Landlord's contractor.

DESCRIPTION OF TENANT'S WORK

Tenant shall be responsible for completing and doing all other work not specifically described under "Description of Landlord's Work" to the Premises including, but not limited to, the items listed below:

1. Tenant shall provide and install floor covering.

2. Tenant shall provide and install partition walls other than those provided for under Description of Landlord's Work.

3. Tenant shall furnish and install all painting and wall covering.

4. Tenant shall provide and install all additional plumbing, electrical, water heater (s) and appurtenances, wall finishes, fixtures, HVAC distribution, ventilation, sanitary facilities, and restrooms required by code. Such facilities shall be located as Landlord desires and shall be in conformance with all applicable building codes and shall require Landlord's approval.

5. Tenant shall be responsible for the complete installation, electrical hookup, and cost of its exterior business name sign as required by Landlord. Tenant's sign (s) shall be designed, constructed, and located in accordance with the procedures established in the Lease and the Signs *Exhibit* and shall be subject to the approval of Landlord's architect and/or Landlord. Tenant shall cause Tenant's signs, at Tenant's expense, to be connected to a J-box (in the canopy) that is connected to the house panel with a common timing device so that all of the signage on Landlord's building of which the Demised Premises is a part is illuminated during uniform hours.

6. Tenant shall complete its electrical system including, but not limited to, all additional wiring, conduits, convenience outlets, controls, connections to Landlord-furnished junction boxes, accent lighting, and other light fixtures not provided by Landlord.

7. Tenant shall furnish and install telephones, music systems, and security devices, if required.

8. Tenant shall furnish and install all fixtures and equipment necessary to open for business.

9. Tenant shall provide covered metal trash containers within the Premises, maintenance facilities, and all fire protection equipment required by rating bureaus, codes, or ordinances in addition to any fire sprinkler system furnished by Landlord.

In the event that Tenant requests Landlord's contractor to supply any materials, or provide any work on items to be paid for by Tenant, such materials and labor shall be set forth on a separate sheet and identified as *Exhibit "B-l"* and attached hereto. Said *Exhibit "B-l"* shall set forth all charges to be made by Landlord's contractor to Tenant and shall total the same and, when approved by Tenant and attached hereto, shall become Tenant's binding agreement to pay the same in an amount of one hundred percent (100%) of the total prior to the time that Landlord's contractor commences to perform the work. Upon receipt of the said *Exhibit "B-l,"* signed by Tenant, Landlord shall secure his contractor's approval and commitment to complete the work and shall notify Tenant of the same.

EXHIBIT "C"

CPI ADJUSTMENT

The Minimum Rent shall be adjusted every year during the term of the Lease and any renewal periods, if any, commencing with the beginning of the second (2nd) year from the date of the commencement of the term based upon A or B below outlined.

A. As used here in increases in the cost of living as provided in this *Exhibit:*

1) "Index" shall mean the Consumer Price Index for All Urban Consumers, United States City Average, Subgroup "All Items" (1982-84=100) and issued by the Bureau of Labor Statistics of the United States Department of Labor. In the event the Index shall hereafter be converted to a different standard reference base or otherwise revised, the determination of the Percentage Increase (defined below) shall be made with the use of such conver-

sion factor, formula, or table for converting the Index as may be published by the Bureau of Labor Statistics or, if said Bureau shall not publish the same, then the use of such conversion factor, formula, or table as may be published by the United States government. In the event the Index shall cease to be published, then there shall be substituted for the Index such other index as most reasonably approximates the Index. It is the intent of the parties that the Minimum Rent adjustment provided for in this *Article* not fail or be ineffective because of the failure to agree upon a new index, and such new index as most reasonably approximates the original Index be used.

2) "Base Index" shall mean the Index in effect in the month immediately preceding the date of the commencement of the term and the same month each year thereafter.

3) "Anniversary Month" shall mean the month preceding the first (1st) anniversary of the month immediately preceding the date of the commencement of the term and the same month each year thereafter.

4) "Percentage Increase" shall mean the percentage equal to the fraction, the numerator of which shall be the Index in the Anniversary Month less the Base Index and the denominator of which shall be the Base Index.

B. If the Index in the Anniversary Month shall exceed the Base Index, then the Minimum Rent payable pursuant to *Article 4* for the ensuing year shall be increased by the Percentage Increase. Landlord shall send Tenant an Index Comparative Statement setting forth (a) the Index in the Anniversary Month preceding the date of the statement, (b) the Base Index, (c) the Percentage Increase, and (d) the increase in the Minimum Rent. Until such time as Tenant receives such statement, Tenant shall continue to pay the Minimum Rent based upon the previous annual amount. In the event Minimum Rent is increased by the Index Comparative Statement, then the increase in the Minimum Rent during the period of time prior to receipt of such Comparative Statement shall be paid by Tenant to Landlord upon receipt of such statement. The Minimum Rent shall only be increased pursuant to the provisions herein and in no event shall the Minimum Rent be decreased.

C. For the purposes of this lease, the Minimum Rent shall be adjusted every year during the term of the Lease and any renewal periods, if any, commencing with the beginning of the second (2nd) year from the date of the commencement of the term. The adjustment shall be five percent (5%) per annum. Said adjustment shall be the same for the option periods outlined in *Article 1* of this lease.

The parties agree hereto to use the adjustment outlined in B herein above.

Tenant ______________________________ Landlord ______________________________

ACKNOWLEDGMENT OF COMMENCEMENT

This Acknowledgment is made as of ______, 20__, with reference to that certain Lease Agreement (hereinafter referred to as the "Lease") dated _____, 20__, by and between ____________________________ as "Landlord" therein, and ____________________________ as "Tenant."

The undersigned hereby confirms the following:

1. That Lessee accepted possession of the Demised Premises (as described in said Lease) on ______________, 20____, and acknowledges that the premises are as represented by Landlord and in good order, condition, and repair, and that the improvements, if any required to be constructed for Tenant by Landlord under this Lease, have been so constructed and are satisfactorily completed in all respects.

2. That all conditions of said Lease to be performed by Landlord prerequisite to the full effectiveness of said Lease have been satisfied and Landlord has fulfilled all of its duties of an inducement nature.

3. That in accordance with the provisions of Paragraph 3 of said Lease the Commencement Date of the term is ______________, 20____ and that, unless sooner terminated, the original term thereof expires on ____________, 20____.

4. That said Lease is in full force and effect and that the same represents the entire agreement between Landlord and Tenant concerning said Lease.

5. That there are no existing defenses which Tenant has against the enforcement of said Lease by Landlord and no offsets or credits against rentals.

6. That the minimum rental obligation of said Lease is presently in effect and that all rents, charges, and other obligations on the part of Tenant under said Lease commenced to accrue on ______.

7. That the undersigned Tenant has no notice of prior assignment, hypothecation, or pledge of said Lease or of rents thereunder.

Landlord: ____________________ Tenant: ________________________

By ________________________ By ____________________________
Signatory Landlord

EXHIBIT "D"

SIGNS

These criteria have been established for the purpose of assuring an outstanding shopping complex and for the mutual benefit of all tenants.

A. GENERAL REQUIREMENTS

1. Tenant shall submit or cause to be submitted to Landlord or Landlord's architect for approval before fabrication at least three copies of detailed drawings indicating the location, site layout, design, and color of the proposed signs, including all lettering and/or graphics.

2. All permits for Tenant's sign(s) and its installation shall be obtained by Tenant or its representative and shall conform to all local building and electrical codes.

3. Tenant's sign(s) shall be constructed and installed at Tenant's expense.

4. Tenant shall be responsible for the fulfillment of all requirements of these criteria.

B. LOCATION OF SIGN(S)

1. Only one exterior sign shall be permitted at the sign area, if any, designated by Landlord or Landlord's architect and shall not be permitted without prior written consent of Landlord.
   a) Tenant shall provide on one facade of the Premises a suitable exterior signboard, sign, or signs of such size, design, and character and in such location only as Landlord or Landlord's architect shall approve in writing at its sole discretion. Size specification shall be provided by Landlord or Landlord's architect.
   b) Tenant's sign(s) shall be located at least thirty-six (36) inches from each lease line.

2. No signs perpendicular to the face of the building or storefront will be permitted.

C. DESIGN REQUIREMENTS

1. Tenant's sign shall have *singly illuminated letters* and shall not have exposed lamps, animated, flashing, audible signs, crossovers, conduit, or brackets. All cabinets, conductors, exposed raceways, ballast boxes, or transformers and other equipment shall be concealed.

2. Tenant's storefront entrance/store name identification designs shall be subject to the approval of Landlord or Landlord's architect. Wording of sign(s) shall not include the product(s) sold except as part of Tenant's trade name or insignia.

3. The design of all signs, including style, placement, and height of lettering, symbols or logos, size, color, type of paint, and materials, method, and amount of illumination shall be subject to the approval of Landlord or Landlord's architect. The brightness of Tenant's sign(s) shall not exceed the brightness of other exterior signs on the fascia where Tenant's sign(s) is located. The depth of letters shall be limited to eight (8) inches unless otherwise approved by Landlord or Landlord's architect. Exposed raceways will not be allowed.

4. Exterior sign(s) shall be pan-channel letters, internally illuminated with neon, fabricated sheet metal with Plexiglas® faces, and shall have a minimum of one (1)-inch trim cap edges.

5. In the event, in Landlord's opinion, the fascia over Tenant's space needs repainting due to the results of stains, corrosion, dirt, rust, or other cause, Landlord may repaint Tenant's fascia and Tenant shall reimburse Landlord for such costs upon demand.

D. CONSTRUCTION REQUIREMENTS

1. Exterior facade sign(s), bolts, fastenings, and clips, if such exterior sign(s) and appurtenances are permitted by Landlord, shall be enameled iron with enamel finish, stainless steel, aluminum, brass, bronze, or other rust-free metal. No black iron materials of any type will be permitted. Any deterioration of the paint used on Tenant's sign will be corrected by Tenant to the satisfaction of Landlord within ten (10) working days after notice to Tenant by Landlord.

2. Exterior facade sign(s), if such exterior sign(s) are permitted by Landlord, exposed to the weather shall be mounted flush to the building to permit proper dirt and water drainage away from the building unless otherwise directed by Landlord or Landlord's architect.

3. Location of all openings for conduits in sign panels and/or letters on building walls shall be indicated by the sign contractor on drawings submitted to Landlord or Landlord's architect. All penetrations of the building structure required for sign installation shall be neatly sealed in a watertight condition. No labels will be permitted on the exposed surface of sign(s) except those required by local ordinance which shall be applied in an inconspicuous location.

E. MISCELLANEOUS REQUIREMENTS

1. Tenant will be permitted to place upon each entrance of its Premise not more than one hundred forty-four (144) square inches of gold leaf or decal application lettering not to exceed two (2) inches in height, indicating hours of business, emergency telephone number, etc. Tenant may install on the store front, if required by the U.S. Post Office, the numbers only for the street address in exact location stipulated by Landlord or Landlord's architect. Size, type, and color of numbers shall be as stipulated by Landlord or Landlord's architect.

2. In the event Tenant has a non-customer door for receiving merchandise only, Tenant's name shall be uniformly applied on said door in a location, as directed by Landlord or Landlord's architect, in two (2)-inch high block letters. Where more than one tenant uses the same door, each name shall be applied.

3. Tenant shall be fully responsible for the operations of Tenant's sign contractors and Tenant shall indemnify, defend, and hold Landlord harmless from any acts or omissions of Tenant's sign contractors.

4. Tenant, its representative, or its sign contractor shall at the termination of this Lease remove Tenant's sign and repair any damage area to its original condition when Tenant's sign was erected.

5. The exterior facade sign may, at Landlord's option, be operated by a central time clock and shall be illuminated during such hours as prescribed by Landlord.

6. Tenant's cost for service and the maintenance, repair, and replacement of such facilities,

including time clocks to Tenant's sign, may be on a pro-rata basis which shall be the proportion of such cost which Tenant's sign bears to the total number of signs contributing toward said service bill with necessary and equitable modification where special or comparatively excessive use of such facilities occurs with respect to or is afforded an individual Tenant and will be billed by Landlord to Tenant on a regular basis and shall be due and payable upon demand. Tenant shall pay to Landlord Tenant's share of said cost within ten (10) days after receipt of billing from Landlord. Tenant's share may be estimated monthly and included with the common area billing, which shall be due the first of each month and periodically adjusted with the common area expenses.

EXHIBIT "E"

TENANT OFFSET AND ESTOPPEL CERTIFICATE

To: ______________________________

RE: Lease dated ___________, 20 ____, by and between ______________________________________ [INSERT LANDLORD'S NAME] as "Landlord" and ____ [INSERT TENANT'S NAME] as "Tenant," on Premises located in _____________ [INSERT PREMISES ADDRESS].

Gentlemen:

The undersigned tenant (the "Tenant") certifies and represents unto the addressee hereof (hereinafter referred to as the "Addressee") and its attorneys and representatives, with respect to the above-described lease, a true and correct copy of which is attached as *Exhibit "A"* hereto (the "Lease"), as follows:

1. All space and improvements covered by the Lease have been completed and furnished to the satisfaction of Tenant, all conditions required under the Lease have been met, and Tenant has accepted and taken possession of and presently occupies the Premises covered by the Lease.

2. The Lease is for the total term of _______ (________) years, ____ (________) months commencing ____, 20 _____, has not been modified, altered, or amended in any respect, and contains the entire agreement between Landlord and Tenant, except as _________ (list amendments and modifications other than those, if any, attached to and forming a part of the attached Lease as well as any verbal agreements, or write "None").

3. As of the date hereof, the Minimum Rent under the Lease, payable in equal monthly installments during the term, is $ _________, subject to the CPI Adjustment escalation and Percentage Rent, in accordance with the terms and provisions of the Lease.

4. No rent has been paid by Tenant in advance under the Lease except for $ _______, which amount represents rent for the period ___________, 20___ and ending ___________, 20___ and

Tenant has no charge or claim of offset under said Lease or otherwise, against rents or other amounts due or to become due thereunder. No "discounts," "free rent," or "discounted rent" have been agreed to or are in effect except for ___________.

5. A Security Deposit of $ ______ has been made and is currently being held by Landlord.

6. Tenant has no claim against Landlord for any deposit or prepaid rent except as provided in paragraphs 4 and 5 above.

7. The Landlord has satisfied all commitments, arrangements, or understandings made to induce Tenant to enter into the Lease, and Landlord is not in any respect in default in the performance of the terms and provisions of the Lease, nor is there now any fact or condition which, with notice or lapse of time or both, would become such a default.

8. Tenant is not in any respect in default under the terms and provisions of the Lease, nor is there now any fact or condition which, with notice or lapse of time or both, would become such a default, and has not assigned, transferred, or hypothecated its interest under the Lease, except as follows: ______________________________________.

9. Except as expressly provided in the Lease or in any amendment or supplement to the Lease, Tenant:

(i) does not have any right to renew or extend the term of the Lease,

(ii) does not have any option or preferential right to purchase all or any part of the Premises or all or any part of the building or premises of which the Premises are a part, and

(iii) does not have any right, title, or interest with respect to the Premises other than as Tenant under the Lease.

There are no understandings, contracts, agreements, subleases, assignments, or commitments of any kind whatsoever with respect to the Lease of the Premises covered thereby except as expressly provided in the Lease or in any amendment or supplement to the Lease set forth in paragraph 2 above, copies of which are attached hereto.

10. The Lease is in full force and effect and Tenant has no defenses, setoffs, or counterclaims against Landlord arising out of the Lease or in any way relating thereto or arising out of any other transaction between Tenant and Landlord.

11. Tenant has not received any notice, directly or indirectly, of a prior assignment, hypothecation, or pledge by Landlord of the rents of the Lease to a person or entity.

12. The current address to which all notices to Tenant as required under the Lease should be sent is: ____.

13. Addressee's rights hereunder shall inure to its successors and assigns.

14. With respect to the Merchant's Promotional Association and/or the Promotional Service, if any, Tenant has no claims, liens, or offsets with regard to any amounts due or to become due thereunder except for ___________. (If Addressee is a purchaser or prospective purchaser of

the Premises and/or the Building, Tenant shall also include the following.)

15. Tenant acknowledges that Addressee is acquiring ownership of the building in which the Premises are located. Tenant agrees that upon Addressee acquiring ownership, Tenant will attorn and does attorn and agrees to recognize and does recognize Addressee as Landlord on the condition that Addressee agrees to recognize the Lease referred to in this document as long as Tenant is not in default thereunder; provided, however, that Addressee shall have no liability or responsibility under or pursuant to the terms of the Lease for any cause of action or matter not disclosed herein or that accrues after Addressee ceases to own a fee interest in the property covered by the Lease.

16. Tenant agrees to execute such documents as Addressee may request for the purpose of subordinating the Lease to any mortgage or deed of trust to be placed upon the property by Addressee from time to time and any estoppel certificates requested by Addressee from time to time in connection with the sale or encumbrance of the Premises.

17. Tenant makes this certificate with the understanding that Addressee is contemplating acquiring the Premises and that if Addressee acquires the Premises, it will do so in material reliance on this certificate and Tenant agrees that the certifications and representations made herein shall survive such acquisition.

Executed on this __________ of ______________, 20____.

Tenant: _____________________________________

By: _____________________________, Title: _________________________

Index

D

E

H

I

N

Q

R

Accompanying CD

This book includes a CD with the following files:

Word

- Agreement of Purchase and Sale and Joint Escrow Instructions.doc (Appendix B)
- Commercial Lease.doc (Appendix C)

Excel

- Appreciation Calculator.xls
- Construction Cost Breakdown.xls
- Critical Path Scheduling Tool.xls
- Five year cash flow projection.xls
- Land Speculation Analysis.xls
- One Page Proformas.xls
- Personal Financial Analysis.xls
- Proposed Investment Schedule.xls
- ROI Single Family Home.xls
- Tenant Information Sheet.xls